SELECTIONS FROM

— THE OLD — TESTAMENT
MADE EASIER

JOURNAL EDITION

PART THREE: 1 KINGS 17 THROUGH JEREMIAH 20

COME, FOLLOW ME VERSION

DAVID J. RIDGES

BEST-SELLING AUTHOR

SELECTIONS FROM

— THE OLD —
TESTAMENT
MADE EASIER

JOURNAL EDITION

PART THREE: 1 KINGS 17 THROUGH JEREMIAH 20

COME, FOLLOW ME VERSION

DAVID J. RIDGES

BEST-SELLING AUTHOR

CFI, AN IMPRINT OF

CEDAR FORT
Publishing & Media

SPRINGVILLE, UTAH

ISBN 13: 978-1-4621-4203-3 (set)

Published by CFI, an imprint of Cedar Fort, Inc.
2373 W. 700 S., Springville, UT, 84663
Distributed by Cedar Fort, Inc., www.cedarfort.com

Cover design by Shawnda T. Craig
Cover design © 2022 Cedar Fort, Inc.

Printed in the United States of America

10 9 8 7 6 5 4 3 2 1

Printed on acid-free paper

Contents

1 Kings 17–19

"If the Lord Be God, Follow Him"

In this reading block for our Come, Follow Me curriculum, you will meet Elijah, the prophet, for the first time in the Old Testament. He will be a prophet to the Northern Kingdom (composed of ten tribes of Israel—the Southern Kingdom consisted of two tribes, Judah and part of Benjamin) where King Ahab and Queen Jezebel have corrupted the people and led them to worship the false god, Baal. We know nothing about Elijah before he appeared on the scene here. As you first meet him, he will command that there be no rain, and a devastating three-year drought and famine will follow that is intended to humble King Ahab and his wicked people. You will see ravens as well as a widow woman who feed Elijah during the famine. In this selection, you will also witness Elijah challenge 450 prophets of Baal to a contest to see which god can light the fire for their sacrifices. And finally, you will be instructed in recognizing the "still, small voice," and your heart will be pained as you feel Elijah's loneliness.

---

1 KINGS 17

NOTES

Selection: all verses

As we continue our study of the Old Testament, we will meet Elijah. He is one of the best-known Old Testament prophets. He comes on the scene in 1 Kings 17:1. It is a time of great apostasy, led by Ahab, wicked king of the northern kingdom (Israel), and Jezebel, his equally wicked wife. These two firmly established Baal worship in their kingdom.

Remember that Baal worship involved sexual immorality as part of its rituals. Things got so bad that Elijah challenged the priests of Baal to a contest. You will see it in 1 Kings 18. As you read about Jezebel's reaction in 1 Kings 19, you will notice that she makes a vow to see that Elijah is killed within twenty-four hours. She does not succeed.

As you read these chapters, you will sense Elijah's loneliness. But his reward for faithful service to the Lord was for him to be translated and taken up to heaven without dying.

First, here in chapter 17, verse 1, Elijah prophesied a three-year drought. Remember, Ahab is the extremely wicked king over the northern ten tribes of Israel at this time.

1 AND **Elijah** the Tishbite, *who was* of the inhabitants of Gilead, **said unto Ahab,** *As* the LORD God of Israel liveth, before whom I stand, **there shall not be dew nor rain these years**, but according to my word [*unless I command otherwise*].

Next, in verses 2–7, Elijah is fed by ravens during the famine caused by the drought.

2 And **the word of the LORD came unto him, saying,**

3 Get thee hence, and turn thee eastward, and **hide thyself by the brook Cherith**, that *is* before Jordan [*east of the Jordan River*].

4 And it shall be, *that* thou shalt **drink of the brook**; and **I have commanded the ravens to feed thee there.**

NOTES

_____
_____
_____
_____
_____
_____
_____
_____
_____
_____
_____
_____
_____
_____
_____
_____
_____
_____
_____
_____
_____
_____
_____
_____
_____
_____
_____
_____
_____
_____
_____
_____

5 So **he** went and **did according unto the word of the LORD**: for he went and dwelt by the brook Cherith, that *is* before Jordan.

6 And **the ravens brought him bread and flesh** [*meat*] in the morning, and bread and flesh in the evening; **and he drank of the brook.**

7 And it came to pass **after a while,** that **the brook dried up,** because there had been no rain in the land.

8 ¶ And **the word of the LORD came** unto him, saying,

9 Arise, **get thee to Zarephath** [*a city on the coast of the Mediterranean Sea, between Tyre and Sidon, in what is now Lebanon*], which *belongeth* to Zidon, and **dwell there**: behold, **I have commanded a widow woman there to sustain thee.**

Next, in verses 10–16, you will see the miracle of the flour and cooking oil.

10 So **he arose and went to Zarephath.** And when he came to the gate of the city, behold, **the widow woman** *was* **there gathering of sticks: and he called to her, and said, Fetch me, I pray thee, a little water in a vessel, that I may drink.**

11 And **as she was going to fetch** *it,* **he called to her, and said, Bring me, I pray thee, a morsel of bread in thine hand.**

12 And **she said,** *As* the LORD thy God liveth, **I have not a cake, but an handful of meal** [*flour*] **in a barrel, and a little oil in a cruse: and, behold, I** *am* **gathering two sticks, that I may go in and dress it for me and my son, that we may eat it, and die.**

13 And **Elijah said unto her, Fear not; go** *and* **do as thou hast said: but make me thereof a little cake first, and bring** *it* **unto me, and after make for thee and for thy son.**

14 For **thus saith the LORD** God of Israel, **The barrel of meal shall not waste** [*run out*]**, neither shall the cruse of oil fail** [*become empty*]**, until the day** *that* **the LORD sendeth rain upon the earth.**

15 And **she went and did according to the saying of Elijah**: and **she, and he, and her house, did eat** *many* days.

16 *And* **the barrel of meal wasted not, neither did the cruse of oil fail, according to the word of the LORD**, which he spake by Elijah.

Next, in verses 17–24, the miracle of raising the widow woman's son from the dead.

17 ¶ And it came to pass **after these things,** *that* **the son of the woman,** the mistress of the house, **fell sick; and his sickness was so sore, that there was no breath left in him.**

Next, it appears that the widow is expressing deep feelings of disappointment and confusion, as she chides Elijah, to the effect that she expected blessings when she fed a
prophet, but, instead, her son is now dead.

18 And **she said unto Elijah**, What have I to do with thee, O thou man of God? **art
thou come unto me to call my sin to remembrance, and to slay my son?**

19 And **he said unto her, Give me thy son. And he** took him out of her bosom, and
carried him up into a loft, where he abode, and laid him upon his own bed.

In verse 20, next, Elijah asks the Lord an honest question.

20 And he cried unto the LORD, and said, **O LORD my God, hast thou also
brought evil upon the widow with whom I sojourn, by slaying her son?**

21 And **he stretched himself upon the child three times, and cried unto the
LORD**, and said, O LORD my God, **I pray thee, let this child's soul come into
him again**.

22 **And the LORD heard the voice of Elijah; and the soul of the child came into
him again, and he revived**.

23 And **Elijah** took the child, and brought him down out of the chamber into the
house, and **delivered him unto his mother: and Elijah said, See, thy son liveth**.

24 ¶ And **the woman said to Elijah, Now by this I know that thou** *art* **a man of
God,** *and* **that the word of the LORD in thy mouth** *is* **truth**.

1 KINGS 18

Selection: all verses

Remember, Ahab is the king of the northern ten tribes of Israel, headquartered in Samaria.
He and his wicked wife, Jezebel, are leading their people in wickedness. They have abandoned the Lord and are especially involved in Baal worship. In this chapter you will read
about the rather well-known challenge of Elijah to the false prophets of Baal to set up a
sacrifice and see whose god will light the fire for the sacrifice.

1 AND it came to pass *after* **many days, that the word of the LORD came to Elijah**
in the third year [*of the drought*], saying, **Go, shew thyself unto Ahab; and I will
send rain upon the earth**.

2 And **Elijah went** to shew himself unto Ahab. And *there was* **a sore** [*extreme*] **famine in Samaria**.

3 And **Ahab called Obadiah, which** *was* **the governor of** *his* **house**. (Now Obadiah
feared the LORD greatly [*was a righteous, God-fearing man*]:

4 For it was *so,* **when Jezebel cut off** [*started killing*] **the prophets of the LORD,
that Obadiah took an hundred prophets, and hid them by fifty in a cave, and fed
them with bread and water**.)

NOTES

_____
_____
_____
_____
_____
_____
_____
_____
_____
_____
_____
_____
_____
_____
_____
_____
_____
_____
_____
_____
_____
_____
_____
_____
_____
_____
_____
_____
_____
_____
_____

NOTES

5 And **Ahab said unto Obadiah, Go into the land**, unto all fountains of water [*to every spring*], and unto all brooks: **peradventure we may find grass to save the horses and mules alive**, that we lose not all the beasts.

6 So they divided the land between them to pass throughout it: **Ahab went one way by himself, and Obadiah went another way by himself.**

7 ¶ **And as Obadiah was in the way** [*going his way*], behold, **Elijah met him**: and he knew him, and fell on his face, and said, *Art* **thou** that my lord **Elijah?**

8 And **he answered him, I** *am:* go, **tell thy lord** [*King Ahab*], Behold, **Elijah** *is here.*

In verse 8, above, Elijah told Obadiah to go tell Ahab that Elijah is here and to come and meet him. But there is a real problem in the mind of Obadiah; namely, that Elijah has a reputation of being taken by the Spirit and disappearing. This could cause Obadiah his life, as explained in verses 9–16.

9 And **he said, What have I sinned, that thou wouldest deliver thy servant into the hand of Ahab, to slay me** [*why do you want to get me killed*]?

10 As the LORD thy God liveth, **there is no nation or kingdom, whither my lord hath not sent to seek thee** [*Ahab has looked everywhere for you*]: and when they said, *He is* not *there;* he took an oath of the kingdom and nation, that **they found thee not.**

11 And **now thou sayest, Go, tell thy lord, Behold, Elijah** *is here.*

12 And it shall come to pass, *as soon as* **I am gone from thee, that the Spirit of the LORD shall carry thee whither I know not;** and *so* **when I come and tell Ahab, and he cannot find thee, he shall slay me**: but I thy servant fear the LORD from my youth.

13 **Was it not told my lord** [*have you not heard*] **what I did when Jezebel slew the prophets of the LORD, how I hid an hundred** men of the LORD's **prophets by fifty in a cave, and fed them with bread and water?**

14 **And now thou sayest, Go, tell thy lord, Behold, Elijah** *is here:* **and he shall slay me.**

15 And **Elijah said,** *As* the LORD of hosts liveth, before whom I stand, **I will surely shew myself unto him to day.**

16 So **Obadiah went to meet Ahab, and told him: and Ahab went to meet Elijah.**

17 ¶ And it came to pass, **when Ahab saw Elijah, that Ahab said unto him,** *Art* **thou he that troubleth Israel?**

18 And **he answered, I have not troubled Israel; but thou, and thy father's house** [*you are the ones who have caused the trouble*], in that **ye have forsaken the commandments of the LORD, and thou hast followed Baalim** [*Baal worship; idol worship*].

Next, Elijah challenges Ahab to gather his 450 prophets of Baal plus the 400 other false prophets Jezebel supports to a contest between their god and his God, to be held at Mount Carmel and to be viewed by all the people.

19 Now therefore send, *and* **gather to me all Israel unto mount Carmel** [*straight west of the Sea of Galilee, near the coast of the Mediterranean Sea*]**, and the prophets of Baal four hundred and fifty, and the prophets of the groves** [*where the Baal worship takes place, including the associated sexual immorality—thus, the groves of trees for seclusion*] **four hundred, which eat at Jezebel's table.**

20 So **Ahab** sent unto all the children of Israel, and **gathered the prophets together unto mount Carmel**.

Verse 21, next, is well known among those who value and read the Bible.

21 And Elijah came unto all the people, and said, **How long halt ye between two opinions? if the LORD *be* God, follow him: but if Baal, *then* follow him**. And the people answered him not a word.

22 **Then said Elijah unto the people, I, *even* I only, remain a prophet of the LORD**; but **Baal's prophets *are* four hundred and fifty** men.

Next, the sacrifices are prepared. Imagine the feeling of drama that attended this scene as the masses looked on!

23 **Let them** therefore **give us two bullocks**; and **let them** [*the priests of Baal*] **choose one bullock for themselves, and cut it in pieces, and lay *it* on wood, and put no fire *under*:** and **I will dress the other bullock, and lay *it* on wood, and put no fire *under*:**

24 And **call ye on the name of your gods, and I will call on the name of the LORD: and the God that answereth by fire, let him be God**. And all the people answered and said, It is well spoken.

25 And **Elijah said unto the prophets of Baal**, Choose you one bullock for yourselves, and **dress *it* first** [*you go first*]; for ye *are* many; and **call on the name of your gods, but put no fire *under*** [*don't cheat by lighting the fire yourselves*].

26 And **they took the bullock** which was given them, **and they dressed *it*,** and **called on the name of Baal from morning even until noon**, saying, **O Baal, hear us. But *there was* no voice, nor any that answered**. And they leaped upon the altar which was made.

27 And it came to pass **at noon, that Elijah mocked them**, and said, **Cry aloud** [*call louder*]: for he *is* a god; **either he is talking**, or he is **pursuing** [*involved with something else*], or he is **in a journey**, *or* peradventure he **sleepeth** [*maybe he is sleeping*], **and must be awaked**.

28 And **they cried aloud, and cut themselves** after their manner **with knives and lancets, till the blood gushed out upon them.**

NOTES

29 And it came to pass, **when midday was past, and they prophesied** [*kept shouting and carrying on*] **until the** *time* **of the offering of the** *evening* **sacrifice**, that *there was* **neither voice, nor any to answer, nor any that regarded**.

No doubt, Elijah had their full attention by now.

30 And **Elijah said unto all the people, Come near unto me**. And all the people came near unto him. And **he repaired the altar of the LORD** *that was* **broken down**.

31 And Elijah **took twelve stones**, according to the number of the tribes of the sons of Jacob, unto whom the word of the LORD came, saying, Israel shall be thy name:

32 And with the stones he **built an altar** in the name of the LORD: and **he made a trench about the altar**, as great as would contain two measures of seed.

33 And **he put the wood in order, and cut the bullock in pieces, and laid** *him* **on the wood**, and said, **Fill four barrels with water, and pour** *it* **on the burnt sacrifice, and on the wood**.

34 **And he said, Do** *it* **the second time**. And they did *it* the second time. And he said, **Do** *it* **the third time**. And they did *it* the third time.

35 And the water ran round about the altar; **and he filled the trench also with water**.

36 And it came to pass at *the time of* the offering of the *evening* sacrifice, that **Elijah the prophet came near, and said, LORD God of Abraham, Isaac, and of Israel, let it be known this day that thou** *art* **God in Israel, and** *that* **I** *am* **thy servant, and** *that* **I have done all these things at thy word**.

37 **Hear me, O LORD, hear me, that this people may know that thou** *art* **the LORD God, and** *that* **thou hast turned their heart back again** [*that Thou art giving them a chance to repent*].

38 **Then the fire of the LORD fell** [*came down*], **and consumed the burnt sacrifice, and the wood, and the stones, and the dust, and licked up the water that** *was* **in the trench**.

39 And **when all the people saw** *it,* **they fell on their faces: and they said, The LORD, he** *is* **the God; the LORD, he** *is* **the God**.

40 And **Elijah said unto them, Take the prophets of Baal; let not one of them escape**. And they took them: **and Elijah** brought them down to the brook Kishon, and **slew them there**.

Next, the drought is over.

41 ¶ And **Elijah said unto Ahab**, Get thee up, eat and drink; for *there is* **a sound of abundance of rain**.

42 So Ahab went up to eat and to drink. And **Elijah went up to the top of Carmel**; and he cast himself down upon the earth, and put his face between his knees,

43 **And said to his servant, Go up now, look toward the sea. And he went up, and looked, and said,** *There is* nothing. **And he said, Go again seven times**.

44 And it came to pass **at the seventh time**, that **he said,** Behold, **there ariseth a little cloud out of the sea,** like a man's hand. And **he said, Go up, say unto Ahab, Prepare** *thy chariot,* **and get thee down, that the rain stop thee not.**

45 And it came to pass **in the mean while,** that **the heaven was black with clouds and wind,** and **there was a great rain.** And Ahab rode, and went to Jezreel.

46 And **the hand of the LORD was on Elijah**; and **he** girded up his loins, and **ran before Ahab to the entrance of Jezreel.**

1 KINGS 19

Selection: all verses

Rather than being convinced of the power of the Lord, Jezebel is now angry at Elijah and swears to get him killed within twenty-four hours. This is yet another reminder that wickedness does not promote rational thought.

1 AND **Ahab told Jezebel all that Elijah had done, and** withal **how he had slain all the prophets with the sword.**

2 **Then Jezebel sent a messenger unto Elijah, saying, So let the gods do** *to me,* **and more also, if I make not thy life as the life of one of them** [*in other words, if I don't succeed in having you killed*] **by to morrow about this time.**

3 And **when he saw** *that,* **he arose, and went for his life** [*NIV, "ran for his life"*], **and came to Beer-sheba** [*about one hundred miles away*], **which** *belongeth* to Judah, and left his servant there.

In the next verses, we see that Elijah was very discouraged by this time.

4 ¶ But **he himself went a day's journey into the wilderness, and came and sat down under a juniper tree: and he requested for himself that he might die**; and said, **It is enough; now, O LORD, take away my life**; for I *am* not better than my fathers.

5 And **as he lay and slept under a juniper tree,** behold, then **an angel touched him, and said unto him, Arise** *and* **eat.**

6 And **he looked**, and, behold, *there was* a cake baken on the coals, and a cruse of water at his head. **And he did eat and drink, and laid him down again.**

7 And **the angel of the LORD came again the second time, and touched him, and said, Arise** *and* **eat; because the journey** *is* **too great for thee.**

NOTES

8 And **he arose, and did eat and drink, and went in the strength of that meat forty days and forty nights unto Horeb** [*Mt. Sinai*] **the mount of God.**

9 ¶ And **he came** thither **unto a cave, and lodged there**; and, behold, **the word of the LORD** *came* **to him, and he said unto him, What doest thou here, Elijah?**

Next, Elijah tells the Lord that he is the only righteous one left, and, thus, is alone and very lonely.

10 And **he said, I have been very jealous** [*faithful*] **for the LORD God of hosts: for the children of Israel have forsaken thy covenant, thrown down thine altars, and slain thy prophets** with the sword; **and I,** *even* **I only, am left; and they seek my life, to take it away.**

Verses 11–12, next, are often-quoted by teachers and Church leaders to remind us that the "still small voice" (the Holy Ghost) is one of the most common ways the Lord communicates with us (as opposed to sometimes hoped for or expected much more spectacular means of communication from on high).

11 And **he said, Go** forth, and **stand upon the mount** before the LORD. **And,** behold, **the LORD passed by, and a great and strong wind** rent the mountains, and brake in pieces the rocks before the LORD; *but* **the LORD** *was* **not in the wind**: and **after the wind an earthquake;** *but* **the LORD** *was* **not in the earthquake:**

12 And **after the earthquake a fire;** *but* **the LORD** *was* **not in the fire**: and **after the fire a still small voice.**

13 And it was *so,* **when Elijah heard** *it,* that **he wrapped his face in his mantle, and went out, and stood in the entering in of the cave.** And, behold, *there came* **a voice** unto him, and **said, What doest thou here, Elijah?**

In verse 14, next, Elijah says basically what he said in verse 10, above.

14 And he said, **I have been very jealous for the LORD God of hosts** [*I have been very faithful to Thee*]: because **the children of Israel have forsaken thy covenant, thrown down thine altars, and slain thy prophets** with the sword; and I, *even* **I only, am left; and they seek my life, to take it away.**

In the previous verses, you can sense that Elijah is feeling that he has failed as a prophet and in being an influence for good. However, the Lord quickly reinstates him as a prophet in his own mind by sending him on several major assignments. In verses 15–16, next, the Lord instructs him to anoint a king for Syria (see Bible Dictionary under "Hazael), to anoint a king for Israel (the northern ten tribes), and also to anoint a prophet to take his place (Elisha).

15 **And the LORD said unto him, Go, return on thy way to the wilderness of Damascus** [*in Syria*]: and when thou comest, **anoint Hazael** *to be* **king over Syria**:

16 **And Jehu** the son of Nimshi **shalt thou anoint** *to be* **king over Israel**: and **Elisha** the son of Shaphat of Abel-meholah **shalt thou anoint** *to be* **prophet in thy room** [*in your place*].

NOTES

17 And it shall come to pass, *that* him that escapeth the sword of Hazael shall Jehu slay: and him that escapeth from the sword of Jehu shall Elisha slay.

Remember, in verses 10 and 14, above, Elijah felt that he was the only one left who was striving to be faithful to Jehovah. However, in verse 18, the Lord will assure Elijah that there are at least 7,000 righteous people left in Israel.

18 **Yet I have left** *me* **seven thousand in Israel**, all the knees **which have not bowed unto Baal**, and every mouth which hath not kissed him.

Next, in verses 19–21, we see the calling of Elisha to be a prophet.

19 ¶ So **he** departed thence, and **found Elisha** the son of Shaphat, who *was* plowing *with* twelve yoke *of oxen* before him, and he with the twelfth: **and Elijah passed by him, and cast his mantle upon him** [*a symbolic gesture, indicating, in that culture, that Elisha was to be the successor to Elijah as a prophet*].

Verses 20–21, next, are a strong reminder to all of us that it often requires the sacrifice of material wealth and position in order to follow the prophet and do God's work. It appears that Elisha's family was quite wealthy and Elisha, himself, was well-off as far as material possessions were concerned. But he leaves it all to serve the Lord.

20 And **he left the oxen**, and **ran after Elijah, and said, Let me, I pray thee, kiss my father and my mother, and** *then* **I will follow thee.** And he said unto him, Go back again: for what have I done to thee [*German Bible: "think, what have I done to you"*]?

21 And **he returned back from him, and took a yoke of oxen, and slew them, and boiled their flesh with the instruments of the oxen** [*he used the wood from his farming implements for the fire*], **and gave unto the people, and they did eat.** Then **he arose, and went after Elijah, and ministered unto him**.

2 Kings 2–7

"There Is a Prophet in Israel"

This reading selection for Come, Follow Me begins by informing us that Elijah was translated, meaning that his mortal body was changed so that he wouldn't die yet, which also happened with the three Nephites (3 Nephi 28). He was taken to heaven in what was described as a chariot of fire in a whirlwind and would later be seen on the Mount of Transfiguration ministering to the Savior about six months before His crucifixion. He was resurrected with the Savior (D&C 133:54–55) and will appear to Joseph Smith and Oliver Cowdery in the Kirtland Temple and restore the keys of work for the dead. As you will read, Elisha will succeed Elijah as prophet. He will perform many miracles, including multiplying the widow's oil. You will meet Gehazi, Elisha's servant, who will become a disappointment to you as you continue to read. One of the best-known Bible stories in this reading block is that of Naaman, the Syrian, who is healed of leprosy when he finally dips himself seven times in the muddy Jordan River as instructed by Elisha.

NOTES

2 KINGS 2

Selection: all verses

As you will see in this chapter, Elijah and Elisha covered a lot of territory, no doubt giving Elisha some fast-track training (verses 1–10) before Elijah was taken up (verse 11) at the end of his earthly mission. Elijah was translated (meaning that he was taken up without dying yet, to die and be resurrected later—similar to the three Nephites—see 3 Nephi 28). He was with the Savior on the Mount of Transfiguration (Matthew 17:1–3) and was resurrected with Jesus Christ (Doctrine & Covenants 133:54–55). He appeared to Joseph Smith and Oliver Cowdery in the Kirtland Temple and restored the keys of the sealing power (Doctrine & Covenants 110).

Verse 1 tells us that the time for Elijah to be translated was rapidly approaching.

1 AND it came to pass, **when the LORD would** [*was getting ready to*] **take up Elijah into heaven** by a whirlwind, that **Elijah went with Elisha from Gilgal** [*just north of Jericho*].

Next, we see that Elisha is nervous about leaving Elijah.

2 And **Elijah said unto Elisha, Tarry** [*wait*] **here**, I pray thee; **for the LORD hath sent me to Beth-el** [*about 12 miles north of Jerusalem*]. **And Elisha said** *unto him, As* the LORD liveth, and *as* thy soul liveth, **I will not leave thee. So they went down to Beth-el.**

The "sons of the prophets," mentioned in verse 3, next, were groups of men living together, under the direction of prophets such as Samuel, Elijah, and Elisha, and who received training and instruction from them—see Bible Dictionary under "Schools of the Prophets." In this verse, they seem to have been told in advance that Elijah is going to be taken up shortly.

3 And **the sons of the prophets** that *were* **at Beth-el came forth to Elisha, and said** unto him, **Knowest thou that the LORD will take away thy master from thy head to day? And he said, Yea, I know** *it;* **hold ye your peace** [*don't worry about it*].

4 And **Elijah said** unto him, **Elisha, tarry here**, I pray thee; **for the LORD hath sent me to Jericho**. And **he said**, *As* the LORD liveth, and *as* thy soul liveth, **I will not leave thee. So they came to Jericho**.

5 And **the sons of the prophets that** *were* **at Jericho came to Elisha, and said** unto him, **Knowest thou that the LORD will take away thy master from thy head to day?** And **he answered, Yea, I know** *it;* **hold ye your peace**.

6 And **Elijah said unto him, Tarry**, I pray thee, **here; for the LORD hath sent me to Jordan**. And **he said**, *As* the LORD liveth, and *as* thy soul liveth, **I will not leave thee. And they two went on**.

7 And **fifty men of the sons of the prophets went, and stood to view afar off**: and they two stood by Jordan [*German Bible, "the Jordan River"*].

Next, Elijah parts the water of the Jordan River.

8 And **Elijah took his mantle** [*cloak*], and wrapped *it* together, **and smote the waters, and they were divided hither and thither, so that they two went over on dry ground**.

Next, Elijah kindly asks if Elisha has any final wishes before Elijah is taken up.

9 ¶ And it came to pass, when they were gone over, that **Elijah said unto Elisha, Ask what I shall do for thee, before I be taken away from thee**. And **Elisha said**, I pray thee, **let a double portion of thy spirit be upon me**.

10 And **he said, Thou hast asked a hard thing:** *nevertheless,* **if thou see me** *when I am* **taken from thee, it shall be so unto thee** [*your wish will be granted*]; but if not, it shall not be *so*.

Verse 11, next, is well known. Many paintings have depicted this scene of Elijah being taken up in a chariot of fire.

11 And it came to pass, as they still went on, and talked, that, behold, *there appeared* **a chariot of fire, and horses of fire**, and parted them both asunder [*separated Elijah from Elisha*]; **and Elijah went up by a whirlwind into heaven**.

12 ¶ And **Elisha saw** *it,* and he cried, My father, my father, the chariot of Israel, and the horsemen thereof. **And he saw him no more**: and he took hold of his own clothes, and rent them in two pieces.

13 **He took** up also **the mantle of Elijah** that fell from him, **and went back, and stood by the bank of Jordan;**

14 And **he took the mantle of Elijah** that fell from him, **and smote the waters**, and said, Where *is* the LORD God of Elijah? **and when he also had smitten the waters, they parted** hither and thither: **and Elisha went over**.

NOTES

15 And when the sons of the prophets which *were* to view at Jericho **saw him, they said, The spirit of Elijah doth rest on Elisha**. And they came to meet him, and bowed themselves to the ground before him.

> Next, in verses 16–18, the fifty students of this "school of the prophets," who don't understand what has just happened, offer to help Elisha find Elijah. He tells them no, but they insist.

16 ¶ And **they said unto him, Behold now, there be with thy servants fifty strong men; let them go, we pray thee, and seek thy master**: lest peradventure the Spirit of the LORD hath taken him up, and cast him upon some mountain, or into some valley. And **he said, Ye shall not send** [*Elisha said not to*].

17 And when **they urged him** till he was ashamed, **he said, Send**. They sent therefore fifty men; **and they sought three days, but found him not**.

18 And **when they came again to him**, (for he tarried at Jericho,) **he said unto them, Did I not say unto you, Go not?**

> Next, in verses 19–22, the men of Jericho approach Elisha, explaining that the water of their well has gone bad and ask him to heal it.

19 ¶ And **the men of the city said unto Elisha**, Behold, I pray thee, **the situation of this city *is* pleasant** [*we are nicely located*], as my lord seeth: **but the water *is* naught** [*bad*], **and the ground barren** [*unproductive*].

20 And **he said, Bring me a new cruse** [*bowl*], **and put salt therein**. And they brought *it* to him.

21 And **he went forth unto the spring of the waters, and cast the salt in there, and said, Thus saith the LORD, I have healed these waters**; there shall not be from thence any more death or barren *land*.

22 **So the waters were healed** unto this day, according to the saying of Elisha which he spake.

> After Elijah had been taken up in the whirlwind into heaven, Elisha became the next prophet in Israel. One day as he was out walking, the Bible tells us that several "little children" mocked him, calling him, in effect, "baldy, baldy, baldy" and taunting him for not being translated like Elijah was (verse 23, next). His response was to curse them. As a result, two female bears attacked them and injured forty-two of them.

23 ¶ And he went up from thence unto Beth-el: and as he was going up by the way, **there came forth little children out of the city, and mocked him**, and said unto him, Go up, thou bald head; go up, thou bald head [*a challenge for him to be translated as Elijah was*].

24 And **he turned back, and looked on them, and cursed them in the name of the LORD**. And there came forth **two she bears** out of the wood, and **tare forty and two children of them**.

The main concern most students of the Bible express is that such a punishment upon little children, who are not even accountable, is unthinkable. The fact is, they were not little children. They were youths, which in that culture could include anyone from late teenage up to thirty years of age, when men officially became adults (see footnote 23a in your Bible). Thus, they were indeed accountable and were intentionally mocking and blaspheming the Lord's prophet.

25 And **he went from thence to mount Carmel,** and from thence **he returned to Samaria.**

2 KINGS 3

Selection: all verses

As we begin this chapter, we see that Elisha has his work cut out for him. King Jehoram of Israel (the northern ten tribes, with headquarters in Samaria) did some good in that he stopped the idol worship of Baal among his people. But, otherwise, he was a wicked king and led his people to be wicked in other ways (verses 1–3).

1 NOW **Jehoram the son of Ahab began to reign over Israel in Samaria** the eighteenth year of Jehoshaphat king of Judah, **and reigned twelve years.**

2 And **he wrought evil in the sight of the LORD**; but not like his father, and like his mother: for **he put away the image of Baal that his father had made.**

3 **Nevertheless he cleaved unto the sins of Jeroboam** the son of Nebat, which made Israel to sin; he departed not therefrom.

In verses 4–5, next, we are told that Mesha, King of Moab (an enemy nation east of the southern half of the Dead Sea), who had been paying heavy taxes to Ahab, king of Israel, decided to quit paying tribute to Jehoram when Ahab died.

4 ¶ And **Mesha king of Moab** was a sheepmaster, and **rendered unto the king of Israel an hundred thousand lambs, and an hundred thousand rams, with the wool.**

5 **But** it came to pass, **when Ahab was dead**, that the king of Moab **rebelled against the king of Israel.**

The kings of Israel and Judah unite to fight Moab.

6 ¶ And **king Jehoram** went out of Samaria the same time, and numbered all Israel.

7 And he **went** and sent **to Jehoshaphat the king of Judah, saying, The king of Moab hath rebelled against me: wilt thou go with me against Moab to battle? And he said, I will go up**: I *am* as thou *art,* my people as thy people, *and* my horses as thy horses.

8 And **he said, Which way shall we go** up? And he answered, The way through the wilderness of Edom.

NOTES

9 So **the king of Israel** went, and **the king of Judah**, and **the king of Edom** [*a nation south of the Dead Sea, whose king joined the kings of Israel and Judah in the battle against Moab*]: and they fetched a compass [*took a circle route*] of seven days' journey: and **there was no water for the host** [*the army*]**, and for the cattle** that followed them.

10 And **the king of Israel said**, Alas! that the LORD hath called these three kings together, to deliver them into the hand of Moab [*we're in big trouble and Moab is going to win*]!

11 **But Jehoshaphat said,** *Is there* **not here a prophet of the LORD**, that we may enquire of the LORD by him? And **one of the king of Israel's servants** answered and **said, Here** *is* **Elisha** the son of Shaphat, which poured water on the hands of Elijah [*he was Elijah's assistant*].

12 And **Jehoshaphat said, The word of the LORD is with him. So the king of Israel and Jehoshaphat and the king of Edom went down to him**.

13 And **Elisha said** unto the king of Israel, What have I to do with thee? **get thee to the prophets of thy father, and to the prophets of thy mother** [*go to the false gods and idols your father, Ahab, and your mother, Jezebel used*]. **And the king of Israel said unto him, Nay**: for the LORD hath called these three kings together, to deliver them into the hand of Moab.

14 And **Elisha said**, *As* the LORD of hosts liveth, before whom I stand, surely, **were it not that I regard** [*respect*] the presence of **Jehoshaphat the king of Judah, I would not look toward thee, nor see thee**.

15 But now **bring me a minstrel** [*NIV, "harpist"*]. And it came to pass, when the minstrel played, that the hand of the LORD came upon him.

16 And **he said, Thus saith the LORD, Make this valley full of ditches**.

17 For **thus saith the LORD, Ye shall not see wind, neither shall ye see rain; yet that valley shall be filled with water, that ye may drink, both ye, and your cattle, and your beasts**.

18 And this is *but* a light thing in the sight of **the LORD**: he **will deliver the Moabites also into your hand**.

Next, Elisha prophesies and instructs that these armies will devastate the land of Moab.

19 And **ye shall smite every fenced city, and every choice city, and shall fell every good tree, and stop all wells of water, and mar every good piece of land with stones**.

20 And it came to pass **in the morning**, when the meat offering was offered, that, behold, there came water by the way of Edom, and **the country was filled with water**.

NOTES

21 ¶ And **when all the Moabites heard that the kings were come up to fight against them, they gathered all that were able to put on armour, and upward, and stood in the border.**

22 And they rose up early in the morning, and the sun shone upon the water, **and the Moabites saw the water on the other side** *as* **red as blood:**

23 And **they said, This** *is* blood: the kings are surely slain, and they have smitten one another: now therefore, Moab, to the spoil.**

24 And when they came to the camp of Israel, **the Israelites rose up and smote the Moabites**, so that **they fled before them**: but they went forward smiting the Moabites, even in *their* country.

25 And **they beat down the cities, and on every good piece of land cast every man his stone, and filled it; and they stopped all the wells of water, and felled all the good trees**: only in Kir-haraseth left they the stones thereof; howbeit the slingers went about *it,* and smote it.

26 ¶ And **when the king of Moab saw that the battle was too sore for him, he took with him seven hundred men** that drew swords, **to break through** *even* unto the king of Edom: **but they could not.**

27 **Then he took his eldest son that should have reigned in his stead, and offered him** *for* **a burnt offering upon the wall.** And there was great indignation against Israel: and they departed from him, and returned to *their own* land.

2 KINGS 4

Selection: all verses

It is likely that you have heard some of the popular Bible stories from this chapter. Elisha multiplies the widow's oil, promises a son to a woman, and, when the child dies, he raises the child back to life. He heals deadly stew and multiplies bread and grain for the hungry people to eat. Elisha is indeed a mighty prophet of the Lord!

1 NOW **there cried a certain woman of the wives of the sons of the prophets unto Elisha, saying,** Thy servant **my husband is dead**; and thou knowest that thy servant did fear the LORD: and **the creditor** [*debt collector*] **is come to take unto him my two sons to be bondmen** [*to be servants to pay the debt*].

2 And **Elisha said unto her, What shall I do for thee? tell me, what hast thou in the house?** And **she said,** Thine handmaid hath not any thing in the house, save **a pot of oil.**

3 Then **he said, Go, borrow thee vessels** abroad **of all thy neighbours,** *even* **empty vessels; borrow not a few.**

4 And **when thou art come in,** thou **shalt shut the door** upon thee and upon thy sons, and shalt **pour out into all those vessels,** and thou shalt **set aside that which is full.**

_____
_____
_____
_____
_____
_____
_____
_____
_____
_____
_____
_____
_____
_____
_____
_____
_____
_____
_____
_____
_____
_____
_____
_____
_____
_____
_____
_____
_____
_____
_____

5 So she went from him, and shut the door upon her and upon her sons, who brought *the vessels* to her; **and she poured** out.

6 And it came to pass, **when the vessels were full**, that **she said unto her son, Bring me yet a vessel**. And **he said** unto her, *There is* **not a vessel more. And the oil stayed** [*NIV, "stopped flowing"*].

7 Then **she came and told the man of God. And he said, Go, sell the oil, and pay thy debt, and live thou and thy children of the rest** [*live on what's left*].

8 ¶ And it fell on a day, that **Elisha passed to Shunem, where** *was* **a great** [*wealthy*] **woman**; and **she constrained** [*imposed on*] **him to eat bread. And** *so* it was, *that* as oft as he passed by, he turned in thither to eat bread.

9 And **she said unto her husband**, Behold now, **I perceive that this** *is* **an holy man of God**, which passeth by us continually.

Next, the wealthy woman and her husband make a place for Elisha to stay each time he comes by.

10 **Let us make a little chamber**, I pray thee, on the wall [*NIV, "a small room on the roof"*]; and **let us set for him there a bed**, and **a table**, and **a stool**, and **a candle-stick**: and it shall be, **when he cometh to us, that he shall turn in thither.**

11 And it fell **on a day, that he came** thither, and **he turned into the chamber, and lay there**.

12 And **he said to Gehazi his servant, Call this Shunammite** [*the wealthy woman who lived in Shunem—see verse 8*]. And when he had called her, she stood before him [*she came*].

13 And he said unto him, **Say now unto her, Behold, thou hast been careful for us with all this care; what** *is* **to be done for thee** [*what can we do to repay you*]? wouldest thou be spoken for to the king, or to the captain of the host? And she answered, I dwell among mine own people.

14 And he said, What then *is* to be done for her? And **Gehazi answered, Verily she hath no child, and her husband is old**.

15 And **he said, Call her**. And when he had called her, she stood in the door.

16 **And he said, About this season, according to the time of life, thou shalt embrace a son**. And **she said**, Nay, my lord, *thou* man of God, **do not lie unto thine handmaid** [*please don't mislead me*].

17 **And the woman conceived, and bare a son** at that season that Elisha had said unto her, according to the time of life.

18 ¶ And **when the child was grown**, it fell on a day, that **he went out to his father to the reapers**.

NOTES

19 And **he said unto his father, My head, my head** [*my head hurts*]. And he said to a lad, **Carry him to his mother**.

20 And when he had taken him, and brought him to his mother, **he sat on her knees till noon, and *then* died**.

21 **And she went up, and laid him on the bed of the man of God**, and shut *the door* upon him, and went out.

22 And **she called unto her husband, and said, Send me, I pray thee, one of the young men, and one of the asses, that I may run to the man of God, and come again**.

23 And **he said, Wherefore wilt thou go to him to day?** *it is* neither new moon, nor sabbath [*how will we know where to find him*]. And she said, *It shall be* well.

24 Then **she saddled an ass, and said to her servant, Drive**, and go forward; slack not *thy* riding for me, except I bid thee.

25 So **she** went and came **unto the man of God to mount Carmel**. And it came to pass, **when the man of God saw her afar off, that he said to Gehazi his servant, Behold, *yonder is* that Shunammite**:

26 **Run now**, I pray thee, to **meet her, and say** unto her, *Is it* well with thee? *is it* well with thy husband? *is it* well with the child? And **she answered, *It is* well**.

27 And **when she came to the man of God** to the hill, **she caught him by the feet: but Gehazi came near to thrust her away**. And the man of God said, **Let her alone; for her soul *is* vexed within her**: and **the LORD** hath hid *it* from me, and **hath not told me**.

28 Then **she said, Did I desire a son of my lord? did I not say, Do not deceive me?**

29 Then **he said to Gehazi**, Gird up thy loins [*get ready*], and **take my staff** in thine hand, and go thy way: if thou meet any man, salute him not; and if any salute thee, answer him not again: **and lay my staff upon the face of the child**.

30 And **the mother of the child said**, *As* the LORD liveth, and *as* thy soul liveth, **I will not leave thee. And he arose, and followed her**.

31 And **Gehazi passed on before them, and laid the staff upon the face of the child; but *there was* neither voice, nor hearing**. Wherefore **he went again to meet him, and told him, saying, The child is not awaked**.

32 And **when Elisha was come into the house**, behold, **the child was dead, *and* laid upon his bed**.

33 **He** went in therefore, and shut the door upon them twain, and **prayed unto the LORD**.

NOTES

34 And **he went up, and lay upon the child, and put his mouth upon his mouth, and his eyes upon his eyes, and his hands upon his hands: and he stretched himself upon the child; and the flesh of the child waxed warm.**

35 Then he returned, and walked in the house to and fro; and went up, and stretched himself upon him: and **the child sneezed seven times, and the child opened his eyes.**

36 And **he called Gehazi**, and said, **Call this Shunammite.** So he called her. And **when she was come in unto him, he said, Take up thy son.**

37 Then **she went in, and fell at his feet, and bowed herself to the ground, and took up her son**, and went out.

Next, Elisha visits the sons of the prophets during a terrible famine.

38 ¶ And **Elisha came again to Gilgal: and** *there was* **a dearth** [*famine*] **in the land; and the sons of the prophets** *were* **sitting before him: and he said unto his servant, Set on the great pot, and seethe pottage** [*cook some stew*] **for the sons of the prophets.**

39 And **one went out into the field to gather herbs, and found a wild vine, and gathered thereof wild gourds his lap full**, and came **and shred** *them* **into the pot of pottage**: for they knew *them* not [*they were not familiar with those gourds*].

Next, they discover that the wild gourds were terrible and they couldn't eat the stew.

40 So **they poured out for the men to eat.** And it came to pass, **as they were eating of the pottage, that they cried out, and said, O** *thou* **man of God,** *there is* **death in the pot**. And they could not eat *thereof.*

41 But **he said, Then bring meal** [*some flour*]. And **he cast** *it* **into the pot; and he said, Pour out for the people, that they may eat. And there was no harm in the pot**.

Finally, in this chapter, Elisha feeds a hundred men with just twenty loaves of bread and some heads of new grain.

42 ¶ And there came **a man** from Baal-shalisha, and **brought the man of God bread** of the firstfruits, twenty loaves of barley, **and full ears of corn in the husk** thereof. And **he said, Give unto the people, that they may eat.**

43 And **his servitor said, What, should I set this before an hundred men? He said again, Give the people, that they may eat: for thus saith the LORD, They shall eat, and shall leave** *thereof* [*and there will be plenty left over*].

44. So he set *it* before them, and they did eat, and left *thereof,* according to the word of the LORD

2 KINGS 5

Selection: all verses

This chapter contains the well-known account of Naaman, the commander-in-chief of the armies of Syria, who had leprosy, as he came to Elisha to be healed. It also has the disappointing and sad account of Gehazi, Elisha's here-to-fore faithful servant, who goes around Elisha's back to dishonestly acquire a gift from Naaman.

1 NOW **Naaman, captain of the host** [*army*] **of the king of Syria**, was a great man with his master, and honourable, because by him the LORD had given deliverance unto Syria: he was also a mighty man in valour, *but he was* **a leper** [*had leprosy*].

2 And **the Syrians** had gone out by companies, and **had brought away captive out of the land of Israel a little maid**; and **she waited on** [*served*] **Naaman's wife.**

Next, the little maid servant, who believed in God and His prophet, Elisha, told Naaman's wife about Elisha.

3 And **she said** unto her mistress, **Would God my lord** *were* **with the prophet that** *is* **in Samaria** [*where the northern ten tribes of Israel lived*]**! for he would recover** [*heal*] **him of his leprosy.**

In verse 5, next, someone heard about this and told the King of Syria.

4 And *one* **went in, and told his lord** [*the king*], saying, Thus and thus said the maid that *is* of the land of Israel.

5 And **the king of Syria said, Go to, go** [*said to Naaman, go to Israel to get healed*], and **I will send a letter unto the king of Israel.** And he departed, and took with him ten talents of silver, and six thousand *pieces* of gold, and ten changes of raiment [*as a gift for Elisha*].

6 And **he brought the letter to the king of Israel, saying, Now when this letter is come unto thee, behold, I have** *therewith* **sent Naaman my servant to thee, that thou mayest recover him of his leprosy.**

7 And it came to pass, **when the king of Israel had read the letter**, that **he rent** [*tore*] **his clothes, and said,** *Am* **I God, to kill and to make alive, that this man doth send unto me to recover** [*heal*] **a man of his leprosy?** wherefore consider, I pray you, and see how he seeketh a quarrel against me [*why is he trying to stir up trouble with me*].

8 ¶ And it was *so,* **when Elisha the man of God had heard that the king of Israel had rent his clothes, that he sent to the king, saying, Wherefore hast thou rent thy clothes? let him come now to me, and he shall know that there is a prophet in Israel.**

9 **So Naaman came** with his horses and with his chariot, **and stood at the door of the house of Elisha.**

NOTES

_____
_____
_____
_____
_____
_____
_____
_____
_____
_____
_____
_____
_____
_____
_____
_____
_____
_____
_____
_____
_____
_____
_____
_____
_____
_____
_____
_____
_____
_____
_____
_____
_____

Notice that Elisha didn't even come to the door to meet Naaman, rather sent his servant. As you will see, this indignity made Naaman mad.

10 And **Elisha sent a messenger unto him, saying, Go and wash in Jordan seven times, and thy flesh shall come again to thee, and thou shalt be clean** [*healed*].

11 But **Naaman was wroth, and went away**, and said, Behold, **I thought, He will surely come out to me, and stand, and call on the name of the LORD his God, and strike his hand over the place, and recover the leper.**

12 *Are* **not** Abana and Pharpar, **rivers of Damascus, better than all the waters of Israel? may I not wash in them, and be clean?** So he turned and went away in a **rage.**

Next, Naaman's servants try to talk some sense into him. He is humble enough to take counsel from those lower than he is in social status.

13 And **his servants came near, and spake unto him, and said, My father** [*a term of respect*], **if the prophet had bid thee** *do some* **great thing, wouldest thou not have done** *it?* **how much rather then, when he saith to thee, Wash, and be clean?**

14 **Then went he down, and dipped himself seven times in Jordan, according to the saying of the man of God: and his flesh came again like unto the flesh of a little child, and he was clean.**

Next, Naaman seeks to express his gratitude to Elisha by giving him some lavish gifts. (As you are well aware, priesthood holders and others in the Church who serve do not accept money or gifts for their services.)

15 ¶ And **he returned to the man of God, he and all his company**, and came, and stood before him: and **he said, Behold, now I know that** *there is* **no God in all earth, but in Israel**: now therefore, **I pray thee, take a blessing of thy servant** [*let me give you a gift to show appreciation*].

16 **But he said,** *As* the LORD liveth, before whom I stand, **I will receive none.** And **he urged him to take** *it;* **but he refused.**

17 And **Naaman said, Shall there not** then, I pray thee, **be given to thy servant two mules' burden of earth** [*may I at least take two mule loads of soil*]? for thy servant will henceforth offer neither burnt offering nor sacrifice unto other gods, but unto the LORD.

18 In this thing the LORD pardon thy servant, *that* **when my master** [*the king of Syria*] **goeth into the house of Rimmon** [*a Syrian god of wind, rain, and storm—see footnote 18a in your Bible*] **to worship there, and he leaneth on my hand, and I bow myself in the house of Rimmon: when I bow down myself in the house of Rimmon, the LORD pardon thy servant in this thing.**

19 And **he** [*Elisha*] **said unto him, Go in peace.** So he departed from him a little way.

Next, Gehazi, sees an opportunity to become a wealthy man himself and secretly catches up to Naaman and his company and lies to him.

20 ¶ **But Gehazi, the servant of Elisha the man of God, said, Behold, my master hath spared Naaman this Syrian, in not receiving at his hands that which he brought: but,** *as* **the LORD liveth, I will run after him, and take somewhat of him.**

21 So Gehazi followed after Naaman. And **when Naaman saw** *him* **running after him, he lighted down from the chariot to meet him, and said,** *Is* **all well?**

22 And **he said, All** *is* **well. My master hath sent me, saying, Behold, even now there be come to me from mount Ephraim two young men of the sons of the prophets: give them, I pray thee, a talent of silver, and two changes of garments.**

23 And **Naaman said**, Be content, **take two talents.** And he urged him, **and bound two talents of silver in two bags, with two changes of garments,** and laid *them* upon two of his servants; and they bare *them* before him.

24 And when he came to the tower, **he took** *them* **from their hand, and bestowed** *them* **in the house**: and he let the men go, and they departed.

Next, Gehazi lies to Elisha.

25 But **he went in, and stood before his master. And Elisha said unto him, Whence** *comest thou,* **Gehazi** [where have you been]**? And he said, Thy servant went no whither.**

In verses 26–27, Elisha, through revelation, tells Gehazi exactly what he has done and pronounces that the leprosy of Naaman will now come upon Gehazi.

26 And **he said unto him, Went not mine heart** *with thee* [I was inspired to know]**, when the man turned again from his chariot to meet thee?** *Is it* **a time to receive money, and to receive garments, and oliveyards, and vineyards, and sheep, and oxen, and menservants, and maidservants?**

27 **The leprosy therefore of Naaman shall cleave unto thee, and unto thy seed for ever. And he went out from his presence a leper** *as white* **as snow.**

2 KINGS 6

Selection: all verses

We are reminded in this chapter that the Lord, in His kindness, blesses us with many mercies in dealing with our daily, mundane needs. In this case, an axe is lost in the water and would be very difficult to replace.

1 AND **the sons of the prophets** [one of several groups in the land who were in a type of schooling by the prophets—see Bible Dictionary under "Schools of the Prophets"] **said unto Elisha, Behold now, the place where we dwell with thee is too strait for us** [there is not enough room for all of us].

_____
_____
_____
_____
_____
_____
_____
_____
_____
_____
_____
_____
_____
_____
_____
_____
_____
_____
_____
_____
_____
_____
_____
_____
_____
_____
_____
_____
_____

2 **Let us go**, we pray thee, **unto Jordan, and take thence every man a beam, and let us make us a place there, where we may dwell.** And **he answered, Go** ye.

3 And **one said**, Be content, I pray thee, and **go with thy servants. And he answered, I will go.**

4 **So he went with them.** And **when they came to Jordan, they cut down wood.**

5 **But as one was felling a beam, the axe head fell into the water**: and **he cried, and said, Alas, master! for it was borrowed.**

6 And **the man of God** [*Elisha*] **said, Where fell it? And he shewed him the place.** And he cut down a stick, and cast *it* in thither; and **the iron did swim** [*floated up*].

7 **Therefore said he, Take** *it* **up to thee. And he put out his hand, and took it.**

8 ¶ **Then the king of Syria warred against Israel**, and took counsel with his servants, saying, In such and such a place *shall be* my camp.

Next, in verse 9, Elisha gives political advice to the king of Israel. This is a straightforward example that our living prophets have every right—indeed the obligation—to give counsel regarding political issues as inspired by the Lord.

9 And **the man of God sent unto the king of Israel, saying, Beware that thou pass not such a place; for thither the Syrians are come down.**

10 And **the king of Israel sent to the place which the man of God told him and warned him of, and saved himself there, not once nor twice.**

11 **Therefore the heart of the king of Syria was sore troubled for this thing**; and **he called his servants, and said unto them, Will ye not shew me which of us** *is* **for the king of Israel** [*who's the traitor among us who keeps revealing to Israel where we are secretly hiding our troops*]?

12 And **one of his servants said, None, my lord, O king: but Elisha, the prophet that** *is* **in Israel, telleth the king of Israel the words that thou speakest in thy bedchamber.**

13 ¶ And **he said, Go and spy where he** *is,* **that I may send and fetch him. And it was told him**, saying, Behold, *he is* **in Dothan.**

14 **Therefore sent he thither horses, and chariots, and a great host: and they came by night, and compassed the city about** [*surrounded the city*].

Verses 15–16 are well known to those who read the Bible. It is a reminder that we are never outnumbered when we strive to be on the Lord's side.

15 And **when the servant of the man of God was risen early, and gone forth**, behold, **an host** [*army*] **compassed the city both with horses and chariots.** And **his servant said unto him, Alas, my master! how shall we do?**

NOTES

16 And **he answered, Fear not**: for **they that** *be* **with us** *are* **more than they that** *be* **with them**.

17 And **Elisha prayed, and said, LORD, I pray thee, open his eyes, that he may see**. And **the LORD opened the eyes of the young man; and he saw: and, behold, the mountain** *was* **full of horses and chariots of fire round about Elisha**.

18 And **when they came down to him, Elisha prayed unto the LORD, and said, Smite this people, I pray thee, with blindness**. And **he smote them with blindness** according to the word of Elisha.

19 ¶ And **Elisha said unto them, This** *is* **not the way, neither** *is* **this the city: follow me, and I will bring you to the man whom ye seek. But he led them to Samaria**.

20 And it came to pass, **when they were come into Samaria**, that **Elisha said, LORD, open the eyes of these** *men,* **that they may see. And the LORD opened their eyes, and they saw; and, behold,** *they were* **in the midst of Samaria**.

21 And **the king of Israel said unto Elisha**, when he saw them, **My father, shall I smite** *them?* **shall I smite** *them?*

22 And **he answered, Thou shalt not smite** *them:* wouldest thou smite those whom thou hast taken captive with thy sword and with thy bow? **set bread and water before them, that they may eat and drink, and go to their master**.

23 And **he prepared great provision** [*meal*] **for them: and when they had eaten and drunk, he sent them away**, and they went to their master. **So the bands of Syria came no more into the land of Israel**.

Remember, in verse 11, above, that the King of Syria (located north of Israel) had determined to secretly attack Israel. But, as you have just read, Elisha foiled that strategy of war. Therefore, King Ben-hadad, of Syria, decided to openly attack Israel (the northern ten tribes, headquartered in Samaria.)

24 ¶ And it came to pass **after this**, that **Ben-hadad king of Syria** gathered all his host [*army*], and went up, and **besieged Samaria**.

You can see how bad the famine had become in Samaria as you read verses 25–29, next.

25 And **there was a great famine in Samaria**: and, behold, they besieged it, until **an ass's head was** *sold* **for fourscore** *pieces* **of silver**, and **the fourth part of a cab of dove's dung** [*for food*] **for five** *pieces* **of silver** [*NIV, about 2 ounces of silver*].

26 And **as the king of Israel was passing by upon the wall, there cried a woman unto him, saying, Help, my lord, O king**.

27 And **he said**, If the LORD do not help thee, **whence shall I help thee?** out of the barnfloor, or out of the winepress?

NOTES

_____
_____
_____
_____
_____
_____
_____
_____
_____
_____
_____
_____
_____
_____
_____
_____
_____
_____
_____
_____
_____
_____
_____
_____
_____
_____
_____

28 And **the king said unto her, What aileth thee? And she answered, This woman said unto me, Give thy son, that we may eat him to day, and we will eat my son to morrow.**

29 **So we boiled my son, and did eat him: and I said unto her on the next day, Give thy son, that we may eat him: and she hath hid her son.**

Tearing one's clothes and wearing sackcloth were signs of extreme concern and mourning in the culture of that day.

30 ¶ And it came to pass, **when the king heard the words of the woman, that he rent his clothes**; and he passed by upon the wall, and the people looked, and, behold, *he had* **sackcloth** within upon his flesh.

31 **Then he** [*the king of Israel*] **said, God do so and more also to me, if the head of Elisha** the son of Shaphat **shall stand on him this day** [*he is vowing to kill Elisha that day*].

32 **But Elisha sat in his house, and the elders sat with him**; and *the king* sent a **man** [*an assassin*] from before him: but ere the messenger came to him, **he said to the elders, See ye how this son of a murderer hath sent to take away mine head?** look, **when the messenger cometh, shut the door, and hold him fast at the door** [*don't let him enter*]: *is* not the sound of his master's feet behind him?

33 And while he yet talked with them, behold, **the messenger came** down unto him: and **he said, Behold, this evil** *is* **of the LORD**; what should I wait for the LORD any longer?

2 KINGS 7

Selection: all verses

In chapter 6, you saw a terrible famine in Samaria. Now, in chapter 7, Elisha prophesies a miraculous end to the famine the next day. It will be fulfilled in verse 16 as the Syrian armies flee in terror the next day and the starving citizens of Israel plunder the food left behind.

1 **THEN Elisha said**, Hear ye the word of the LORD; **Thus saith the LORD, To morrow about this time** *shall* **a measure** [*NIV, "about seven quarts"*] **of fine flour** *be sold* **for a shekel** [*very cheap*], and **two measures of barley for a shekel**, in the gate of Samaria.

2 **Then a lord on whose hand the king leaned** answered the man of God, and **said,** Behold, *if* **the LORD would make windows in heaven, might this thing be?** And **he** [*Elisha*] **said, Behold, thou shalt see** *it* **with thine eyes, but shalt not eat thereof.**

3 ¶ And **there were four leprous men at the entering in of the gate**: and **they said one to another, Why sit we here until we die?**

4 **If we say, We will enter into the city, then the famine** *is* **in the city, and we shall die there: and if we sit still here, we die also.** Now therefore **come, and let us fall**

unto the host of the Syrians: **if they save us alive, we shall live; and if they kill us, we shall but die.**

5 And **they rose up in the twilight, to go unto the camp of the Syrians: and when they were come to the uttermost part** [*outskirts*] **of the camp of Syria, behold,** *there was* **no man there.**

6 **For the Lord had made the host of the Syrians to hear a noise of chariots, and a noise of horses,** *even* **the noise of a great host: and they said one to another, Lo, the king of Israel hath hired against us the kings of the Hittites, and the kings of the Egyptians, to come upon us.**

7 Wherefore **they arose and fled** in the twilight, and **left their tents, and their horses, and their asses, even the camp as it** *was,* **and fled for their life.**

8 And **when these lepers came to the uttermost part** [*outer edge*] **of the camp, they** went into one tent, and **did eat and drink, and carried thence silver, and gold, and raiment, and went and hid** *it;* and came again, **and entered into another tent, and carried thence** *also,* **and went and hid** *it.*

9 Then **they said one to another,** We do not well: this day *is* a day of good tidings, and we hold our peace: **if we tarry till the morning light, some mischief will come upon us:** now therefore **come, that we may go and tell the king's household.**

10 **So they came and called unto the porter of the city: and they told them, saying,** We came to the camp of the Syrians, and, behold, *there was* no man there, neither voice of man, but horses tied, and asses tied, and the tents as they *were.*

11 And **he called the porters; and they told** *it* **to the king's house** within.

The king of Israel thinks it is a trick, an ambush to draw them to their empty camp and then ambush them.

12 ¶ And **the king arose in the night, and said** unto his servants, **I will now shew you what the Syrians have done to us.** They know that we *be* hungry; therefore are **they gone out of the camp to hide themselves in the field, saying, When they come out of the city, we shall catch them alive, and get into the city.**

13 And **one of his servants answered and said,** Let *some* take, I pray thee, five of the horses that remain, which are left in the city, (behold, they *are* as all the multitude of Israel that are left in it: behold, *I say,* they *are* even as all the multitude of the Israelites that are consumed:) and **let us send and see.**

14 They took therefore two chariot horses; and **the king sent after the host of the Syrians, saying, Go and see.**

15 And **they went after them unto Jordan** [*to the Jordan River*]: and, **lo, all the way** *was* full of garments and vessels, which the Syrians had cast away in their haste. And **the messengers returned, and told the king.**

NOTES

16 **And the people went out, and spoiled the tents of the Syrians. So a measure of fine flour was** *sold* **for a shekel, and two measures of barley for a shekel, according to the word of the LORD** [*just as Elisha had prophesied*].

> Next, as the starving people in the city hear that the Syrian army has fled and that they left all their food and stuff behind, they stampede and trample to death the King's officer left at the gate to control things. Thus, Elisha's prophecy, given in verse 2, above, about him, was fulfilled.

17 ¶ And **the king appointed the lord on whose hand he leaned to have the charge of the gate: and the people trode upon him in the gate, and he died, as the man of God had said**, who spake when the king came down to him.

> Verses 18–20 are a review of the above prophecies as they were fulfilled.

18 **And it came to pass as the man of God had spoken** to the king, saying, **Two measures of barley for a shekel, and a measure of fine flour for a shekel, shall be to morrow** about this time in the gate of Samaria:

19 And **that lord** [*officer*] **answered** the man of God, and said, Now, behold, *if* the LORD should make windows in heaven, **might such a thing be** [*how could such a prophecy of plenty of food possibly come about in one day*]? **And he** [*Elisha*] **said, Behold, thou shalt see it with thine eyes, but shalt not eat thereof.**

20 **And so it fell out unto him** [*and so the prophecy was fulfilled*]: **for the people trode upon him in the gate, and he died.**

> Because of space limitations, we will now skip ahead to 2 Kings, chapter 17, to continue our study. Suffice it to say that the kingdom of Israel, the northern ten tribes, continued on a path of wickedness, including idol worship, especially worshiping the false god, Baal. Finally, in chapter 17, the Assyrian armies attack and carry the northern ten tribes away into captivity. Thus, we have the "lost ten tribes" who will return, as prophesied, sometime before the Second Coming of Christ.

2 Kings 17–25

"He Trusted in the Lord God of Israel"

The main event for the Northern Kingdom in this reading selection for Come, Follow Me is that these ten tribes of Israel will be carried away into captivity by the Assyrians in about 722–721 BC because of their wickedness. They are known to us today as the "Lost Ten Tribes." In the rest of this curriculum reading block, you will be introduced to a righteous king over the Southern Kingdom, with headquarters in Jerusalem. His name is Hezekiah. Watch as he works diligently to undo the damage his wicked father, Elah, did while he was king of Judah. Also, watch as the Assyrian armies, having successfully conquered the ten tribes of Northern Israel and carried most of them away into captivity, now seek to conquer Jerusalem. You will see righteous King Hezekiah seek counsel from Isaiah, the prophet, and follow it. Because of this, Jerusalem will be spared. You will also see more wicked and righteous kings of Judah and the results of each upon the people.

2 KINGS 17

NOTES

Selection: all verses

As we begin this chapter, remember that the twelve tribes of Israel split up into two kingdoms over two hundred years ago. The southern kingdom, headquartered in Jerusalem, was called Judah and consisted of the tribes of Judah, Levi (some of Levi were with the northern kingdom), and about half of the tribe of Benjamin, as well as some from the other tribes who had migrated to the Jerusalem area. The northern kingdom, consisting of ten tribes, was known as Israel, with headquarters in Samaria.

The main focus of this chapter will be on the wickedness of these two nations and the eventual conquest of the northern kingdom and their being carried away captive by the Assyrians (located basically where Iraq is today).

Verse 1 gives us the names of the kings of these two rival kingdoms among the children of Israel, and verse 21 tells us that Hoshea, king of Israel, was very wicked.

1 IN the twelfth year of **Ahaz king of Judah** began **Hoshea** the son of Elah to reign in Samaria **over Israel** nine years.

2 And **he** [*Hoshea*] **did *that which was* evil in the sight of the LORD**, but not as the kings of Israel that were before him.

Verses 3–4, next, summarize the fact that, initially, Hoshea made a pact with Assyria that Assyria would not attack Israel if Israel paid tribute.

3 ¶ **Against him came up Shalmaneser king of Assyria; and Hoshea became his servant, and gave him presents** [*tribute; payments for protection*].

But Hoshea, king of Israel, violated their agreement by turning to the king of Egypt for protection against Assyria and stopping tribute payments to Assyria.

4 And **the king of Assyria found conspiracy in Hoshea: for he had sent messengers to So king of Egypt**, and brought no present [*stopped tribute payments*] **to the**

27

NOTES

king of Assyria, as *he had done* year by year: **therefore the king of Assyria shut him up, and bound him in prison**.

Verses 5–6, next, tell us that the northern ten tribes were attacked and carried away into Assyrian captivity. The year was about 722 or 721 B.C. Thus, we have the lost ten tribes.

5 ¶ Then **the king of Assyria** came up throughout all the land, and **went up to Samaria, and besieged it three years**.

6 ¶ **In the ninth year** [*722–721 B.C.*] **of Hoshea** the king of **Assyria took Samaria, and carried Israel away into Assyria**, and placed them in Halah and in Habor *by* the river of Gozan, and in the cities of the Medes.

Verses 7–23 review the terrible sins and wickedness of both houses of Israel, the northern tribes and the southern tribes.

7 For *so* it was, **that the children of Israel had sinned against the LORD their God**, which had brought them up out of the land of Egypt, from under the hand of Pharaoh king of Egypt, **and had feared** [*worshipped*] **other gods**,

8 And **walked in the statutes** [*false rites and worship*] **of the heathen**, whom the LORD cast out from before the children of Israel, and of the kings of Israel, which they had made.

9 And **the children of Israel did secretly** *those* things that *were* not right against **the LORD** their God, and **they built them high places** [*places for idol worship*] in all their cities, from the tower of the watchmen to the fenced city.

10 And **they set them up images and groves in every high hill, and under every green tree** [*remember that most idol worship involved sexual immorality with temple prostitutes, both male and female, and the groves and trees provided seclusion for that*]:

11 And there **they burnt incense in all the high places, as** *did* **the heathen** whom the LORD carried away before them; **and wrought wicked things to provoke the LORD to anger**:

12 For **they served idols**, whereof **the LORD had said unto them, Ye shall not do this thing**.

Verse 13, next, is a reminder that the Lord gave them fair warning.

13 Yet **the LORD testified against Israel, and against Judah, by all the prophets,** *and by* **all the seers** [*another name for prophets*]**, saying, Turn ye from your evil ways, and keep my commandments** *and* **my statutes**, according to all the law which I commanded your fathers, and which I sent to you by my servants the prophets.

14 Notwithstanding **they would not hear**, but **hardened their necks** [*would not bow their heads in humility and accept correction from God*], like to the neck of their fathers, that did not believe in the LORD their God.

NOTES

15 And **they rejected his statutes, and his covenant** that he made with their fathers, and his testimonies which he testified against them; and **they followed vanity, and became vain**, and went after the heathen that *were* round about them, *concerning* whom the LORD had charged them, that they should not do like them.

16 And **they left all the commandments of the LORD** their God, and **made them molten images** [*idols*], *even* two calves, and made a grove, **and worshipped all the host of heaven** [*the sun, moon, and stars, which Moses had forbidden—see Deuteronomy 4:19, 17:3*], and **served Baal.**

17 And **they caused their sons and their daughters to pass through the fire** [*sacrificed their children to fire god idols*], and **used divination and enchantments** [*the occult*], and **sold themselves to do evil in the sight of the LORD, to provoke him to anger.**

18 **Therefore the LORD was very angry with Israel**, and **removed them out of his sight** [*allowed the Assyrians to take Israel away into captivity*]: **there was none left but the tribe of Judah only.**

19 Also Judah kept not the commandments of the LORD their God, but walked in the statutes of Israel which they made.

20 And **the LORD rejected** all the seed of **Israel, and afflicted them, and delivered them into the hand of spoilers** [*enemy armies; Assyrians*], **until he had cast them out of his sight.**

21 For **he rent** [*tore*] **Israel from the house of David** [*Judah*]; and **they** [*the ten tribes*] **made Jeroboam** [*he was of the tribe of Ephraim*] the son of Nebat **king: and Jeroboam drave Israel from following the LORD, and made them sin a great sin.**

22 For **the children of Israel walked in all the sins of Jeroboam** which he did; they departed not from them;

23 **Until the LORD removed Israel out of his sight**, as he had said by all his servants the prophets. **So was Israel carried away out of their own land to Assyria** unto this day.

Verses 17–24 tell us about the origins of the Samaritans, who were despised and avoided by the Jews in the New Testament. This is a bit of background for the parable of the good Samaritan in the New Testament.

As you can see, in verse 24, next, the king of Assyria brought non-Israelites from his subjects in foreign countries and resettled them in Samaria. They eventually intermarried with the citizens of Israel who were left behind (not all the Israelites were successfully captured and taken away). Thus, they were despised and avoided by the Jews in Judah.

24 ¶ And **the king of Assyria brought** *men* **from Babylon, and from Cuthah, and from Ava, and from Hamath, and from Sepharvaim, and placed** *them* **in the cities of Samaria instead of** [*in the place of*] **the children of Israel: and they possessed Samaria, and dwelt in the cities thereof.**

NOTES

25 And *so* it was at the beginning of their dwelling there, *that* they feared not the LORD [*didn't have the same religion as the Israelites who remained*]: therefore the LORD sent lions among them, which slew *some* of them.

Next, in verses 26–41, we see that the King of Assyria imported a priest of Israel from the captives back to Samaria in an attempt to help those he resettled there learn how to worship the God of the Israelites in order to appease the Israelite God so He wouldn't be angry with them. Thus, we see a sort of hodge-podge of religion. Eventually, the Samaritans had enough similarities to the religious practices in Jerusalem that they considered themselves to have the true religion.

26 **Wherefore they** [*the new settlers*] **spake to the king of Assyria, saying, The nations which thou hast removed, and placed in the cities of Samaria, know not the manner of the God of the land**: therefore he hath sent lions among them, and, behold, they slay them, because they know not the manner of the God of the land.

27 Then **the king of Assyria commanded**, saying, **Carry thither** [*to Samaria*] **one of the priests whom ye brought from thence**; and let them go and dwell there, and **let him teach them the manner of the God of the land**.

28 **Then one of the priests** whom they had carried away from Samaria **came and dwelt in Beth-el, and taught them how they should fear** [*worship*] **the LORD**.

29 **Howbeit** [*however*] **every nation made gods of their own**, and put *them* in the houses of the high places which the Samaritans had made, every nation in their cities wherein they dwelt.

30 And the men of Babylon made Succoth-benoth, and the men of Cuth made Nergal, and the men of Hamath made Ashima,

31 And the Avites made Nibhaz and Tartak, and the Sepharvites burnt their children in fire to Adrammelech and Anammelech, the gods of Sepharvaim.

32 **So they feared the LORD, and made unto themselves of the lowest of them priests** of the high places, which sacrificed for them in the houses of the high places.

33 **They feared the LORD, and served their own gods**, after the manner of the nations whom they carried away from thence.

34 **Unto this day they do after the former manners: they fear not the LORD, neither do they after their statutes, or after their ordinances, or after the law and commandment which the LORD commanded the children of Jacob, whom he named Israel**;

35 **With whom the LORD had made a covenant**, and charged them, saying, Ye shall not fear other gods, nor bow yourselves to them, nor serve them, nor sacrifice to them:

36 **But the LORD**, who brought you up out of the land of Egypt with great power and a stretched out arm, **him shall ye fear, and him shall ye worship**, and to him shall ye do sacrifice.

NOTES

37 **And the statutes, and the ordinances, and the law, and the commandment, which he wrote for you, ye shall observe to do** for evermore; and ye shall not fear other gods.

38 And **the covenant that I have made with you ye shall not forget; neither shall ye fear other gods**.

39 **But the LORD your God ye shall fear**; and he shall deliver you out of the hand of all your enemies.

40 **Howbeit they did not hearken, but they did after their former manner**.

41 **So these nations feared the LORD, and served their graven images**, both their children, and their children's children: as did their fathers, so do they unto this day.

2 KINGS 18

Selection: all verses

In 726 B.C., about five years before the northern kingdom (Israel) was taken away into Assyrian captivity, righteous Hezekiah became king over the southern kingdom (Judah), headquartered in Jerusalem. He ruled for twenty-nine years. He did much to bring his people back to the Lord. Watch now and see what he did to destroy idolatry among his people. As a result, his kingdom and people were protected from the Assyrians.

1 NOW it came to pass in the third year of Hoshea son of Elah king of Israel, *that* **Hezekiah** the son of Ahaz **king of Judah began to reign**.

2 **Twenty and five years old was he when he began to reign; and he reigned twenty and nine years** in Jerusalem. His mother's name also *was* Abi, the daughter of Zachariah.

   Hezekiah was righteous.

3 And **he did** *that which was* **right in the sight of the LORD**, according to all that David his father did.

   He destroyed the idols and the places and shrines built for the purpose of worshiping the idols.

4 ¶ **He removed the high places**, and **brake the images** [*broke the idols*], and **cut down the groves**, and **brake in pieces the brasen serpent that Moses had made**: for unto those days **the children of Israel did burn incense to it** [*had turned it into an idol*]: and he called it Nehushtan.

5 **He trusted in the LORD God of Israel**; so that after him was none like him among all the kings of Judah, nor *any* that were before him.

6 For **he clave to the LORD, *and* departed not from following him, but kept his commandments**, which the LORD commanded Moses [*lived the law of Moses faithfully*].

NOTES

7 And **the LORD was with him**; *and* he prospered whithersoever he went forth: and **he rebelled against the king of Assyria** [*Sennacherib*], **and served him not**.

You will see more about this rebellion starting with verse 13.

8 **He smote the Philistines** [*successfully fought the Philistines—enemies to the southwest of Jerusalem*], *even* unto Gaza, and the borders thereof, from the tower of the watchmen to the fenced city.

Verses 9–12 are a review of the Assyrian captivity of Israel, the northern kingdom, the northern ten tribes, about 722–721 B.C.

9 ¶ And it came to pass **in the fourth year of king Hezekiah**, which *was* the seventh year of Hoshea son of Elah king of Israel, *that* **Shalmaneser king of Assyria came up against Samaria, and besieged it**.

10 **And at the end of three years they took it**: *even* in the sixth year of Hezekiah, that *is* the ninth year of Hoshea king of Israel, Samaria was taken.

11 And **the king of Assyria did carry away Israel unto Assyria**, and put them in Halah and in Habor *by* the river of Gozan, and in the cities of the Medes:

12 **Because they obeyed not the voice of the LORD their God, but transgressed his covenant**, *and* all that Moses the servant of the LORD commanded, and would not hear *them*, nor do *them*.

Now back to the account of the Assyrians' attempted attack on Jerusalem about ten years later. King Sennacherib's Assyrian forces will successfully conquer several cities of the southern kingdom, Judah, leading right up to the walls of Jerusalem.

13 ¶ Now **in the fourteenth year of king Hezekiah did Sennacherib king of Assyria come up against all the fenced cities of Judah, and took them**.

Next, in verses 14–16, King Hezekiah offers to stop rebelling against the king of Assyria (see verse 7, above) and start paying tribute in order to avoid being attacked in Jerusalem.

14 **And Hezekiah king of Judah sent to the king of Assyria to Lachish** [*about fifteen miles southwest of Jerusalem*], saying, **I have offended; return from me** [*back off from attacking Jerusalem*]: **that which thou puttest on me will I bear** [*whatever tribute, ransom, you require, that will I pay*]. And **the king of Assyria appointed** [*demanded*] unto Hezekiah king of Judah **three hundred talents** [*NIV, "about 11 tons"*] **of silver and thirty talents** [*NIV, "about 1 ton"*] **of gold**.

15 And **Hezekiah gave** *him* **all the silver that was found in the house of the LORD** [*the temple at Jerusalem*], **and in the treasures of the king's house**.

16 At that time did **Hezekiah cut off** *the gold from* **the doors of the temple** of the LORD, **and** *from* **the pillars** which Hezekiah king of Judah had overlaid, and gave it to the king of Assyria.

Despite the tribute paid, the Assyrian king still sends his forces to attack Jerusalem. They will come up to Jerusalem and camp there just outside the city. In a shouting match back and forth between the Assyrian generals and King Hezekiah's people, the Assyrians will mock and do everything they can to demoralize Hezekiah and his people.

17 ¶ And **the king of Assyria sent Tartan and Rabsaris and Rab-shakeh from Lachish to king Hezekiah with a great host** [*army*] **against Jerusalem**. And **they** went up and **came to Jerusalem**. And when they were come up, they came and stood by the conduit of the upper pool, which *is* in the highway of the fuller's field.

Hezekiah sends three of his most trusted men to negotiate with the Assyrian generals.

18 And when they had called to the king, there came out to them **Eliakim** the son of Hilkiah, which *was* over the household, and **Shebna** the scribe, and **Joah** the son of Asaph the recorder.

19 And **Rab-shakeh** [*one of the Assyrian generals*] **said unto them, Speak ye now to Hezekiah, Thus saith** the great king, **the king of Assyria, What confidence *is* this wherein thou trustiest** [*on what are you basing your confidence against us; why should we not attack you*]?

20 Thou sayest, (but *they are but* vain words,) *I have* counsel and strength for the war. **Now on whom dost thou trust, that thou rebellest against me?**

You will see the answer to this question in verses 21 and 22. They are trusting in an alliance with Egypt and ultimately, they are trusting Jehovah to rescue them.

21 Now, behold, **thou trustest** upon the staff of this bruised reed, *even* **upon Egypt**, on which if a man lean, it will go into his hand, and pierce it [*a sarcastic statement that Egypt is so weak and powerless it is like a broom straw to lean on and it would just poke through your hand if you did lean on it*]: so *is* Pharaoh king of Egypt unto all that trust on him.

22 **But if ye say unto me, We trust in the LORD our God:** *is* not that he, whose **high places and whose altars Hezekiah hath taken away, and hath said to Judah and Jerusalem, Ye shall worship before this altar in Jerusalem** [*didn't your king, Hezekiah, destroy all your idols and gods on whom you could depend for protection and now all you have left is the God you worship at your temple in Jerusalem*]?

Next, the Assyrian general offers to give the Jews in Jerusalem two thousand horses for their men to ride, taunting them that even if they could find two thousand men to ride these horses into battle against the Assyrian forces, the least of his captains could defeat them.

23 Now therefore, I pray thee, **give pledges to** [*make a deal with*] **my lord the king of Assyria**, and **I will deliver thee two thousand horses, if thou be able on thy part to set riders upon them.**

24 **How then wilt thou turn away the face of one captain of the least of my master's servants**, and put thy trust on Egypt for chariots and for horsemen?

Next, the Assyrian general claims that the Jew's own god told the Assyrians to attack them.

25 Am I now come up without the LORD against this place to destroy it? **The LORD said to me, Go up against this land** [*Judah*]**, and destroy it.**

Hezekiah's three emissaries reply. They request that they use the Syrian language to talk back and forth because they don't want the Jewish citizens on the walls of Jerusalem to understand the embarrassing taunts and ridicule that the Assyrians are hurling at them.

26 **Then said Eliakim** the son of Hilkiah, and **Shebna, and Joah**, unto Rab-shakeh, **Speak**, I pray thee, to thy servants **in the Syrian language; for we understand** *it:* and **talk not with us in the Jews' language in the ears of the people that** *are* **on the wall.**

Of course, Rab-shakeh, the Assyrian general delights in ignoring their request and speaks more loudly and continues to talk in the Jewish language. He invites the Jews to ignore Hezekiah's counsel to depend on the Lord and surrender and eventually be carried captive to a foreign land where they will be well off.

27 **But Rab-shakeh said unto them, Hath my master sent me to thy master, and to thee, to speak these words?** *hath he* not *sent me* **to the men which sit on the wall**, that they may eat their own dung, and drink their own piss with you [*so they are aware of the horrible conditions they will soon face*]?

28 **Then Rab-shakeh stood and cried with a loud voice in the Jews' language**, and spake, saying, Hear the word of the great king, the king of Assyria:

29 **Thus saith the king, Let not Hezekiah deceive you: for he shall not be able to deliver you out of his hand**:

30 **Neither let Hezekiah make you trust in the LORD** [*Jehovah*], saying, The LORD will surely deliver us, and this city shall not be delivered into the hand of the king of Assyria.

31 **Hearken not to Hezekiah**: for **thus saith the king of Assyria** [*a mockery of "thus saith the LORD"*], **Make** *an agreement* [*a treaty*] **with me** by a present, and **come out to me** [*surrender*], and *then* eat ye every man of his own vine, and every one of his fig tree, and drink ye every one the waters of his cistern:

32 **Until I come and take you away to a land like your own land**, a land of corn and wine, a land of bread and vineyards, a land of oil olive and of honey, **that ye may live, and not die**: and **hearken not unto Hezekiah, when he persuadeth you, saying, The LORD will deliver us**.

33 **Hath any of the gods of the nations delivered at all his land out of the hand of the king of Assyria** [*have any of the idols, in other words, gods, of the surrounding cities we conquered on the way to Jerusalem, saved them*]?

34 Where *are* the gods of Hamath, and of Arpad? where *are* the gods of Sepharvaim, Hena, and Ivah? **have they delivered Samaria out of mine hand?**

35 **Who** *are* **they among all the gods of the countries, that have delivered their country out of mine hand, that the LORD should deliver Jerusalem out of mine hand** [*what makes you think that Jehovah can save you*]?

36 **But the people held their peace**, and **answered him not a word**: for the king's [*Hezekiah's*] commandment was, saying, Answer him not.

37 **Then came Eliakim** the son of Hilkiah, which *was* over the household, and **Shebna** the scribe, **and Joah** the son of Asaph the recorder, **to Hezekiah with** *their* **clothes rent, and told him the words of Rab-shakeh.**

2 KINGS 19

Selection: all verses

This is an exciting chapter. Watch now as righteous King Hezekiah seeks counsel and help from Isaiah, the prophet. Isaiah prophesies defeat for the Assyrians and the death of their king, Sennacherib. Hezekiah does what he can by praying fervently for the Lord's help.

1 AND it came to pass, **when king Hezekiah heard** *it,* **that he rent his clothes, and covered himself with sackcloth, and went into the house of the LORD.**

2 **And he sent Eliakim**, which *was* over the household, **and Shebna** the scribe, **and the elders of the priests**, covered with sackcloth, **to Isaiah the prophet** the son of Amoz.

3 And **they said unto him, Thus saith Hezekiah, This day** *is* **a day of trouble, and of rebuke, and blasphemy**: for the children are come to the birth, and *there is* not strength to bring forth [*we are doomed, like when a woman is in hard labor but the baby doesn't come*].

4 **It may be the LORD thy God will hear all the words of Rab-shakeh**, whom the king of Assyria his master hath sent to reproach the living God; **and will reprove the words which the LORD thy God hath heard**: wherefore **lift up** *thy* **prayer for the remnant that are left.**

5 **So the servants of king Hezekiah came to Isaiah.**

6 ¶ And **Isaiah said unto them, Thus shall ye say to your master, Thus saith the LORD, Be not afraid of the words which thou hast heard**, with which the servants of the king of Assyria have blasphemed me.

7 Behold, **I will send a blast upon him** [*I will change his frame of mind and make him nervous*]**, and he shall hear a rumour** [*he will hear bad news from home*]**, and shall return to his own land**; and **I will cause him to fall by the sword in his own land** [*he will be killed in his own land*].

8 ¶ **So Rab-shakeh returned, and found the king of Assyria warring against Libnah** [*southwest of Jerusalem*]: for he had heard that he was departed from Lachish.

NOTES

Next, the king of Assyria is worried about the approaching Egyptian armies and sends messengers to press Hezekiah for a quick surrender.

9 And **when he heard say of Tirhakah king of Ethiopia** [*the Egyptian army*], **Behold, he is come out to fight against thee: he sent messengers again unto Hezekiah, saying,**

10 Thus shall ye **speak to Hezekiah king of Judah, saying, Let not thy God in whom thou trustest deceive thee, saying, Jerusalem shall not be delivered into the hand of the king of Assyria.**

11 Behold, **thou hast heard what the kings of Assyria have done to all lands, by destroying them utterly: and shalt thou be delivered?**

12 **Have the gods of the nations delivered them** which my fathers have destroyed; *as* Gozan, and Haran, and Rezeph, and the children of Eden which *were* in Thelasar?

13 **Where *is* the king of Hamath,** and **the king of Arpad,** and the king of the city of **Sepharvaim, of Hena, and Ivah?** [*The gods of these cities did not save them.*]

14 ¶ And **Hezekiah received the letter** of the hand of the messengers, and read it: and Hezekiah **went up into the house of the LORD, and spread it before the LORD**.

15 And **Hezekiah prayed** before the LORD, and said, O LORD God of Israel, which dwellest *between* the cherubims [*carvings of cherubim on the lid of the Ark of the Covenant, where the Lord often came to commune with His people*], **thou art the God, *even* thou alone** [*Thou art the only true God*], of all the kingdoms of the earth: thou hast made heaven and earth.

16 **LORD, bow down thine ear, and hear: open, LORD, thine eyes, and see**: and hear **the words of Sennacherib,** which hath sent him to reproach the living God [*listen to what the Assyrian general said as he mocked Thee*].

17 **Of a truth, LORD, the kings of Assyria have destroyed the nations and their lands,**

18 And **have cast their gods into the fire: for they *were* no gods,** but the work of men's hands, wood and stone: therefore they have destroyed them.

19 Now **therefore, O LORD our God,** I beseech thee, **save thou us out of his hand,** that all the kingdoms of the earth may know that thou *art* the LORD God, *even* thou only.

20 ¶ **Then Isaiah** the son of Amoz **sent to Hezekiah, saying, Thus saith the LORD God of Israel, *That* which thou hast prayed to me against Sennacherib king of Assyria I have heard.**

Next, you will see three words and phrases for Jerusalem.

21 **This *is* the word that the LORD hath spoken concerning him** [*the king of Assyria*]; **The virgin the daughter of Zion** [*Jerusalem*] **hath despised thee,** *and* laughed thee to scorn; **the daughter of Jerusalem** hath shaken her head at thee.

22 **Whom hast thou reproached and blasphemed?** and against whom hast thou exalted [*raised your voice and shouted insults*] *thy* voice, and lifted up thine eyes on high? *even* **against the Holy *One* of Israel** [*Jehovah*].

Next, trees are often symbolic of people in biblical symbolism.

23 **By thy messengers thou hast reproached the Lord, and hast said** [*boasted*], With the multitude of my chariots I am come up to the height of the mountains, to the sides of Lebanon, and will cut down the tall cedar trees thereof, *and* the choice fir trees thereof: and I will enter into the lodgings of his borders, *and into* the forest of his Carmel.

24 **I have digged and drunk strange waters** [*I have conquered many foreign countries*], and with the sole of my feet have I dried up all the rivers of besieged places.

25 Hast thou not heard long ago *how* **I have done it,** *and* of ancient times that I have formed it? now have I brought it to pass, that thou shouldest be to lay waste fenced cities *into* ruinous heaps.

26 Therefore **their inhabitants were of small power,** they were dismayed and confounded; **they were *as* the grass of the field,** and *as* the green herb, *as* the grass on the housetops, and *as corn* blasted before it be grown up.

Next, the Lord replies to the boasting of the king of Assyria, above.

27 **But I** [*the Lord*] **know thy abode, and thy going out, and thy coming in** [*I know everything about you*], **and thy rage against me**.

28 Because thy rage against me and thy tumult is come up into mine ears, **therefore I will put my hook in thy nose, and my bridle in thy lips, and I will turn thee back by the way by which thou camest** [*I will stop you cold and send you back home*].

The topic now turns to Hezekiah and his people who have been extremely worried by the planned siege of the Assyrian armies against Jerusalem.

29 And **this *shall be* a sign unto thee, Ye shall eat this year such things as grow of themselves** [*because of the Assyrian siege, you have not been able to plant crops, but you will be all right this year because of the "volunteer" grain that will grow*], **and in the second year that which springeth of the same** [*volunteer grain will keep you in food okay*]; and **in the third year sow ye, and reap, and plant vineyards, and eat the fruits thereof** [*in the third year, you will be back to normal*].

30 And **the remnant that is escaped of the house of Judah shall yet again take root downward, and bear fruit upward** [*a remnant of Judah will flourish again*].

NOTES

31 **For out of Jerusalem shall go forth a remnant**, and they that escape out of mount Zion: **the zeal** [*power and watchful care*] **of the LORD** *of hosts* **shall do this**.

Verse 32, next, is an absolute, very specific prophecy about the Assyrian armies just outside the walls of Jerusalem!

32 Therefore thus saith the LORD concerning the king of Assyria, **He shall not come into this city, nor shoot an arrow there, nor come before it with shield, nor cast a bank** [*a dirt wall for purposes of laying siege*] **against it**.

33 By **the way that he came, by the same shall he return, and shall not come into this city, saith the LORD**.

34 **For I will defend this city**, to save it, for mine own sake, and for my servant David's sake.

The above prophecies were fulfilled in verses 35–37, next.

35 ¶ And it came to pass that night, that **the angel of the LORD went out, and smote in the camp of the Assyrians an hundred fourscore and five thousand** [*185,000*]: and when they arose early in the morning, behold, **they** *were* **all dead** corpses.

36 So **Sennacherib king of Assyria** departed, and went and **returned, and dwelt at Nineveh** [*his home city in Assyria*].

Verse 37, next took place about twenty years later.

37 And it came to pass, **as he was worshipping in the house of Nisroch his god**, that Adrammelech and Sharezer **his sons smote** [*killed*] **him with the sword**: and they escaped into the land of Armenia. And Esarhaddon his son reigned in his stead.

2 KINGS 20

Selection: all verses

This chapter appears to be out of order chronologically and probably takes place sometime before. In this chapter, you will see the sun come back up ten degrees as a sign to righteous King Hezekiah that the Lord will heal him and give him fifteen more years of life. Also, Isaiah will prophesy the future Babylonian captivity of the Jews. First, we see Hezekiah on his deathbed.

1 **IN those days was Hezekiah sick unto death**. And the prophet **Isaiah** the son of Amoz **came to him, and said** unto him, Thus saith the LORD, **Set thine house in order; for thou shalt die, and not live**.

2 Then **he turned his face to the wall, and prayed unto the LORD, saying**,

3 **I beseech thee, O LORD, remember now how I have walked before thee in truth and with a perfect heart, and have done** *that which is* **good in thy sight**. And **Hezekiah wept** sore.

4 And it came to pass, afore Isaiah was gone out into the middle court, that the word of the LORD came to him, saying,

There is a major message here; namely that when it is in harmony with the will of the Lord, the mighty prayers of the faithful can change the plan temporarily.

5 **Turn again, and tell Hezekiah** the captain of my people, Thus saith the LORD, the God of David thy father, **I have heard thy prayer, I have seen thy tears: behold, I will heal thee**: on the third day thou shalt go up unto the house of the LORD.

6 And **I will add unto thy days fifteen years**; and **I will deliver thee and this city out of the hand of the king of Assyria**; and I will defend this city for mine own sake, and for my servant David's sake.

Apparently, Hezekiah had a boil that was causing terrible pain at this time also, and Isaiah gave him a remedy.

7 And Isaiah said, **Take a lump of figs. And they took and laid** *it* on the boil, and **he recovered**.

Next, Hezekiah righteously asks for a sign that he won't die now, as indicated in verse 1.

8 ¶ And **Hezekiah said unto Isaiah, What** *shall be* the sign that the LORD will **heal me**, and that I shall go up into the house of the LORD the third day?

9 And **Isaiah said, This sign shalt thou have of the LORD**, that the LORD will do the thing that he hath spoken: **shall the shadow** [*on the sun dial*] **go forward ten degrees, or go back ten degrees?**

10 And **Hezekiah answered, It is a light thing** [*easy*] **for the shadow to go down ten degrees**: nay, **but let the shadow return backward ten degrees**.

11 And **Isaiah the prophet cried** [*earnestly prayed*] **unto the LORD**: and **he brought the shadow ten degrees backward**, by which it had gone down in the dial of Ahaz [*on the sundial that Hezekiah's father, Ahaz, had made*].

Next, in verses 12–13, Hezekiah makes a very unwise mistake. He shows the messengers of the son of the king of Babylon all of his treasures.

12 ¶ At that time Berodach-baladan, **the son of Baladan, king of Babylon, sent letters and a present unto Hezekiah**: for he had heard that Hezekiah had been sick.

13 And **Hezekiah** hearkened unto them, and **shewed them all the house of his precious things**, the silver, and the gold, and the spices, and the precious ointment, and *all* the house of his armour, and all that was found in his treasures: there was nothing in his house, nor in all his dominion, that Hezekiah shewed them not.

14 ¶ **Then came Isaiah the prophet unto king Hezekiah, and said** unto him, **What said these men? and from whence came they unto thee?** And **Hezekiah said, They are come from a far country**, *even* **from Babylon.**

NOTES

_____
_____
_____
_____
_____
_____
_____
_____
_____
_____
_____
_____
_____
_____
_____
_____
_____
_____
_____
_____
_____
_____
_____
_____
_____
_____
_____
_____
_____
_____
_____
_____
_____
_____
_____
_____
_____
_____

NOTES

_____
_____
_____
_____
_____
_____
_____
_____
_____
_____
_____
_____
_____
_____
_____
_____
_____
_____
_____
_____
_____
_____
_____
_____
_____
_____
_____
_____
_____
_____

15 And **he said, What have they seen in thine house?** And **Hezekiah answered, All** *the things* that *are* **in mine house** have they seen: there is nothing among my treasures that I have not shewed them.

16 And **Isaiah said unto Hezekiah, Hear the word of the LORD**.

Next, Isaiah prophesies of the future Babylonian captivity of the Jews. It will start a little before 600 B.C. and will be completed about 589 B.C. Lehi and his family will flee from Jerusalem in 600 B.C.

17 Behold, **the days come, that all that** *is* **in thine house**, and that which thy fathers have laid up in store unto this day, **shall be carried into Babylon: nothing shall be left, saith the LORD**.

18 And of **thy sons** that shall issue from thee, which thou shalt beget, **shall they take away; and they shall be eunuchs in the palace of the king of Babylon**.

19 **Then said Hezekiah unto Isaiah, Good** *is* **the word of the LORD** which thou hast spoken. And he said, *Is it* not *good,* if peace and truth be in my days?

Next, we see another book mentioned that is missing from the Bible.

20 ¶ And the rest of the acts of Hezekiah, and all his might, and how he made a pool, and a conduit, and brought water into the city [*Hezekiah's tunnel*], *are* they not written in **the book of the chronicles of the kings of Judah**?

21 And **Hezekiah slept with his fathers** [*died*]: and Manasseh his son reigned in his stead.

2 KINGS 21

Selection: all verses

In this chapter, we are introduced to righteous Hezekiah's wicked son, Manasseh who became king of Judah after the death of his father. He reminds us of King Noah in the Book of Mormon, who undid much of the good his father, Zeniff, did (see Mosiah 11). Manasseh was twelve years old when he became king.

1 **MANASSEH** *was* **twelve years old when he began to reign, and reigned fifty and five years in Jerusalem**. And his mother's name *was* Hephzi-bah.

2 And **he did** *that which was* **evil in the sight of the LORD**, after the abominations of the heathen, whom the LORD cast out before the children of Israel.

He promoted idol worship.

3 For **he built up again the high places** [*shrines and locations for idolatry*] **which Hezekiah his father had destroyed**; and he **reared up altars for Baal** [*a major false god*], **and made a grove** [*planted a grove of trees where temple prostitutes could serve patrons, especially those who were worshiping Baal*], **as did Ahab king of Israel**; and **worshipped all the host of heaven** [*the sun, moon, and stars*], and served them.

He blasphemed and desecrated the temple by putting altars in it for worshipping idols and false gods.

4 And **he built altars in the house of the LORD**, of which the LORD said, In Jerusalem will I put my name.

5 And **he built altars for all the host of heaven** [*for worshiping the sun, moon, and stars*] **in the two courts of the house of the LORD**.

He sacrificed one of his sons to a fire god.

6 And **he made his son pass through the fire**, and observed times, and used enchantments, and dealt with familiar spirits and wizards [*he promoted the occult among his people*]: **he wrought much wickedness** in the sight of the LORD, to provoke *him* to anger.

7 And **he set a graven image** of the grove that he had made **in the house** [*the temple*], of which the LORD said to David, and to Solomon his son, In this house, and in Jerusalem, which I have chosen out of all tribes of Israel, will I put my name for ever:

8 Neither will I make the feet of Israel move any more out of the land [*I will protect My people from being taken away captive to foreign countries*] which I gave their fathers; **only if they will observe to do according to all that I have commanded them**, and according to all the law that my servant Moses commanded them.

9 **But they hearkened not**: and **Manasseh seduced them to do more evil than did the nations whom the LORD destroyed before the children of Israel.**

Remember, Manasseh was king for fifty-five years.

10 ¶ And **the LORD spake by his servants the prophets, saying,**

11 **Because Manasseh king of Judah hath done these abominations, *and* hath done wickedly** above all that the Amorites did, which *were* before him, and hath made Judah also to sin with his idols:

12 **Therefore** thus saith the LORD God of Israel, Behold, **I *am* bringing *such* evil upon Jerusalem and Judah, that whosoever heareth of it, both his ears shall tingle.**

13 And I will stretch over Jerusalem the line [*"measuring tape"*] of Samaria, and the plummet [*plum line*] of the house of Ahab [*I will see how they measure up against other wicked people*]: and **I will wipe Jerusalem as *a man* wipeth a dish, wiping *it,* and turning *it* upside down.**

14 And **I will** forsake the remnant of mine inheritance, and **deliver them into the hand of their enemies**; and they shall become a prey and a spoil to all their enemies;

15 **Because they have done *that which was* evil in my sight, and have provoked me to anger**, since the day their fathers came forth out of Egypt, even unto this day.

NOTES

NOTES

16 Moreover **Manasseh shed innocent blood very much, till he had filled Jerusalem from one end to another**; beside his sin wherewith **he made Judah to sin**, in doing *that which was* evil in the sight of the LORD.

Next, we see the same missing book from the Bible as mentioned in chapter 20, verse 20.

17 ¶ Now the rest of the acts of Manasseh, and all that he did, and his sin that he sinned, *are* they not written in **the book of the chronicles of the kings of Judah?**

18 And **Manasseh slept with his fathers**, and was buried in the garden of his own house, in the garden of Uzza: and **Amon his son reigned in his stead.**

19 ¶ **Amon** *was* **twenty and two years old when he began to reign, and he reigned two years in Jerusalem**. And his mother's name *was* Meshullemeth, the daughter of Haruz of Jotbah.

20 And **he did** *that which was* **evil** in the sight of the LORD, as his father Manasseh did.

21 And **he walked in all the way that his father walked in, and served the idols that his father served, and worshipped them**:

22 And **he forsook the LORD** God of his fathers, **and walked not in the way of the LORD**.

23 ¶ **And the servants of Amon conspired against him, and slew the king in his own house**.

Next, in verses 24 and 26, we meet another king of Judah who was righteous; namely, Josiah. He can remind us of Limhi, in the Book of Mormon, who became king in place of his father, wicked King Noah (Mosiah 19:16).

24 And **the people of the land slew all them that had conspired against king Amon**; and **the people of the land made Josiah his son king in his stead.**

25 Now **the rest of the acts of Amon** which he did, *are* **they not written in the book of the chronicles of the kings of Judah?**

26 And he was buried in his sepulchre in the garden of Uzza: and **Josiah his son reigned in his stead.**

2 KINGS 22

Selection: all verses

Righteous King Josiah will help his people repent and turn back to God, in chapters 22–23. It shows us how important it is to have righteous leaders for a nation.

1 **JOSIAH** *was* **eight years old when he began to reign, and he reigned thirty and one years in Jerusalem**. And his mother's name *was* Jedidah, the daughter of Adaiah of Boscath.

2 And **he did** *that which was* **right in the sight of the LORD**, and walked in all the way of David his father [*ancestor*], and turned not aside to the right hand or to the left.

In the next verses, righteous king Josiah will determine to repair the temple in Jerusalem. We will watch as he allocates money for that purpose.

3 ¶ And it came to **pass in the eighteenth year of king Josiah**, *that* **the king sent Shaphan** the son of Azaliah, the son of Meshullam, the scribe, **to the house of the LORD** [*the temple*]**, saying,**

4 **Go up to Hilkiah the high priest, that he may sum** [*count*] **the silver** which is brought into the house of the LORD, which the keepers of the door have gathered of the people [*the offerings the people have given as they come to the temple to worship*]:

Next, he instructs that this money is to be given to workers who are to use it to pay those who repair the temple.

5 And **let them deliver it into the hand of the doers of the work**, that have the oversight of the house of the LORD: and let them give it to the doers of the work which *is* in the house of the LORD, **to repair the breaches of the house,**

6 Unto carpenters, and **builders**, and **masons**, and **to buy timber and hewn stone to repair the house**.

Verse 7, next, says, in effect, that there was no need for an accounting for the money given because they were all trustworthy men.

7 **Howbeit there was no reckoning made with them of the money** that was delivered into their hand, **because they dealt faithfully**.

Next, we suspect that, because of gross and widespread wickedness, the scriptures had long been lost. So, when a set of scriptures was found during the repair work on the temple (some Bible scholars think it was Deuteronomy, others think it was all five books of the Pentateuch—Genesis, Exodus, Leviticus, Numbers, and Deuteronomy), there was great rejoicing among Josiah and his close associates.

8 ¶ And **Hilkiah the high priest said unto Shaphan the scribe, I have found the book of the law in the house of the LORD. And Hilkiah gave the book to Shaphan, and he read it**.

9 **And Shaphan** the scribe **came to the king**, and brought the king word again, and said, Thy servants have gathered the money that was found in the house, and have delivered it into the hand of them that do the work, that have the oversight of the house of the LORD.

10 And **Shaphan the scribe shewed the king, saying, Hilkiah the priest hath delivered me a book. And Shaphan read it before the king.**

NOTES

NOTES

_____
_____
_____
_____
_____
_____
_____
_____
_____
_____
_____
_____
_____
_____
_____
_____
_____
_____
_____
_____
_____
_____
_____
_____
_____
_____
_____
_____
_____
_____
_____

11 And it came to pass, **when the king had heard the words of the book of the law**, that **he rent** [*tore*] **his clothes** [*a sign of deep concern and anguish in his culture*].

The tearing of his clothes on the part of the king, in verse 11, above, is quite likely because he realized more than ever the terrible apostasy among his people, especially under his father and grandfather's rule, that had led to the loss of the scriptures among them.

12 And **the king commanded** Hilkiah the priest, and Ahikam the son of Shaphan, and Achbor the son of Michaiah, and Shaphan the scribe, and Asahiah a servant of the king's, saying,

13 **Go ye, enquire of the LORD for me, and for the people, and for all Judah, concerning the words of this book that is found**: for **great** *is* **the wrath of the LORD that is kindled against us, because our fathers have not hearkened unto the words of this book**, to do according unto all that which is written concerning us.

Next, these leaders, under the direction of King Josiah, go to a woman named Huldah, who obviously had the gift of prophecy (one of the gifts of the Spirit—see D&C 46:22), to seek counsel from the Lord. (We know nothing else about her, other than these verses.)

14 **So Hilkiah** the priest, and **Ahikam**, and **Achbor**, and **Shaphan**, and **Asahiah**, **went unto Huldah the prophetess**, the wife of Shallum the son of Tikvah, the son of Harhas, keeper of the wardrobe; (now she dwelt in Jerusalem in the college [*a major section of Jerusalem*];) **and they communed with her**.

15 ¶ And **she said unto them, Thus saith the LORD God of Israel, Tell the man** [*King Josiah*] **that sent you to me**,

16 **Thus saith the LORD, Behold, I will bring evil upon this place, and upon the inhabitants thereof,** *even* all the words of the book which the king of Judah hath read:

17 **Because they have forsaken me**, and have burned incense unto other gods, that they might provoke me to anger with all the works of their hands; therefore my wrath shall be kindled against this place, and shall not be quenched.

18 **But to the king of Judah which sent you** to enquire of the LORD, thus shall **ye say to him**, Thus saith the LORD God of Israel, *As touching* the words which thou hast heard;

19 **Because thine heart was tender, and thou hast humbled thyself before the LORD**, when thou heardest what I spake against this place, and against the inhabitants thereof, that they should become a desolation and a curse, **and hast rent thy clothes, and wept before me; I also have heard** *thee,* **saith the LORD**.

20 Behold **therefore**, I will gather thee unto thy fathers, and **thou shalt be gathered into thy grave in peace; and thine eyes shall not see all the evil which I will bring upon this place**. And they brought the king word again.

2 KINGS 23

NOTES

Selection: all verses

In this chapter, we watch as King Josiah strives to influence his people to repent and return to the Lord. He reads the newly found book of scripture to them ("the book of the law" that was found in the temple during the renovation work—see 2 Kings 22:8). This could remind us of Alma 31:5, where Alma and his missionary companions determined to use the "preaching of the word" to reclaim the apostate Zoramites.

1 AND **the king** sent, and they **gathered unto him all the elders** of Judah and of Jerusalem.

2 And **the king went up into the house of the LORD** [*the temple*], and **all the men of Judah and all the inhabitants of Jerusalem with him**, and the priests, and the prophets, and all the people, both small and great: and **he read in their ears all the words of the book of the covenant** [*was called "the book of the law," in 2 Kings 22:8*] which was found in the house of the LORD.

3 ¶ And **the king** stood by a pillar, and **made a covenant before the LORD, to walk after the LORD, and to keep his commandments and his testimonies and his statutes with all** *their* **heart and all** *their* **soul**, to perform the words of this covenant that were written in this book. **And all the people stood to the covenant**.

Next, King Josiah commands that the idols and idol worship support materials be removed from the temple and destroyed.

4 And **the king commanded** Hilkiah the high priest, and the priests of the second order [*the next rank*], and the keepers of the door, **to bring forth out of the temple of the LORD all the vessels that were made for Baal, and for the grove, and for all the host of heaven** [*materials for worshiping the sun, moon, and stars*]: **and he burned them without** [*outside of*] **Jerusalem** in the fields of Kidron, and carried the ashes of them unto Beth-el.

5 And **he put down the idolatrous priests**, whom the kings of Judah had ordained to burn incense in the high places in the cities of Judah, and in the places round about Jerusalem; them also that burned incense unto Baal, to the sun, and to the moon, and to the planets, and to all the host of heaven.

6 And **he brought out the grove** [*a shrine used for worshiping Asherah, a fertility goddess—see 2 Kings 23:6, footnote 6a in your Bible*] **from the house of the LORD**, without [*outside of*] Jerusalem, unto the brook Kidron, **and burned it** at the brook Kidron, and stamped *it* small to powder, and cast the powder thereof upon the graves of the children of the people.

7 And **he brake down the houses of the sodomites** [*NIV, "male shrine prostitutes"*], that *were* by the house of the LORD [*that were by the Jerusalem Temple*], where the women wove hangings for the grove.

8 And **he brought all the priests** [*false priests*] **out of the cities of Judah, and defiled** [*destroyed*] **the high places where the priests had burned incense** [*as part of idol worship*], **from Geba** [*about ten miles northeast of Jerusalem*] **to Beer-sheba** [*in the*

NOTES

_____
_____
_____
_____
_____
_____
_____
_____
_____
_____
_____
_____
_____
_____
_____
_____
_____
_____
_____
_____
_____
_____
_____
_____
_____
_____
_____
_____
_____
_____
_____
_____
_____
_____

far southern part of Judah], **and brake down the high places** of the gates that *were* in the entering in of the gate of Joshua the governor of the city, which *were* on a man's left hand at the gate of the city.

9 Nevertheless the [*apostate*] priests of the high places came not up to the altar of the LORD in Jerusalem [*they had not been serving at the altar in Jerusalem*], but **they did eat of the unleavened bread among their brethren** [*they were still associating with other priests (likewise leading the Jews to participate in idol worship)*].

10 And **he defiled** [*destroyed*] **Topheth** [*a spot in a valley south of Jerusalem where human sacrifices, including children, were offered to the fire god, Molech—see Bible Dictionary under "Topeth"*], which *is* in the valley of the children of Hinnom, **that no man might make his son or his daughter to pass through the fire to Molech** [*so that no one could sacrifice their children to the fire god, Molech*].

11 And **he took away the horses that the kings of Judah had given to the sun** [*sun worship*], at the entering in of the house of the LORD [*near the temple*], by the chamber of Nathan-melech the chamberlain, which *was* in the suburbs, **and burned the chariots of the sun with fire.**

12 And **the altars that** *were* **on the top of the upper chamber of Ahaz, which the kings of Judah had made, and the altars which Manasseh had made** in the two courts of the house of the LORD, **did the king beat down**, and brake *them* down from thence, and cast the dust of them into the brook Kidron.

> Next, we are reminded that King Solomon was led by his many foreign-born wives to support them in their heathen idol worship and to become involved in idol worship himself—see 1 Kings 11:3–8.

13 And **the high places** [*shrines for idol worship*] **that** *were* **before Jerusalem** [*NIV, "east of Jerusalem"*], which *were* on the right hand of the mount of corruption, **which Solomon the king of Israel had builded for Ashtoreth** [*a fertility goddess*] the abomination of the Zidonians, **and for Chemosh** the abomination [*false god*] of the Moabites, **and for Milcom** the abomination of the children of Ammon, did the king defile.

14 And **he brake in pieces the images, and cut down the groves**, and filled their places with the bones of men.

15 ¶ **Moreover the altar that** *was* **at Beth-el,** *and* **the high place** which Jeroboam the son of Nebat, who made Israel to sin, had made, both that altar and the high place **he brake down, and burned the high place,** *and* **stamped** *it* **small to powder, and burned the grove**.

16 And as Josiah turned himself, **he spied the sepulchres that** *were* **there in the mount, and sent, and took the bones out of the sepulchres, and burned** *them* **upon the altar** [*an altar for worshiping one of the idols*], **and polluted it** [*made it so that the superstitious idol worshipers would not want to use it and the ground around it for idolatry any more*], according to the word of the LORD which the man of God proclaimed, who proclaimed these words.

NOTES

In verses 7–8, next, we are told of an unknown prophet whose bones Josiah did not allow to be disturbed.

17 Then he said, What title *is* that that I see? And the men of the city told him, **It is the sepulchre of the man of God**, which came from Judah, and proclaimed these things that thou hast done against the altar of Beth-el.

18 And **he said, Let him alone; let no man move his bones**. So they let his bones alone, with the bones of **the prophet that came out of Samaria**.

19 And **all the houses also of the high places that** *were* **in the cities of Samaria**, which the kings of Israel had made to provoke *the LORD* to anger, **Josiah took away, and did to them according to all the acts that he had done in Beth-e**l.

20 And **he slew all the priests of the high places that** *were* **there upon the altars, and burned men's bones upon them**, and returned to Jerusalem.

21 ¶ And **the king commanded all the people, saying, Keep the passover** unto the LORD your God, as *it is* written in the book of this covenant.

This was an amazing Passover!

22 **Surely there was not** holden **such a passover** from the days of the judges that judged Israel, nor in all the days of the kings of Israel, nor of the kings of Judah;

23 **But in the eighteenth year of king Josiah,** *wherein* **this passover was holden to the LORD in Jerusalem**.

Next, Josiah does away with the occult among his people.

24 ¶ Moreover **the** *workers with* **familiar spirits** [*seances*]**, and the wizards**, and the images, and the idols, and all the abominations that were spied in the land of Judah and in Jerusalem, **did Josiah put away**, that he might perform the words of the law which were written in the book that Hilkiah the priest found in the house of the LORD.

In verse 25, next, we are told that King Josiah was indeed a truly righteous man and king. This tribute to him would be a worthy goal for any of us who strive to stay on the covenant path.

25 And **like unto him was there no king before** him, that **turned to the LORD with all his heart, and with all his soul, and with all his might**, according to all the law of Moses; neither after him arose there *any* like him.

In spite of all the purging and cleansing of idol worship and its accompanying wickedness, we know from experience that external force does not usually lead to internal conversion. We see this in verses 26–27, next, where the Lord indicates that the people were still wicked in their minds and hearts.

26 ¶ **Notwithstanding** [*in spite of all the reforms that King Josiah commanded and carried out*] **the LORD turned not from the fierceness of his great wrath**, wherewith his

NOTES

anger was kindled **against Judah**, because of all the provocations [*wickedness*] that Manasseh [*Josiah's grandfather*] had provoked him withal.

27 And **the LORD said, I will remove Judah** [*the coming Babylonian captivity, which will come in various waves of Babylonian armies, starting in about 605 B.C. and finishing in 587 B.C*] also out of my sight, **as I have removed Israel** [*the Assyrian captivity, about 722–721 B.C.*], and will cast off this city Jerusalem which I have chosen, and the house of which I said, My name shall be there.

Next, another reference to this book of scripture that is missing from the Bible.

28 Now the rest of the acts of Josiah, and all that he did, *are* they not written in **the book of the chronicles of the kings of Judah?**

Next, in verses 29–30, Josiah brings his military forces against the Egyptian armies who have come north to fight Assyrian forces. King Josiah is killed.

29 ¶ **In his days** [*in Josiah's day*] **Pharaoh-nechoh king of Egypt went up against the king of Assyria** to the river Euphrates: and **king Josiah went against him**; and he [*the king of Egypt*] slew him [*King Josiah*] at Megiddo [*Near Mt. Carmel, about forty miles northwest of Jerusalem*], when he had seen him.

30 **And his** [*King Josiah*] **servants** carried him in a chariot dead from Megiddo, and **brought him to Jerusalem, and buried him in his own sepulchre**. And the people of the land took Jehoahaz the son of Josiah, and anointed him, and made him king in his father's stead.

Another wicked king takes over.

31 ¶ **Jehoahaz** *was* twenty and three years old when he began to reign; and he **reigned three months in Jerusalem**. And his mother's name *was* Hamutal, the daughter of Jeremiah of Libnah.

32 And **he did** *that which was* **evil in the sight of the LORD**, according to all that his fathers had done.

33 And **Pharaoh-nechoh** [*king of Egypt*] **put him in bands** at Riblah in the land of Hamath, **that he might not reign in Jerusalem**; and **put the land to a tribute of an hundred talents of silver** [*NIV, "about 3¾ tons"*]**, and a talent of gold** [*NIV, "about 75 pounds"*].

34 And **Pharaoh-nechoh made Eliakim the son of Josiah king** in the room of [*in place of*] Josiah his father, **and turned** [*changed*] **his name to Jehoiakim**, and took Jehoahaz away: and he came to Egypt, and died there.

35 And **Jehoiakim gave the silver and the gold to Pharaoh; but he taxed the land to give the money** according to the commandment of Pharaoh: he exacted the silver and the gold of the people of the land, of every one according to his taxation, to give *it* unto Pharaoh-nechoh.

NOTES

36 ¶ **Jehoiakim** *was* **twenty and five years old when he began to reign; and he reigned eleven years in Jerusalem**. And his mother's name *was* Zebudah, the daughter of Pedaiah of Rumah.

37 And **he did** *that which was* **evil in the sight of the LORD**, according to all that his fathers had done.

Chapters 24–25, next, contain the account of the fall and Babylonian captivity of the Jews in the Jerusalem area. Remember that Lehi and his family fled Jerusalem during this period in history, in 600 B.C.

2 KINGS 24

Selection: all verses

In this chapter, the Babylonians attack Jerusalem and carry away captives to Babylon. This takes place in three waves or attacks over several years. Daniel was taken in the first wave, about 605 B.C., and served in the court of King Nebuchadnezzar. Ezekiel was taken in the second wave, about 601–597 B.C., along with about 10,000 of the more important and capable citizens of Judah, and served among the Jewish captives along the river Chebar in Babylon. The third and final wave came about 587 B.C., in which wicked King Zedekiah, king of Judah, was taken captive. We will read about him in this chapter and in chapter 25. Jeremiah was one of the Lord's prophets in Jerusalem at the time Lehi and his family fled the Jerusalem area in 600 B.C.

Verses 1–4 are a summary leading up to verse 5. At this time, Jehoiakim, king of Judah, was paying tribute to Egypt for protection against the Babylonians.

1 **IN his** [*Jehoiakim's*] **days Nebuchadnezzar king of Babylon came up, and Jehoiakim became his servant three years: then he turned and rebelled against him.**

2 And **the LORD sent against him bands of the Chaldees**, and bands of the **Syrians**, and bands of the **Moabites**, and bands of the **children of Ammon** [*Ammonites*], and sent them **against Judah to destroy it, according to the word of the LORD, which he spake by his servants the prophets.**

3 Surely at the commandment of the LORD came *this* upon Judah, to remove *them* out of his sight, **for the sins of Manasseh**, according to all that he did;

4 And also **for the innocent blood that he shed: for he filled Jerusalem with innocent blood; which the LORD would not pardon.**

5 ¶ Now the rest of the acts of Jehoiakim, and all that he did, *are* they not written **in the book of the chronicles of the kings of Judah?**

Next, Jehoiakim dies and is replaced by his son, Jehoiachin, who rules as king only three months (verse 8).

6 So **Jehoiakim slept with his fathers** [*died*]: **and Jehoiachin his son reigned in his stead.**

7 And **the king of Egypt came not again any more out of his land:** for **the king of Babylon had taken** from the river of Egypt unto the river Euphrates **all that pertained to the king of Egypt.**

8 ¶ **Jehoiachin** *was* **eighteen years old when he began to reign**, and he **reigned in Jerusalem three months**. And his mother's name *was* Nehushta, the daughter of Elnathan of Jerusalem.

9 And **he did** *that which was* **evil** in the sight of the LORD, according to all that his father had done.

10 ¶ At that time **the servants of Nebuchadnezzar king of Babylon came up against Jerusalem**, and the city was besieged [*surrounded and cut it off from outside support*].

11 And Nebuchadnezzar king of Babylon came against the city, and **his servants** [*armies*] **did besiege it**.

12 And **Jehoiachin the king of Judah** [*the wicked, eighteen–year-old king of Judah in Jerusalem who lasted only three months before he was captured by Nebuchadnezzar and taken to Babylon and replaced by his uncle, Zedekiah, who was twenty-one years old and treated the Prophet Jeremiah with disrespect and cruelty*] went out to the king of Babylon, **he, and his mother, and his servants, and his princes, and his officers**: and the **king of Babylon took him** [*Jehoiachin*] **in the eighth year of his** [*Nebuchadnezzar's*] **reign**.

13 **And he** [*the King of Babylon*] **carried out thence** [*from there*] **all the treasures of the house of the Lord** [*the temple in Jerusalem*], **and the treasures of the king's house**, and cut in pieces all the vessels of gold which Solomon king of Israel had made in the temple of the Lord, as the Lord had said.

> Next, in verses 14–16, we are told that Nebuchadnezzar also took the most capable and educated Jews, including skilled craftsmen, metal workers, and the like captive back to Babylon. It is likely that this group included young Ezekiel. Daniel, also relatively young, had been taken captive in an earlier wave of Jewish exiles to Babylon.

14 **And he** [*the King of Babylon*] **carried away all Jerusalem** [*not "all"; rather, all the best, most highly skilled and educated*], and **all the princes, and all the mighty men of valour, even ten thousand captives, and all the craftsmen and smiths**: none remained, **save** [*except*] **the poorest sort of the people of the land**.

15 And **he carried away Jehoiachin** [*the young King of Judah spoken of in verse 12*] **to Babylon, and the king's mother, and the king's wives, and his officers, and the mighty of the land**, those carried he into captivity from Jerusalem to Babylon.

16 And all **the men of might**, even seven thousand, **and craftsmen and smiths** a thousand, **all that were strong and apt for war, even them the king of Babylon brought captive to Babylon**.

17 ¶ And **the king of Babylon made Mattaniah** his father's brother **king in his stead** [*in place of Jehoiachin*], and **changed his name to Zedekiah**.

18 **Zedekiah was twenty and one years old when he began to reign**, and **he reigned eleven years in Jerusalem** [*he was king of Judah in Jerusalem when Lehi and*

his family fled the Jerusalem area in 600 B.C.]. And his mother's name was Hamutal, the daughter of Jeremiah of Libnah.

19 And **he did** *that which was* **evil** in the sight of the LORD, according to all that Jehoiakim had done.

20 For through the anger of the LORD it came to pass in Jerusalem and Judah, until he had cast them out from his presence, that **Zedekiah rebelled against the king of Babylon**.

2 KINGS 25

Selection: all verses

In this chapter, you will see the last wave of Babylonian armies finalize the conquest of Jerusalem, including the capture of King Zedekiah and his sons. He will be forced to watch as his sons are killed, and then his eyes will be put out. He will be taken as a trophy to Babylon. By the way, the Book of Mormon informs us that one of his sons was not killed. He somehow got away and was brought to the Americas. His name was Mulek (Mosiah 25:2; Helaman 6:10, 8:21.)

1 AND it came to pass **in the ninth year of his reign** [*Zedekiah's rule as king of Judah*], in the tenth month, in the tenth *day* of the month, *that* **Nebuchadnezzar king of Babylon came, he, and all his host, against Jerusalem**, and pitched against it; and they built forts against it round about.

2 And **the city was besieged** unto the eleventh year of king Zedekiah.

3 And on the ninth *day* of the *fourth* month the **famine prevailed** in the city, and there was **no bread for the people of the land**.

Next, Zedekiah, along with others, attempts to escape Jerusalem by night.

4 ¶ And the city was broken up, and all the men of war *fled* by night by the way of the gate between two walls, which *is* by the king's garden: (now the Chaldees *were* against the city round about:) and *the king* **went the way toward the plain** [*toward Jericho*].

5 **And the army of the Chaldees** [*another name for Babylonians*] **pursued after the king, and overtook him in the plains of Jericho**: and all his army were scattered from him.

6 **So they took the king, and brought him up to the king of Babylon to Riblah** [*way up north by Syria*]; and they gave judgment upon him.

7 And **they slew the sons of Zedekiah before his eyes**, and **put out the eyes of Zedekiah**, and **bound him with fetters of brass, and carried him to Babylon**.

8 ¶ And **in the fifth month, on the seventh** *day* of the month, which *is* **the nineteenth year of king Nebuchadnezzar** king of Babylon, **came Nebuzar-adan**, captain of the guard, a servant of the king of Babylon, **unto Jerusalem**:

NOTES

_____
_____
_____
_____
_____
_____
_____
_____
_____
_____
_____
_____
_____
_____
_____
_____
_____
_____
_____
_____
_____
_____
_____
_____
_____
_____
_____
_____

9 And **he burnt the house of the LORD** [*the temple*], and **the king's house** [*the palace*], and **all the houses of Jerusalem**, and **every great** *man's* **house** burnt he with fire.

10 And all **the army of the Chaldees** [*Babylonians*], that *were with* the captain of the guard, **brake down the walls of Jerusalem** round about.

11 Now **the rest of the people** *that were* **left in the city, and the fugitives** that fell away to the king of Babylon, with the remnant of the multitude, **did Nebuzar-adan the captain of the guard carry away.**

Next, in verse 12, we see that not all the citizens of Judah were carried away to Babylon. The poorer citizens were intentionally left behind.

12 But **the captain of the guard left of the poor of the land** *to be* **vinedressers and husbandmen** [*to work in the vineyards and in the fields*].

The temple was ransacked.

13 And **the pillars of brass that** *were* **in the house of the LORD**, and **the bases**, and the **brasen sea** [*the brass font—7½ feet high, 15 feet in diameter, placed on the backs of twelve oxen, about a hand's width thick—see 1 Kings 7:23–26—which was used for baptisms for the living according to Bruce R. McConkie in* Mormon Doctrine, *pages 103–4*] that *was* in the house of the LORD, **did the Chaldees break in pieces, and carried the brass of them to Babylon.**

14 **And the pots, and the shovels, and the snuffers, and the spoons, and all the vessels of brass wherewith they ministered, took they away.**

15 And **the firepans, and the bowls,** *and* such things as *were* **of gold,** *in* gold, **and of silver,** *in* silver, **the captain of the guard took away.**

16 The two pillars, one sea, and the bases which Solomon had made for the house of the LORD; **the brass of all these vessels was without weight** [*was more than they could weigh*].

17 The **height of the one pillar** *was* **eighteen cubits** [*27 feet—remember, a cubit was about 18 inches*], **and the chapiter** [*the bronze decoration on top of each pillar*] upon it *was* **brass**: and the height of the chapiter three cubits; and the wreathen work, and pomegranates upon the chapiter round about, all of brass: and like unto these had the second pillar with wreathen work.

18 ¶ And **the captain of the guard took** [*as prisoners*] **Seraiah the chief priest**, and **Zephaniah** the second priest, **and the three keepers of the door**:

Next, in verses 19–21, several important men of the Jews will be taken to where the King of Babylon was staying temporarily in Syria and will be executed by his orders.

19 And **out of the city he took** an officer that was set over the men of war, and five men of them that were in the king's presence, which were found in the city, and the

principal scribe of the host, which mustered the people of the land, and threescore men of the people of the land *that were* found in the city:

20 And Nebuzar-adan captain of the guard took these, **and brought them to the king of Babylon to Riblah**:

21 And **the king of Babylon smote them, and slew them at Riblah** in the land of Hamath. So Judah was carried away out of their land.

> In verses 22–26, we see that King Nebuchadnezzar of Babylon set up a puppet ruler over those who were left in Judah in Palestine. However, he is assassinated in a mutiny, and those responsible flee to Egypt for protection. (As you can see, these are very brief summaries of events that took a long time to play out.)

22 ¶ And *as for* **the people that remained in the land of Judah**, whom Nebuchadnezzar king of Babylon had left, even over them **he made Gedaliah** the son of Ahikam, the son of Shaphan, **ruler**.

23 And **when all the captains of the armies, they and their men, heard that the king of Babylon had made Gedaliah governor, there came to Gedaliah** to Mizpah, even **Ishmael** the son of Nethaniah, **and Johanan** the son of Careah, **and Seraiah** the son of Tanhumeth the Netophathite, **and Jaazaniah** the son of a Maachathite, **they and their men**.

24 And **Gedaliah sware to** [*promised*] **them**, and to their men, and said unto them, **Fear not to be the servants of the Chaldees** [*the Babylonians*]: **dwell in the land, and serve the king of Babylon; and it shall be well with you**.

25 **But** it came to pass **in the seventh month**, that **Ishmael** the son of Nethaniah, the son of Elishama, **of the seed royal, came, and ten men with him, and smote Gedaliah, that he died, and the Jews and the Chaldees that were with him at Mizpah** [*about ten miles north and a bit west of Jerusalem*].

26 And **all the people, both small and great, and the captains of the armies, arose, and came to Egypt**: for they were afraid of the Chaldees.

> Next, a new king in Babylon releases Jehoiachin, a former king of Judah, from his prison in Babylon and allows him to live in comfort for the rest of his life in Babylon after thirty-seven years in prison.

27 ¶ And it came to pass in the seven and thirtieth year of the captivity of Jehoiachin king of Judah, in the twelfth month, on the seven and twentieth *day* of the month, *that* **Evil-merodach king of Babylon** in the year that he began to reign **did lift up the head of Jehoiachin king of Judah out of prison**;

28 And **he spake kindly to him**, and **set his throne above the throne of the kings** [*other captive kings*] **that** *were* **with him in Babylon**;

29 And **changed his prison garments**: and **he did eat bread continually before him** [*he ate at the king's table*] **all the days of his life**.

NOTES

30 And **his allowance** *was* **a continual allowance given him of the king, a daily rate for every day, all the days of his life**.

2 CHRONICLES

The books of First and Second Chronicles summarize from the creation down to the return of the Jews to Jerusalem after the proclamation of Cyrus the Persian giving permission for their return, in 538 B.C. Many genealogies are included. The two books of Chronicles repeat much of what is recorded in the books of Samuel as well as the books of Kings.

As you have no doubt noticed, righteous kings cause much good and wicked kings cause much damage and evil as their people follow their example. We will take time to look at King Hezekiah, of Judah, who is an example of a good king. Before his reign, the temple in Jerusalem had come into terrible neglect. He cleaned it up and restored its proper use.

2 CHRONICLES 29

Selection: verses 1–11

Hezekiah's father, Ahaz, left a legacy of wickedness, but Hezekiah determined to serve the Lord and not follow the evil example of his father. As you know, this is very rare.

1 **HEZEKIAH began to reign when he was five and twenty years old**, and he reigned nine and twenty years in Jerusalem. And his mother's name was Abijah, the daughter of Zechariah.

2 And **he did that which was right in the sight of the LORD**, according to all that David his father had done.

> We suspect that the last phrase of verse 2, above, refers to the first part of David's life, where he lived righteously.

3 ¶ **He** in the first year of his reign, in the first month, **opened the doors of the house of the LORD** [*the temple*], **and repaired them**.

4 And **he brought in the priests and the Levites, and gathered them together** into the east street,

5 And said unto them, Hear me, ye Levites, **sanctify now yourselves, and sanctify the house of the LORD God of your fathers, and carry forth the filthiness out of the holy place**.

6 **For our fathers have trespassed, and done that which was evil in the eyes of the LORD** our God, and have forsaken him, and have turned away their faces from the habitation of the LORD, and turned their backs.

7 Also they have shut up the doors of the porch, and put out the lamps, and have not burned incense nor offered burnt offerings in the holy place unto the God of Israel.

8 Wherefore the wrath of the LORD was upon Judah and Jerusalem, and he hath delivered them to trouble, to astonishment, and to hissing, as ye see with your eyes.

NOTES

9 For, lo, our fathers have fallen by the sword, and our sons and our daughters and our wives are in captivity for this.

10 **Now it is in mine heart to make a covenant with the LORD God of Israel, that his fierce wrath may turn away from us.**

11 My sons, be not now negligent: for the LORD hath chosen you to stand before him, to serve him, and that ye should minister unto him, and burn incense [*start up proper worship again*].

2 CHRONICLES 30

Selection: verses 26–27

The return of righteousness and respect to the temple during King Hezekiah's reign brought happiness to the people.

26 So **there was great joy in Jerusalem**: for since the time of Solomon the son of David king of Israel *there was* not the like in Jerusalem.

27 ¶ Then the priests the Levites arose and blessed the people: and their voice was heard, and their prayer came *up* to his holy dwelling place, *even* unto heaven.

NOTE: Isaiah was the prophet during Hezekiah's reign. At one point, righteous King Hezekiah was sick and was on his deathbed. We will quote from Isaiah to see what happened.

Isaiah 38:1–22

1 **In those days** [*about 705–703 BC*] **was Hezekiah sick unto death.** And **Isaiah** the prophet the son of Amoz **came unto him, and said** unto him, Thus saith the LORD, **Set thine house in order** [*get ready*]: **for thou shalt die, and not live.**

2 **Then Hezekiah** turned his face toward the wall, and **prayed unto the LORD,**

3 And said, **Remember** now, O LORD, I beseech thee, **how I have walked before thee in truth and with a perfect heart, and have done that which is good** in thy sight [*in other words, I have lived a good life*]. And Hezekiah wept sore [*bitterly*].

4 **Then came the word of the LORD to Isaiah, saying,**

5 **Go, and say to Hezekiah**, Thus saith the LORD, the God of David thy father [*ancestor*], **I have heard thy prayer, I have seen thy tears: behold, I will add unto thy days fifteen years** [*I will add fifteen years to your life*].

Major Message

When they are in harmony with the will of the Lord, the mighty prayers of the faithful can change the Lord's plan temporarily.

6 And **I will deliver thee and this city out of the hand of the king of Assyria**: and I will defend this city [*this would seem to place Hezekiah's illness sometime during the Assyrian threats to Jerusalem as described in chapters 36 and 37*].

7 And this **shall be a sign unto thee** from the LORD, that the LORD will do this thing that he hath spoken;

8 Behold, **I will bring again the shadow of the degrees** [*the shadow on the sundial*], which is gone down in the sun dial of Ahaz, **ten degrees backward**. So the sun returned ten degrees, by which degrees it was gone down [*the sun came back up ten degrees; in other words, time was turned backward*].

9 [*Hezekiah is healed and gives thanks and praise to the Lord for his miraculous recovery.*] **The writing** [*psalm*] **of Hezekiah** king of Judah, **when he had been sick, and was recovered** of his sickness [*after he had been sick and had recovered*]:

Righteous King Hezekiah now tells us what he said, expressing the thoughts of his heart when he was blessed with another fifteen years of life by the Lord.

First, he tells us what was going through his mind when he knew he was going to die.

10 **I** [*Hezekiah*] **said** in the cutting off of my days [*when I was on my deathbed*], I shall go to the gates of the grave [*I am doomed*]: I am deprived of the residue [*remainder*] of my years [*I am too young to die*].

11 I said, I shall not see the LORD, even the LORD, in the land of the living [*I am about to leave this mortal life*]: I shall behold man no more with the inhabitants of the world [*I won't be around anymore to associate with my fellow men*].

12 Mine age is departed [*German Bible: my time is up*], and is removed from me as a shepherd's tent [*they are taking down my tent*]: I have [*Thou hast*] cut off like a weaver my life [*Thou hast "clipped my threads" as a weaver does when the rug is finished*]: he will cut me off with pining sickness [*fatal illness is how the Lord is sending me out of this life*]: from day even to night wilt thou make an end of me [*I will die very shortly*].

13 I reckoned till morning [*German Bible: I thought, "If I could just live until morning!"*], that, as a lion, so will he break all my bones [*I can't stop the Lord if he wants me to die anymore than I could stop a lion*]: from day even to night wilt thou make an end of me [*my time is short*].

14 Like a crane or a swallow, so did I chatter [*German Bible: whimper*]: I did mourn as a dove: mine eyes fail with looking upward [*falter as I look up to heaven*]: O LORD, I am oppressed [*German Bible: suffering*]; undertake [*German: sooth, moderate my condition*] for me [*be Thou my help, security*].

Next, Hezekiah tells us how he felt when he found out he was not going to die.

15 What shall I say [*how can I express my gratitude*]? he hath both spoken unto me, and himself hath done it [*JST: "healed me"*]: I shall go softly [*German Bible: in humility*] all my years [*JST: "that I may not walk"*] in the bitterness of my soul.

16 O Lord, by these things men live, and in all these things is the life of my spirit [*JST: "thou who art the life of my spirit, in whom I live"*]: so wilt thou recover [*heal*] me, and make me to live [*JST: "and in all these things I will praise thee"*].

17 Behold, for peace I had great bitterness [*JST: "Behold, I had great bitterness instead of peace"*]: but thou hast in love to my soul delivered it [*JST: "saved me"*] from the pit of corruption [*from rotting in the grave*]: for thou hast cast all my sins behind thy back [*the effect of the Atonement*].

18 For the grave cannot praise [*German Bible: Hell does not praise*] thee, death can not celebrate thee: they [*people in spirit prison*] that go down into the pit [*hell; see Isaiah 14:15*] cannot hope for thy truth [*see Alma 34:32–34*].

19 The living, the living, he shall praise thee, as I do this day [*I am very happy to still be alive*]: the father to the children shall make known thy truth [*I will testify to my family and others of Thy kindness to me*].

20 The LORD was ready to save me: therefore we [*I and my family*] will sing my songs to the stringed instruments [*we will put my words of praise to music*] all the days of our life in the house of the LORD.

Next, Hezekiah refers to something Isaiah instructed him to do in order to be healed.

21 **For Isaiah had said, Let them take a lump of figs, and lay it for a plaister** [*plaster*] **upon the boil, and he shall recover** [*perhaps the lump of figs served the same purpose as the lump of clay to heal the blind man in John 9:6–7, i.e., faith obedience*].

22 Hezekiah also had said, What is the sign that I shall go up to the house of the LORD? [*This verse fits after verse 6—see 2 Kings 20:8.*]

NOTES

Ezra 1; 3–7; Nehemiah 2; 4–6; 8

"I Am Doing a Great Work"

About 130 years after the ten tribes were carried away captive by the Assyrians in about 722–721 BC, the Southern Kingdom, headquartered in Jerusalem, which consisted of the tribe of Judah (the Jews) and part of the tribe of Benjamin, were conquered by invaders from Babylon and carried away captive into Babylon. This took place in various waves, with the final group of captives taken to Babylon about 587 BC. After 70 years of Babylonian captivity, Cyrus, king of Persia (who by now had conquered Babylon) was inspired to let the Jews return to Jerusalem and rebuild Jerusalem and their temple. You will read about this in the Come, Follow Me reading block for this week. Watch as the Samaritans volunteer to help these Jews but are rejected by them and, consequently, harass them to the point that the work is stopped for a time. Also, as you read and study, pay attention to the value of having written copies of the scriptures.

NOTES

EZRA AND NEHEMIAH

These two books fit into the Old Testament chronology after the Jews who were taken captive to Babylon (605–587 B.C.) were released to return to Jerusalem (about 538 B.C.). They tell the story of Israel from the time of their return, when they began to rebuild Jerusalem and the temple, to the end of Nehemiah's second term as governor of Judah, about 400 B.C.

In these books you will find a remarkable effort to return to the laws of Moses and a strong reformation in the people's lives. Pay special attention to Nehemiah 8:5–18, where Ezra reads the book containing the laws of God, and the people listen to it day after day for many days.

EZRA 1

Selection: all verses

King Cyrus of Persia successfully conquered Babylon, including the huge city of Babylon, in about 539–538 B.C. One of his first decrees was to allow the Jews to return to Jerusalem and the surrounding area if they wanted to. He even returned the things that had been looted from the temple by the Babylonian armies under King Nebuchadnezzar.

1 NOW **in the first year of Cyrus king of Persia**, that the word of the LORD by the mouth of Jeremiah might be fulfilled, **the LORD stirred up the spirit of Cyrus king of Persia, that he made a proclamation** throughout all his kingdom, and *put it* also in writing, **saying,**

> Verse 2, next, gives evidence that God inspired Cyrus to allow the Jews to return home to the Holy Land.

2 Thus saith Cyrus king of Persia, **The LORD God of heaven** hath given me all the kingdoms of the earth; and he **hath charged me to build him an house at Jerusalem, which** *is* **in Judah.**

NOTES

In verse 3, next, Cyrus invites any Jews who so desire to return to Jerusalem and re-build the temple. Not all of them will want to return. They have been living in Babylon now for around fifty years and many of them are doing quite well in their business pur-suits. In fact, less than half of them will return.

3 **Who** *is there* **among you** of all his people? his God be with him, **and let him go up to Jerusalem**, which *is* in Judah, **and build the house of the LORD God of Israel**, (he *is* the God,) **which** *is* **in Jerusalem**.

4 **And whosoever** remaineth in any place where he sojourneth [*where the Jews live*], **let the men of his place help him** with silver, and with gold, and with goods, and with beasts [*any neighbors of Jews who are returning to Jerusalem are to give money and supplies to them to assist in this work*], beside the freewill offering for the house of God that *is* in Jerusalem.

5 ¶ **Then rose up the chief of the fathers of Judah and Benjamin** [*the leaders of the tribes of Judah and Benjamin*]**, and the priests, and the Levites**, with all *them* whose spirit God had raised, **to go up to build the house of the LORD which** *is* **in Jerusalem**.

6 And **all they that** *were* **about them strengthened their hands with vessels of silver, with gold, with goods, and with beasts, and with precious things**, beside all *that* was **willingly offered**.

Next, Cyrus returns the treasures stolen from the Jerusalem temple by the Babylonian armies. He has his "secretary of the treasury" collect them and deliver them to one of the Jewish leaders.

7 ¶ Also **Cyrus the king brought forth the vessels of the house of the LORD, which Nebuchadnezzar had brought forth** [*stolen*] **out of Jerusalem**, and had put them in the house of his gods [*the shrines of his idols*];

8 Even those did Cyrus king of Persia bring forth by the hand of **Mithredath the treasurer**, and **numbered them unto Sheshbazzar, the prince of Judah**.

In verses 9–11, next, we are given a list of the treasures and equipment Cyrus arranged to be sent back to the temple in Jerusalem with those who returned.

9 And **this** *is* **the number of them**: thirty chargers of gold, a thousand chargers of silver, nine and twenty knives,

10 Thirty basons of gold, silver basons of a second *sort* four hundred and ten, *and* other vessels a thousand.

11 All the vessels of gold and of silver *were* five thousand and four hundred. **All** *these* **did Sheshbazzar bring up with** *them of* **the captivity that were brought up from Babylon unto Jerusalem**.

We will not include chapter 2 because of space limitations, but you can read it in your Bible. It gives a list of the Jews who did return. If you do read it, you will find that around fifty thousand Jews returned with their animals and equipment (Ezra 2:64–67).

EZRA 3

Selection: all verses

This chapter briefly summarizes the rebuilding of the altar of sacrifice in the courtyard just outside of the temple. As they complete this work, they will reinstitute sacrifices required by the law of Moses. They will also lay the foundations of the temple as they begin rebuilding it.

1 AND when the seventh month was come, and the children of Israel *were* in the cities, **the people gathered themselves together** as one man [*in unity*] **to Jerusalem**.

2 Then stood up **Jeshua** the son of Jozadak, **and his brethren the priests, and Zerubbabel** the son of Shealtiel, **and his brethren, and builded the altar of the God of Israel, to offer burnt offerings thereon, as** *it is* **written in the law of Moses** the man of God.

3 And **they set the altar upon his bases**; for fear *was* upon them because of the people of those countries: **and they offered burnt offerings thereon unto the LORD,** *even* **burnt offerings morning and evening**.

4 **They kept also the feast of tabernacles**, as *it is* written, **and** *offered* **the daily burnt offerings** by number, according to the custom, as the duty of every day required [*the daily number of offerings required by the law of Moses*];

5 And **afterward** *offered* **the continual burnt offering**, both of the new moons, and of all the set feasts of the LORD that were consecrated, and of every one that willingly offered a freewill offering unto the LORD.

6 From the first day of the seventh month began they to offer burnt offerings unto the LORD. **But the foundation of the temple of the LORD was not** *yet* **laid**.

The Jews who returned gave donations to help with rebuilding the temple.

7 **They gave money** also unto the masons, and to the carpenters; and meat, and drink, and oil, unto them of Zidon, and to them of Tyre, to bring cedar trees from Lebanon to the sea of Joppa, according to the grant that they had of Cyrus king of Persia.

In the second year after their return, they began work on the temple.

8 ¶ Now **in the second year of their coming unto the house of God at Jerusalem**, in the second month, **began** Zerubbabel the son of Shealtiel, and Jeshua the son of Jozadak, and the remnant of their brethren the priests and the Levites, and all they that were come out of the captivity unto Jerusalem; and appointed the Levites, from twenty years old and upward, **to set forward the work of the house of the LORD**.

9 Then stood Jeshua *with* his sons and his brethren, Kadmiel and his sons, the sons of Judah, together, to set forward the workmen in the house of God: the sons of Henadad, *with* their sons and their brethren the Levites.

In verses 10–14, next, we see a great celebration after the laying of the foundation for the rebuilding of the temple. We also feel the depth of emotion among the older Jews who had personally seen the temple before it was destroyed by the Babylonians.

10 And **when the builders laid the foundation of the temple of the LORD**, they set the priests in their apparel with **trumpets**, and the Levites the sons of Asaph with **cymbals**, to praise the LORD, after the ordinance of David king of Israel [*according to instructions given by King David*].

11 And **they sang together** by course in praising and giving thanks unto the LORD; because *he is* good, for his mercy *endureth* for ever toward Israel. And **all the people shouted with a great shout, when they praised the LORD, because the foundation of the house of the LORD was laid**.

12 **But many of the priests and Levites and chief of the fathers,** *who were* **ancient men, that had seen the first house**, when the foundation of this house was laid before their eyes, **wept with a loud voice; and many shouted aloud for joy:**

13 So that **the people could not discern the noise of the shout of joy from the noise of the weeping** of the people: for the people shouted with a loud shout, and the noise was heard afar off.

EZRA 4

Selection: all verses

Unfortunately, the animosity and hatred between the Samaritans and the Jews shows up in this chapter. Remember that around 180 years ago, the Assyrians conquered the nation of Israel (the northern ten tribes, headquartered in Samaria) and carried them away into captivity in about 722–721 B.C. These are the lost ten tribes. However, the Assyrians did not take all the Israelites. They left the poorer class behind. Consequently, the occupational armies intermarried with the Israelites, contrary to the law of Moses, thus "polluting" the chosen people. Because of this, the Jews and Samaritans harbored deep feelings of hatred toward each other. By the way, because their history included basics of the Jewish faith, including sacrifices offered according to the law of Moses (but mixed with paganism), the Samaritans offered to help rebuild the Jerusalem temple. We see this in verses 1–2, next.

1 NOW **when the adversaries** [*the Samaritans*] **of Judah and Benjamin** [*the two tribes mainly making up the Jews in Judah*] **heard that the children of the captivity builded the temple** unto the LORD God of Israel;

2 Then **they came to Zerubbabel** [*the leader of this group of Jewish immigrants*], and to the chief of the fathers, **and said** unto them, **Let us build with you**: for we seek your God, as ye *do;* and we do sacrifice unto him since the days of Esar-haddon king of Assur, which brought us up hither.

3 **But Zerubbabel, and Jeshua, and the rest of the chief of the fathers of Israel, said unto them, Ye have nothing to do with us to build an house unto our God**; but we ourselves together will build unto the LORD God of Israel, as king Cyrus the king of Persia hath commanded us.

Zerubbabel and his fellow leaders flatly rejected the Samaritan's offer (verse 3, above), which caused deep feelings such that the Samaritans began to sabotage the project.

4 **Then the people of the land** [*the Samaritans and others*] **weakened the hands of the people of Judah, and troubled them in building,**

5 **And hired counsellors against them, to frustrate their purpose,** all the days of Cyrus king of Persia, even until the reign of Darius king of Persia.

6 And in the reign of Ahasuerus, in the beginning of his reign, wrote **they *unto him* an accusation against the inhabitants of Judah and Jerusalem**.

Next, in verses 7–24, the disgruntled Samaritans write a letter to the new Persian king accusing the Jews of various things designed to get the new king to stop the Jews from working on their temple. Thus, the Samaritans succeeded in delaying the work on rebuilding the temple for several years.

7 ¶ And **in the days of Artaxerxes** [*the new Persian king*] wrote Bishlam, Mithredath, Tabeel, and the rest of their companions [*Samaritans and others*], unto Artaxerxes king of Persia; and the writing of the letter *was* written in the Syrian tongue, and interpreted in the Syrian tongue.

8 Rehum the chancellor and Shimshai the scribe **wrote a letter against Jerusalem to Artaxerxes the king** in this sort:

9 Then *wrote* Rehum the chancellor, and Shimshai the scribe, and the rest of their companions; the Dinaites, the Apharsathchites, the Tarpelites, the Apharsites, the Archevites, the Babylonians, the Susanchites, the Dehavites, *and* the Elamites,

10 And the rest of the nations whom the great and noble Asnappar brought over, and set in the cities of Samaria, and the rest *that are* on this side the river, and at such a time.

11 ¶ **This *is* the copy of the letter that they sent unto him, *even* unto Artaxerxes the king**; Thy servants the men on this side the river, and at such a time.

12 **Be it known unto the king**, that **the Jews** which came up from thee to us **are** come unto Jerusalem, **building the rebellious and the bad city**, and have set up the walls *thereof,* and joined the foundations.

13 Be it known now unto the king, that, **if this city be builded, and the walls set up** *again, then* **will they not pay toll, tribute, and custom**, and *so* thou shalt endamage the revenue of the kings.

14 Now **because we have maintenance from *the king's* palace** [*because we are supported by you*], and **it was not meet for us to see the king's dishonour**, therefore have we sent and certified the king;

15 That search may be made in the book of the records of thy fathers: so shalt thou find in the book of the records, and know that **this city *is* a rebellious city, and**

hurtful unto kings and provinces, and that **they have moved sedition** within the same of old time: **for which cause was this city destroyed**.

16 **We certify the king that, if this city be builded** *again,* and the walls thereof set up, by this means **thou shalt have no portion on this side the river**.

17 ¶ *Then* **sent the king an answer unto** Rehum the chancellor, and *to* Shimshai the scribe, and *to* the rest of their companions **that dwell in Samaria**, and *unto* the rest beyond the river, Peace, and at such a time.

18 **The letter which ye sent unto us hath been plainly read before me**.

19 And I commanded, and search hath been made, and **it is found that this city** [*Jerusalem*] **of old time hath made insurrection against kings, and** *that* **rebellion and sedition have been made therein**.

20 **There have been mighty kings also over Jerusalem**, which have ruled over all *countries* beyond the river; **and toll, tribute, and custom, was paid unto them**.

Next, the new king of Persia commands these enemies of the Jews to do what is necessary to stop the work on the temple.

21 **Give ye now commandment to cause these men to cease**, and that this city be not builded, until *another* commandment shall be given from me [*until I send you further orders*].

22 Take heed now that ye **fail not to do this**: why should damage grow to the hurt of the kings?

23 ¶ **Now when the copy of king Artaxerxes' letter** *was* **read** before Rehum, and Shimshai the scribe, and their companions, **they went up in haste to Jerusalem unto the Jews, and made them to cease by force and power**.

The work on rebuilding the temple was stopped for about 15–17 years.

24 **Then ceased the work of the house of God which** *is* **at Jerusalem**. So it ceased unto the second year of the reign of Darius king of Persia.

EZRA 5

Selection: all verses

After many years of delays in rebuilding the temple (see Ezra 4:24) the Lord raised up two prophets, Haggai and Zechariah, who prophesied that the Jews should resume work on the temple. They did, as you will see in verses 1–2.

1 THEN **the prophets, Haggai** the prophet, **and Zechariah** the son of Iddo, **prophesied unto the Jews that** *were* **in Judah and Jerusalem** in the name of the God of Israel, *even* unto them.

_____
_____
_____
_____
_____
_____
_____
_____
_____
_____
_____
_____
_____
_____
_____
_____
_____
_____
_____
_____
_____
_____
_____
_____
_____
_____
_____
_____
_____
_____
_____

2 **Then rose up Zerubbabel** the son of Shealtiel, **and Jeshua** the son of Jozadak, **and began to build the house of God which** is **at Jerusalem**: and **with them** were **the prophets of God helping them**.

Next, some of the leaders of the opposition to rebuilding the temple approached and challenged those supervising the work on the temple.

3 ¶ **At the same time came to them Tatnai**, governor on this side the river [*an important governor over a territory on this side of the Euphrates River under the king of Persia*], **and Shethar-boznai, and their companions, and said** thus unto them, **Who hath commanded you to build this house, and to make up this wall?**

4 Then said we unto them after this manner, **What are the names of the men that make this building?**

In verse 5, we see that the Jews refused to be intimidated by the threats of these men and kept working until they could send a letter to Darius, now king of Persia, explaining the whole situation and receive word back from him.

5 **But the eye of their God was upon the elders of the Jews, that they could not cause them to cease**, till the matter came to Darius: and then they returned answer by letter concerning this *matter*.

Next, in verses 6–10 plus the first phrase of verse 11, you will see a copy of the letter sent by the opposition forces to King Darius, basically tattling on the Jews. The rest of the letter they sent records the answer the Jews gave (verses 11–17) upon being asked, "Who commanded you to build this house?" (See verse 9.)

6 ¶ **The copy of the letter that Tatnai**, governor on this side the river, **and Shethar-boznai, and his companions** the Apharsachites, which *were* on this side the river, **sent unto Darius the king**:

7 They sent a letter unto him, wherein was written thus; **Unto Darius the king, all peace**.

8 Be it known unto the king, that **we went into the province of Judea, to the house of the great God**, which is builded with great stones, and timber is laid in the walls, **and this work goeth fast** on, and prospereth in their hands.

9 **Then asked we those elders,** *and* said unto them thus, **Who commanded you to build this house, and to make up these walls?**

10 **We asked their names also,** to certify thee, that we might write the names of the men that *were* the chief of them.

11 And thus **they** [*the Jews*] **returned us answer**, saying, **We are the servants of the God of heaven and earth, and build the house that was builded these many years ago, which a great king of Israel builded and set up.**

12 But after that our fathers [*ancestors*] **had provoked the God of heaven unto wrath, he gave them into the hand of Nebuchadnezzar the king of Babylon,** the Chaldean, **who destroyed this house, and carried the people away into Babylon.**

13 But in the first year of Cyrus the king of Babylon *the same* king **Cyrus made a decree to build this house of God.**

14 And the vessels also of gold and silver of the house of God, which Nebuchadnezzar took out of the temple that *was* in Jerusalem, and brought them into the temple of Babylon, those **did Cyrus the king take out of the temple of Babylon, and they were delivered unto** *one,* **whose name** *was* **Sheshbazzar,** whom he had made governor;

15 And said unto him, Take these vessels, go, carry them into the temple that *is* **in Jerusalem, and let the house of God be builded in his place.**

16 Then came the same Sheshbazzar, *and* laid the foundation of the house of God which *is* in Jerusalem: and **since that time even until now hath it been in building, and** *yet* **it is not finished.**

Finally, this letter sent to King Darius of Persia by the Samaritans and others attempting to stop the work on the temple includes a request from the Jews that King Darius authorize a search in the treasury in Babylon for the original decree by King Cyrus (now dead) authorizing the rebuilding of the temple in Jerusalem.

17 Now therefore, **if** *it seem* good to the king, let there be search made in the king's treasure house, which** *is* **there at Babylon, whether it be** *so,* **that a decree was made of Cyrus the king to build this house of God at Jerusalem, and let the king send his pleasure to us concerning this matter.**

EZRA 6

Selection: all verses

King Darius, who had a reputation of being more fair and gentle to foreign captives under his rule, requested a search be made for such a decree by his predecessor, Cyrus. It was found (verses 1–2) and the details contained in it are given (verses 3–5.)

1 THEN **Darius the king made a decree, and search was made** in the house of the rolls, where the treasures were laid up in Babylon.

2 And **there was found** at Achmetha, in the palace that *is* in the province of the Medes, **a roll** [*scroll*], **and therein** *was* **a record** thus written:

3 **In the first year of Cyrus the king** *the same* Cyrus **the king made a decree concerning the house of God at Jerusalem, Let the house be builded,** the place where they offered sacrifices, and let the foundations thereof be strongly laid; the height thereof threescore cubits, *and* the breadth thereof threescore cubits;

4 *With* three rows of great stones, and a row of new timber: **and let the expenses be given out of the king's house:**

NOTES

_____
_____
_____
_____
_____
_____
_____
_____
_____
_____
_____
_____
_____
_____
_____
_____
_____
_____
_____
_____
_____
_____
_____
_____
_____
_____
_____
_____
_____
_____
_____

5 And **also let the golden and silver vessels of the house of God**, which Nebuchadnezzar took forth out of the temple which *is* at Jerusalem, and brought unto Babylon, **be restored, and brought again unto the temple which *is* at Jerusalem**, *every one* to his place, **and place** *them* **in the house of God.**

Next, King Darius commands the opposition forces to leave the Jews alone as they rebuild the temple and restore their sacrifices and worship rites.

6 Now *therefore,* Tatnai, governor beyond the river, Shethar-boznai, and your companions the Apharsachites, which *are* beyond the river, be ye far from thence:

7 Let the work of this house of God alone; let the governor of the Jews and the elders of the Jews build this house of God in his place.

8 Moreover I make a decree what ye shall do to the elders of these Jews for the building of this house of God: that of the king's goods, *even* of the tribute beyond the river, forthwith expenses be given unto these men, that they be not hindered.

9 And that which they have need of, both young bullocks, and rams, and lambs, for the burnt offerings of the God of heaven, wheat, salt, wine, and oil, according to the appointment of the priests which *are* at Jerusalem, let it be given them day by day without fail:

10 That they may offer sacrifices of sweet savours unto the God of heaven, and pray for the life of the king, and of his sons.

As you can see, in verse 11, next, King Darius is serious about having his orders carried out.

11 **Also I have made a decree**, that **whosoever shall alter this word, let timber be pulled down from his house, and being set up, let him be hanged thereon**; and **let his house be made a dunghill for this**.

12 And the God that hath caused his name to dwell there destroy all kings and people, that shall put to their hand to alter *and* to destroy this house of God which *is* at Jerusalem. **I Darius have made a decree; let it be done with speed.**

13 ¶ **Then Tatnai, governor** on this side the river, **Shethar-boznai, and their companions**, according to that which Darius the king had sent, so **they did speedily**.

14 **And the elders of the Jews** builded, and they prospered through the prophesying of Haggai the prophet and Zechariah the son of Iddo. And they **builded, and finished** *it,* **according to the commandment of the God of Israel, and according to the commandment of Cyrus, and Darius, and Artaxerxes king of Persia.**

15 **And this house was finished** on the third day of the month Adar, which was **in the sixth year of the reign of Darius the king.**

16 ¶ **And the children of Israel**, the priests, and the Levites, and the rest of the children of the captivity, **kept the dedication of this house of God with joy,**

As you can see, in verses 17–18, next, the dedication of the temple was a huge celebration.

17 **And offered** at the dedication of this house of God **an hundred bullocks, two hundred rams, four hundred lambs**; and for a sin offering for all Israel, **twelve he goats, according to the number of the tribes of Israel**.

18 And **they set the priests in their divisions, and the Levites in their courses**, for the service of God, which *is* at Jerusalem; **as it is written in the book of Moses**.

They kept the Passover once again in Jerusalem, as instructed by Moses. Can you imagine their joy as they did this?

19 **And the children of the captivity** [*the Jews who had returned from Babylonian captivity*] **kept the passover** upon the fourteenth *day* of the first month.

20 For the priests and the Levites were purified together, all of them *were* pure, **and killed the Passover** [*killed a male lamb, without blemish—one per family or one for two small families*] **for all the children of the captivity**, and for their brethren the priests, and for themselves.

21 **And the children of Israel**, which were come again out of captivity, and all such as had separated themselves unto them from the filthiness of the heathen of the land, to seek the LORD God of Israel, **did eat**,

22 **And kept the feast of unleavened bread seven days with joy**: for the LORD had made them joyful, and turned the heart of the king of Assyria unto them, to strengthen their hands in the work of the house of God, the God of Israel.

EZRA 7

Selection: all verses

In this chapter we are given information as to who Ezra was and how he came to return to Jerusalem from Babylonian captivity and exile. First of all, "he was a famous priest and scribe who brought back part of the exiles from captivity" (see Bible Dictionary under "Ezra"). In 458 B.C., Ezra was given permission from Artaxerxes, King of Persia, to lead this second group of Jewish exiles back to Jerusalem. Along with this permission, the Persian king gave him authority, as a scribe, to organize and strengthen the legal system among the Jews in Jerusalem. This was designed to give the Jews certain rights and privileges under the law. He organized a system of scribes who became the interpreters of the law of Moses among the Jews.

First, we are given the genealogy of Ezra back to Aaron, showing that he was fully qualified by lineage to be a priest in the Aaronic Priesthood as well as a scribe.

1 NOW after these things, **in the reign of Artaxerxes king of Persia, Ezra the son of Seraiah**, the son of Azariah, the son of Hilkiah,

2 The son of Shallum, the son of Zadok, the son of Ahitub,

3 The son of Amariah, the son of Azariah, the son of Meraioth,

NOTES

_____
_____
_____
_____
_____
_____
_____
_____
_____
_____
_____
_____
_____
_____
_____
_____
_____
_____
_____
_____
_____
_____
_____
_____
_____
_____
_____
_____

4 The son of Zerahiah, the son of Uzzi, the son of Bukki,

5 The son of Abishua, the son of Phinehas, **the son of Eleazar, the son of Aaron the chief priest**:

> Verse 6 implies that Ezra had made a request to King Artaxerxes for permission to lead a group of Jews back to Jerusalem.

6 This **Ezra went up from Babylon**; and **he** _was_ **a ready scribe in the law of Moses**, which the LORD God of Israel had given: and **the king granted him all his request**, according to the hand of the LORD his God upon him.

7 **And there went up** _some_ **of the children of Israel**, and of the priests, and the Levites, and the singers, and the porters, and the Nethinims, **unto Jerusalem**, in the seventh year of Artaxerxes the king [_about 458 B.C._].

8 And **he came to Jerusalem** in the fifth month, which _was_ in the seventh year of the king.

9 For upon the first _day_ of the first month began he to go up from Babylon, and on the first _day_ of the fifth month came he to Jerusalem [_about a four-month journey_], according to the good hand of his God upon him.

> Ezra was well-prepared spiritually to do this important work. He is a good example for us to follow as we seek to do the Lord's work in our callings in the Church as well as in our families.

10 For **Ezra had prepared his heart** to seek the law of the LORD, and to do _it,_ and to teach in Israel statutes and judgments.

> Next, in verses 11–26, we are provided a copy of the edict that the King gave to Ezra.

11 ¶ Now **this** _is_ **the copy of the letter that the king Artaxerxes gave unto Ezra** the priest, the scribe, _even_ a scribe of the words of the commandments of the LORD, and of his statutes to Israel.

12 **Artaxerxes, king of kings, unto Ezra** the priest, a scribe of the law of the God of heaven, perfect _peace,_ and at such a time.

13 **I make a decree**, that all they of the people of Israel, and _of_ his priests and Levites, in my realm, which are minded of their own freewill to go up to Jerusalem [_who want to return to Jerusalem_], go with thee.

14 Forasmuch as **thou art sent of the king, and of his seven counsellors**, to enquire concerning Judah and Jerusalem, according to the law of thy God which _is_ in thine hand;

15 And **to carry the silver and gold**, which the king and his counsellors have freely offered unto the God of Israel, whose habitation _is_ in Jerusalem,

NOTES

16 And all the silver and gold that thou canst find in all the province of Babylon, with the freewill offering of the people, and of the priests, offering willingly for the house of their God which *is* in Jerusalem:

17 That thou mayest buy speedily with this money bullocks, rams, lambs, with their meat offerings and their drink offerings, and offer them upon the altar of the house of your God which *is* in Jerusalem.

18 And whatsoever shall seem good to thee, and to thy brethren, to do with the rest of the silver and the gold, that do after the will of your God [*do according to inspiration from your God*].

19 The vessels also that are given thee for the service of the house of thy God, *those* **deliver** thou **before the God of Jerusalem**.

The Persian king is willing to subsidize these efforts of Ezra and his people, as needed.

20 And whatsoever more shall be needful for the house of thy God, which thou shalt have occasion to bestow, **bestow** *it* **out of the king's treasure house**.

21 And I, *even* **I Artaxerxes the king, do make a decree to all the treasurers which** *are* **beyond the river, that whatsoever Ezra the priest, the scribe of the law of the God of heaven, shall require of you, it be done speedily,**

In verse 21, the king orders all the people in charge of government funds throughout his territories west and south of the Euphrates River, clear to the Jerusalem area, to provide funding for Ezra and his people as needed, up to a certain limit (verse 22).

22 Unto [*up to*] **an hundred talents of silver** [*NIV, "about 3¾ tons"*], and to **an hundred measures of wheat** [*NIV, "about 600 bushels"*], and to an hundred baths of **wine**, and to an hundred baths of **oil**, and **salt** without prescribing *how much* [*without a specific limit on salt*].

According to verse 23, next, the Persian king clearly respects the God of the Jews.

23 Whatsoever is commanded by the God of heaven, let it be diligently done for the house of the God of heaven: for why should there be wrath against the realm of the king and his sons?

24 Also we certify you, that touching [*concerning*] any of the priests and Levites, singers, porters, Nethinims, or ministers of this house of God, **it shall not be lawful to impose toll, tribute, or custom, upon them**.

Next, Ezra is given authority to organize a judicial system among the Jews in Jerusalem and Judah, according to the laws of God.

25 And thou, Ezra, after the wisdom of thy God, that *is* in thine hand, **set magistrates and judges, which may judge all the people** that *are* beyond the river, **all such as know the laws of thy God; and teach ye them that know** *them* not.

NOTES

26 And **whosoever will not do the law of thy God, and the law of the king, let judgment be executed speedily upon him, whether** *it be* **unto death, or to banishment, or to confiscation of goods, or to imprisonment**.

Verses 27–28, next, appear to be written by Ezra himself.

27 ¶ **Blessed** *be* **the LORD God of our fathers, which hath put** *such a thing* **as this in the king's heart**, to beautify the house of the LORD which *is* in Jerusalem:

28 And hath extended mercy unto me before the king, and his counsellors, and before all the king's mighty princes. And **I was strengthened as the hand of the LORD my God** *was* **upon me, and I gathered together out of Israel chief men to go up with me** [*to Jerusalem*].

NEHEMIAH

Nehemiah was a Jew, "either a Levite or of the tribe of Judah" (Bible Dictionary under "Nehemiah"). He was a later governor of Judah who led the rebuilding the wall around Jerusalem. He was sent to Jerusalem by the same Persian king who sent Ezra and his people to Jerusalem earlier; namely, Artaxerxes. Due to space limitations, we will only study chapters 2, 4–6, and 8. We can learn much about facing opposition from Nehemiah and his people.

NEHEMIAH 2

Selection: all verses

In verses 1–8, we are introduced to Nehemiah, who was a cupbearer for the king (see verse 1), a position of great trust since he was in charge of making sure the king's food was safe and protected from assassination attempts. Nehemiah was obviously on friendly terms with the king, because he appears before the king of Persia and asks a huge favor; namely, that he and his associates be allowed to return to Jerusalem and rebuild the walls of the city. On this particular day, Nehemiah was sad, and the king noticed it.

1 AND it came to pass in the month Nisan, in the twentieth year of Artaxerxes the king, *that* wine *was* before him: and **I took up the wine, and gave** *it* **unto the king. Now I had not been** *beforetime* **sad in his presence**.

2 Wherefore **the king said unto me, Why** *is* **thy countenance sad**, seeing thou *art* not sick? this *is* nothing *else* but sorrow of heart. **Then I was very sore afraid,**

3 **And said unto the king**, Let the king live for ever: **why should not my countenance be sad**, when the city, the place of my fathers' sepulchres [*ancestor's graves, tombs*], *lieth* waste, and the gates thereof are consumed with fire?

4 **Then the king said unto me, For what dost thou make request?** So I prayed to the God of heaven.

5 **And I said unto the king, If it please the king**, and if thy servant have found favour in thy sight, that thou wouldest **send me unto Judah, unto the city of my fathers' sepulchres, that I may build it.**

6 **And the king said unto me**, (the queen also sitting by him,) **For how long** shall thy journey be? **and when wilt thou return?** So **it pleased the king to send me**; and I set him a time.

7 **Moreover I said unto the king**, If it please the king, **let letters be given me to the governors beyond the river, that they may convey me over till I come into Judah**;

8 **And a letter unto Asaph the keeper of the king's forest, that he may give me timber** to make beams for the gates of the palace which *appertained* to the house, and for the wall of the city, and for the house that I shall enter into. **And the king granted me, according to the good hand of my God upon me**.

9 ¶ **Then I came to the governors beyond the river** [*the governors of Persian territories south and west of the Euphrates River*], **and gave them the king's letters**. Now the king had sent captains of the army and horsemen with me [*the king has sent soldiers and cavalry with Nehemiah*].

Next, Sanballat, the governor of Samaria and other nearby provinces under Persian rule, is deeply opposed to letting more Jews return to Jerusalem.

10 **When Sanballat** the Horonite, **and Tobiah** the servant, **the Ammonite** [*the Ammonites were long-time enemies of the Jews who lived across the Jordan River to the east of Jericho*], **heard *of it,* it grieved them exceedingly** that there was come a man to seek the welfare of the children of Israel.

11 **So I** [*Nehemiah*] **came to Jerusalem**, and **was there three days**.

12 ¶ And **I arose in the night, I and some few men with me**; neither told I *any* man what my God had put in my heart to do at Jerusalem: neither *was there any* beast with me, save the beast that I rode upon.

13 And **I went out by night** by the gate of the valley, even before the dragon well, and to the dung port, **and viewed the walls of Jerusalem, which were broken down, and the gates thereof were consumed with fire**.

14 **Then I went on to the gate of the fountain, and to the king's pool**: but *there was* no place for the beast *that was* under me to pass.

15 **Then went I up in the night by the brook, and viewed the wall**, and turned back, and entered by the gate of the valley, and *so* returned.

16 And **the rulers knew not whither I went, or what I did; neither had I as yet told *it*** to the Jews, nor to the priests, nor to the nobles, nor to the rulers, nor to the rest that did the work.

17 ¶ **Then said I unto them**, Ye see the distress that we *are* in, how Jerusalem *lieth* waste, and the gates thereof are burned with fire: **come, and let us build up the wall of Jerusalem**, that we be no more a reproach [*that we no longer be disgraced by it*].

NOTES

_____
_____
_____
_____
_____
_____
_____
_____
_____
_____
_____
_____
_____
_____
_____
_____
_____
_____
_____
_____
_____
_____
_____
_____
_____
_____
_____
_____
_____
_____
_____
_____
_____

NOTES

18 **Then I told them of the hand of my God** which was good upon me; as **also the king's words** that he had spoken unto me. **And they said, Let us rise up and build**. So they strengthened their hands for *this* good *work*.

Next, the leaders of some neighboring provinces of Persia accuse them of rebelling against the king of Persia.

19 **But when Sanballat** the Horonite, **and Tobiah** the servant, **the Ammonite**, and **Geshem the Arabian, heard** *it,* **they laughed us to scorn**, and despised us, **and said, What** *is* **this thing that ye do? will ye rebel against the king?**

20 **Then answered I them, and said unto them, The God of heaven, he will prosper us**; therefore we his servants will arise and build: but ye have no portion, nor right, nor memorial, in Jerusalem [*you have no say in what we do in Jerusalem*].

NEHEMIAH 4

Selection: all verses

This chapter documents efforts of neighboring nations to interrupt the work that Nehemiah and his fellow patriots are attempting to do. But they forge ahead despite the opposition.

1 BUT it came to pass, that **when Sanballat heard that we builded the wall, he was wroth, and took great indignation, and mocked the Jews**.

2 And **he spake before his brethren and the army of Samaria, and said, What do these feeble Jews** [*what are these weaklings trying to do*]? will they fortify themselves? will they sacrifice? will they make an end in a day? will they revive the stones out of the heaps of the rubbish which are burned?

The Syrian governor, Sanballat, is joined by the leader of the Ammonites, Tobiah, in mocking and ridiculing the efforts of the Jews. Tobiah says that the wall they are building is so bad that a fox could easily knock it down.

3 Now **Tobiah the Ammonite** *was* **by him**, and he said, **Even that which they build, if a fox go up, he shall even break down their stone wall**.

Next, Nehemiah prays.

4 **Hear, O our God**; for we are despised: and turn their reproach [*insults*] upon their own head, and give them for a prey in the land of captivity:

5 And **cover not their iniquity, and let not their sin be blotted out from before thee**: for they have provoked *thee* to anger before the builders.

6 **So built we the wall**; and all the wall was joined together unto the half thereof [*we had built the wall to half of its final height*]: for the people had a mind to work.

7 ¶ **But** it came to pass, *that* **when Sanballat**, and **Tobiah**, and **the Arabians**, and the **Ammonites**, and the **Ashdodites, heard that the walls of Jerusalem were made up,** *and* **that the breaches began to be stopped,** then **they were very wroth,**

8 **And conspired all of them together to come** *and* **to fight against Jerusalem, and to hinder it.**

9 **Nevertheless we made our prayer unto our God, and set a watch against them day and night,** because of them.

In verse 10, next, the Jews are worried that the strength of the workers on the wall is giving out and there is too much rubble from the former wall in the way.

10 And **Judah** [*the people of Judah*] **said, The strength of the bearers of burdens is decayed,** and *there is* **much rubbish; so that we are not able to build the wall.**

The surrounding enemies threaten to infiltrate the workers on the wall and kill them.

11 And **our adversaries said,** They shall not know, neither see [*we will do this in secret and catch them off guard*], till **we come in the midst among them, and slay them, and cause the work to cease.**

Jews who live near these enemies hear of their plans and warn their fellow Jews over and over that they are coming.

12 And it came to pass, that **when the Jews which dwelt by them came, they said unto us ten times,** From all places whence ye shall return unto us *they will be upon you*.

In verse 13, next, Nehemiah tells us what he did to protect the workers so the work could proceed.

13 ¶ **Therefore** set **I** in the lower places behind the wall, *and* on the higher places, I even **set the people after their families with their swords, their spears, and their bows.**

14 And I looked, and rose up, **and said** unto the nobles, and to the rulers, and to the rest of the people, **Be not ye afraid of them**: remember the Lord, *which is* great and terrible, and **fight for your brethren, your sons, and your daughters, your wives, and your houses** [*this reminds us of the things Captain Moroni wrote on the Title of Liberty as he rallied his people. See Alma 46:12*].

15 And it came to pass, **when our enemies heard that it was known unto us, and God had brought their counsel to nought, that we returned all of us to the wall, every one unto his work.**

16 And it came to pass **from that time forth,** *that* the **half of my servants wrought in the work** [*worked on the wall*], and **the other half of them held both the spears, the shields, and the bows, and the habergeons** [*protected the workers*]; and the rulers *were* behind all the house of Judah [*the officers of the Jews posted themselves nearby so they could help watch over the workers*].

NOTES

_____
_____
_____
_____
_____
_____
_____
_____
_____
_____
_____
_____
_____
_____
_____
_____
_____
_____
_____
_____
_____
_____
_____
_____
_____
_____
_____
_____
_____
_____

17 **They which builded on the wall**, and **they that bare burdens** [*carried materials for building*], with those that laded, *every one* **with one of his hands wrought in the work, and with the other** *hand* **held a weapon.**

18 For **the builders, every one had his sword girded by his side, and** *so* **builded.** And he that sounded the trumpet *was* by me.

Next, in verses 19–20, since the workers were widely separated as they worked, there was a clear danger that their enemies could easily pick them off. So, Nehemiah devised a plan. When danger approached a small group of workers, a trumpet was blown nearby and other workers and their guards came running.

19 ¶ And **I said** unto the nobles, and to the rulers, and to the rest of the people, **The work** *is* **great and large, and we are separated upon the wall, one far from another.**

20 **In what place** *therefore* **ye hear the sound of the trumpet, resort ye thither unto us** [*come to our aid*]: our God shall fight for us.

21 So we laboured in the work: and **half of them held the spears from the rising of the morning till the stars appeared.**

22 Likewise at the same time said I unto the people, **Let every one with his servant lodge within Jerusalem, that in the night they may be a guard to us, and labour on the day.**

23 So neither I, nor my brethren, nor my servants, nor the men of the guard which followed me, **none of us put off our clothes,** *saving that* **every one put them off for washing.**

NEHEMIAH 5

Selection: all verses

In this chapter, we gain insights into the personal attributes of Nehemiah. He was a great man, righteous and full of integrity. He was much like King Benjamin in the Book of Mormon in that he refused to be paid by taxes on the people; rather, he used his own money to live on. Many of his people were poverty-stricken because of taxes imposed by previous rulers. Many were still in bondage because of unpaid loans to other Jews, or as slaves to other Jews, and so on. He will also stop the practice of charging interest on loans to other Jews (usury).

In verses 1–5, the Jews complain loudly because of these perceived injustices perpetrated by their own people.

1 AND **there was a great cry of the people and of their wives against their brethren the Jews.**

2 For **there were that said, We, our sons, and our daughters,** *are* **many**: therefore we take up corn [*try to get enough grain*] *for them,* that we may eat, and live.

3 *Some* also there were that said, **We have mortgaged our lands, vineyards, and houses, that we might buy corn**, because of the dearth [*famine, drought*].

4 There were also that said, **We have borrowed money for the king's tribute, *and that upon* our lands and vineyards** [*we have taken out loans on our lands and vineyards in order to pay the required tribute to the king*].

5 Yet now **our flesh *is* as the flesh of our brethren, our children as their children** [*we are all one people*]: **and, lo** [*and yet*], **we bring into bondage our sons and our daughters to be servants**, and *some* of our daughters are brought unto bondage *already:* **neither *is it* in our power *to redeem them*; for other men have our lands and vineyards**.

Nehemiah is outraged at what he is hearing.

6 ¶ And **I was very angry when I heard their cry and these words**.

7 **Then I consulted with myself** [*considered these things in my own mind*], and **I rebuked the nobles, and the rulers**, and said unto them, **Ye exact usury, every one of his brother.** And I set a great assembly against them [*called an assembly of officials to discuss these complaints*].

8 **And I said** unto them, **We** after our ability **have redeemed our brethren the Jews, which were sold unto the heathen; and will ye even sell your brethren?** or shall they be sold unto us? **Then held they their peace, and found nothing *to answer*.**

9 Also **I said, It *is* not good that ye do: ought ye not to walk in the fear of our God** because of the reproach of the heathen our enemies?

10 I likewise, *and* my brethren, and my servants, might exact of them money and corn: **I pray you, let us leave off this usury.**

11 **Restore**, I pray you, to them, **even this day, their lands, their vineyards, their oliveyards, and their houses**, also **the hundredth *part* of the money, and of the corn, the wine, and the oil, that ye exact of them** [*which is the rate of usury (interest) they were charging*] .

12 **Then said they, We will restore *them,* and will require nothing of them**; so will we do as thou sayest. **Then I called the priests, and took an oath of them, that they should do according to this promise.**

13 Also **I shook my lap** [*NIV, "shook out the folds of my robe"*], **and said, So God shake out every man from his house, and from his labour, that performeth not this promise**, even thus be he shaken out, and emptied. **And all the congregation said, Amen**, and praised the LORD. And the people did according to this promise.

14 ¶ **Moreover from the time that I was appointed to be their governor** in the land of Judah, from the twentieth year even unto the two and thirtieth year of Artaxerxes the king, *that is,* twelve years, **I and my brethren have not eaten the bread of the governor** [*we have earned our own living*].

NOTES

15 But **the former governors that** *had been* **before me were chargeable unto the people** [*had laid heavy taxes and burdens upon the people*], and had taken of them bread and wine, beside forty shekels of silver; yea, even their servants bare rule over the people: **but so did not I, because of the fear of God** [*because I respect and honor God*].

16 Yea, **also I continued in the work of this wall**, neither bought we any land: and all my servants *were* gathered thither unto the work.

17 **Moreover** *there were* **at my table an hundred and fifty of the Jews and rulers, beside those that came unto us from among the heathen that** *are* **about us** [*Nehemiah provided food and support for all these additional people besides for himself*].

18 Now *that* which was prepared *for me* daily *was* one ox *and* six choice sheep; **also fowls** were prepared for me, and once in ten days store of all sorts of wine: **yet for all this required not I the bread of the governor** [*I did not require taxes, rather paid for it out of my own pocket*], because the bondage was heavy upon this people.

19 **Think upon me, my God, for good,** *according* **to all that I have done for this people**.

NEHEMIAH 6

Selection: all verses

In this chapter, we see Sanballat, a leader of the Samaritan opposition to Nehemiah, make another attempt to interfere with his work by making several false accusations against him and the Jews. In spite of the opposition, the work is finished.

1 NOW it came to pass, **when Sanballat**, and **Tobiah**, and **Geshem the Arabian, and the rest of our enemies, heard that I had builded the wall**, and *that* there was no breach left therein; (though at that time I had not set up the doors upon the gates;)

2 That **Sanballat and Geshem sent unto me**, saying, Come, **let us meet together in** *some one of* the villages in the plain of Ono. But **they thought to do me mischief** [*to interfere or harm me in some way*].

3 And **I sent messengers unto them, saying, I** *am* **doing a great work, so that I cannot come down**: why should the work cease, whilst I leave it, and come down to you?

4 **Yet they sent unto me four times** after this sort**; and I answered them after the same** manner.

5 **Then sent Sanballat his servant unto me in like manner the fifth time with an open letter in his hand;**

6 **Wherein** *was* **written, It is reported among the heathen**, and Gashmu saith *it, that* **thou and the Jews think to rebel: for which cause thou buildest the wall** [*that's why you are building the wall*]**, that thou mayest be their king,** according to these words.

7 And **thou hast also appointed prophets to preach of thee at Jerusalem, saying,** *There is* **a king in Judah**: and now shall it be reported to the king according to these words [*word of this Jewish rebellion will get to the king of Persia*]. **Come now therefore, and let us take counsel together** [*let's talk this over together*].

8 **Then I sent unto him**, saying, **There are no such things done as thou sayest**, but thou feignest them out of thine own heart [*you are making these things up because you have ulterior motives*].

9 For **they all made us afraid, saying, Their hands shall be weakened from the work**, that it be not done. Now therefore, *O God*, **strengthen my hands**.

Next, in verses 10–14, some enemies hatch a plot to lure Nehemiah to the temple to hide from an alleged plot to take his life, in order to discredit him before his people. He visited a fellow named Shemaiah at his house who was part of the plot.

10 Afterward **I came unto the house of Shemaiah** the son of Delaiah the son of Mehetabeel, who *was* shut up [*was at home*]; and **he said, Let us meet together in the house of God, within the temple**, and **let us shut the doors of the temple: for they will come to slay thee; yea, in the night will they come to slay thee.**

11 And **I said, Should such a man as I flee?** and who *is there*, that, *being* as I *am,* would go into the temple to save his life? **I will not go in.**

12 And, lo, **I perceived that God had not sent him**; but that he pronounced this prophecy against me: for **Tobiah and Sanballat had hired him.**

13 **Therefore** *was* **he hired, that I should be afraid, and do so**, and sin, and *that* **they might have** *matter* **for an evil report, that they might reproach me** [*that they might make me look bad in front of my people*].

14 **My God, think thou upon Tobiah** and **Sanballat** according to these their works [*their plots to stop our work in Jerusalem*], **and on the prophetess Noadiah**, and **the rest of the prophets** [*false prophets*], **that would have put me in fear** [*tried to intimidate me*].

15 ¶ **So the wall was finished** in the twenty and fifth *day* of *the month* Elul, in fifty and two days.

16 And it came to pass, that **when all our enemies heard** *thereof,* **and all the heathen that** *were* **about us saw** *these things,* **they were much cast down** [*they were depressed and discouraged*] in their own eyes: for **they perceived that this work was wrought of our God** [*they finally saw that this work was done under the protection of our God*].

17 ¶ Moreover **in those days the nobles of Judah sent many letters unto Tobiah** [*a ruler of the Ammonite nation, across the Jordon River east of Jericho*], and *the letters* of Tobiah came unto them.

NOTES

_____
_____
_____
_____
_____
_____
_____
_____
_____
_____
_____
_____
_____
_____
_____
_____
_____
_____
_____
_____
_____
_____
_____
_____
_____
_____
_____
_____

NOTES

Next, in verses 18–19, we see that there were many Jewish nobles in Jerusalem who were secretly loyal to Tobiah (see verse 17, above) and who kept him informed as to Nehemiah's activities.

18 For *there were* **many in Judah sworn unto him** [*loyal to him*], because he *was* the son in law of Shechaniah the son of Arah; and his son Johanan had taken the daughter of Meshullam the son of Berechiah.

19 **Also they reported his good deeds before me** [*trying to get me to trust him*], and uttered my words to him. *And* **Tobiah sent letters to put me in fear** [*tried to intimidate me*].

NEHEMIAH 8

Selection: all verses

It appears that in the seventy years or so of Babylonian captivity, many of the Jewish exiles and their children and grandchildren lost much of their ability to speak the Hebrew language. Plus, their religious rites and rituals according to the law of Moses were forbidden by their captors. Thus, they lost their familiarity with these also. In other words, over the course of many years in captivity, they mostly lost their language, their scriptures, and their religion.

In this chapter, Nehemiah has built a synagogue and undertakes to have Ezra read a book of scripture from the law of Moses to the people. But they run into a problem. Some of the people can still understand Hebrew, but the majority of them can't. So Nehemiah has some Levite priests translate into the Babylonian language so the people can understand. These priests also explain the meaning and application of these scriptures.

1 AND **all the people gathered themselves together** as one man into the street that *was* before the water gate; and **they spake unto Ezra the scribe to bring the book of the law of Moses,** which the LORD had commanded to Israel.

2 **And Ezra the priest brought the law before the congregation both of men and women, and all that could hear with understanding,** upon the first day of the seventh month.

3 And **he read** therein before the street that *was* before the water gate **from the morning until midday,** before the men and the women, and those that could understand; and the ears of **all the people** *were attentive* **unto the book of the law.**

4 And **Ezra the scribe stood upon a pulpit of wood,** which they had made for the purpose; and **beside him stood Mattithiah, and Shema, and Anaiah, and Urijah, and Hilkiah, and Maaseiah, on his right hand**; and **on his left** hand, **Pedaiah, and Mishael, and Malchiah, and Hashum, and Hashbadana, Zechariah,** *and* **Meshullam.**

5 And **Ezra opened the book in the sight of all the people**; (for he was above all the people;) and when he opened it, **all the people stood up**:

6 And **Ezra blessed the LORD, the great God. And all the people answered, Amen, Amen,** with **lifting up their hands**: and they bowed their heads, and worshipped the LORD with *their* faces to the ground.

NOTES

Next, in verses 7–8, certain men, including some Levites, translated and explained the meaning.

7 Also Jeshua, and Bani, and Sherebiah, Jamin, Akkub, Shabbethai, Hodijah, Maaseiah, Kelita, Azariah, Jozabad, Hanan, Pelaiah, and the Levites, **caused the people to understand the law**: and the people *stood* in their place.

8 So they read in the book in the law of God distinctly, **and gave the sense, and caused *them* to understand the reading**.

9 ¶ And **Nehemiah**, which *is* **the Tirshatha** [*another word for governor of the Jews in Jerusalem*], **and Ezra the priest the scribe, and the Levites that taught the people**, said unto all the people, This day *is* holy unto the LORD your God; mourn not, nor weep. For all the people wept, when they heard the words of the law.

Next, Nehemiah asks the people to go and feast, and also to make sure the poor among them have plenty to eat.

10 **Then he said** unto them, **Go your way, eat the fat** [*the best food*]**, and drink the sweet** [*the best drink*], and **send portions unto them** [*the poor*] **for whom nothing is prepared**: for *this* day *is* holy unto our Lord: neither be ye sorry; for the joy of the LORD is your strength [*in other words, rejoice*].

11 **So the Levites stilled all the people** [*calmed them down*], saying, Hold your peace, for the day *is* holy; neither be ye grieved.

12 And **all the people went their way to eat, and to drink, and to send portions, and to make great mirth, because they had understood the words that were declared unto them**.

Next, a major feast under the law of Moses will be restored. It is the feast of tabernacles (see under "Feasts" in your Bible Dictionary). The Jewish leaders go to Ezra seeking to be taught more about the law of Moses.

13 ¶ And **on the second day were gathered together** the chief of the fathers of all the people, the priests, and the Levites, **unto Ezra the scribe, even to understand the words of the law**.

14 And **they found written in the law which the LORD had commanded by Moses, that the children of Israel should dwell in booths** [*part of celebrating the feast of tabernacles*] **in the feast of the seventh month**:

15 And that they should publish and proclaim in all their cities, and in Jerusalem, saying, Go forth unto the mount, and fetch olive branches, and pine branches, and myrtle branches, and palm branches, and branches of thick trees, to **make booths**, as *it is* written.

16 ¶ **So the people** went forth, and brought *them,* and **made themselves booths**, every one upon the roof of his house, and in their courts, and in the courts of the house of God, and in the street of the water gate, and in the street of the gate of Ephraim.

NOTES

_____
_____
_____
_____
_____
_____
_____
_____
_____
_____
_____
_____
_____
_____
_____
_____
_____
_____
_____
_____
_____
_____
_____
_____
_____
_____
_____
_____
_____
_____
_____

17 And **all the congregation** of them **that were come again out of the captivity made booths, and sat under the booths**: for since the days of Jeshua [*Joshua, the prophet who took over after Moses*] the son of Nun unto that day had not the children of Israel done so. **And there was very great gladness**.

18 Also **day by day**, from the first day unto the last day, **he read in the book of the law of God**. And they kept the feast seven days; and **on the eighth day** *was* **a solemn assembly**, according unto the manner.

Esther

"Thou Art Come . . . for Such a Time as This"

Esther is a favorite Bible story for young and old. It takes place somewhere around 482 BC to 478 BC in Persia. It is helpful to know that many Jews in captivity opted not to return to Jerusalem when Cyrus, King of Persia, made it possible for them to do so. In fact, many Jews were prospering and comfortable in Babylon (now part of the Persian Empire) and did not want to uproot and go back to the homeland of the Jews. As you read and study, you will see many gospel themes at work as you follow the story of Esther, a beautiful, righteous, orphaned Jewish girl who, under heaven-directed circumstances, became queen of Persia and saved all the Jews in Persia from being executed. You will meet Mordecai, Esther's cousin and a righteous man, who has adopted her and taken care of her as he would his own daughter. You will be introduced to Haman, a man full of evil and malice toward the Jews. Esther will replace Vashti, the queen, who rebels against the king. Watch as moral strength, personal integrity, and loyalty to God overcome evil.

The beautiful story of the courage and faith of Esther fits chronologically with Ezra 7:1. Most Bible scholars place this account between 482 and 478 B.C. It is basically the story of an orphaned Jewish girl among the Jewish exiles in Babylon, which was now ruled by the King of Persia, Ahasuerus. Esther eventually became queen and was instrumental in saving her people, the Jews, from a plot in which they were to be slaughtered.

In the Book of Esther, we meet

Ahasuerus, King of Persia and Media, who at this time rules over numerous provinces, including Babylon.

Vashti, the queen who refuses to come to a banquet when the king requests it, and, consequently is deposed as queen.

Esther, the beautiful orphaned Jewish girl who becomes queen.

Mordecai, Esther's cousin (their fathers were brothers), who adopted Esther when her parents died, and raised her in his home.

Haman, the chief minister in King Ahasuerus's court, who plotted to get all the Jews in exile killed.

ESTHER 1

Selection: all verses

First, we are told that King Ahasuerus ruled over a vast empire consisting of 127 provinces.

1 NOW it came to pass **in the days of Ahasuerus,** (this *is* Ahasuerus **which reigned,** from India even unto Ethiopia, *over* **an hundred and seven and twenty provinces:)**

2 *That* in those days, when the king **Ahasuerus sat on the throne of his kingdom, which** *was* **in Shushan** [*located in modern Iran today*] the palace,

NOTES

_____
_____
_____
_____
_____
_____
_____
_____
_____
_____
_____
_____
_____
_____
_____
_____
_____
_____
_____
_____
_____
_____
_____
_____
_____
_____
_____
_____
_____
_____

3 **In the third year of his reign, he made a feast unto all his princes and his servants; the power of Persia and Media, the nobles and princes of the provinces,** *being* before him:

He showed off his wealth for 180 days.

4 When he shewed the riches of his glorious kingdom and the honour of his excellent majesty many days, ***even*** an hundred and fourscore days.

At the end of this extravaganza, he held a seven-day feast.

5 And **when these days were expired, the king made a feast unto all the people** that were present **in Shushan the palace**, both unto great and small, **seven days**, in the court of the garden of the king's palace;

The palace was elaborately decorated.

6 *Where were* white, green, and blue, *hangings,* fastened with cords of fine linen and purple to silver rings and pillars of marble: the beds *were of* gold and silver, upon a pavement of red, and blue, and white, and black, marble.

7 And **they gave** *them* **drink in vessels of gold**, (the vessels being diverse one from another,) **and royal wine in abundance**, according to the state of the king.

8 And the drinking *was* according to the law; none did compel: for so the king had appointed to all the officers of his house, that they should do **according to every man's pleasure**.

9 Also **Vashti the queen made a feast for the women** *in* **the royal house** which *belonged* to king Ahasuerus.

10 ¶ **On the seventh day, when the heart of the king was merry with wine** [*when everyone was good and drunk*], **he commanded** Mehuman, Biztha, Harbona, Bigtha, and Abagtha, Zethar, and Carcas, **the seven chamberlains** that served in the presence of Ahasuerus the king,

11 **To bring Vashti the queen before the king** with the crown royal, **to shew the people and the princes her beauty: for she** *was* **fair to look on**.

Perhaps, we should not blame Queen Vashti too harshly for refusing to appear before such a group of drunken revelers who, after seven days of drinking, no doubt, would be crude and vulgar to her. But, in that culture, it was a deep insult to the king to refuse his request.

12 **But the queen Vashti refused to come at the king's commandment** by *his* chamberlains: **therefore was the king very wroth, and his anger burned in him.**

13 ¶ **Then the king said to the wise men**, which knew the times, (for so *was* the king's manner toward all that knew law and judgment:

14 And the next unto him *was* Carshena, Shethar, Admatha, Tarshish, Meres, Marsena, *and* Memucan, the seven princes of Persia and Media, which saw the king's face, *and* which sat the first in the kingdom;)

15 **What shall we do unto the queen Vashti according to law, because she hath not performed the commandment of the king** Ahasuerus by the chamberlains?

16 And **Memucan answered** before the king and the princes, **Vashti the queen hath not done wrong to the king only, but also to all the princes, and to all the people that** *are* **in all the provinces of the king Ahasuerus.**

17 **For** *this* **deed of the queen shall come abroad unto all women, so that they shall despise their husbands in their eyes, when it shall be reported, The king Ahasuerus commanded Vashti the queen to be brought in before him, but she came not** [*her bad example could cause all of us a lot of trouble, when word gets out*].

18 *Likewise* **shall the ladies of Persia and Media say** this day unto all the king's princes, which have heard of the deed of the queen. **Thus** *shall there arise* **too much contempt and wrath.**

19 If it please the king, **let there go a royal commandment from him**, and let it be written among the laws of the Persians and the Medes, that it be not altered, **That Vashti come no more before king Ahasuerus; and let the king give her royal estate unto another that is better than she** [*depose the queen and choose another to take her place*].

20 And **when the king's decree** which he shall make **shall be published throughout all his empire**, (for it is great,) **all the wives shall give to their husbands honour**, both to great and small.

21 And **the saying pleased the king** and the princes; and **the king did according to the word of Memucan:**

22 For **he sent letters into all the king's provinces**, into every province according to the writing thereof, and to every people after their language, **that every man should bear rule in his own house**, and that *it* should be published according to the language of every people.

ESTHER 2

Selection: all verses

Next, the king seeks a new queen. Mordecai, who apparently served in the king's court, introduces Esther to the king.

1 **AFTER these things, when the wrath of king Ahasuerus was appeased, he remembered Vashti, and what she had done, and what was decreed against her.**

2 **Then said the king's servants** that ministered unto him, **Let there be fair young virgins sought for the king:**

————————————
————————————
————————————
————————————
————————————
————————————
————————————
————————————
————————————
————————————
————————————
————————————
————————————
————————————
————————————
————————————
————————————
————————————
————————————
————————————
————————————
————————————
————————————
————————————
————————————
————————————
————————————
————————————
————————————

3 And **let the king appoint officers in all the provinces of his kingdom, that they may gather together all the fair young virgins unto Shushan the palace**, to the house of the women, unto the custody of Hege the king's chamberlain [*NIV, "the king's eunuch"*], keeper of the women; and let their things for purification [*NIV, "beauty treatments"*] be given *them:*

4 And **let the maiden which pleaseth the king be queen instead of Vashti**. And **the thing pleased the king; and he did so**.

5 ¶ *Now* in Shushan the palace there was a certain Jew, whose name *was* **Morde-cai**, the son of Jair, the son of Shimei, the son of Kish, a Benjamite;

6 Who had been carried away from Jerusalem with the captivity which had been carried away with Jeconiah king of Judah, whom Nebuchadnezzar the king of Babylon had carried away.

7 And **he brought up Hadassah** [*another name for Esther*], **that *is,* Esther, his uncle's daughter**: for she had neither father nor mother, and the maid [*virgin*] *was* fair and beautiful; whom Mordecai, when her father and mother were dead, took for his own daughter [*Mordecai adopted her and raised her*].

8 ¶ So it came to pass, when the king's commandment and his decree was heard, and when **many maidens were gathered together unto Shushan the palace**, to the custody of Hegai, that **Esther was brought also unto the king's house**, to the custody of Hegai, keeper of the women.

9 And **the maiden** [*Esther*] **pleased him** [*the king*], and she obtained kindness of him; and **he speedily gave her her things for purification** [*beauty supplies*], with such things as belonged to her, **and seven maidens** [*servants*], *which were* meet to be given her, out of the king's house: and **he preferred** [*moved*] **her and her maids unto the best *place* of the house of the women**.

Mordecai had counseled her, as indicated in verse 10, next, not to tell anyone that she was a Jew. Jews were looked down upon by the general population and it would ruin her chances to become queen.

10 **Esther had not shewed her people nor her kindred** [*disclosed that she was a Jew*]: for Mordecai had charged her that she should not shew *it*.

11 And **Mordecai walked every day before the court of the women's house, to know how Esther did**, and what should become of her.

12 ¶ Now **when every maid's turn was come to go in to king Ahasuerus, after** that **she had been twelve months**, according to the manner of the women [*had had twelve months of training and beauty treatments*], (for so were the days of their purifications accomplished, *to wit,* **six months with oil of myrrh**, and **six months with sweet odours, and with *other* things for the purifying of the women;**)

13 Then **thus came *every* maiden unto the king**; whatsoever she desired was given her to go with her out of the house of the women unto the king's house.

14 **In the evening she went, and on the morrow she returned into the second house of the women, to the custody of** Shaashgaz, **the king's chamberlain, which kept the concubines: she came in unto the king no more, except the king delighted in her, and that she were called by name.**

15 ¶ **Now when the turn of Esther**, the daughter of Abihail the uncle of Mordecai, who had taken her for his daughter, **was come** to go in unto the king, she required nothing but what Hegai the king's chamberlain, the keeper of the women, appointed. And **Esther obtained favour in the sight of all them that looked upon her.**

16 **So Esther was taken unto king Ahasuerus** into his house royal in the tenth month, which *is* the month Tebeth, in the seventh year of his reign.

17 **And the king loved Esther above all the women**, and she obtained grace and favour in his sight more than all the virgins; **so that he set the royal crown upon her head, and made her queen instead of Vashti.**

18 **Then the king made a great feast unto all his princes and his servants,** *even* **Esther's feast**; and he made a release to the provinces, and gave gifts, according to the state of the king.

19 **And when the virgins were gathered together the second time, then Mordecai sat in the king's gate.**

20 **Esther had not** *yet* **shewed her kindred nor her people** [*had not yet disclosed that she was a Jew*]; as Mordecai had charged her: for **Esther did the commandment of Mordecai** [*followed his counsel faithfully*], like as when she was brought up with him.

Next, Mordecai overhears two of the king's close, personal doorkeepers discussing a plot to assassinate the king.

21 ¶ In those days, **while Mordecai sat in the king's gate, two of the king's chamberlains**, Bigthan and Teresh, of those which kept the door, **were wroth, and sought to lay hand on the king Ahasuerus.**

Mordecai told Esther and she told the king, telling him that Mordecai was the one who found out about it and told her to tell the king.

22 And the thing was known to **Mordecai**, who **told** *it* unto **Esther** the queen; and **Esther certified the king** *thereof* **in Mordecai's name.**

23 And **when inquisition was made of the matter, it was found out; therefore they were both hanged on a tree**: and it was written in the book of the chronicles before the king.

ESTHER 3

Selection: all verses

In this chapter, we watch as the king promotes a man named Haman to a position above all the other leaders in his kingdom. Everyone was commanded to bow to him when he

NOTES

came by or when entering his presence. This will be a problem for Mordecai because he is a Jew and his religion requires that he not bow down to any but God. Also, Haman hates all the Jews in the kingdom as a matter of deep personal prejudice.

1 **AFTER these things** [*after the events in chapters 1 and 2*] did **king Ahasuerus promote Haman** the son of Hammedatha the Agagite, and **advanced him, and set his seat above all the princes** [*leaders*] that *were* with him.

2 And **all the king's servants**, that *were* in the king's gate, **bowed, and reverenced Haman**: for the king had so commanded concerning him. **But Mordecai bowed not, nor did *him* reverence**.

3 Then **the king's servants**, which *were* in the king's gate, **said unto Mordecai, Why transgressest thou the king's commandment** [*why won't you bow to Haman*]?

4 Now it came to pass, when **they spake daily unto him, and he hearkened not unto them**, that **they told Haman, to see whether Mordecai's matters would stand: for he had told them that he *was* a Jew.**

5 And **when Haman saw that Mordecai bowed not, nor did him reverence, then was Haman full of wrath**.

Next, we are told that Haman scorned the idea of only killing Mordecai; rather, since Mordecai was a Jew, he would arrange to have all the Jews in the kingdom killed.

6 And **he thought scorn to lay hands on Mordecai alone**; for they had shewed him the people of Mordecai: **wherefore Haman sought to destroy all the Jews** that *were* throughout the whole kingdom of Ahasuerus, *even* the people of Mordecai.

Esther was the queen for three years before Hamon put his plot to work to kill all the Jews. Then, he and his fellow conspirators cast lots to determine when to carry out the plot. Fortunately for Mordecai and Ester, the day the lot fell on was some distance in the future, which allowed them time to counteract the plot.

7 ¶ In the first month, that *is,* the month Nisan, in the twelfth year of king Ahasuerus, **they cast Pur, that *is*, the lot**, before Haman from day to day, and from month to month, *to* the twelfth *month, that is,* the month Adar.

8 ¶ And **Haman said unto king Ahasuerus, There is a certain people** scattered abroad and dispersed among the people **in all the provinces of thy kingdom**; and **their laws *are* diverse from all people; neither keep they the king's laws**: therefore **it *is* not for the king's profit to suffer** [*tolerate*] them.

9 **If it please the king, let it be written that they may be destroyed**: and I will pay ten thousand talents of silver to the hands of those that have the charge of the business, to bring *it* into the king's treasuries.

10 **And the king took his ring from his hand, and gave it unto Haman** [*a symbol that the king had given Haman great authority*] the son of Hammedatha the Agagite, **the Jews' enemy**.

11 **And the king said unto Haman,** The silver *is* given to thee, the people also, to **do with them as it seemeth good to thee** [*do what you want with the Jews*].

12 Then were the king's scribes called on the thirteenth day of the first month, and **there was written according to all that Haman had commanded** unto the king's lieutenants, and to the governors that *were* over every province, and **to the rulers of every people of every province** according to the writing thereof, and *to* every people after their language; in the name of king Ahasuerus was it written, **and sealed with the king's ring**.

13 And the letters were sent by posts into all the king's provinces, to destroy, to kill, and **to cause to perish, all Jews, both young and old, little children and women, in one day,** *even* **upon the thirteenth** *day* **of the twelfth month, which** *is* **the month Adar, and** *to take* **the spoil of them for a prey** [*and those who killed the Jews could plunder the Jews' belongings and keep them for themselves*].

14 **The copy of the writing** for a commandment to be given in every province **was published unto all people**, that they should be ready against that day [*so they could be ready to kill the Jews on that specific day*].

15 **The posts** [*written edicts*] **went out**, being hastened by the king's commandment, and the decree was given in Shushan the palace. And the king and Haman sat down to drink; but the city Shushan was perplexed.

ESTHER 4

Selection: all verses

Imagine the terror among the Jews upon hearing this horrifying news! The news of the king's edict also reached Mordecai and Esther at the palace. Esther defied normal palace protocol and, at peril of her life, went to the king uninvited to plead for the Jews.

1 **WHEN Mordecai perceived all that was done, Mordecai rent** [*tore*] **his clothes, and put on sackcloth** [*coarse, burlap-like fabric*] **with ashes** [*a sign of deep mourning and anguish in his culture*], **and went out into the midst of the city, and cried with a loud and a bitter cry**;

2 **And came even before the king's gate**: for none *might* enter into the king's gate clothed with sackcloth.

3 And **in every province, whithersoever the king's commandment and his decree came,** *there was* **great mourning among the Jews**, and fasting, and weeping, and wailing; and many lay in sackcloth and ashes.

4 ¶ So **Esther's maids and her chamberlains came and told** *it* **her** [*that Mordecai was in front of the palace gate clothed in sackcloth and ashes*]. **Then was the queen exceedingly grieved; and she sent raiment** [*clothing*] **to clothe Mordecai**, and to take away his sackcloth from him: **but he received** *it* **not** [*he refused it*].

Next, Esther sends word to Mordecai to see what is going on.

5 **Then called Esther for Hatach,** *one* of the king's chamberlains [*eunuchs*], whom he had appointed to attend upon her, **and gave him a commandment to Mordecai, to know what it** *was,* **and why it** *was.*

6 So **Hatach went forth to Mordecai** unto the street of the city, which *was* before the king's gate.

7 And **Mordecai told him of all that had happened unto him, and of the sum of the money that Haman had promised to pay to the king's treasuries for the Jews, to destroy them.**

8 **Also he gave him the copy of the writing of the decree that was given at Shushan to destroy them, to shew** *it* **unto Esther,** and to declare *it* unto her, **and to charge her that she should go in unto the king, to make supplication unto him, and to make request before him for her people.**

9 And **Hatach came and told Esther the words of Mordecai.**

Esther sends instructions back to Mordecai, including her concern about going to the king without being invited.

10 ¶ Again **Esther spake unto Hatach, and gave him commandment unto Mordecai;**

11 **All the king's servants,** and the people of the king's provinces, do **know, that whosoever,** whether man or woman, **shall come unto the king into the inner court, who is not called,** *there is* **one law of his to put** *him* **to death, except such to whom the king shall hold out the golden sceptre, that he may live:** but I have not been called to come in unto the king these thirty days.

12 And **they told to Mordecai Esther's words.**

13 **Then Mordecai commanded to answer Esther, Think not with thyself that thou shalt escape in the king's house, more than all the Jews** [*don't think that just because you are in the palace, you will escape death when all other Jews are killed*].

The last phrase of verse 14, next, has been used in many, many talks and lessons.

14 For if thou altogether holdest thy peace at this time, *then* shall there enlargement and deliverance arise to the Jews from another place; but thou and thy father's house shall be destroyed: and who knoweth whether thou art come to the kingdom **for** *such* **a time as this**?

15 ¶ **Then Esther bade** *them* **return Mordecai** *this answer,*

Esther's courage and faith is strongly revealed in the last phrase of this verse.

16 **Go, gather together all the Jews that are present in Shushan, and fast ye for me, and neither eat nor drink three days, night or day: I also and my maidens**

will fast likewise; **and so will I go in unto the king**, which *is* not according to the law: and **if I perish, I perish.**

17 So **Mordecai went his way, and did according to all that Esther had commanded him**.

ESTHER 5

Selection: all verses

In this chapter, Esther risks her life by going to the king uninvited. He holds out his golden scepter to her, indicating that she may continue coming toward him. She invites him and Haman to a banquet and Haman makes plans to have Mordecai hanged.

1 NOW it came to pass on the third day, that **Esther put on** *her* royal *apparel* [*clothing*]**, and stood in the inner court of the king's house** [*palace*]**,** over against the king's house [*NIV, "in front of the king's hall"*]: and **the king sat upon his royal throne** in the royal house, over against the gate of the house.

2 And it was so, **when the king saw Esther the queen standing in the court,** *that* **she obtained favour in his sight: and the king held out to Esther the golden sceptre** that *was* in his hand. **So Esther drew near, and touched the top of the sceptre.**

3 **Then said the king** unto her, **What wilt thou, queen Esther?** and **what** *is* **thy request? it shall be even given thee to the half of the kingdom.**

4 And **Esther answered, If** *it seem* **good unto the king, let the king and Haman come this day unto the banquet that I have prepared for him.**

5 Then the king said, Cause Haman to make haste, that he may do as Esther hath said. **So the king and Haman came to the banquet that Esther had prepared.**

6 ¶ And **the king said unto Esther at the banquet** of wine, **What** *is* **thy petition? and it shall be granted thee**: and what *is* thy request? even to the half of the kingdom it shall be performed.

7 **Then answered Esther,** and said, My petition and **my request** *is;*

8 If I have found favour in the sight of the king, and if it please the king to grant my petition, and to perform my request, **let the king and Haman come to the banquet that I shall prepare for them, and I will do to morrow as the king hath said** [*I will tell you tomorrow what my request is*].

9 ¶ **Then went Haman forth that day joyful and with a glad heart: but when Haman saw Mordecai in the king's gate, that he stood not up, nor moved for him, he was full of indignation against Mordecai.**

10 **Nevertheless Haman refrained himself** [*didn't do anything to Mordecai at that time*]**: and when he came home, he sent and called for his friends, and Zeresh his wife.**

_____
_____
_____
_____
_____
_____
_____
_____
_____
_____
_____
_____
_____
_____
_____
_____
_____
_____
_____
_____
_____
_____
_____
_____
_____
_____
_____

11 And **Haman told them** of the glory of his riches, and the multitude of his children, and all *the things* wherein the king had promoted him, and how he had advanced him above the princes and servants of the king.

12 **Haman said moreover, Yea, Esther the queen did let no man come in with the king unto the banquet that she had prepared but myself; and to morrow am I invited unto her also with the king.**

13 **Yet all this availeth me nothing, so long as I see Mordecai the Jew sitting at the king's gate.**

Next, Haman's wife and friends exultantly suggest that Haman should build a 75-foot-high gallows upon which to hang Mordecai, in anticipation of more honors from the king to be bestowed upon Haman.

14 ¶ **Then said Zeresh his wife and all his friends unto him, Let a gallows be made of fifty cubits high, and to morrow speak thou unto the king that Mordecai may be hanged thereon**: then go thou in merrily with the king unto the banquet. **And the thing pleased Haman; and he caused the gallows to be made.**

ESTHER 6

Selection: all verses

Chapter 6 tells us that on the next day, Haman follows the suggestions of his wife and friends. He goes to the king to ask for permission to hang Mordecai. In the meantime, though, the king had a sleepless night and to pass the time, he had records of recent events in the kingdom read to him by some of his servants. In so doing, he discovered that Mordecai was the one who had exposed the plot by two doorkeepers to assassinate him. He then asks what has been done to reward and honor Mordecai. The answer, nothing. So, when Haman arrives, the king asks him what he thinks should be done to honor a certain man who has done much for the king. Haman thinks he is talking about him.

Enjoy the rest of the story as told in this chapter.

1 **ON that night could not the king sleep**, and he commanded to bring **the book of records** of the chronicles; and they **were read before the king**.

2 And **it was found written, that Mordecai had told of** Bigthana and Teresh, **two of the king's chamberlains, the keepers of the door, who sought to lay hand on the king Ahasuerus** [*assassinate him*].

3 And **the king said, What honour and dignity hath been done to Mordecai for this?** Then said the king's servants that ministered unto him, **There is nothing done for him.**

Next, Haman enters the hall, requesting an audience with the king.

4 ¶ And **the king said, Who** *is* **in the court?** Now **Haman was come into the outward court of the king's house, to speak unto the king to hang Mordecai** on the gallows that he had prepared for him.

5 And **the king's servants said unto him, Behold, Haman standeth in the court. And the king said, Let him come in.**

6 **So Haman came in.** And **the king said unto him, What shall be done unto the man whom the king delighteth to honour?** Now **Haman thought in his heart**, To whom would the king delight to do honour more than to **myself?**

7 And **Haman answered** the king, For the man whom the king delighteth to honour,

8 **Let the royal apparel be brought which the king** *useth* **to wear, and the horse that the king rideth upon, and the crown royal which is set upon his head:**

9 And let this apparel and horse be delivered to the hand of one of the king's most noble princes, that they may array the man *withal* whom the king delighteth to honour, **and bring him on horseback through the street of the city, and proclaim before him** [*have runners go ahead of him announcing him to the people*], Thus shall it be done to the man whom the king delighteth to honour.

10 **Then the king said to Haman**, Make haste, *and* take the apparel and the horse, as thou hast said, and **do even so to Mordecai the Jew**, that sitteth at the king's gate: let nothing fail of all that thou has spoken [*don't leave out any of the things you mentioned*].

11 **Then took Haman the apparel and the horse, and arrayed Mordecai, and brought him on horseback through the street of the city, and proclaimed before him**, Thus shall it be done unto the man whom the king delighteth to honour.

Imagine how Haman felt as he returned home. Certainly, there is a lesson for us here to avoid pridefully building ourselves up at the expense of others.

12 ¶ And Mordecai came again to the king's gate. But **Haman hasted to his house mourning, and having his head covered.**

13 And **Haman told Zeresh his wife and all his friends every** *thing* that had befallen him. **Then said his wise men and Zeresh his wife unto him, If Mordecai** *be* **of the seed of the Jews, before whom thou hast begun to fall, thou shalt not prevail against him, but shalt surely fall before him** [*since Mordecai is a Jew, there is no way you can carry out your plot to kill the Jews, and, you are in big trouble*].

14 And **while they** *were* **yet talking with him, came the king's chamberlains**, and hasted **to bring Haman unto the banquet that Esther had prepared.**

ESTHER 7

Selection: all verses

In this chapter, Esther reveals that she is a Jew and that Haman's plot is designed to get her and her people all killed.

1 **SO the king and Haman came to banquet with Esther the queen.**

NOTES

_____
_____
_____
_____
_____
_____
_____
_____
_____
_____
_____
_____
_____
_____
_____
_____
_____
_____
_____
_____
_____
_____
_____
_____
_____
_____
_____
_____
_____
_____
_____

2 And **the king said again unto Esther** on the second day at the banquet of wine, **What** *is* **thy petition, queen Esther?** and it shall be granted thee: and what *is* thy request? and it shall be performed, *even* to the half of the kingdom.

3 Then **Esther the queen answered** and said, **If I have found favour in thy sight**, O king, and if it please the king, **let my life be given me at my petition, and my people at my request**:

> Next, Esther explains the plot to kill the Jews to the king.

4 **For we are sold, I and my people, to be destroyed, to be slain, and to perish**. But if we had been sold for bondmen and bondwomen, I had held my tongue, although the enemy could not countervail the king's damage [*German Bible, if this plot were only to sell us as slaves, I would have kept quiet about it because it would not have done you, as king, so much damage*].

5 ¶ **Then the king** Ahasuerus answered and **said unto Esther** the queen, **Who is he, and where is he, that durst presume in his heart to do so?**

6 And **Esther said, The adversary and enemy** *is* **this wicked Haman**. Then Haman was afraid before the king and the queen.

7 ¶ **And the king arising from the banquet** of wine **in his wrath** [*anger*] *went* **into the palace garden**: and **Haman stood up to make request for his life** [*pled for his life*] **to Esther the queen**; for **he saw that there was evil determined against him by the king**.

8 Then the king returned out of the palace garden into the place of the banquet of wine; and **Haman was fallen upon the bed whereon Esther** *was*. Then **said the king, Will he force** [*molest*] **the queen also before me in the house?** As the word went out of the king's mouth, **they covered Haman's face**.

9 And Harbonah, **one of the chamberlains, said** before the king, **Behold** [*take a good look at*] **also, the gallows fifty cubits high, which Haman had made for Mordecai**, who had spoken good for the king, **standeth in the house of Haman**. Then **the king said, Hang him thereon**.

10 **So they hanged Haman on the gallows that he had prepared for Mordecai**. Then was the king's wrath pacified.

ESTHER 8

Selection: all verses

In this chapter we see the courage and faith of Queen Esther pay off as Mordecai is given the signet ring that the king had given to Haman and the king reverses the decree to kill the Jews. Certainly, we learn that "after much tribulation come the blessings" (D&C 58:4).

1 **ON that day did the king Ahasuerus give the house** [*entire estate*] **of Haman the Jews' enemy unto Esther the queen. And Mordecai came before the king**; for **Esther had told what he** *was* **unto her** [*how she was related to him*].

2 And **the king took off his ring, which he had taken from Haman, and gave it unto Mordecai**. And Esther set Mordecai over the house of Haman.

Next, Esther pleads with the king to reverse the edict to kill the Jews.

3 ¶ And **Esther spake yet again before the king, and fell down at his feet, and besought him with tears to put away the mischief of Haman** the Agagite, and his device [*plot*] that he had devised against the Jews.

4 Then **the king held out the golden sceptre toward Esther. So Esther arose, and stood before the king**.

5 And said, If it please the king, and if I have found favour in his sight, and the thing *seem* right before the king, and I *be* pleasing in his eyes, **let it be written to reverse the letters devised by Haman** the son of Hammedatha the Agagite, **which he wrote to destroy the Jews which *are* in all the king's provinces**:

6 For **how can I endure to see the evil that shall come unto my people?** or how can I endure to see the destruction of my kindred?

7 ¶ **Then the king Ahasuerus said unto Esther the queen and to Mordecai the Jew**, Behold, I have given Esther the house of Haman, and him they have hanged upon the gallows, because he laid his hand upon the Jews.

8 **Write ye also for the Jews, as it liketh you, in the king's name, and seal *it* with the king's ring**: for the writing which is written in the king's name, and sealed with the king's ring, may no man reverse.

9 **Then were the king's scribes called** at that time in the third month, that *is,* the month Sivan, on the three and twentieth *day* thereof; **and it was written according to all that Mordecai commanded** unto the Jews, and to the lieutenants, and the deputies and rulers of the provinces which *are* from India unto Ethiopia, an hundred twenty and seven provinces, unto every province according to the writing thereof, and unto every people after their language, and to the Jews according to their writing, and according to their language.

10 And **he wrote in the king Ahasuerus' name, and sealed *it* with the king's ring, and sent letters by posts on horseback, *and* riders on mules, camels, *and* young dromedaries** [*camels*]:

11 Wherein **the king granted the Jews which *were* in every city to gather themselves together, and to stand for their life**, to destroy, to slay, and to cause to perish, all the power of the people and province that would assault them, *both* little ones and women, and *to take* the spoil of them for a prey,

12 Upon one day in all the provinces of king Ahasuerus, *namely,* upon the thirteenth *day* of the twelfth month, which *is* the month Adar.

NOTES

NOTES

_____
_____
_____
_____
_____
_____
_____
_____
_____
_____
_____
_____
_____
_____
_____
_____
_____
_____
_____
_____
_____
_____
_____
_____
_____
_____
_____
_____
_____
_____

13 **The copy of the writing for a commandment** to be given in every province *was* **published unto all people**, and **that the Jews should be ready against that day to avenge themselves on their enemies**.

14 *So* the posts that rode upon mules *and* camels went out, being hastened and pressed on by the king's commandment. **And the decree was given at** Shushan **the palace**.

15 ¶ And **Mordecai went out from the presence of the king in royal apparel** of blue and white, and **with a great crown of gold**, and with **a garment of fine linen and purple**: and the city of Shushan rejoiced and was glad.

16 **The Jews had light, and gladness, and joy, and honour**.

17 And in every province, and in every city, whithersoever the king's commandment and his decree came, **the Jews had joy and gladness, a feast and a good day**. And **many of the people of the land became Jews**; for the fear of the Jews fell upon them.

ESTHER 9

Selection: all verses

In this chapter, we will see a great feast and joyful celebration held by the Jews in the Persian Empire as they celebrated their freedom from Hamon's plot. In fact, it was perpetuated in the years to come as a yearly feast and celebration and is still held and celebrated today. It is called Purim.

First, in verses 1–11, the Jews carry out the permission from the king to slay those who were preparing to kill them.

1 **NOW in the twelfth month**, that *is,* the month Adar, on the thirteenth day of the same, when the king's commandment and his decree drew near to be put in execution, **in the day that the enemies of the Jews hoped to have power over them**, (though it was turned to the contrary, that the Jews had rule over them that hated them;)

2 **The Jews gathered themselves together in their cities throughout all the provinces of the king Ahasuerus, to lay hand on such as sought their hurt**: and no man could withstand them; for the fear of them fell upon all people.

3 And **all the rulers of the provinces**, and the lieutenants, and the deputies, and officers of the king, **helped the Jews; because the fear of Mordecai fell upon them**.

4 **For Mordecai** *was* **great in the king's house, and his fame went out throughout all the provinces**: for this man Mordecai waxed greater and greater.

5 **Thus the Jews smote all their enemies with the stroke of the sword, and slaughter, and destruction, and did what they would unto those that hated them**.

6 And in Shushan **the palace the Jews slew and destroyed five hundred men**.

7 And Parshandatha, and Dalphon, and Aspatha,

8 And Poratha, and Adalia, and Aridatha,

9 And Parmashta, and Arisai, and Aridai, and Vajezatha,

10 **The ten sons of Haman** [*named above in verses 7–9*] the son of Hammedatha, **the enemy of the Jews, slew they; but on the spoil laid they not their hand** [*but they did not plunder their belongings*].

11 On that day the number of those that were slain in Shushan the palace was brought before the king.

Verses 12–16, next, appear to be a review, giving a bit more detail for the above verses.

12 ¶ And **the king said unto Esther** the queen, **The Jews have slain and destroyed five hundred men in Shushan the palace, and the ten sons of Haman; what have they done in the rest of the king's provinces?** now **what** *is* **thy petition?** and it shall be granted thee: or **what** *is* **thy request further? and it shall be done**.

13 **Then said Esther**, If it please the king, let it be granted to the Jews which *are* in Shushan to do to morrow also according unto this day's decree, and **let Haman's ten sons be hanged upon the gallows**.

14 And **the king commanded it so to be done**: and the decree was given at Shushan; and **they hanged Haman's ten sons**.

15 For **the Jews that** *were* **in Shushan** [*the palace*] gathered themselves together on the fourteenth day also of the month Adar, and **slew three hundred men at Shushan; but on the prey they laid not their hand** [*but did not pillage and plunder*].

16 But **the other Jews that** *were* **in the king's provinces** gathered themselves together, and stood for their lives, and had rest from their enemies, and **slew of their foes seventy and five thousand, but they laid not their hands on the prey**,

Next, we see the beginning of the feast of Purim, as explained above in the heading to this chapter.

17 On the thirteenth day of the month Adar; and on the fourteenth day of **the same rested they, and made it a day of feasting and gladness**.

18 But **the Jews that** *were* **at Shushan** assembled together on the thirteenth *day* thereof, and on the fourteenth thereof; and on the fifteenth *day* of the same they **rested, and made it a day of feasting and gladness**.

19 **Therefore the Jews of the villages**, that dwelt in the unwalled towns, **made the fourteenth day of the month Adar** *a day of* **gladness and feasting, and a good day, and of sending portions one to another**.

NOTES

_____
_____
_____
_____
_____
_____
_____
_____
_____
_____
_____
_____
_____
_____
_____
_____
_____
_____
_____
_____
_____
_____
_____
_____
_____
_____
_____
_____
_____
_____
_____

20 ¶ And **Mordecai wrote these things, and sent letters unto all the Jews that** _were_ **in all the provinces** of the king Ahasuerus, _both_ nigh and far,

21 **To stablish** _this_ **among them, that they should keep the fourteenth day of the month Adar, and the fifteenth day of the same, yearly** [_instructing them to make it an annual feast and celebration_],

22 As the days wherein the Jews rested from their enemies, and the month which was turned unto them from sorrow to joy, and from mourning into a good day: **that they should make them days of feasting and joy, and of sending portions one to another, and gifts to the poor**.

23 **And the Jews undertook to do as they had begun, and as Mordecai had writ-ten unto them**;

In verses 24–32, we have a review and additional explanation of how Purim came to be a yearly celebration. As mentioned above, "Pur" means to cast lots. When Haman cast lots to determine which day on the calendar the Jews were to be killed, the lot fell on a day quite far in the future, thus giving Esther and Mordecai time to stop Haman's plot to kill all the Jews in the kingdom.

24 **Because Haman** the son of Hammedatha, the Agagite, **the enemy of all the Jews, had devised against the Jews to destroy them**, and **had cast Pur, that** _is_, **the lot**, to consume them, and to destroy them;

25 **But when** _Esther_ **came before the king, he commanded by letters that his wicked device, which he devised against the Jews, should return upon his own head, and that he and his sons should be hanged on the gallows**.

26 **Wherefore they called these days Purim** after the name of Pur. Therefore for all the words of this letter, and _of that_ which they had seen concerning this matter, and which had come unto them,

27 **The Jews ordained**, and took upon them, and upon their seed, and upon all such as joined themselves unto them, so as it should not fail, **that they would keep these two days** according to their writing, and according to their _appointed_ time **every year**;

28 **And** _that_ **these days** _should be_ **remembered and kept throughout every gener-ation, every family, every province, and every city; and** _that_ **these days of Purim should not fail from among the Jews, nor the memorial of them perish from their seed**.

29 Then **Esther the queen**, the daughter of Abihail, **and Mordecai the Jew, wrote with all authority, to confirm this second letter of Purim**.

30 And **he sent the letters unto all the Jews, to the hundred twenty and seven provinces of the kingdom** of Ahasuerus, _with_ **words of peace and truth**,

31 **To confirm these days of Purim** in their times *appointed,* according as Mordecai the Jew and Esther the queen had enjoined them, and as they had decreed for themselves and for their seed, the matters of the fastings and their cry.

32 **And the decree of Esther confirmed these matters of Purim; and it was written in the book**.

ESTHER 10

Selection: all verses

Finally, in this very short chapter, we have a summary of Mordecai's rise to power in a very large empire. It can remind us of Joseph who was sold into Egypt and his rise to be second in command in all Egypt, directly under Pharaoh.

1 AND the **king Ahasuerus laid a tribute** [*laid taxes*] **upon the land, and** *upon* **the isles of the sea** [*all the providences in his kingdom*].

Next, we see that the things we have been reading about in the Book of Esther are recorded in other histories.

2 And **all the acts of his power and of his might, and the declaration of the greatness of Mordecai,** whereunto the king advanced him, *are* **they not written in the book of the chronicles of the kings of Media and Persia?**

And, finally, a summary of Mordecai. It will be interesting to meet him someday in the next life.

3 For **Mordecai the Jew** *was* **next unto king Ahasuerus, and great among the Jews, and accepted of the multitude of his brethren, seeking the wealth of his people, and speaking peace to all his seed.**

NOTES

Job 1–3; 12–14; 19; 21–24; 38–40; 42

"Yet Will I Trust in Him"

As you will likely see, the storyline of Job is relatively easy to understand as you read along. For this reason and because of limited space, I have chosen not to do much by way of commentary in this journal format, but I've included several chapters of Job that go along with our Come, Follow Me curriculum just as they stand in the Bible. I'm hoping that the training you've already received in this study guide in understanding the language of the Old Testament will be a great help to you in comprehending the book of Job. It may be helpful to know that the book of Job is considered poetry. Hebrew poetry like this, as well as in Psalms, Proverbs, parts of Isaiah, Jeremiah, and Amos, does not involve rhyming of words as it does in most of our English poetry. Rather, it involves repetition of ideas for emphasis that is often called "parallelism." Doctrinally, two of the most important references in Job are Job 19:25–27, which bears witness of our literal resurrection, and Job 38:4–7, which bears witness of the literal nature of our premortality and our attendance in the grand council held in heaven during our premortal existence.

NOTES

Job contains several major messages. One is that bad things happen to good people. Another is that the only sure strength during times of trial and adversity is personal righteousness and integrity, combined with deep faith in God. Yet another is the value of patience when things keep going wrong.

One definite message provided at the end of the book is that ultimately, personal righteousness pays off in ways beyond our ability to comprehend. The ending of the account of Job (Job 42:10–17) can be considered to be a "type" of exaltation.

Because Job is fairly easy to read as it stands in the Bible, and because I have limited time, I will spend it on the more difficult books in the Old Testament, like Isaiah and Ezekiel. I will therefore not go through Job verse-by-verse; rather, I will include the headings from our Bible to assist you in your study. We will use bold font in Job 19:25–26 and 38:7.

JOB 1

Job, a just and perfect man, is blessed with great riches—Satan obtains leave from the Lord to tempt and try Job—His property and children are destroyed, and yet he praises and blesses the Lord.

1 THERE was a man in the land of Uz, whose name *was* Job; and that man was perfect and upright, and one that feared God, and eschewed evil.

2 And there were born unto him seven sons and three daughters.

3 His substance also was seven thousand sheep, and three thousand camels, and five hundred yoke of oxen, and five hundred she asses, and a very great household; so that this man was the greatest of all the men of the east.

4 And his sons went and feasted *in their* houses, every one his day; and sent and called for their three sisters to eat and to drink with them.

5 And it was so, when the days of *their* feasting were gone about, that Job sent and sanctified them, and rose up early in the morning, and offered burnt offerings

according to the number of them all: for Job said, It may be that my sons have sinned, and cursed God in their hearts. Thus did Job continually.

6 ¶ Now there was a day when the sons of God came to present themselves before the LORD, and Satan came also among them.

7 And the LORD said unto Satan, Whence comest thou? Then Satan answered the LORD, and said, From going to and fro in the earth, and from walking up and down in it.

8 And the LORD said unto Satan, Hast thou considered my servant Job, that *there is* none like him in the earth, a perfect and an upright man, one that feareth God, and escheweth evil?

9 Then Satan answered the LORD, and said, Doth Job fear God for nought?

10 Hast not thou made an hedge about him, and about his house, and about all that he hath on every side? thou hast blessed the work of his hands, and his substance is increased in the land.

11 But put forth thine hand now, and touch all that he hath, and he will curse thee to thy face.

12 And the LORD said unto Satan, Behold, all that he hath *is* in thy power; only upon himself put not forth thine hand. So Satan went forth from the presence of the LORD.

13 ¶ And there was a day when his sons and his daughters *were* eating and drinking wine in their eldest brother's house:

14 And there came a messenger unto Job, and said, The oxen were plowing, and the asses feeding beside them:

15 And the Sabeans fell *upon them,* and took them away; yea, they have slain the servants with the edge of the sword; and I only am escaped alone to tell thee.

16 While he *was* yet speaking, there came also another, and said, The fire of God is fallen from heaven, and hath burned up the sheep, and the servants, and consumed them; and I only am escaped alone to tell thee.

17 While he *was* yet speaking, there came also another, and said, The Chaldeans made out three bands, and fell upon the camels, and have carried them away, yea, and slain the servants with the edge of the sword; and I only am escaped alone to tell thee.

18 While he *was* yet speaking, there came also another, and said, Thy sons and thy daughters *were* eating and drinking wine in their eldest brother's house:

NOTES

NOTES

19 And, behold, there came a great wind from the wilderness, and smote the four corners of the house, and it fell upon the young men, and they are dead; and I only am escaped alone to tell thee.

20 Then Job arose, and rent his mantle, and shaved his head, and fell down upon the ground, and worshipped,

21 And said, Naked came I out of my mother's womb, and naked shall I return thither: the LORD gave, and the LORD hath taken away; blessed be the name of the LORD.

22 In all this Job sinned not, nor charged God foolishly.

JOB 2

Satan obtains leave from the Lord to afflict Job physically—He is smitten with boils—Eliphaz, Bildad, and Zophar come to comfort him.

1 AGAIN there was a day when the sons of God came to present themselves before the LORD, and Satan came also among them to present himself before the LORD.

2 And the LORD said unto Satan, From whence comest thou? And Satan answered the LORD, and said, From going to and fro in the earth, and from walking up and down in it.

3 And the LORD said unto Satan, Hast thou considered my servant Job, that *there is* none like him in the earth, a perfect and an upright man, one that feareth God, and escheweth evil? and still he holdeth fast his integrity, although thou movedst me against him, to destroy him without cause.

4 And Satan answered the LORD, and said, Skin for skin, yea, all that a man hath will he give for his life.

5 But put forth thine hand now, and touch his bone and his flesh, and he will curse thee to thy face.

6 And the LORD said unto Satan, Behold, he *is* in thine hand; but save his life.

7 ¶ So went Satan forth from the presence of the LORD, and smote Job with sore boils from the sole of his foot unto his crown.

8 And he took him a potsherd to scrape himself withal; and he sat down among the ashes.

9 ¶ Then said his wife unto him, Dost thou still retain thine integrity? curse God, and die.

10 But he said unto her, Thou speakest as one of the foolish women speaketh. What? shall we receive good at the hand of God, and shall we not receive evil? In all this did not Job sin with his lips.

11 ¶ Now when Job's three friends heard of all this evil that was come upon him, they came every one from his own place; Eliphaz the Temanite, and Bildad the Shuhite, and Zophar the Naamathite: for they had made an appointment together to come to mourn with him and to comfort him.

12 And when they lifted up their eyes afar off, and knew him not, they lifted up their voice, and wept; and they rent every one his mantle, and sprinkled dust upon their heads toward heaven.

13 So they sat down with him upon the ground seven days and seven nights, and none spake a word unto him: for they saw that *his* grief was very great.

JOB 3

Job curses the day and services of his birth. He asks: Why died I not from the womb?

1 AFTER this opened Job his mouth, and cursed his day.

2 And Job spake, and said,

3 Let the day perish wherein I was born, and the night *in which* it was said, There is a man child conceived.

4 Let that day be darkness; let not God regard it from above, neither let the light shine upon it.

5 Let darkness and the shadow of death stain it; let a cloud dwell upon it; let the blackness of the day terrify it.

6 *As for* that night, let darkness seize upon it; let it not be joined unto the days of the year, let it not come into the number of the months.

7 Lo, let that night be solitary, let no joyful voice come therein.

8 Let them curse it that curse the day, who are ready to raise up their mourning.

9 Let the stars of the twilight thereof be dark; let it look for light, but *have* none; neither let it see the dawning of the day:

10 Because it shut not up the doors of my *mother's* womb, nor hid sorrow from mine eyes.

11 Why died I not from the womb? *why* did I *not* give up the ghost when I came out of the belly?

12 Why did the knees prevent me? or why the breasts that I should suck?

13 For now should I have lain still and been quiet, I should have slept: then had I been at rest,

NOTES

NOTES

14 With kings and counsellors of the earth, which built desolate places for themselves;

15 Or with princes that had gold, who filled their houses with silver:

16 Or as an hidden untimely birth I had not been; as infants *which* never saw light.

17 There the wicked cease *from* troubling; and there the weary be at rest.

18 *There* the prisoners rest together; they hear not the voice of the oppressor.

19 The small and great are there; and the servant *is* free from his master.

20 Wherefore is light given to him that is in misery, and life unto the bitter *in* soul;

21 Which long for death, but it *cometh* not; and dig for it more than for hid treasures;

22 Which rejoice exceedingly, *and* are glad, when they can find the grave?

23 *Why is light given* to a man whose way is hid, and whom God hath hedged in?

24 For my sighing cometh before I eat, and my roarings are poured out like the waters.

25 For the thing which I greatly feared is come upon me, and that which I was afraid of is come unto me.

26 I was not in safety, neither had I rest, neither was I quiet; yet trouble came.

JOB 12

Job says: The souls of all things are in the hands of the Lord; and, With the ancient is wisdom; and, The Lord governs in all things.

1 AND Job answered and said,

2 No doubt but ye *are* the people, and wisdom shall die with you.

3 But I have understanding as well as you; I *am* not inferior to you: yea, who knoweth not such things as these?

4 I am *as* one mocked of his neighbour, who calleth upon God, and he answereth him: the just upright *man is* laughed to scorn.

5 He that is ready to slip with *his* feet *is as* a lamp despised in the thought of him that is at ease.

6 The tabernacles of robbers prosper, and they that provoke God are secure; into whose hand God bringeth *abundantly*.

7 But ask now the beasts, and they shall teach thee; and the fowls of the air, and they shall tell thee:

8 Or speak to the earth, and it shall teach thee: and the fishes of the sea shall declare unto thee.

9 Who knoweth not in all these that the hand of the LORD hath wrought this?

10 In whose hand *is* the soul of every living thing, and the breath of all mankind.

11 Doth not the ear try words? and the mouth taste his meat?

12 With the ancient *is* wisdom; and in length of days understanding.

13 With him *is* wisdom and strength, he hath counsel and understanding.

14 Behold, he breaketh down, and it cannot be built again: he shutteth up a man, and there can be no opening.

15 Behold, he withholdeth the waters, and they dry up: also he sendeth them out, and they overturn the earth.

16 With him *is* strength and wisdom: the deceived and the deceiver *are* his.

17 He leadeth counsellors away spoiled, and maketh the judges fools.

18 He looseth the bond of kings, and girdeth their loins with a girdle.

19 He leadeth princes away spoiled, and overthroweth the mighty.

20 He removeth away the speech of the trusty, and taketh away the understanding of the aged.

21 He poureth contempt upon princes, and weakeneth the strength of the mighty.

22 He discovereth deep things out of darkness, and bringeth out to light the shadow of death.

23 He increaseth the nations, and destroyeth them: he enlargeth the nations, and straiteneth them *again*.

24 He taketh away the heart of the chief of the people of the earth, and causeth them to wander in a wilderness *where there is* no way.

25 They grope in the dark without light, and he maketh them to stagger like *a* drunken *man*.

NOTES

NOTES

_____
_____
_____
_____
_____
_____
_____
_____
_____
_____
_____
_____
_____
_____
_____
_____
_____
_____
_____
_____
_____
_____
_____
_____
_____
_____
_____
_____
_____

JOB 13

Job testifies of his confidence in the Lord, and says: Though he slay me, yet will I trust in him; and, He also shall be my salvation.

1 LO, mine eye hath seen all *this,* mine ear hath heard and understood it.

2 What ye know, *the same* do I know also: I *am* not inferior unto you.

3 Surely I would speak to the Almighty, and I desire to reason with God.

4 But ye *are* forgers of lies, ye *are* all physicians of no value.

5 O that ye would altogether hold your peace! and it should be your wisdom.

6 Hear now my reasoning, and hearken to the pleadings of my lips.

7 Will ye speak wickedly for God? and talk deceitfully for him?

8 Will ye accept his person? will ye contend for God?

9 Is it good that he should search you out? or as one man mocketh another, do ye *so* mock him?

10 He will surely reprove you, if ye do secretly accept persons.

11 Shall not his excellency make you afraid? and his dread fall upon you?

12 Your remembrances *are* like unto ashes, your bodies to bodies of clay.

13 Hold your peace, let me alone, that I may speak, and let come on me what *will.*

14 Wherefore do I take my flesh in my teeth, and put my life in mine hand?

15 Though he slay me, yet will I trust in him: but I will maintain mine own ways before him.

16 He also *shall be* my salvation: for an hypocrite shall not come before him.

17 Hear diligently my speech, and my declaration with your ears.

18 Behold now, I have ordered *my* cause; I know that I shall be justified.

19 Who *is* he *that* will plead with me? for now, if I hold my tongue, I shall give up the ghost.

20 Only do not two *things* unto me: then will I not hide myself from thee.

21 Withdraw thine hand far from me: and let not thy dread make me afraid.

22 Then call thou, and I will answer: or let me speak, and answer thou me.

23 How many *are* mine iniquities and sins? make me to know my transgression and my sin.

24 Wherefore hidest thou thy face, and holdest me for thine enemy?

25 Wilt thou break a leaf driven to and fro? and wilt thou pursue the dry stubble?

26 For thou writest bitter things against me, and makest me to possess the iniquities of my youth.

27 Thou puttest my feet also in the stocks, and lookest narrowly unto all my paths; thou settest a print upon the heels of my feet.

28 And he, as a rotten thing, consumeth, as a garment that is moth eaten.

JOB 14

Job testifies of the shortness of life, the certainty of death, and the guarantee of a resurrection—He asks: If a man die, shall he live again?—He answers that he will await the Lord's call to come forth from the grave.

1 MAN *that is* born of a woman *is* of few days, and full of trouble.

2 He cometh forth like a flower, and is cut down: he fleeth also as a shadow, and continueth not.

3 And dost thou open thine eyes upon such an one, and bringest me into judgment with thee?

4 Who can bring a clean *thing* out of an unclean? not one.

5 Seeing his days *are* determined, the number of his months *are* with thee, thou hast appointed his bounds that he cannot pass;

6 Turn from him, that he may rest, till he shall accomplish, as an hireling, his day.

7 For there is hope of a tree, if it be cut down, that it will sprout again, and that the tender branch thereof will not cease.

8 Though the root thereof wax old in the earth, and the stock thereof die in the ground;

9 *Yet* through the scent of water it will bud, and bring forth boughs like a plant.

10 But man dieth, and wasteth away: yea, man giveth up the ghost, and where *is* he?

11 As the waters fail from the sea, and the flood decayeth and drieth up:

12 So man lieth down, and riseth not: till the heavens *be* no more, they shall not awake, nor be raised out of their sleep.

13 O that thou wouldest hide me in the grave, that thou wouldest keep me secret, until thy wrath be past, that thou wouldest appoint me a set time, and remember me!

14 If a man die, shall he live *again*? all the days of my appointed time will I wait, till my change come.

15 Thou shalt call, and I will answer thee: thou wilt have a desire to the work of thine hands.

16 For now thou numberest my steps: dost thou not watch over my sin?

17 My transgression *is* sealed up in a bag, and thou sewest up mine iniquity.

18 And surely the mountain falling cometh to nought, and the rock is removed out of his place.

19 The waters wear the stones: thou washest away the things which grow *out* of the dust of the earth; and thou destroyest the hope of man.

20 Thou prevailest for ever against him, and he passeth: thou changest his countenance, and sendest him away.

21 His sons come to honour, and he knoweth *it* not; and they are brought low, but he perceiveth *it* not of them.

22 But his flesh upon him shall have pain, and his soul within him shall mourn.

JOB 19

Job tells of the ills that have befallen him, and then testifies: I know that my Redeemer liveth—He prophesies of his own resurrection and that in his flesh he shall see God.

1 THEN Job answered and said,

2 How long will ye vex my soul, and break me in pieces with words?

3 These ten times have ye reproached me: ye are not ashamed *that* ye make yourselves strange to me.

4 And be it indeed *that* I have erred, mine error remaineth with myself.

5 If indeed ye will magnify *yourselves* against me, and plead against me my reproach:

6 Know now that God hath overthrown me, and hath compassed me with his net.

7 Behold, I cry out of wrong, but I am not heard: I cry aloud, but *there is* no judgment.

8 He hath fenced up my way that I cannot pass, and he hath set darkness in my paths.

9 He hath stripped me of my glory, and taken the crown *from* my head.

10 He hath destroyed me on every side, and I am gone: and mine hope hath he removed like a tree.

11 He hath also kindled his wrath against me, and he counteth me unto him as one of his enemies.

12 His troops come together, and raise up their way against me, and encamp round about my tabernacle.

13 He hath put my brethren far from me, and mine acquaintance are verily estranged from me.

14 My kinsfolk have failed, and my familiar friends have forgotten me.

15 They that dwell in mine house, and my maids, count me for a stranger: I am an alien in their sight.

16 I called my servant, and he gave *me* no answer; I intreated him with my mouth.

17 My breath is strange to my wife, though I intreated for the children's *sake* of mine own body.

18 Yea, young children despised me; I arose, and they spake against me.

19 All my inward friends abhorred me: and they whom I loved are turned against me.

20 My bone cleaveth to my skin and to my flesh, and I am escaped with the skin of my teeth.

21 Have pity upon me, have pity upon me, O ye my friends; for the hand of God hath touched me.

22 Why do ye persecute me as God, and are not satisfied with my flesh?

23 Oh that my words were now written! oh that they were printed in a book!

24 That they were graven with an iron pen and lead in the rock for ever!

25 For I know that my redeemer liveth, and that he shall stand at the latter day upon the earth:

NOTES

NOTES

26 **And though after my skin worms destroy this body, yet in my flesh shall I see God** [*we will be resurrected*]:

27 Whom I shall see for myself, and mine eyes shall behold, and not another; *though* my reins be consumed within me.

28 But ye should say, Why persecute we him, seeing the root of the matter is found in me?

29 Be ye afraid of the sword: for wrath *bringeth* the punishments of the sword, that ye may know *there is* a judgment.

JOB 21

Job admits that the wicked sometimes prosper in this life—Then he testifies that their judgment shall be hereafter in the day of wrath and destruction.

1 BUT Job answered and said,

2 Hear diligently my speech, and let this be your consolations.

3 Suffer me that I may speak; and after that I have spoken, mock on.

4 As for me, *is* my complaint to man? and if *it were so,* why should not my spirit be troubled?

5 Mark me, and be astonished, and lay *your* hand upon *your* mouth.

6 Even when I remember I am afraid, and trembling taketh hold on my flesh.

7 Wherefore do the wicked live, become old, yea, are mighty in power?

8 Their seed is established in their sight with them, and their offspring before their eyes.

9 Their houses *are* safe from fear, neither *is* the rod of God upon them.

10 Their bull gendereth, and faileth not; their cow calveth, and casteth not her calf.

11 They send forth their little ones like a flock, and their children dance.

12 They take the timbrel and harp, and rejoice at the sound of the organ.

13 They spend their days in wealth, and in a moment go down to the grave.

14 Therefore they say unto God, Depart from us; for we desire not the knowledge of thy ways.

NOTES

15 What *is* the Almighty, that we should serve him? and what profit should we have, if we pray unto him?

16 Lo, their good *is* not in their hand: the counsel of the wicked is far from me.

17 How oft is the candle of the wicked put out! and *how oft* cometh their destruction upon them! God distributeth sorrows in his anger.

18 They are as stubble before the wind, and as chaff that the storm carrieth away.

19 God layeth up his iniquity for his children: he rewardeth him, and he shall know *it*.

20 His eyes shall see his destruction, and he shall drink of the wrath of the Almighty.

21 For what pleasure *hath* he in his house after him, when the number of his months is cut off in the midst?

22 Shall *any* teach God knowledge? seeing he judgeth those that are high.

23 One dieth in his full strength, being wholly at ease and quiet.

24 His breasts are full of milk, and his bones are moistened with marrow.

25 And another dieth in the bitterness of his soul, and never eateth with pleasure.

26 They shall lie down alike in the dust, and the worms shall cover them.

27 Behold, I know your thoughts, and the devices *which* ye wrongfully imagine against me.

28 For ye say, Where *is* the house of the prince? and where *are* the dwelling places of the wicked?

29 Have ye not asked them that go by the way? and do ye not know their tokens,

30 That the wicked is reserved to the day of destruction? they shall be brought forth to the day of wrath.

31 Who shall declare his way to his face? and who shall repay him *what* he hath done?

32 Yet shall he be brought to the grave, and shall remain in the tomb.

33 The clods of the valley shall be sweet unto him, and every man shall draw after him, as *there are* innumerable before him.

34 How then comfort ye me in vain, seeing in your answers there remaineth falsehood?

NOTES

JOB 22

Eliphaz accuses Job of divers sins and exhorts him to repent.

1 THEN Eliphaz the Temanite answered and said,

2 Can a man be profitable unto God, as he that is wise may be profitable unto himself?

3 *Is it* any pleasure to the Almighty, that thou art righteous? or *is it* gain *to him,* that thou makest thy ways perfect?

4 Will he reprove thee for fear of thee? will he enter with thee into judgment?

5 *Is* not thy wickedness great? and thine iniquities infinite?

6 For thou hast taken a pledge from thy brother for nought, and stripped the naked of their clothing.

7 Thou hast not given water to the weary to drink, and thou hast withholden bread from the hungry.

8 But *as for* the mighty man, he had the earth; and the honourable man dwelt in it.

9 Thou hast sent widows away empty, and the arms of the fatherless have been broken.

10 Therefore snares *are* round about thee, and sudden fear troubleth thee;

11 Or darkness, *that* thou canst not see; and abundance of waters cover thee.

12 *Is* not God in the height of heaven? and behold the height of the stars, how high they are!

13 And thou sayest, How doth God know? can he judge through the dark cloud?

14 Thick clouds *are* a covering to him, that he seeth not; and he walketh in the circuit of heaven.

15 Hast thou marked the old way which wicked men have trodden?

16 Which were cut down out of time, whose foundation was overflown with a flood:

17 Which said unto God, Depart from us: and what can the Almighty do for them?

18 Yet he filled their houses with good *things:* but the counsel of the wicked is far from me.

19 The righteous see *it,* and are glad: and the innocent laugh them to scorn.

20 Whereas our substance is not cut down, but the remnant of them the fire consumeth.

21 Acquaint now thyself with him, and be at peace: thereby good shall come unto thee.

22 Receive, I pray thee, the law from his mouth, and lay up his words in thine heart.

23 If thou return to the Almighty, thou shalt be built up, thou shalt put away iniquity far from thy tabernacles.

24 Then shalt thou lay up gold as dust, and the *gold* of Ophir as the stones of the brooks.

25 Yea, the Almighty shall be thy defence, and thou shalt have plenty of silver.

26 For then shalt thou have thy delight in the Almighty, and shalt lift up thy face unto God.

27 Thou shalt make thy prayer unto him, and he shall hear thee, and thou shalt pay thy vows.

28 Thou shalt also decree a thing, and it shall be established unto thee: and the light shall shine upon thy ways.

29 When *men* are cast down, then thou shalt say, *There is* lifting up; and he shall save the humble person.

30 He shall deliver the island of the innocent: and it is delivered by the pureness of thine hands.

JOB 23

Job seeks the Lord and asserts his own righteousness—He says: When the Lord has tried me, I shall come forth as gold.

1 THEN Job answered and said,

2 Even to day *is* my complaint bitter: my stroke is heavier than my groaning.

3 Oh that I knew where I might find him! *that* I might come *even* to his seat!

4 I would order *my* cause before him, and fill my mouth with arguments.

5 I would know the words *which* he would answer me, and understand what he would say unto me.

6 Will he plead against me with *his* great power? No; but he would put *strength* in me.

7 There the righteous might dispute with him; so should I be delivered for ever from my judge.

8 Behold, I go forward, but he *is* not *there;* and backward, but I cannot perceive him:

9 On the left hand, where he doth work, but I cannot behold *him:* he hideth himself on the right hand, that I cannot see *him:*

10 But he knoweth the way that I take: *when* he hath tried me, I shall come forth as gold.

11 My foot hath held his steps, his way have I kept, and not declined.

12 Neither have I gone back from the commandment of his lips; I have esteemed the words of his mouth more than my necessary *food.*

13 But he *is* in one *mind,* and who can turn him? and *what* his soul desireth, even *that* he doeth.

14 For he performeth *the thing that is* appointed for me: and many such *things are* with him.

15 Therefore am I troubled at his presence: when I consider, I am afraid of him.

16 For God maketh my heart soft, and the Almighty troubleth me:

17 Because I was not cut off before the darkness, *neither* hath he covered the darkness from my face.

JOB 24

Murderers, adulterers, those who oppress the poor, and wicked people in general often go unpunished.

1 WHY, seeing times are not hidden from the Almighty, do they that know him not see his days?

2 *Some* remove the landmarks; they violently take away flocks, and feed *thereof.*

3 They drive away the ass of the fatherless, they take the widow's ox for a pledge.

4 They turn the needy out of the way: the poor of the earth hide themselves together.

5 Behold, *as* wild asses in the desert, go they forth to their work; rising betimes for a prey: the wilderness *yieldeth* food for them *and* for *their* children.

6 They reap *every one* his corn in the field: and they gather the vintage of the wicked.

7 They cause the naked to lodge without clothing, that *they have* no covering in the cold.

8 They are wet with the showers of the mountains, and embrace the rock for want of a shelter.

9 They pluck the fatherless from the breast, and take a pledge of the poor.

10 They cause *him* to go naked without clothing, and they take away the sheaf *from* the hungry;

11 *Which* make oil within their walls, *and* tread *their* winepresses, and suffer thirst.

12 Men groan from out of the city, and the soul of the wounded crieth out: yet God layeth not folly *to them.*

13 They are of those that rebel against the light; they know not the ways thereof, nor abide in the paths thereof.

14 The murderer rising with the light killeth the poor and needy, and in the night is as a thief.

15 The eye also of the adulterer waiteth for the twilight, saying, No eye shall see me: and disguiseth *his* face.

16 In the dark they dig through houses, *which* they had marked for themselves in the daytime: they know not the light.

17 For the morning *is* to them even as the shadow of death: if *one* know *them, they are in* the terrors of the shadow of death.

18 He *is* swift as the waters; their portion is cursed in the earth: he beholdeth not the way of the vineyards.

19 Drought and heat consume the snow waters: *so doth* the grave *those which* have sinned.

20 The womb shall forget him; the worm shall feed sweetly on him; he shall be no more remembered; and wickedness shall be broken as a tree.

21 He evil entreateth the barren *that* beareth not: and doeth not good to the widow.

22 He draweth also the mighty with his power: he riseth up, and no *man* is sure of life.

23 *Though* it be given him *to be* in safety, whereon he resteth; yet his eyes *are* upon their ways.

24 They are exalted for a little while, but are gone and brought low; they are taken out of the way as all *other,* and cut off as the tops of the ears of corn.

NOTES

NOTES

25 And if *it be* not *so* now, who will make me a liar, and make my speech nothing worth?

JOB 38

God asks Job where he was when the foundations of the earth were laid, when the morning stars sang together, and all the sons of God shouted for joy—The phenomena of nature show greatness of God and weakness of man.

1 THEN the LORD answered Job out of the whirlwind, and said,

2 Who *is* this that darkeneth counsel by words without knowledge?

3 Gird up now thy loins like a man; for I will demand of thee, and answer thou me.

4 Where wast thou when I laid the foundations of the earth? declare, if thou hast understanding.

5 Who hath laid the measures thereof, if thou knowest? or who hath stretched the line upon it?

6 Whereupon are the foundations thereof fastened? or who laid the corner stone thereof;

7 **When the morning stars sang together, and all the sons of God shouted for joy** [*our reaction as spirits in the premortal council when we were taught of the Father's plan of salvation for us*]**?**

8 Or *who* shut up the sea with doors, when it brake forth, *as if* it had issued out of the womb?

9 When I made the cloud the garment thereof, and thick darkness a swaddlingband for it,

10 And brake up for it my decreed *place,* and set bars and doors,

11 And said, Hitherto shalt thou come, but no further: and here shall thy proud waves be stayed?

12 Hast thou commanded the morning since thy days; *and* caused the dayspring to know his place;

13 That it might take hold of the ends of the earth, that the wicked might be shaken out of it?

14 It is turned as clay *to* the seal; and they stand as a garment.

15 And from the wicked their light is withholden, and the high arm shall be broken.

16 Hast thou entered into the springs of the sea? or hast thou walked in the search of the depth?

17 Have the gates of death been opened unto thee? or hast thou seen the doors of the shadow of death?

18 Hast thou perceived the breadth of the earth? declare if thou knowest it all.

19 Where *is* the way *where* light dwelleth? and *as for* darkness, where *is* the place thereof,

20 That thou shouldest take it to the bound thereof, and that thou shouldest know the paths *to* the house thereof?

21 Knowest thou *it,* because thou wast then born? or *because* the number of thy days *is* great?

22 Hast thou entered into the treasures of the snow? or hast thou seen the treasures of the hail,

23 Which I have reserved against the time of trouble, against the day of battle and war?

24 By what way is the light parted, *which* scattereth the east wind upon the earth?

25 Who hath divided a watercourse for the overflowing of waters, or a way for the lightning of thunder;

26 To cause it to rain on the earth, *where* no man *is; on* the wilderness, wherein *there is* no man;

27 To satisfy the desolate and waste *ground;* and to cause the bud of the tender herb to spring forth?

28 Hath the rain a father? or who hath begotten the drops of dew?

29 Out of whose womb came the ice? and the hoary frost of heaven, who hath gendered it?

30 The waters are hid as *with* a stone, and the face of the deep is frozen.

31 Canst thou bind the sweet influences of Pleiades, or loose the bands of Orion?

32 Canst thou bring forth Mazzaroth in his season? or canst thou guide Arcturus with his sons?

33 Knowest thou the ordinances of heaven? canst thou set the dominion thereof in the earth?

NOTES

_____

_____

_____

_____

_____

_____

_____

_____

_____

_____

_____

_____

_____

_____

_____

_____

_____

_____

_____

_____

_____

_____

_____

_____

_____

_____

_____

NOTES

_____
_____
_____
_____
_____
_____
_____
_____
_____
_____
_____
_____
_____
_____
_____
_____
_____
_____
_____
_____
_____
_____
_____
_____
_____
_____
_____
_____
_____
_____
_____
_____

34 Canst thou lift up thy voice to the clouds, that abundance of waters may cover thee?

35 Canst thou send lightnings, that they may go, and say unto thee, Here we *are?*

36 Who hath put wisdom in the inward parts? or who hath given understanding to the heart?

37 Who can number the clouds in wisdom? or who can stay the bottles of heaven,

38 When the dust groweth into hardness, and the clods cleave fast together?

39 Wilt thou hunt the prey for the lion? or fill the appetite of the young lions,

40 When they couch in *their* dens, *and* abide in the covert to lie in wait?

41 Who provideth for the raven his food? when his young ones cry unto God, they wander for lack of meat.

JOB 39

Man's weakness and ignorance compared with God's mighty works—Does man even know how the laws of nature operate?

1 KNOWEST thou the time when the wild goats of the rock bring forth? *or* canst thou mark when the hinds do calve?

2 Canst thou number the months *that* they fulfil? or knowest thou the time when they bring forth?

3 They bow themselves, they bring forth their young ones, they cast out their sorrows.

4 Their young ones are in good liking, they grow up with corn; they go forth, and return not unto them.

5 Who hath sent out the wild ass free? or who hath loosed the bands of the wild ass?

6 Whose house I have made the wilderness, and the barren land his dwellings.

7 He scorneth the multitude of the city, neither regardeth he the crying of the driver.

8 The range of the mountains *is* his pasture, and he searcheth after every green thing.

9 Will the unicorn be willing to serve thee, or abide by thy crib?

10 Canst thou bind the unicorn with his band in the furrow? or will he harrow the valleys after thee?

NOTES

11 Wilt thou trust him, because his strength *is* great? or wilt thou leave thy labour to him?

12 Wilt thou believe him, that he will bring home thy seed, and gather *it into* thy barn?

13 *Gavest thou* the goodly wings unto the peacocks? or wings and feathers unto the ostrich?

14 Which leaveth her eggs in the earth, and warmeth them in dust,

15 And forgetteth that the foot may crush them, or that the wild beast may break them.

16 She is hardened against her young ones, as though *they were* not hers: her labour is in vain without fear;

17 Because God hath deprived her of wisdom, neither hath he imparted to her understanding.

18 What time she lifteth up herself on high, she scorneth the horse and his rider.

19 Hast thou given the horse strength? hast thou clothed his neck with thunder?

20 Canst thou make him afraid as a grasshopper? the glory of his nostrils *is* terrible.

21 He paweth in the valley, and rejoiceth in *his* strength: he goeth on to meet the armed men.

22 He mocketh at fear, and is not affrighted; neither turneth he back from the sword.

23 The quiver rattleth against him, the glittering spear and the shield.

24 He swalloweth the ground with fierceness and rage: neither believeth he that *it is* the sound of the trumpet.

25 He saith among the trumpets, Ha, ha; and he smelleth the battle afar off, the thunder of the captains, and the shouting.

26 Doth the hawk fly by thy wisdom, *and* stretch her wings toward the south?

27 Doth the eagle mount up at thy command, and make her nest on high?

28 She dwelleth and abideth on the rock, upon the crag of the rock, and the strong place.

29 From thence she seeketh the prey, *and* her eyes behold afar off.

30 Her young ones also suck up blood: and where the slain *are,* there *is* she.

NOTES

JOB 40

The Lord challenges Job, and Job replies humbly—The Lord speaks of his power to Job—He asks: Hast thou an arm like God?—He points to his power in behemoth.

1 MOREOVER the LORD answered Job, and said,

2 Shall he that contendeth with the Almighty instruct *him*? he that reproveth God, let him answer it.

3 ¶ Then Job answered the LORD, and said,

4 Behold, I am vile; what shall I answer thee? I will lay mine hand upon my mouth.

5 Once have I spoken; but I will not answer: yea, twice; but I will proceed no further.

6 ¶ Then answered the LORD unto Job out of the whirlwind, and said,

7 Gird up thy loins now like a man: I will demand of thee, and declare thou unto me.

8 Wilt thou also disannul my judgment? wilt thou condemn me, that thou mayest be righteous?

9 Hast thou an arm like God? or canst thou thunder with a voice like him?

10 Deck thyself now *with* majesty and excellency; and array thyself with glory and beauty.

11 Cast abroad the rage of thy wrath: and behold every one *that is* proud, and abase him.

12 Look on every one *that is* proud, *and* bring him low; and tread down the wicked in their place.

13 Hide them in the dust together; *and* bind their faces in secret.

14 Then will I also confess unto thee that thine own right hand can save thee.

15 ¶ Behold now behemoth, which I made with thee; he eateth grass as an ox.

16 Lo now, his strength *is* in his loins, and his force *is* in the navel of his belly.

17 He moveth his tail like a cedar: the sinews of his stones are wrapped together.

18 His bones *are as* strong pieces of brass; his bones *are* like bars of iron.

19 He *is* the chief of the ways of God: he that made him can make his sword to approach *unto him.*

NOTES

20 Surely the mountains bring him forth food, where all the beasts of the field play.

21 He lieth under the shady trees, in the covert of the reed, and fens.

22 The shady trees cover him *with* their shadow; the willows of the brook compass him about.

23 Behold, he drinketh up a river, *and* hasteth not: he trusteth that he can draw up Jordan into his mouth.

24 He taketh it with his eyes: *his* nose pierceth through snares.

JOB 42

Job repents in dust and ashes—He sees the Lord with his eyes—The Lord chastises Job's friends, accepts him, and blesses him, and makes his latter end greater than his beginning.

1 THEN Job answered the LORD, and said,

2 I know that thou canst do every *thing,* and *that* no thought can be withholden from thee.

3 Who *is* he that hideth counsel without knowledge? therefore have I uttered that I understood not; things too wonderful for me, which I knew not.

4 Hear, I beseech thee, and I will speak: I will demand of thee, and declare thou unto me.

5 I have heard of thee by the hearing of the ear: but now mine eye seeth thee.

6 Wherefore I abhor *myself,* and repent in dust and ashes.

7 ¶ And it was *so,* that after the LORD had spoken these words unto Job, the LORD said to Eliphaz the Temanite, My wrath is kindled against thee, and against thy two friends: for ye have not spoken of me *the thing that is* right, as my servant Job *hath.*

8 Therefore take unto you now seven bullocks and seven rams, and go to my servant Job, and offer up for yourselves a burnt offering; and my servant Job shall pray for you: for him will I accept: lest I deal with you *after your* folly, in that ye have not spoken of me *the thing which is* right, like my servant Job.

9 So Eliphaz the Temanite and Bildad the Shuhite *and* Zophar the Naamathite went, and did according as the LORD commanded them: the LORD also accepted Job.

10 And the LORD turned the captivity of Job, when he prayed for his friends: also the LORD gave Job twice as much as he had before.

NOTES

_____
_____
_____
_____
_____
_____
_____
_____
_____
_____
_____
_____
_____
_____
_____
_____
_____
_____
_____
_____
_____
_____
_____
_____
_____
_____
_____
_____
_____
_____
_____
_____
_____

11 Then came there unto him all his brethren, and all his sisters, and all they that had been of his acquaintance before, and did eat bread with him in his house: and they bemoaned him, and comforted him over all the evil that the LORD had brought upon him: every man also gave him a piece of money, and every one an earring of gold.

12 So the LORD blessed the latter end of Job more than his beginning: for he had fourteen thousand sheep, and six thousand camels, and a thousand yoke of oxen, and a thousand she asses.

13 He had also seven sons and three daughters.

14 And he called the name of the first, Jemima; and the name of the second, Kezia; and the name of the third, Keren-happuch.

15 And in all the land were no women found so fair as the daughters of Job: and their father gave them inheritance among their brethren.

16 After this lived Job an hundred and forty years, and saw his sons, and his sons' sons, *even* four generations.

17 So Job died, *being* old and full of days.

Psalms 1–2; 8; 19–33; 40; 46

"The Lord Is My Shepherd"

The Psalms are songs of praise to God that were usually set to music. One of the best-known Psalms is the 23rd, in which David proclaims, "The Lord is my shepherd; I shall not want." Many Christians have this Psalm memorized. The 24th, with its clear message of the importance of being clean and pure, is an example of the many brief, to-the-point teachings contained in this book. As was the case with the Book of Job, I have included the Psalms with their Bible headings that are referenced in our Come, Follow Me curriculum for your convenience, but I've not added much commentary because of space limitations. The commentary for these chapters given in the Come, Follow Me manual will be helpful to you as you read and study these chapters. It will be helpful as you study Psalms to know that "Blessed," as used in Psalm 1:1, often carries the meaning "happy is" along with being blessed. Note also in Psalm 8:4–8 the importance of man relative to all of God's creations. Many people get this wrong and consider humans to be no more important than animals and other forms of life. One last thing: "preventest," as used in Psalm 21:3, means to "precede" or "go before" rather than to "stop" or "restrain." It comes from the Latin "prae," meaning "before," plus "venire," meaning "to come." It is used fifteen times in the King James Version of the Old Testament, and two times in the King James Version of the New Testament. You will see it, for example, in Psalm 119:147, where it means "I arose before dawn," and in Matthew 17:25, where it means that Jesus spoke first.

The Psalms were written by many different authors, David being one of the main ones. We will include a list of the 150 Psalms that appear in our Bible by their author, where known. The quote below and the list come from the Old Testament Student Manual, page 310.

"There is a great debate among biblical scholars about the authorship of the Psalms. Superscriptions on many of the Psalms themselves attribute them to various ancient authors:

Psalms with no superscription	18
Psalms attributed to David	70
Psalms attributed to Solomon	2
Psalms attributed to Asaph (a musician in David's court)	12
Psalms attributed to the sons of Korah (Levites)	10
Psalms attributed to Heman (a leader of the temple music)	1
Psalms attributed to Ethan (a leader of the temple music)	1
Psalms attributed to Moses	1
Psalms with song titles	4
Hallelujah ('Praise Ye Jehovah') Psalms	18
Psalms of degree	13
Total:	150"

NOTES

_____
_____
_____
_____
_____
_____
_____
_____
_____
_____
_____
_____
_____
_____
_____
_____
_____
_____

NOTES

_____
_____
_____
_____
_____
_____
_____
_____
_____
_____
_____
_____
_____
_____
_____
_____
_____
_____
_____
_____
_____
_____
_____
_____
_____
_____
_____
_____
_____
_____

We will include selections from Psalms for your convenience that are referenced in Come, Follow Me.

Note that Psalm 51 was written by David after he had committed adultery with Bathsheba. You can feel his anguish as you read it. One concern with it is that his thinking is not exactly straight on some issues. For example:

Psalm 51:4

4 Against thee [*the Lord—see verse 1*], thee only, have I sinned, and done this evil in thy sight: that thou mightest be justified when thou speakest, and be clear when thou judgest.

That is not correct doctrine. David sinned against Bathsheba, against her husband, against his other wives and children, against the citizens of his kingdom, and so forth. It is often the claim of the sinner that he has done damage only to himself.

PSALM 1

Blessed are the righteous—The ungodly shall perish.

1 BLESSED *is* the man that walketh not in the counsel of the ungodly, nor standeth in the way of sinners, nor sitteth in the seat of the scornful.

2 But his delight *is* in the law of the LORD; and in his law doth he meditate day and night.

3 And he shall be like a tree planted by the rivers of water, that bringeth forth his fruit in his season; his leaf also shall not wither; and whatsoever he doeth shall prosper.

4 The ungodly *are* not so: but *are* like the chaff which the wind driveth away.

5 Therefore the ungodly shall not stand in the judgment, nor sinners in the congregation of the righteous.

6 For the LORD knoweth the way of the righteous: but the way of the ungodly shall perish.

PSALM 2

A Messianic Psalm—The heathen shall rage against the Lord's anointed—The Lord speaks of his Son whom he has begotten.

1 WHY do the heathen rage, and the people imagine a vain thing?

2 The kings of the earth set themselves, and the rulers take counsel together, against the LORD, and against his anointed, *saying,*

3 Let us break their bands asunder, and cast away their cords from us.

4 He that sitteth in the heavens shall laugh: the Lord shall have them in derision.

5 Then shall he speak unto them in his wrath, and vex them in his sore displeasure.

6 Yet have I set my king upon my holy hill of Zion.

7 I will declare the decree: the LORD hath said unto me, Thou *art* my Son; this day have I begotten thee.

8 Ask of me, and I shall give *thee* the heathen *for* thine inheritance, and the uttermost parts of the earth *for* thy possession.

9 Thou shalt break them with a rod of iron; thou shalt dash them in pieces like a potter's vessel.

10 Be wise now therefore, O ye kings: be instructed, ye judges of the earth.

11 Serve the LORD with fear, and rejoice with trembling.

12 Kiss the Son, lest he be angry, and ye perish *from* the way, when his wrath is kindled but a little. Blessed *are* all they that put their trust in him.

PSALM 8

A Messianic Psalm of David—He says that babes and sucklings praise the Lord—He asks: What is man, that thou art mindful of him?

To the chief Musician upon Gittith, A Psalm of David.

1 O LORD our Lord, how excellent *is* thy name in all the earth! who hast set thy glory above the heavens.

2 Out of the mouth of babes and sucklings hast thou ordained strength because of thine enemies, that thou mightest still the enemy and the avenger.

3 When I consider thy heavens, the work of thy fingers, the moon and the stars, which thou hast ordained;

4 What is man, that thou art mindful of him? and the son of man, that thou visitest him?

5 For thou hast made him a little lower than the angels, and hast crowned him with glory and honour.

6 Thou madest him to have dominion over the works of thy hands; thou hast put all *things* under his feet:

7 All sheep and oxen, yea, and the beasts of the field;

—————————————
—————————————
—————————————
—————————————
—————————————
—————————————
—————————————
—————————————
—————————————
—————————————
—————————————
—————————————
—————————————
—————————————
—————————————
—————————————
—————————————
—————————————
—————————————
—————————————
—————————————
—————————————
—————————————
—————————————
—————————————
—————————————
—————————————
—————————————
—————————————
—————————————
—————————————

8 The fowl of the air, and the fish of the sea, *and whatsoever* passeth through the paths of the seas.

9 O LORD our Lord, how excellent *is* thy name in all the earth!

PSALM 19

David testifies: The heavens declare the glory of God—Also: the law of the Lord is perfect—And: The judgments of the Lord are true and righteous altogether.

To the chief Musician, A Psalm of David.

1 THE heavens declare the glory of God; and the firmament sheweth his handywork.

2 Day unto day uttereth speech, and night unto night sheweth knowledge.

3 *There is* no speech nor language, *where* their voice is not heard.

4 Their line is gone out through all the earth, and their words to the end of the world. In them hath he set a tabernacle for the sun,

5 Which *is* as a bridegroom coming out of his chamber, *and* rejoiceth as a strong man to run a race.

6 His going forth *is* from the end of the heaven, and his circuit unto the ends of it: and there is nothing hid from the heat thereof.

7 The law of the LORD *is* perfect, converting the soul: the testimony of the LORD *is* sure, making wise the simple.

8 The statutes of the LORD *are* right, rejoicing the heart: the commandment of the LORD *is* pure, enlightening the eyes.

9 The fear of the LORD *is* clean, enduring for ever: the judgments of the LORD *are* true *and* righteous altogether.

10 More to be desired *are they* than gold, yea, than much fine gold: sweeter also than honey and the honeycomb.

11 Moreover by them is thy servant warned: *and* in keeping of them *there is* great reward.

12 Who can understand *his* errors? cleanse thou me from secret *faults.*

13 Keep back thy servant also from presumptuous *sins;* let them not have dominion over me: then shall I be upright, and I shall be innocent from the great transgression.

14 Let the words of my mouth, and the meditation of my heart, be acceptable in thy sight, O LORD, my strength, and my redeemer.

PSALM 20

David prays that the Lord will hear in time of trouble—The Lord saves his anointed.

To the chief Musician, A Psalm of David.

1 THE LORD hear thee in the day of trouble; the name of the God of Jacob defend thee;

2 Send thee help from the sanctuary, and strengthen thee out of Zion;

3 Remember all thy offerings, and accept thy burnt sacrifice; Selah.

4 Grant thee according to thine own heart, and fulfil all thy counsel.

5 We will rejoice in thy salvation, and in the name of our God we will set up *our* banners: the LORD fulfil all thy petitions.

6 Now know I that the LORD saveth his anointed; he will hear him from his holy heaven with the saving strength of his right hand.

7 Some *trust* in chariots, and some in horses: but we will remember the name of the LORD our God.

8 They are brought down and fallen: but we are risen, and stand upright.

9 Save, LORD: let the king hear us when we call.

PSALM 21

A Messianic Psalm of David—He tells of the glory of the great King—He shall triumph over all his enemies—Their evil designs shall fail.

To the chief Musician, A Psalm of David.

1 THE king shall joy in thy strength, O LORD; and in thy salvation how greatly shall he rejoice!

2 Thou hast given him his heart's desire, and hast not withholden the request of his lips. Selah.

3 For thou preventest him with the blessings of goodness: thou settest a crown of pure gold on his head.

4 He asked life of thee, *and* thou gavest *it* him, *even* length of days for ever and ever.

5 His glory *is* great in thy salvation: honour and majesty hast thou laid upon him.

NOTES

_____

_____

_____

_____

_____

_____

_____

_____

_____

_____

_____

_____

_____

_____

_____

_____

_____

_____

_____

_____

_____

_____

_____

_____

_____

_____

_____

_____

6 For thou hast made him most blessed for ever: thou hast made him exceeding glad with thy countenance.

7 For the king trusteth in the LORD, and through the mercy of the most High he shall not be moved.

8 Thine hand shall find out all thine enemies: thy right hand shall find out those that hate thee.

9 Thou shalt make them as a fiery oven in the time of thine anger: the LORD shall swallow them up in his wrath, and the fire shall devour them.

10 Their fruit shalt thou destroy from the earth, and their seed from among the children of men.

11 For they intended evil against thee: they imagined a mischievous device, *which* they are not able *to perform*.

12 Therefore shalt thou make them turn their back, *when* thou shalt make ready *thine arrows* upon thy strings against the face of them.

13 Be thou exalted, LORD, in thine own strength: *so* will we sing and praise thy power.

PSALM 22

A Messianic Psalm of David—He foretells events in Messiah's life—Messiah says: My God, my God, why hast thou forsaken me?—They pierce his hands and feet—He shall yet govern among all nations.

To the chief Musician upon Aijeleth Shahar, A Psalm of David.

1 MY God, my God, why hast thou forsaken me? *why art thou so* far from helping me, *and from* the words of my roaring?

2 O my God, I cry in the daytime, but thou hearest not; and in the night season, and am not silent.

3 But thou *art* holy, *O thou* that inhabitest the praises of Israel.

4 Our fathers trusted in thee: they trusted, and thou didst deliver them.

5 They cried unto thee, and were delivered: they trusted in thee, and were not confounded.

6 But I *am* a worm, and no man; a reproach of men, and despised of the people.

7 All they that see me laugh me to scorn: they shoot out the lip, they shake the head, *saying,*

8 He trusted on the LORD *that* he would deliver him: let him deliver him, seeing he delighted in him.

9 But thou *art* he that took me out of the womb: thou didst make me hope *when I was* upon my mother's breasts.

10 I was cast upon thee from the womb: thou *art* my God from my mother's belly.

11 Be not far from me; for trouble *is* near; for *there is* none to help.

12 Many bulls have compassed me: strong *bulls* of Bashan have beset me round.

13 They gaped upon me *with* their mouths, *as* a ravening and a roaring lion.

14 I am poured out like water, and all my bones are out of joint: my heart is like wax; it is melted in the midst of my bowels.

15 My strength is dried up like a potsherd; and my tongue cleaveth to my jaws; and thou hast brought me into the dust of death.

16 For dogs have compassed me: the assembly of the wicked have inclosed me: they pierced my hands and my feet.

17 I may tell all my bones: they look *and* stare upon me.

18 They part my garments among them, and cast lots upon my vesture.

19 But be not thou far from me, O LORD: O my strength, haste thee to help me.

20 Deliver my soul from the sword; my darling from the power of the dog.

21 Save me from the lion's mouth: for thou hast heard me from the horns of the unicorns.

22 I will declare thy name unto my brethren: in the midst of the congregation will I praise thee.

23 Ye that fear the LORD, praise him; all ye the seed of Jacob, glorify him; and fear him, all ye the seed of Israel.

24 For he hath not despised nor abhorred the affliction of the afflicted; neither hath he hid his face from him; but when he cried unto him, he heard.

25 My praise *shall be* of thee in the great congregation: I will pay my vows before them that fear him.

26 The meek shall eat and be satisfied: they shall praise the LORD that seek him: your heart shall live for ever.

NOTES

NOTES

27 All the ends of the world shall remember and turn unto the LORD: and all the kindreds of the nations shall worship before thee.

28 For the kingdom *is* the LORD's: and he *is* the governor among the nations.

29 All *they that be* fat upon earth shall eat and worship: all they that go down to the dust shall bow before him: and none can keep alive his own soul.

30 A seed shall serve him; it shall be accounted to the Lord for a generation.

31 They shall come, and shall declare his righteousness unto a people that shall be born, that he hath done *this*.

PSALM 23

David acclaims: The Lord is my shepherd.

A Psalm of David.

1 THE LORD *is* my shepherd; I shall not want.

2 He maketh me to lie down in green pastures: he leadeth me beside the still waters.

3 He restoreth my soul: he leadeth me in the paths of righteousness for his name's sake.

4 Yea, though I walk through the valley of the shadow of death, I will fear no evil: for thou *art* with me; thy rod and thy staff they comfort me.

5 Thou preparest a table before me in the presence of mine enemies: thou anointest my head with oil; my cup runneth over.

6 Surely goodness and mercy shall follow me all the days of my life: and I will dwell in the house of the LORD for ever.

PSALM 24

David testifies: The earth is the Lord's, and the fulness thereof—He that hath clean hands and a pure heart shall ascend unto the hill of the Lord—The Lord of hosts is the King of glory.

A Psalm of David.

1 THE earth *is* the LORD's, and the fulness thereof; the world, and they that dwell therein.

2 For he hath founded it upon the seas, and established it upon the floods.

3 Who shall ascend into the hill of the LORD? or who shall stand in his holy place?

4 He that hath clean hands, and a pure heart; who hath not lifted up his soul unto vanity, nor sworn deceitfully.

5 He shall receive the blessing from the LORD, and righteousness from the God of his salvation.

6 This *is* the generation of them that seek him, that seek thy face, O Jacob. Selah.

7 Lift up your head, O ye gates; and be ye lift up, ye everlasting doors; and the King of glory shall come in.

8 Who *is* this King of glory? The LORD strong and mighty, the LORD mighty in battle.

9 Lift up your heads, O ye gates; even lift *them* up, ye everlasting doors; and the King of glory shall come in.

10 Who is this King of glory? The LORD of hosts, he *is* the King of glory. Selah.

PSALM 25

David pleads for truth and asks for pardon—Mercy and truth are for those who keep the commandments.

A Psalm of David.

1 UNTO thee, O LORD, do I lift up my soul.

2 O my God, I trust in thee: let me not be ashamed, let not mine enemies triumph over me.

3 Yea, let none that wait on thee be ashamed: let them be ashamed which transgress without cause.

4 Shew me thy ways, O LORD; teach me thy paths.

5 Lead me in thy truth, and teach me: for thou *art* the God of my salvation; on thee do I wait all the day.

6 Remember, O LORD, thy tender mercies and thy lovingkindnesses; for they *have been* ever of old.

7 Remember not the sins of my youth, nor my transgressions: according to thy mercy remember thou me for thy goodness' sake, O LORD.

8 Good and upright *is* the LORD: therefore will he teach sinners in the way.

NOTES

NOTES

9 The meek will he guide in judgment: and the meek will he teach his way.

10 All the paths of the LORD *are* mercy and truth unto such as keep his covenant and his testimonies.

11 For thy name's sake, O LORD, pardon mine iniquity; for it *is* great.

12 What man *is* he that feareth the LORD? him shall he teach in the way *that* he shall choose.

13 His soul shall dwell at ease; and his seed shall inherit the earth.

14 The secret of the LORD *is* with them that fear him; and he will shew them his covenant.

15 Mine eyes *are* ever toward the LORD; for he shall pluck my feet out of the net.

16 Turn thee unto me, and have mercy upon me; for I *am* desolate and afflicted.

17 The troubles of my heart are enlarged: *O* bring thou me out of my distresses.

18 Look upon mine affliction and my pain; and forgive all my sins.

19 Consider mine enemies; for they are many; and they hate me with cruel hatred.

20 O keep my soul, and deliver me: let me not be ashamed; for I put my trust in thee.

21 Let integrity and uprightness preserve me; for I wait on thee.

22 Redeem Israel, O God, out of all his troubles.

PSALM 26

David says he has walked in integrity and obedience—He loves the Lord's house.

A Psalm of David.

1 JUDGE me, O LORD; for I have walked in mine integrity: I have trusted also in the LORD; *therefore* I shall not slide.

2 Examine me, O LORD, and prove me; try my reins and my heart.

3 For thy lovingkindness *is* before mine eyes: and I have walked in thy truth.

4 I have not sat with vain persons, neither will I go in with dissemblers.

5 I have hated the congregation of evil doers; and will not sit with the wicked.

6 I will wash mine hands in innocency: so will I compass thine altar, O LORD:

7 That I may publish with the voice of thanksgiving, and tell of all thy wondrous works.

8 LORD, I have loved the habitation of thy house, and the place where thine honour dwelleth.

9 Gather not my soul with sinners, nor my life with bloody men:

10 In whose hands *is* mischief, and their right hand is full of bribes.

11 But as for me, I will walk in mine integrity: redeem me, and be merciful unto me.

12 My foot standeth in an even place: in the congregations will I bless the LORD.

PSALM 27

David says: The Lord is my light and my salvation—He desires to dwell in the house of the Lord forever—He counsels: Wait on the Lord and be of good courage.

A Psalm of David.

1 THE LORD *is* my light and my salvation; whom shall I fear? the LORD *is* the strength of my life; of whom shall I be afraid?

2 When the wicked, *even* mine enemies and my foes, came upon me to eat up my flesh, they stumbled and fell.

3 Though an host should encamp against me, my heart shall not fear: though war should rise against me, in this *will* I *be* confident.

4 One *thing* have I desired of the LORD, that will I seek after; that I may dwell in the house of the LORD all the days of my life, to behold the beauty of the LORD, and to enquire in his temple.

5 For in the time of trouble he shall hide me in his pavilion: in the secret of his tabernacle shall he hide me; he shall set me up upon a rock.

6 And now shall mine head be lifted up above mine enemies round about me: therefore will I offer in his tabernacle sacrifices of joy; I will sing, yea, I will sing praises unto the LORD.

7 Hear, O LORD, *when* I cry with my voice: have mercy also upon me, and answer me.

8 *When thou saidst,* Seek ye my face; my heart said unto thee, Thy face, LORD, will I seek.

NOTES

_____
_____
_____
_____
_____
_____
_____
_____
_____
_____
_____
_____
_____
_____
_____
_____
_____
_____
_____
_____
_____
_____
_____
_____
_____
_____
_____

9 Hide not thy face *far* from me; put not thy servant away in anger: thou hast been my help; leave me not, neither forsake me, O God of my salvation.

10 When my father and my mother forsake me, then the LORD will take me up.

11 Teach me thy way, O LORD, and lead me in a plain path, because of mine enemies.

12 Deliver me not over unto the will of mine enemies: for false witnesses are risen up against me, and such as breathe out cruelty.

13 *I had fainted,* unless I had believed to see the goodness of the LORD in the land of the living.

14 Wait on the LORD: be of good courage, and he shall strengthen thine heart: wait, I say, on the LORD.

PSALM 28

David pleads with the Lord to hear his voice and grant his petitions—He prays: Save thy people, and bless thine inheritance.

A Psalm of David.

1 UNTO thee will I cry, O LORD my rock; be not silent to me: lest, *if* thou be silent to me, I become like them that go down into the pit.

2 Hear the voice of my supplications, when I cry unto thee, when I lift up my hands toward thy holy oracle.

3 Draw me not away with the wicked, and with the workers of iniquity, which speak peace to their neighbours, but mischief *is* in their hearts.

4 Give them according to their deeds, and according to the wickedness of their endeavours: give them after the work of their hands; render to them their desert.

5 Because they regard not the works of the LORD, nor the operation of his hands, he shall destroy them, and not build them up.

6 Blessed *be* the LORD, because he hath heard the voice of my supplications.

7 The LORD *is* my strength and my shield; my heart trusted in him, and I am helped: therefore my heart greatly rejoiceth; and with my song will I praise him.

8 The LORD *is* their strength, and he *is* the saving strength of his anointed.

9 Save thy people, and bless thine inheritance: feed them also, and lift them up for ever.

PSALM 29

David counsels: Worship the Lord in the beauty of holiness—He sets forth the wonder and power of the voice of the Lord.

A Psalm of David.

1 GIVE unto the LORD, O ye mighty, give unto the LORD glory and strength.

2 Give unto the LORD the glory due unto his name; worship the LORD in the beauty of holiness.

3 The voice of the LORD *is* upon the waters: the God of glory thundereth: the LORD *is* upon many waters.

4 The voice of the LORD *is* powerful; the voice of the LORD *is* full of majesty.

5 The voice of the LORD breaketh the cedars; yea, the LORD breaketh the cedars of Lebanon.

6 He maketh them also to skip like a calf; Lebanon and Sirion like a young unicorn.

7 The voice of the LORD divideth the flames of fire.

8 The voice of the LORD shaketh the wilderness; the LORD shaketh the wilderness of Kadesh.

9 The voice of the LORD maketh the hinds to calve, and discovereth the forests: and in his temple doth every one speak of *his* glory.

10 The LORD sitteth upon the flood; yea, the LORD sitteth King for ever.

11 The LORD will give strength unto his people; the LORD will bless his people with peace.

PSALM 30

David sings praises and gives thanks to the Lord—He pleads for mercy.

A Psalm *and* Song *at* the dedication of the house of David.

1 I WILL extol thee, O LORD; for thou hast lifted me up, and hast not made my foes to rejoice over me.

2 O LORD my God, I cried unto thee, and thou hast healed me.

3 O LORD, thou hast brought up my soul from the grave: thou hast kept me alive, that I should not go down to the pit.

NOTES

4 Sing unto the LORD, O ye saints of his, and give thanks at the remembrance of his holiness.

5 For his anger *endureth but* a moment; in his favour *is* life: weeping may endure for a night, but joy *cometh* in the morning.

6 And in my prosperity I said, I shall never be moved.

7 LORD, by thy favour thou hast made my mountain to stand strong: thou didst hide thy face, *and* I was troubled.

8 I cried to thee, O LORD; and unto the LORD I made supplication.

9 What profit *is there* in my blood, when I go down to the pit? Shall the dust praise thee? shall it declare thy truth?

10 Hear, O LORD, and have mercy upon me: LORD, be thou my helper.

11 Thou hast turned for me my mourning into dancing: thou hast put off my sackcloth, and girded me with gladness;

12 To the end that *my* glory may sing praise to thee, and not be silent. O LORD my God, I will give thanks unto thee for ever.

PSALM 31

David trusts in the Lord and rejoices in his mercy—Speaking Messianically he says: Into thine hand I commit my spirit—He counsels: O love the Lord, all ye his saints, for the Lord preserveth the faithful.

To the chief Musician, A Psalm of David.

1 IN thee, O LORD, do I put my trust; let me never be ashamed: deliver me in thy righteousness.

2 Bow down thine ear to me; deliver me speedily: be thou my strong rock, for an house of defence to save me.

3 For thou *art* my rock and my fortress; therefore for thy name's sake lead me, and guide me.

4 Pull me out of the net that they have laid privily for me: for thou *art* my strength.

5 Into thine hand I commit my spirit: thou hast redeemed me, O LORD God of truth.

6 I have hated them that regard lying vanities: but I trust in the LORD.

7 I will be glad and rejoice in thy mercy: for thou hast considered my trouble; thou hast known my soul in adversities;

8 And hast not shut me up into the hand of the enemy: thou hast set my feet in a large room.

9 Have mercy upon me, O LORD, for I am in trouble: mine eye is consumed with grief, *yea,* my soul and my belly.

10 For my life is spent with grief, and my years with sighing: my strength faileth because of mine iniquity, and my bones are consumed.

11 I was a reproach among all mine enemies, but especially among my neighbours, and a fear to mine acquaintance: they that did see me without fled from me.

12 I am forgotten as a dead man out of mind: I am like a broken vessel.

13 For I have heard the slander of many: fear *was* on every side: while they took counsel together against me, they devised to take away my life.

14 But I trusted in thee, O LORD: I said, Thou *art* my God.

15 My times *are* in thy hand: deliver me from the hand of mine enemies, and from them that persecute me.

16 Make thy face to shine upon thy servant: save me for thy mercies' sake.

17 Let me not be ashamed, O LORD; for I have called upon thee: let the wicked be ashamed, *and* let them be silent in the grave.

18 Let the lying lips be put to silence; which speak grievous things proudly and contemptuously against the righteous.

19 *Oh* how great *is* thy goodness, which thou hast laid up for them that fear thee; *which* thou hast wrought for them that trust in thee before the sons of men!

20 Thou shalt hide them in the secret of thy presence from the pride of man: thou shalt keep them secretly in a pavilion from the strife of tongues.

21 Blessed *be* the LORD: for he hath shewed me his marvellous kindness in a strong city.

22 For I said in my haste, I am cut off from before thine eyes: nevertheless thou heardest the voice of my supplications when I cried unto thee.

23 O love the LORD, all ye his saints: *for* the LORD preserveth the faithful, and plentifully rewardeth the proud doer.

NOTES

24 Be of good courage, and he shall strengthen your heart, all ye that hope in the LORD.

PSALM 32

David says: Blessed is the man unto whom the Lord imputeth not iniquity—He acknowledges his sin—He recommends that the righteous be glad in the Lord and rejoice.

A Psalm of David, Maschil.

1 BLESSED *is he whose* transgression *is* forgiven, *whose* sin *is* covered.

2 Blessed *is* the man unto whom the LORD imputeth not iniquity, and in whose spirit *there is* no guile.

3 When I kept silence, my bones waxed old through my roaring all the day long.

4 For day and night thy hand was heavy upon me: my moisture is turned into the drought of summer. Selah.

5 I acknowledged my sin unto thee, and mine iniquity have I not hid. I said, I will confess my transgressions unto the LORD; and thou forgavest the iniquity of my sin. Selah.

6 For this shall every one that is godly pray unto thee in a time when thou mayest be found: surely in the floods of great waters they shall not come nigh unto him.

7 Thou *art* my hiding place; thou shalt preserve me from trouble; thou shalt compass me about with songs of deliverance. Selah.

8 I will instruct thee and teach thee in the way which thou shalt go: I will guide thee with mine eye.

9 Be ye not as the horse, *or* as the mule, *which* have no understanding: whose mouth must be held in with bit and bridle, lest they come near unto thee.

10 Many sorrows *shall be* to the wicked: but he that trusteth in the LORD, mercy shall compass him about.

11 Be glad in the LORD, and rejoice, ye righteous: and shout for joy, all *ye that are* upright in heart.

PSALM 33

Rejoice in the Lord—Sing unto him a new song—He loveth righteousness and judgment—Blessed is the nation whose God is the Lord.

1 REJOICE in the LORD, O ye righteous: *for* praise is comely for the upright.

2 Praise the LORD with harp: sing unto him with the psaltery *and* an instrument of ten strings.

3 Sing unto him a new song; play skilfully with a loud noise.

4 For the word of the LORD *is* right; and all his works *are done* in truth.

5 He loveth righteousness and judgment: the earth is full of the goodness of the LORD.

6 By the word of the LORD were the heavens made; and all the host of them by the breath of his mouth.

7 He gathereth the waters of the sea together as an heap: he layeth up the depth in storehouses.

8 Let all the earth fear the LORD: let all the inhabitants of the world stand in awe of him.

9 For he spake, and it was *done;* he commanded, and it stood fast.

10 The LORD bringeth the counsel of the heathen to nought: he maketh the devices of the people of none effect.

11 The counsel of the LORD standeth for ever, the thoughts of his heart to all generations.

12 Blessed *is* the nation whose God *is* the LORD: *and* the people *whom* he hath chosen for his own inheritance.

13 The LORD looketh from heaven; he beholdeth all the sons of men.

14 From the place of his habitation he looketh upon all the inhabitants of the earth.

15 He fashioneth their hearts alike; he considereth all their works.

16 There is no king saved by the multitude of an host: a mighty man is not delivered by much strength.

17 An horse *is* a vain thing for safety: neither shall he deliver *any* by his great strength.

18 Behold, the eye of the LORD *is* upon them that fear him, upon them that hope in his mercy;

19 To deliver their soul from death, and to keep them alive in famine.

20 Our soul waiteth for the LORD: he *is* our help and our shield.

NOTES

NOTES

_____
_____
_____
_____
_____
_____
_____
_____
_____
_____
_____
_____
_____
_____
_____
_____
_____
_____
_____
_____
_____
_____
_____
_____
_____
_____
_____
_____

21 For our heart shall rejoice in him, because we have trusted in his holy name.

22 Let thy mercy, O LORD, be upon us, according as we hope in thee.

PSALM 40

A Messianic Psalm of David—The Messiah shall come and preach righteousness—He shall declare salvation—The righteous shall say: The Lord be magnified.

To the chief Musician, A Psalm of David.

1 I WAITED patiently for the LORD; and he inclined unto me, and heard my cry.

2 He brought me up also out of an horrible pit, out of the miry clay, and set my feet upon a rock, *and* established my goings.

3 And he hath put a new song in my mouth, *even* praise unto our God: many shall see *it,* and fear, and shall trust in the LORD.

4 Blessed *is* that man that maketh the LORD his trust, and respecteth not the proud, nor such as turn aside to lies.

5 Many, O LORD my God, *are* thy wonderful works *which* thou hast done, and thy thoughts *which are* to us-ward: they cannot be reckoned up in order unto thee: *if* I would declare and speak *of them,* they are more than can be numbered.

6 Sacrifice and offering thou didst not desire; mine ears hast thou opened: burnt offering and sin offering hast thou not required.

7 Then said I, Lo, I come: in the volume of the book *it is* written of me,

8 I delight to do thy will, O my God: yea, thy law *is* within my heart.

9 I have preached righteousness in the great congregation: lo, I have not refrained my lips, O LORD, thou knowest.

10 I have not hid thy righteousness within my heart; I have declared thy faithfulness and thy salvation: I have not concealed thy lovingkindness and thy truth from the great congregation.

11 Withhold not thou thy tender mercies from me, O LORD: let thy lovingkindness and thy truth continually preserve me.

12 For innumerable evils have compassed me about: mine iniquities have taken hold upon me, so that I am not able to look up; they are more than the hairs of mine head: therefore my heart faileth me.

13 Be pleased, O LORD, to deliver me: O LORD, make haste to help me.

14 Let them be ashamed and confounded together that seek after my soul to destroy it; let them be driven backward and put to shame that wish me evil.

15 Let them be desolate for a reward of their shame that say unto me, Aha, aha.

16 Let all those that seek thee rejoice and be glad in thee: let such as love thy salvation say continually, The LORD be magnified.

17 But I *am* poor and needy; *yet* the Lord thinketh upon me: thou *art* my help and my deliverer; make no tarrying, O my God.

PSALM 46

God is our refuge and strength—He dwells in his city, doeth marvelous things, and saith: Be still and know that I am God.

To the chief Musician for the sons of Korah, A Song upon Alamoth.

1 GOD *is* our refuge and strength, a very present help in trouble.

2 Therefore will not we fear, though the earth be removed, and though the mountains be carried into the midst of the sea;

3 *Though* the waters thereof roar *and* be troubled, *though* the mountains shake with the swelling thereof. Selah.

4 *There is* a river, the streams whereof shall make glad the city of God, the holy *place* of the tabernacles of the most High.

5 God *is* in the midst of her; she shall not be moved: God shall help her, *and that* right early.

6 The heathen raged, the kingdoms were moved: he uttered his voice, the earth melted.

7 The LORD of hosts *is* with us; the God of Jacob *is* our refuge. Selah.

8 Come, behold the works of the LORD, what desolations he hath made in the earth.

9 He maketh wars to cease unto the end of the earth; he breaketh the bow, and cutteth the spear in sunder; he burneth the chariot in the fire.

10 Be still, and know that I *am* God: I will be exalted among the heathen, I will be exalted in the earth.

11 The LORD of hosts *is* with us; the God of Jacob *is* our refuge. Selah.

NOTES

Psalms 49–51; 61-66; 69–72; 77–78; 85–86

"I Will Declare What He Hath Done for My Soul"

As mentioned in the introductory paragraph for last week's reading block, space limitations for this four-volume study guide for Old Testament did not allow for much commentary. However, the Come, Follow Me materials and suggestions will be helpful to you as you read and study the chapters of Psalms that were selected for this section, and you can put your own notes and commentary in the space provided in the margins. As you study these selections from Psalms, note the reference to the Second Coming in Psalm 50:3, the importance of gratitude in receiving blessings in Psalm 50:14–15, the brief review of the Lord's dealings with the children of Israel while they were in the wilderness in Psalm 78, and the prophecy of the coming forth of the Book of Mormon in Psalm 85:11.

NOTES

PSALM 49

Men cannot be ransomed or redeemed by wealth—God alone can redeem a soul from the grave—The glory of a rich man ceases with his death.

To the chief Musician, A Psalm for the sons of Korah.

1 HEAR this, all *ye* people; give ear, all *ye* inhabitants of the world:

2 Both low and high, rich and poor, together.

3 My mouth shall speak of wisdom; and the meditation of my heart *shall be* of understanding.

4 I will incline mine ear to a parable: I will open my dark saying upon the harp.

5 Wherefore should I fear in the days of evil, *when* the iniquity of my heels shall compass me about?

6 They that trust in their wealth, and boast themselves in the multitude of their riches;

7 None *of them* can by any means redeem his brother, nor give to God a ransom for him:

8 (For the redemption of their soul *is* precious, and it ceaseth for ever:)

9 That he should still live for ever, *and* not see corruption.

10 For he seeth *that* wise men die, likewise the fool and the brutish person perish, and leave their wealth to others.

11 Their inward thought *is, that* their houses *shall continue* for ever, *and* their dwelling places to all generations; they call *their* lands after their own names.

12 Nevertheless man *being* in honour abideth not: he is like the beasts *that* perish.

13 This their way *is* their folly: yet their posterity approve their sayings. Selah.

14 Like sheep they are laid in the grave; death shall feed on them; and the upright shall have dominion over them in the morning; and their beauty shall consume in the grave from their dwelling.

15 But God will redeem my soul from the power of the grave: for he shall receive me. Selah.

16 Be not thou afraid when one is made rich, when the glory of his house is increased;

17 For when he dieth he shall carry nothing away: his glory shall not descend after him.

18 Though while he lived he blessed his soul: and *men* will praise thee, when thou doest well to thyself.

19 He shall go to the generation of his fathers; they shall never see light.

20 Man *that is* in honour, and understandeth not, is like the beasts *that* perish.

PSALM 50

Asaph speaks of the Second Coming—The Lord accepts the sacrifices of the righteous and will deliver them—Those whose conduct is right shall see the salvation of God.

A Psalm of Asaph.

1 THE mighty God, *even* the LORD, hath spoken, and called the earth from the rising of the sun unto the going down thereof.

2 Out of Zion, the perfection of beauty, God hath shined.

3 Our God shall come, and shall not keep silence: a fire shall devour before him, and it shall be very tempestuous round about him.

4 He shall call to the heavens from above, and to the earth, that he may judge his people.

5 Gather my saints together unto me; those that have made a covenant with me by sacrifice.

6 And the heavens shall declare his righteousness: for God *is* judge himself. Selah.

NOTES

7 Hear, O my people, and I will speak; O Israel, and I will testify against thee: I *am* God, *even* thy God.

8 I will not reprove thee for thy sacrifices or thy burnt offerings, *to have been* continually before me.

9 I will take no bullock out of thy house, *nor* he goats out of thy folds.

10 For every beast of the forest *is* mine, *and* the cattle upon a thousand hills.

11 I know all the fowls of the mountains: and the wild beasts of the field *are* mine.

12 If I were hungry, I would not tell thee: for the world *is* mine, and the fulness thereof.

13 Will I eat the flesh of bulls, or drink the blood of goats?

14 Offer unto God thanksgiving; and pay thy vows unto the most High:

15 And call upon me in the day of trouble: I will deliver thee, and thou shalt glorify me.

16 But unto the wicked God saith, What hast thou to do to declare my statutes, or *that* thou shouldest take my covenant in thy mouth?

17 Seeing thou hatest instruction, and castest my words behind thee.

18 When thou sawest a thief, then thou consentedst with him, and hast been partaker with adulterers.

19 Thou givest thy mouth to evil, and thy tongue frameth deceit.

20 Thou sittest *and* speakest against thy brother; thou slanderest thine own mother's son.

21 These *things* hast thou done, and I kept silence; thou thoughtest that I was altogether *such an one* as thyself: *but* I will reprove thee, and set *them* in order before thine eyes.

22 Now consider this, ye that forget God, lest I tear *you* in pieces, and *there be* none to deliver.

23 Whoso offereth praise glorifieth me: and to him that ordereth *his* conversation *aright* will I shew the salvation of God.

PSALM 51

David pleads for forgiveness after he went in to Bath-sheba—He pleads: Create in me a clean heart, and renew a right spirit within me.

To the chief Musician, A Psalm of David, when Nathan the prophet came unto him, after he had gone in to Bath-sheba.

1 HAVE mercy upon me, O God, according to thy lovingkindness: according unto the multitude of thy tender mercies blot out my transgressions.

2 Wash me throughly from mine iniquity, and cleanse me from my sin.

3 For I acknowledge my transgressions: and my sin *is* ever before me.

4 Against thee, thee only, have I sinned, and done *this* evil in thy sight: that thou mightest be justified when thou speakest, *and* be clear when thou judgest.

5 Behold, I was shapen in iniquity; and in sin did my mother conceive me.

6 Behold, thou desirest truth in the inward parts: and in the hidden *part* thou shalt make me to know wisdom.

7 Purge me with hyssop, and I shall be clean: wash me, and I shall be whiter than snow.

8 Make me to hear joy and gladness; *that* the bones *which* thou hast broken may rejoice.

9 Hide thy face from my sins, and blot out all mine iniquities.

10 Create in me a clean heart, O God; and renew a right spirit within me.

11 Cast me not away from thy presence; and take not thy holy spirit from me.

12 Restore unto me the joy of thy salvation; and uphold me *with thy* free spirit.

13 *Then* will I teach transgressors thy ways; and sinners shall be converted unto thee.

14 Deliver me from bloodguiltiness, O God, thou God of my salvation: *and* my tongue shall sing aloud of thy righteousness.

15 O Lord, open thou my lips; and my mouth shall shew forth thy praise.

16 For thou desirest not sacrifice; else would I give *it:* thou delightest not in burnt offering.

17 The sacrifices of God *are* a broken spirit: a broken and a contrite heart, O God, thou wilt not despise.

18 Do good in thy good pleasure unto Zion: build thou the walls of Jerusalem.

19 Then shalt thou be pleased with the sacrifices of righteousness, with burnt offering and whole burnt offering: then shall they offer bullocks upon thine altar.

PSALM 61

David finds shelter in the Lord; abides in his presence; and keeps his own vows.

To the chief Musician upon Neginah, *A Psalm* of David.

1 HEAR my cry, O God; attend unto my prayer.

2 From the end of the earth will I cry unto thee, when my heart is overwhelmed: lead me to the rock *that* is higher than I.

3 For thou hast been a shelter for me, *and* a strong tower from the enemy.

4 I will abide in thy tabernacle for ever: I will trust in the covert of thy wings. Selah.

5 For thou, O God, hast heard my vows: thou hast given *me* the heritage of those that fear thy name.

6 Thou wilt prolong the king's life: *and* his years as many generations.

7 He shall abide before God for ever: O prepare mercy and truth, *which* may preserve him.

8 So will I sing praise unto thy name for ever, that I may daily perform my vows.

PSALM 62

David extols God as his defence, his rock, and his salvation—The Lord judges men according to their works.

To the chief Musician, to Jeduthun, A Psalm of David.

1 TRULY my soul waiteth upon God: from him *cometh* my salvation.

2 He only *is* my rock and my salvation; *he is* my defence; I shall not be greatly moved.

3 How long will ye imagine mischief against a man? ye shall be slain all of you: as a bowing wall *shall ye be, and as* a tottering fence.

4 They only consult to cast *him* down from his excellency: they delight in lies: they bless with their mouth, but they curse inwardly. Selah.

5 My soul, wait thou only upon God; for my expectation *is* from him.

6 He only *is* my rock and my salvation: *he is* my defence; I shall not be moved.

7 In God *is* my salvation and my glory: the rock of my strength, *and* my refuge, *is* in God.

8 Trust in him at all times; ye people, pour out your heart before him: God *is* a refuge for us. Selah.

9 Surely men of low degree *are* vanity, *and* men of high degree *are* a lie: to be laid in the balance, they *are* altogether *lighter* than vanity.

10 Trust not in oppression, and become not vain in robbery: if riches increase, set not your heart *upon them.*

11 God hath spoken once; twice have I heard this; that power *belongeth* unto God.

12 Also unto thee, O Lord, *belongeth* mercy: for thou renderest to every man according to his work.

PSALM 63

David thirsts for God, whom he praises with joyful lips.

A Psalm of David, when he was in the wilderness of Judah.

1 O GOD, thou *art* my God; early will I seek thee: my soul thirsteth for thee, my flesh longeth for thee in a dry and thirsty land, where no water is;

2 To see thy power and thy glory, so *as* I have seen thee in the sanctuary.

3 Because thy lovingkindness *is* better than life, my lips shall praise thee.

4 Thus will I bless thee while I live: I will lift up my hands in thy name.

5 My soul shall be satisfied as *with* marrow and fatness; and my mouth shall praise *thee* with joyful lips:

6 When I remember thee upon my bed, *and* meditate on thee in the *night* watches.

7 Because thou hast been my help, therefore in the shadow of thy wings will I rejoice.

8 My soul followeth hard after thee: thy right hand upholdeth me.

9 But those *that* seek my soul, to destroy *it,* shall go into the lower parts of the earth.

10 They shall fall by the sword: they shall be a portion for foxes.

11 But the king shall rejoice in God; every one that sweareth by him shall glory: but the mouth of them that speak lies shall be stopped.

NOTES

PSALM 64

David prays for safety—The righteous shall be glad in heart.

To the chief Musician, A Psalm of David.

1 HEAR my voice, O God, in my prayer: preserve my life from fear of the enemy.

2 Hide me from the secret counsel of the wicked; from the insurrection of the workers of iniquity:

3 Who whet their tongue like a sword, *and* bend *their bows to shoot* their arrows, *even* bitter words:

4 That they may shoot in secret at the perfect: suddenly do they shoot at him, and fear not.

5 They encourage themselves *in* an evil matter: they commune of laying snares privily; they say, Who shall see them?

6 They search out iniquities; they accomplish a diligent search: both the inward *thought* of every one *of them,* and the heart, *is* deep.

7 But God shall shoot at them *with* an arrow; suddenly shall they be wounded.

8 So they shall make their own tongue to fall upon themselves: all that see them shall flee away.

9 And all men shall fear, and shall declare the work of God; for they shall wisely consider of his doing.

10 The righteous shall be glad in the LORD, and shall trust in him; and all the upright in heart shall glory.

PSALM 65

David speaks of the blessedness of God's chosen—The Lord sends rain and good things upon the earth.

To the chief Musician, A Psalm *and* Song of David.

1 PRAISE waiteth for thee, O God, in Sion: and unto thee shall the vow be performed.

2 O thou that hearest prayer, unto thee shall all flesh come.

3 Iniquities prevail against me: *as for* our transgressions, thou shalt purge them away.

4 Blessed *is the man whom* thou choosest, and causest to approach *unto thee, that* he may dwell in thy courts: we shall be satisfied with the goodness of thy house, *even* of thy holy temple.

5 *By* terrible things in righteousness wilt thou answer us, O God of our salvation; *who art* the confidence of all the ends of the earth, and of them that are afar off *upon* the sea:

6 Which by his strength setteth fast the mountains; *being* girded with power:

7 Which stilleth the noise of the seas, the noise of their waves, and the tumult of the people.

8 They also that dwell in the uttermost parts are afraid at thy tokens: thou makest the outgoings of the morning and evening to rejoice.

9 Thou visitest the earth, and waterest it: thou greatly enrichest it with the river of God, *which* is full of water: thou preparest them corn, when thou hast so provided for it.

10 Thou waterest the ridges thereof abundantly: thou settlest the furrows thereof: thou makest it soft with showers: thou blessest the springing thereof.

11 Thou crownest the year with thy goodness; and thy paths drop fatness.

12 They drop *upon* the pastures of the wilderness: and the little hills rejoice on every side.

13 The pastures are clothed with flocks; the valleys also are covered over with corn; they shout for joy, they also sing.

PSALM 66

Praise and worship the Lord—He tests and tries men—Sacrifices to be offered in his house.

To the Chief Musician, A Song *or* Psalm.

1 MAKE a joyful noise unto God, all ye lands:

2 Sing forth the honour of his name: make his praise glorious.

3 Say unto God, How terrible *art thou in* thy works! through the greatness of thy power shall thine enemies submit themselves unto thee.

4 All the earth shall worship thee, and shall sing unto thee; they shall sing *to* thy name. Selah.

5 Come and see the works of God: *he is* terrible *in his* doing toward the children of men.

6 He turned the sea into dry *land:* they went through the flood on foot: there did we rejoice in him.

7 He ruleth by his power for ever; his eyes behold the nations: let not the rebellious exalt themselves. Selah.

8 O bless our God, ye people, and make the voice of his praise to be heard:

9 Which holdeth our soul in life, and suffereth not our feet to be moved.

10 For thou, O God, hast proved us: thou hast tried us, as silver is tried.

11 Thou broughtest us into the net; thou laidst affliction upon our loins.

12 Thou hast caused men to ride over our heads; we went through fire and through water: but thou broughtest us out into a wealthy *place.*

13 I will go into thy house with burnt offerings: I will pay thee my vows,

14 Which my lips have uttered, and my mouth hath spoken, when I was in trouble.

15 I will offer unto thee burnt sacrifices of fatlings, with the incense of rams; I will offer bullocks with goats. Selah.

16 Come *and* hear, all ye that fear God, and I will declare what he hath done for my soul.

17 I cried unto him with my mouth, and he was extolled with my tongue.

18 If I regard iniquity in my heart, the Lord will not hear *me:*

19 *But* verily God hath heard *me;* he hath attended to the voice of my prayer.

20 Blessed *be* God, which hath not turned away my prayer, nor his mercy from me.

PSALM 69

A Messianic Psalm of David—The zeal of the Lord's house hath eaten him up—Reproach has broken his heart—He is given gall and vinegar to drink—He is persecuted—He will save Zion.

To the chief Musician upon Shoshannim, *A Psalm* of David.

1 SAVE me, O God; for the waters are come in unto *my* soul.

NOTES

2 I sink in deep mire, where *there is* no standing: I am come into deep waters, where the floods overflow me.

3 I am weary of my crying: my throat is dried: mine eyes fail while I wait for my God.

4 They that hate me without a cause are more than the hairs of mine head: they that would destroy me, *being* mine enemies wrongfully, are mighty: then I restored *that* which I took not away.

5 O God, thou knowest my foolishness; and my sins are not hid from thee.

6 Let not them that wait on thee, O Lord GOD of hosts, be ashamed for my sake: let not those that seek thee be confounded for my sake, O God of Israel.

7 Because for thy sake I have borne reproach; shame hath covered my face.

8 I am become a stranger unto my brethren, and an alien unto my mother's children.

9 For the zeal of thine house hath eaten me up; and the reproaches of them that reproached thee are fallen upon me.

10 When I wept, *and chastened* my soul with fasting, that was to my reproach.

11 I made sackcloth also my garment; and I become a proverb to them.

12 They that sit in the gate speak against me; and I *was* the song of the drunkards.

13 But as for me, my prayer *is* unto thee, O LORD, *in* an acceptable time: O God, in the multitude of thy mercy hear me, in the truth of thy salvation.

14 Deliver me out of the mire, and let me not sink: let me be delivered from them that hate me, and out of the deep waters.

15 Let not the waterflood overflow me, neither let the deep swallow me up, and let not the pit shut her mouth upon me.

16 Hear me, O LORD; for thy lovingkindness *is* good: turn unto me according to the multitude of thy tender mercies.

17 And hide not thy face from thy servant; for I am in trouble: hear me speedily.

18 Draw nigh unto my soul, *and* redeem it: deliver me because of mine enemies.

19 Thou hast known my reproach, and my shame, and my dishonour: mine adversaries *are* all before thee.

20 Reproach hath broken my heart; and I am full of heaviness: and I looked *for some* to take pity, but *there was* none; and for comforters, but I found none.

21 They gave me also gall for my meat; and in my thirst they gave me vinegar to drink.

22 Let their table become a snare before them: and *that which should have been* for *their* welfare, *let it become* a trap.

23 Let their eyes be darkened, that they see not; and make their loins continually to shake.

24 Pour out thine indignation upon them, and let thy wrathful anger take hold of them.

25 Let their habitation be desolate; *and* let none dwell in their tents.

26 For they persecute *him* whom thou hast smitten; and they talk to the grief of those whom thou hast wounded.

27 Add iniquity unto their iniquity: and let them not come into thy righteousness.

28 Let them be blotted out of the book of the living, and not be written with the righteous.

29 But I *am* poor and sorrowful: let thy salvation, O God, set me up on high.

30 I will praise the name of God with a song, and will magnify him with thanksgiving.

31 *This* also shall please the LORD better than an ox *or* bullock that hath horns and hoofs.

32 The humble shall see *this, and* be glad: and your heart shall live that seek God.

33 For the LORD heareth the poor, and despiseth not his prisoners.

34 Let the heaven and earth praise him, the seas, and everything that moveth therein.

35 For God will save Zion, and will build the cities of Judah: that they may dwell there, and have it in possession.

36 The seed also of his servants shall inherit it: and they that love his name shall dwell therein.

PSALM 70

David proclaims: Let God be magnified.

To the chief Musician, *A Psalm* of David, to bring to remembrance.

1 MAKE haste, O God, to deliver me; make haste to help me, O LORD.

NOTES

2 Let them be ashamed and confounded that seek after my soul: let them be turned backward, and put to confusion, that desire my hurt.

3 Let them be turned back for a reward of their shame that say, Aha, aha.

4 Let all those that seek thee rejoice and be glad in thee: and let such as love thy salvation say continually, Let God be magnified.

5 But I *am* poor and needy: make haste unto me, O God: thou *art* my help and my deliverer; O LORD, make no tarrying.

PSALM 71

David praises God with thanksgiving—Who is like unto the Lord!

1 IN thee, O LORD, do I put my trust: let me never be put to confusion.

2 Deliver me in thy righteousness, and cause me to escape: incline thine ear unto me, and save me.

3 Be thou my strong habitation, whereunto I may continually resort: thou hast given commandment to save me; for thou *art* my rock and my fortress.

4 Deliver me, O my God, out of the hand of the wicked, out of the hand of the unrighteous and cruel man.

5 For thou *art* my hope, O Lord GOD: *thou art* my trust from my youth.

6 By thee have I been holden up from the womb: thou art he that took me out of my mother's bowels: my praise *shall be* continually of thee.

7 I am as a wonder unto many; but thou *art* my strong refuge.

8 Let my mouth be filled *with* thy praise *and with* thy honour all the day.

9 Cast me not off in the time of old age; forsake me not when my strength faileth.

10 For mine enemies speak against me; and they that lay wait for my soul take counsel together,

11 Saying, God hath forsaken him: persecute and take him; for *there is* none to deliver *him*.

12 O God, be not far from me: O my God, make haste for my help.

13 Let them be confounded *and* consumed that are adversaries to my soul; let them be covered *with* reproach and dishonour that seek my hurt.

14 But I will hope continually, and will yet praise thee more and more.

15 My mouth shall shew forth thy righteousness *and* thy salvation all the day; for I know not the numbers *thereof.*

16 I will go in the strength of the Lord GOD: I will make mention of thy righteousness, *even* of thine only.

17 O God, thou hast taught me from my youth: and hitherto have I declared thy wondrous works.

18 Now also when I am old and grayheaded, O God, forsake me not; until I have shewed thy strength unto *this* generation, *and* thy power to every one *that* is to come.

19 Thy righteousness also, O God, *is* very high, who hast done great things: O God, who *is* like unto thee!

20 *Thou,* which hast shewed me great and sore troubles, shalt quicken me again, and shalt bring me up again from the depths of the earth.

21 Thou shalt increase my greatness, and comfort me on every side.

22 I will also praise thee with the psaltery, *even* thy truth, O my God: unto thee will I sing with the harp, O thou Holy One of Israel.

23 My lips shall greatly rejoice when I sing unto thee; and my soul, which thou hast redeemed.

24 My tongue also shall talk of thy righteousness all the day long: for they are confounded, for they are brought unto shame, that seek my hurt.

PSALM 72

David speaketh of Solomon, who is made a type of Christ—He shall have dominion—His name shall endure forever—All nations shall call him blessed—The whole earth shall be filled with his glory.

A Psalm for Solomon.

1 GIVE the king thy judgments, O God, and thy righteousness unto the king's son.

2 He shall judge thy people with righteousness, and thy poor with judgment.

3 The mountains shall bring peace to the people, and the little hills, by righteousness.

4 He shall judge the poor of the people, he shall save the children of the needy, and shall break in pieces the oppressor.

5 They shall fear thee as long as the sun and moon endure, throughout all generations.

6 He shall come down like rain upon the mown grass: as showers *that* water the earth.

7 In his days shall the righteous flourish; and abundance of peace so long as the moon endureth.

8 He shall have dominion also from sea to sea, and from the river unto the ends of the earth.

9 They that dwell in the wilderness shall bow before him; and his enemies shall lick the dust.

10 The kings of Tarshish and of the isles shall bring presents: the kings of Sheba and Seba shall offer gifts.

11 Yea, all kings shall fall down before him: all nations shall serve him.

12 For he shall deliver the needy when he crieth; the poor also, and *him* that hath no helper.

13 He shall spare the poor and needy, and shall save the souls of the needy.

14 He shall redeem their soul from deceit and violence: and precious shall their blood be in his sight.

15 And he shall live, and to him shall be given of the gold of Sheba: prayer also shall be made for him continually; *and* daily shall he be praised.

16 There shall be an handful of corn in the earth upon the top of the mountains; the fruit thereof shall shake like Lebanon: and *they* of the city shall flourish like grass of the earth.

17 His name shall endure for ever: his name shall be continued as long as the sun: and *men* shall be blessed in him: all nations shall call him blessed.

18 Blessed *be* the LORD God, the God of Israel, who only doeth wondrous things.

19 And blessed *be* his glorious name for ever: and let the whole earth be filled *with* his glory; Amen, and Amen.

20 The prayers of David the son of Jesse are ended.

PSALM 77

The righteous cry unto the Lord—They remember the wonders of old, how he redeemed the sons of Jacob, and led Israel like a flock.

To the chief Musician, to Jeduthun, A Psalm of Asaph.

NOTES

_____
_____
_____
_____
_____
_____
_____
_____
_____
_____
_____
_____
_____
_____
_____
_____
_____
_____
_____
_____
_____
_____
_____
_____
_____
_____
_____
_____
_____
_____
_____
_____
_____

1 I CRIED unto God with my voice, *even* unto God with my voice; and he gave ear unto me.

2 In the day of my trouble I sought the Lord: my sore ran in the night, and ceased not: my soul refused to be comforted.

3 I remembered God, and was troubled: I complained, and my spirit was overwhelmed. Selah.

4 Thou holdest mine eyes waking: I am so troubled that I cannot speak.

5 I have considered the days of old, the years of ancient times.

6 I call to remembrance my song in the night: I commune with mine own heart: and my spirit made diligent search.

7 Will the Lord cast off for ever? and will he be favourable no more?

8 Is his mercy clean gone for ever? doth *his* promise fail for evermore?

9 Hath God forgotten to be gracious? hath he in anger shut up his tender mercies? Selah.

10 And I said, This *is* my infirmity: *but I will remember* the years of the right hand of the most High.

11 I will remember the works of the LORD: surely I will remember thy wonders of old.

12 I will meditate also of all thy work, and talk of thy doings.

13 Thy way, O God, *is* in the sanctuary: who *is so* great a God as *our* God?

14 Thou *art* the God that doest wonders: thou hast declared thy strength among the people.

15 Thou hast with *thine* arm redeemed thy people, the sons of Jacob and Joseph. Selah.

16 The waters saw thee, O God, the waters saw thee; they were afraid: the depths also were troubled.

17 The clouds poured out water: the skies sent out a sound: thine arrows also went abroad.

18 The voice of thy thunder *was* in the heaven: the lightnings lightened the world: the earth trembled and shook.

19 Thy way *is* in the sea, and thy path in the great waters, and thy footsteps are not known.

20 Thou leddest thy people like a flock by the hand of Moses and Aaron.

PSALM 78

Israel to teach the Lord's law to their children—Disobedient Israel provokes the Lord in the wilderness—Egyptian plagues recounted—The Lord chooses and blesses Judah and David.

Maschil of Asaph.

1 GIVE ear, O my people, *to* my law: incline your ears to the words of my mouth.

2 I will open my mouth in a parable: I will utter dark sayings of old:

3 Which we have heard and known, and our fathers have told us.

4 We will not hide *them* from their children, shewing to the generation to come the praises of the LORD, and his strength, and his wonderful works that he hath done.

5 For he established a testimony in Jacob, and appointed a law in Israel, which he commanded our fathers, that they should make them known to their children:

6 That the generation to come might know *them, even* the children *which* should be born; *who* should arise and declare *them* to their children:

7 That they might set their hope in God, and not forget the works of God, but keep his commandments:

8 And might not be as their fathers, a stubborn and rebellious generation; a generation *that* set not their heart aright, and whose spirit was not stedfast with God.

9 The children of Ephraim, *being* armed, *and* carrying bows, turned back in the day of battle.

10 They kept not the covenant of God, and refused to walk in his law;

11 And forgat his works, and his wonders that he had shewed them.

12 Marvellous things did he in the sight of their fathers, in the land of Egypt, *in* the field of Zoan.

13 He divided the sea, and caused them to pass through; and he made the waters to stand as an heap.

14 In the daytime also he led them with a cloud, and all the night with a light of fire.

NOTES

15 He clave the rocks in the wilderness, and gave *them* drink as *out of* the great depths.

16 He brought streams also out of the rock, and caused waters to run down like rivers.

17 And they sinned yet more against him by provoking the most High in the wilderness.

18 And they tempted God in their heart by asking meat for their lust.

19 Yea, they spake against God; they said, Can God furnish a table in the wilderness?

20 Behold, he smote the rock, that the waters gushed out, and the streams overflowed; can he give bread also? can he provide flesh for his people?

21 Therefore the LORD heard *this,* and was wroth: so a fire was kindled against Jacob, and anger also came up against Israel;

22 Because they believed not in God, and trusted not in his salvation:

23 Though he had commanded the clouds from above, and opened the doors of heaven,

24 And had rained down manna upon them to eat, and had given them of the corn of heaven.

25 Man did eat angels' food: he sent them meat to the full.

26 He caused an east wind to blow in the heaven: and by his power he brought in the south wind.

27 He rained flesh also upon them as dust, and feathered fowls like as the sand of the sea:

28 And he let *it* fall in the midst of their camp, round about their habitations.

29 So they did eat, and were well filled: for he gave them their own desire;

30 They were not estranged from their lust. But while their meat *was* yet in their mouths,

31 The wrath of God came upon them, and slew the fattest of them, and smote down the chosen *men* of Israel.

32 For all this they sinned still, and believed not for his wondrous works.

33 Therefore their days did he consume in vanity, and their years in trouble.

34 When he slew them, then they sought him: and they returned and enquired early after God.

35 And they remembered that God *was* their rock, and the high God their redeemer.

36 Nevertheless they did flatter him with their mouth, and they lied unto him with their tongues.

37 For their heart was not right with him, neither were they stedfast in his covenant.

38 But he, *being* full of compassion, forgave *their* iniquity, and destroyed *them* not: yea, many a time turned he his anger away, and did not stir up all his wrath.

39 For he remembered that they *were but* flesh; a wind that passeth away, and cometh not again.

40 How oft did they provoke him in the wilderness, *and* grieve him in the desert!

41 Yea, they turned back and tempted God, and limited the Holy One of Israel.

42 They remembered not his hand, *nor* the day when he delivered them from the enemy.

43 How he had wrought his signs in Egypt, and his wonders in the field of Zoan:

44 And had turned their rivers into blood; and their floods, that they could not drink.

45 He sent divers sorts of flies among them, which devoured them; and frogs, which destroyed them.

46 He gave also their increase unto the caterpiller, and their labour unto the locust.

47 He destroyed their vines with hail, and their sycomore trees with frost.

48 He gave up their cattle also to the hail, and their flocks to hot thunderbolts.

49 He cast upon them the fierceness of his anger, wrath, and indignation, and trouble, by sending evil angels *among them.*

50 He made a way to his anger; he spared not their soul from death, but gave their life over to the pestilence;

51 And smote all the firstborn in Egypt; the chief of *their* strength in the tabernacles of Ham:

52 But made his own people to go forth like sheep, and guided them in the wilderness like a flock.

NOTES

NOTES

_____
_____
_____
_____
_____
_____
_____
_____
_____
_____
_____
_____
_____
_____
_____
_____
_____
_____
_____
_____
_____
_____
_____
_____
_____
_____
_____

53 And he led them on safely, so that they feared not: but the sea overwhelmed their enemies.

54 And he brought them to the border of his sanctuary, *even to* this mountain, *which* his right hand had purchased.

55 He cast out the heathen also before them, and divided them an inheritance by line, and made the tribes of Israel to dwell in their tents.

56 Yet they tempted and provoked the most high God, and kept not his testimonies:

57 But turned back, and dealt unfaithfully like their fathers: they were turned aside like a deceitful bow.

58 For they provoked him to anger with their high places, and moved him to jealousy with their graven images.

59 When God heard *this,* he was wroth, and greatly abhorred Israel:

60 So that he forsook the tabernacle of Shiloh, the tent *which* he placed among men;

61 And delivered his strength into captivity, and his glory into the enemy's hand.

62 He gave his people over also unto the sword; and was wroth with his inheritance.

63 The fire consumed their young men; and their maidens were not given to marriage.

64 Their priests fell by the sword; and their widows made no lamentation.

65 Then the Lord awaked as one out of sleep, *and* like a mighty man that shouteth by reason of wine.

66 And he smote his enemies in the hinder parts: he put them to a perpetual reproach.

67 Moreover he refused the tabernacle of Joseph, and chose not the tribe of Ephraim:

68 But chose the tribe of Judah, the mount Zion which he loved.

69 And he built his sanctuary like high *palaces,* like the earth which he hath established for ever.

70 He chose David also his servant, and took him from the sheepfolds:

71 From following the ewes great with young he brought him to feed Jacob his people, and Israel his inheritance.

72 So he fed them according to the integrity of his heart; and guided them by the skilfulness of his hands.

PSALM 85

The Lord speaks peace to his people—Truth shall spring out of the earth (the Book of Mormon), and righteousness look down from heaven.

To the chief Musician, A Psalm for the sons of Korah.

1 LORD, thou hast been favourable unto thy land: thou hast brought back the captivity of Jacob.

2 Thou hast forgiven the iniquity of thy people, thou hast covered all their sin. Selah.

3 Thou hast taken away all thy wrath: thou hast turned *thyself* from the fierceness of thine anger.

4 Turn us, O God of our salvation, and cause thine anger toward us to cease.

5 Wilt thou be angry with us for ever? wilt thou draw out thine anger to all generations?

6 Wilt thou not revive us again: that thy people may rejoice in thee?

7 Shew us thy mercy, O LORD, and grant us thy salvation.

8 I will hear what God the LORD will speak: for he will speak peace unto his people, and to his saints: but let them not turn again to folly.

9 Surely his salvation *is* nigh them that fear him; that glory may dwell in our land.

10 Mercy and truth are met together; righteousness and peace have kissed *each other.*

11 Truth shall spring out of the earth; and righteousness shall look down from heaven.

12 Yea, the LORD shall give *that which is* good; and our land shall yield her increase.

13 Righteousness shall go before him; and shall set *us* in the way of his steps.

PSALM 86

David implores God for mercy and is saved from the lowest hell—The Lord is good and plenteous in mercy—All nations shall worship before him.

A Prayer of David.

1 BOW down thine ear, O LORD, hear me: for I *am* poor and needy.

NOTES

NOTES

_____

_____

_____

_____

_____

_____

_____

_____

_____

_____

_____

_____

_____

_____

_____

_____

_____

_____

_____

_____

_____

_____

_____

_____

_____

_____

_____

_____

2 Preserve my soul; for I *am* holy: O thou my God, save thy servant that trusteth in thee.

3 Be merciful unto me, O Lord: for I cry unto thee daily.

4 Rejoice the soul of thy servant: for unto thee, O Lord, do I lift up my soul.

5 For thou, Lord, *art* good, and ready to forgive; and plenteous in mercy unto all them that call upon thee.

6 Give ear, O LORD, unto my prayer; and attend to the voice of my supplications.

7 In the day of my trouble I will call upon thee: for thou wilt answer me.

8 Among the gods *there is* none like unto thee, O Lord; neither *are there any* works like unto thy works.

9 All nations whom thou hast made shall come and worship before thee, O Lord; and shall glorify thy name.

10 For thou *art* great, and doest wondrous things: thou *art* God alone.

11 Teach me thy way, O LORD; I will walk in thy truth: unite my heart to fear thy name.

12 I will praise thee, O Lord my God, with all my heart: and I will glorify thy name for evermore.

13 For great *is* thy mercy toward me: and thou hast delivered my soul from the lowest hell.

14 O God, the proud are risen against me, and the assemblies of violent *men* have sought after my soul; and have not set thee before them.

15 But thou, O Lord, *art* a God full of compassion, and gracious, longsuffering, and plenteous in mercy and truth.

16 O turn unto me, and have mercy upon me; give thy strength unto thy servant, and save the son of thine handmaid.

17 Shew me a token for good; that they which hate me may see *it,* and be ashamed: because thou, LORD, hast holpen me, and comforted me.

Psalms 102–103; 110; 116–119; 127–128; 135–139; 146–150

"Let Every Thing That Hath Breath Praise the Lord"

See the introductions to the last two weeks' scripture reading blocks in this study guide to see why I did not add much commentary for Psalms. By the way, it will be helpful for you to know that "judgment," as used in Psalm 103:6 and elsewhere, can often mean "fairness." Another thing: You will find wonderful reviews of history such as in Psalm 105 regarding Abraham and the covenant people. You will see the value of the perspectives received from living the gospel as taught in Psalm 119:165. The priceless value of having children is taught in Psalm 127. The precious value of God's mercy is taught in Psalm 136. It helps to know that "right hand" is the covenant hand and is symbolic of covenants, as you will see in Psalm 139:10. And know that "horn," as used in Psalm 148:14, means "power."

PSALM 102

NOTES

A prayer of the afflicted—Zion shall be built up when the Lord appears in his glory—Though heaven and earth perish, the Lord who created them shall endure forever.

A Prayer of the afflicted, when he is overwhelmed, and poureth out his complaint before the LORD.

1 HEAR my prayer, O LORD, and let my cry come unto thee.

2 Hide not thy face from me in the day *when* I am in trouble; incline thine ear unto me: in the day *when* I call answer me speedily.

3 For my days are consumed like smoke, and my bones are burned as an hearth.

4 My heart is smitten, and withered like grass; so that I forget to eat my bread.

5 By reason of the voice of my groaning my bones cleave to my skin.

6 I am like a pelican of the wilderness: I am like an owl of the desert.

7 I watch, and am as a sparrow alone upon the house top.

8 Mine enemies reproach me all the day; *and* they that are mad against me are sworn against me.

9 For I have eaten ashes like bread, and mingled my drink with weeping,

10 Because of thine indignation and thy wrath: for thou hast lifted me up, and cast me down.

NOTES

11 My days *are* like a shadow that declineth; and I am withered like grass.

12 But thou, O LORD, shalt endure for ever; and thy remembrance unto all generations.

13 Thou shalt arise, *and* have mercy upon Zion: for the time to favour her, yea, the set time, is come.

14 For thy servants take pleasure in her stones, and favour the dust thereof.

15 So the heathen shall fear the name of the LORD, and all the kings of the earth thy glory.

16 When the LORD shall build up Zion, he shall appear in his glory.

17 He will regard the prayer of the destitute, and not despise their prayer.

18 This shall be written for the generation to come: and the people which shall be created shall praise the LORD.

19 For he hath looked down from the height of his sanctuary; from heaven did the LORD behold the earth;

20 To hear the groaning of the prisoner; to loose those that are appointed to death;

21 To declare the name of the LORD in Zion, and his praise in Jerusalem;

22 When the people are gathered together, and the kingdoms, to serve the LORD.

23 He weakened my strength in the way; he shortened my days.

24 I said, O my God, take me not away in the midst of my days: thy years *are* throughout all generations.

25 Of old hast thou laid the foundation of the earth: and the heavens *are* the work of thy hands.

26 They shall perish, but thou shalt endure: yea, all of them shall wax old like a garment; as a vesture shalt thou change them, and they shall be changed:

27 But thou *art* the same, and thy years shall have no end.

28 The children of thy servants shall continue, and their seed shall be established before thee.

PSALM 103

David exhorts the saints to bless the Lord for his mercy—The Lord is merciful unto those who keep his commandments.

A Psalm of David.

NOTES

1 BLESS the LORD, O my soul: and all that is within me, *bless* his holy name.

2 Bless the LORD, O my soul, and forget not all his benefits:

3 Who forgiveth all thine iniquities; who healeth all thy diseases;

4 Who redeemeth thy life from destruction; who crowneth thee with lovingkindness and tender mercies;

5 Who satisfieth thy mouth with good *things; so that* thy youth is renewed like the eagle's.

6 The LORD executeth righteousness and judgment for all that are oppressed.

7 He made known his ways unto Moses, his acts unto the children of Israel.

8 The LORD *is* merciful and gracious, slow to anger, and plenteous in mercy.

9 He will not always chide: neither will he keep *his anger* for ever.

10 He hath not dealt with us after our sins; nor rewarded us according to our iniquities.

11 For as the heaven is high above the earth, *so* great is his mercy toward them that fear him.

12 As far as the east is from the west, *so* far hath he removed our transgressions from us.

13 Like as a father pitieth *his* children, *so* the LORD pitieth them that fear him.

14 For he knoweth our frame; he remembereth that we *are* dust.

15 *As for* man, his days *are* as grass: as a flower of the field, so he flourisheth.

16 For the wind passeth over it, and it is gone; and the place thereof shall know it no more.

17 But the mercy of the LORD *is* from everlasting to everlasting upon them that fear him, and his righteousness unto children's children;

18 To such as keep his covenant, and to those that remember his commandments to do them.

19 The LORD hath prepared his throne in the heavens; and his kingdom ruleth over all.

20 Bless the LORD, ye his angels, that excel in strength, that do his commandments, hearkening unto the voice of his word.

21 Bless ye the LORD, all *ye* his hosts; *ye* ministers of his, that do his pleasure.

22 Bless the LORD, all his works in all places of his dominion: bless the LORD, O my soul.

PSALM 110

A Messianic Psalm of David—Christ shall sit on the Lord's right hand—He shall be a priest forever after the order of Melchizedek.

A Psalm of David.

1 THE LORD said unto my Lord, Sit thou at my right hand, until I make thine enemies thy footstool.

2 The LORD shall send the rod of thy strength out of Zion: rule thou in the midst of thine enemies.

3 Thy people *shall be* willing in the day of thy power, in the beauties of holiness from the womb of the morning: thou hast the dew of thy youth.

4 The LORD hath sworn, and will not repent, Thou *art* a priest for ever after the order of Melchizedek.

5 The Lord at thy right hand shall strike through kings in the day of his wrath.

6 He shall judge among the heathen, he shall fill *the places* with the dead bodies; he shall wound the heads over many countries.

7 He shall drink of the brook in the way: therefore shall he lift up the head.

PSALM 116

Gracious is the Lord, and righteous—Precious in the sight of the Lord is the death of his saints.

1 I LOVE the LORD, because he hath heard my voice *and* my supplications.

2 Because he hath inclined his ear unto me, therefore will I call upon *him* as long as I live.

3 The sorrows of death compassed me, and the pains of hell gat hold upon me: I found trouble and sorrow.

4 Then called I upon the name of the LORD; O LORD, I beseech thee, deliver my soul.

5 Gracious *is* the LORD, and righteous; yea, our God *is* merciful.

6 The LORD preserveth the simple: I was brought low, and he helped me.

7 Return unto thy rest, O my soul; for the LORD hath dealt bountifully with thee.

8 For thou hast delivered my soul from death, mine eyes from tears, *and* my feet from falling.

9 I will walk before the LORD in the land of the living.

10 I believed, therefore have I spoken: I was greatly afflicted:

11 I said in my haste, All men *are* liars.

12 What shall I render unto the LORD *for* all his benefits toward me?

13 I will take the cup of salvation, and call upon the name of the LORD.

14 I will pay my vows unto the LORD now in the presence of all his people.

15 Precious in the sight of the LORD *is* the death of his saints.

16 O LORD, truly I *am* thy servant; I *am* thy servant, *and* the son of thine handmaid: thou hast loosed my bonds.

17 I will offer to thee the sacrifice of thanksgiving, and will call upon the name of the LORD.

18 I will pay my vows unto the LORD now in the presence of all his people,

19 In the courts of the LORD's house, in the midst of thee, O Jerusalem. Praise ye the LORD.

PSALM 117

Praise the Lord for his mercy and truth.

1 O PRAISE the LORD, all ye nations: praise him, all ye people.

2 For his merciful kindness is great toward us: and the truth of the LORD *endureth* for ever. Praise ye the LORD.

PSALM 118

A Messianic Psalm—Let all Israel say of the Lord: His mercy endureth forever—The Stone which the builders refused is become the head stone of the corner—Blessed is he that cometh in the name of the Lord.

NOTES

NOTES

_____

_____

_____

_____

_____

_____

_____

_____

_____

_____

_____

_____

_____

_____

_____

_____

_____

_____

_____

_____

_____

_____

_____

_____

_____

_____

_____

_____

_____

_____

_____

1 O GIVE thanks unto the LORD; for *he is* good: because his mercy *endureth* for ever.

2 Let Israel now say, that his mercy *endureth* for ever.

3 Let the house of Aaron now say, that his mercy *endureth* for ever.

4 Let them now that fear the LORD say, that his mercy *endureth* for ever.

5 I called upon the LORD in distress: the LORD answered me, *and set me* in a large place.

6 The LORD *is* on my side; I will not fear: what can man do unto me?

7 The LORD taketh my part with them that help me: therefore shall I see *my desire* upon them that hate me.

8 *It is* better to trust in the LORD than to put confidence in man.

9 *It is* better to trust in the LORD than to put confidence in princes.

10 All nations compassed me about: but in the name of the LORD will I destroy them.

11 They compassed me about; yea, they compassed me about: but in the name of the LORD I will destroy them.

12 They compassed me about like bees; they are quenched as the fire of thorns: for in the name of the LORD I will destroy them.

13 Thou hast thrust sore at me that I might fall: but the LORD helped me.

14 The LORD *is* my strength and song, and is become my salvation.

15 The voice of rejoicing and salvation *is* in the tabernacles of the righteous: the right hand of the LORD doeth valiantly.

16 The right hand of the LORD is exalted: the right hand of the LORD doeth valiantly.

17 I shall not die, but live, and declare the works of the LORD.

18 The LORD hath chastened me sore: but he hath not given me over unto death.

19 Open to me the gates of righteousness: I will go into them, *and* I will praise the LORD:

20 This gate of the LORD, into which the righteous shall enter.

21 I will praise thee: for thou hast heard me, and art become my salvation.

22 The stone *which* the builders refused is become the head *stone* of the corner.

23 This is the LORD's doing; it *is* marvellous in our eyes.

24 This *is* the day *which* the LORD hath made; we will rejoice and be glad in it.

25 Save now, I beseech thee, O LORD: O LORD, I beseech thee, send now prosperity.

26 Blessed *be* he that cometh in the name of the LORD: we have blessed you out of the house of the LORD.

27 God *is* the LORD, which hath shewed us light: bind the sacrifice with cords, *even* unto the horns of the altar.

28 Thou *art* my God, and I will praise thee: *thou art* my God, I will exalt thee.

29 O give thanks unto the LORD; for *he is* good: for his mercy *endureth* for ever.

PSALM 119

א ALEPH

Blessed are they who keep the commandments.

1 BLESSED *are* the undefiled in the way, who walk in the law of the LORD.

2 Blessed *are* they that keep his testimonies, *and that* seek him with the whole heart.

3 They also do no iniquity: they walk in his ways.

4 Thou hast commanded *us* to keep thy precepts diligently.

5 O that my ways were directed to keep thy statutes!

6 Then shall I not be ashamed, when I have respect unto all thy commandments.

7 I will praise thee with uprightness of heart, when I shall have learned thy righteous judgments.

8 I will keep thy statutes: O forsake me not utterly.

ב BETH

PSALM 127

Children are an heritage from the Lord.

NOTES

A Song of degrees for Solomon.

1 EXCEPT the LORD build the house, they labour in vain that build it: except the LORD keep the city, the watchman waketh *but* in vain.

2 *It is* vain for you to rise up early, to sit up late, to eat the bread of sorrows: *for* so he giveth his beloved sleep.

3 Lo, children *are* an heritage of the LORD: *and* the fruit of the womb *is his* reward.

4 As arrows *are* in the hand of a mighty man; so *are* children of the youth.

5 Happy *is* the man that hath his quiver full of them: they shall not be ashamed, but they shall speak with the enemies in the gate.

PSALM 128

Blessed are those who fear the Lord and walk in his ways.

A Song of degrees.

1 BLESSED *is* every one that feareth the LORD; that walketh in his ways.

2 For thou shalt eat the labour of thine hands: happy *shalt* thou *be,* and *it shall be* well with thee.

3 Thy wife *shall be* as a fruitful vine by the sides of thine house: thy children like olive plants round about thy table.

4 Behold, that thus shall the man be blessed that feareth the LORD.

5 The LORD shall bless thee out of Zion: and thou shalt see the good of Jerusalem all the days of thy life.

6 Yea, thou shalt see thy children's children, *and* peace upon Israel.

PSALM 135

Praise and bless the Lord—Our Lord is above all gods; and idols can neither see, nor hear, nor speak.

1 PRAISE ye the LORD. Praise ye the name of the LORD; praise *him,* O ye servants of the LORD.

2 Ye that stand in the house of the LORD, in the courts of the house of our God,

3 Praise the LORD; for the LORD *is* good: sing praises unto his name; for *it is* pleasant.

4 For the LORD hath chosen Jacob unto himself, *and* Israel for his peculiar treasure.

5 For I know that the LORD *is* great, and *that* our Lord *is* above all gods.

6 Whatsoever the LORD pleased, *that* did he in heaven, and in earth, in the seas, and all deep places.

7 He causeth the vapours to ascend from the ends of the earth; he maketh lightnings for the rain; he bringeth the wind out of his treasuries.

8 Who smote the firstborn of Egypt, both of man and beast.

9 *Who* sent tokens and wonders into the midst of thee, O Egypt, upon Pharaoh, and upon all his servants.

10 Who smote great nations, and slew mighty kings;

11 Sihon king of the Amorites, and Og king of Bashan, and all the kingdoms of Canaan:

12 And gave their land *for* an heritage, an heritage unto Israel his people.

13 Thy name, O LORD, *endureth* for ever; *and* thy memorial, O LORD, throughout all generations.

14 For the LORD will judge his people, and he will repent himself concerning his servants.

15 The idols of the heathen *are* silver and gold, the work of men's hands.

16 They have mouths, but they speak not; eyes have they, but they see not;

17 They have ears, but they hear not; neither is there *any* breath in their mouths.

18 They that make them are like unto them: *so is* every one that trusteth in them.

19 Bless the LORD, O house of Israel: bless the LORD, O house of Aaron:

20 Bless the LORD, O house of Levi: ye that fear the LORD, bless the LORD.

21 Blessed be the LORD out of Zion, which dwelleth at Jerusalem. Praise ye the LORD.

PSALM 136

Give thanks unto God for all things, for his mercy endureth forever.

1 O GIVE thanks unto the LORD; for *he is* good: for his mercy *endureth* for ever.

NOTES

NOTES

2 O give thanks unto the God of gods: for his mercy *endureth* for ever.

3 O give thanks to the Lord of lords: for his mercy *endureth* for ever.

4 To him who alone doeth great wonders: for his mercy *endureth* for ever.

5 To him that by wisdom made the heavens: for his mercy *endureth* for ever.

6 To him that stretched out the earth above the waters: for his mercy *endureth* for ever.

7 To him that made great lights: for his mercy *endureth* for ever:

8 The sun to rule by day: for his mercy *endureth* for ever:

9 The moon and stars to rule by night: for his mercy *endureth* for ever.

10 To him that smote Egypt in their firstborn: for his mercy *endureth* for ever:

11 And brought out Israel from among them: for his mercy *endureth* for ever:

12 With a strong hand, and with a stretched out arm: for his mercy *endureth* for ever.

13 To him which divided the Red sea into parts: for his mercy *endureth* for ever:

14 And made Israel to pass through the midst of it: for his mercy *endureth* for ever:

15 But overthrew Pharaoh and his host in the Red sea: for his mercy *endureth* for ever.

16 To him which led his people through the wilderness: for his mercy *endureth* for ever.

17 To him which smote great kings: for his mercy *endureth* for ever:

18 And slew famous kings: for his mercy *endureth* for ever:

19 Sihon king of the Amorites: for his mercy *endureth* for ever:

20 And Og the king of Bashan: for his mercy *endureth* for ever:

21 And gave their land for an heritage: for his mercy *endureth* for ever:

22 *Even* an heritage unto Israel his servant: for his mercy *endureth* for ever.

23 Who remembered us in our low estate: for his mercy *endureth* for ever:

24 And hath redeemed us from our enemies: for his mercy *endureth* for ever.

25 Who giveth food to all flesh: for his mercy *endureth* for ever.

26 O give thanks unto the God of heaven: for his mercy *endureth* for ever.

PSALM 137

While in captivity, the Jews wept by the rivers of Babylon—Because of sorrow, they could not bear to sing the songs of Zion.

1 BY the rivers of Babylon, there we sat down, yea, we wept, when we remembered Zion.

2 We hanged our harps upon the willows in the midst thereof.

3 For there they that carried us away captive required of us a song; and they that wasted us *required of us* mirth, *saying,* Sing us *one* of the songs of Zion.

4 How shall we sing the LORD's song in a strange land?

5 If I forget thee, O Jerusalem, let my right hand forget *her cunning.*

6 If I do not remember thee, let my tongue cleave to the roof of my mouth; if I prefer not Jerusalem above my chief joy.

7 Remember, O LORD, the children of Edom in the day of Jerusalem; who said, Rase *it,* rase *it, even* to the foundation thereof.

8 O daughter of Babylon, who art to be destroyed; happy *shall he be,* that rewardeth thee as thou hast served us.

9 Happy *shall he be,* that taketh and dasheth thy little ones against the stones.

PSALM 138

David praises the Lord for his lovingkindness and truth—He worships toward the holy temple.

A Psalm of David.

1 I WILL praise thee with my whole heart: before the gods will I sing praise unto thee.

2 I will worship toward thy holy temple, and praise thy name for thy lovingkindness and for thy truth: for thou hast magnified thy word above all thy name.

3 In the day when I cried thou answeredst me, *and* strengthenedst me *with* strength in my soul.

NOTES

NOTES

4 All the kings of the earth shall praise thee, O LORD, when they hear the words of thy mouth.

5 Yea, they shall sing in the ways of the LORD: for great *is* the glory of the LORD.

6 Though the LORD *be* high, yet hath he respect unto the lowly: but the proud he knoweth afar off.

7 Though I walk in the midst of trouble, thou wilt revive me: thou shalt stretch forth thine hand against the wrath of mine enemies, and thy right hand shall save me.

8 The LORD will perfect *that which* concerneth me: thy mercy, O LORD, *endureth* for ever: forsake not the works of thine own hands.

PSALM 139

David says the Lord knows all man's thoughts and doings—He asks: Whither shall man go to escape from the spirit and presence of the Lord? —Man is fearfully and wonderfully made.

To the chief Musician, A Psalm of David.

1 O LORD, thou hast searched me, and known *me.*

2 Thou knowest my downsitting and mine uprising, thou understandest my thought afar off.

3 Thou compassest my path and my lying down, and art acquainted *with* all my ways.

4 For *there is* not a word in my tongue, *but,* lo, O LORD, thou knowest it altogether.

5 Thou hast beset me behind and before, and laid thine hand upon me.

6 *Such* knowledge *is* too wonderful for me; it is high, I cannot *attain* unto it.

7 Whither shall I go from thy spirit? or whither shall I flee from thy presence?

8 If I ascend up into heaven, thou *art* there: if I make my bed in hell, behold, thou *art there.*

9 *If* I take the wings of the morning, *and* dwell in the uttermost parts of the sea;

10 Even there shall thy hand lead me, and thy right hand shall hold me.

11 If I say, Surely the darkness shall cover me; even the night shall be light about me.

12 Yea, the darkness hideth not from thee; but the night shineth as the day: the darkness and the light *are* both alike *to thee.*

13 For thou hast possessed my reins: thou hast covered me in my mother's womb.

14 I will praise thee; for I am fearfully *and* wonderfully made: marvellous *are* thy works; and *that* my soul knoweth right well.

15 My substance was not hid from thee, when I was made in secret, *and* curiously wrought in the lowest parts of the earth.

16 Thine eyes did see my substance, yet being unperfect; and in thy book all *my members* were written, *which* in continuance were fashioned, when *as yet there was* none of them.

17 How precious also are thy thoughts unto me, O God! how great is the sum of them!

18 *If* I should count them, they are more in number than the sand: when I awake, I am still with thee.

19 Surely thou wilt slay the wicked, O God: depart from me therefore, ye bloody men.

20 For they speak against thee wickedly, *and* thine enemies take *thy name* in vain.

21 Do not I hate them, O LORD, that hate thee? and am not I grieved with those that rise up against thee?

22 I hate them with perfect hatred: I count them mine enemies.

23 Search me, O God, and know my heart: try me, and know my thoughts:

24 And see if *there be any* wicked way in me, and lead me in the way everlasting.

PSALM 146

Happy are they whose hope is in the Lord—The Lord looseth the prisoners, loveth the righteous, and reigneth forever.

1 PRAISE ye the LORD. Praise the LORD, O my soul.

2 While I live will I praise the LORD: I will sing praises unto my God while I have any being.

3 Put not your trust in princes, *nor* in the son of man, in whom *there is* no help.

4 His breath goeth forth, he returneth to his earth; in that very day his thoughts perish.

NOTES

_____
_____
_____
_____
_____
_____
_____
_____
_____
_____
_____
_____
_____
_____
_____
_____
_____
_____
_____
_____
_____
_____
_____
_____
_____
_____

5 Happy *is he* that *hath* the God of Jacob for his help, whose hope *is* in the LORD his God:

6 Which made heaven, and earth, the sea, and all that therein *is:* which keepeth truth for ever:

7 Which executeth judgment for the oppressed: which giveth food to the hungry. The LORD looseth the prisoners:

8 The LORD openeth *the eyes of* the blind: the LORD raiseth them that are bowed down: the LORD loveth the righteous:

9 The LORD preserveth the strangers; he relieveth the fatherless and widow: but the way of the wicked he turneth upside down.

10 The LORD shall reign for ever, *even* thy God, O Zion, unto all generations. Praise ye the LORD.

PSALM 147

Praise the Lord for his power—His understanding is infinite—He sends his commandments, his word, his statutes, and his judgments unto Israel.

1 PRAISE ye the LORD: for *it is* good to sing praises unto our God; for *it is* pleasant; *and* praise is comely.

2 The LORD doth build up Jerusalem: he gathereth together the outcasts of Israel.

3 He healeth the broken in heart, and bindeth up their wounds.

4 He telleth the number of the stars; he calleth them all by *their* names.

5 Great *is* our Lord, and of great power: his understanding *is* infinite.

6 The LORD lifteth up the meek: he casteth the wicked down to the ground.

7 Sing unto the LORD with thanksgiving; sing praise upon the harp unto our God:

8 Who covereth the heaven with clouds, who prepareth rain for the earth, who maketh grass to grow upon the mountains.

9 He giveth to the beast his food, *and* to the young ravens which cry.

10 He delighteth not in the strength of the horse: he taketh not pleasure in the legs of a man.

11 The LORD taketh pleasure in them that fear him, in those that hope in his mercy.

12 Praise the LORD, O Jerusalem; praise thy God, O Zion.

13 For he hath strengthened the bars of thy gates; he hath blessed thy children within thee.

14 He maketh peace *in* thy borders, *and* filleth thee with the finest of the wheat.

15 He sendeth forth his commandment *upon* earth: his word runneth very swiftly.

16 He giveth snow like wool: he scattereth the hoarfrost like ashes.

17 He casteth forth his ice like morsels: who can stand before his cold?

18 He sendeth out his word, and melteth them: he causeth his wind to blow, *and* the waters flow.

19 He sheweth his word unto Jacob, his statutes and his judgments unto Israel.

20 He hath not dealt so with any nation: and *as for his* judgments, they have not known them. Praise ye the LORD.

PSALM 148

Let all things praise the Lord: men and angels, the heavenly bodies, the elements and the earth, and all things thereon.

1 PRAISE ye the LORD. Praise ye the LORD from the heavens: praise him in the heights.

2 Praise ye him, all his angels: praise ye him, all his hosts.

3 Praise ye him, sun and moon: praise him, all ye stars of light.

4 Praise him, ye heavens of heavens, and ye waters that *be* above the heavens.

5 Let them praise the name of the LORD: for he commanded, and they were created.

6 He hath also stablished them for ever and ever: he hath made a decree which shall not pass.

7 Praise the LORD from the earth, ye dragons, and all deeps:

8 Fire, and hail; snow, and vapour; stormy wind fulfilling his word:

9 Mountains, and all hills; fruitful trees, and all cedars:

10 Beasts, and all cattle; creeping things, and flying fowl:

11 Kings of the earth, and all people; princes, and all judges of the earth:

NOTES

12 Both young men, and maidens; old men, and children:

13 Let them praise the name of the LORD: for his name alone is excellent; his glory *is* above the earth and heaven.

14 He also exalteth the horn of his people, the praise of all his saints; *even* of the children of Israel, a people near unto him. Praise ye the LORD.

PSALM 149

Praise the Lord in the congregation of the saints—He will beautify the meek with salvation.

1 PRAISE ye the LORD. Sing unto the LORD a new song, *and* his praise in the congregation of saints.

2 Let Israel rejoice in him that made him: let the children of Zion be joyful in their King.

3 Let them praise his name in the dance: let them sing praises unto him with the timbrel and harp.

4 For the LORD taketh pleasure in his people: he will beautify the meek with salvation.

5 Let the saints be joyful in glory: let them sing aloud upon their beds.

6 *Let* the high *praises* of God *be* in their mouth, and a twoedged sword in their hand;

7 To execute vengeance upon the heathen, *and* punishments upon the people;

8 To bind their kings with chains, and their nobles with fetters of iron;

9 To execute upon them the judgment written: this honour have all his saints. Praise ye the LORD.

PSALM 150

Praise God in his sanctuary—Let everything that hath breath praise the Lord.

1 PRAISE ye the LORD. Praise God in his sanctuary: praise him in the firmament of his power.

2 Praise him for his mighty acts: praise him according to his excellent greatness.

3 Praise him with the sound of the trumpet: praise him with the psaltery and harp.

4 Praise him with the timbrel and dance: praise him with stringed instruments and organs.

5 Praise him upon the loud cymbals: praise him upon the high sounding cymbals.

6 Let every thing that hath breath praise the LORD. Praise ye the LORD.

NOTES

Proverbs 1–4; 15–16; 22; 31; Ecclesiastes 1–3; 11–12

"The Fear of the Lord Is the Beginning of Wisdom"

Again, because of limited space, I will not add commentary to Proverbs. Rather, I will use the available space to add verse-by-verse commentary to what are considered more difficult Old Testament books, such as Isaiah, Jeremiah, and Ezekiel, as well as to Habakkuk and others of the so-called "minor" prophets. You will find excellent help in the Come, Follow Me curriculum. Solomon wrote many of the Proverbs. Some content of Proverbs can lead to deep spiritual contemplation, and some of it is pretty-much confined to human wisdom. You will see as you read and study that some verses of Proverbs do not connect with verses before or after but instead stand alone. It is likely that you will find several verses of Proverbs to be somewhat familiar. For example, Proverbs 3:5–6; 16:18, 22:6, 23:7; 26:11, 29:18, and 31:10–28.

NOTES

PROVERBS

Proverbs is sometimes referred to as "wisdom literature." We will quote from the Bible Dictionary to provide a general background for this book of the Bible.

BIBLE DICTIONARY

PROVERBS

The Heb. word rendered proverb is mashal, a similitude or parable, but the book contains many maxims and sayings not properly so called, and also connected poems of considerable length. There is much in it that does not rise above the plane of worldly wisdom, but throughout it is taken for granted that "the fear of the Lord is the beginning of wisdom" (1:7; 9:10). The least spiritual of the Proverbs are valuable as reminding us that the voice of Divine Inspiration does not disdain to utter homely truths. The first section, Chs. 1–9, is the most poetic and contains an exposition of true wisdom. Chapters 10–24 contain a collection of proverbs and sentences about the right and wrong ways of living. Chapters 25–29 contain the proverbs of Solomon that the men of Hezekiah, king of Judah, copied out. Chapters 30 and 31 contain the "burden" of Agur and Lemuel, the latter including a picture of the ideal wife, arranged in acrostic form. The book is frequently quoted in the New Testament, the use of chapter 3 being especially noteworthy.

Again, because of limited time and space, I will not add commentary to Proverbs; rather, I will use my time to add commentary to what are considered more difficult Old Testament books such as Isaiah, Jeremiah, Ezekiel, Habakkuk, and others.

PROVERBS 1

The fear of the Lord is the beginning of knowledge—If sinners entice thee, consent thou not—Those who hearken to wisdom shall dwell safely.

1 THE proverbs of Solomon the son of David, king of Israel;

2 To know wisdom and instruction; to perceive the words of understanding;

3 To receive the instruction of wisdom, justice, and judgment, and equity;

4 To give subtilty to the simple, to the young man knowledge and discretion.

5 A wise *man* will hear, and will increase learning; and a man of understanding shall attain unto wise counsels:

6 To understand a proverb, and the interpretation; the words of the wise, and their dark sayings.

7 ¶ The fear of the LORD *is* the beginning of knowledge: *but* fools despise wisdom and instruction.

8 My son, hear the instruction of thy father, and forsake not the law of thy mother:

9 For they *shall be* an ornament of grace unto thy head, and chains about thy neck.

10 ¶ My son, if sinners entice thee, consent thou not.

11 If they say, Come with us, let us lay wait for blood, let us lurk privily for the innocent without cause:

12 Let us swallow them up alive as the grave; and whole, as those that go down into the pit:

13 We shall find all precious substance, we shall fill our houses with spoil:

14 Cast in thy lot among us; let us all have one purse:

15 My son, walk not thou in the way with them; refrain thy foot from their path:

16 For their feet run to evil, and make haste to shed blood.

17 Surely in vain the net is spread in the sight of any bird.

18 And they lay wait for their *own* blood; they lurk privily for their *own* lives.

19 So *are* the ways of every one that is greedy of gain; *which* taketh away the life of the owners thereof.

20 ¶ Wisdom crieth without; she uttereth her voice in the streets:

21 She crieth in the chief place of concourse, in the openings of the gates: in the city she uttereth her words, *saying,*

22 How long, ye simple ones, will ye love simplicity? and the scorners delight in their scorning, and fools hate knowledge?

NOTES

_____
_____
_____
_____
_____
_____
_____
_____
_____
_____
_____
_____
_____
_____
_____
_____
_____
_____
_____
_____
_____
_____
_____
_____
_____
_____
_____
_____
_____
_____
_____
_____
_____
_____
_____
_____
_____

23 Turn you at my reproof: behold, I will pour out my spirit unto you, I will make known my words unto you.

24 ¶ Because I have called, and ye refused; I have stretched out my hand, and no man regarded;

25 But ye have set at nought all my counsel, and would none of my reproof:

26 I also will laugh at your calamity; I will mock when your fear cometh;

27 When your fear cometh as desolation, and your destruction cometh as a whirl-wind; when distress and anguish cometh upon you.

28 Then shall they call upon me, but I will not answer; they shall seek me early, but they shall not find me:

29 For that they hated knowledge, and did not choose the fear of the LORD:

30 They would none of my counsel: they despised all my reproof.

31 Therefore shall they eat of the fruit of their own way, and be filled with their own devices.

32 For the turning away of the simple shall slay them, and the prosperity of fools shall destroy them.

33 But whoso hearkeneth unto me shall dwell safely, and shall be quiet from fear of evil.

PROVERBS 2

The Lord giveth wisdom, knowledge, and understanding—Walk in the way of good men.

1 MY son, if thou wilt receive my words, and hide my commandments with thee;

2 So that thou incline thine ear unto wisdom, *and* apply thine heart to understanding;

3 Yea, if thou criest after knowledge, *and* liftest up thy voice for understanding;

4 If thou seekest her as silver, and searchest for her as *for* hid treasures;

5 Then shalt thou understand the fear of the LORD, and find the knowledge of God.

6 For the LORD giveth wisdom: out of his mouth *cometh* knowledge and under-standing.

7 He layeth up sound wisdom for the righteous: *he is* a buckler to them that walk uprightly.

8 He keepeth the paths of judgment, and preserveth the way of his saints.

9 Then shalt thou understand righteousness, and judgment, and equity; *yea,* every good path.

10 ¶ When wisdom entereth into thine heart, and knowledge is pleasant unto thy soul;

11 Discretion shall preserve thee, understanding shall keep thee:

12 To deliver thee from the way of the evil *man,* from the man that speaketh froward things;

13 Who leave the paths of uprightness, to walk in the ways of darkness;

14 Who rejoice to do evil, *and* delight in the frowardness of the wicked;

15 Whose ways *are* crooked, and *they* froward in their paths:

16 To deliver thee from the strange woman, *even* from the stranger *which* flattereth with her words;

17 Which forsaketh the guide of her youth, and forgetteth the covenant of her God.

18 For her house inclineth unto death, and her paths unto the dead.

19 None that go unto her return again, neither take they hold of the paths of life.

20 That thou mayest walk in the way of good *men,* and keep the paths of the righteous.

21 For the upright shall dwell in the land, and the perfect shall remain in it.

22 But the wicked shall be cut off from the earth, and the transgressors shall be rooted out of it.

PROVERBS 3

Write mercy and truth upon the tablet of thy heart—Trust in the Lord—Honor him with thy substance—Whom the Lord loveth he correcteth—Happy is the man that findeth wisdom.

1 MY son, forget not my law; but let thine heart keep my commandments:

2 For length of days, and long life, and peace, shall they add to thee.

3 Let not mercy and truth forsake thee: bind them about thy neck; write them upon the table of thine heart:

NOTES

4 So shalt thou find favour and good understanding in the sight of God and man.

5 ¶ Trust in the LORD with all thine heart; and lean not unto thine own understanding.

6 In all thy ways acknowledge him, and he shall direct thy paths.

7 ¶ Be not wise in thine own eyes: fear the LORD, and depart from evil.

8 It shall be health to thy navel, and marrow to thy bones.

9 Honour the LORD with thy substance, and with the firstfruits of all thine increase:

10 So shall thy barns be filled with plenty, and thy presses shall burst out with new wine.

11 ¶ My son, despise not the chastening of the LORD; neither be weary of his correction:

12 For whom the LORD loveth he correcteth; even as a father the son *in whom* he delighteth.

13 ¶ Happy *is* the man *that* findeth wisdom, and the man *that* getteth understanding.

14 For the merchandise of it *is* better than the merchandise of silver, and the gain thereof than fine gold.

15 She *is* more precious than rubies: and all the things thou canst desire are not to be compared unto her.

16 Length of days *is* in her right hand; *and* in her left hand riches and honour.

17 Her ways *are* ways of pleasantness, and all her paths *are* peace.

18 She *is* a tree of life to them that lay hold upon her: and happy *is every one* that retaineth her.

19 The LORD by wisdom hath founded the earth; by understanding hath he established the heavens.

20 By his knowledge the depths are broken up, and the clouds drop down the dew.

21 ¶ My son, let not them depart from thine eyes: keep sound wisdom and discretion:

22 So shall they be life unto thy soul, and grace to thy neck.

23 Then shalt thou walk in thy way safely, and thy foot shall not stumble.

24 When thou liest down, thou shalt not be afraid: yea, thou shalt lie down, and thy sleep shall be sweet.

25 Be not afraid of sudden fear, neither of the desolation of the wicked, when it cometh.

26 For the LORD shall be thy confidence, and shall keep thy foot from being taken.

27 ¶ Withhold not good from them to whom it is due, when it is in the power of thine hand to do *it.*

28 Say not unto thy neighbour, Go, and come again, and to morrow I will give; when thou hast it by thee.

29 Devise not evil against thy neighbour, seeing he dwelleth securely by thee.

30 ¶ Strive not with a man without cause, if he have done thee no harm.

31 ¶ Envy thou not the oppressor, and choose none of his ways.

32 For the froward *is* abomination to the LORD: but his secret *is* with the righteous.

33 ¶ The curse of the LORD *is* in the house of the wicked: but he blesseth the habitation of the just.

34 Surely he scorneth the scorners: but he giveth grace unto the lowly.

35 The wise shall inherit glory: but shame shall be the promotion of fools.

PROVERBS 4

Keep the Lord's commandments and live—With all thy getting get understanding—Go not in the way of evil men.

1 HEAR, ye children, the instruction of a father, and attend to know understanding.

2 For I give you good doctrine, forsake ye not my law.

3 For I was my father's son, tender and only *beloved* in the sight of my mother.

4 He taught me also, and said unto me, Let thine heart retain my words: keep my commandments, and live.

5 Get wisdom, get understanding: forget *it* not; neither decline from the words of my mouth.

6 Forsake her not, and she shall preserve thee: love her, and she shall keep thee.

NOTES

NOTES

_____

_____

_____

_____

_____

_____

_____

_____

_____

_____

_____

_____

_____

_____

_____

_____

_____

_____

_____

_____

_____

_____

_____

_____

_____

_____

_____

NOTES

7 Wisdom _is_ the principal thing; _therefore_ get wisdom: and with all thy getting get understanding.

8 Exalt her, and she shall promote thee: she shall bring thee to honour, when thou dost embrace her.

9 She shall give to thine head an ornament of grace: a crown of glory shall she deliver to thee.

10 Hear, O my son, and receive my sayings; and the years of thy life shall be many.

11 I have taught thee in the way of wisdom; I have led thee in right paths.

12 When thou goest, thy steps shall not be straitened; and when thou runnest, thou shalt not stumble.

13 Take fast hold of instruction; let _her_ not go: keep her; for she _is_ thy life.

14 ¶ Enter not into the path of the wicked, and go not in the way of evil _men._

15 Avoid it, pass not by it, turn from it, and pass away.

16 For they sleep not, except they have done mischief; and their sleep is taken away, unless they cause _some_ to fall.

17 For they eat the bread of wickedness, and drink the wine of violence.

18 But the path of the just _is_ as the shining light, that shineth more and more unto the perfect day.

19 The way of the wicked _is_ as darkness: they know not at what they stumble.

20 ¶ My son, attend to my words; incline thine ear unto my sayings.

21 Let them not depart from thine eyes; keep them in the midst of thine heart.

22 For they _are_ life unto those that find them, and health to all their flesh.

23 ¶ Keep thy heart with all diligence; for out of it _are_ the issues of life.

24 Put away from thee a froward mouth, and perverse lips put far from thee.

25 Let thine eyes look right on, and let thine eyelids look straight before thee.

26 Ponder the path of thy feet, and let all thy ways be established.

27 Turn not to the right hand nor to the left: remove thy foot from evil.

PROVERBS 15

A soft answer turneth away wrath—A wise son maketh a glad father—The thoughts of the wicked are an abomination to the Lord—Before honor is humility.

1 A SOFT answer turneth away wrath: but grievous words stir up anger.

2 The tongue of the wise useth knowledge aright: but the mouth of fools poureth out foolishness.

3 The eyes of the LORD *are* in every place, beholding the evil and the good.

4 A wholesome tongue *is* a tree of life: but perverseness therein *is* a breach in the spirit.

5 A fool despiseth his father's instruction: but he that regardeth reproof is prudent.

6 In the house of the righteous *is* much treasure: but in the revenues of the wicked is trouble.

7 The lips of the wise disperse knowledge: but the heart of the foolish *doeth* not so.

8 The sacrifice of the wicked *is* an abomination to the LORD: but the prayer of the upright *is* his delight.

9 The way of the wicked *is* an abomination unto the LORD: but he loveth him that followeth after righteousness.

10 Correction *is* grievous unto him that forsaketh the way: *and* he that hateth reproof shall die.

11 Hell and destruction *are* before the LORD: how much more then the hearts of the children of men?

12 A scorner loveth not one that reproveth him: neither will he go unto the wise.

13 A merry heart maketh a cheerful countenance: but by sorrow of the heart the spirit is broken.

14 The heart of him that hath understanding seeketh knowledge: but the mouth of fools feedeth on foolishness.

15 All the days of the afflicted *are* evil: but he that is of a merry heart *hath* a continual feast.

16 Better *is* little with the fear of the LORD than great treasure and trouble therewith.

17 Better *is* a dinner of herbs where love is, than a stalled ox and hatred therewith.

18 A wrathful man stirreth up strife: but *he that is* slow to anger appeaseth strife.

19 The way of the slothful *man is* as an hedge of thorns: but the way of the righteous *is* made plain.

20 A wise son maketh a glad father: but a foolish man despiseth his mother.

21 Folly *is* joy to *him that is* destitute of wisdom: but a man of understanding walketh uprightly.

22 Without counsel purposes are disappointed: but in the multitude of counsellors they are established.

23 A man hath joy by the answer of his mouth: and a word *spoken* in due season, how good *is it!*

24 The way of life *is* above to the wise, that he may depart from hell beneath.

25 The LORD will destroy the house of the proud: but he will establish the border of the widow.

26 The thoughts of the wicked *are* an abomination to the LORD: but *the words* of the pure *are* pleasant words.

27 He that is greedy of gain troubleth his own house; but he that hateth gifts shall live.

28 The heart of the righteous studieth to answer: but the mouth of the wicked poureth out evil things.

29 The LORD *is* far from the wicked: but he heareth the prayer of the righteous.

30 The light of the eyes rejoiceth the heart: *and* a good report maketh the bones fat.

31 The ear that heareth the reproof of life abideth among the wise.

32 He that refuseth instruction despiseth his own soul: but he that heareth reproof getteth understanding.

33 The fear of the LORD *is* the instruction of wisdom; and before honour *is* humility.

PROVERBS 16

It is better to get wisdom than gold—Pride goeth before destruction—The hoary head of the righteous is a crown of glory.

1 THE preparations of the heart in man, and the answer of the tongue, *is* from the LORD.

2 All the ways of a man *are* clean in his own eyes; but the LORD weigheth the spirits.

3 Commit thy works unto the LORD, and thy thoughts shall be established.

4 The LORD hath made all *things* for himself: yea, even the wicked for the day of evil.

5 Every one *that is* proud in heart *is* an abomination to the LORD: *though* hand *join* in hand, he shall not be unpunished.

6 By mercy and truth iniquity is purged: and by the fear of the LORD *men* depart from evil.

7 When a man's ways please the LORD, he maketh even his enemies to be at peace with him.

8 Better *is* a little with righteousness than great revenues without right.

9 A man's heart deviseth his way: but the LORD directeth his steps.

10 A divine sentence *is* in the lips of the king: his mouth transgresseth not in judgment.

11 A just weight and balance *are* the LORD's: all the weights of the bag *are* his work.

12 *It is* an abomination to kings to commit wickedness: for the throne is established by righteousness.

13 Righteous lips *are* the delight of kings; and they love him that speaketh right.

14 The wrath of a king *is as* messengers of death: but a wise man will pacify it.

15 In the light of the king's countenance *is* life; and his favour *is* as a cloud of the latter rain.

16 How much better *is it* to get wisdom than gold! and to get understanding rather to be chosen than silver!

17 The highway of the upright *is* to depart from evil: he that keepeth his way preserveth his soul.

18 Pride *goeth* before destruction, and an haughty spirit before a fall.

19 Better *it is to be* of an humble spirit with the lowly, than to divide the spoil with the proud.

20 He that handleth a matter wisely shall find good: and whoso trusteth in the LORD, happy *is* he.

NOTES

21 The wise in heart shall be called prudent: and the sweetness of the lips increaseth learning.

22 Understanding *is* a wellspring of life unto him that hath it: but the instruction of fools *is* folly.

23 The heart of the wise teacheth his mouth, and addeth learning to his lips.

24 Pleasant words *are as* an honeycomb, sweet to the soul, and health to the bones.

25 There is a way that seemeth right unto a man, but the end thereof *are* the ways of death.

26 He that laboureth laboureth for himself; for his mouth craveth it of him.

27 An ungodly man diggeth up evil: and in his lips *there is* as a burning fire.

28 A froward man soweth strife: and a whisperer separateth chief friends.

29 A violent man enticeth his neighbour, and leadeth him into the way *that is* not good.

30 He shutteth his eyes to devise froward things: moving his lips he bringeth evil to pass.

31 The hoary head *is* a crown of glory, *if* it be found in the way of righteousness.

32 *He that is* slow to anger *is* better than the mighty; and he that ruleth his spirit than he that taketh a city.

33 The lot is cast into the lap; but the whole disposing thereof *is* of the LORD.

PROVERBS 22

A good name is better than riches—Train up a child in the way he should go.

1 A *GOOD* name *is* rather to be chosen than great riches, *and* loving favour rather than silver and gold.

2 The rich and poor meet together: the LORD *is* the maker of them all.

3 A prudent *man* foreseeth the evil, and hideth himself: but the simple pass on, and are punished.

4 By humility *and* the fear of the LORD *are* riches, and honour, and life.

5 Thorns *and* snares *are* in the way of the froward: he that doth keep his soul shall be far from them.

6 Train up a child in the way he should go: and when he is old, he will not depart from it.

7 The rich ruleth over the poor, and the borrower *is* servant to the lender.

8 He that soweth iniquity shall reap vanity: and the rod of his anger shall fail.

9 He that hath a bountiful eye shall be blessed; for he giveth of his bread to the poor.

10 Cast out the scorner, and contention shall go out; yea, strife and reproach shall cease.

11 He that loveth pureness of heart, *for* the grace of his lips the king *shall be* his friend.

12 The eyes of the LORD preserve knowledge, and he overthroweth the words of the transgressor.

13 The slothful *man* saith, *There is* a lion without, I shall be slain in the streets.

14 The mouth of strange women *is* a deep pit: he that is abhorred of the LORD shall fall therein.

15 Foolishness *is* bound in the heart of a child; *but* the rod of correction shall drive it far from him.

16 He that oppresseth the poor to increase his *riches, and* he that giveth to the rich, *shall* surely *come* to want.

17 Bow down thine ear, and hear the words of the wise, and apply thine heart unto my knowledge.

18 For *it is* a pleasant thing if thou keep them within thee; they shall withal be fitted in thy lips.

19 That thy trust may be in the LORD, I have made known to thee this day, even to thee.

20 Have not I written to thee excellent things in counsels and knowledge,

21 That I might make thee know the certainty of the words of truth; that thou mightest answer the words of truth to them that send unto thee?

22 Rob not the poor, because he *is* poor: neither oppress the afflicted in the gate:

23 For the LORD will plead their cause, and spoil the soul of those that spoiled them.

24 Make no friendship with an angry man; and with a furious man thou shalt not go:

25 Lest thou learn his ways, and get a snare to thy soul.

NOTES

26 Be not thou *one* of them that strike hands, *or* of them that are sureties for debts.

27 If thou hast nothing to pay, why should he take away thy bed from under thee?

28 Remove not the ancient landmark, which thy fathers have set.

29 Seest thou a man diligent in his business? he shall stand before kings; he shall not stand before mean *men.*

PROVERBS 31

Wine and strong drink condemned—Plead the cause of the poor and needy—A virtuous woman is priced above rubies.

1 THE words of king Lemuel, the prophecy that his mother taught him.

2 What, my son? and what, the son of my womb? and what, the son of my vows?

3 Give not thy strength unto women, nor thy ways to that which destroyeth kings.

4 *It is* not for kings, O Lemuel, *it is* not for kings to drink wine; nor for princes strong drink:

5 Lest they drink, and forget the law, and pervert the judgment of any of the afflicted.

6 Give strong drink unto him that is ready to perish, and wine unto those that be of heavy hearts.

7 Let him drink, and forget his poverty, and remember his misery no more.

8 Open thy mouth for the dumb in the cause of all such as are appointed to destruction.

9 Open thy mouth, judge righteously, and plead the cause of the poor and needy.

10 ¶ Who can find a virtuous woman? for her price *is* far above rubies.

11 The heart of her husband doth safely trust in her, so that he shall have no need of spoil.

12 She will do him good and not evil all the days of her life.

13 She seeketh wool, and flax, and worketh willingly with her hands.

14 She is like the merchants' ships; she bringeth her food from afar.

15 She riseth also while it is yet night, and giveth meat to her household, and a portion to her maidens.

16 She considereth a field, and buyeth it: with the fruit of her hands she planteth a vineyard.

17 She girdeth her loins with strength, and strengtheneth her arms.

18 She perceiveth that her merchandise *is* good: her candle goeth not out by night.

19 She layeth her hands to the spindle, and her hands hold the distaff.

20 She stretcheth out her hand to the poor; yea, she reacheth forth her hands to the needy.

21 She is not afraid of the snow for her household: for all her household *are* clothed with scarlet.

22 She maketh herself coverings of tapestry; her clothing *is* silk and purple.

23 Her husband is known in the gates, when he sitteth among the elders of the land.

24 She maketh fine linen, and selleth *it;* and delivereth girdles unto the merchant.

25 Strength and honour *are* her clothing; and she shall rejoice in time to come.

26 She openeth her mouth with wisdom; and in her tongue *is* the law of kindness.

27 She looketh well to the ways of her household, and eateth not the bread of idleness.

28 Her children arise up, and call her blessed; her husband *also,* and he praiseth her.

29 Many daughters have done virtuously, but thou excellest them all.

30 Favour *is* deceitful, and beauty *is* vain: *but* a woman *that* feareth the LORD, she shall be praised.

31 Give her of the fruit of her hands; and let her own works praise her in the gates.

ECCLESIASTES

The word "Ecclesi-astes," is a Greek translation of a Hebrew word that means "one who convenes a congregation" (see Bible Dictionary, under "Ecclesiastes"). As you can see in your Bible, at the beginning of this book, Ecclesiastes has also come to be known as "The Preacher." In effect, the book gathers us together as a congregation of readers and preaches to us about life.

We do not know for sure who wrote Ecclesiastes; however, many Bible scholars suggest that it was probably written by Solomon because of considerable evidence within the book that leads to this conclusion. Solomon was the son of King David and Bathsheba. The evidence, for example, in Ecclesiastes 1:1, 12, 16; 2:4–10; and 12:9, seems to point to Solomon as the author.

NOTES

NOTES

Perhaps the most well known verses of Ecclesiastes are 3:1–8, which begin with "To every thing there is a season, and a time to every purpose under the heaven."

An important key to understanding Ecclesiastes is the word "vanity," as used in one form or another five times in chapter 1, verse 2, and at least thirty-two times elsewhere within the book. If you define the word as "pride," or "self-aggrandizement," you will not understand Ecclesiastes. However, if you correctly understand that in Ecclesiastes "vanity" means a state or situation that is "temporary," "transitory," or "fleeting," (see Bible Dictionary, under "Ecclesiastes"), and thus means "the temporary or transitory nature of mortality," then you will get much more out of it. In fact, look at verse 2 of chapter 1 right now. What it is saying, in effect, is that everything associated with mortal life is fleeting and temporary.

Many students become a bit confused as they study Ecclesiastes because it seems that at one moment, the author is being pessimistic, cynical, bitter, and depicting the philosophies of the world. And then in the next sentence or verse, he seems to be preaching true gospel concepts.

For example, in 9:5, we read, "the dead know not any thing," and 9:10, "there is no work, nor device, nor knowledge, nor wisdom, in the grave." These statements would lead most readers to conclude that there is no life after death. But, in 12:7, we read, "the spirit shall return unto God who gave it." And in 12:14, we see, "God shall bring every work into judgment, with every secret thing, whether it be good, or whether it be evil," which certainly indicates that there is life beyond the grave!

So, what is going on here? Answer: The author of Ecclesiastes (most likely Solomon) appears on the one hand to be presenting the pessimistic, cynical outlook or philosophy of the "natural man"—in other words, the ideas of people of the world who do not believe in God. They do not believe in life beyond the grave and consequently see life as being essentially meaningless. In fact, they look at people who do believe in God and in life beyond the grave as being foolish, perhaps weak, needing religion as a crutch because they can't handle the reality of the futility of life.

On the other hand, the author reminds everyone, including those who believe in God, that life is brief and that it is vital to keep God in mind, separating the important from the relatively unimportant. Chapters 11 and 12, as a whole, are the most spiritual of the book, and teach that obedience to God and His commandments provides lasting value and permanence to mortal souls.

In summary, much of what we are seeing in Ecclesiastes is how people who do not believe in God see life. Their outlook, although not reflecting the truth, is what the author is depicting. If you keep this in mind as you read, it will make much more sense. Putting it another way, the book can be seen as a study in comparison and contrast between the unbelieving "natural man" and those who do believe in God. Life is often dismal and pessimistic for those who do not believe in God nor in life after death, and thus view life only from a worldly point of view (see more on this in Bible Dictionary, under "Ecclesiastes"). Also, mortality is brief and fleeting for all, including the believers.

One approach to understanding Ecclesiastes is to read chapter 1, verses 3–11, which present the outlook or view of the natural man, and then read chapter 12, verses 13–14, which present the view of those who believe in God, and conclude that all people are accountable to Him and will face Him on the day of final judgment. In effect, these two sets of verses form "bookends" to Ecclesiastes, the one bookend being the pessimism and cynicism of the natural man and the other bookend representing the truth that there is a God and that life has meaning and will continue beyond the grave. Between the "bookends," we see the comparison and contrast between the thinking of the natural man and the thoughts of the believers, with most of the emphasis being placed on the natural man.

One of the major messages of the book is that all people—believers and unbelievers—are subject to the trials and tribulations of mortality.

Another message is the obvious warning to avoid relying too much on the things of the world for satisfaction and fulfillment.

Yet another major message is that, by design, mortality is intended to provide many opportunities to enjoy the good things provided by a pleasant, merciful Creator. In other words, the blessings of the earth are provided for all to enjoy. For example, in 2:24 we read (bold added for emphasis): "There is nothing better for a man, than that he should eat and drink, and that he should make his soul enjoy good in his labour. This also I saw, that it was from the hand of God."

In other words, there is indeed much to be enjoyed in life (compare with 2 Nephi 2:25). This message is repeated again in 3:12–13.

By the way, Ecclesiastes is read by Jews at their annual Feast of Tabernacles (see Bible Dictionary, under "Feasts") as a sobering reminder of the fleeting nature of mortality.

We will now proceed with our study of Ecclesiastes. Keep in mind that there are many ways to study and interpret this book. We will present some possibilities. You will no doubt see others also, both positive and negative.

Bold will be used for teaching emphasis, suggesting things you may wish to underline or otherwise mark in your own scriptures.

ECCLESIASTES 1

Selection: all verses

1 The words of the Preacher [*possibly Solomon*], the son of David, king in Jerusalem.

2 **Vanity of vanities** [*fleeting and temporary*], saith the Preacher, **vanity of vanities** [*temporary and fleeting*]; **all** *is* **vanity** [*everything in mortality is temporary*].

One way to look at verses 3–11, next, is to consider them to be the viewpoint of the natural man, the one who neither believes in God or in life after death. You will see that for such people, there is no ultimate purpose or meaning to mortal life. It is a rather pessimistic and dismal view of things. Life, to them, is essentially meaningless.

3 **What profit hath a man of all his labour** [*what good does all the work do*] which he taketh **under the sun** [*which mankind does upon the earth*]?

4 *One* generation passeth away, and *another* generation cometh [*people come and go; we all end up dying*]: but the earth abideth for ever.

5 The sun also ariseth, and the sun goeth down, and hasteth to his place where he arose.

6 The wind goeth toward the south, and turneth about unto the north; it whirleth about continually, and the wind returneth again according to his circuits [*everything remains the same; there is no ultimate purpose nor goal*].

7 All the rivers run into the sea; yet the sea *is* not full; unto the place from whence the rivers come, thither [*there*] they return again.

8 **All things** *are* **full of labour** [*everything requires tiresome work*]; man cannot utter it [*more than words can express*]: the eye is not satisfied with seeing, nor the ear filled with hearing [*nothing really satisfies*].

NOTES

9 The thing that hath been, it *is that* which shall be [*the past will be repeated*]; and that which is done *is* that which shall be done [*everything is mere repetition*]: and **there is no new *thing* under the sun** [*nothing is new*].

10 **Is there *any* thing whereof it may be said, See, this *is* new?** it hath been already of old time, which was before us [*answer: nothing is new*].

11 ***There is* no remembrance of former *things*** [*nobody remembers the past*]; neither shall there be *any* remembrance of *things* that are to come with *those* that shall come after [*neither will the future be remembered by those who come after it; in other words, nothing changes*].

By the way, you can probably see that verses 9–11, above, could also be interpreted as saying, in effect, that nobody ever seems to learn from the past, which in many ways would be true of worldly societies and people.

12 ¶ I the Preacher was king over Israel in Jerusalem [*probably Solomon referring to himself*].

In verses 13–18, the author of Ecclesiastes sadly seems to take a pessimistic view of the benefits of wisdom. This outlook could also reflect the viewpoint of the natural man and those who do not believe in God nor in an afterlife.

13 And **I gave my heart to seek and search out by wisdom** concerning **all *things*** that are done **under heaven** [*I dedicated myself to applying my wisdom to the study of all things*]: this sore travail [*heavy burden*] hath God given to the sons of man to be exercised therewith [*in other words, wisdom becomes a heavy burden upon those who possess it*].

14 **I have seen all the works that are done under the sun** [*in the world*]; and, behold, all *is* vanity and vexation of spirit [*everything in the world is fleeting, meaningless, and frustrating*].

15 *That which is* crooked cannot be made straight [*nothing can be fixed*]: and that which is wanting [*lacking*] cannot be numbered [*counted*].

Another interpretation of verse 15, above, might depict pessimism in dealing with people. It could be saying that people never learn their lessons, and that their foolishness seems to be infinite.

Verses 16–18, next, appear to be Solomon speaking about himself.

16 I communed with mine own heart, saying [*I said to myself*], Lo, I am come to great estate [*I have become great—see footnote 16a in your Bible*], and have gotten more wisdom than all *they* that have been before me in Jerusalem [*Solomon was given great wisdom as a gift from God—see 1 Kings 3:12*]: yea, my heart had great experience of wisdom and knowledge.

17 And I gave my heart [*I dedicated myself*] to know wisdom, and to know [*recognize*] madness and folly: I perceived that this also is vexation of spirit [*this was also frustrating*].

18 For [*because*] in much wisdom *is* much grief: and he that increaseth knowledge increaseth sorrow.

ECCLESIASTES 2

Selection: all verses

As mentioned at the end of the introductory notes to Ecclesiastes, in this study guide, there are many different ways to approach this particular book of the Bible. One of the major messages of Ecclesiastes can be the warning not to trust too much in the things of the world for satisfaction. For chapter 2, however, the author seems to be pointing out that the Lord has indeed provided many things in this world that are designed to provide appropriate pleasure and enjoyment to mankind. Solomon (assuming he is the author) seems to come to this conclusion at the end of the chapter.

As the chapter progresses, we see a series of things that Solomon samples in order to evaluate their worth. Having investigated them, he draws conclusions about them. We will bold several of them as we go along.

1 I said in mine heart, Go to now, I will prove thee with **mirth** [*laughter and merriment*], therefore enjoy **pleasure**: and, behold, this also *is* vanity [*conclusion: this is temporary, fleeting; it doesn't last*].

2 I said of **laughter**, *It is* mad [*crazy*]: and of **mirth**, What doeth it [*what does it accomplish*]?

In verses 3–10, next, Solomon discusses his experiences with several things in this world to which people turn for satisfaction. He will give his conclusion about them in verse 11.

3 I sought in mine heart to give myself unto **wine**, yet acquainting mine heart with wisdom; and to lay hold on **folly**, till I might see what *was* that good for the sons of men, which they should do under the heaven all the days of their life.

4 I made me **great works**; I builded me **houses**; I planted me **vineyards**:

5 I made me **gardens** and **orchards**, and I planted trees in them of all *kind of* fruits:

6 I made me **pools of water**, to water therewith the wood that bringeth forth trees:

7 I got *me* **servants and maidens**, and had servants born in my house; also I had **great possessions** of great and small cattle above all that were in Jerusalem before me:

8 I gathered me also **silver and gold**, and the peculiar **treasure** of kings and of the provinces: I gat me **men singers and women singers**, and the delights of the sons of men, *as* **musical instruments**, and that **of all sorts**.

9 **So I was great**, and increased more than all that were before me in Jerusalem: **also my wisdom remained with me.**

NOTES

_____
_____
_____
_____
_____
_____
_____
_____
_____
_____
_____
_____
_____
_____
_____
_____
_____
_____
_____
_____
_____
_____
_____
_____
_____
_____
_____
_____
_____
_____

NOTES

10 And **whatsoever mine eyes desired I kept not from them, I withheld not my heart from any joy**; for my heart rejoiced in all my labour: and this was my portion of all my labour.

11 **Then I looked on all the works that my hands had wrought** [*accomplished, built, made*], and on the labour that I had laboured to do: **and, behold, all** *was* **vanity and vexation of spirit** [*it was all ultimately of no lasting value, and brought more frustration than it was worth*], and there was no profit under the sun [*I found that there is no lasting value in worldly things*].

12 ¶ And I turned myself to behold wisdom, and madness, and folly: for what *can* the man *do* that cometh after the king [*what can my successor do*]? *even* that which hath been already done.

In the next verses, we see more of Solomon's conclusions.

13 Then **I saw that wisdom excelleth folly**, as far **as light excelleth darkness**.

14 **The wise man's eyes** *are* **in his head; but the fool walketh in darkness**: and I myself perceived also that **one event happeneth to them all** [*life is essentially the same for all people*].

15 Then said I in my heart, As it happeneth to the fool, so it happeneth even to me; and why was I then more wise? Then I said in my heart, that this also *is* vanity.

16 For *there is* no remembrance of the wise more than of the fool for ever; seeing that which now *is* in the days to come shall all be forgotten. And how dieth the wise *man?* as the fool [*ultimately, the wise man dies just the same as the fool dies*].

Solomon had concluded, at this point, that he had no basic advantage over any other person in life. He would eventually die and leave all his wealth and possessions behind (see verse 18). This was frustrating to him (verse 17) but reminded him of the temporary nature of worldly possessions.

17 **Therefore I hated life**; because the work that is wrought **under the sun** [*"from a worldly point of view"—see Bible Dictionary, under "Ecclesiastes"*] *is* grievous unto me: for all *is* vanity [*fleeting, temporary*] and vexation of spirit [*frustration*].

18 ¶ Yea, **I hated all my labour** which I had taken under the sun [*I despised all my worldly accomplishments*]: **because I should leave it unto the man that shall be after me**.

19 And who knoweth whether he shall be a wise *man* or a fool? yet shall he have rule over all my labour wherein I have laboured, and wherein I have shewed myself wise under the sun. This *is* also vanity.

Next, we see that Solomon despaired because of what he had observed (verses 20–23). However, he will come to a valuable conclusion for all of us in verse 24.

20 **Therefore I went about to cause my heart to despair** of all the labour which I took under the sun.

21 For there is a man whose labour *is* in wisdom, and in knowledge, and in equity; yet to a man that hath not laboured therein shall he leave it *for* his portion [*I will leave all my worldly possessions and accomplishments to someone who has not worked for it as I did*]. This also *is* vanity and a great evil.

22 For what hath man of all his labour, and of the vexation of his heart, wherein he hath laboured under the sun [*what is the ultimate value of worldly pursuits*]?

23 For all his days *are* sorrows, and his travail [*labor, work*] grief; yea, his heart taketh not rest in the night. This is also vanity [*temporary, fleeting*].

There are some philosophies and many religious creeds that teach that mankind should avoid physical pleasures because they are inherently evil. In verse 24, next, Solomon concludes that the Lord has provided many things to be enjoyed in life by His children here on earth, and that it is proper to enjoy them. Obviously, he is not endorsing sin and wickedness but rather the proper enjoyment of the good things of the earth created to "please the eye and gladden the heart" (Doctrine & Covenants 59:18).

24 ¶ *There is* **nothing better** for a man, ***than* that he should eat and drink, and *that* he should make his soul enjoy good in his labour** [*derive satisfaction from his work*]. This also **I saw, that it *was* from the hand of God.**

The same conclusion is drawn elsewhere.

Ecclesiastes 3:13

13 And also that every man should **eat** and **drink**, and **enjoy the good of all his labour**, it *is* **the gift of God**.

25 For who can eat, or who else can hasten *hereunto,* more than I [*can't I enjoy these things just as much as anyone else*]?

In verse 26, next, Solomon teaches that God gives righteous people wisdom, knowledge, and also joy.

The last phrase of the verse seems to apply to the "sinner" who will ultimately lose any benefit from that which he has "gathered and heaped up."

26 For ***God* giveth** to a man that *is* good in his sight [*a man who is righteous*] **wisdom, and knowledge, and joy**: but to the sinner [*the wicked*] he giveth travail, to gather and to heap up, that he may give to *him that is* good before God. This also *is* vanity and vexation of spirit.

ECCLESIASTES 3

Selection: all verses

As we mentioned in the introductory notes to Ecclesiastes, in this study guide, verses 1–8 are probably the most-quoted verses in Ecclesiastes. They remind us that timing plays a major role in our mortal lives. The ability to wisely discern between these "seasons" (verse 1) and act accordingly, is one of the signs of spiritual maturity and wisdom. We will go ahead with these eight verses now. Notice that they focus primarily upon everything that takes place "under the heaven" (verse 1), in other words, during mortality.

NOTES

1 **To every** *thing there is* **a season, and a time to every purpose under the heaven:**

2 **A time to be born, and a time to die; a time to plant, and a time to pluck up** *that which is* **planted;**

3 **A time to kill, and a time to heal; a time to break down, and a time to build up;**

4 **A time to weep, and a time to laugh; a time to mourn, and a time to dance;**

5 **A time to cast away stones, and a time to gather stones together; a time to embrace, and a time to refrain from embracing;**

6 **A time to get, and a time to lose; a time to keep, and a time to cast away;**

7 **A time to rend [***tear***], and a time to sew; a time to keep silence, and a time to speak;**

8 **A time to love, and a time to hate; a time of war, and a time of peace.**

The word "hate" in verse 8 above does not reflect proper gospel living in terms of forgiving others. Remember, though, that much of Ecclesiastes reflects the thinking of the natural man, who is "an enemy to God" (Mosiah 3:19). People who are living in the natural man "mode" are often given to hating others deeply, much to the detriment of their own souls as well as of society in general.

As you have no doubt noticed, the author of Ecclesiastes keeps asking hard questions. For the unbeliever, few if any of the questions have answers. For the believer, many of the questions have answers but some still do not because we do not comprehend the mind and will of God in all things.

Continuing with chapter 3, we see that the preacher asks a question in verse 9, makes an observation in verse 10, and then states in verse 11 that it is only through an eternal perspective that we can make sense out of mortality.

9 **What profit hath he that worketh** in that wherein he laboureth [*what benefit does a worker gain from his labor*]?

10 I have seen the travail [*work*], which God hath given to the sons of men to be exercised in it [*to be kept busy by it*].

11 He [*the Lord*] hath made every *thing* beautiful in his [*its*] time [*all things in nature have their time to be beautiful*]: also he [*the Lord*] hath set the world in their heart [*Hebrew: "hath set the eternal in their heart without which man cannot find out the work that God hath done"—see footnote 11b in your Bible*], so that no man can find out the work that God maketh from the beginning to the end.

12 I know that *there is* no good in them, but for *a man* to rejoice, and to do good in his life [*the thing that makes life good is being happy and doing good*].

NOTES

Next, in verse 13, the preacher concludes that the Lord has given us much that is designed by Him for us to enjoy during our mortal years. In other words, it is okay to be happy and enjoy the good things of life appropriately.

<u>Major Message</u>

By design, mortality is intended to provide many opportunities to enjoy the good things provided by a pleasant, merciful Creator.

13 And also **that every man should eat and drink, and enjoy the good of all his labour,** it *is* **the gift of God**.

Next, in verse 14, we are taught that God's work is eternal and unchanging. In other words, He is completely dependable and we can always rely on Him and His gospel.

14 I know that, **whatsoever God doeth, it shall be for ever: nothing can be put to it, nor any thing taken from it**: and God doeth *it,* that *men* should fear before him.

15 That which hath been is now; and that which is to be hath already been; and God requireth that which is past.

Verse 17 seems to suggest that an appropriate interpretation of verse 16, next, is that it contains the doctrine of final judgment. All who are accountable will ultimately answer to God for their mortal choices.

16 ¶ And moreover I saw under the sun **the place of judgment,** *that* wickedness *was* there [*the wicked were there*]; and the place of righteousness [*the righteous were there*], *that* iniquity *was* there [*"the filthy were filthy still"—see 2 Nephi 9:16*].

17 I said in mine heart, **God shall judge the righteous and the wicked**: for *there is* a time there for every purpose and for every work.

One way to look at verses 18–21 next, is that they represent the incorrect thinking of those who do not believe in God, many of whom conclude that people are simply animals of a higher order and that we are no more important than animals. The Savior provided true doctrine about this. He taught:

<u>Matthew 6:26</u>

26 Behold the fowls of the air: for they sow not, neither do they reap, nor gather into barns; yet your heavenly Father feedeth them. **Are ye not much better than they?**

18 I said in mine heart **concerning the estate of the sons of men,** that God might manifest them, and that they might see that **they themselves are beasts**.

19 For **that which befalleth** [*happens to*] **the sons of men befalleth beasts**; even one thing befalleth them: as the one dieth, so dieth the other; yea, they have all one breath; so that **a man hath no preeminence above a beast**: for all *is* vanity.

20 All go unto one place; all are of the dust, and all turn to dust again.

Verse 21, next, poses a rather interesting question. We do have an answer, which we will give after the verse.

21 **Who knoweth the spirit of man** that **goeth upward, and the spirit of the beast** that **goeth downward to the earth** [*who knows if there is a heaven and the spirits of men go up to it and the spirits of animals do not*]?

The answer to one question that arises from verse 21 (do animals resurrect?) is given in the Doctrine and Covenants. The answer is yes.

Doctrine & Covenants 29:23–25

23 And the end shall come, and the heaven and the earth shall be consumed and pass away, and there shall be a new heaven and a new earth.

24 For all old things shall pass away, and **all things shall become new** [*will be resurrected*], even the heaven and the earth, and all the fulness thereof [*everything that is in it*], both **men** and **beasts**, the **fowls** of the air, and the **fishes** of the sea;

25 And not one hair, neither mote, shall be lost, for it is the workmanship of mine hand.

Among other things, verse 22, next, can be looked at from the viewpoint of the natural man and also from the perspective of the believers. If viewed as the thinking of the natural man, we might conclude that it means that, since life is basically meaningless, we might as well at least enjoy what we are able to accomplish.

If viewed from the standpoint of those who believe in God, we might say that it misses the mark. There is much more to life than just what we can accomplish as mortals. We ought to rejoice in the marvelous works of God and in the availability of eternal life.

22 Wherefore **I perceive that** *there is* **nothing better, than that a man should rejoice in his own works; for that** *is* **his portion**: for who shall bring him to see what shall be after him?

ECCLESIASTES 4

Selection: all verses

One of our purposes as we study Ecclesiastes is to help you see that there are actually many ways to approach understanding it. One way is to simply read through Ecclesiastes and, on the one hand, mark the verses that seem to be the viewpoint of those who do not believe in God, who do not believe that life has any ultimate purpose, and whose views often reflect pessimism. On the other hand, while reading through it you could also mark the verses that represent the viewpoint of the believer, those that point out the good in mortal life and give an eternal perspective to it.

We will use this approach in chapter 4, realizing that many verses could go either way. Thus, you could go through it using the same approach as we do and come up with quite different results. We will use two headings for this approach:

Pessimist: representing the natural man and those who do not believe in God.

The Positive Approach: representing the viewpoint of those who see things in an eternal perspective, through their belief in God. They are often optimists.

Pessimist (verses 1–5)

1 So I returned, and considered **all the oppressions** that are done under the sun [*in mortality*]: and behold the **tears** of *such as were* oppressed, and they had **no comforter**; and **on the side of their oppressors** *there was* **power** [*life is not fair; the power in daily life lies with those who oppress others*]; but they had **no comforter**.

2 Wherefore [*as a result*] **I praised the dead** which are already dead **more than the living which are yet alive** [*people who are dead are the lucky ones*].

3 Yea, **better** *is he* **than** both **they**, which hath not yet been, **who hath not seen the evil work that is done under the sun** [*the unborn are better off than both the dead and the living, because they have seen none of the evils of mortality*].

4 ¶ Again, **I considered all travail, and every right work, that for this a man is envied of his neighbour** [*everything that is supposedly good has its downside; all achievement comes as a result of people envying their neighbors*]. **This** *is* also **vanity** [*meaningless, transitory*] **and vexation of spirit** [*frustrating*].

5 **The fool** foldeth his hands together, and **eateth his own flesh** [*makes decisions leading to his own destruction*].

The Positive Approach (verse 6)

6 **Better** *is* **an handful** *with* **quietness, than both the hands full** *with* **travail and vexation of spirit** [*better to be satisfied with what you have than to be constantly striving for more and getting frustrated*].

Pessimist (verses 7–8)

7 ¶ Then I returned, and **I saw vanity under the sun** [*everything in mortal life is fleeting, meaningless*].

8 **There is one** *alone*, **and** *there is* **not a second** [*we are all basically alone in life*]; yea, he hath neither child nor brother: yet *is* **there no end of all his labour** [*life is basically one big struggle to survive*]; **neither is his eye satisfied with riches**; neither *saith he*, For whom do I labour, and bereave my soul of good? This *is* also vanity, yea, it *is* a sore travail [*it is a miserable life*].

The Positive Approach (verses 9–12)

9 ¶ **Two** *are* **better than one**; because they have a good reward for their labour.

10 For **if they fall, the one will lift up his fellow**: but woe to him *that is* alone when he falleth; for *he hath* not another to help him up.

11 Again, **if two lie together, then they have heat: but how can one be warm** *alone?*

NOTES

NOTES

12 And **if one prevail against him, two shall withstand him; and a threefold cord is not quickly broken**.

> Verse 13, next, is a wise saying, and doesn't really fit under the pessimist heading nor the positive heading.

13 ¶ **Better** *is* **a poor and a wise child than an old and foolish king, who will no more be admonished** [*who will not take counsel*].

Pessimist (verses 14–16)

14 For out of prison he cometh to reign; whereas also *he that is* born in his kingdom becometh poor.

15 I considered [*I thought about*] all the living which walk under the sun [*who live on the earth*], with the second child that shall stand up in his stead [*I looked at the successor to the current ruler*].

16 *There is* **no end of all the people,** *even* of all that have been before them: **they** also that come after **shall not rejoice in him** [*basically, all are oppressed by their rulers, including the successors to the rulers*]. Surely **this also** *is* **vanity and vexation of spirit**.

ECCLESIASTES 5

Selection: all verses

We will continue the approach we used in chapter 4 as we consider chapter 5. You will see that there are many more positives than negatives in this chapter. As usual, we will use bold to point things out.

Perspective and Wisdom from the Viewpoint of the Believer (verses 1–10)

1 Keep thy foot **when thou goest to the house of God**, and **be more ready to hear, than to give the sacrifice of fools**: for they consider not that they do evil.

2 **Be not rash with thy mouth, and let not thine heart be hasty to utter** *any* **thing before God: for God** *is* **in heaven, and thou upon earth: therefore let thy words be few**.

3 For a dream cometh through the multitude of business; and **a fool's voice** *is known* **by multitude of words**.

4 **When thou vowest a vow unto God, defer not to pay it**; for *he hath* no pleasure in fools: **pay that which thou hast vowed**.

5 **Better** *is it* **that thou shouldest not vow, than that thou shouldest vow and not pay** [*it is better not to make a covenant with God than to make and then break it*]**.**

6 **Suffer not thy mouth to cause thy flesh to sin**; neither say thou before the angel [*the officiator in the temple; see New International Version*], that it *was* an error [*that you*

made a mistake in making a vow]: wherefore should God be angry at thy voice, and destroy the work of thine hands?

7 For in the multitude of dreams and many words [*much dreaming and many empty words*] *there are* also *divers* vanities [*amount to nothing*]: but **fear thou God** [*live in respect and awe of God*].

8 ¶ If thou seest the oppression of the poor, and violent perverting of judgment and justice in a province [*in the government of a particular region*], marvel not at the matter [*don't be surprised that such things take place*]: for *he that is* **higher than the highest regardeth** [*God is watching everything*]; and *there be* higher than they [*God is indeed higher than mortal government officials*].

9 ¶ Moreover **the profit of the earth is for all** [*God intends the bounties of the earth to bless all people*]: the king *himself* is served by the field [*is benefited by the crops of the field*].

10 **He that loveth silver shall not be satisfied with silver;** nor he that loveth abundance with increase [*one whose heart is set on wealth is never satisfied with his income*]: this *is* also vanity [*meaningless, temporary*].

Verse 11, next, probably fits best in the "pessimist" category.

Pessimist (verse 11)

11 **When goods increase, they are increased that eat them** [*if your income increases, there will just be more mouths to feed*]: and what good *is there* to the owners thereof, saving the beholding *of them* with their eyes?

Perspective and Wisdom from the Viewpoint of the Believer (verses 12–13)

12 **The sleep of a labouring man *is* sweet, whether he eat little or much:** but **the abundance** [*wealth*] **of the rich will not suffer** [*allow*] **him to sleep.**

13 There is a sore [*grievous, serious*] evil *which* I have seen **under the sun** [*among people who view things "from a worldly point of view"—see Bible Dictionary, under "Ecclesiastes"*] *namely,* **riches kept for** [*hoarded by*] **the owners thereof to their hurt** [*in other words, wealth often ruins worldly people*].

Pessimist (verses 14–17)

14 But those riches perish by evil travail: and **he begetteth a son, and *there is* nothing in his hand**.

15 **As he came forth of his mother's womb, naked shall he return to go as he came, and shall take nothing of his labour,** which he may carry away in his hand [*this life is meaningless*].

16 And **this also** *is* **a sore evil,** *that* **in all points as he came, so shall he go**: and what profit hath he that hath laboured for the wind? [*One interpretation of verses 15–16 is that life on earth has basically no real value.*]

Depending on how you look at it, verse 16, above could also be saying that people who spend all their lives only pursuing material things (last half of the verse) have labored for nothing of real value.

17 **All his days also he eateth in darkness** [*his whole life is spent not knowing what life is about*], and *he hath* **much sorrow** and wrath with his sickness.

Perspective and Wisdom from the Viewpoint of the Believer (verses 18–20)

18 ¶ Behold *that* which I have seen [*here is what I have concluded*]: *it is* **good and comely** [*appropriate*] *for one* **to eat and to drink, and to enjoy the good of all his labour** that he taketh under the sun [*during mortality*] **all the days of his life, which God giveth him**: for it *is* his portion [*it is God's gift to him*].

19 Every man also to whom God hath given riches and wealth, and hath given him power to eat thereof, and to take his portion, and to rejoice in his labour; **this** *is* **the gift of God**.

20 For **he shall not much remember the days of his life; because God answereth** *him* **in the joy of his heart** [*in other words, with an eternal perspective, mortal life passes quickly and one has much joy because of the goodness of God*].

By now you have seen that there are many different ways to look at Ecclesiastes—and even at individual verses within the book. So far, we have given some possible approaches and perspectives for your consideration. We hope this will be helpful to you as you read the rest of Ecclesiastes. We will examine a few more verses and then finish with considerable detail on the last two chapters.

First, we will skip to chapter 7, where the preacher (another name for the author of Ecclesiastes) asks, in effect, "Why do the righteous suffer while the wicked seem to prosper?"

Question

Why do the righteous suffer while the wicked continue to prosper? (Chapter 7, verse 15)

Ecclesiastes 7:15

15 All *things* have I seen in the days of my vanity: **there is a just** *man* **that perisheth in his righteousness, and there is a wicked** *man* **that prolongeth** *his life* **in his wickedness.**

Answer (Chapter 7, verse 18)

The answer can be seen only with an eternal perspective. With that perspective, you will see that in the eternities, the righteous prosper and the unrepentant wicked will suffer.

Ecclesiastes 7:18

18 *It is* good that thou shouldest **take hold of this** [*perhaps meaning the counsel about to be given*]; yea, also from this withdraw not thine hand: for **he that feareth God shall come forth of them all** [*in other words, those who honor God and live the gospel will rise above all others (exaltation) in the next life*].

The above answer is confirmed in chapter 8.

Ecclesiastes 8:12–13

12 ¶ **Though a sinner do evil an hundred times, and his** *days* **be prolonged** [*even if the wicked live a long life*], yet surely **I know that it shall be well with them that fear** [*respect, honor, obey*] **God, which fear before him**:

13 **But it shall not be well with the wicked**, neither shall he prolong *his* days, *which are* as a shadow [*which are fleeting, temporary*]; because he feareth not before God.

The same message is again confirmed in the last chapter of Ecclesiastes.

Ecclesiastes 12:13–14

13 ¶ **Let us hear the conclusion of the whole matter: Fear God, and keep his commandments**: for this *is* the whole *duty* of man.

14 For **God shall bring every** *work* **into judgment, with every secret thing, whether** *it be* **good, or whether** *it be* **evil**.

The false doctrines and beliefs of the natural man, who neither believes in God or in life after death, are exemplified in the following verses:

Ecclesiastes 9:5 & 10

5 For the living know that they shall die: but **the dead know not any thing**, neither have they any more a reward; for the memory of them is forgotten.

10 Whatsoever thy hand findeth to do, do *it* with thy might; for *there is* **no work, nor device, nor knowledge, nor wisdom, in the grave, whither thou goest** [*in other words, once you die, that is the end*].

Some people use verses 5 and 10, above, taken out of context, to attempt to prove from the Bible that there is no life after death. This is what is known as "wresting the scriptures"—taking something in the scriptures out of context in order to attempt to prove a falsehood.

We will now conclude our study of Ecclesiastes by examining chapters 11 and 12 verse-by-verse. Keep in mind, as previously stated, that there is more than one way to look at what the "preacher" (probably Solomon) teaches. What we present in these last two chapters is just one approach.

NOTES

ECCLESIASTES 11

Selection: all verses

One message of this chapter seems to be to plant wisely so that we have a good harvest, despite troubles and difficulties along the way. In other words, we should live wisely and keep the commandments of God as we move through mortality, in order to have a pleasant harvest as we stand before God on Judgment Day.

1 **Cast thy bread upon the waters: for thou shalt find it after many days** [*what you do now will come back to you in the future*].

2 **Give a portion to seven, and also to eight; for thou knowest not what evil shall be upon the earth** [*perhaps meaning that if you prepare well, future downturns will not be as damaging to you*].

3 **If the clouds be full of rain, they empty** *themselves* **upon the earth** [*what you fill your life with will come out in the end*]: and **if the tree fall toward the south, or toward the north, in the place where the tree falleth, there it shall be** [*when you die, you will remain what you are at the time*].

4 **He that observeth the wind** [*pays too much attention to the wind*] **shall not sow** [*will not plant*]; and **he that regardeth the clouds** [*is afraid there won't be enough rain to grow a newly-planted crop*] **shall not reap** [*a person who worries too much about planting will never get a harvest; in other words, a pessimist lives in fear of the future, therefore never gets anything done*].

> Verses 5–6, next, seem to be saying that even though there are many things we do not understand about life and about God, we should still proceed with planting and working toward goals.

5 As thou knowest not what *is* the way of the spirit, *nor* how the bones *do grow* in the womb of her that is with child: even so thou knowest not the works of God who maketh all.

6 **In the morning sow thy seed**, and in the evening **withhold not thine hand** [*keep working*]: for **thou knowest not whether** [*which of your efforts or works*] **shall prosper**, either this or that, or whether they both *shall be* alike good.

> Among other things, verses 7–8, next, remind us that we run into both good and evil during our mortal lives.

7 ¶ Truly the light *is* sweet, and **a pleasant** *thing it is* **for the eyes to behold the sun** [*a beautiful day with sunlight is pleasant to see*]:

8 But if a man live many years, *and* rejoice in them all; yet let him remember **the days of darkness** [*there will be bad times too*]; for they shall be many. **All that cometh** *is* **vanity** [*passing, temporary*].

9 ¶ Rejoice, O young man, in thy youth; and let thy heart cheer thee in the days of thy youth, and walk in the ways of thine heart, and in the sight of thine eyes: but **know**

thou, that for all these *things* God will bring thee into judgment [*remember, you will someday stand before God to account for your life*].

10 Therefore **remove sorrow from thy heart** [*be happy*], and **put away evil from thy flesh** [*avoid the sins common to mortals*]: for **childhood and youth *are* vanity** [*temporary, fleeting*].

ECCLESIASTES 12

Selection: all verses

As mentioned earlier, verses 13 and 14 are "the conclusion of the whole matter" for the "preacher" (the author of Ecclesiastes, probably Solomon). Throughout the previous chapters of Ecclesiastes, he has asked many questions, emphasized the temporary nature of mortality, presented many things from the viewpoint of the "natural man," pointed out that there is much to be appropriately enjoyed here on earth, and taught that an eternal perspective is essential for us in order to make sense of mortal life.

Now, in this final chapter, he counsels us to be wise in our earlier mortal days, while future accountability before God is far off (verses 1–6). He teaches the doctrine that, upon our mortal deaths, our spirits return to God (verse 7), in other words, there is indeed life after death. He once again reminds us that mortality is temporary and fleeting (verse 8). After that, he adds a personal note, explaining that he has taught his people and given them many wise sayings, through much study on his part (verses 9–12). At the end of the chapter, he gives us his final conclusion and counsel about mortality (verses 13–14).

We will use bold to point these things out.

1 **Remember** now **thy Creator in the days of thy youth**, while the evil days come not [*before old age comes to you*], nor the years draw nigh, when thou shalt say, I have no pleasure in them [*before you get so old that you no longer find pleasure in the things of youth*];

2 While the sun, or the light, or the moon, or the stars, be not darkened [*while you are still young, before old age catches up to you and dims your senses*], nor the clouds return after the rain:

3 In the day when the keepers of the house shall tremble, and the strong men shall bow themselves, and the grinders cease because they are few, and those that look out of the windows be darkened,

4 And the doors shall be shut in the streets, when the sound of the grinding is low, and he shall rise up at the voice of the bird, and all the daughters of musick shall be brought low;

5 Also *when* they shall be afraid of *that which is* high, and fears *shall be* in the way, and the almond tree shall flourish, and the grasshopper shall be a burden [*just like the grasshopper—whose life is also temporary—finally grows old and drags slowly to his death*], and desire shall fail: because man goeth to his long home [*because he finally dies*], and the mourners go about the streets:

Verse 6, next, uses several different idiomatic sayings from the culture of ancient Israel, which in this context all say, in effect, the day eventually comes to all of us in which we will die. We have many such idiomatic phrases in our modern language that likewise

NOTES

refer to death. Some of them are, "We will all bite the dust," "kick the bucket," "give up the ghost," "cash in," or "our ticker will stop."

6 Or ever **the silver cord be loosed** [*death comes; mortal life comes to an end*], or **the golden bowl be broken** [*death come*], or **the pitcher be broken** at the fountain [*mortal life comes to an end; the source of mortal life—the spirit—leaves*], or **the wheel broken** at the cistern [*the well of life ceases to sustain mortal life*].

7 **Then shall the dust** [*mortal body*] **return to the earth** as it was: **and the spirit shall return unto God who gave it**.

The word "return" in the last half of verse 7, above, is an important doctrinal reminder that we did have a premortal life with Heavenly Father.

8 ¶ Vanity [*temporary*] of vanities, saith the preacher; **all** *is* **vanity** [*everything in mortality is temporary*].

Next, the preacher adds a personal note about his attempts to share his knowledge and wisdom with his people.

9 And moreover [*in addition*], **because the preacher was wise, he** still **taught the people knowledge**; yea, he gave good heed, and sought out, *and* set in order **many proverbs** [*wise sayings*].

10 **The preacher sought to find out acceptable words** [*he worked hard to find the right words to communicate his wisdom*]: and *that which was* written *was* upright, *even* words of truth.

11 **The words of the wise** *are* **as goads** [*sharp-pointed sticks—see footnote 11a in your Bible; cattle prods*], and **as nails fastened** *by* **the masters of assemblies** [*the words of the wise are like a collection of goads assembled by masters of wisdom*], **which** **are given from one shepherd** [*which ultimately come from one source*].

12 And further, **by these, my son, be admonished** [*allow yourself to be taught by these collections of wisdom*]: of making many books *there is* no end [*there is no end to the possibilities for writing wise sayings*]; and much study *is* a weariness of the flesh [*much study can make a body tired*].

There is another possible interpretation of verse 12, above, that is quite different from the possibility we gave above. We will include it as a reminder that there are many disagreements as to how to correctly interpret ancient languages.

Verse 12, repeated

12 And further, **by these, my son, be admonished** [*"be warned about anything in addition to"—NIV Bible and German Bible (Martin Luther translation)*]: of making many books *there is* no end [*there is no end to the writing of books*]; and much study *is* a weariness of the flesh [*much study can make a body tired*].

The Conclusion (verses 13–14)

13 ¶ Let us hear the conclusion of the whole matter: **Fear** [*honor, respect, obey*] **God, and keep his commandments**: for this *is* the whole *duty* of man.

14 For **God shall bring every** *work* [*act, deed*] **into judgment**, with every secret thing, whether *it be* good, or whether *it be* evil [*we will all ultimately stand before God to account for our lives*].

THE SONG OF SOLOMON

The Song of Solomon is thought by some to have been written by Solomon but many Bible scholars consider its authorship to be unknown. Some consider it to be a simple love song while others look at its imagery as being symbolic of the love that God has for His people.

Because of some of its content, some students wonder how such a book as this even made it into the Bible. In fact, over the ages, the Song of Solomon has generated quite a bit of controversy. A statement by the Prophet Joseph Smith is helpful. You will see a note in your Bible, after footnote 1a in chapter one of Song of Solomon, which quotes the manuscript for the Joseph Smith Translation of the Bible (the JST) as saying: "The Songs of Solomon are not inspired writings." As a result of the Prophet's statement, we will not do more with the Song of Solomon in this study guide.

Isaiah 1–12

"God Is My Salvation"

Many members of the Church approach the study of Isaiah with what could easily be termed as "fear and trepidation." The same goes for the Isaiah chapters in 2 Nephi. As you read and study these Come, Follow Me selections for this week, it is my hope that the direction provided in this verse-by-verse study guide, along with the guidance of the Holy Ghost, will prove helpful and enable you to actually understand and appreciate Isaiah's writing to at least some degree. In Isaiah chapter 1, you will see this prophet severely chastise the Jews who have rebelled against the Lord. He explains that they are spiritually sick and don't even know it. Despite their being so far from God in their daily thoughts and actions, he tenderly invites them to repent, even though their sins are like "scarlet," which is a color-fast dye used by the Jews and others in dying fabric. His message is basically that even though they might consider themselves beyond the reach of the Savior's Atonement, such is not the case. They can still repent. Chapter 3 prophesies that when women become as wicked as men, the nation is doomed. Chapter 5 prophesies that in the last days, people will "call evil good, and good evil." Chapter 6 tells about Isaiah's feelings of deep inadequacy when he receives his call to serve as a prophet. Chapter 12 prophesies about the Millennium.

NOTES

ISAIAH

We will include every verse of Isaiah, with notes and commentary, in this study guide. Isaiah began his ministry about 740 BC (see chronology chart in the Bible Dictionary in the back of your Latter-day Saint Bible). He continued until about 701 BC. He is one of the greatest prophets who ever lived. You can read a summary about him in the Bible Dictionary under "Isaiah." We will quote one portion of that summary here:

Isaiah

"The Lord is salvation. Son of Amoz, a prophet in Jerusalem during 40 years, 740–701 BC He had great religious and political influence during the reign of Hezekiah, whose chief advisor he was. Tradition states that he was "sawn asunder" during the reign of Manasseh; for that reason he is often represented in art holding a saw."

The Savior quoted Isaiah more often than He quoted any other prophet in the Old Testament. This fact alone testifies of the importance of the writings and teachings of Isaiah. During the Savior's ministry to the Nephites on the American continent, He quoted Isaiah (in 3 Nephi 22) and then said (bold added for emphasis):

3 Nephi 23:1

1 AND now, behold, I say unto you, that **ye ought to search these things. Yea, a commandment I give unto you that ye search these things diligently; for great are the words of Isaiah**.

There are obviously many reasons that the teachings of Isaiah are vital to us. We will quote again from the Book of Mormon to see two major reasons to study Isaiah, according to Nephi. We will use bold to point out Nephi's reasons for quoting Isaiah to his people, including his wayward brothers Laman and Lemuel.

1 Nephi 19:23–24

23 And I did read many things unto them which were written in the books of Moses; but that I might **more fully persuade them to believe in the Lord their Redeemer** I did read unto them that which was written by the prophet Isaiah; for I did liken all scriptures unto us, that it might be for our profit and learning.

24 Wherefore I spake unto them, saying: Hear ye the words of the prophet, ye who are a remnant of the house of Israel, a branch who have been broken off; hear ye the words of the prophet, which were written unto all the house of Israel, and liken them unto yourselves, **that ye may have hope** as well as your brethren from whom ye have been broken off; for after this manner has the prophet written.

Thus we are taught that Isaiah's teachings can greatly strengthen our testimonies of Jesus Christ, our Redeemer, and provide wonderful hope and assurance in our hearts that we can be found among those who are saved.

Knowing what Isaiah can do for us is one thing, but for many members of the Church, understanding the writings of Isaiah is quite another thing. Many years ago when I first remember reading 3 Nephi 23:1 (quoted above), I thought to myself, "If the Savior says that the words of Isaiah are great, then there must be something wrong with me because I don't understand most of them. Perhaps I am not spiritual enough, or the Holy Ghost can't work with me, or whatever." At any rate, it was a concern to me that I found Isaiah so difficult to understand.

Several years later, I attended a summer class for seminary and institute of religion teachers that was being taught by Brother Ellis Rasmussen of the BYU religion department. With Brother Rasmussen's first words, Isaiah came alive for me. As I recall, he quoted the first line of Isaiah 53:1 where Isaiah says, "Who hath believed our report?" And then he explained that it is just another way of saying, "Who believes us prophets anyway?"

Just like that, the key for understanding Isaiah was turned for me. It was possible to understand it! I listened with rapt attention and made many tiny, short notes in my scriptures during Brother Rasmussen's classes.

My intent is to make Isaiah "easier," not necessarily "easy," for students of the scriptures. The notes provided are intentionally brief, for two main reasons. One: They allow you to read the actual Bible text, with minimal interruption, and get a quick threshold understanding of Isaiah's teachings. Two: You may wish to write some of these brief notes in your own scriptures.

In order to keep the notes brief and somewhat conversational, considerable license has been taken with respect to capitalization and punctuation. The explanations and interpretations provided are not intended to be the final word on Isaiah. I am hopeful that readers will begin to see many other possibilities for interpretation and application of this great prophet's words, for the symbolism and messages of Isaiah do indeed lend themselves to multiple interpretations in various settings.

By the way, the references for the notes in brackets that say "German" are a reference to the translation found in the Martin Luther edition of the German Bible.

We will now proceed with our study of Isaiah.

ISAIAH 1

Selection: all verses

Chapter 1 is a preface to the whole book of Isaiah, much like Doctrine and Covenants, section one, is to the whole Doctrine and Covenants, or like the superscription at the beginning of First Nephi is, which says "An account of Lehi . . ."

1 **The vision of Isaiah** the son of Amoz, which he saw **concerning Judah and Jerusalem** in the days of Uzziah, Jotham, Ahaz, and Hezekiah, kings of Judah [*The kings mentioned above reigned from about 740 BC to 701 BC*].

Isaiah states the main problem, in verses 2–4, next.

NOTES

NOTES

_____
_____
_____
_____
_____
_____
_____
_____
_____
_____
_____
_____
_____
_____
_____
_____
_____
_____
_____
_____
_____
_____
_____
_____
_____
_____
_____
_____
_____
_____
_____
_____
_____
_____

2 Hear, O heavens, and give ear, O earth: for the Lord hath spoken, **I have nourished and brought up children, and they have rebelled against me**.

3 The ox knoweth his owner, and the ass his master's crib [*manger*]: but **Israel doth not know** [*know God*], my people doth not consider [*think seriously, Israel—animals are wiser than you are!*].

4 Ah **sinful nation**, a **people laden with iniquity** [*loaded down with wickedness*], a seed of evildoers, children that are **corrupters**: they **have forsaken the Lord**, they have provoked the Holy One of Israel unto anger, they **are gone away backward** [*retrogressing; they are "in the world" and "of the world"*].

5 ¶ **Why should ye be stricken any more** [*why do you keep asking for more punishment*]? ye will revolt more and more: **the whole head** [*leadership*] **is sick**, and the whole heart [*the people*] faint [*is diseased; in other words, the whole nation is spiritually sick*].

Isaiah continues the theme that the whole nation is riddled with wickedness and is thus spiritually sick. He uses repetition to drive home the point.

6 **From the sole of the foot even unto the head there is no soundness in it** [*you are completely sick*]; but **wounds, and bruises, and putrifying** [*filled with pus*] **sores** [*symbolically saying that the people are spiritually beaten and infected with sin*]: **they have not been closed, neither bound up, neither mollified with ointment** [*you are sick and you don't even care; you won't try the simplest first aid (the Atonement of Christ)*].

Old Testament prophets often spoke prophetically of the future as if it had already taken place. Isaiah uses this technique next, as he prophesies of the impending captivity of these wicked people.

7 **Your country is desolate**, your cities are **burned** with fire: your land, strangers [*foreigners*] devour it in your presence, and it is desolate as overthrown by strangers [*foreigners, specifically the Assyrians*].

8 And **the daughter of Zion** [*Israel*] **is left as a cottage** [*temporary shade structure built of straw and leaves*] in a vineyard, as a lodge [*same as cottage*] in a garden of cucumbers, as a besieged city [*you are about as secure as a flimsy shade shack in a garden*].

9 **Except the Lord of hosts had left unto us a very small remnant** [*if God hadn't intervened and saved a few of Israel*], **we should have been as Sodom**, and we should have been like unto Gomorrah [*completely destroyed*].

10 ¶ **Hear the word of the Lord, ye rulers of Sodom** [*"Listen up, you wicked leaders!"*]; **give ear unto the law of our God, ye people of Gomorrah** [*Sodom and Gomorrah symbolize total wickedness*].

11 **To what purpose is the multitude of your sacrifices unto me** [*what good are your insincere, empty rituals*]? saith the Lord: I am full [*"I've had it to here!"*] of the burnt offerings of rams, and the fat of fed beasts; and I delight not in the blood of bullocks, or of lambs, or of he goats.

NOTES

12 When ye come to appear before me, who **hath required this at your hand, to tread my courts** [*who authorized you hypocrites to act religious and pretend to worship Me*]?

13 **Bring no more vain** [*useless*] **oblations** [*offerings*]; incense is an abomination unto me; the new moons [*special Sabbath ritual at beginning of month—see Bible Dictionary under "New Moon"*] and sabbaths, the calling of assemblies, I cannot [*"I can't stand it!"*] away with; it is iniquity, even the solemn meeting [*solemn assembly*].

14 **Your new moons and your appointed feasts** [*your hypocritical worship*] **my soul hateth**: they are a trouble unto me; I am weary to bear them.

15 And **when ye spread forth your hands** [*when you pray*], **I will hide mine eyes from you**: yea, when ye make many prayers, **I will not hear**: your hands are full of blood [*bloodshed; murder—see verse 21*].

Next, in spite of the gross wickedness of these people, as described by Isaiah, they are invited by a merciful Savior to repent and return to Him.

Major Message

If you want to repent but you think your sins have put you beyond the reach of the Savior's Atonement, think again.

16 ¶ **Wash you** [*be baptized*], make you clean; put away the evil of your doings from before mine eyes [*repent*]; cease to do evil;

17 **Learn to do well** [*don't just cease to do evil but replace evil with good in your lives*]; seek judgment [*be fair in your dealings with others*], relieve the oppressed, judge the fatherless [*be kind and fair to them*], plead for [*stand up for, defend*] the widow.

Verse 18, next, is among the most well known of all quotes from Isaiah. With verses 1–15 as a backdrop, this verse wonderfully and clearly teaches the power of the Atonement of Jesus Christ to cleanse and heal completely.

18 Come now, and let us reason together, saith the Lord: **though your sins be as scarlet** [*cloth dyed with scarlet, a colorfast dye*], **they shall be as white as snow** [*even though you think your sins are "colorfast," the Atonement can cleanse you*]; **though they be red like crimson, they shall be as wool** [*a long process is required to get wool white, but it can be done*].

19 **If ye be willing** [*agency, choice*] **and obedient**, ye shall eat the good of the land [*you will prosper*]:

20 **But if ye refuse and rebel**, ye shall be devoured with the sword: for the mouth of the Lord hath spoken it.

The word "harlot" (or prostitute), in verse 21, next, is a play on the imagery of a husband whose wife commits adultery against him. In the symbolism of the Bible, the husband represents Christ, and the wife represents Israel. They are bound together by covenant, but Israel cheats on her husband by being loyal to false gods, including wickedness and self-indulgence.

21 ¶ **How is** [*did*] **the faithful city** [*Jerusalem*] **become an harlot** [*unfaithful to the Lord; a willful sinner*]! it was full of judgment [*justice*]; righteousness lodged in it; but now murderers.

22 Thy silver is become dross [*surface scum on molten metal*] thy wine mixed with water [*you are polluted!*]:

23 **Thy princes** [*leaders, rulers*] **are rebellious**, and companions of thieves: **every one loveth gifts** [*bribes*], and followeth after rewards: they judge not [*do not do justice to*] the fatherless, neither doth the cause of the widow come unto them [*never penetrates their hearts*].

24 **Therefore saith the Lord**, the Lord of hosts, the mighty One of Israel, Ah, **I will ease me of** [*be rid of*] **mine adversaries**, and avenge me of mine enemies [*in other words, the Lord will turn the wicked people of Israel over to the law of justice, since they have chosen to become His enemies*]:

25 ¶ And **I will turn my hand upon thee** [*repeatedly chastise you*], and purely purge away thy dross, and take away all thy tin [*slag; I will refine thee; in other words, put you through the refiner's fire to burn your impurities and sins out of you*]:

26 And **I will restore thy judges as at the first** [*among other things, a reference to the future when the gospel is restored by Joseph Smith*], and thy counsellors as at the beginning: **afterward thou shalt be called, The city of righteousness, the faithful city** [*the future gathering of Israel*].

27 **Zion shall be redeemed** [*a prophetic fact*] with judgment, and her converts with righteousness [*message of hope*].

28 **And the destruction of the transgressors and of the sinners shall be together** [*at the same time*], and they that forsake the Lord shall be consumed [*at the Second Coming*].

29 For **they shall be ashamed of** [*put to shame because of*] the oaks [*trees and gardens used in their idol worship*] which ye have desired, and **ye shall be confounded for the** [*because of the*] **gardens** [*used in idol worship*] that ye have chosen.

30 For **ye shall be as an oak whose leaf fadeth, and as a garden that hath no water** [*drought; destruction will come upon you because of your wickedness*].

31 And **the strong** [*the mighty wicked among you*] **shall be as tow** [*as a tuft of inflammable fibers*], and the maker of it as a spark, and **they shall both burn together, and none shall quench them** [*destruction of the wicked is sure to happen*].

ISAIAH 2

Selection: all verses

Chapters 2, 3, and 4 go together. Chapter 2 is a multi-faceted prophecy of the latter-day gathering to the tops of the Rocky Mountains (Salt Lake City), the building of latter-day temples, the Millennium, and the destruction of the wicked at the Second Coming. Isaiah saw these things in vision (as stated in verse 1).

1 **The word that Isaiah the son of Amoz saw** concerning Judah and Jerusalem.

2 And it shall come to pass **in the last days**, that **the mountain** of the Lord's house shall be established in the top of the mountains [*"high place"—temples will be established; also, the Church will be established in the tops of the mountains in the last days*], and shall be exalted above the hills [*symbolism: you can get higher, closer to God in the temples than on the highest mountains*]; and **all nations shall flow unto it** [*the gathering of Israel in the last days, coming to the true gospel, with headquarters in the "top of the mountains"*].

3 And **many people shall go and say, Come ye, and let us go up to the mountain of the Lord**, to the house [*temples*] of the God of Jacob; and **he will teach us of his ways, and we will walk in his paths**: for out of Zion shall go forth the law, and the word of the Lord from Jerusalem [*"law" and "word" are synonyms; this seems to be a reference to the Millennium, when there will be two headquarters of Christ's kingdom, Zion (the New Jerusalem), built in Independence, Missouri, and Old Jerusalem; the Lord's word will go out from both cities*].

Verse 4, next, is a direct reference to the Millennium.

4 **And he** [*Christ*] **shall judge** [*rule*] **among the nations**, and shall rebuke many people: and **they shall beat their swords into plowshares, and their spears into pruninghooks** [*there will be peace*]: **nation shall not lift up sword against nation, neither shall they learn war any more** [*Millennium*].

Isaiah now switches from the future back to his own time and people. It is a common practice (and somewhat confusing to us) for Isaiah to switch from the future to the past, or the present, and then back and forth, with no notice. It is part of "the manner of prophesying among the Jews" (2 Nephi 25:1).

Having told the people what will happen to their descendants in the far-distant future, and given them a glimpse of the beautiful peace and joy of living with the Savior during the Millennium, he now invites them to repent and prepare themselves to be worthy of living with Him forever.

5 **O house of Jacob** [*another name for Israel*], **come ye, and let us walk in the light of the Lord**.

Next, Isaiah reminds these wicked people why they are not currently enjoying the blessings of the Lord.

6 Therefore [*this is why*] thou [*the Lord*] hast forsaken thy people the house of Jacob [*the Israelites*], **because they be replenished from the east** [*they are adopting false*

eastern religions], **and are soothsayers** [*are into witchcraft, sorcery, and so forth*] like the Philistines, and **they please themselves in the children of strangers** [*are mixing with and marrying foreigners, people not of covenant Israel*].

7 **Their land also is full of silver and gold, neither is there any end of their treasures** [*they have become materialistic*]; **their land is also full of horses,** neither is there any end of their **chariots** [*horses and chariots represent armaments of war*]:

8 **Their land also is full of idols**; they worship the work of their own hands, that which their own fingers have made [*Isaiah is pointing out how absurd worshiping idols is*]:

The Book of Mormon adds a very important word in two places in verse 9, next. The Book of Mormon passages of Isaiah came from the brass plates and were thus of much earlier date and accuracy than the manuscripts from which our Old Testament is taken.

9 And the **mean man** [*poor, low in social status*] **boweth** [*not, see 2 Nephi 12:9*] down, **and the great** [*high in social status and influence*] **man humbleth himself** [*not*]: therefore forgive them not [*no one is humble*].

The main message in verse 10, next, is that it is impossible to hide from God.

10 **Enter into the rock** [*go ahead and try to find a place to hide from the Lord in the rocks, you wicked people*], **and hide thee in the dust,** for fear of the Lord and for [*2 Nephi 12:10 does not have "for"*] the glory of his majesty [*2 Nephi 12:10 adds "shall smite thee"*].

One other thing we learn from verse 10, above, with the Book of Mormon additions, is that the wicked will be destroyed by the glory of the coming Savior, at the time of the Second Coming (compare with Doctrine & Covenants 5:19).

11 **The lofty looks of man** [*pride*] **shall be humbled,** and the haughtiness of men shall be bowed down, and **the Lord alone shall be exalted in that day** [*the Lord will demonstrate power over all things at the Second Coming*].

Verse 12, next, is yet another reminder to you that Isaiah uses repetition to emphasize a point he wishes to make.

12 **For the day of the Lord of hosts** [*Second Coming*] **shall be upon** [*against*] **every one that is proud** and lofty, and upon [*against*] every one that is lifted up [*full of pride*]; and he shall be brought low [*humbled*]:

Trees are often used by Isaiah and other Old Testament prophets to represent people. We see this technique in verse 13, next.

13 And **upon all the cedars** [*people*] of Lebanon, **that are high and lifted up,** and upon all the oaks [*people*] of Bashan,

14 And upon all the high mountains, and upon all the hills that are lifted up,

15 And upon every high tower, and upon every fenced wall [*man-made defenses*],

16 And **upon all the ships of Tarshish** [*symbolic of materialism and earthly power; noted for ability to travel long distances and carry large cargoes, and for their strength as warships*], **and upon all pleasant pictures** [*pleasure craft upon which the wealthy traveled*].

17 And **the loftiness** [*pride*] **of man shall be bowed down**, and the haughtiness of men shall be made low: and **the Lord alone shall be exalted in that day** [*at the time of the Second Coming*].

18 And **the idols he shall utterly abolish**.

> The terror in the hearts of the wicked at the time of the Second Coming is depicted in verses 19 and 21, next.

19 And **they** [*the wicked*] **shall go into the holes of the rocks** [*caves*], and into the caves of the earth, **for fear of the Lord, and for the glory of his majesty**, when he ariseth to shake terribly the earth [*at the time of the Second Coming*].

20 **In that day** [*Second Coming*] **a man shall cast his idols** of silver, and his idols of gold, which they made each one for himself to worship [*a reminder that idol worship is completely absurd*], **to the moles and to the bats** [*a play on words, pointing out that wicked people live in "darkness" also*];

21 **To go into the clefts of the rocks, and into the tops of the ragged rocks, for fear of the Lord**, and for the glory of his majesty, when he ariseth to shake terribly the earth [*at the time of the Second Coming*].

22 **Cease ye from man** [*stop trusting in man*], **whose breath is in his nostrils** [*who is mortal*]: **for wherein is he to be accounted of** [*in other words, why trust in man rather than God*]?

ISAIAH 3

Selection: all verses

In this chapter Isaiah describes the downfall of Jerusalem because of wickedness. In a significant way, it is a pattern that applies to any nation or society in which personal sin and wickedness become a way of life for the majority of citizens.

Beginning with verse 16 and continuing to the end of the chapter, Isaiah points out, in effect, that women are generally the last stronghold against the downfall of a nation, and that when they also turn to pride and personal wickedness as a lifestyle, the nation is doomed.

We will be introduced to an ancient writing technique in this chapter called "chiasmus." It is a writing form in which the author says certain things and then intentionally repeats them in reverse order for emphasis.

Chiasmus was not discovered by scholars until after the time the Book of Mormon was published. This is significant because the Book of Mormon has several passages in which chiasmus is used (for example, 2 Nephi 29:13, Mosiah 3:18–19, and Alma 36). Such use of chiasmus as a writing style in the Book of Mormon is strong evidence that it is of ancient origin, which of course it is. We will include one example from the Book of Mormon. You will in fact see two short chiastic structures within this one verse. In this case, the structure consists of A B C C' B' A,' and it is repeated twice.

NOTES

2 Nephi 29:13

<u>13</u> And it shall come to pass that the <u>Jews</u> **[A]** shall have the <u>words</u> **[B]** of the <u>Nephites</u> **[C]**, and the <u>Nephites</u> **[C']** shall have the <u>words</u> **[B']** of the <u>Jews</u> **[A]**; and the <u>Nephites and the Jews</u> **[A]** shall have the <u>words</u> **[B]** of the <u>lost tribes of Israel</u> **[C]**; and the <u>lost tribes of Israel</u> **[C]** shall have the <u>words</u> **[B']** of the <u>Nephites and the Jews</u> **[A']**.

Often, but not necessarily always, the pivot point or midpoint of the chiasmus is the main message. For example, in the chiasmus used by Isaiah here in the first eight verses, the main message is found in verse 5, where he emphasizes that when a society collapses because of wickedness, everyone is persecuted and oppressed by everyone else.

We will now proceed with this chapter. The chiastic structure begins in verse 1 and ends at the beginning of verse 8. You may wish to read only the words of the chiasmus (in underlined bold), and then come back and read the complete verses. It will help you get the feel of a chiasmus.

1 For, behold, the Lord, the Lord of hosts, doth <u>take away from Jerusalem</u> **[A]** and from Judah the stay [*supply*] and the staff [*support*], the whole stay of <u>bread</u> **[B]**, and the whole stay of water [*the Lord is going to pull the props out and the whole thing will collapse*],

2 The <u>mighty man</u> **[C]** [*the powerful leader*], and the man of war [*your military power will crumble*], the judge, and the prophet, and the prudent, and the ancient,

3 The captain of fifty, and <u>the honourable man, and the counsellor</u> **[D]** [*no competent leaders*], and the cunning artificer [*skilled craftsman*], and the eloquent orator [*all the stable, dependable people who are the mainstays of a stable society will be gone*].

4 And I will give <u>children to be their princes</u> **[E]** [*leaders*], and babes [*immature people*] shall rule over them [*immature, irresponsible leaders will take over*].

5 And <u>the people shall be oppressed, every one by another</u> **[F]**, [*this is the pivot point of this chiasmus*] and every one by his neighbour [*anarchy*]: the <u>child shall behave himself proudly against the ancient</u> **[E']**, and the base [*crude and rude*] against the honourable [*no respect for authority; public acceptance of coarseness, crudeness, rudeness*].

Economic conditions will become so bad that people will be asked to serve as leaders if they happen to have a decent set of clothes.

6 When a man shall take hold of his brother of the house of his father, saying, <u>Thou hast clothing, be thou our ruler</u> **[D']**, and let [*let not; see 2 Nephi 13:6*] this ruin be under thy hand [*be our leader, don't let this happen to us*]:

7 In that day shall he [*the man asked to be the leader in verse 6, above*] swear [*protest*], saying, <u>I will not be an healer</u> **[C']** [*I can't lead you and fix your problems!*]; for in my house is neither <u>bread</u> **[B']** nor clothing: make me not a ruler of the people [*I can't solve your problems. I've got my own problems*].

8 For <u>Jerusalem is ruined</u> **[A']**, and Judah is fallen: because their tongue and their doings are against the Lord, to provoke the eyes of his glory [*in word and actions, the people are completely against the Lord*].

Next, Isaiah tells us that the faces of the truly wicked and evil "radiate" their wickedness to all.

9 ¶ **The shew of their countenance doth witness against them**; and **they declare their sin as Sodom, they hide it not** [*blatant sin; they show no embarrassment nor shame for what they are doing*]. **Woe unto their soul!** for they have rewarded evil unto themselves [*they are sinning against themselves, preparing an evil harvest for themselves*].

Next, the Lord assures the righteous among the wicked that they will reap the sweet harvest of their goodness.

The bolded text in verses 10 and 11, next, summarizes a major message found throughout Isaiah's teachings.

10 **Say ye to the righteous, that it shall be well with him**; for they shall eat the fruit of their doings [*righteousness will pay off*].

11 **Woe unto the wicked! it shall be ill with him**: for the reward of his hands shall be given him. [*"As ye sow, so shall ye reap."*]

12 ¶ As for my people, **children are their oppressors, and women rule over them** [*breakdown of traditional family; men are weak leaders, women have to fill in; can also reflect the deep bitterness and powerful influence of many women when they turn wicked*]. O my people, **they which lead thee cause thee to err**, and destroy the way of thy paths [*leadership without basic gospel values can be devastating*].

13 **The Lord standeth up to plead** [*to try your case as in a court of law; implying that the evidence is against you*], and standeth to judge the people.

14 **The Lord will enter into judgment** [*in effect, you will stand before the Lord to answer for your behaviors*] with the ancients of his people, and the princes [*leaders*] thereof: for **ye have eaten up the vineyard; the spoil of** [*things you have taken from*] **the poor is in your houses** [*you were supposed to protect them but instead you preyed on them*].

15 **What mean ye** [*what have you got to say for yourselves*] that **ye beat my people to pieces, and grind the faces of the poor**? saith the Lord God of hosts.

Isaiah now says that society is lost when women also turn to evil. From this we can better understand the devil's strategy in our day as he works to convince women to join in the evils of men and pull away from home and family.

16 ¶ Moreover the Lord saith, **Because the daughters of Zion** [*women of the Church particularly, and women in general*] **are haughty** [*full of pride*], and **walk with stretched forth necks** [*prideful*] and **wanton eyes** [*lustful*], walking and **mincing as they go** [*walking in such a way as to attract men's lustful thoughts*], and **making a tinkling with their feet** [*a reference to wearing expensive, high-fashion shoes (in Isaiah's day) with little bells on them to attract attention to their wealthy status*]:

NOTES

NOTES

17 **Therefore** [*for these reasons*] **the Lord will smite** with a scab the crown of the head [*will take away their beauty*] of **the daughters of Zion**, and the Lord will discover [*uncover*] their secret parts [*expose their evil deeds*].

> Scholars do not always agree on the nature of the female ornaments mentioned in verses 18–23, next. We will supply definitions from a variety of sources, realizing that many of them are simply best guesses.

18 **In that day** [*when destruction comes*] **the Lord will take away** the bravery [*beauty*] of their tinkling **ornaments** about their feet, and their **cauls**, and their **round tires like the moon** [*possibly crescent-shaped necklaces*],

19 The **chains**, and the **bracelets**, and the **mufflers** [*veils*],

20 The **bonnets**, and the **ornaments** of the legs, and the *headbands,* and the **tablets** [*perfume boxes*], and the **earrings**,

21 The **rings**, and **nose jewels**,

22 The **changeable suits of apparel** [*beautiful clothing*], and the *mantles,* and the **wimples** [*shawls*], and the crisping pins [*money purses*],

23 The **glasses** [*see-through clothing; see Isaiah 3:23, footnote a in your Bible*], and the **fine linen**, and the **hoods** [*turbans*], and the **vails**. [*Isaiah has described female high-society fashions, accompanied by arrogance and materialism, in terms of such things in his day.*]

24 **And it shall come to pass, that instead** [*in place of*] **of sweet smell there shall be stink** [*from corpses of people killed by invading armies*]; and instead of a girdle [*high-fashion clothing*] a **rent** [*torn clothing, rags*], and instead of well set hair **baldness** [*invading armies customarily shaved the heads of captives whom they enslaved for the purposes of humiliation, identification, and sanitation*]; and instead of a **stomacher** [*nice robe*] a girding of sackcloth [*coarse clothing worn by slaves and the poor class*]; and burning [*branding; conquerors often branded their slaves*] instead of [*in the place of*] beauty.

25 **Thy men shall fall by the sword**, and thy mighty in the war [*invasion*].

> The above-mentioned slaughter of men will set the stage for the plural marriage mentioned in Isaiah 4:1. With so few men left, the widows and other women in Jerusalem will plead with men to marry several wives, so that they can have a proper place in society. They will offer to pay their own way so they will not become a financial burden on their husbands. Remember that plural marriage was common in that culture at the time.

26 **And her** [*Jerusalem's*] **gates shall lament and mourn**; and **she** being desolate [*empty, defeated*] **shall sit upon the ground** [*a sign of defeat and humility*].

ISAIAH 4

NOTES

Selection: all verses

Both the Joseph Smith Translation and the Hebrew Bible put verse one of chapter 4 at the end of chapter 3, which puts it in the context of Jerusalem's destruction and the scarcity of men resulting from the war prophesied in Isaiah 3:25–26. Footnote 4:1a in your Bible, says "because of scarcity of men due to wars. See 3:25." Footnote b likewise refers the reader to chapter 3.

Verses 2–6 deal with the Millennium.

1 **And in that day** [*the time of the destruction of Jerusalem spoken of in Isaiah 3:25–26*] **seven women shall take hold of one man, saying,** We will eat our own bread, and wear our own apparel [*we will pay our own way*]: only let us be called by thy name [*please marry us*], to take away our reproach [*the stigma in that society of being unmarried and childless*].

Verse 2, next, starts a new topic; namely, conditions during the Millennium.

2 **In that day** [*Millennium*] **shall the branch of the Lord** [*Christ—see Jeremiah 23:5*] **be beautiful and glorious**, and the fruit of the earth shall be excellent and comely [*pleasant to look at*] for them that are escaped of Israel [*for those who have escaped wickedness—the righteous remnant of Israel*].

3 And it shall come to pass, that **he that is left in Zion, and he that remaineth in Jerusalem, shall be called holy,** even every one that is written among the living [*those saved by approval of the Messiah*] in Jerusalem:

4 **When the Lord shall have washed away the filth of the daughters of Zion** [*after the Lord has cleansed the earth of the wicked at the Second Coming*], and shall have purged the blood of Jerusalem from the midst thereof by the spirit of judgment, and by the spirit of burning [*earth will be cleansed by fire*].

The angel Moroni quoted verses 5 and 6 to Joseph Smith in reference to the last days. (See Messenger and Advocate, April 1835, page 110.) The imagery in verse five can symbolize the presence of the Lord in the meetings of the saints as well as upon the homes of the righteous in the last days, as well as the presence of the Lord on earth during the Millennium.

It is very encouraging to know that, in spite of the gross wickedness upon the earth in the final days before the Second Coming, the righteous can be assured of having the presence of the Lord in their homes and in their church meetings.

5 And **the Lord will create upon every dwelling place** [*homes*] **of mount Zion** [*faithful covenant people*]**, and upon her assemblies** [*meetings, sacrament meetings, stake conferences, mission conferences, general conferences, and so forth*]**, a cloud and smoke by day** [*represent the presence of the Lord as in Exodus 19:16–18*], and the shining of a **flaming fire by night**: for upon all the glory shall be a defence.

6 And **there shall be a tabernacle** [*shelter*] **for a shadow** [*shade*] in the daytime from the heat, and for a place of refuge, and **for a covert** [*protection*] from storm and from rain [*peace and protection*].

NOTES

_____
_____
_____
_____
_____
_____
_____
_____
_____
_____
_____
_____
_____
_____
_____
_____
_____
_____
_____
_____
_____
_____
_____
_____
_____
_____
_____
_____
_____
_____
_____
_____
_____
_____
_____

ISAIAH 5

Selection: all verses

In this chapter we will see Isaiah's marvelous intellect and poetic talent at work as he composes a song or poetic parable of a vineyard, symbolizing God's mercy and Israel's unresponsiveness to Him.

1 **Now will I sing** [*compose a song or poetic parable*] to my wellbeloved **a song of my beloved** [*Christ*] touching **his vineyard** [*Israel—see verse 7*]. My wellbeloved hath a vineyard in a fruitful hill [*in a place where they have great potential to grow and produce the desired fruit*]:

2 And **he fenced it, and gathered out the stones thereof** [*took away the stumbling blocks and obstacles to progression*], **and planted it with the choicest vine** [*the men of Judah—see verse 7; symbolic of His covenant people*], and **built a tower** [*set prophets*] in the midst of it, and also **made a winepress therein** [*planning for a good harvest*]: and **he looked that it should bring forth grapes** [*the desired product, faithful people*], **and it brought forth wild grapes** [*apostasy*].

3 And now, O inhabitants of Jerusalem, and men of Judah, **judge, I pray you, betwixt me and my vineyard** [*I'll give you the facts; you be the judge*].

4 **What could have been done more** to my vineyard, **that I have not done** in it [*the main question—compare with Jacob 5:47, 49*]? **wherefore** [*why*], when I looked [*planned*] that it should bring forth grapes [*the desired result, faithful people*], **brought it forth wild grapes** [*wicked people; apostasy*]?

5 And now go to; **I will tell you what I will do to my vineyard** [*Israel*]: **I will take away the hedge** [*divine protection*] thereof, **and it shall be eaten up** [*destroyed*]; and **break down the wall** [*protection*] thereof, **and it shall be trodden down** [*by enemies*]:

6 And **I will lay it waste: it shall not be pruned** [*will not have sins, false doctrines, and so forth pruned out of the lives of its people by living prophets*], **nor digged** [*nourished; the Spirit withdraws, no prophets*]; **but there shall come up briers and thorns** [*apostate doctrines and behaviors*]: I will also command the clouds that they rain **no rain** upon it [*famine*].

Next, in verse 7, Isaiah defines some of the symbolism in this parable.

7 For **the vineyard** of the Lord of hosts **is the house of Israel**, and the **men of Judah his pleasant plant**: and **he looked for judgment** [*fairness, honesty, and so forth*], **but behold oppression; for righteousness, but behold a cry** [*found riotous living instead*].

Verse 8, next, has actually been misinterpreted on occasions to mean that building row houses and condominiums is sinful. Of course, such is not the meaning but it is interesting how far astray things can go.

8 ¶ **Woe unto them** [*the powerful, wealthy*] that join house to house [*cheat the poor and unfortunate out of their homes and take them from them*], **that lay field to field, till there**

be no place, that they [the poor] may be placed alone in the midst of the earth [those in power push the poor farmers off their land by unscrupulous means].

9 In mine ears said the Lord of hosts, Of a truth **many houses shall be desolate**, even great and fair [the homes and palaces of the great and powerful wicked], without inhabitant [troubles are coming because of your wickedness].

Next, Isaiah uses stark imagery to prophesy that a famine is coming.

10 Yea, **ten acres of vineyard shall yield one bath** [about 8¼ U.S. gallons], and **the seed of an homer** [6½ bushel of seed] **shall yield an ephah** [½ bushel of harvest; in other words, famine is coming].

Next, we see a warning against riotous living, which generally accompanies sin and wickedness in society.

11 ¶ **Woe unto them that rise up early in the morning, that they may follow strong drink; that continue until night**, till wine inflame them!

Next, in verse 12, Isaiah points out that these people "go to church" and go through all the motions of the true religion (Law of Moses, for them), but they are hypocrites and do not live the gospel in their daily lives.

12 And **the harp**, and the **viol** [lyre], the **tabret** [drums], and **pipe** [instruments associated with worship of the Lord in Bible times], and **wine**, are in their feasts: **but they regard not the work of the Lord** [their worship is empty, hypocritical], neither consider the operation of his hands [they do not actually acknowledge God].

Next, Isaiah speaks prophetically of the future as if it has already happened. This way of speaking is quite common in Old Testament prophecies.

13 ¶ **Therefore** [that is why] **my people are gone into captivity, because they have no knowledge** [Amos 8:11–12 famine of hearing words of the Lord]: and **their honourable men are famished, and their multitude dried up** with thirst [the prophesied destructions and famine have taken their toll].

14 **Therefore** [that is why] **hell hath enlarged herself** [they've had to add on to hell to make room for you], and opened her mouth without measure [more than anyone thought possible]: **and their glory, and their multitude, and their pomp, and he that rejoiceth** [in wickedness and riotous living], **shall descend into it**.

15 And **the mean** [poor] **man shall be brought down** [humbled], and **the mighty man shall be humbled**, and the eyes of the lofty shall be humbled [everyone needs humbling]:

16 **But the Lord of hosts shall be exalted in judgment** [you will see that the Lord is correct], and God that is holy shall be sanctified in righteousness [the Lord will triumph].

17 **Then** [after the destruction that is coming to Israel] **shall the lambs feed** [graze where the Lord's vineyard once stood—destruction is complete] after their manner, **and the**

waste places [*ruins*] **of the fat ones** [*the former prosperous inhabitants*] shall strangers [*foreigners*] eat [*in other words, foreign enemies will take over your land*].

Next, in verse 18, Isaiah uses yet another image to describe the bondage of sin among the covenant people of Israel.

18 **Woe unto them that draw iniquity with cords of vanity, and sin as it were with a cart rope** [*you are tethered to your sins; they follow you like a cart follows the animal pulling it*]:

19 **That say, Let him** [*the Lord*] make speed, and **hasten his work, that we may see it** [*it is up to God to prove to us that He exists*]: and **let the counsel** [*plans*] **of the Holy One of Israel** [*the Lord*] draw nigh and come [*come to pass*], that we may know it [*if He wants us to know Him, He will have to be more obvious about His existence*]!

Verse 20, next, is well known and often used in our lessons and sermons. We see much of this switching of things around in the world today.

20 ¶ **Woe unto them that call evil good, and good evil**; that **put darkness for light, and light for darkness**; that put bitter for sweet, and sweet for bitter!

21 **Woe unto them that are wise in their own eyes** [*full of evil pride*], and prudent in their own sight!

22 **Woe unto them that are mighty to drink wine**, and men of strength to mingle strong drink:

23 **Which justify the wicked for reward** [*bribes, corrupt judicial system*], **and take away the righteousness of the righteous from him** [*ruin the good reputations of righteous people*]!

Next, in verse 24, Isaiah describes serious ultimate consequences of rebellion and sin.

24 Therefore as the fire devoureth the stubble, and the flame consumeth the chaff, so **their root shall be as rottenness, and their blossom shall go up as dust** [*shall not bear fruit, shall have no posterity in the next life and destruction of many in this life*]: **because they have cast away the law of the Lord** of hosts, and despised the word of the Holy One of Israel.

The unfathomable depth of the love and mercy that the Savior has for us is brought out at the end of verse 25, next. In this we see the power of the Atonement of Jesus Christ to cleanse and heal. You may wish to reread Isaiah 1:18 as you read this verse.

25 **Therefore** [*for these reasons*] **is the anger of the Lord kindled against his people** [*covenant Israel*], and **he hath stretched forth his hand against them**, and hath smitten them: and the hills did tremble, and their carcases were torn in the midst of the streets [*great destruction is coming*]. For all this [*because of all this wickedness*] his anger is not turned away, **but his hand is stretched out still** [*you can still repent— compare with Jacob 6:4*].

In verses 26–30, next, we see a prophecy of the gathering of Israel in the last days. We see modern transportation bringing members and new converts great distances to gather together as Saints. Isaiah's imagery shows us that none will stop the work of the Lord and the gathering of Israel in these marvelous times. Surely, we are witnessing this in our day.

26 ¶ And **he will lift up an ensign** [*flag, rallying point; the true gospel*] **to the nations from far**, and will hiss [*whistle; a signal to gather*] unto them from the end of the earth: and, behold, **they shall come with speed swiftly** [*modern transportation*]:

27 **None shall be weary nor stumble** among them; **none shall slumber nor sleep**; neither shall the girdle of their loins be loosed [*change clothes*], nor the latchet of their shoes be broken [*they will travel so fast that they won't need to change clothes or even take their shoes off*]:

28 **Whose arrows are sharp, and all their bows bent** [*perhaps describing the body of a sleek airliner, like an arrow, and the swept back wings like a bow*], **their horses' hoofs shall be counted like flint** [*making sparks like the wheels on a train?*], and their wheels like a whirlwind [*airplanes, trains?*]:

29 **Their roaring shall be like a lion** [*the noise of airplanes, trains, and so on?*], they shall roar like young lions: yea, they shall roar, and **lay hold of the prey** [*take in their passengers?*], **and shall carry it away safe, and none shall deliver it** [*the converts—none will stop the gathering of Israel in the last days*].

30 **And in that day** [*the last days*] they shall roar against them like the roaring of the sea: and **if one look unto the land, light is darkened in the heavens thereof** [*conditions in the last days: war, smoke, pollution, spiritual darkness?*].

ISAIAH 6

Selection: all verses

Chapter 6 contains rich Atonement symbolism, especially verses 6 and 7. Without an understanding of symbolism, these two verses seem strange and mysterious. With it, they show the wonderful power of the Atonement of Christ to cleanse and heal, and to enable us to accept difficult callings with assurance and faith.

Most scholars agree that this chapter is an account of Isaiah's call to serve as a prophet of the Lord. Some feel that it is a later calling to a major assignment. Either way, Isaiah feels completely inadequate and overwhelmed (verse 5).

Verse 1 identifies the date of this revelation to Isaiah.

1 **In the year that king Uzziah died** [*about 740 BC*] **I** [*Isaiah*] **saw** also **the Lord** [*Jesus—see footnote 6c in your Bible*] **sitting upon a throne, high and lifted up** [*exalted*], and **his train** [*skirts of his robe; authority; power. Hebrew: wake, light*] **filled the temple** [*symbolic of heaven—see Revelation 21:22, where the celestial kingdom does not need a temple but, in effect, is a temple itself*].

2 **Above it** [*the throne*] **stood the seraphims** [*angelic beings*]: **each one had six wings** [*wings are symbolic of power to move, act, and so forth, in God's work—see Doctrine & Covenants 77:4*]; **with twain** [*two*] **he covered his face** [*symbolic of a veil, which shows*

———————————
———————————
———————————
———————————
———————————
———————————
———————————
———————————
———————————
———————————
———————————
———————————
———————————
———————————
———————————
———————————
———————————
———————————
———————————
———————————
———————————
———————————
———————————
———————————
———————————
———————————
———————————
———————————
———————————

reverence and respect toward God in biblical culture], and **with twain he covered his feet**, and **with twain he did fly**.

3 And **one cried unto another, and said, Holy, holy, holy, is the Lord of hosts** [a word repeated three times forms the superlative in Hebrew, meaning the very best]: **the whole earth is full of his glory**.

4 **And the posts of the door moved** [shook] at the voice of him that cried, **and the house was filled with smoke** [shaking and smoke are symbolic of God's presence in biblical culture, as at Sinai, Exodus 19:18].

Next, Isaiah tells us that he was completely overwhelmed by the experience of seeing the Savior.

5 ¶ **Then said I, Woe is me! for I am undone** [completely overwhelmed]; because **I am a man of unclean lips** [I am so imperfect], and I dwell in the midst of a people of unclean lips: **for mine eyes have seen the King, the Lord of hosts**.

6 **Then flew one of the seraphims unto me, having a live coal** [symbolic of the Atonement; also symbolic of the Holy Ghost who guides us to the Atonement; we often say that the Holy Ghost "cleanses by fire"] **in his hand**, which he had taken with the tongs **from** off **the altar** [the "altar cross," representing the Savior's sacrifice for our sins]:

7 **And he laid it** [the Atonement] **upon my mouth** [inadequacies, sins, imperfections], **and said, Lo, this** [the Atonement] **hath touched thy lips** [Isaiah's sins and imperfections—see verse 5, above]; and **thine iniquity is taken away, and thy sin purged** [the results of the Atonement].

Watch now as the blessings of the Atonement give Isaiah confidence to accept his mission from the Lord. It can do the same for us in our callings.

8 Also [then] **I heard the voice of the Lord, saying, Whom shall I send, and who will go for us? Then said I** [Isaiah], **Here am I; send me** [the cleansing power of the Atonement and help of the Spirit gave Isaiah the needed confidence to accept the call].

Next, in verses 9–12, the Savior gives Isaiah an idea of the kinds of people he will be working with as a prophet. It will be a tough assignment. We will use a quote from Isaiah in the Book of Mormon to help with verse 9.

9 ¶ **And he** [the Lord] **said, Go** [this is the official call], **and tell this people, Hear** ye indeed, but understand not; **and see** ye indeed, but perceive not.

The Book of Mormon makes significant changes to the above verse of Isaiah.

2 Nephi 16:9

9 And he said: Go and tell this people—Hear ye indeed, but they understood not; and see ye indeed, but they perceived not [Isaiah's task will not be easy with that kind of people].

In verse 10, next, (which contains a chiasmus—see notes in chapter 3 of this study guide) the Lord gives Isaiah some additional insights as to the type of people he will be preaching to. In effect, the Savior appears to be telling him to imagine this type of people in his mind's eye.

10 [*In your imagination*] Make the heart **[A]** of this people fat [*unfeeling, insulated from truth*], and make their ears **[B]** heavy [*deaf to spiritual matters*], and shut their eyes **[C]** [*spiritually blind*]; lest they see with their eyes **[C']**, and hear with their ears **[B']**, and understand with their heart **[A']**, and convert, and be healed.

There is a quote in Matthew in which the Savior basically quoted the above verse of Isaiah. Note that Matthew records that the people have refused to hear the gospel message.

Matthew 13:15

15 For this people's heart is waxed gross, and their ears are dull of hearing, and their eyes they have closed; lest at any time they should see with their eyes, and hear with their ears, and should understand with their heart, and should be converted, and I should heal them.

The Lord's description of the people with whom Isaiah would be working appears to have startled and concerned him somewhat, causing him to ask the following question:

11 **Then said I, Lord, how long** [*will people be like this*]? And **he answered,** Until the cities be wasted without inhabitant, and the houses without man, and the land be utterly desolate [*in other words, as long as people are around*],

12 **And the Lord have removed men far away** [*people are gone*], and there be a great forsaking [*many deserted cities*] in the midst of the land.

In verse 13, next, Isaiah is assured that the time will never come when there are no more people, as mentioned in the scenario given in verses 11–12, above. Instead, a remnant of Israel will survive and will be pruned by the Lord and gathered.

13 ¶ **But yet in it** [*the land*] **shall be a tenth** [*a remnant*]**, and it** [*Israel*] **shall return** [*includes the concept of repenting*]**, and shall be eaten** [*in other words, pruned—as by animals eating the limbs, leaves, and branches; in other words, the Lord "prunes" his vineyard or cuts out old apostates, false doctrines, and so forth; He destroys old unrighteous generations so new may have a chance to grow*]**: as a teil** [*lime?*] **tree, and as an oak, whose substance** [*sap*] **is in them, when they cast their leaves** [*trees that shed the old, non-functioning leaves and look dead in winter but are still alive*]**: so the holy seed shall be the substance thereof** [*Israel may look dead, but there is still life in it*].

ISAIAH 7

Selection: all verses

In this chapter, we see a plot by Israel (the northern ten tribes who became the "lost ten tribes," also known as "Ephraim" at this time in history) and Syria to attack Judah (Jerusalem and the surrounding area). Their plan is to conquer Judah and place a puppet king on the throne in Jerusalem who will be loyal to them.

You will see different names used to refer to Syria, the northern kingdom (Israel) and the southern kingdom (Judah), and this can be confusing. We will list some of these plus the names of kings, to help you keep things straight:

- Syria

- Damascus (the capital city of Syria)

- Rezin (the king)

- Israel (the ten tribes)

- Ephraim

- Samaria (the capitol city of Israel)

- Pekah (the king)

- Judah (the tribes of Judah and Benjamin)

- House of David

- Jerusalem

- Ahaz (the king)

In verse 1, next, we are told that this plot took place about 734 BC, which is about twelve years before the Assyrians conquered Israel and carried them away captive (thus they became the lost ten tribes).

1 And **it came to pass in the days of Ahaz** [*about 734 BC*] the son of Jotham, the son of Uzziah, **king of Judah**, that Rezin **the king of Syria, and** Pekah **the** son of Remaliah, **king of Israel** [*the ten tribes in northern Israel*], **went up toward Jerusalem to war against it**, but could not prevail against it [*didn't win, but they did kill 120,000 men of Judah and take 200,000 captives in one day; see 2 Chronicles 28:6–15*].

Next, in verse 2, we learn that the inhabitants of Judah found out about the plot against them.

2 And **it was told the house of David** [*Judah, Jerusalem*], saying, **Syria is confederate** [*joining forces*] **with Ephraim** [*Israel, the northern ten tribes*]. **And his** [*King Ahaz's*] **heart was moved** [*shaken*], **and the heart of his people, as the trees of the wood are moved with the wind** [*they were "shaking in their boots"; scared*].

Next, the Lord sends Isaiah to wicked King Ahaz to tell him not to worry about the plot, because it will not amount to anything.

3 **Then said the Lord unto Isaiah, Go forth now to meet Ahaz** [*king in Jerusalem*], thou, and Shear-jashub [*Hebrew: "the remnant shall return"*] thy son, at the end of the conduit of the upper pool **in the highway of the fuller's field** [*where the women wash clothes—Ahaz is hiding among the women*];

4 **And say unto him**, Take heed, and **be quiet** [*settle down*]; **fear not**, neither be faint-hearted [*don't worry about continued threats from Syria and Israel*] **for** [*because of*] **the two tails of these smoking firebrands** [*these two kings who think they are really something but are nothing but smoldering stubs of firewood*], for [*because of*] the fierce anger of Rezin with Syria, and of the son of Remaliah [*referring to Pekah, king of Israel*].

5 **Because Syria, Ephraim** [*the ten tribes*], and the son of Remaliah [*the ten tribes' king*], **have taken evil counsel** [*have evil plans*] **against thee, saying,**

6 **Let us go up against Judah**, and vex [*cause trouble for*] it, **and let us** make a breach therein for us, and **set a king in the midst of it** [*set up our own king in Jerusalem*], even the son of Tabeal [*the name of the fellow they had in mind to install as a puppet king*]:

7 **Thus saith the Lord God, It shall not stand, neither shall it come to pass** [*the plot will fail, so don't worry about it*].

8 For **the head** [*capital city*] **of Syria is Damascus, and the head** [*leader*] **of Damascus is Rezin**; and **within threescore and five years** [*sixty-five years*] **shall Ephraim** [*the ten tribes*] be **broken**, that it be not a people [*in sixty-five years, the ten tribes will be lost; apparently it took several years after Assyria captured the ten tribes (about 722 BC) until they were lost to the knowledge of other people*].

9 And **the head** [*capital city*] **of Ephraim is Samaria, and the head** [*leader*] **of Samaria is Remaliah's son** [*Pekah; apparently Isaiah had such disdain for Pekah that he refused to use his name, preferring instead to call him "Remaliah's boy"*]. **If ye** [*Ahaz and his people, the tribe of Judah*] **will not believe** [*in the Lord*], surely **ye shall not be established** [*not be saved by the Lord's power*].

Next, the Lord has Isaiah invite King Ahaz to ask for a sign to prove that what Isaiah has told him about the plot is true. Watch how this weak king reacts to this rare invitation from the Lord.

10 ¶ **Moreover** the Lord spake again unto Ahaz, saying,

11 **Ask thee a sign** [*to strengthen your faith*] **of the Lord** thy God; ask it either in the depth, or in the height above [*ask anything you want*].

12 **But Ahaz said, I will not ask, neither will I tempt** [*test*] **the Lord** [*refuses to follow prophet's counsel; he is deliberately evasive, and is already secretly depending on Assyria for help*].

13 **And he** [*Isaiah*] **said, Hear ye now, O house of David** [*Ahaz and his people, Judah*]; Is it a small thing for you to weary men, but **will ye weary my God also** [*try the patience of God*]?

Next, Isaiah prophesies of the coming of Jesus Christ in the meridian of time—see heading to chapter 7 in your Bible. Verse 14 emphasizes that because of their wickedness, these people desperately need the Savior.

14 **Therefore** [*because of your disobedience*] the Lord himself shall give you a sign; Behold, **a virgin shall conceive, and bear a son, and shall call his name Immanuel** [*the day will come when the Savior will be born*].

15 **Butter and honey** [*curd and honey, the only foods available to the poor at times*] **shall he eat, that he may know to refuse the evil, and choose the good**.

Next, in verse 16, Isaiah explains that in the same number of years it will take the future Savior to grow from an infant to the point of being able to choose between right and wrong, the kings of Syria and Israel will fall from power.

16 For **before the child shall know to refuse the evil, and choose the good** [*before he is old enough to choose right from wrong—in just a few years*], **the land** [*both Israel and Syria*] **that thou abhorrest** [*that causes you fear*] **shall be forsaken of both her kings**.

17 **The Lord shall bring upon thee** [*Ahaz*], **and upon thy people, and upon thy father's house** [*the royal family*], days that have not come [*trouble like never before*], from the day that Ephraim departed from Judah [*when the ten tribes comprising Israel split into the northern kingdom under Jeroboam I, and the tribes of Judah and Benjamin under Rehoboam, about 975 BC*]; even **the king of Assyria** [*the king of Assyria and his armies will come upon you*].

18 And it shall come to pass **in that day, that the Lord shall hiss** [*signal, call for*] **for the fly** [*associated with plagues, troubles and so forth*] **that is in the uttermost part of the rivers of Egypt, and for the bee that is in the land of Assyria**.

19 And **they shall come, and shall rest** all of them **in the desolate valleys, and in the holes of the rocks, and upon all thorns, and upon all bushes** [*you will have enemies in your land like flies; they will overrun the land*].

Verse 20, next, says, in effect, that the people of Judah will become slaves.

20 In the same day shall the Lord shave with a razor [*fate of captives, slaves—who are shaved for humiliation, sanitation, identification*] that is hired [*Assyria will be "hired" to do this to Judah*], namely, by them beyond the river, by the king of Assyria, the head, and the hair of the feet: and it shall also consume the beard [*they will shave you clean—conquer you; beards were a sign of dignity in ancient Israel*].

The imagery used by Isaiah in verses 21–25, next, shows us that, after the conquering enemy armies have done their work, the land will be relatively empty of inhabitants.

21 And **it shall come to pass in that day** [*after much devastation in Judah*], **that a man shall nourish a young cow, and two sheep**;

22 And it shall come to pass, **for the abundance of milk that they** [*the domestic animals*] **shall give he shall eat butter**: for butter and honey shall every one eat that is left in the land [*not many people left, so a few animals can supply them well*].

23 And it shall come to pass in that day, that every place shall be, **where there were a thousand vines at a thousand silverlings** [*worth a thousand pieces of silver*], **it shall even be for briers and thorns** [*uncultivated land where it used to be cultivated and productive; symbolic of apostasy*].

24 **With arrows and bows shall men come thither**; because all the land shall become briers and thorns [*previously cultivated land will become wild and overgrown so hunters will hunt wild beasts there*].

25 **And on all hills that shall be digged** [*that were once cultivated*] with the mattock [*hoe*] there [*you*] shall not come thither [*because of*] the fear of briers and thorns: but **it shall be for the sending forth** [*pasturing*] **of oxen, and for the treading of lesser cattle** [*sheep or goats*].

ISAIAH 8

Selection: all verses

We mentioned in Isaiah 7:12 that King Ahaz was secretly planning on alliances and treaties for protection, rather than repenting and turning to the Lord for help. In this chapter, we will see the Lord warn Judah against such alliances.

Isaiah will have the uncomfortable and very unpopular role of telling the people that such treaties will do no good, and that they should repent instead and thus qualify for the help of the Lord.

Isaiah will also prophesy of the coming destruction of Syria and Israel (verse 4).

As the chapter begins, we see Isaiah's use of imagery and symbolism to carry his message. In verse 1, he is told that he and Sister Isaiah will have a son. They are to give him a name (verse 3) that means that enemy armies will carry swift destruction upon the cities of Judah (except Jerusalem).

1 Moreover **the Lord said unto me, Take thee a great** [*large*] **roll** [*scroll*]**, and write in it** with a man's pen **concerning Maher-shalal-hash-baz** [*"to speed to the spoil, he hasteneth the prey"—see footnote 1d in your Bible*].

Isaiah invites two men to witness this prophecy, as it is written upon the scroll.

2 And I [*Isaiah*] took unto me faithful **witnesses** to record, **Uriah** the priest, and **Zechariah** the son of Jeberechiah.

3 And I went unto the prophetess [*Isaiah's wife*]; and she conceived, and bare a son. **Then said the Lord to me, Call his name Maher-shalal-hash-baz.**

4 For **before the child shall have knowledge to cry, My father, and my mother** [*before their son is old enough to talk*]**, the riches of Damascus** [*Syria*] and **the spoil** [*wealth*] **of Samaria** [*northern Israel; the ten tribes*] **shall be taken away before the king of Assyria** [*before Isaiah's son is old enough to say "Daddy," "Mommy," Assyria will attack and ravage northern Israel and Syria*].

Now the topic turns to the people of Judah, with Jerusalem as their capital city.

5 The Lord spake also unto me again, saying,

6 **Forasmuch as** [*since*] **this people** [*Judah, Jerusalem*] **refuseth the waters of Shiloah** [*the gentle help of Christ, John 4:14*] that go softly, **and rejoice in Rezin** [*heed Syria instead of the Lord*] **and Remaliah's son** [*northern Israel's king*];

7 Now **therefore**, behold, **the Lord bringeth up upon them the waters of the river, strong** [*terrifying*] **and many** [*armies and so forth*], even the king of Assyria, and all his glory [*pomp fanfare and ceremony of coming enemy armies*]: and **he shall come up over all his channels, and go over all his banks** [*you'll be "flooded" with Assyrians*]:

8 And **he** [*Assyria*] **shall pass through Judah**; he shall overflow and go over, he shall reach even to the neck [*to Jerusalem*]; and the stretching out of his wings shall fill the breadth of thy land, O Immanuel [*or, the land of the future birth of Christ*].

NOTES

9 ¶ **Associate yourselves** [*if you form political alliances for protection rather than turning to God*], **O ye people, and ye shall be broken in pieces**; and **give ear, all ye of far countries** [*listen up, foreign nations who might rise against Judah*]: **gird yourselves** [*prepare for war against Judah*], **and ye shall be broken in pieces;** gird yourselves, and ye shall be broken in pieces [*note that "broken in pieces" is repeated three times for emphasis; repeating something three times indicates the Hebrew superlative*].

Perhaps you have noticed that Isaiah makes considerable use of repetition as a means of emphasizing his messages. This is a common part of the "manner of prophesying among the Jews" (2 Nephi 25:1). We see an example of this type of repetition in verse 10, next.

10 **Take counsel together, and it shall come to nought** [*your plans to destroy Judah will not succeed ultimately*]; **speak the word** [*make decrees*], **and it shall not stand**: for God is with us [*Judah won't be destroyed completely*].

Next, beginning with verse 11, Isaiah is given the difficult task of taking a stand opposite to that which was popular among the people. It was politically popular among the people at this time to advocate making alliances for safety with other nations, especially Assyria. Isaiah tells them this is a mistake.

11 ¶ For **the Lord spake thus to me** [*Isaiah*] **with a strong hand** [*firmly*], **and instructed me that I should not walk in the way of this people** [*that I should not go along with popular opinion among the people of Judah*], **saying,**

12 **Say ye not, A confederacy** [*be allies with Assyria*], to all them to whom this people shall say, A confederacy; **neither fear ye their fear, nor be afraid.** [*"Isaiah, don't endorse Judah's plan for confederacy with Assyria. Don't tell them what they want to hear."*]

13 **Sanctify the Lord of hosts himself; and let him be your fear, and let him be your dread.** [*"Isaiah, you rely on the Lord, not public approval."*]

14 **And he** [*the Lord*] **shall be for a sanctuary** [*for you, Isaiah*]; **but for a stone of stumbling and for a rock of offence to** [*the Lord will stand in the way of*] **both the houses of Israel** [*Israel (the northern ten tribes) and Judah*], for a gin [*a trap*] and for **a snare to the inhabitants of Jerusalem.**

Note Isaiah's great skill with words as he describes the downfall of Judah with hammer-like driving force, next, in verse 15.

15 And many among them [*Judah*] shall **stumble**, and **fall**, and be **broken**, and be **snared**, and be **taken**.

16 **Bind up the testimony** [*record your testimony against these wicked people, Isaiah*], seal the law among my disciples [*followers*].

Next, in verses 17–18, Isaiah pledges his loyalty to the Lord, in the face of much public opposition.

17 **And I** [*Isaiah*] **will wait upon the Lord** [*I will trust the Lord*], **that hideth his face from the house of Jacob** [*who has had to withdraw His blessings from the house of Israel*], and I will look for him [*will watch for His blessings and guidance in my life*].

18 **Behold, I and the children whom the Lord hath given me are for signs and for wonders in Israel from the Lord of hosts**, which dwelleth in mount Zion [*in other words, Isaiah and his family serve as a witness of the Lord among these Israelites*].

Many people turn to the occult for messages from beyond the veil. It seems to be easier to do this than to repent and gain revelation from the Lord. Isaiah speaks of this turning to the dark side in verse 19, next.

19 ¶ And **when they** [*the wicked*] **shall say unto you, Seek unto them** [*spiritualists, mediums, and so forth*] **that have familiar spirits, and unto wizards that peep** [*into their crystal balls and so forth*], **and that mutter: should not a people seek unto their God?** for the living to the dead [*why consult the dead on behalf of the living*]?

20 **To the law and to the testimony** [*the scriptures*]: **if they** [*sorcerers, wizards, mediums, and so forth*] **speak not according to this word** [*the scriptures*], it is because there *is no light in them.*

Next, Isaiah foretells what will happen to these people if they continue in the direction they are heading.

21 **And they** [*Israel, who will be taken into captivity*] **shall pass through it** [*the land*], **hardly bestead** [*severely distressed*] **and hungry**: and it shall come to pass, that when they shall be hungry, **they shall fret themselves** [*become enraged*], **and curse their king and their God, and look upward** [*be cocky, defiant; not humbled by their troubles*].

22 **And they shall look unto the earth** [*will look around them*]; **and behold** [*see only*] **trouble and darkness, dimness of anguish** [*gloom*]; **and they shall be driven to darkness** [*thrust into utter despair; spiritual darkness as the result of wickedness*].

ISAIAH 9

Selection: all verses

This is a continuation of the topic in chapter 8. King Ahaz of Judah ignored the Lord's counsel and made an alliance with Assyria anyway. Symbolism here can include that Assyria would represent the devil and his evil, prideful ways. King Ahaz could symbolize foolish and wicked people who make alliances with the devil or his evil ways and naively think that they are thus protected from destruction spiritually and often physically.

In this chapter, Isaiah gives one of the most famous and beautiful of all his messianic prophecies. He prophesies that Christ will come. Handel's "Messiah" puts some of this chapter to magnificent music. You will likely recognize verse 6.

Verse 1 is positioned as the last verse of chapter 8 in the Hebrew Bible. It serves as a transition from the end of chapter 8 to the topic of the Savior's mortal mission, in chapter 9.

Verse 1 is somewhat complex and basically prophesies that the Savior will come to earth and prepare a way for people to escape from spiritual darkness and despair. It helps to know that two of the twelve tribes of Israel, the tribes of Zebulun and Naphtali, were located in

NOTES

what became known as Galilee in the Savior's day. Thus, verse 1 says that the humbling of haughty Israel, which took place when the Assyrians swept down upon them, will someday be softened when the Savior walks and teaches there during His mortal mission.

1 **Nevertheless the dimness** [*the despair and spiritual darkness referred to in 8:22*] **shall not be such as was in her vexation** [*distress*], **when at the first** [*Assyrian attacks in Isaiah's day*] **he lightly afflicted** [*NIV: "humbled"*] **the land of Zebulun** [*in northern Israel*] **and the land of Naphtali** [*in northern Israel*], **and afterward did more grievously afflict** [*Hebrew: gloriously bless; German: bring honor to*] **her** [*NIV: Galilee*] by the way of the sea, beyond Jordan, **in Galilee** of the nations [*blessed her via Jesus walking and teaching in Galilee*].

Next, Isaiah speaks prophetically of the future as if it has already happened. As we mentioned before, this was a common form of prophesying among the Jews.

2 **The people that walked in darkness** [*apostasy and captivity*] **have seen a great light** [*the Savior and His teachings*]: they that dwell in the land of the shadow of death, **upon them hath the light shined.**

3 **Thou hast multiplied the nation, and** not [*"not" is a mistake in translation and doesn't belong here; see 2 Nephi 19:3 where it is rendered correctly in this chapter of Isaiah as found in the Book of Mormon*] **increased the joy**: they joy before thee according to the joy in harvest, and as men rejoice when they divide the spoil [*Christ and His faithful followers will ultimately triumph*].

4 **For thou hast broken the yoke of his burden** [*Thou hast set them free*], and the staff of his shoulder, the rod [*symbolic of power*] of his oppressor, as in the day of Midian [*just like with Gideon and his three hundred; Judges 7:22*].

Next, Isaiah looks ahead to the destruction of the wicked at the time of the Second Coming and points out that their destruction will be different than that found in a normal battle.

5 For **every battle of the warrior** [*of man against man*] **is with confused noise, and garments rolled in blood** [*normal battles involve much noise and bloodshed*]; **but this** [*the final freedom from the wicked*] **shall be with burning** and fuel of fire [*the burning at the Second Coming*].

6 **For unto us a child** [*Christ*] **is born, unto us a son is given: and the government shall be upon his shoulder: and his name shall be called Wonderful, Counsellor, The mighty God, The everlasting Father, The Prince of Peace.**

7 **Of the increase of his government and peace there shall be no end, upon the throne of David** [*during the Millennium, Christ will rule on earth*], and upon his kingdom, to order it, and to establish it with judgment [*fairness*] and with justice from henceforth even for ever. The zeal [*energy, power*] of the Lord of hosts will perform this.

The topic now switches back to Isaiah's day as he prophesies of the pride and wickedness that will continue to plague the northern ten tribes, often referred to at this point in history as "Israel" or "northern Israel." You will see that Isaiah uses several different ways of referring to the ten tribes.

8 **The Lord sent a word into Jacob** [*Israel*], and it hath lighted upon Israel.

9 And **all the people shall know**, even Ephraim [*northern Israel*] and the inhabitant of Samaria [*northern Israel*], **that say in the pride and stoutness of heart**,

Next, in verse 10, Isaiah points out how full of pride rebellious Israel is. In effect, they boast that God's punishments won't humble them. They don't need God and they are not afraid of Him. They are basically saying to the Lord, "Go ahead and tear down our cities. We will simply rebuild them and with better materials than ever!"

10 **The bricks are fallen down, but we will build with hewn stones** [*boastful northern Israel claims they can't be destroyed but would simply rebuild with better materials than before*]: **the sycomores are cut down, but we will change them into cedars** [*we will rebuild with better wood than before*].

11 **Therefore the Lord shall set** up the adversaries of Rezin [*Syria*] **against him** [*Israel*], and join his enemies together [*the enemies of Syria will also come against Israel*];

One of the most important and consistent messages of Isaiah is that the wicked can still repent. We see this sweet message at the end of verse 12, next.

Major Message

The wicked can still repent. It is not too late for these wicked Israelites.

12 **The Syrians before** [*on the east*], and **the Philistines behind** [*on the west*]; **and they shall devour Israel with open mouth.** For all this his anger is not turned away, **but his hand is stretched out still** [*the Lord will still let you repent if you will turn to Him. Compare with Jacob 6:4–5*].

Sadly, as Isaiah prophesies next, these people refuse the offer of freedom through repentence.

13 ¶ For **the people turneth not unto him** [*the Lord*] that smiteth them [*who is punishing them*], **neither do they seek the Lord of hosts**.

14 **Therefore the Lord will cut off from Israel head** [*leaders*] and **tail** [*false prophets*], **branch** [*palm branch, meaning triumph and victory in Hebrew culture*] and **rush** [*reed, meaning people low in social status in the Hebrew culture*], in one day [*it will happen fast*].

Next, Isaiah defines some of the terms he used in verse 14, above, which were familiar to people in his day but not to us.

15 **The ancient and honourable, he is the head**; and the [*false*] **prophet that teacheth lies, he is the tail.**

16 For **the leaders of this people cause them to err; and they that are led of them are destroyed**.

Verse 17, next, shows us that the entire society was corrupt through and through.

17 **Therefore the Lord shall have no joy** [*pleasure, satisfaction*] **in their young men, neither shall have mercy on their fatherless and widows** [*all levels of society have gone bad*]: for **every one is an hypocrite** and an **evildoer**, and **every mouth speaketh folly** [*evil, corruption*]. For all this his anger is not turned away, but **his hand is stretched out still** [*please repent!*].

18 For **wickedness burneth as the fire** [*wickedness destroys like wildfire*]: it shall devour the **briers and thorns** [*the people of apostate Israel*], and **shall kindle in the thickets of the forest** [*destroy the people*], and they shall mount up like the lifting up of smoke.

19 **Through the wrath of the Lord of hosts is the land darkened** [*awful conditions*], and the people shall be as the fuel of the fire: **no man shall spare his brother**.

Wickedness inevitably destroys a society and nation. Verse 20, next, describes the desperate conditions that eventually overtake a wicked people.

20 And **he** [*the wicked*] **shall snatch on the right hand, and be hungry**; and he shall eat on the left hand, and **they shall not be satisfied: they shall eat every man the flesh of his own arm** [*the wicked will turn on each other*]:

Verse 21, next, speaks of the civil wars between the northern ten tribes and the people of Judah, which Isaiah has been discussing.

21 **Manasseh, Ephraim** [*Israel, the ten tribes*]; and Ephraim, Manasseh: and they together **shall be against Judah**. For all this his anger is not turned away, **but his hand is stretched out still** [*you can still repent; please do!*]

ISAIAH 10

Selection: all verses

In the heading to chapter 10 in your Bible, you find the phrase, "Destruction of Assyria is a type of destruction of the wicked at the Second Coming." The word "type" means something that is symbolic of something else. For example, both Joseph who was sold into Egypt and Isaac were "types" of Christ; in other words, many things that happened to them were symbolic of the Savior. The following charts show some of the ways in which these great prophets were "types" of Christ:

Joseph in Egypt	Christ
Was sold for the price of a common slave	Was sold for the price of a common slave
Was thirty years old when he began his mission as prime minister to save his people	Was thirty years old when He began His formal mission to save His people
Gathered food for seven years to save his people	Used seven "days" to create the earth in which to offer salvation to us
Forgave his persecutors	Forgave His persecutors

Isaac	Christ
Was the only begotten of Abraham and Sarah	Is the Only Begotten of the Father
Was to be sacrificed by his father	Was allowed to be sacrificed by His Father
Carried the wood for his sacrifice	Carried the cross for His sacrifice
Volunteered to give his life (Abraham was too old to restrain him.)	Gave His life voluntarily

Another example of a "type" of Christ is found in Leviticus 14 where the priest is a "type" of Christ as he presents the privilege of being cleansed to the leper (who is a "type" of all sinners—that is to say, the leper can be symbolic of the need we all have to be cleansed from sin). We will include Leviticus 14:1–9 here as a brief lesson on the power of understanding the use of "types" in the scriptures.

Leviticus 14:1–9

1 And the LORD spake unto Moses, saying,

2 This shall be **the law of the leper** [*the rules for being made clean; symbolic of serious sin and great need for help and cleansing*] **in the day of his cleansing** [*symbolic of the desire to be made spiritually clean and pure*]: **He shall be brought unto the priest** [*authorized servant of God; bishop, stake president, who holds the keys of authority to act for God*]:

3 And **the priest shall go forth out of the camp** [*the person with leprosy did not have fellowship with the Lord's people and was required to live outside the main camp of the children of Israel; the bishop symbolically goes out of the way to help sinners who want to repent*]; and **the priest shall look, and, behold,** *if* **the plague of leprosy be healed in the leper** [*the bishop serves as a judge to see if the repentant sinner is ready to return to full membership privileges*];

4 Then shall the priest command to take for him that is to be cleansed [*the person who has repented*] **two birds** [*one represents the Savior during His mortal mission, the other represents the person who has repented*] alive *and* clean, and **cedar wood** [*symbolic of the cross*], and **scarlet** [*associated with mocking Christ before his crucifixion, Mark 15:17*], and **hyssop** [*associated with Christ on the cross, John 19:29*]:

5 And the priest shall command that **one of the birds** [*symbolic of the Savior*] be **killed in an earthen vessel** [*Christ was sent to earth to die for us*] **over running water** [*Christ offers "living water," the gospel of Jesus Christ—John 7:37–38—which cleanses us when we come unto Him*]:

6 **As for the living bird** [*representing the person who has repented*], **he** [*the priest; symbolic of the bishop, stake president, one who holds the keys of judging*] **shall take it** [*the living bird*], **and the cedar wood**, and the **scarlet**, and the **hyssop** [*all associated with the Atonement*], **and shall dip them and the living bird in the blood of the bird** *that was* **killed over the running water** [*representing the cleansing power of the Savior's blood, which was shed for us*]:

7 And he shall **sprinkle upon him that is to be cleansed from the leprosy** [*symbolically, being cleansed from sin*] **seven times** [*seven is the number that, in biblical numeric symbolism, represents completeness, perfection*], **and shall pronounce him clean** [*he has been forgiven*], **and shall let the living bird** [*the person who has repented*] **loose into**

the open field [*representing the wide open opportunities again available in the kingdom of God for the person who truly repents*].

8 And **he that is to be cleansed shall wash his clothes** [*symbolic of cleaning up your life from sinful ways and pursuits—compare with Isaiah 1:16*], and **shave off all his hair** [*symbolic of becoming like a newborn baby; "born again;" fresh start*], and **wash himself in water** [*symbolic of baptism*], **that he may be clean** [*cleansed from sin*]: and **after that he shall come into the camp** [*rejoin the Lord's covenant people*], and shall tarry abroad out of his tent seven days.

9 But it shall be on the seventh day, that he shall shave all his hair off his head and his beard and his eyebrows, even all his hair he shall shave off [*symbolic of being "born again"*]: and he shall wash his clothes [*clean up his life*], also he shall wash his flesh in water [*symbolic of baptism*], and he shall be clean [*a simple fact, namely that we can truly be cleansed and healed by the Savior's Atonement*].

Having considered the use of "types" (sometimes called "types and shadows") in the scriptures, we will now proceed with chapter 10 and watch as Assyria is used as a "type" of the destruction of the wicked at the Second Coming.

1 **Woe unto them that decree unrighteous decrees** [*unrighteous laws*], and that write grievousness [*oppression*] which they have prescribed;

2 **To turn aside the needy from judgment** [*fair treatment*], and to **take away the right from the poor of my people, that widows may be their prey** [*victims*], and **that they may rob the fatherless!**

3 And **what will ye do in the day of visitation** [*punishment*], and in the desolation which shall come from far [*from Assyria*]? to whom will ye flee for help? and where will ye leave your glory [*wealth and so forth*]?

4 **Without me** [*the Lord*] **they shall bow down under the prisoners** [*huddle among the prisoners*], and **they shall fall under the slain**. For all this his anger is not turned away, but **his hand is stretched out still** [*you can still repent*].

Have you noticed how often, in Isaiah's writings, the Lord says that "His hand is stretched out still"? It means that they can still repent. This is one of the major themes in the Lord's teachings through His prophet, Isaiah. We will quote from the Book of Mormon to verify that this is the meaning of that phrase:

Jacob 6:4–5

4 And how merciful is our God unto us, for he remembereth the house of Israel, both roots and branches; and **he stretches forth his hands unto them all the day long**; and they are a stiffnecked and a gainsaying people [*always opposing God*]; but as many as will not harden their hearts shall be saved in the kingdom of God.

5 Wherefore, my beloved brethren, I beseech of you in words of soberness that ye would **repent**, and come with full purpose of heart, and cleave unto God as he cleaveth unto you. And **while his arm of mercy is extended towards you** in the light of the day, harden not your hearts.

5 ¶ **O Assyrian, the rod of mine anger** [*the tool of destruction used by the Lord to "hammer" Israel*], and the staff in their hand is mine indignation.

NOTES

6 **I will send him** [*Assyria*] **against an hypocritical nation** [*Israel*], and against the people of my wrath will I give him a charge, to take the spoil, and **to take the prey, and to tread them** [*Israel*] **down** like the mire of the streets.

7 **Howbeit** [*however*] **he meaneth not so**, neither doth his heart think so [*king of Assyria doesn't realize he is a tool in God's hand, thinks he's very important on his own*]; but it is in his heart to destroy and cut off nations not a few.

Isaiah depicts the boasting and bragging of the prideful king of Assyria, in verse 8, next.

8 For **he** [*Assyrian king*] **saith** [*brags*], Are not my princes [*commanders*] altogether kings [*just like kings in other countries*]?

Next, Isaiah depicts the king boasting about cities his armies have already conquered.

9 Is not **Calno** as **Carchemish**? is not **Hamath** as **Arpad**? is not **Samaria** as **Damascus?** [*Assyria has already taken these cities.*]

Next, the king boastfully declares that the gods of the above cities were powerless to save them, and they were more powerful than the God of Judah and Israel.

10 As my hand hath found the kingdoms of **the idols, and** whose **graven images did excel** [*were more powerful than*] **them of Jerusalem and of Samaria**;

11 **Shall I not, as I have done unto Samaria and her idols, so do to Jerusalem and her idols** [*a boast; I'll do the same to Jerusalem*]?

In verse 12, next, Isaiah explains what the Lord will do to the king of Assyria and his armies, when He is through using him to punish His rebellious covenant people.

12 Wherefore it shall come to pass, that **when the Lord hath performed his whole work upon mount Zion and on Jerusalem, I will punish** the fruit of the stout heart of **the king of Assyria**, and the glory of his high looks [*when I'm through using Assyria against Israel, then Assyria will get its just punishments*].

13 **For he** [*Assyrian king*] **saith, By the strength of my hand I have done it**, and by my wisdom; for I am prudent: and I have removed the bounds of the people, and have robbed their treasures, and I have put down the inhabitants like a valiant man [*bragging*]:

14 **And my hand hath found as a nest the riches of the people**: and as one gathereth eggs that are left, have I gathered all the earth; and **there was none that moved the wing, or opened the mouth, or peeped** [*everybody is afraid of me!*].

15 **Shall the axe** [*Assyria*] **boast itself against him** [*the Lord*] **that heweth therewith** [*is it reasonable for the ax to claim that it swings itself*]? or shall the saw magnify itself against him that shaketh it [*uses it*]? as if the rod should shake itself against them that lift it up, or as if the staff should lift up itself, as if it were no wood [*how foolish for people to say they don't need the Lord*].

NOTES

_____
_____
_____
_____
_____
_____
_____
_____
_____
_____
_____
_____
_____
_____
_____
_____
_____
_____
_____
_____
_____
_____
_____
_____
_____
_____
_____
_____
_____
_____

16 **Therefore shall the Lord, the Lord of hosts, send among his fat ones** [*Assyria's powerful armies*] **leanness** [*trouble is coming*]; and under his [*Assyria's*] glory **he** [*Christ*] **shall kindle a burning like the burning of a fire** [*the fate of Assyria*].

17 And **the light of Israel** [*Christ*] **shall be for a fire**, and his Holy One [*Christ*] for a flame: and **it shall burn and devour his** [*Assyria's*] **thorns and his briers** [*armies*] **in one day** [*Example: 185,000 Assyrians died of devastating sickness in one night as they prepared to attack Jerusalem; see 2 Kings 19:35–37*];

18 **And shall consume the glory of his forest** [*symbolic of his armies, people*], and of his fruitful field, both soul and body: and they shall be **as when a standardbearer fainteth** [*as when the last flag-carrying soldier falls and the flag with him, the Assyrians will waste away, be destroyed*].

Next, Isaiah uses an interesting image to foretell that the Assyrians will be reduced to few people, so few that a small child who is just learning how to count and write numbers could count them and write the number down.

19 **And the rest of the trees** [*people*] **of his forest shall be few, that a child may write them**.

Attention now turns to the remnant of Israel remaining after the Assyrians are through with them. It is a prophecy of the gathering of Israel in the last days.

20 ¶ And it shall come to pass **in that day** [*the last days*], that **the remnant of Israel**, and such as are escaped of the house of Jacob [*Israel*], **shall no more again stay** [*depend*] **upon him** [*Assyria; symbolic of Satan and his evil front organizations*] that smote them; **but shall stay upon the Lord, the Holy One of Israel, in truth**.

21 **The remnant shall return**, even the remnant of Jacob, **unto the mighty God** [*1. A remnant remains in the land after Assyrian destruction. 2. A future righteous remnant*].

22 For though thy people Israel be as the sand of the sea, yet **a remnant of them shall return**: the consumption decreed [*at end of the world*] shall overflow with righteousness [*Christ; the glory of the Savior will consume the wicked at the Second Coming; see Doctrine & Covenants 5:19; 2 Nephi 12:10*].

23 **For the Lord God of hosts** [*Jehovah, Jesus Christ*] **shall make a consumption**, even determined, in the midst of all the land.

The topic now turns again to the fate of the Assyrians.

24 ¶ Therefore thus saith the Lord God of hosts, O my people that dwellest in Zion, **be not afraid of the Assyrian: he shall smite thee with a rod, and shall lift up his staff against thee**, after the manner of Egypt [*like Egypt did in earlier times*].

25 **For yet a very little while**, and the indignation shall cease, and mine anger in their destruction [*then the Assyrian kingdom will fall via the anger of the Lord*].

26 And **the Lord of hosts shall stir up a scourge for him** according to the slaughter of Midian at the rock of Oreb: and as his rod was upon the sea [*the parting of the*

NOTES

Red Sea], so shall he lift it up after the manner of Egypt [*God will stop Assyria like he stopped the Egyptians*].

27 And it shall come to pass **in that day**, that **his burden** [*Assyria's rule; Satan's oppression*] **shall be taken away from off thy shoulder**, and his yoke from off thy neck, and **the yoke shall be destroyed because of the anointing** [*the Savior*].

Beginning with verse 28, next, Isaiah foretells how the Assyrian armies will gobble up city after city, and will come right up to the gates of Jerusalem, and then will be stopped in their tracks by the Lord. What remains of their army will then go home.

Isaiah speaks of the future as if it has already happened. He is a master at building dramatic tension.

28 **He** [*Assyria*] **is come to Aiath**, he is passed **to Migron**: at **Michmash** he hath laid up his carriages [*horses and chariots are symbolic of military might in biblical symbolism*].

29 They are gone over the passage: they have taken up their lodging at **Geba**; **Ramah** is afraid; **Gibeah** of Saul is fled.

30 Lift up thy voice, O daughter of **Gallim**: cause it to be heard unto **Laish**, O poor **Anathoth** [*Jeremiah's hometown; see Jeremiah 1:1*].

31 **Madmenah** is removed; the inhabitants of **Gebim** gather themselves to flee.

32 As **yet shall he** [*Assyria*] **remain at Nob** that day [*Assyria will take city after city, getting closer and closer to Jerusalem until they come to Nob, just outside Jerusalem*]: **he shall shake his hand** [*threaten*] **against** the mount of the daughter of Zion [*Jerusalem*], the hill of **Jerusalem**.

33 **Behold, the Lord, the Lord of hosts, shall lop** [*cut off*] **the bough with terror** [*when the Assyrian armies get right to Jerusalem, the Lord will "trim them down to size," "clip their wings," and stop them in their tracks*]: **and the high ones of stature** [*leaders of Assyrian armies*] **shall be hewn down, and the haughty shall be humbled.**

34 **And he shall cut down the thickets of the forest** [*the Assyrians*] **with iron** [*an axe*], and Lebanon shall fall by a mighty one [*see 2 Kings 19:32*].

ISAIAH 11

Selection: all verses

Joseph Smith recorded that Moroni quoted this chapter, saying that it was about to be fulfilled. We find this statement in the Pearl of Great Price, Joseph Smith—History, as follows:

Joseph Smith–History 1:40

40 In addition to these, **he quoted the eleventh chapter of Isaiah, saying that it was about to be fulfilled.** He quoted also the third chapter of Acts, twenty-second and twenty-third verses, precisely as they stand in our New Testament. He said that that prophet was Christ; but the day had not yet come when "they who would not hear his voice should be cut off from among the people," but soon would come.

NOTES

In Isaiah, chapter 11, we are taught that powerful leaders will come forth in the last days to lead the gathering of Israel. We are instructed in Christlike qualities of leadership. We will be shown the peace that will abound during the Millennium and Isaiah will also teach about the gathering of Israel in the last days.

1 And **there shall come forth a rod** [*Hebrew: twig or branch; Doctrine & Covenants 113:3–4 defines this "rod" as "a servant in the hands of Christ"*] **out of the stem** [*root*] **of Jesse** [*Christ—see heading to this chapter in your Bible*], and a Branch shall grow out of his roots:

Perhaps, the imagery here in verse 1 grows out of the last two verses of chapter 10, where the wicked leaders end up, in effect, as "stumps" and have been destroyed. In the last days, new, righteous, powerful leaders will be brought forth to replace the "stumps" of the past and will have their origins in the "roots" of Christ. Roots can symbolically represent being solid and firmly rooted in God.

Next, we see a description of Christlike qualities of leadership.

2 And the spirit of the Lord shall rest upon him, the **spirit of wisdom** and **understanding**, the spirit of **counsel** and **might**, the spirit of **knowledge** and of the **fear of** [*respect, honoring of*] **the Lord**;

3 And shall make him of **quick understanding in the fear of the Lord**: and **he shall not judge after the sight of his eyes, neither reprove after the hearing of his ears**:

Verse 4, next, makes a transition into describing powers held exclusively by the Savior.

4 But **with righteousness shall he judge the poor**, and **reprove with equity** for the meek of the earth: and he shall **smite the earth** with the rod of his mouth, and with the breath of his lips shall he **slay the wicked**.

5 And **righteousness shall be the girdle of his loins** [*He will be clothed in righteousness*], and faithfulness the girdle of his reins [*desires, thoughts*].

Next, we are taken into the Millennium, where we are shown conditions of peace.

6 **The wolf also shall dwell with the lamb,** and **the leopard shall lie down with the kid** [*young goat*]; and **the calf and the young lion** and the fatling together; **and a little child shall lead** [*herd*] **them** [*Millennial conditions*].

7 And **the cow and the bear shall feed** [*graze*]; their young ones shall lie down together: and **the lion shall eat straw like the ox**.

8 And **the sucking** [*nursing*] **child shall play on the hole of the asp** [*viper*], and the weaned child shall put his hand on the cockatrice' [*venomous serpent's*] den.

9 **They shall not hurt nor destroy in all my holy mountain** [*throughout the earth*]: for **the earth shall be full of the knowledge of** [*Hebrew: "devotion to"*] **the Lord**, as the waters cover the sea.

10 **And in that day there shall be a root of Jesse** [*probably Joseph Smith—see Doctrine and Covenants Student Manual for Institutes of Religion of the Church, page 284*], **which shall stand for an ensign** [*a rallying point for gathering*] of the people; **to it shall the Gentiles seek**: and his rest shall be glorious.

11 And it shall come to pass in that day, that **the Lord shall set his hand again the second time** [*dual meaning: after Babylonian captivity; also last days*] **to recover** [*gather*] **the remnant of his people**, which shall be left, from Assyria, and from Egypt, and from Pathros, and from Cush, and from Elam, and from Shinar, and from Hamath, and from the islands of the sea [*in other words, Israel will be gathered throughout the earth*].

12 And **he shall set up an ensign** [*the Church in the last days*] for the nations, **and shall assemble the outcasts of Israel, and gather together the dispersed of Judah** from the four corners of the earth.

13 The envy also of Ephraim shall depart, and the adversaries of Judah shall be cut off: **Ephraim shall not envy Judah, and Judah shall not vex Ephraim** [*the United States and others will work with the Jews*].

14 **But they** [*the Jews with Ephraim's help*] **shall fly upon the shoulders of the Philistines toward the west** [*will attack the western slopes that were Philistine territory*]; **they shall spoil them of the east** together: they shall lay their hand upon Edom and Moab; and the children of Ammon shall obey them [*the Jews will be powerful in the last days rather than easy prey for their enemies*].

15 **And the Lord shall utterly destroy the tongue of the Egyptian sea** [*perhaps meaning that the productivity of the Nile River will be ruined; see Isaiah 19:5–10*]; **and with his mighty wind shall he shake his hand over the river** [*perhaps the river referred to in Revelation 16:12; symbolically, the Euphrates, representing preparation for the Battle of Armageddon*], and shall smite it in the seven streams, and make men go over dryshod.

16 And **there shall be an highway** [*God will prepare a way for them to return; gathering*] **for the remnant of his people**, which shall be left, from Assyria; like as it was to Israel in the day that he came up out of the land of Egypt.

ISAIAH 12

Selection: all verses

This short but beautiful chapter refers to the Millennium. It describes the faithful who survive the destruction at the Second Coming of Christ as praising the Lord and rejoicing at the salvation that has come to them.

1 And **in that day** [*during the Millennial reign of the Savior*] **thou** [*Israel*] **shalt say**, O Lord, I will praise thee: though thou wast angry with me [*in times past, because of my rebellions*], thine anger is turned away, and thou comfortedst me.

2 Behold, God is my salvation; I will trust, and not be afraid: for **the Lord JEHOVAH** [*Jesus Christ*] **is my strength and my song**: he also is become my salvation.

NOTES

_____
_____
_____
_____
_____
_____
_____
_____
_____
_____
_____
_____
_____
_____
_____
_____
_____
_____
_____
_____
_____
_____
_____
_____
_____
_____
_____
_____
_____

3 **Therefore** [*because Christ is your King during the Millennium*] **with joy shall ye draw water** [*"living water"; see John 4:10, 7:38–39*] **out of the wells of salvation.**

4 And **in that day shall ye say, Praise the Lord**, call upon his name, declare his doings among the people, make mention that his name is exalted.

5 **Sing unto the Lord; for he hath done excellent things**: this is known in all the earth [*knowledge of the gospel will permeate the whole earth during the Millennium*].

6 **Cry out** [*sing it out with great joy*] **and shout**, thou inhabitant of Zion [*the people who dwell on earth during the Millennium*]: **for great is the Holy One of Israel** [*Christ*] **in the midst of thee** [*the Savior will be on earth among the people during the Millennium*].

Isaiah 13–14; 24–30; 35

"A Marvellous Work and a Wonder"

In Isaiah 13, you will see that in the last days—our day—the Lord will gather His righteous armies to fight the forces of evil. We are seeing this now and are participating in it as we strive to remain solidly on the covenant path. In chapter 14, Isaiah teaches us about the premortal rebellion of Lucifer and his being cast out of heaven. In chapters 24–30, Isaiah will teach us many things, including the destruction of the wicked at the Second Coming, the restoration of the Church, the resurrection of the Savior, the successful gathering of Israel in the last days, and how the Holy Ghost works with us "line upon line, here a little and there a little." Chapter 29 is a major prophecy about the coming forth of the Book of Mormon. You may find yourself somewhat familiar with it. Chapter 30 is a prophecy of the scattering of Israel and then the gathering of Israel in the last days. We are watching this now. As you study chapter 35, you will see that Isaiah prophesies the restoration of the Church and the gathering of Israel in the last days along with the joy and happiness of those who participate in it.

ISAIAH 13

NOTES

Selection: all verses

In chapter 10, the destruction of Assyria was described as a "type" of (meaning "symbolic of") the destruction of the wicked at the Second Coming of Christ. We discussed the definition of "type" in the notes at the beginning of that chapter. In this chapter, the destruction of Babylon is likewise a "type" of the destruction of Satan's kingdom at the time of the Second Coming.

It will be helpful for you to understand that the ancient city of Babylon was a huge city full of wickedness and evil. Over time, Babylon has come to symbolize the wickedness of the world. A brief description of Babylon is given in your Bible Dictionary under "Babylon" as follows (bold added for emphasis):

BIBLE DICTIONARY: BABYLON

The capital of Babylonia. According to Gen. 10:8–10 it was founded by Nimrod, and was one of the oldest cities of the land of Shinar; in 11:1–9 we have the record of the Tower of Babel and the "Confusion of Tongues." (See Ether 1:3–5, 34–35.) During the Assyrian supremacy (see *Assyria*) it became part of that empire, and was destroyed by Sennacherib. After the downfall of Assyria, Babylon became Nebuchadnezzar's capital. He built an enormous city, of which the ruins still remain. The city was square, and the Euphrates ran through the middle of it. According to Herodotus **the walls were 56 miles in circumference, 335 feet high, and 85 feet wide**. A large part of the city consisted of beautiful parks and gardens. The chief building was the famous temple of Bel. Inscriptions that have been recently deciphered show that the Babylonians had accounts of the Creation and the Deluge in many ways similar to those given in the book of Genesis. Other inscriptions contain accounts of events referred to in the Bible histories of the kingdoms of Israel and Judaea, and also give valuable information as to the chronology of these periods.

You can find a brief sketch of the history of the Babylonian empire in the Bible Dictionary, under "Assyria."

In verse 1, Isaiah tells us that this prophecy is essentially a message of doom to Babylon, which he saw in vision. It applies to ancient Babylon, as a nation, and to the "Babylon" of evil in the last days before the Second Coming.

NOTES

_____
_____
_____
_____
_____
_____
_____
_____
_____
_____
_____
_____
_____
_____
_____
_____
_____
_____
_____
_____
_____
_____
_____
_____

1 **The burden of Babylon** [*message of doom to Babylon*], which Isaiah the son of Amoz did see.

In verses 2–5, next, Isaiah explains that The Lord will gather his righteous forces (as stated in verse 4) in the last days to do battle with the forces of evil (Babylon).

2 **Lift ye up a banner upon the high mountain** [*raise up an ensign to the righteous*], **exalt** [*raise*] **the voice unto them** [*the righteous*], **shake the hand** [*wave to them; signal to them*], **that they may go into the gates of the nobles** [*gather with the righteous*].

Next, Isaiah speaks of the future as if it had already happened. The Book of Mormon makes a significant change to verse 3, next.

3 **I have commanded my sanctified ones** [*the righteous who are worthy to be in the presence of the Lord*], **I have also called my mighty ones for mine anger** [*2 Nephi 23:3 adds "is not upon them"*], **even them that rejoice in my highness** [*exalted and glorious status*].

4 **The noise of a multitude in the mountains** [*gathering*], like as of **a great people**; a tumultuous noise of the **kingdoms** of **nations gathered together**: **the Lord of hosts mustereth the host of the battle** [*the Lord rallies the righteous together to do battle with evil*].

5 **They come from a far country, from the end of heaven, even the Lord, and the weapons of his indignation**, to destroy the whole land [*the wicked*].

Next, in effect, Isaiah suggests that the wicked in the last days would do well to begin practicing their howling and screaming in preparation for the Second Coming.

6 ¶ **Howl ye** [*the wicked*]; **for the day of the Lord** [*the Second Coming*] **is at hand** [*is getting close*]; it shall come as a destruction from the Almighty.

7 **Therefore shall all hands be faint** [*hang limp*], **and every man's heart shall melt** [*wicked men's courage will falter*]:

8 And **they shall be afraid**: pangs and sorrows shall take hold of them; they shall be in pain as a woman that travaileth [*like a woman in labor, they can't get out of it now*]: **they shall be amazed** [*will look in fear*] one at another; **their faces shall be as flames** [*burn with shame at the thought of facing the Lord*].

9 **Behold, the day of the Lord** [*Second Coming*] **cometh, cruel** [*as viewed by the wicked*] both with wrath and fierce anger, to lay the land desolate: **and he shall destroy the sinners thereof out of it** [*a purpose of the Second Coming*].

Next, Isaiah mentions a few signs of the times, which will precede the Second Coming.

10 For **the stars of heaven** and the constellations thereof **shall not give their light: the sun shall be darkened** in his going forth, and **the moon shall not** cause her light to **shine**.

NOTES

11 And **I will punish the world for their evil**, and the wicked for their iniquity; and **I will cause the arrogancy of the proud to cease**, and will lay low the haughtiness of the terrible [*will humble the tyrants; typical Isaiah repetition to drive home a point*].

12 **I will make a man** [*survivor of the burning at the Second Coming*] **more precious** [*scarce*] **than fine gold**; even a man than the golden wedge of Ophir [*a land rich in gold, possibly in southern Arabia; in other words, there will be relatively few survivors of the Second Coming because of widespread wickedness at the time*].

13 **Therefore** [*because of gross wickedness on earth*] **I will shake the heavens, and the earth shall remove out of her place**, in the wrath of the Lord of hosts, and in the day of his fierce anger.

In verse 14, next, Isaiah turns his attention back to the nation of Babylon in ancient times. But the prophecy can also refer to the wicked in general. Huge numbers of the wicked, including foreigners, had gravitated to Babylon because of the opportunity for wickedness there.

14 **And it** [*dual meaning: Babylon; also the wicked in general*] **shall be as the chased roe** [*hunted deer*], **and as a sheep that no man taketh up** [*no shepherd, no one defending them*]: **they shall every man turn to his own people, and flee every one into his own land** [*foreigners who have had safety in Babylon because of Babylon's great power will return back to their homelands because Babylon is no longer powerful and safe*].

15 **Every one that is found** [*"everyone that is proud," 2 Nephi 23:15*] **shall be thrust through** [*with the sword*]; and **every one that is joined unto them** [*who has gathered with the wicked in Babylon*] **shall fall by the sword**.

16 **Their children also shall be dashed to pieces before their eyes** [*refers only to conditions in Babylon and among the wicked before the Second Coming, not at the Second Coming; young children will not be harmed by the Second Coming of the Savior*]; **their houses shall be spoiled, and their wives ravished** [*the fate of Babylon; conditions among the wicked in the last days*].

Next, Isaiah prophesies that the Medes will be the army that conquers the ancient city of Babylon.

17 Behold, **I will stir up the Medes against them** [*a specific prophecy; Medes from Persia conquered Babylon easily in 538 BC*], **which shall not regard silver; and as for gold, they shall not delight in it** [*you Babylonians will not be able to bribe the Medes not to destroy you*].

18 **Their bows also shall dash the young men to pieces; and they shall have no pity on the fruit of the womb** [*babies*]; their eye shall not spare children.

19 **And Babylon** [*a huge city with 335–foot high walls; see Bible Dictionary, under "Babylon"*], the glory of kingdoms, the beauty of the Chaldees' excellency [*Babylonian's pride*], **shall be as** when God overthrew **Sodom and Gomorrah** [*Babylon will be completely destroyed and never inhabited again*].

NOTES

20 **It shall never be inhabited**, neither shall it be dwelt in from generation to generation: neither shall the Arabian pitch tent there; neither shall the shepherds make their fold there.

21 **But wild beasts of the desert shall lie there**; and their houses [*the ruins of ancient Babylon*] shall be full of doleful creatures [*lonely, solitary creatures*]; and **owls shall dwell there**, and satyrs [*male goats; can also mean demons—see footnote 21b in your Bible*] shall dance [*leap about*] there.

Have you noticed that whenever Isaiah desires to communicate the complete destruction of a city, people, or nation, he describes the ruins that are left as places where owls live? Owls tend to prefer to live in lonely places, away from human habitation.

22 And **the wild beasts of the islands** [*NIV: "hyenas"*] **shall cry** [*howl*] **in their desolate houses** [*the ruins*], and dragons [*hyenas, wild dogs, jackals*] in their pleasant [*in their once-pleasant*] palaces: and **her time is near to come, and her days shall not be prolonged** [*Babylon's time is nearly up, her days are almost over*].

The rest of verse 22, above, was apparently left out of the Bible. We will turn to the Book of Mormon for it.

2 Nephi 23:22

22 And the wild beasts of the islands shall cry in their desolate houses, and dragons in their pleasant palaces; and her time is near to come, and her day shall not be prolonged. For I will destroy her speedily; yea, for I will be merciful unto my people, but the wicked shall perish.

ISAIAH 14

Selection: all verses

In this chapter, Isaiah uses colorful style and imagery as he prophesies concerning the future downfall of the King of Babylon and, symbolically, the downfall of Satan's kingdom. Verse 12 is a particularly well-known verse.

There are several possible fulfillments of verse 1, next.

1 **For the Lord will have mercy on Jacob** [*Israel*], and will yet choose Israel [*bless Israel; another definition of "choose" is to "elect for eternal happiness"; see 1828 Noah Webster's Dictionary, under "choose"*], **and set them in their own land** [*One historical fulfillment was when Cyrus the Great of Persia allowed captives in Babylon to return in 538 BC; another group returned in 520 BC. This is also being fulfilled in our day.*]: **and the strangers shall be joined with them** [*foreigners will live with them*], and they shall cleave to the house of Jacob [*possibly meaning that Gentiles will join with Israel in the last days*].

2 **And the people** [*many nations who will help Israel return*] **shall take them** [*Israel*], **and bring them to their place: and the house of Israel shall possess them** [*nations who used to dominate Israel*] in the land of the Lord for servants and handmaids: **and they** [*Israel*] **shall take them** [*nations who used to dominate Israel*] **captives**, whose captives they [*Israel*] were; **and they shall rule over their oppressors** [*the tables will be turned in the last days*].

In verse 3, next, we are taught that righteous Israel will finally have peace during the Millennium.

3 And **it shall come to pass in the day** [*"in that day," 2 Nephi 24:3*] **that the Lord shall give thee rest from thy sorrow, and from thy fear, and from the hard bondage** wherein thou wast made to serve [*Israel will finally be free from subjection by foreigners and enemies during the Millennium*],

Several of the verses that follow now can be considered as dual in meaning. Many of them can refer to the king of Babylon. And they can also refer to Satan, as his kingdom comes to an end for a thousand years at the time of the Second Coming.

Verse 4 is a continuation of verse 3, with Isaiah holding forth the thought to Israel, in order to make a point, that when they are set free by the fall of Babylon, and ultimately by the fall of Satan and his kingdom, they will be in a position to taunt their former adversaries. The message is that ultimately, the righteous will triumph over all their enemies, because they have sided with the Lord.

4 That thou shalt take up this proverb [*a taunting*] against the king of Babylon [*dual: literally King of Babylon. Refers to Satan also, plus any wicked leader*], and say, How hath the oppressor ceased [*what happened to you!*]! the golden city ceased [*your unconquerable city, kingdom, is gone!*]!

The answer to the question in verse 4, above, is found in verse 5, next. One of the important doctrines in the answer is that God has power over Satan and any members of his evil kingdom.

5 **The Lord hath broken the staff of the wicked**, and the sceptre [*power*] of the rulers.

6 *He* [*Babylon; Satan*] **who smote the people in wrath with a continual stroke** [*constantly*], **he that ruled the nations in anger, is persecuted** [*punished*], **and none hindereth** [*nobody can stop it*].

7 **The whole earth is at rest, and is quiet: they break forth into singing** [*during the Millennium*].

8 Yea, **the fir trees** [*cyprus trees; symbolic of people*] **rejoice** at thee, and the cedars [*people*] of Lebanon, saying, **Since thou art laid down** [*since you got chopped down; compare with Isaiah 10:33–34*], **no feller** [*tree cutter; destruction*] **is come up against us.**

9 **Hell** [*spirit prison*] **from beneath is moved for thee** [*is getting ready to receive you*] to meet thee at thy coming: it stirreth up the dead for thee, even all the chief ones of the earth [*wicked leaders*]; it hath raised up from their thrones all the kings of the nations.

In verses 9 and 10, Isaiah creates a scene in our minds wherein all the wicked leaders of the earth (who by the time this vision is foretelling are in spirit prison) are taunting the devil and the king of Babylon at the time they arrive in hell.

10 **All they shall speak and say unto thee, Art thou also become weak as we** [*What happened to your power, Satan; king of Babylon*]? **art thou become like unto us** [*how is it that you are no better off than we are*]?

NOTES

11 **Thy pomp is brought down to the grave** [*was destroyed with you*], and the noise of thy viols [*royal harp music*]: **the worm is spread under thee, and the worms cover thee** [*your dead body is covered with maggots just like ours were; you're no better off here in hell than we are, so ha, ha, ha! (refers to the king of Babylon, since Satan has no physical body)*].

12 **How art thou fallen from heaven, O Lucifer** [*what happened to you; how were you dethroned*], son of the morning [*one who was high in authority—compare with Doctrine & Covenants 76:25–26*]! **how art thou cut down to the ground, which didst weaken the nations** [*how did you get cut down to this; you used to destroy nations, now your power is destroyed*]!

Next, in verses 13–14, Isaiah explains to us Lucifer's motives that led to his rebellion.

13 For **thou hast said in thine heart** [*these were your motives*], I will ascend into heaven, **I will exalt my throne above the stars of God** [*I will be the highest*]: I will sit also upon the mount of the congregation, in the sides of the north [*mythical mountain in the north where gods assemble*]:

14 I will ascend above the heights of the clouds; **I will be like the most High** [*as described in Moses 4:1–3*].

We will quote from the scene given in Moses, in the Pearl of Great Price, in which Lucifer rebelled, and will add **bold** to point things out:

<u>Moses 4:1–3</u>

1 And I, the Lord God, spake unto Moses, saying: That **Satan**, whom thou hast commanded in the name of mine Only Begotten, is the same which was from the beginning, and he **came before me, saying**—Behold, here am I, **send me, I will be thy son** [*the Redeemer*], and I will redeem all mankind, that one soul shall not be lost, and surely I will do it; **wherefore give me thine honor**.

2 But, behold, my Beloved Son, which was my Beloved and Chosen from the beginning, said unto me—Father, thy will be done, and the glory be thine forever.

3 Wherefore, because that **Satan** rebelled against me, and **sought** to destroy the agency of man, which I, the Lord God, had given him, and also, **that I should give unto him mine own power**; by the power of mine Only Begotten, I caused that he should be cast down;

We will now continue with Isaiah's teaching as to what will become of Satan when his kingdom (referred to as "the kingdom of the devil" in 1 Nephi 22:22) is brought down by the power of God.

15 **Yet thou** [*Lucifer*] **shalt be brought down to hell, to the sides of the pit** [*to the lowest part of the world of the dead, outer darkness*].

16 **They** [*the residents of hell*] **that see thee** [*Lucifer; King of Babylon*] **shall narrowly look upon thee** [*look at you with contorted faces and sneers*], and consider thee, **saying** [*with sarcasm*], **Is this the man that made the earth to tremble, that did shake kingdoms;**

NOTES

17 **That made the world as a wilderness, and destroyed the cities thereof**; that opened not the house of his prisoners [*who never freed his prisoners*]?

18 **All the kings of the nations**, even all of them, **lie in glory, every one in his own house** [*all other kings have magnificent tombs*].

19 **But thou** [*dual meaning: King of Babylon literally; Satan figuratively because he doesn't even have a physical body*] **art cast out of thy grave like an abominable branch** [*cut off and walked upon*], and as the raiment of those that are slain, thrust through with a sword [*ruined and discarded*], that go down to the stones of the pit [*the very bottom*]; as a carcase trodden under feet.

20 **Thou** [*King of Babylon/Satan*] **shalt not be joined with them in burial** [*you will not have a magnificent tomb like they do. Satan will not get a tomb because he does not have a physical body*], because thou hast destroyed thy land, and slain thy people: the seed of evildoers shall never be renowned [*none of your (king of Babylon) evil family will survive*].

21 **Prepare slaughter for his** [*king of Babylon's*] **children for** [*because of*] **the iniquity of their fathers** [*parents and ancestors*]; that they do not rise, nor possess the land, nor fill the face of the world with cities [*none of your children will rule the earth like you have*].

22 **For I will rise up against them**, saith the Lord of hosts, **and cut off from Babylon the name, and remnant, and son, and nephew** [*I will destroy Babylon completely; Satan's kingdom on earth completely*], saith the Lord.

23 **I will also make it** [*Babylon*] **a possession for the bittern** [*owls*], and pools of water: and I will sweep it with the besom [*broom*] of destruction [*a "clean sweep"*], saith the Lord of hosts.

Next, beginning with verse 24, Isaiah begins a new topic. It is a prophecy concerning the fate of Assyria. Remember that Isaiah served as a prophet from about 740 BC to 701 BC, which means that he was still alive when the Assyrians attacked and conquered the northern ten tribes (known as Israel during this period of history) in about 722 BC. The Assyrian army will suffer a major defeat in Judah about 701 BC.

His prophecy about the downfall of Babylon (the first part of this chapter) was for future fulfillment (about 538 BC).

24 **The Lord of hosts hath sworn** [*covenanted, promised*], **saying**, Surely as I have thought [*planned*], so shall it come to pass [*here is something else I will do*]; and as I have purposed, so shall it stand [*it will happen*]:

25 That **I will break the Assyrian** [*the Assyrian army*] **in my land** [*Judah*], **and upon my mountains** [*the mountains of Judah*] **tread him** [*the Assyrians*] **under foot**: then shall his yoke [*bondage*] **depart from off them** [*my people*], and his burden depart from off their shoulders [*dual meaning: the Assyrian downfall in Judah in 701 BC; the forces of the wicked will be destroyed at the Second Coming and again, after the final battle at the end of the Millennium, when Satan and his followers will be cast out permanently; see Doctrine & Covenants 88:111–15*].

NOTES

_____
_____
_____
_____
_____
_____
_____
_____
_____
_____
_____
_____
_____
_____
_____
_____
_____
_____
_____
_____
_____
_____
_____
_____
_____
_____
_____
_____
_____
_____

26 **This is the purpose** [*the plan*] **that is purposed upon the whole earth**: and this is **the hand** [*the hand of the Lord*] **that is stretched out upon all the nations** [*the eventual fate of all wicked nations*].

27 **For the Lord of hosts hath purposed, and who shall disannul it** [*prevent it*]? **and his hand is stretched out, and who shall turn it back?**

Beginning with verse 28, next, the topic again changes, this time to the fate of the Philistines, who have also been enemies to the Lord's people.

28 **In the year that king Ahaz died** [*about 720 BC*] **was this burden** [*prophetic message of doom to the Philistines*].

29 **Rejoice not** [*don't start celebrating*], **whole Palestina** [*Philistia*], **because the rod** [*power*] **of him** [*Shalmaneser, King of Assyria from 727–722 BC*] **that smote thee is broken: for out of the serpent's root** [*"snakes lay eggs"—from the same source, Assyria*] **shall come forth a cockatrice** [*one "snake" is dead (Shalmaneser) and a worse one will yet come (Sennacherib, King of Assyria, 705–687 BC). The Philistines rejoiced when Sargon, King of Assyria from 722–705 BC took over at Shalmaneser's death. Sargon was not as hard on them as his predecessor was.*], **and his** [*Sennacherib's*] **fruit shall be a fiery flying serpent.**

Next, in verse 30, the Lord describes the two options that are before the Philistines at this point.

30 **And the firstborn of the poor shall feed, and the needy shall lie down in safety** [*if you Philistines will repent and join with the Lord, you too can enjoy peace and safety, otherwise . . .*]: **and I will kill thy** [*Philistines'*] **root with famine, and he shall slay thy remnant** [*you will be utterly destroyed, if you don't repent*].

Next, Isaiah speaks prophetically of the future, as if it had already happened.

31 **Howl, O gate; cry, O city; thou whole Palestina** [*Philistia*], **art dissolved** [*reduced to nothing*]: **for there shall come from the north a smoke** [*cloud of dust made by an enemy army*], **and none shall be alone in his appointed times** [*the enemy army will have no cowards in it*].

32 **What shall one then answer the messengers of the nation** [*Philistia—what will one say when people ask, "What happened to the Philistines"?*] [*Answer:*] **That the Lord hath founded Zion, and the poor of his people shall trust in it** [*the Lord is the one who caused the destruction of the wicked and established Zion*].

ISAIAH 15

Selection: all verses

Next, we see a message of doom to the country of Moab, located east of the Dead Sea and named after the son of Lot's oldest daughter. There was constant warfare between the Moabites and the Israelites.

One of the major messages of these chapters of "doom" for the enemies of Israel is that all enemies of the Lord and His covenant people will ultimately fall. In other words, all members of Satan's kingdom, whose ultimate goal it is to destroy righteousness and the agency of others, will be overcome by the power of the Lord.

1 **The burden** [*message of doom*] **of Moab** [*descendants of Lot and his eldest daughter; see Genesis 19:37*]. Because in the night [*suddenly? unexpectedly?*] Ar of Moab [*a city in Moab*] is laid waste, and brought to silence; because in the night, Kir [*another city*] of Moab is laid waste, and brought to silence;

2 He [*Moab, the country east of the Dead Sea*] is gone up to Bajith [*a city*], and to Dibon, [*a city*], the high places [*pagan places of worship*], to weep: **Moab shall howl** over Nebo [*Mt. Nebo, north of Moab*], and over Medeba [*a city*]: **on all their heads shall be baldness** [*symbolic of slavery, captivity, and mourning*], and every beard cut off [*disgrace, slavery, captivity, and mourning*].

3 **In their streets they shall gird** [*dress*] **themselves with sackcloth** [*symbolic of deep tragedy and mourning*]: on the tops of their houses [*flat-roofed buildings used like we use decks, etc.*], and **in their streets, every one shall howl, weeping abundantly**.

4 And Heshbon [*a city in Moab*] shall cry, and Elealeh [*a city*]: their voice shall be heard even unto Jahaz [*a city*]: therefore [*for this reason*] **the armed soldiers of Moab shall cry out**; his life shall be grievous [*miserable*] unto him.

5 **My heart shall cry out for Moab**; his fugitives shall flee unto Zoar [*a border city just south of the Dead Sea*], an heifer [*young cow*] of three years old [*Moab, including Zoar, is being destroyed in its prime*]: for by the mounting up of Luhith [*where you start climbing up to get to Luhith*] **with weeping shall they go** it up; for in the way of Horonaim they shall raise up a cry of destruction.

6 For **the waters of Nimrim shall be desolate** [*dried up*]: for **the hay is withered away, the grass faileth, there is no green thing** [*there will be a drought and resulting famine*].

7 Therefore the abundance they have gotten, and that which they have laid up, shall they carry away to the brook of the willows [*probably the border between Moab and Edom—land directly south of Moab*].

Again, as previously mentioned several times in this study guide, Isaiah is speaking of the future as if it had already happened. This is part of "the manner of prophesying among the Jews" mentioned by Nephi in 2 Nephi 25:1.

8 For **the cry is gone round about the borders of Moab** [*they are completely surrounded*]; the howling thereof unto Eglaim, and the howling thereof unto Beer-elim.

9 For the waters of Dimon shall be full of blood: for **I will bring more upon Dimon, lions upon him that escapeth of Moab**, and upon the remnant of the land [*those who manage to escape the enemy armies will be destroyed by other means, including lions.*]

NOTES

NOTES

ISAIAH 16

Selection: all verses

A mood change now occurs. Isaiah indicates the time will come when Moab will come under the protection of Jerusalem, probably symbolic of the Savior, during the Millennium (verses 1–5).

1 **Send ye the lamb** [*send an appeal for help*] to the ruler of the land from Sela [*about sixty miles south of the Dead Sea*] to the wilderness, unto the mount of the daughter of Zion [*Jerusalem*].

2 For it shall be, that, **as a wandering bird cast out of the nest, so the daughters of Moab shall be** at the fords of Arnon [*a river on the northern border of Moab. Moab will have gone through some rough times.*]

Isaiah now prophesies that Moab will appeal to Judah for help. Their plea to Judah for help is given in verse 3, next. This could take place at a future time when harmony exists between them.

3 Take counsel, execute judgment [*kindness and fairness*]; make thy shadow [*symbolic of protection and help*] as the night in the midst of the noonday; **hide the outcasts** [*protect the inhabitants of Moab*]; bewray [*betray*] not him that wandereth.

4 **Let mine outcasts dwell with thee, Moab** [*should say "Judah"; NIV: "Let the Moabite fugitives stay with you"*]; **be thou a covert** [*protection*] **to them** [*Moab's inhabitants*] from the face of the spoiler [*German: destroyer*]; **for the extortioner** [*persecutor*] **is at an end, the spoiler ceaseth, the oppressors are consumed out of the land** [*thanks to help from Judah. Could also refer to destruction of wicked at Second Coming.*].

5 And **in mercy shall the throne be established: and he** [*Christ—see heading to this chapter in your Bible*] **shall sit upon it in truth in the tabernacle of David, judging, and seeking judgment, and hasting righteousness.** [*Conditions during the Millennium. Could also refer to Judah in the last days.*]

Isaiah now returns to troubles to come upon Moab back then.

6 **We have heard of the pride of Moab; he is very proud**; even of his **haughtiness**, and his **pride**, and his **wrath**: but his **lies** shall not be so. [*Moab's unfounded boasts of strength and well-being will not work out in fact.*]

In the background notes accompanying Isaiah chapter 3 in this study guide, we introduced a writing technique called "chiasmus." You may wish to go back and reread those notes, because Isaiah uses chiastic structure again here, in verses 7 through 11. In this case, he lists several cities in order and then lists them in reverse order (the basic structure of a chiasmus). The last two cities of the chiasmus are out of order, but it still works.

7 Therefore [*because of these sins listed in verse 6*] shall Moab howl for <u>Moab</u> **[A]**, every one shall howl: for the foundations of <u>Kir-hareseth</u> **[B]** shall ye mourn; surely they are stricken.

8 For the fields of Heshbon **[C]** languish, and the vine of Sibmah **[D]**: the lords of the heathen [*enemy nations—Assyrians*] have broken down the principal plants thereof [*the Assyrians ruined terraced vineyards when they attacked Moab*], they are come even unto Jazer **[E]**, they wandered through the wilderness: her branches are stretched out, they are gone over the sea.

9 ¶ Therefore [*this is why*] I will bewail with the weeping of Jazer **[E']** the vine of Sibmah **[D']**: I will water thee with my tears, O Heshbon **[C']**, and Elealeh: for the shouting for thy summer fruits and for thy harvest is fallen.

10 And gladness is taken away, and joy out of the plentiful field; and in the vineyards there shall be no singing, neither shall there be shouting [*in other words, there will be great sadness*]: the treaders shall tread out no wine in their presses [*because the grapes and vines have been destroyed by the enemy soldiers*]; I have made their vintage shouting to cease.

11 Wherefore my bowels [*symbolic in Hebrew of the center of feeling and emotion*] shall sound like an harp for Moab **[A']**, and mine inward parts for Kir-haresh **[B']**.

12 ¶ **And it shall come to pass, when it is seen that Moab is weary on the high place** [*places of worshipping idols and false gods*], that **he shall come to his sanctuary to pray; but he shall not prevail** [*won't get the help he needs from his false gods*].

13 **This is the word that the Lord hath spoken concerning Moab since that time** [*the Lord has warned Moab through past prophets too*].

14 But now the Lord hath spoken, saying, **Within three years**, as the years of an hireling, and **the glory of Moab shall be contemned** [*scorned*], with all that great multitude; **and the remnant shall be very small and feeble** [*in three years, there won't be much left of Moab*].

ISAIAH 17

Selection: all verses

Isaiah now tells what will happen to Syria and says a few more things about Israel.

1 **The burden** [*message of doom*] **of Damascus** [*a major city in Syria*]. Behold, **Damascus is taken away from being a city, and it shall be a ruinous heap** [*worthless pile of rubble*].

Isaiah is speaking prophetically of the future as if it had already taken place.

2 **The cities of Aroer** [*area near Damascus*] **are forsaken**: they shall be for flocks, which shall lie down, and none shall make them afraid [*animals will graze where cities now stand*].

3 **The fortress** [*fortified city*] **also shall cease from Ephraim** [*northern Israel, the northern ten tribes*], and the kingdom from Damascus, and the remnant of Syria: **they shall be as the glory of the children of Israel** [*will be cut down like Israel will be*], saith the Lord of hosts.

NOTES

The topic now turns to Israel's coming troubles.

4 And in that day it shall come to pass, that **the glory of Jacob** [*Israel*] **shall be made thin**, and the fatness of his flesh [*his prosperity*] shall wax lean [*bad times are coming*].

5 And **it shall be as when the harvestman gathereth the corn** [*grain*], and reapeth the ears with his arm; and it shall be as he that gathereth ears in the valley of Rephaim [*a fertile valley northwest of Jerusalem well known for good harvests—Israel will be "harvested," plucked up*].

6 ¶ **Yet gleaning grapes shall be left in it** [*a small remnant will be left after Assyria's attack on Israel*], as the shaking of an olive tree, two or three berries [*olives*] in the top of the uppermost bough, four or five in the outmost fruitful branches thereof, saith the Lord God of Israel [*remnants scattered here and there*].

7 **At that day shall a man look to his Maker** [*people will repent*], **and his eyes shall have respect to the Holy One of Israel** [*Jesus*].

8 **And he shall not look to the altars** [*of false gods*], **the work of his hands** [*idols he has made*], neither shall respect [*worship*] that which his fingers have made, either the groves [*locations used for idol worship*], or the images [*idols*]. [*This probably refers also to the last days and into the Millennium.*]

9 ¶ **In that day shall his** [*Syria's*] **strong cities be as a forsaken bough** [*limb*], and an uppermost branch, which they left because of the children of Israel: and there shall be desolation [*in Syria*].

10 **Because** [*this is why you have these problems*] **thou hast forgotten** the **God** of thy salvation, and hast not been mindful of the rock of thy strength [*the Lord*], therefore shalt thou plant pleasant plants [*continue idol worship*], and shalt set it with strange slips [*cuttings for grafting, symbolic of imported gods or idols*]:

11 **In the day** [*while things are going well*] **shalt thou make thy plant to grow** [*continue worshiping idols*], and in the morning shalt thou make thy seed to flourish: **but the harvest** [*results of idol worship*] **shall be a heap** [*worthless*] in the day of grief and of desperate sorrow [*your false gods will not help you*].

12 **Woe to the multitude of many people** [*nations, including Assyria, who attack the Lord's people*], which make a noise like the noise of the seas [*powerful*]; and to **the rushing of nations**, that make a rushing like the rushing of mighty waters!

13 **The nations shall rush like the rushing of many waters: but God shall rebuke them** [*will stop them*], and they shall flee far off, and shall be chased as the chaff of the mountains before the wind, and like a rolling thing [*tumbleweeds, etc.*] before the whirlwind [*wicked enemy nations are nothing compared to God's power; when the time is right, the Lord will stop them*].

14 And behold **at eveningtide trouble; and before the morning** [*unexpected, sudden disaster*] **he is not** [*the wicked are gone, destroyed; can refer to the destruction at the time of the Second Coming also*]. **This is the portion** [*the lot; in other words, they will get what*

is coming to them] **of them that spoil us** [*the Lord's people*], and the lot of them that rob us.

ISAIAH 18

Selection: all verses

This chapter uses symbolism to depict the gathering of Israel in the last days. You will see the missionaries (verse 2) going forth throughout the world, inviting all people to gather into the gospel fold. This is, in effect, the final pruning (verse 5) before the Second Coming.

As we begin with verse 1, we see a mistranslation with the first word.

1 **Woe** [*this is a mistranslation in the King James Version. The Hebrew word means "hark" or "greetings" and has no negative connotation—see footnote 1a in your Bible*] **to the land** [*most likely America*] **shadowing** [*overshadowed with God's protecting Spirit*] **with wings** [*wings often represent shelter or protection, as in the hen gathering her chicks under her wings in Matthew 23:37, and so forth. Wings also represent power in Doctrine & Covenants 77:4; Also, North and South America look somewhat like wings*], **which is beyond the rivers of Ethiopia** [*America is beyond the "rivers" or oceans beyond Africa*].

2 **That sendeth ambassadors** [*missionaries*] by the sea, even in vessels of bulrushes upon the waters, **saying, Go, ye swift** [*modern transportation?*] **messengers, to a nation scattered** [*scattered Israel*] **and peeled**, to a people terrible from their beginning hitherto [*German: once powerful, perhaps meaning once righteous*]; **a nation meted out and trodden down** [*scattered Israel*], whose land the rivers [*symbolic of enemy nations in Isaiah 8:7, 17:12*] have spoiled!

3 **All ye inhabitants of the world, and dwellers on the earth, see ye** [*pay attention*], **when he** [*the Lord*] **lifteth up an ensign** [*a signal to gather; the restored gospel*] **on the mountains** [*can symbolize Church headquarters; see Isaiah 2:2; also can symbolize temples*]; and when he bloweth a trumpet [*a clear, unmistakable sound, easy to distinguish from other sounds—the gospel message*], **hear ye.**

4 **For so the Lord said unto me** [*Isaiah*], I will take my rest, and I will consider in my dwelling place like a clear heat [*nourishing rays of light and truth*] upon herbs, and like a cloud of dew [*nourishing water*] in the heat of harvest [*right when it is needed*].

5 **For afore** [*before*] **the harvest** [*at the time of the Second Coming*], when the bud is perfect, and the sour grape [*immature grape*] is ripening in the flower, **he** [*the Lord*] **shall both cut off the sprigs with pruning hooks, and take away and cut down the branches** [*just before the millennial harvest, a final "pruning" will take place—the wicked will be destroyed, pruned away so the righteous can develop to their full potential*].

6 **They** [*the wicked*] **shall be left together** [*completely*] **unto the fowls of the mountains** [*birds of prey*], and to the beasts of the earth: and the fowls shall summer upon them, and all the beasts of the earth shall winter upon them.

Isaiah now prophesies that the remnant, scattered Israel, will be gathered and brought back to the Lord, a righteous nation.

NOTES

7 ¶ **In that time** [*probably the last days*] **shall the present** [*gift, gathered Israel*] **be brought unto the Lord** of hosts of a people scattered and peeled, and from a people terrible from their beginning hitherto; a nation meted out and trodden under foot, whose land the rivers have spoiled [*see verse 2*], to the place of the name of the Lord of hosts, the mount Zion [*the remnant, scattered Israel, will be gathered and brought back to the Lord a righteous nation; see verse 1*].

ISAIAH 19

Selection: all verses

This chapter contains a rather detailed prophecy about Egypt, including civil war (verse 2). Of particular interest to us in modern times is the prophecy of the destruction that will occur against the productivity of the Nile River in the last days (verses 5–10). The building of the Aswan Dam, beginning in 1960, may be a substantial contributor to the fulfilling of this prophecy, because of the severe problems it caused downstream.

A beautiful prophecy, beginning with verse 18, informs us that the day will come when our Egyptian brothers and sisters will have the gospel of Jesus Christ, and that Egypt and Assyria will join together with Israel as covenant people of the Lord.

1 **The burden** [*message of doom*] **of Egypt.** Behold, the Lord rideth upon a swift cloud [*trouble coming quickly*], and shall come into Egypt: and the idols [*false religions*] of Egypt shall be moved at his presence, and the heart [*courage*] of Egypt shall melt in the midst of it [*they will be terrified*].

2 And **I will set the Egyptians against the Egyptians** [*civil war*]: and they shall fight every one against his brother, and every one against his neighbor; city against city, and kingdom against kingdom.

3 And **the spirit of Egypt shall fail** [*great despair*] in the midst thereof; and I will destroy the counsel [*plans*] thereof: and **they shall seek to the idols** [*they will seek help from their false gods*], and to the charmers, **and to them that have familiar spirits** [*spiritualists who claim to contact the dead*], and to the wizards [*the occult*].

4 **And the Egyptians will I give over into the hand of a cruel lord** [*hard masters*]; and **a fierce king shall rule over them** [*we don't know who this is or was*], saith the Lord, the Lord of hosts.

5 And the waters shall fail from the sea, and **the river shall be wasted** and dried up [*the Nile River will be ruined*].

6 And **they** [*the Egyptians*] **shall turn the rivers far away** [*will ruin their own rivers*]; and the brooks of defence shall be emptied and dried up: the reeds and flags shall wither.

7 **The paper reeds** [*papyrus*] by the brooks, by the mouth of the brooks, **and every thing sown** [*planted*] **by the brooks, shall wither**, be driven away, and be no more [*the papyrus industry, crops, and so forth will be devastated*].

8 **The fishers also shall mourn**, and all they that cast angle [*fishhooks*] into the brooks shall lament, **and they that spread nets upon the waters shall languish** [*fishing industry will be ruined*].

9 **Moreover** [*in addition*] **they that work in fine flax** [*linen fabric is made from flax plant fibers*], **and they that weave networks** [*fine linen*], **shall be confounded** [*stopped; in other words, the textile industry will be ruined*].

10 **And they shall be broken** in the purposes [*will have no success*] thereof, all **that make sluices** [*dams*] **and ponds for fish.**

11 **Surely the princes** [*nobles; leaders*] of Zoan [*Tanis, ancient capital of the Nile Delta*] **are fools**, the **counsel** of the wise counsellors of Pharaoh **is become brutish** [*absurd; Pharaoh has received bad counsel from those who are supposed to be wise*]: **how say ye unto Pharaoh, I am the son of the wise, the son of ancient kings** [*how do you counselors to Pharaoh dare to claim to be wise*]?

12 Where are they? **where are thy wise men** [*to whom you have turned instead of the Lord*]**? and let them tell thee now**, and let them know what the Lord of hosts hath purposed upon [*against*] Egypt.

13 **The princes** [*leaders*] **of Zoan are become fools**, the princes of Noph [*Memphis, capital of northern Egypt*] are deceived; **they have also seduced Egypt** [*led her astray*], even they that are the stay [*support*] of the tribes thereof.

14 The Lord hath mingled [*has allowed, because of agency*] a perverse spirit in the midst thereof: and **they have caused Egypt to err in every work thereof**, as a drunken man staggereth in his vomit.

15 **Neither shall there be any work for Egypt**, which the head [*leaders, high society*] or tail [*poor, low society*], branch [*palm branch, high society*] or rush [*papyrus reed, low society, poor*], may do.

16 **In that day** [*the last days*] **shall Egypt be like unto women** [*the worst insult in Egyptian culture of that day*]**: and** it [*Egypt*] **shall be afraid and fear because of the shaking of the hand of the Lord** of hosts, which he shaketh over it.

Next, in verse 17, Isaiah tells us that, in the last days, the Jews will become a terror to Egypt. This is the exact opposite of what the situation has been throughout history, where the Egyptians were a terrifying power in the eyes of the Jews.

17 And **the land of Judah shall be a terror unto Egypt** [*a complete turnabout; tremendous prophecy!*], every one that maketh mention thereof shall be afraid in himself, because of the counsel [*plan*] of the Lord of hosts, which he hath determined against it [*Egypt*].

Next, Isaiah prophesies that the day will come when relations will improve between Egypt and Israel. He also foretells the day in which the Egyptians will have the true gospel and will make covenants with the Lord.

NOTES

18 **In that day** [*last days*] **shall five** [*several*] **cities in the land of Egypt speak the language of Canaan** [*Israel; a prophecy of greatly improved relationship between Egypt and Judah in the last days*], **and swear** [*make covenants*] **to the Lord of Hosts** [*make covenants with Jesus Christ*]; one shall be called, The city of destruction [*not a good translation; could be "city of the sun"*].

Verse 19, next, tends to make us think that there will someday be a temple to the Lord built in Egypt.

19 **In that day** [*last days*] **shall there be an altar** [*a temple?*] **to the Lord in the midst of the land of Egypt**, and a pillar [*symbolic of a temple*] at the border thereof to the Lord.

20 **And it** [*the altar and the pillar*] **shall be for a sign and for a witness** [*reminder*] **unto** [*of*] **the Lord of hosts in the land of Egypt**: for they [*Egyptians*] shall cry [*pray*] unto the Lord because of the oppressors, and **he shall send them a saviour**, and a great one, **and he shall deliver them** [*the Egyptians will hear and live the gospel*].

21 **And the Lord shall be known to Egypt, and the Egyptians shall know the Lord in that day** [*the last days*], and shall do sacrifice [*3 Nephi 9:20; broken heart and contrite spirit*] and oblation [*Doctrine & Covenants 59:12*]; yea, **they shall vow a vow** [*make covenants*] **unto the Lord, and perform it** [*and will be faithful to them*].

Often, the Lord has to first humble people and then heal them. Otherwise they won't listen to Him. We see this in verse 22, next.

22 And **the Lord shall smite Egypt**: he shall smite **and heal it** [*first humble it, then heal it*]: **and they shall return even to the Lord**, and he shall be intreated [*prayed to*] of [*by*] them, and shall heal them [*wonderful blessings are in store for Egypt*].

23 ¶ **In that day shall there be a highway out of Egypt to Assyria** [*Iraq?*], and the Assyrian shall come into Egypt, and the Egyptian into Assyria, and **the Egyptians shall serve** [*the Lord; see verse 25*] **with the Assyrians.**

24 **In that day** [*the last days*] **shall Israel be the third with Egypt and with Assyria** [*all three will be allied, with Israel as a blessing in the midst of them*], even a blessing in the midst of the land:

25 Whom the Lord of hosts shall bless, saying, **Blessed be Egypt my people, and Assyria the work of my hands, and Israel mine inheritance** [*all three nations will worship the true God and be part of the Lord's people*].

ISAIAH 20

Selection: all verses

Isaiah 20 seems to have no particular references to the future. It deals with ancient Egypt and is a prophecy that Assyria will overrun Egypt.

1 **In the year** [*about 711 BC*] **that Tartan** [*an Assyrian general*] **came unto Ashdod** [*when Sargon the king of Assyria sent him, Ashdod was a coastal city about forty miles west of Jerusalem*] **and fought against Ashdod** [*the center of a revolt against Assyria*], **and took it;**

In verse 2, next, Isaiah uses a rather dramatic method of communicating what is in store for Egypt, when the Assyrians attack them.

2 At the same time [*about 711 BC—see verse 1*] **spake the Lord by Isaiah** the son of Amoz, **saying, Go and loose the sackcloth** [*symbolic of mourning already*] **from off thy loins, and put off thy shoe from thy foot.** And he did so, walking naked [*without an upper garment; symbolic of slavery and exile; see verse 4*] and barefoot [*like a slave*].

3 **And the Lord said, Like as my servant Isaiah hath walked naked** [*stripped to the waist*] **and barefoot three years** [*we don't know whether this means constantly during the three years, or occasionally during the three years to remind the people of the message*] **for a sign and wonder upon Egypt and upon Ethiopia** [*symbolic of what will happen to Egypt and Ethiopia*];

4 **So shall the king of Assyria lead away the Egyptians prisoners**, and the Ethiopians captives, young and old, naked and barefoot, even with their buttocks [*upper thighs*] uncovered, to the shame of Egypt.

The Jews at this time had been depending on Egypt and Ethiopia for protection from Assyria, rather than repenting and turning to the Lord for help, as counseled by their prophets. In verse 5, next, the Lord tells them that their hopes are in vain.

5 **And they** [*Judah*] **shall be afraid and ashamed of** [*disappointed by*] **Ethiopia their expectation** [*hope*], **and of Egypt their glory** [*as mentioned above, Judah was hoping for protection from Egypt and Ethiopia, rather than repenting and turning to God*].

6 And **the inhabitant of this isle** [*nation; in other words, Jerusalem, Judah*] **shall say in that day, Behold, such is our expectation** [*our hope is destroyed!*], **whither we flee for help to be delivered from the king of Assyria**: and how shall we escape [*if that can happen to Ethiopia and Egypt, our "protection" from Assyria, what do we do now*]?

ISAIAH 21

Selection: all verses

This chapter is another prophecy about the destruction of Babylon. As mentioned in verses 2–4, this was a particularly difficult vision for Isaiah to watch.

1 **The burden** [*message of doom*] **of the desert of the sea** [*Babylon*]. As whirlwinds [*which are devastating in the desert*] in the south pass through; so it cometh from the desert, from a terrible land.

2 **A grievous vision is declared unto me** [*Isaiah; this was extra hard for Isaiah to watch*]; the treacherous dealer dealeth treacherously, and the spoiler spoileth. Go up, O Elam [*a country east of Babylon*]: **besiege** [*attack*], **O Media** [*a country northeast of Babylon; the Medes conquered Babylon in about 538 BC*]; **all the sighing thereof** [*groaning Babylon has caused*] **have I** [*the Lord*] **made to cease.**

3 **Therefore are my** [*Isaiah's*] **loins** [*whole being*] **filled with pain**: pangs have taken hold upon me, as the pangs of a woman that travaileth [*is in labor*]: **I was bowed down at the hearing of it** [*the vision*]; **I was dismayed at the seeing of it** [*this vision of the destruction of Babylon overwhelmed Isaiah*].

4 **My heart panted** [*faltered*], fearfulness affrighted me [*made me tremble*]: **the night of my pleasure hath he turned into fear unto me** [*I can't get to sleep at night*].

5 Prepare the table, watch in the watchtower, eat, drink: arise, ye princes, and anoint the shield [*oil your shields, get ready for action*].

6 For thus hath the Lord said unto me [*Isaiah*], **Go, set a watchman, let him declare what he seeth.**

7 **And he saw** a chariot with a couple of horsemen, a chariot of asses, and a chariot of camels; **and he hearkened diligently with much heed** [*paid close attention to what he saw*]:

8 And he cried, A lion: My lord, I stand continually [*day after day*] upon the watchtower in the daytime, and I am set in my ward whole nights [*I am keeping watch constantly like You told me to*]:

9 And, behold, here cometh a chariot of men, with a couple of horsemen [*messengers*]. **And he answered and said, Babylon is fallen, is fallen** [*dual meaning: Babylon has fallen; Satan's kingdom will likewise eventually fall*]; and all the graven images of her gods he hath broken unto the ground [*the Medes joined the Persians and Elamites and conquered Babylon, about 538 BC*].

10 **O my threshing** [*O my crushed one*], and the corn [*grain*] of my floor [*the son of my threshing floor, that is, the Israelites who will survive Babylon's downfall*]: **that which I have heard of the Lord of hosts, the God of Israel, have I declared unto you.**

　　It seems that no wicked nation is escaping Isaiah's prophecies of destruction. Next, we see the message of doom to the Edomites in Dumah.

11 **The burden of Dumah** [*message of doom to the Edomites who live in Dumah, a desert oasis about 250 miles southeast of the Dead Sea*]. **He calleth to me out of Seir** [*mountain range southeast of the Dead Sea*], **Watchman, what of the night** [*how long until daylight? In other words, how long will this oppression last*]? Watchman, what of the night?

12 The watchman said, **The morning cometh, and also the night** [*the end of Babylonian captivity will come but another oppressor will follow*]: if ye will enquire, enquire ye [*ask for more information later*]: return, come.

13 **The burden upon Arabia** [*difficulties caused Arabia by the Babylonian conquests*]. In the forest [*oasis*] in Arabia shall ye lodge, O ye travelling companies of Dedanim [*an area about 150 miles east of the Sea of Galilee*].

14 **The inhabitants of the land of Tema** [*about 250 miles south of Jerusalem, in the Arabian Desert*] **brought water to him** [*Kedar, that is, refugees from Kedar*] **that was thirsty, they prevented** [*met; "prevent" is used seventeen times in King James Version,*

always in the obsolete sense of "go before," "meet," "precede," and so forth. See Psalm 119:147, where "prevented" means "got up before dawn." See also Matthew 17:25, where Jesus spoke first, before Peter spoke] **with their bread him that fled** [*refugees from Kedar fleeing the Babylonians, Dedan and Tema need to prepare to take care of later refugees from Kedar*].

15 **For they** [*refugees from Kedar*] **fled from the swords**, from the drawn sword, and from the bent bow, and from the grievousness of war.

16 For thus hath the Lord said unto me [*Isaiah*], **Within a year**, according to the years of an hireling [*a wage earner, who can be fired for poor performance just as Kedar, in one year, will be "fired" for poor performance with respect to God*], and **all the glory of Kedar shall fail.**

17 And **the residue of the number of archers, the mighty men** of the children of Kedar, **shall be diminished** [*Kedar will be devastated and have few warriors left*]: **for the Lord God of Israel hath spoken it**.

ISAIAH 22

Selection: all verses

This prophecy deals with the wicked inhabitants of Jerusalem. If you read the heading to this chapter in your Bible, you see that it prophesies of the coming captivity of the Jews. It also deals with the power of Christ to free captives from sin.

1 **The burden of the valley of vision** [*message of doom to Jerusalem*]. **What aileth thee now, that thou art wholly gone up to the housetops** [*"What's wrong with you! Can't you see what's coming? How can you be so insensitive, always partying when your future is so bleak!"*]?

2 **Thou that art full of stirs** [*noise*], **a tumultuous city, a joyous city** [*always partying; false sense of security*]: **thy slain men are not slain with the sword**, nor dead in battle [*are easily captured and killed*].

Remember, as in many cases previously pointed out in this study guide, Isaiah is speaking prophetically of the future as if it has already taken place. We see that the partying and lack of vigilance on the part of the Jewish soldiers has made it easy for the enemy to capture them.

3 **All thy rulers are fled together, they are bound by the archers** [*captured easily; tied up by the archers, who don't normally do the actual hand-to-hand combat and capturing*]: all that are found in thee are bound together, which have fled from far.

4 **Therefore said I** [*this is the reason Isaiah said*], **Look away from me** [*don't try to get me to party with you*]; **I will weep bitterly, labour not to comfort me** [*don't try to comfort me because I see what's coming*], **because of the spoiling of the daughter of my people** [*Jerusalem*].

NOTES

5 For **it is a day of trouble**, and of treading down, and of perplexity by the Lord God of hosts in the valley of vision [*Jerusalem*], breaking down the walls, and of crying to the mountains.

6 And **Elam bare the quiver with chariots** [*symbolic of war*] **of men and horsemen** [*horse is symbolic of conquering, victory*], **and Kir uncovered the shield** [*Jerusalemites hope the soldiers of Elam and Kir—on the main road between Elam and Babylon—will defeat the Assyrians before they reach Jerusalem*].

Isaiah is pointing out the futility of the efforts of the Jews to defend themselves against these enemies. They have been weakened by wickedness and riotous living. Their only effective defense is to repent and turn to the Lord (verse 11).

7 ¶ And it shall come to pass, that **thy choicest valleys shall be full of chariots**, and the horsemen shall set themselves in array at the gate [*enemy soldiers will be everywhere in your land*].

8 And **he discovered** [*stripped off*] **the covering** [*defense*] **of Judah**, and thou didst look in that day to the armour of the house of the forest [*Jerusalem's defense is inadequate*].

9 **Ye have seen also the breaches** [*cracks, breaks in the wall*] **of the city of David** [*Jerusalem*], **that they are many** [*Isaiah points out weaknesses in Jerusalem's defenses*]: and ye gathered together the waters of the lower pool [*Hezekiah's tunnel; you dug a tunnel to bring water into the city during siege*].

10 **And ye have numbered** [*taken stock of things*] **the houses of Jerusalem, and the houses have ye broken down to fortify the wall** [*dismantled houses for stone to fortify city walls and so forth*].

11 Ye made also a ditch between the two walls for the water of the old pool: but **ye have not looked unto the maker thereof** [*the Lord*], **neither had respect unto him that fashioned it long ago** [*you have not turned to the Lord and repented, wherein your only reliable protection lies*].

Verse 12 again reminds them that humility and repentance are the only way out of the coming destruction.

12 **And in that day did the Lord God of hosts call to weeping**, and to **mourning**, and to **baldness**, and to **girding with sackcloth** [*God said, "Repent, humble yourselves!"*]:

13 **And behold** [*instead of repenting and humbly turning to the Lord for protection, the people continued in*] **joy and gladness** [*partying*], **slaying oxen, and killing sheep, eating flesh, and drinking wine**: let us **eat and drink; for to morrow we shall die** [*people ignore God, don't repent, continue riotous living*].

14 And it was revealed in mine ears by the Lord of hosts, **Surely this iniquity shall not be purged from you till ye die**, saith the Lord God of hosts [*the way you're heading, you will die in your sins*].

Next, Isaiah illustrates the negative influence that foreign lifestyles, philosophies and religions, and so forth, are having upon the Lord's people at this time.

15 **Thus saith the Lord God of hosts, Go, get thee unto** [*go see*] **this treasurer, even unto Shebna** [*leader of the king's court, probably a foreigner; perhaps symbolic of foreign religions, lifestyles, and so forth, taking hold of Jews but eventually driven out by the Messiah; see verses 19–20*], **which is over the house, and say,**

16 **What hast thou here? and whom hast thou here, that thou hast hewed thee out a sepulchre here** [*foreign influences attempting to become permanent; Shebna is a vain man carving out a great monument to himself*], as he that heweth him out a sepulchre on high, and that graveth an habitation for himself in a rock?

17 Behold, the Lord will carry thee away with a mighty captivity, and will surely cover thee [*you won't be famous*].

18 **He will surely violently turn and toss thee like a ball into a large country: there shalt thou die** [*you will die in a foreign land (likely Assyria—see footnote 18a in your Bible), symbolic of the fate of Jerusalem's inhabitants as they are carried away into a foreign land*], and there the chariots of thy glory shall be the shame of thy lord's house.

19 And **I will drive thee from thy station**, and from thy state shall he pull thee down.

20 And it shall come to pass **in that day**, that **I will call my servant Eliakim** [*a real person in Jerusalem, symbolic of the Messiah—see footnote 20a in your Bible*] the son of Hilkiah:

21 And **I will clothe him with thy robe, and strengthen him with thy girdle** [*he will take your place*], **and I will commit thy government into his hand**: and he [*Messiah*] shall be a father to the inhabitants of Jerusalem, and to the house of Judah.

22 And **the key of the house of David will I lay upon his shoulder; so he shall open, and none shall shut; and he shall shut, and none shall open** [*symbolic of Christ's power*].

23 And **I will fasten him as a nail in a sure place** [*the Messiah is absolutely reliable*]; and he shall be for a glorious throne to his father's house [*dual meaning: Eliakim's family depends on him for their temporal salvation; we depend on Christ for our spiritual salvation*].

24 **And they shall hang upon him all the glory of his father's house, the offspring and the issue**, all vessels of small quantity, from the vessels of cups, even to all the vessels of flagons [*dual meaning: Eliakim's relatives, small and great, depend on him; Christ carries all mankind, small and great, upon the cross; Atonement*].

The symbolism in verse 25, next, does not apply to the Savior, rather, only to Eliakim.

25 **In that day, saith the Lord of hosts, shall the nail that is fastened in the sure place be removed**, and be cut down, and fall; and the burden that was upon it shall be cut off: for the Lord hath spoken it [*Eliakim will eventually fall from office and his family with him*].

NOTES

_____
_____
_____
_____
_____
_____
_____
_____
_____
_____
_____
_____
_____
_____
_____
_____
_____
_____
_____
_____
_____
_____
_____
_____
_____
_____
_____
_____
_____

ISAIAH 23

Selection: all verses

This is the last of the set of prophecies against foreign nations that began with chapter 13.

1 **The burden** [*prophecy of doom*] **of Tyre** [*located about 120 miles north of Jerusalem, on the coast of the Mediterranean Sea; a leading sea power of Isaiah's time*]. **Howl, ye ships of Tarshish** [*large ships of trade*]; **for it** [*Tyre*] **is laid waste**, so that there is no house, no entering [*harbor*] in: from the land of Chittim [*Cyprus*] it is revealed to them.

2 **Be still** [*stunned*], ye inhabitants of the isle [*seaport of Tyre or Cyprus?*]; thou whom the merchants of Zidon, that pass over the sea, have replenished [*made rich*].

3 And by great waters the seed [*grain from the Nile*] of Sihor [*city in Egypt*], the harvest of the river, is her revenue; and she is a mart [*marketplace*] of nations.

4 **Be thou ashamed** [*German: terrified—Sidon's commerce will be interrupted via Tyre's downfall*], **O Zidon**: for the sea hath spoken, even the strength of the sea, saying, I travail not, nor bring forth children, neither do I nourish up young men, nor bring up virgins [*Tyre is not producing anymore*].

5 **As at the report concerning Egypt** [*as the report comes to Egypt*], **so shall they** [*the Egyptians*] **be sorely pained at the report of Tyre** [*Egypt will be in anguish upon hearing what has happened to Tyre*].

6 Pass ye over to Tarshish [*probably in Spain*]; howl, ye inhabitants of the isle.

7 **Is this your joyous** [*riotous*] **city**, whose antiquity is of ancient days? **her own feet shall carry her afar off to sojourn** [*she creates her own downfall like we do when we go against God*].

8 **Who hath taken this counsel** [*who is planning this*] **against Tyre**, the crowning city, whose merchants are princes [*mighty leaders*], whose traffickers [*traders*] are the honourable [*famous*] of the earth?

   Verse 9, next, has the answer to the question posed by Isaiah, in verse 8, above.

9 **The Lord of hosts hath purposed** [*planned*] **it**, to stain the pride of all glory, and to bring into contempt [*to humble*] all the honourable [*unrighteous famous*] of the earth.

10 Pass through thy land as a river, O daughter of Tarshish : **there is no more strength** [*you are ruined*].

11 **He** [*the Lord*] **stretched out his hand over the sea, he shook the kingdoms: the Lord hath given a commandment against the merchant city** [*Tyre*], to destroy the strong holds thereof [*merchandising networks; Tyre is doomed*].

12 And he said, **Thou shalt no more rejoice**, O thou oppressed virgin [*unconquered until the fulfillment of this prophesy*], daughter of Zidon: arise, pass over to Chittim [*Cyprus*]; **there also shalt thou have no rest** [*Tyre's downfall ruins other economies too*].

13 **Behold** [*look at*] **the land of the Chaldeans** [*Babylon*]; **this people was not, till** [*was not ruined, until*] **the Assyrian founded it** [*set it up*] **for them** [*desert creatures*] **that dwell in the wilderness** [*the Assyrians destroyed Babylon to the point that it is now nothing more than a place for desert creatures to live*]: they set up the towers [*siege towers*] thereof, they raised [*razed; destroyed*] up the palaces thereof; and he [*Assyria*] brought it to ruin.

14 **Howl, ye ships of Tarshish: for your strength is laid waste** [*via Tyre's downfall*].

15 And it shall come to pass in that day, that **Tyre shall be forgotten seventy years,** according to the days of one king: **after the end of seventy years shall Tyre sing as an harlot** [*will "prostitute" the ways of God again*].

16 Take an harp, go about the city, thou harlot that hast been forgotten; make sweet melody, sing many songs, that thou mayest be remembered.

17 And it shall come to pass **after the end of seventy years,** that the Lord will visit **Tyre,** and she **shall turn** [*return*] **to her hire** [*wicked ways*], **and shall commit fornication** [*symbolic of intense and total disloyalty to God; see Bible Dictionary, under "Adultery"*] **with all the kingdoms of the world upon the face of the earth** [*Tyre will be an evil influence to many nations*].

18 **And her merchandise and her hire shall be holiness to the Lord** [*perhaps referring to the future when the wicked will be gone and the good things and wealth of the earth will be for the righteous and the building up of the kingdom of God*]: it shall not be treasured nor laid up; for her merchandise shall be for them that dwell before the Lord [*the righteous*], to eat sufficiently, and for durable clothing [*righteousness blesses people for eternity*].

ISAIAH 24

Selection: all verses

In the first part of this chapter, Isaiah emphasizes the consequences of wickedness. The punishment for sin (if they don't repent) will eventually come upon all, regardless of social status (verse 3). Isaiah will again use chiasmus (see notes in the background for chapter 3 in this study guide) as a means of providing emphasis. It will be a simple chiasmus, consisting of A, B, C, B,' A.'

Other messages in this chapter also include the seriousness of breaking covenants (beginning with verse 5), and the burning of the wicked at the time of the Second Coming.

We will begin our study now by noting the chiasmus, which begins in verse 1.

1 Behold, the Lord **[A]** maketh the earth empty **[B]**, and maketh it waste, and turneth it upside down, and scattereth abroad the inhabitants thereof.

NOTES

2 And it shall be, as with the <u>people</u> **[C]**, so with the priest; as with the servant, so with his master; as with the maid, so with her mistress; as with the buyer, so with the seller; as with the lender, so with the borrower; as with the taker of usury [*interest on loans*], so with the giver of usury to him [*no one who is wicked will escape, regardless of social status*].

3 The <u>land shall be utterly emptied</u> **[B']**, and utterly spoiled: for <u>the Lord</u> **[A']** hath spoken this word.

Verse 4, next, reminds us that pride is a devastating sin for individuals and nations.

4 The earth mourneth and fadeth away, **the world languisheth** [*wastes away*] and fadeth away, **the haughty** [*prideful*] **people of the earth do languish**.

The main problem that is causing the people of the world (verse 4) to waste away is described by Isaiah in verse 5.

5 **The earth** also **is defiled** under the inhabitants thereof; **because they have transgressed the laws, changed the ordinance, broken the everlasting covenant** [*they have gone into apostasy*].

In verse 6, next, Isaiah explains that apostasy with its accompanying personal and national wickedness will be the cause of the burning at the Second Coming.

6 **Therefore** [*this is why*] **hath the curse** [*the punishments of God*] **devoured the earth**, and they that dwell therein are desolate: **therefore** [*this is why*] **the inhabitants of the earth are burned, and few men left** [*at the Second Coming*].

The glory of the Lord will be the source of the burning at the Second Coming, according to Doctrine & Covenants 5:19 and 2 Nephi 12:10, 19, and 21.

In verses 7–12, next, Isaiah uses several different ways to say, in effect, that the party is over for the wicked.

7 **The new wine mourneth** [*fails, runs out*], the vine languisheth [*fails*], **all the merryhearted do sigh** [*"the party's over!"*].

8 **The mirth** [*merriment*] **of tabrets** [*drums; tambourines*] **ceaseth**, the noise of them that rejoice [*party, revel in riotous living*] endeth, the joy of the harp ceaseth.

9 **They shall not drink wine with a song** [*drunken singing*]; strong drink shall be bitter to them that drink it.

10 **The city of confusion is broken down** [*towns are broken down*]: every house is shut up, that no man may come in.

11 **There is a crying for wine in the streets** [*people still want their wicked lifestyle*]; all joy is darkened, the mirth of the land is gone.

12 In the city is left desolation, and the gate is smitten with destruction [*Isaiah has "painted" a verbal picture that the "party" is very over, in verses 7–12. This is an excellent example of his inspired brilliance and use of repetition in his prophesying*].

13 When thus it shall be in the midst of the land among the people [*nations*], **there shall be as the shaking of an olive tree, and as the gleaning grapes when the vintage is done** [*a few righteous will be separated, or gleaned from the wicked*].

14 They [*the relatively few righteous*] **shall lift up their voice, they shall sing** [*praises*] **for the majesty of the Lord**, they shall cry aloud from the sea.

15 Wherefore glorify ye the Lord in the fires [*probably should say "islands," see footnote 15a in your Bible*], even the name of the Lord God of Israel in the isles of the sea [*nations of the earth; a few righteous, a remnant, are scattered throughout the earth*].

16 From the uttermost part of the earth have we heard songs, even glory to the righteous. But I [*Isaiah*] said, My leanness, my leanness [*my inability to change things!*], woe unto me! the treacherous dealers have dealt very treacherously; yea, the treacherous dealers have dealt treacherously [*wickedness continues despite Isaiah's efforts to warn them and get them to change*].

17 Fear [*terror*], and **the pit** [*a trap*], and **the snare** [*a trap*], **are upon thee, O inhabitant** [*wicked people*] **of the earth**.

In verse 18, next, Isaiah teaches that, ultimately, there is no escape for the wicked.

18 And it shall come to pass, that **he who fleeth from the noise of the fear shall fall into the pit** [*as stated in verse 17, above*]; **and he that cometh up out** [*escapes*] **of the midst of the pit shall be taken in the snare** [*sometimes the wicked think that they have escaped the justice of God, but they haven't*]: **for the windows from on high are open** [*heaven is watching*], and the foundations of the earth do shake.

19 The earth is utterly broken down, the earth is clean dissolved, the earth is moved exceedingly [*will "reel to and fro"; see verse 20*].

20 The earth shall reel to and fro like a drunkard, and shall be removed like a cottage [*flimsy temporary shade structure built in a garden; see Isaiah 1:8*]; and the transgression thereof shall be heavy upon it; and it shall fall, and not rise again [*German: not remain standing*].

21 And it shall come to pass **in that day, that the Lord shall punish the host of the high ones** [*wicked, proud*] that are on high, and the kings of the earth upon the earth [*the wicked will be punished*].

The doctrine of missionary work in the postmortal spirit world prison is clearly taught in verse 22, next.

22 And **they shall be gathered together, as prisoners are gathered in the pit** [*spirit prison—see footnotes 22a and 22b in your Bible*], and shall be shut up in the prison, **and after many days shall they be visited** [*by missionaries who come to the spirit prison; see Doctrine & Covenants 138*].

NOTES

_____
_____
_____
_____
_____
_____
_____
_____
_____
_____
_____
_____
_____
_____
_____
_____
_____
_____
_____
_____
_____
_____
_____
_____
_____
_____
_____

Next, in verse 23, Isaiah explains to us that the glory of the Savior, as He comes to earth at the time of His Second Coming, will be beyond anything we have ever experienced.

23 **Then the moon shall be confounded, and the sun ashamed** [*moon and sun's majesty are nothing compared to radiant glory and majesty of Christ when He comes; see Doctrine & Covenants 133:49*], **when the Lord of hosts shall reign in mount Zion, and in Jerusalem** [*during the Millennium*], and before his ancients gloriously.

ISAIAH 25

Selection: all verses

One of the major messages in this chapter is that it is worth being righteous. Those who are worthy to be with the Savior will receive the very best of blessings and enjoy the results of their righteous efforts.

As we begin, we see the righteous praising God for the plan of salvation.

1 **O Lord, thou art my God**; I will exalt thee, **I will praise thy name**; for thou hast done wonderful things; **thy counsels of old** [*plans made in Council in Heaven*] are faithfulness and truth.

Next, the righteous praise and acknowledge the Lord for His power over the wicked. This is an important doctrine, since some people are of the opinion that the forces of evil, with Satan at the helm, have a chance to ultimately triumph over the Savior. They don't.

2 For **thou hast made of a** [*wicked*] **city an heap** [*pile of rubble*]; **of a defenced city a ruin**: **a palace of strangers** [*symbolic of kingdoms of the wicked*] **to be no city**; it shall never be built [*rebuilt; symbolic of the fall of Babylon, and the eventual fall of Satan's kingdom*].

3 **Therefore shall** [*this is why*] **the strong** [*powerful wicked*] **people glorify** [*acknowledge*] **thee**, the city of the terrible [*tyrant; German: powerful Gentile*] nations shall fear thee [*God has power over the wicked*].

4 **For thou hast been a strength to the poor, a strength to the needy in his distress, a refuge from the storm, a shadow** [*shade; protection*] **from the heat, when the blast of the terrible ones** [*the wicked*] **is as a storm against the wall** [*you have helped the righteous poor and needy*].

5 **Thou shalt bring down** [*humble*] **the noise** [*unrighteous revelry*] of strangers [*foreigners; people whose lifestyle is "foreign" to the gospel*], as the heat in a dry place [*strangers who have been fierce like the heat in the desert against the righteous*]; even the heat with the shadow [*shade*] of a cloud [*God subdues the wicked like He subdues desert heat with clouds*]: **the branch** [*German Bible: victory song of tyrants*] **of the terrible ones** [*tyrants*] **shall be brought low** [*humbled*].

6 ¶ **And in this mountain** [*mount Zion—see heading to this chapter in your Bible; probably a reference to the Millennium—see Doctrine & Covenants 133:56*] **shall the Lord of hosts make unto all people** [*nations; the righteous*] **a feast of fat things** [*the best*], a

feast of wines on the lees [*thickest, best part of the wine, in other words, the best blessings of the gospel are made available to the righteous*], of fat things full of marrow, of wines on the lees well refined.

7 And **he will destroy** in this mountain the face of the covering [*veil*] cast over all people, and **the vail that is spread over all nations** [*veil of spiritual darkness will be taken away*].

We see the blessed and happy state of the righteous, because of the resurrection and Atonement of Jesus Christ, highlighted in verse 8, next.

8 **He** [*Christ*] **will swallow up death in victory** [*the resurrection*]; **and the Lord God will wipe away tears from off all faces** [*through the Atonement come happiness and eternal life for the righteous; sharp contrast with the fate of wicked in verses 2, 10, 11, 12, and so forth*]; and the rebuke [*troubles, persecutions, problems*] of his people shall he take away from off all the earth: for **the Lord hath spoken it** [*it will happen!*].

9 **And it shall be said in that day** [*future*], **Lo, this is our God; we have waited for him, and he will save** [*has saved*] **us: this is the Lord; we have waited for him, we will be** [*are*] **glad** and rejoice in his salvation.

In verses 10–12, next, Isaiah yet again emphasizes the fact that the Lord will triumph over the wicked.

10 **For in this mountain shall the hand of the Lord rest, and Moab** [*symbolic of the wicked*] **shall be trodden down under him,** even as straw is trodden down for the dunghill [*fate of the wicked*].

11 And **he shall spread forth his hands in the midst of them** [*the wicked*], as he that swimmeth spreadeth forth his hands to swim: and **he shall bring down their pride** together with the spoils of their hands [*He will humble the wicked and take away their ill-gotten gain*].

12 **And the fortress of the high fort** [*supposedly invincible domains of the wicked*] of thy walls **shall he** [*the Lord*] **bring down, lay low, and bring to the ground, even to the dust** [*kingdoms of the wicked destroyed completely!*].

ISAIAH 26

Selection: all verses

This chapter consists of a message of encouragement to the righteous and a warning against wickedness. It depicts the righteous singing and praising Jehovah.

1 **In that day** [*last days*] **shall this song** [*of praise to the Lord*] **be sung in the land of Judah**; We have a strong city; **salvation will God appoint for walls and bulwarks** [*"salvation is all around us"*].

2 **Open ye the gates** [*several possible meanings: implies peaceful times when the city gates can be left open; can mean the gates of heaven; "gate" can also mean baptism*], **that the righteous nation** [*the righteous people*] **which keepeth the truth may enter in.**

NOTES

_____
_____
_____
_____
_____
_____
_____
_____
_____
_____
_____
_____
_____
_____
_____
_____
_____
_____
_____
_____
_____
_____
_____
_____
_____
_____
_____
_____
_____
_____
_____
_____
_____
_____
_____
_____
_____

3 **Thou wilt keep him** [*the righteous nation; individual*] **in perfect peace, whose mind is stayed** [*based, supported, supplied by*] **on thee**: because he trusteth in thee.

4 **Trust ye in the Lord for ever: for in the Lord JEHOVAH** [*the Savior*] **is everlasting strength**.

5 ¶ **For he** [*JEHOVAH in verse 4, above*] **bringeth down** [*humbles*] **them that dwell on high** [*the "high and mighty," that is, the proud wicked*]; the lofty city, he layeth it low; he layeth it low, even to the ground; he bringeth it even to the dust [*will completely destroy the wicked*].

6 **The foot shall tread it** [*the lofty city, that is, the wicked*] **down,** even the feet of the poor, and the steps of the needy [*the tables are turned; the oppressed now triumph and the wicked get their just dues*].

7 The way of the just [*righteous*] is uprightness: **thou, most upright** [*Christ*], **dost weigh the path of the just** [*make the path smooth, bless the righteous*].

8 Yea, **in the way of thy judgments, O Lord, have we waited for thee** [*we've been living righteously*]; **the desire of our soul is to thy name** [*our hearts are right; see Doctrine & Covenants 64:22*], and to the remembrance of thee.

9 **With my soul have I desired thee in the night; yea, with my spirit within me will I seek thee early** [*I seek Thee day and night, in other words, always*]; for when thy judgments [*teachings and commandments*] are in the earth, the inhabitants of the world will learn righteousness.

Next, in verse 10, Isaiah points out to us that the problem with the wicked is that they do not want to do right.

10 **Let favour be shewed to the wicked, yet will he not** [*does not want to*] **learn righteousness**: in the land of uprightness [*among the righteous*] will he deal unjustly [*the wicked are always looking for ways to cheat the righteous*], and **will not** [*does not want to*] **behold the majesty of the Lord** [*even when the Lord shows kindness to the wicked, they don't repent because they don't desire righteousness; their hearts are not right*].

11 **Lord, when thy hand is lifted up** [*when Your power and existence are obvious*], **they** [*the wicked*] **will not see** [*don't want to see*]: **but they shall see** [*every knee shall bow and every tongue confess; see Doctrine & Covenants 76:110*], **and be ashamed** [*put to shame*] for their envy at the people [*because of thy zeal for thy people*]; yea, **the fire of** [*reserved for*] **thine enemies shall devour them** [*the wicked; Second Coming*].

12 ¶ Lord, thou wilt ordain peace for us: for **thou also hast wrought all our works in us** [*all we have is from Thee; gratitude—compare with Doctrine & Covenants 59:21*].

13 O Lord our God, **other lords** [*secular leaders, including wicked rulers*] beside thee **have had dominion over us: but by thee only will we make mention of thy name** [*Thou only do we honor and worship*].

Next, Isaiah speaks of the fact that the wicked will not be resurrected with the righteous. He speaks of the future as if it had already happened.

14 They [*the wicked rulers*] **are dead, they shall not live** [*until the resurrection of the wicked at the end of the Millennium—see Doctrine & Covenants 88:101*]; they are deceased, **they shall not rise** [*their power is ended*]: **therefore** [*because of their wickedness*] **hast thou visited** [*punished*] **and destroyed them**, and made all their memory to perish.

15 Thou hast increased the nation [*the righteous—see verse 2*], O Lord, thou hast increased the nation: **thou art glorified: thou hadst** [*hast*] **removed** [*spread*] **it far unto all the ends of the earth** [*there will be a tremendous increase in the number of righteous during the Millennium*].

16 Lord, in trouble have they [*the righteous*] **visited thee** [*come unto thee*], **they poured out a prayer when thy chastening was upon them** [*the righteous turn to God in times of trouble*].

17 Like as a woman with child, that draweth near the time of her delivery, is in pain, and crieth out in her pangs: so have we been in thy sight, O Lord [*when unavoidable trouble came, we turned to thee*].

Next, Israel, in effect, confesses that they have not always acted like the Lord's covenant people, which includes the responsibility of blessing others with the gospel and taking the gospel and the priesthood to all the world (see Abraham 2:9–11).

18 We have been with child [*we have had pain and suffering as part of our mortal probation*], **we have been in pain, we have as it were brought forth wind** [*nothing—sometimes we have turned from Thee, and pain and suffering have not produced desired results, fruits of righteousness in our lives*], **we have not wrought any deliverance in the earth** [*we have not brought salvation to people of the earth like we were called to do as Thy covenant people*]; neither have the inhabitants of the world fallen [*been humbled*].

Next, in verse 19, the Savior teaches that the righteous, who have died before His resurrection, will be resurrected with Him (see also Doctrine & Covenants 133:54–55).

19 Thy dead men shall live [*be resurrected*], **together with my** [*Christ's*] **dead body shall they arise** [*they will be resurrected with Christ*]. **Awake and sing, ye that dwell in dust** [*lie in graves*]: for thy dew is as the dew of herbs, and **the earth shall cast out the dead** [*resurrection*].

20 ¶ Come, my people [*the righteous, Isaiah 19:25*], **enter thou into thy chambers, and shut thy doors about thee: hide thyself as it were for a little moment, until the indignation** [*cleansing of the earth*] **be overpast.** [*This verse is full of Passover symbolism. The Israelites closed their doors and put lamb's blood (symbolic of the Atonement) on doorposts, which provided them safety from the Lord's destruction among the Egyptians. Through righteous homes where the gospel is lived and the Atonement used, we can be spared God's punishments. God punishes only those who merit punishment.*]

21 For, behold, the Lord cometh out of his place [*heaven*] **to punish the inhabitants of the earth for their iniquity** [*the destruction of the wicked at the Second Coming as well as many destructions of the wicked previous to that time*]: **the earth also shall disclose her blood, and shall no more cover her slain** [*the bloodshed and crimes of the wicked will be exposed and punishment given out*].

NOTES

ISAIAH 27

Selection: all verses

This chapter is a prophecy of the gathering of Israel in the last days. The Church will flourish and spread throughout the earth (verse 6), as prophesied in Daniel 2:35, 44–45. The "kingdom of the devil" spoken of in 1 Nephi 22:22, will ultimately be destroyed by Christ.

1 **In that day** [*spoken of in chapter 26, above*] **the Lord with his sore** [*hard, fierce*] **and great and strong sword shall punish leviathan** [*Satan; can also include all forces of evil, all who serve Satan*] the piercing serpent, even leviathan **that crooked serpent** [*the devil—see Revelation 12:9*]; **and he shall slay the dragon** that is in the sea [*Leviathan was a legendary sea monster representing evil*].

2 **In that day sing ye unto her** [*Israel*], **A vineyard of red wine** [*symbolizing a productive people to the Lord*].

3 **I the Lord do keep it** [*my vineyard, Israel*]; **I will water it every moment: lest any hurt it, I will keep it night and day** [*so that it will flourish as described in verse 6*].

4 Fury is not in me: **who would set the briers and thorns** [*the wicked*] **against me in battle** [*who dares to fight against the Lord*]? I would go through them, **I would burn them together** [*all of them*].

5 **Or let him** [*Israel*] **take hold of my strength** [*repent and come unto Me*], that he may make peace with me; and **he shall make peace with me** [*prophetic!*].

6 **He** [*God*] **shall cause them** [*Israel*] **that come of Jacob** [*the father of the twelve sons who became the twelve tribes of Israel*] **to take root** [*Israel will be restored*]: **Israel shall blossom and bud, and fill the face of the world with fruit** [*the blessings of righteousness and salvation*].

Without help, the pronouns in verse 7, next, can be quite confusing.

7 ¶ Hath **he** [*God*] smitten **him** [*Israel*], as **he** [*God*] smote **those** [*Israel's enemies*] that smote **him** [*Israel*]? or is **he** [*Israel*] slain according to [*like*] the slaughter of **them** [*Israel's enemies*] that are slain by **him** [*God*]? [*Has God been as hard on his people, Israel, as on her enemies? Answer: No!*]

8 **In measure** [*moderation*], **when it** [*Israel*] **shooteth forth, thou wilt debate with it** [*prune it, discipline it*]: **he** [*God*] **stayeth his rough wind in the day of the east wind** [*God could destroy you with a really "rough" wind, but instead he sends the terrible east wind, a hot, dry wind off the Arabian Desert that devastates crops and helps humble you. In German, this says "You mete to them what is needed to set them straight so You can set them free." Jeremiah 30:11 in the King James Version says the same thing and is much clearer than the King James translation of verse 8, above.*]

We will include Jeremiah 30:11 here, so you can read it along with verse 8, above:

Jeremiah 30:11

11 For I am with thee, saith the LORD, to save thee: though I make a full end of all nations whither I have scattered thee, yet will I not make a full end of thee [*you will not be destroyed completely*]: but I will correct [*discipline*] thee in measure, and will not leave thee altogether unpunished.

9 **By this** [*the rough times, refiner's fire referred to in verse 8*] **therefore shall the iniquity** [*wickedness*] **of Jacob** [*Israel*] **be purged** [*rooted out*]; **and this is all the fruit** [*the product of Israel's wickedness—the consequences designed by God to purge wickedness out of them*] **to take away his** [*Israel's*] **sin;** when he [*God*] maketh all the stones of the altar [*used in idol worship*] as chalkstones that are beaten in sunder [*into pieces*], the groves [*used in idol worship*] and images [*used in idol worship*] shall not stand up [*your false religions, upon which you have relied, will crumble*].

10 **Yet** [*the time will come that*] **the defenced city** [*established wickedness*] **shall be desolate**, and the habitation forsaken [*abandoned*], and left like a wilderness: **there shall the calf feed** [*in effect, where you once lived will become a place for animals to live*], and there shall he [*the calf*] lie down, and consume the branches thereof [*nothing will be left of you and your wickedness*].

11 When the boughs thereof are withered, they shall be broken off: the women come, and set them on fire [*women will use what is left for cooking fires; symbolically, wickedness will be destroyed completely by fire*]: for **it is a people of no understanding** [*of the gospel, because they don't want it*]: **therefore** [*that is why*] **he that made them will not have mercy on them**, and he [*God*] that formed them will shew them no favour.

Isaiah now switches topics somewhat, and prophesies of the latter-day gathering of Israel, "one by one."

12 ¶ And **it shall come to pass in that day** [*the last days*], that the Lord shall beat [*glean*] off from the channel of the river [*from Mesopotamia*] unto the stream of Egypt [*the Nile River; gather Israel out of the whole world*], and **ye shall be gathered one by one**, O ye children of Israel [*the righteous shall be gathered to Christ from the whole earth*].

13 And it shall come to pass **in that day**, that **the great trumpet shall be blown** [*to signal the gathering*], **and they shall come which were ready to perish in the land of Assyria** [*symbolic of the wicked world*], and the outcasts in the land of Egypt [*the righteous, who have been "outcasts" in the wicked world*], **and shall worship the Lord in the holy mount at Jerusalem** [*in the holy temples*].

ISAIAH 28

Selection: all verses

Isaiah speaks to Israel (the northern ten tribes in his day, also referred to as "Ephraim") in verses 1–4. This message came probably somewhere around 724 BC, before the ten tribes were taken captive by the Assyrians in 722 BC.

1 **Woe to the crown of pride** [*the haughty Ephraimites at Samaria, capital city of Israel, who have not yet come under Assyrian control and have boasted about their invincibility*], **to the drunkards of Ephraim** [*northern Israel is "drunk," out of control with wickedness*],

———————————
———————————
———————————
———————————
———————————
———————————
———————————
———————————
———————————
———————————
———————————
———————————
———————————
———————————
———————————
———————————
———————————
———————————
———————————
———————————
———————————
———————————
———————————
———————————
———————————
———————————
———————————
———————————
———————————
———————————
———————————
———————————
———————————

whose glorious beauty is a fading flower [*on the way out*]**,** which are on the head of the fat valleys [*rich, productive land area in Samaria*] of them that are overcome with wine [*you are out of control with wickedness*]!

2 **Behold, the Lord hath a mighty and strong one** [*Shalmaneser, the Assyrian king and his armies*]**, which as a tempest of hail and a destroying storm, as a flood of mighty waters overflowing** [*compare with Isaiah 8:7*]**, shall cast down** to the earth with the hand [*the Assyrians will flood your land and conquer you*].

3 **The crown of pride, the drunkards of Ephraim, shall be trodden under feet** [*Israel, the northern ten tribes, will be destroyed; this happens in 722 BC via Assyria*]:

We have mentioned several times that one of the techniques used by ancient prophets was repetition. We are seeing another example of that in the verses that follow.

4 **And the glorious beauty, which is on the head of the fat valley, shall be a fading flower,** and **as the hasty fruit** [*early fruit; the first ripe fruit on the tree*] **before the summer; which when he that looketh upon it seeth, while it is yet in his hand he eateth it up** [*it doesn't last long once someone has spotted it, in other words, you will be "gobbled up" quickly like the first ripe fruit of the season*].

5 **In that day** [*last days or Millennium*] **shall the Lord of hosts be for a crown of glory, and for a diadem** [*crown*] **of beauty, unto the residue** [*the righteous who are left*] **of his people** [*the Savior will lead you, as opposed to the proud, haughty drunkards referred to in verse 1*]**,**

6 And for a spirit of judgment to him that sitteth in judgment, and **for strength to them that turn the battle to the gate** [*Christ will provide strength to overcome all enemies and "push them back to where they came from"*].

7 ¶ **But they** [*Israel's leaders*] **also have erred** through wine, and through strong drink are out of the way; the [*false*] **priest** and the [*false*] **prophet** have erred through strong drink, they are swallowed up of wine, they are out of the way through strong drink; **they err in vision,** they **stumble in judgment** [*apostasy; out of control literally and symbolically*].

8 For **all tables are full of vomit and filthiness, so that there is no place clean** [*apostasy has completely penetrated the nation*].

9 ¶ **Whom shall he** [*the Lord*] **teach knowledge** [*of the gospel*]**? and whom shall he make to understand doctrine?** [*answer:*] them that are weaned from the milk, and drawn from the breasts [*toddlers; in other words, start teaching them while very young*].

Verse 10, next, is a rather well-known quote from Isaiah.

10 For precept must be upon precept, **precept upon precept; line upon line, line upon line; here a little, and there a little** [*a lifelong process starting very young*]:

11 **For with stammering** [*not understandable*] **lips and another tongue** [*a tongue "foreign" to the wicked; in other words, through the Holy Ghost*] **will he speak to this people.**

12 **To whom he said,** This is the rest [*peace of God*] wherewith ye may cause the weary to rest; and **this is the refreshing** [*available from God through righteous living*]: **yet they** [*Israel*] **would not** [*didn't want to*] **hear** [*in verse 10, the Lord tells them how he would help them bit by bit, not overwhelm them, but they don't want to hear such stuff*].

Next, in verse 13, Isaiah repeats again that the stubborn people of the northern ten tribes (Israel) had plenty of opportunity to hear and understand the gospel. They were given the opportunity so that they would be accountable for the consequences when they rebelled. This is the law of justice in action.

Remember that at this point in history, the northern ten tribes are called "Israel," and the southern two tribes (Judah and Benjamin) are called "Judah."

13 But **the word of the Lord was unto them precept upon precept**, precept upon precept; **line upon line**, line upon line; here a little, and there a little; **that they might go, and fall backward** [*apostasy isn't just "falling"; it is retrogressing—falling backward*], and **be broken**, and **snared**, and **taken** [*by Satan; in other words, when ignored, the word of God condemns*].

Next, Isaiah turns his attention to the haughty people of Judah.

14 ¶ **Wherefore hear the word of the Lord, ye scornful men** [*scoffers*], **that rule this people** which is in Jerusalem [*Isaiah now speaks to the people in Jerusalem in his day*].

15 **Because ye have said** [*boasted*], **We have made a covenant with death, and with hell are we at agreement** [*we have an "agreement" with death and hell*]; **when the overflowing scourge** [*that all the prophets keep saying will come*] **shall pass through, it shall not come unto us: for we have made lies our refuge** [*we have found that wickedness **does** pay!*], and **under falsehood have we hid ourselves** [*we will live wickedly and get away with it!*]:

16 ¶ **Therefore** [*because of your wickedness, boasting, and so forth*] **thus saith the Lord God, Behold, I lay in Zion for a foundation a stone** [*the Savior*], **a tried** [*proven reliable*] **stone, a precious corner stone** [*Ephesians 2:20*], **a sure foundation** [*the Lord is the only one with whom you can strike agreements and have guaranteed results*]: **he that believeth shall not make haste** [*will not flee; he that lives righteously will not have to flee before the face of the Lord*].

17 **Judgment also will I lay to the line** [*carpenter's line, used to build straight and true*], **and righteousness to the plummet** [*plumb bob (carpenter's tool used to build precisely); symbolic of the fact that all things about the Savior and His gospel are exact and true*]: and the hail shall sweep away the refuge of lies [*in other words, you won't get away with your boast in verse 15*], and the waters [*can refer to the Assyrians, see 8:7; could also refer to Christ as "living water," as in John 4:10*] shall overflow the hiding place [*of the wicked*].

18 ¶ And **your covenant with death** [*verse 15*] **shall be disannulled** [*cancelled*], and **your agreement with hell shall not stand**; when the overflowing scourge [*referred to boastfully in verse 15*] shall pass through, then **ye shall be trodden down** by it [*the wicked will be destroyed*].

NOTES

19 **From the time that it** [*the punishment of God*] **goeth forth it shall take you: for morning by morning shall it pass over, by day and by night** [*continuously*]: and it shall be a vexation [*pure terror*] only to understand the report [*God's judgments*].

Isaiah now refers to the proud boast in verse 15 that they could be comfortable and protected in sin. He uses the imagery of a bed that is too short for the person trying to sleep in it.

20 For **the bed is shorter than that a man can stretch himself on it** [*you can't ever get completely comfortable in the bed of sin you've made for yourselves to lie in*]: **and the covering** [*the blanket of lies you made for yourselves*] **narrower than that he can wrap himself in it** [*you can't get completely comfortable in your blanket of sin!*].

21 **For the Lord shall rise up as in mount Perazim** [*David attacked and smote the Philistines there, with the Lord's help*], **he shall be wroth as in the valley of Gibeon** [*where the Lord killed Joshua's enemies, the Amorites, with huge hailstones*], that he may do his work, his strange work; and bring to pass his act, his strange [*unusual*] act.

Next, Isaiah issues a strong warning to these arrogant people.

22 **Now therefore be ye not mockers** [*don't scoff at God's word*], **lest your bands be made strong** [*lest you be totally enslaved by wickedness*]: **for I** [*Isaiah*] **have heard from the Lord God of hosts a consumption, even determined upon the whole earth** [*I've heard God will annihilate the wicked*].

23 ¶ **Give ye ear, and hear my voice; hearken, and hear my speech**.

24 **Doth the plowman** [*farmer; symbolic of God*] **plow all day to sow** [*getting ready to plant*]: **doth he open and break the clods of his ground** [*continuously*]? [*Does the Lord just keep plowing, preparing and preparing the ground forever, or does he go on to the next steps, planting, harvesting, and so forth? In other words, "Do you think Judgment Day will never come, that the Lord will never get around to harvest time?"*]

Isaiah answers his own question in verse 25, next.

25 **When he** [*the farmer*] **hath made plain the face thereof** [*has the ground plowed and leveled*], **doth he not cast abroad** [*plant, throw the seeds by hand*] the fitches [*dill seeds*], and scatter the cummin, and cast in the principal wheat [*the main crop*] and the appointed [*planned on*] barley and the rie in their place [*doesn't the farmer plan carefully and then work his plan*]?

26 For **his** [*the plowman's*] **God doth instruct him to discretion, and doth teach him**.

Next, Isaiah uses some different methods of harvesting used in his day to illustrate that the Lord carefully applies differing harvesting methods to harvest His people, depending on their personalities.

27 For **the fitches** [*a plant producing small seeds that were harvested and used like we use pepper*] **are not threshed with a threshing instrument, neither is a cart wheel** [*used in harvesting larger grain seeds such as wheat*] **turned about** [*around and around*]

upon the cummin [*very small seeds*]; but the fitches are beaten out with a staff, and the cummin with a rod [*God will use appropriate methods to "harvest" all the righteous out from the wicked, according to their personalities, aptitudes, talents, and so forth*].

28 Bread corn [*cereal grain*] is bruised [*ground in a mill*]; because he will not ever [*forever*] be threshing it, nor break it with the wheel of his cart, nor bruise it with his horsemen. [*In the Martin Luther German Bible, this verse says basically that cereal grain is ground to make bread, not threshed to the point of destruction when it is threshed with wagon wheels and horses.*]

29 **This also cometh forth from the Lord of hosts** [*this is how the Lord goes about harvesting the righteous*], which is wonderful in counsel [*who is wonderful in how He plans His work; see Isaiah 19:3, 25:1*], and excellent in working [*German: carries it out wonderfully*].

ISAIAH 29

Selection: all verses

This chapter compares with 2 Nephi 27 in the Book of Mormon. The Book of Mormon rendition provides many changes for this chapter in the Bible. We will draw heavily from it as we proceed.

This prophecy was given by Isaiah about 700 BC, near the end of his ministry. It deals with the last days, including the restoration of the gospel through the Prophet Joseph Smith, giving many specific details about the coming forth of the Book of Mormon. It is a chapter of scripture that bears extra strong witness of the truthfulness of prophecies given by the Lord through His chosen servants, such as Isaiah.

Isaiah begins by prophesying about the out-of-control wickedness that will prevail among all peoples upon the earth in the last days.

1 **Woe to Ariel** [*Jerusalem; Zion in 2 Nephi 27:3*], to Ariel, **the city where David dwelt**! add ye year to year; let them kill sacrifices [*keep right on going as you are with your wickedness and empty rituals; it will do you no good!*].

2 **Yet I will** [*I will continue to*] **distress Ariel**, and there shall be heaviness and sorrow: and **it shall be unto me as Ariel** [*it shall become a proper Zion*].

3 And **I will camp against thee** [*the Lord will humble his rebellious covenant people*] round about, and will lay siege against thee with a mount [*mound of dirt*], and I will raise forts against thee [*as is the case in a planned military action; in other words, you will be chastened until you repent*].

4 **And thou** [*Ariel*] **shalt be brought down** [*humbled*], and shalt speak out of the ground, and **thy speech shall be low out of the dust**, and **thy voice shall be, as of one** that hath a familiar spirit [*a dead relative speaking from the spirit world*], **out of the ground**, and thy speech shall whisper out of the dust [*the Book of Mormon came "out of the ground" and in it, the Nephites, our dead Israelite "relatives" who came from Ariel; in other words, Jerusalem, speak to us as from the dust*].

5 Moreover **the multitude of thy strangers** [*the number of your enemies*] **shall be like small dust** [*countless*], and the multitude of the terrible ones [*tyrants*] shall be as

NOTES

_____
_____
_____
_____
_____
_____
_____
_____
_____
_____
_____
_____
_____
_____
_____
_____
_____
_____
_____
_____
_____
_____
_____
_____
_____
_____
_____
_____
_____
_____

chaff that passeth away [*that blows away in the wind, in other words, countless*]: yea, **it shall be at an instant suddenly** [*the things that humble you; see first part of verse 4; will catch you off guard so that you will hardly be able to believe they are happening so rapidly and nobody is stopping them*].

6 **Thou shalt be visited of** [*disciplined or punished by*] **the Lord** of hosts with thunder, and with earthquake, and great noise, with storm and tempest, and the flame of devouring fire.

In verses 7–8, next, Isaiah describes the ultimate failure and frustration of the wicked who fight against the work of the Lord.

7 ¶ And the multitude of **all the nations that fight against Ariel** [*the Lord's people; Zion, 2 Nephi 27:3*], even all that fight against her and her munition, and that distress her, **shall be as a dream of a night vision**.

8 **It** [*their persecution of the Saints*] **shall even be** [*unto them, 2 Nephi 27:3—enemy nations*] **as when an hungry man dreameth, and, behold, he eateth; but he awaketh, and his soul is empty** [*he is still hungry*]: or as when a thirsty man dreameth, and, behold, he drinketh [*in his dream*]; but he awaketh, and, behold, he is faint, and his soul hath appetite: **so shall the multitude of all the nations be, that fight against mount Zion** [*persecutors of the Saints never feel satisfied, are still "hungry and thirsty" for more, can't leave us alone*].

9 ¶ **Stay yourselves, and wonder** [*you wicked people, stop and think*]; **cry ye out**, and cry: **they** [*the wicked, 2 Nephi 27:4*] **are drunken** [*out of control*], **but not with wine**; they stagger [*stumble around*], but not with strong drink [*in other words, they are "drunk" with wickedness, out of control because they have no prophets to lead them, as mentioned in verse 10, next*].

The Book of Mormon makes an important doctrinal correction to the Bible, in verse 10, next. It is not the Lord who causes spiritual darkness to come upon people; rather, it is the people themselves who close their eyes to truth and light and who are the cause of spiritual darkness.

10 **For the Lord hath poured out upon you the spirit of deep sleep** [*spiritual darkness*], and hath closed [*"ye have closed," 2 Nephi 27:5*] **your eyes: the prophets and your rulers, the seers hath he covered** [*"because of your iniquity," 2 Nephi 27:5*].

Next, Isaiah begins a marvelous prophecy about the coming forth of the Book of Mormon in the last days. He gives an amazing amount of specific detail, which, as you will see, was fulfilled.

11 And **the vision of all** [*German: the vision of all the prophets, in other words, all of the scripture*] **is become unto you** [*Israelites who are spiritually dead*] **as the words of a book** [*Book of Mormon—see footnote 11a in your Bible*] **that is sealed** [*because you refuse to hearken to the scriptures, they might just as well be sealed and unreadable to you, like the copy of characters from the Book of Mormon plates*], **which men** [*Martin Harris, with the help of Joseph Smith*] **deliver to one that is learned** [*Professor Charles Anthon of Colombia College in New York City, February 1828*], **saying, Read this, I pray thee: and he** [*Charles Anthon*] **saith, I cannot; for it is sealed:**

You can read the account of Martin Harris and Charles Anthon, prophesied above, in the Pearl of Great Price, Joseph Smith—History 1:63–65.

12 And the book [*the gold plates*] **is delivered to him** [*Joseph Smith*] **that is not learned** [*educated, like Professor Anthon*], **saying, Read this, I pray thee: and he saith, I am not learned** [*I can't translate it without God's help*].

13 ¶ Wherefore the Lord said, **Forasmuch as this people draw near me with their mouth, and with their lips do honour me, but have removed their heart far from me** [*they are spiritually dead*], **and their fear toward me is taught by the precept** [*traditions*] **of men** [*people have gone far astray from truth*]:

14 Therefore, behold, **I will proceed to do a marvellous work** among this people, even **a marvellous** [*"astonishing" as used in Old Testament Hebrew*] **work and a wonder** [*the Restoration of the gospel*]: for **the wisdom of their wise men shall perish** [*revealed truth cuts through falsehood*], and the understanding of their prudent men shall be hid [*false philosophies and false scientific conclusions fade away in light of truth*].

15 Woe unto them [*the wicked*] **that seek deep to hide their counsel** [*plans*] **from the Lord**, and **their works are in the dark**, and **they say, Who seeth us? and who knoweth us?** [*We can get away with wickedness without getting exposed—typical thinking of wicked people.*]

16 Surely your turning of things upside down [*foolish perversion of the truth*] **shall be esteemed as** [*is the same as*] **the potter's clay**: for shall the work [*the pot*] say of him that made it [*the potter*], He made me not? or shall the thing framed say of him that framed it, He had no understanding? [*He doesn't know me; I have successfully hidden from God. In other words, you wicked are just as foolish as the potter's clay that claims it made itself into a pot and has no responsibility to its maker.*]

Next, beginning with verse 17, Isaiah tells us that the coming forth of the Book of Mormon will be the key event signaling the beginning of the Restoration of the gospel in the last days and the fulfilling of the many prophecies that will culminate with the Second Coming. Included in these prophecies are the gathering of the Jews and their establishment as a nation again in the Holy Land.

17 Is it not yet a very little while [*after the Book of Mormon comes forth*], **and Lebanon** [*the Holy Land*] **shall be turned into a fruitful field, and the fruitful field shall be esteemed as a forest?** [*In other words, Israel will blossom with forests and in other ways (including eventual spiritual conversion) after the Restoration.*]

18 ¶ **And in that day** [*the time of the Restoration of the gospel, with the Book of Mormon leading the way*] **shall the** [*spiritually*] **deaf hear the words of the book, and the eyes of the** [*spiritually*] **blind shall see out of obscurity, and out of darkness** [*as a result of the Book of Mormon and the Restoration, the spiritually deaf and blind will be healed*].

19 The meek also shall increase their joy in the Lord, and the poor among men shall rejoice in the Holy One of Israel [*the righteous will know the Savior again*].

NOTES

20 For the terrible one [*tyrant*] **is brought to nought, and the scorner** [*scoffer*] **is consumed, and all that watch for iniquity are cut off** [*the restored truth will expose wickedness and eventually overthrow it*]:

In verse 21, next, Isaiah describes the crippling corruption in governments and judicial systems in the last days.

21 That make a man an offender for a word [*via unjust lawsuits, corrupt judicial system, and so forth*], **and lay a snare for him that reproveth in the gate** [*try to eliminate honest people in government, and those who try to expose corruption in government*], **and turn aside the just for a thing of nought** [*destroy the effectiveness of honest government and judicial leaders; replace truth and honesty with lies*].

Next, Isaiah uses his great skill as a writer to create in our minds a picture of a rather embarrassed Jacob (the father of the twelve sons who became the twelve tribes of Israel). In the past, he has been embarrassed by the behaviors of his posterity, rebellious Israel. However, because of the restoration of the gospel in the last days and the gathering of Israel, they will finally become a righteous people. He is no longer embarrassed to be their "father;" rather, he is humbly proud of them.

22 Therefore thus saith the Lord, who redeemed Abraham, **concerning the house of Jacob** [*Israel; implies "I redeemed Abraham and I can and will redeem you."*], **Jacob shall not now be ashamed, neither shall his face now wax pale** [*Father Jacob, Israel, will no longer have to be embarrassed by the behavior of his posterity*].

23 But when he [*Jacob*] **seeth his children** [*his posterity*], **the work of mine hands** [*who are now finally righteous—"My people"*], in the midst of him, **they shall sanctify my name, and sanctify the Holy One of Jacob** [*the Savior*], **and shall fear** [*respect*] **the God of Israel**. [*Isaiah here has said, in many ways, that in the last days' Israel will return to God.*]

In concluding this vision, Isaiah summarizes the marvelous effects of the Book of Mormon and the Restoration of the gospel through the Prophet Joseph Smith.

24 They also that erred in spirit shall come to understanding, and they that murmured shall learn doctrine [*through the Book of Mormon and the Restoration of the Church of Jesus Christ*].

ISAIAH 30

Selection: all verses

In this chapter, we will see the scattering of Israel because they rejected their prophets. Then we will see the gathering and eventual coming of the Savior and the destruction of the wicked.

The historical setting is 705–701 BC. King Sargon II, of Assyria, has died. Judah joins the Philistines and Phoenicians in rebellion against Assyria. Judah makes a treaty for protection with Egypt (which sometimes is used to symbolize Satan's kingdom in Old Testament writings).

In verse 1, Isaiah points out that Judah has turned to political alliances for protection from her enemies, rather than repenting and turning to God for protection.

NOTES

1 **Woe to the rebellious children**, saith the LORD, **that take counsel** [*make political plans*], **but not of me; and that cover with a covering** [*alliance*], **but not of my spirit** [*not approved by God*], that they may add sin to sin [*add insult to injury; make things worse*]:

2 **That walk to go down into Egypt** [*turn to Egypt for help*], **and have not asked at my mouth** [*haven't asked My permission*]; to strengthen themselves in the strength of Pharaoh, and to trust in the shadow [*protection*] of Egypt!

3 **Therefore** [*because you have done this*] **shall the strength of Pharaoh be your shame** [*downfall*], and the trust in the shadow [*protection*] of Egypt your confusion [*your pact with Egypt will lead to your ruin; you should have turned to God rather than man for help*].

4 **For his** [*Pharaoh's*] **princes** [*leaders*] **were at Zoan** [*Tanis*], **and his ambassadors came to Hanes** [*leaders from one end of Egypt to the other worked out the treaty with Judah*].

5 **They** [*Judah*] **were** [*will be*] **all ashamed of** [*disappointed by*] **a people** [*Egypt*] **that could not** [*can not*] **profit them**, nor be an help nor profit, but a shame, and also a reproach [*this deal with Egypt will bring shame and scorn to Judah*].

6 **The burden of** [*message of doom for those of Judah who travel with loads of gifts on animals toward Egypt, verses 2–7*] **the beasts of the south: into the land of trouble and anguish**, from whence come the young and old lion, the viper and fiery flying serpent, **they** [*Judah*] **will carry their riches upon the shoulders of young asses, and their treasures upon the bunches of camels, to a people** [*Egypt*] **that shall not profit them.**

7 **For the Egyptians shall help in vain, and to no purpose**: therefore have I cried concerning this, Their strength is to sit still [*Egypt won't help you at all!*].

Next, the Lord instructs Isaiah to be sure to write this prophecy and warning down as a written witness against these wicked people.

8 ¶ **Now go, write it before them in a table, and note it in a book** [*which will eventually become scripture*], **that it may be for the time to come for ever and ever** [*write this down as a witness against Judah*]:

9 **That this** [*Judah*] **is a rebellious people, lying children, children that will not hear the law of the LORD:**

10 **Which say to the seers, See not; and to the prophets, Prophesy not** unto us **right things, speak unto us smooth things** [*comfortable false doctrines*], **prophesy deceits:**

11 Get you out of the way, turn aside out of the path, **cause the Holy One of Israel to cease from before us** [*tell God to quit bothering us*].

NOTES

12 **Wherefore thus saith the Holy One of Israel, Because ye despise** [*spurn, intentionally ignore*] **this word**, and trust in oppression [*German: wickedness*] and perverseness, and stay [*depend*] thereon:

13 **Therefore this iniquity shall be to you as a breach** [*broken section in a protective wall*] **ready to fall**, swelling [*bulging*] out in a high wall, whose breaking cometh suddenly at an instant [*you are living on borrowed time; you have broken the covenant that could protect you like a wall by making covenants with Egypt rather than God*].

14 **And he** [*Christ*] **shall break it as the breaking of the potters' vessel that is broken in pieces; he shall not spare**: so that there shall not be found in the bursting of it a sherd [*fragment*] to take fire from the hearth, or to take water withal out of the pit [*there won't be a piece big enough left to take a fire start from the fireplace or to dip a little water from the well; nothing usable remains*].

Next, the Lord tells these rebellious people how they could be saved from the fate just described.

15 For **thus saith the Lord** GOD, the Holy One of Israel; **In returning** [*to God*] **and rest shall ye be saved** [*German: you could be saved*]; **in quietness** [*peacefulness*] **and in confidence** [*faith in God*] **shall be your strength**: and ye would not.

16 **But ye said** [*bragged*], **No**; for we will flee [*into battle against Assyria*] upon horses [*symbolize victory*]; therefore [*because of your rebellion*] shall ye flee [*from Assyria's armies*]: and, We will ride upon the swift [*Judah bragged*]; therefore shall they [*Assyrians*] that pursue you be swift [*it will be exactly opposite of what you brag, Judah*].

17 **One thousand** [*of Judah*] **shall flee at the rebuke of one** [*Assyrian*]; at the rebuke of five [*Assyrians*] shall [*German: all of you*] ye flee: till ye be left as a beacon upon the top of a mountain, and as an ensign on an hill [*lonely, nobody left, scattered*].

18 ¶ And **therefore will the LORD wait** [*because of your wickedness, the Lord will have to wait*], **that he may be gracious unto you** [*at a future time*], and therefore will he be exalted, that he may have mercy upon you: for the LORD is a God of judgment [*justice*]: **blessed are all they that wait for** [*German: trust in*] **him**.

Isaiah now describes the ultimate in paradisiacal conditions for those who do trust in the Lord.

19 For the people shall dwell in Zion at Jerusalem: **thou shalt weep no more: he will be very gracious unto thee at the voice of thy cry; when he shall hear it, he will answer thee**.

20 And **though the Lord give you the bread of adversity, and the water of affliction** [*even though you go through some trying times*], yet shall not thy teachers [*thy teacher, the Lord*] be removed into a corner any more, **but thine eyes shall see thy teachers**:

21 And **thine ears shall hear a word behind thee, saying, This is the way, walk ye in it**, when ye turn to the right hand, and when ye turn to the left [*you will be surrounded with guidance and truth*].

22 **Ye shall defile** [*cease to worship*] **also the covering of thy graven images of silver** [*your graven images covered with silver*], and the ornament of thy molten images of gold: thou shalt cast them away as a menstruous cloth [*they will be totally repulsive to you*]; thou shalt say unto it, Get thee hence [*you will shudder at the thought of idol worship*].

23 **Then shall he give the rain of thy seed, that thou shalt sow the ground withal** [*you will prosper*]; and bread of the increase of the earth, and it shall be fat and plenteous: in that day shall thy cattle feed in large pastures [*things will go well when Israel repents and is gathered*].

24 **The oxen likewise and the young asses that ear the ground** [*work the ground in agriculture*] shall eat clean provender [*hay*], which hath been winnowed with the shovel and with the fan.

25 And **there shall be** upon every high mountain, and upon every high hill, **rivers and streams of waters** in the day of the great slaughter, when the towers fall [*when your enemies have been destroyed*].

26 **Moreover the light of the moon shall be as the light of the sun, and the light of the sun shall be sevenfold, as the light of seven days** [*everything will be better than you can imagine*], in the day that the LORD bindeth up the breach of his people, and healeth the stroke of their wound [*Christ heals when people repent*].

27 ¶ Behold, the name of **the LORD cometh from far, burning with his anger,** and the burden thereof is heavy: his lips are full of indignation, and his tongue as a devouring fire [*the wicked are destroyed*]:

28 And **his breath, as an overflowing stream** [*flood*], shall reach to the midst of the neck, **to sift** [*German: destroy*] **the nations** [*the wicked*] with the sieve of vanity [*German: until they are all filtered out, destroyed, gone*]: and there shall be a bridle in the jaws of the people, causing them to err [*they have allowed wickedness to take control of them; that's why they are destroyed*].

29 **Ye** [*the righteous survivors*] **shall have a song,** as in the night when a holy solemnity is kept; **and gladness of heart,** as when one goeth with a pipe [*German: flute*] to come into the mountain of the LORD, to the mighty One of Israel [*the Savior*].

30 **And the LORD shall cause his glorious voice to be heard, and shall shew the lighting down of his arm** [*will come crashing down upon the wicked*], with the indignation of his anger, and with the flame of a devouring fire, with scattering, and tempest, and hailstones.

31 For **through the voice** [*power*] **of the LORD shall the Assyrian** [*the enemy now threatening Judah*] **be beaten down,** which smote [*Israel*] with a rod.

32 And in every place where the grounded staff shall pass [*every stroke of the rod of punishment*], which the LORD shall lay upon him [*Assyria*], it shall be with tabrets and harps: and in battles of shaking [*several "waves" of battle*] will he fight with it.

NOTES
_____
_____
_____
_____
_____
_____
_____
_____
_____
_____
_____
_____
_____
_____
_____
_____
_____
_____
_____
_____
_____
_____
_____
_____
_____
_____
_____
_____
_____
_____
_____
_____
_____
_____
_____

33 **For Tophet** [the "Place of Burning," hell] **is ordained of old** [was planned for in the beginning]; yea, **for the king** [of Assyria] **it is prepared**; he [God] hath made it deep and large [there is plenty of room in hell for the Assyrians and all other wicked]: the pile thereof is fire and much wood [plenty of fuel to burn them]; the breath of the LORD, like a stream of brimstone [fiery molten sulfur], doth kindle it [the Lord is prepared to destroy the wicked].

ISAIAH 31

Selection: all verses

In chapter 30, we learned that the nation of Judah had determined to turn to Egypt for help against Assyria. In this chapter, Isaiah continues to warn them about this mistake.

1 **Woe to them** [Judah] **that go down to Egypt for help**; and stay [rely] on horses, and trust in chariots [the military might of Egypt], **because they** [Egyptian soldiers] **are many**; and in horsemen, because they are very strong; **but they look not unto the Holy One of Israel, neither seek the LORD** [Judah should turn to the Lord instead of Egypt for help]!

2 **Yet he** [the Lord] also **is wise**, and **will bring evil** [calamity upon the wicked], **and will not call back** [retract] **his words: but will arise against the house of the evil-doers, and against the help** [helpers] **of them that work iniquity.**

3 **Now the Egyptians are men, and not God**; and their horses flesh, and not spirit. When the LORD shall stretch out his hand, both he that helpeth shall fall, and he that is holpen [helped] shall fall down, and they all shall fail together [Egypt and Judah will both fail].

Next, Isaiah reminds the Jews that the Lord does indeed have power to protect them against their enemies.

4 For **thus hath the LORD spoken unto me** [Isaiah], **Like as the lion** and the young lion roaring on his prey, **when a multitude of shepherds is called forth against him**, he will not be afraid of their voice, nor abase himself for the noise of them: **so shall the LORD of hosts come down to fight for mount Zion, and for the hill thereof** [the Lord will be as unstoppable among the wicked as a lion among sheep].

5 **As birds flying** [hovering over their young, protecting them], **so will the LORD of hosts defend Jerusalem**; defending also he will deliver it; and passing over he will preserve it.

6 **Turn ye unto him** [the Lord] from whom the children of Israel have deeply revolted [please repent].

7 For **in that day** [if and when you repent] **every man shall cast away his idols of silver, and his idols of gold**, which your own hands have made unto you for a sin [turn away from your sinful idol worship].

8 ¶ **Then shall the Assyrian fall** with the sword, not of a mighty man; and the sword, not of a mean [*poor*] man, shall devour him: but he shall flee from the sword, and his young men shall be discomfited [*put in slavery; God, not men, will overthrow Assyria*].

9 **And he shall pass over to his strong hold for fear** [*will retreat in fear*], and his princes shall be afraid of the ensign, saith the LORD, whose fire is in Zion, and his furnace in Jerusalem [*the power of the Lord can protect Zion, Jerusalem*].

ISAIAH 32

Selection: all verses

In this chapter, Isaiah prophesies that the day will come when Jesus Christ will rule and reign, but in the meantime, until the restoration of the gospel and the gathering of Israel, the land of Israel will be a wilderness.

1 Behold, **a king** [*Jesus*] **shall reign in righteousness, and princes** [*His leaders*] **shall rule in judgment** [*justice, fairness*].

2 **And a man** [*Jesus*] **shall be as an hiding place from the wind, and a covert** [*protection*] **from the tempest**; as rivers of water in a dry place, as the shadow of a great rock in a weary land [*Jesus will be our refuge and protection*].

Next, Isaiah teaches what the effects of the Savior and His gospel will be upon those who listen, who have previously been spiritually blind and deaf.

3 **And the eyes of them that see shall not be dim** [*the spiritual eyes of those who see the gospel, who were previously spiritually blind, shall no longer be dim*], **and the ears of them that hear shall hearken** [*people will be blessed with understanding and discernment*].

4 **The heart** [*mind*] also **of the rash** [*impulsive*] **shall understand** knowledge [*have good judgment*], **and the tongue of the stammerers shall be ready to speak plainly** [*those who previously could not explain the purposes of life according to the gospel will now discuss the gospel plainly*].

5 **The vile person** [*villain*] **shall be no more called liberal** [*noble*], **nor the churl** [*miser; cruel financier*] **said to be bountiful** [*people will be recognized for what they really are, not what they appear to be*].

In verses 6–8, Isaiah describes what the motives of people alluded to in verse 5 really are like.

6 For **the vile person will speak villany,** and his heart **will work iniquity,** to practise **hypocrisy,** and to **utter error against the LORD,** to make empty the soul of the hungry [*oppress the poor and needy*], and he will cause the drink of the thirsty to fail.

7 **The instruments** [*devices*] also of the churl [*wicked moneylenders*] **are evil: he deviseth wicked devices to destroy the poor with lying words** [*trickery*], even when the needy speaketh right [*is in the right*].

NOTES

8 But **the liberal** [*noble*] **deviseth liberal** [*honorable, righteous*] **things**; and by liberal things shall he stand [*German: he will hold to honorable thoughts and actions*].

Next, Isaiah warns the women against the spiritual dangers that confront them.

9 ¶ **Rise up, ye women** [*German: proud women*] **that are at ease** [*overconfident about their safety; see 2 Nephi 28:24*]; **hear my voice, ye careless daughters** [*overconfident, complacent, too secure to change your ways*]; give ear unto my speech [*message*].

10 **Many days and years shall ye be troubled, ye careless women**: for the vintage [*vineyard*] shall fail [*not produce*], the gathering [*harvest*] shall not come [*famine*].

11 **Tremble, ye women that are at ease**; be troubled, ye careless ones: **strip you** [*of pride*], **and make you bare, and gird sackcloth upon your loins** [*humble yourselves*].

In verses 12–14, Isaiah tells of a long period of destruction soon to come upon unsuspecting Israelites.

12 **They shall lament for the teats** [*beat upon the breast in mourning*], **for the pleasant fields, for the fruitful vine** [*they will long for the good times*].

13 **Upon the land of my people shall come up thorns and briers**; yea, upon all the houses of joy in the joyous city [*rough times are coming because of wickedness*]:

14 **Because the** [*your*] **palaces shall be forsaken; the multitude of the city shall be left** [*deserted*]; the forts and towers shall be for dens [*places of habitation for wild beasts*] for ever, a joy of wild asses, a pasture of flocks [*you will be scattered and your lands left lonely and desolate*];

Isaiah now mentions the peaceful conditions to come upon Israel in a future day of righteousness.

15 **Until the spirit be poured upon us from on high, and the wilderness be** [*become*] **a fruitful field, and the fruitful field be counted for a forest.**

16 **Then judgment** [*justice, fairness*] **shall dwell in the wilderness** [*in formerly apostate Israel*], and righteousness remain in the fruitful field.

17 **And the work** [*result*] **of righteousness shall be peace**; and the effect [*result*] of righteousness quietness [*lack of turmoil*] and assurance [*security*] for ever.

18 **And my people shall dwell in a peaceable habitation**, and in sure [*safe*] dwellings, and in quiet resting places [*German: splendid peace*];

19 **When it shall hail** [*destruction upon the wicked*], **coming down on the forest** [*wicked people?*]; **and the city** [*probably the proud and wicked*] **shall be low in a low place** [*brought down, humbled*].

20 **Blessed** [*happy*] **are ye** [*the righteous*] **that sow beside all waters** [*German: everywhere*], that send forth thither [*everywhere*] the feet of the ox and the ass [*perhaps saying that there will be peace everywhere for the righteous*].

ISAIAH 33

Selection: all verses

Isaiah will now prophesy of great wickedness before the Second Coming of the Lord. Israel will be gathered. There will be great destruction among the wicked. The wicked will ultimately be destroyed by fire and the Savior will rule as our King during the Millennium.

The issue in verse 1 is that it seems as though the wicked often get away with sin without consequences. They don't.

1 **Woe to thee** [*probably Sennacherib, king of Assyria, Isaiah 36:1; symbolic of all wicked who seem to get away with wickedness*] **that spoilest, and thou wast not spoiled; and dealest treacherously, and they dealt not treacherously with thee!** when thou shalt cease to spoil, **thou shalt be spoiled**; and when thou shalt make an end to deal treacherously, they shall deal treacherously with thee [*after the Lord is through using you to punish other wicked nations, you will get your just reward*].

2 **O LORD, be gracious unto us** [*Israel*]; **we have waited for thee: be thou their** [*our*] **arm** [*symbolic of power in biblical language*] every morning, our salvation also in the time of trouble.

3 At the noise of the tumult the people fled [*flee*]; at the lifting up of thyself [*Christ*] the nations were [*are*] scattered.

4 **And your spoil** [*Israel's remnants*] **shall be gathered** [*by missionaries*] like the gathering of the caterpiller: as the running to and fro of locusts [*perhaps describing missionaries going everywhere in the last days*] shall he [*they*] run [*collect*] upon them [*Israel*].

5 The LORD is exalted; for he dwelleth on high: he hath filled Zion with judgment and righteousness.

Next, Isaiah teaches that the restored gospel will provide stability in the lives of those who embrace it.

6 And **wisdom and knowledge shall be the stability of thy times, and strength of salvation**: the fear of the LORD is his treasure [*results of the Restoration*].

Verses 7–9 refer back to the Assyrian attack.

7 **Behold, their** [*wicked Israel's*] **valiant ones** [*wicked heroes*] **shall cry without** [*outside of Zion*]: **the ambassadors of peace shall weep bitterly.**

8 **The highways lie waste, the wayfaring man ceaseth** [*there are no more travelers*]: **he hath broken the covenant**, he hath despised the cities, he regardeth no man.

NOTES

9 **The earth mourneth and languisheth: Lebanon is ashamed** [*the Holy Land is severely distressed*] **and hewn down**: Sharon is like a wilderness; and Bashan and Carmel shake off their fruits.

10 **Now will I rise, saith the LORD; now will I be exalted**; now will I lift up myself [*the time will come when God will take over from the wicked*].

11 **Ye shall conceive chaff, ye shall bring forth stubble** [*the end result of wicked lifestyles is nothing of value*]: **your breath, as fire, shall devour you** [*sow evil, harvest misery*].

12 **And the people shall be** as the burnings of lime: **as thorns cut up** [*as useless branches cut up for burning*] **shall they be burned in the fire**.

13 ¶ **Hear, ye that are far off** [*everybody in the whole world, listen up and acknowledge*], **what I have done**; and, ye that are near, acknowledge my might [*in the future the whole world will know God*].

14 **The sinners in Zion are afraid; fearfulness hath surprised** [*seized*] **the hypocrites**. Who among us shall dwell with the devouring fire? who among us shall dwell with everlasting burnings [*who will not be burned, destroyed—who can survive the presence of God*]?

In verses 15–22, plus 24, next, Isaiah answers the question he posed in verse 14, above.

15 **He that walketh righteously, and speaketh uprightly**; he that despiseth the gain of oppressions [*unrighteous profit at the expense of others*], that shaketh his hands from holding of bribes [*refuses bribes*], that stoppeth his ears from hearing of blood, and shutteth his eyes from seeing evil [*does not participate in evils*];

16 **He** [*the righteous*] **shall dwell on high**: his place of defence shall be the munitions [*fortress*] of rocks: bread shall be given him; his waters shall be sure [*reward to the righteous*].

17 **Thine eyes shall see the king** [*the Savior*] in his beauty: they shall behold the land that is very far off [*heaven?*].

18 **Thine heart shall meditate** [*soften, put down*] **terror**. Where is the scribe [*Assyrian tallyman, conqueror*]? where is the receiver? where is he that counted the towers [*Assyrian army? In other words, where are the wicked now?*]?

19 **Thou shalt not see a fierce people** [*foreign invaders*], a people of a deeper speech than thou canst perceive; of a stammering tongue, that thou canst not understand [*enemies who speak foreign languages*].

20 Look upon Zion, the city of our solemnities: **thine eyes shall see Jerusalem a quiet habitation**, a tabernacle that shall not be taken down; not one of the stakes thereof shall ever be removed, neither shall any of the cords thereof be broken [*the future has glorious things in store for the righteous*].

21 **But there the glorious LORD will be unto us a place of broad rivers and streams**; wherein shall go no galley [*enemy ships*] with oars, neither shall gallant ship pass thereby.

22 **For the LORD is our judge, the LORD is our lawgiver, the LORD is our king; he will save us**.

In verse 23, next, Isaiah describes the shutting down of the power of the wicked and compares it to the stopping of a ship.

23 **Thy** [*the wicked's*] **tacklings** [*ship's rigging*] **are loosed; they could not well strengthen their mast, they could not spread the sail** [*the wicked will be shut down*]: then is the prey of a great spoil divided; **the lame** [*the righteous; the wicked have considered the righteous to be lame, weak*] **take the prey** [*the wicked*].

24 And the inhabitant shall not say, I am sick: **the people that dwell therein shall be forgiven their iniquity**.

ISAIAH 34

Selection: all verses

This chapter speaks of the Second Coming and the destruction of the wicked. It contains Isaiah's harshest words against the wicked. It is a review of earlier chapters and is a companion chapter to chapter 35.

1 **Come near, ye nations** [*speaking to the whole world*], **to hear**; and hearken, ye people: let the earth hear, and all that is therein; the world, and all things that come forth of it.

Isaiah now speaks of the future as if it has already happened.

2 For **the indignation** [*righteous anger*] **of the LORD is upon all nations** [*all the wicked*], and his fury upon all their armies: **he hath utterly destroyed them**, he hath delivered them to the slaughter [*future; ultimate fate of the wicked*].

3 Their slain also shall be cast out, and their stink shall come up out of their carcases, and **the mountains shall be melted** [*soaked*] **with their blood**.

4 And all the host [*stars?*] of heaven shall be dissolved, and **the heavens shall be rolled together as a scroll** [*compare with Doctrine & Covenants 88:95, which speaks of the Second Coming*]: and all their host [*starry host?*] shall fall down, as the leaf falleth off from the vine, and as a falling fig from the fig tree [*perhaps goes with Doctrine & Covenants 133:49 and 88:95; Second Coming*].

5 For **my sword shall be bathed in heaven** [*bathed in blood*]: behold, **it shall come down upon Idumea** [*Edom; the world, see Doctrine & Covenants 1:36; connotes the wicked world*], and **upon the people of my curse** [*upon the wicked*], to judgment.

6 **The sword of the LORD is filled with blood** [*bathed in blood*], it is made fat with fatness [*covered with fat like a knife used in animal sacrifices*], and with the blood of lambs and goats, with the fat of the kidneys of rams: for the LORD hath a sacrifice

in Bozrah [*the capital of Edom, a kingdom south of the Dead Sea*], and a great slaughter in the land of Idumea [*the wicked world; the sword of the Lord is going to come crashing down on the wicked of the world*].

7 And the unicorns [*wild oxen*] shall come down with them, and the bullocks [*bull calves*] with the bulls; and **their land shall be soaked with blood**, and their dust [*land*] made fat with fatness [*covered with fat trimmed away by sword of justice*].

8 For **it is the day of the LORD's vengeance** [*it is time for the law of justice to take over*], and the year of recompences [*deserved rewards*] for the controversy [*German: avenging*] of Zion [*a day of avenging the wrongs done against Zion throughout the history of the world*].

9 **And the streams thereof** [*of Edom, the wicked*] **shall be turned into pitch** [*goes up in flames easily*], **and** the dust thereof into **brimstone** [*burning sulfur*], **and the land thereof shall become burning pitch** [*the wicked of the world will be destroyed by fire*].

10 **It shall not be quenched night nor day** [*no one can stop the destruction of the wicked*]; the smoke thereof shall go up for ever: from generation to generation it shall lie waste; none shall pass through it for ever and ever [*wickedness will be destroyed completely*].

Isaiah often uses the imagery that now follows to emphasize the theme that the wicked will all be gone.

11 **But the cormorant and the bittern** [*lonely desert creatures*] **shall possess it; the owl also** and the raven shall dwell in it: and he [*the Lord*] shall stretch out upon it the line [*measuring tape*] of confusion, and the stones [*plumb line*] of emptiness [*Edom, the wicked, will not "measure up."*].

12 **They shall call the nobles** [*leaders*] thereof to the kingdom, **but none shall be there**, and all her [*Edom's*] princes [*leaders*] shall be nothing [*German: they will be people without a kingdom, will have nothing to rule over*].

13 And **thorns shall come up in her palaces**, nettles and brambles in the fortresses thereof: and **it shall be an habitation of dragons** [*jackals*], **and a court** [*home*] **for owls** [*none of the wicked will remain*].

14 The wild beasts of the desert shall also meet with the wild beasts [*hyenas*] of the island [*in other words, the wicked will all be gone, and the ruins where they once lived will be inhabited by creatures that don't like to live around people*], and the satyr [*wild goat*] shall cry to his fellow; the screech owl also shall rest there, and find for herself a place of rest.

15 **There shall the great owl make her nest**, and lay, and hatch, and gather under her shadow: there shall the vultures also be gathered, every one with her mate [*each of the animals mentioned above were considered unclean by the Israelites*].

16 ¶ **Seek ye out of the book of the LORD, and read** [*this is the word of God*]: no one of these [*unclean creatures*] shall fail, none shall want [*lack*] her mate: for my mouth it hath commanded, and his spirit it hath gathered them.

NOTES

17 **And he hath cast the lot** [*voted*] **for them, and his hand hath divided it unto them by line: they shall possess it for ever, from generation to generation shall they dwell therein** [*If the Lord takes such good care of these "unclean" creatures, think how much more the righteous will get; a transition to chapter 35*].

ISAIAH 35

Selection: all verses

This chapter is a continuation of the prophecy in chapter 34 (see background note for chapter 34). However, in this, we are given a prophetic picture of the beauty and peace that the righteous will receive.

1 **The wilderness and the solitary place shall be glad for them** [*the righteous who return*]; and **the desert shall rejoice, and blossom as the rose** [*a paradise awaits the righteous*].

2 **It shall blossom abundantly**, and rejoice even with joy and singing: the glory of Lebanon [*the Holy Land; symbolic of anywhere the righteous gather*] shall be given unto it, the excellency of Carmel and Sharon, **they shall see the glory of the LORD, and the excellency of our God**.

The Lord will strengthen the righteous, who have become weary in fighting evil.

3 ¶ **Strengthen ye the weak** [*German: tired*] **hands, and confirm** [*German: revive*] **the feeble** [*German: stumbling*] **knees.**

4 **Say to them** [*the righteous*] **that are of a fearful** [*German: discouraged*] **heart, Be strong, fear not: behold, your God will come with vengeance** [*upon the wicked*], even God with a recompence; he will come and save you [*the righteous*].

5 **Then the eyes of the** [*spiritually*] **blind shall be opened, and the ears of the** [*spiritually*] **deaf shall be unstopped** [*the restored gospel heals spiritual blindness and deafness*].

6 **Then shall the lame man leap as an hart** [*deer*], **and the tongue of the dumb** [*people who can't talk; symbolic of those who didn't know the gospel previously*] **sing: for in the wilderness shall waters break out, and streams in the desert** [*literal; also symbolic of "living water," the gospel*].

7 **And the parched ground** [*symbolic of apostate Israel; see Isaiah 53:2, Mosiah 14:2*] **shall become a pool, and the thirsty land springs of water** [*through the Restoration of the gospel*]: in the habitation of dragons [*jackals; Isaiah has used this imagery before (see Isaiah 13:22; 34:13–15) to depict the barrenness left when the wicked are destroyed. Here, he depicts the barrenness, apostate "wilderness," and so forth, being replaced with lush growth symbolizing the Restoration of the gospel*] **where each lay, shall be grass with reeds and rushes** [*restored productivity*].

8 **And an highway** [*perhaps literal highways upon which various groups have returned or will return; symbolically, the path to God—the gospel, "strait and narrow" way, temple covenants, baptismal covenants, and so forth*] **shall be there**, and a way, and it shall

NOTES

be called **The way of holiness**; the unclean [*the wicked*] shall not pass over it; but it shall be for those: the wayfaring men, though fools [*JST (Joseph Smith Translation of the Bible): "though they are accounted fools"—though men might consider the righteous to be fools*], shall not err therein.

9 **No lion shall be there, nor any ravenous beast** [*enemies of Israel's return; forces of evil*] **shall go up thereon, it shall not be found there** [*perhaps looking ahead to millennial conditions*]; **but the redeemed shall walk there:**

10 **And the ransomed of the LORD** [*those who have been redeemed by the Lord's Atonement*] **shall return, and come to Zion** with songs and everlasting joy upon their heads: **they shall obtain joy and gladness, and sorrow and sighing shall flee away** [*see Revelation 21:4; 7:17; the final state of the righteous*].

ISAIAH 36

Selection: all verses

Many of the chapters of Isaiah we have studied so far have dealt with the future. This chapter is an account of what happened when the Assyrians approached Judah with the goal of conquering Jerusalem and the cities of Judah. This took place near the end of Isaiah's service as a prophet.

1 Now it came to pass **in the fourteenth year** [*about 701 BC*] **of king Hezekiah** [*righteous king of Judah*], that **Sennacherib king of Assyria came up against all the defenced cities of Judah, and took them** [*perhaps as many as forty-six cities*].

Having conquered many cities in Judah, the Assyrian king now sends one of his chief officers to the outskirts of Jerusalem to harass King Hezekiah and his people in preparation for conquering them.

2 And **the king of Assyria sent Rabshakeh** [*a title meaning "chief of the officers"—see footnote 2a in your Bible*] from Lachish [*about thirty-five miles southwest of Jerusalem*] **to Jerusalem unto king Hezekiah with a great army**. And he [*Rabshakeh*] stood by the conduit of the upper pool in the highway of the fuller's field [*where fullers bleached cloth*].

Next, righteous King Hezekiah sends some trusted leaders to engage in talks with Rabshakeh.

3 **Then came forth unto him** [*Rabshakeh*] **Eliakim** [*prime minister of Judah*], Hilkiah's son, which was over the house, **and Shebna** the scribe, **and Joah**, Asaph's son, the recorder.

4 ¶ **And Rabshakeh said unto them, Say ye now to Hezekiah, Thus saith the great king** [*sarcastically mimicking "Thus saith the Lord"*], **the king of Assyria, What confidence is this wherein thou trustest?** [*you are fools to trust Egypt for protection*]

5 **I say, sayest thou,** [*but they are but vain words*] **I have counsel** [*plans with Egypt*] **and strength for war** [*Egypt is our ally*]: **now on whom dost thou** [*Hezekiah/Judah*] **trust, that thou rebellest against me** [*Assyria*]?

6 Lo, **thou trustest in the staff** ["*scepter," power*] **of this broken reed** ["*broken broom straw"*], **on Egypt**; whereon if a man lean, it will go into his hand, and pierce it ["*Egypt is so weak, so thin that if you were to lean on it with your hand it would poke right through"*]: **so is Pharaoh king of Egypt to all that trust in him** [*Egypt never could protect anyone*].

Next, Rabshakeh takes a poke at the worship of God, which Hezekiah has centralized in Jerusalem.

7 **But if thou say to me, We trust in the LORD our God: is it not he** [*the Lord*], **whose high places and whose altars** [*places of worship*] **Hezekiah hath taken away** [*King Hezekiah did away with local sites of worship and required the Jews to worship at the temple in Jerusalem*], **and said to Judah and to Jerusalem, Ye shall worship before this altar** [*worship at the temple in Jerusalem*]?

8 **Now therefore give pledges** ["*Let's make a bet."*], I pray thee, **to my master the king of Assyria, and I will give thee two thousand horses, if thou be able on thy part to set riders upon them** ["*if I give you two thousand horses, I'll bet you can't find two thousand able-bodied soldiers in all of Judah to ride them"*].

9 **How then wilt thou turn away** the face of **one captain of the least of my master's servants**, and put thy trust on Egypt for chariots and for horsemen [*you'll get no help from puny Egypt!*]?

Next, in verse 10, Rabshakeh claims that the God of Israel, Jehovah, sent him to conquer Jerusalem.

10 And am I now come up without the LORD against this land to destroy it? **the LORD said unto me, Go up against this land, and destroy it** ["*your God told me to come up and destroy you!" A lie, but sometimes an effective intimidation strategy*].

Next, the emissaries sent by King Hezekiah timidly ask Rabshakeh to speak in a language all the public, who have gathered on the wall of Jerusalem to hear, can't understand.

11 **Then said Eliakim and Shebna and Joah unto Rabshakeh, Speak,** I [*we*] pray thee [*please*], **unto thy servants** [*us, King Hezekiah's representatives*] **in the Syrian language; for we understand it:** and **speak not to us in the Jews' language, in the ears of the people that are on the wall.** ["*Can't we discuss this in a language our citizens don't understand? This is too embarrassing."*]

12 **But Rabshakeh said,** Hath my master sent me to thy master and to thee to speak these words? hath he not sent me to the men that sit upon the wall, that they may eat their own dung, and drink their own piss with you [*Before Assyria is through with you, you'll be that bad off*]?

13 **Then Rabshakeh stood, and cried with a loud voice in the Jews' language** [*intentionally so the citizens could easily hear*], and said, **Hear ye the words of the great king, the king of Assyria.**

NOTES

14 Thus saith the king, **Let not Hezekiah deceive you: for he shall not be able to deliver you**.

15 **Neither let Hezekiah make you trust in the LORD, saying, The LORD will surely deliver us**: this city shall not be delivered into the hand of the king of Assyria.

16 **Hearken not to Hezekiah**: for **thus saith the king of Assyria, Make an agreement with me** by a present [*via a payment*], and **come out to me** [*surrender*]: and eat ye every one of his vine, and every one of his fig tree, and drink ye every one the waters of his own cistern [*in effect, stay on your own land for a while in peace, until I make arrangements to transport you elsewhere—see verse 17, next*];

17 **Until I come and take you away to a land like your own land**, a land of corn [*grain*] and wine, a land of bread and vineyards [*you'll like where I take you*].

18 **Beware lest Hezekiah persuade you** [*don't let your foolish king fast-talk you into resisting us Assyrians*], **saying, The LORD will deliver us**. Hath any of the gods of the nations delivered his land out of the hand of the king of Assyria? [*no other gods in other lands have been able to stop us and yours won't either!*]

19 **Where are the gods of Hamath** [*part of modern Syria*] and **Arphad** [*part of modern Syria*]? where are the gods of **Sepharvaim** [*part of modern Syria*]? and have they delivered **Samaria** [*headquarters for the ten tribes, which the Assyrians conquered about twenty-one years earlier, in 722 BC*] out of my hand?

Next, Rabshakeh says, in effect, if the gods of all these other places could not hold us back from conquering them, what makes you think your Jehovah could possibly stop us?

20 **Who are they among all the gods of these lands, that have delivered their land out of my hand** [*which of their gods stopped us*], **that the LORD should deliver Jerusalem out of my hand?**

21 **But they** [*Hezekiah's three men*] **held their peace, and answered him not a word**: for the king's commandment was, saying, Answer him not.

22 **Then came Eliakim**, the son of Hilkiah, that was over the household, **and Shebna** the scribe, **and Joah**, the son of Asaph, the recorder, **to Hezekiah with their clothes rent** [*torn; a sign in their culture that they were very distraught*], **and told him the words of Rabshakeh.**

ISAIAH 37

<u>**Selection: all verses**</u>

This chapter is a continuation of the tense situation reported in chapter 36. Righteous King Hezekiah will send to Isaiah the prophet, for counsel as to how to deal with the situation.

1 And it came to pass, **when king Hezekiah heard it** [*the report from his emissaries in Isaiah 36:22*], that **he rent** [*tore*] **his clothes** [*as a sign of extreme worry*], **and covered himself with sackcloth, and went into the house of the LORD** [*the temple*].

Have you noticed that the word "LORD" (end of verse 1, above, and elsewhere), as printed in your King James version of the Bible, is spelled with a large capital "L" and small caps "ORD"? This is the King James Version of the Bible's way of pointing out that it is "Jehovah" about whom they are speaking. We know from Isaiah 43:1–3, 11, 14, and elsewhere that Jehovah is the premortal Jesus Christ, who is the God of the Old Testament.

2 **And he sent Eliakim** [*his prime minister*], who was over the household, **and Shebna** the [*royal*] scribe, **and the elders** [*older priests*] of the priests covered with sackcloth [*a sign of deep distress and mourning in their culture*], **unto Isaiah** the prophet the son of Amoz.

3 **And they said unto him**, Thus saith Hezekiah, **This day is a day of trouble, and of rebuke** [*we're in big trouble*], **and of blasphemy** [*the Assyrians speak totally disrespectfully of the Lord*]: for the children are come to the birth, and there is not strength to bring forth [*we're doomed, like when a woman is in hard labor, but the baby doesn't come*].

4 **It may be the LORD thy God will hear** [*has heard*] **the words of Rabshakeh** [*Assyria's representative*], whom the king of Assyria his master hath sent to reproach [*blaspheme*] the living God, **and will reprove the words** [*of Rabshakeh*] which the LORD thy God hath heard [*we hope the Lord will not let them get away with such talk*]: wherefore lift up thy prayer for the remnant that is left.

5 So the servants of king Hezekiah came to Isaiah.

6 ¶ And **Isaiah said** unto them, Thus shall ye **say unto your master**, Thus saith the LORD, **Be not afraid of the words that thou hast heard**, wherewith the servants of the king of Assyria have blasphemed me [*the Lord*].

7 **Behold, I** [*the Lord*] **will send a blast upon him** [*I will change his frame of mind, make him nervous*], and **he shall hear a rumour** [*bad news from home*], **and return to his own land; and I will cause him to fall by the sword in his own land.**

8 ¶ **So Rabshakeh returned, and found the king of Assyria warring against Libnah** [*southwest of Jerusalem*]: **for he** [*Rabshakeh*] **had heard that he** [*the King of Assyria*] **was departed from Lachish.**

9 **And he** [*the Assyrian King*] **heard** say **concerning Tirhakah king of Ethiopia** [*the Egyptian army*], He is come forth to make war with thee. **And when he** [*King of Assyria*] **heard it, he sent messengers to Hezekiah, saying** [*the King of Assyria, worried about approaching Egyptian armies, now presses King Hezekiah for quick surrender*],

10 Thus shall ye speak to Hezekiah king of Judah, saying, **Let not thy God, in whom thou trustest, deceive thee, saying, Jerusalem shall not be given into the hand of the king of Assyria** [*your God can't help you; you will be powerless before the Assyrians*].

NOTES

11 Behold, **thou hast heard what the kings of Assyria have done to all lands by destroying them utterly; and shalt thou be delivered** [*what makes you think you'll be different*]?

12 **Have the gods of the nations delivered** them which my fathers have destroyed, as **Gozan** [*Iraq*], and **Haran** [*Turkey*], and **Rezeph** [*Iraq*], and the children of Eden which were in **Telassar** [*Iraq*]?

13 Where is the king of **Hamath** [*Syria*], and the king of Arphad [*Syria*], and the king of the city of **Sepharvaim** [*Syria*], **Hena** [*unknown*], and **Ivah** [*unknown*]?

14 And **Hezekiah received the letter** from the hand of the messengers, and read it: **and** Hezekiah **went up unto the house of the LORD, and spread it before the LORD.**

15 **And Hezekiah prayed unto the LORD, saying,**

16 **O LORD of hosts**, God of Israel, that dwellest between [*German: above*] the cherubims, **thou art the God, even thou alone,** of all the kingdoms of the earth: **thou hast made heaven and earth.**

17 **Incline thine ear, O LORD, and hear**; open thine eyes, O LORD, and see: and **hear all the words of Sennacherib** [*King of Assyria*], **which hath sent to reproach** [*blaspheme*] **the living God.**

18 **Of a truth** [*it is true*], LORD, **the kings of Assyria have laid waste all the nations, and their countries** [*just as the letter in verse 14 says*],

19 **And have cast their gods** [*idols*] **into the fire: for they were no gods** [*weren't real gods*], but the work of men's hands, wood and stone: **therefore they have destroyed them** [*that's why Assyria was able to conquer those cities and nations*].

20 **Now therefore, O LORD our God, save us from his hand, that all the kingdoms of the earth may know that thou art the LORD, even thou only.**

Next, the Lord answers Hezekiah's prayer through Isaiah, the prophet. This is often the case today, as the Lord answers many of our prayers through our living prophets.

21 ¶ **Then Isaiah the son of Amoz sent unto Hezekiah, saying, Thus saith the LORD** God of Israel, **Whereas thou hast prayed to me against Sennacherib king of Assyria:**

22 **This is the word** which the LORD hath spoken concerning him [*this is the answer to Sennacherib*]; **The virgin, the daughter of Zion** [*the unconquered people of Jerusalem*], **hath despised thee, and laughed thee to scorn;** the daughter of Jerusalem hath shaken her head at thee [*not afraid of you Assyrians*].

23 **Whom hast thou reproached and blasphemed?** and against whom hast thou exalted thy voice, and lifted up thine eyes on high? even against the Holy One of Israel [*you chose the wrong one to offend this time; you have mocked the true God*].

24 **By thy servants** [*including Rabshakeh—see Isaiah 36:4*] **hast thou reproached** [*blasphemed*] **the Lord**, and hast said [*bragged*], By the multitude of my chariots am I come up to the height of the mountains, to the sides [*west*] of Lebanon; and I will [*have*] cut down the tall cedars thereof, and the choice fir trees thereof: and I will enter [*have entered*] into the height of his border, and the forest of his Carmel.

25 **I have digged** [*wells*], **and drunk water** [*in many a conquered land*]; and with the sole of my feet have I dried up all the rivers of the besieged places [*end of quoting the Assyrian King's boasts*].

26 Hast thou [*King of Assyria*] not heard long ago ["*Haven't you heard by now?*"], how I [*the Lord*] have done [*allowed*] it; and of ancient times, that I have formed it? now have I brought it to pass, that thou shouldest be to lay waste defenced cities into ruinous heaps [*I, the Lord, allowed you to do these things, otherwise you would never have had such power*].

27 **Therefore** [*that is why*] **their inhabitants were of small power** [*were weak before your armies*], they were dismayed and confounded: they were as the grass of the field, and as the green herb, as the grass on the housetops, and as corn [*grain*] blasted before it be grown up.

28 **But I** [*the Lord*] **know thy abode** [*I know you well*], **and thy going out, and thy coming in, and thy rage against me**.

29 Because thy rage against me, and thy tumult, is come up into mine ears, **therefore will I put my hook in thy nose** [*such as a ring in the nose of a wild animal with which to control it*], **and my bridle in thy lips** [*I will control you, King of Assyria*], and I will turn thee back by the way [*road*] by which thou camest [*I will stop you cold*].

The topic now turns to the word of the Lord to Hezekiah and his people, who have been worrying because of the siege against them by the Assyrians.

30 **And this shall be a sign unto thee** [*Hezekiah and his people*], Ye shall eat this year such as groweth of itself [*because of the Assyrian siege, you have not had time to plant crops normally, yet you will harvest some "volunteer" crops from plants that grew from seeds spilled during last year's harvest; in other words, you'll be okay food wise*]; and the second year that which springeth of the same: and in the third year sow ye, and reap, and plant vineyards, and eat the fruit thereof [*you'll be back to normal planting and harvesting by the third year from now*].

31 And **the remnant that is escaped of the house of Judah shall again take root downward, and bear fruit upward** [*a remnant of Judah will flourish again*]:

32 For **out of Jerusalem shall go forth a remnant**, and they that escape out of mount Zion: the zeal of the LORD of hosts shall do this [*a remnant will flourish again via God's intervention*].

Verse 33 is a specific prophecy and most comforting to King Hezekiah. The Assyrians, despite their boasting, will not shoot so much as one arrow into Jerusalem!

NOTES

33 **Therefore thus saith the LORD** concerning the king of Assyria, **He shall not come into this city, nor shoot an arrow there, nor come before it with shields, nor cast a bank** [*a mound of dirt around it thrown up from trenches dug in order to lay siege*] **against it.**

34 **By the way** [*road*] **that he** [*the Assyrian king and his armies*] **came, by the same shall he return** [*he will retreat*]**, and shall not come into this city, saith the LORD.**

35 For **I will defend this city** to save it for mine own sake, and for my servant David's sake.

Next, we see how the Lord stopped the Assyrian armies dead in their tracks.

36 **Then** [*after the Assyrian armies had come to the outskirts of Jerusalem and were ready to attack*] **the angel of the LORD went forth, and smote in the camp of the Assyrians a hundred and fourscore and five thousand**: and when they [*the few survivors*] arose early in the morning, behold, **they were all dead corpses** [*185,000 Assyrians were dead the following morning*].

37 ¶ **So Sennacherib king of Assyria departed, and went and returned, and dwelt at Nineveh** [*went home to his headquarters*].

38 **And** it came to pass, as he was worshipping in the house of Nisroch his god, that **Adrammelech and Sharezer his sons smote** [*killed*] **him with the sword**; and they escaped into the land of Armenia: and Esar-haddon his son reigned in his stead [*this happened about twenty years after his retreat from Jerusalem*].

ISAIAH 38

Selection: all verses

Chapters 38 and 39 fit historically before chapters 36 and 37 and could be considered "flashbacks" to 705–703 BC.

Isaiah was the prophet during Hezekiah's reign. At one point, righteous King Hezekiah was sick and on his deathbed.

1 **In those days** [*about 705–703 BC*] **was Hezekiah sick unto death. And Isaiah** the prophet the son of Amoz **came unto him, and said** unto him, Thus saith the LORD, **Set thine house in order** [*get ready*]: **for thou shalt die, and not live.**

2 **Then Hezekiah** turned his face toward the wall, and **prayed unto the LORD,**

3 And said, **Remember** now, O LORD, I beseech thee, **how I have walked before thee in truth and with a perfect heart, and have done that which is good** in thy sight [*in other words, I have lived a good life*]. And Hezekiah wept sore [*bitterly*].

4 ¶ **Then came the word of the LORD to Isaiah, saying,**

NOTES

5 **Go, and say to Hezekiah**, Thus saith the LORD, the God of David thy father [*ancestor*], **I have heard thy prayer, I have seen thy tears: behold, I will add unto thy days fifteen years** [*I will add fifteen years to your life*].

Major Message

When it is in harmony with the will of the Lord, the mighty prayers of the faithful can change the plan temporarily.

6 And **I will deliver thee and this city out of the hand of the king of Assyria**: and I will defend this city [*this would seem to place Hezekiah's illness sometime during the Assyrian threats to Jerusalem as described in chapters 36 and 37*].

7 And this **shall be a sign unto thee** from the LORD, that the LORD will do this thing that he hath spoken;

8 Behold, **I will bring again the shadow of the degrees** [*the shadow on the sundial*], which is gone down in the sun dial of Ahaz, **ten degrees backward**. So the sun returned ten degrees, by which degrees it was gone down [*the sun came back up ten degrees; in other words, time was turned backward*].

Hezekiah was healed and now gives thanks and praise to the Lord for his miraculous recovery.

9 ¶ **The writing** [*psalm*] **of Hezekiah** king of Judah, **when he had been sick, and was recovered** of his sickness [*after he had been sick and had recovered*]:

Righteous King Hezekiah now tells us what he said, expressing the thoughts of his heart, when he was blessed with another fifteen years of life by the Lord.

First, he tells us what was going through his mind when he knew he was going to die.

10 **I** [*Hezekiah*] **said** in the cutting off of my days [*when I was on my deathbed*], I shall go to the gates of the grave [*I am doomed*]: I am deprived of the residue [*remainder*] of my years [*I am too young to die*].

11 I said, I shall not see the LORD, even the LORD, in the land of the living [*I am about to leave this mortal life*]: I shall behold man no more with the inhabitants of the world [*I won't be around anymore to associate with my fellow men*].

12 Mine age is departed [*German Bible: my time is up*], and is removed from me as a shepherd's tent [*they are taking down my tent*]: I have [*Thou hast*] cut off like a weaver my life [*Thou hast "clipped my threads" like a weaver does when the rug is finished*]: he will cut me off with pining sickness [*fatal illness is how the Lord is sending me out of this life*]: from day even to night wilt thou make an end of me [*I will die shortly*].

13 I reckoned till morning [*German: I thought, If I could just live until morning*], that, as a lion, so will he break all my bones [*I can't stop the Lord if He wants me to die any more than I could stop a lion*]: from day even to night wilt thou make an end of me [*I'm doomed; my time is short*].

NOTES

14 Like a crane or a swallow, so did I chatter [*German: whimper*]: I did mourn as a dove: mine eyes fail with looking upward [*falter as I look up to heaven*]: O LORD, I am oppressed [*German: suffering*]; undertake [*German: soothe, moderate my condition*] for me [*be Thou my help, security*].

Next, Hezekiah tells us how he felt when he found out he was not going to die.

The Joseph Smith Translation of the Bible helps us considerably with verses 15–17, next.

15 **What shall I say** [*how can I express my gratitude*]? he hath both spoken unto me, and himself hath done it [*JST: healed me*]: I shall go softly [*German: in humility*] all my years [*JST: that I may not walk*] in the bitterness of my soul.

16 O Lord, by these things men live, and in all these things is the life of my spirit [*JST: "thou who art the life of my spirit, in whom I live"*]: so wilt thou recover [*heal*] me, and make me to live [*JST: "and in all these things I will praise thee"*].

17 Behold, for peace I had great bitterness [*JST: "Behold, I had great bitterness instead of peace"*]: but thou hast in love to my soul delivered it [*JST: "saved me"*] from the pit of corruption [*from rotting in the grave*]: for thou hast cast all my sins behind thy back [*the effect of the Atonement*].

18 For the grave cannot praise [*German: hell does not praise*] thee, death can not celebrate thee: they [*people in spirit prison*] that go down into the pit [*hell; see Isaiah 14:15*] cannot hope for thy truth [*see Alma 34:32–34*].

19 The living, the living, he shall praise thee, as I do this day [*I am very happy to still be alive*]: the father to the children shall make known thy truth [*I will testify to my family and others of Thy kindness to me*].

20 The LORD was ready to save me: therefore we [*I and my family*] will sing my songs to the stringed instruments [*we will put my words of praise to music*] all the days of our life in the house of the LORD.

Next, Hezekiah refers to something Isaiah instructed him to do in order to be healed.

21 **For Isaiah had said, Let them take a lump of figs, and lay it for a plaister** [*plaster*] **upon the boil, and he shall recover** [*perhaps the lump of figs served the same purpose as the lump of clay to heal the blind man in John 9:6–7; faith obedience*].

22 Hezekiah also had said, What is the sign that I shall go up to the house of the LORD? [*This verse fits after verse 6. See 2 Kings 20:8.*]

ISAIAH 39

Selection: all verses

As you have perhaps noticed, these chapters are not particularly in chronological order. This chapter records events that took place before chapters 36–37. It appears that King Hezekiah, King of Judah with headquarters in Jerusalem, as a gesture of good faith, showed emissaries from Babylon the great treasures in the temple and in the palace at Jerusalem (verse 2). In about one hundred years, Babylon will be an enemy to Judah and will carry them away into captivity.

1 **At that time** [*about 705–703 BC*] **Merodach-baladan**, the son of Baladan, **king of Babylon, sent letters and a present to Hezekiah: for he had heard that he had been sick**, and was recovered.

2 **And Hezekiah** was glad of them, and **shewed them** [*the Babylonian delegation who brought the letters and present*] **the house of his precious things**, the silver, and the gold, and the spices, and the precious ointment, and all the house of his armour, and all that was found in his treasures: **there was nothing in his house, nor in all his dominion, that Hezekiah shewed them not**.

Next, Isaiah comes to Hezekiah and expresses concern about what he has shown to the delegation from Babylon. It sets the stage for a prophecy about the future Babylonian captivity of the Jews.

3 ¶ **Then came Isaiah the prophet unto king Hezekiah, and said** unto him, **What said these men? and from whence came they** unto thee? **And Hezekiah said, They are come from a far country unto me, even from Babylon**.

4 **Then said he** [*Isaiah*], **What have they seen in thine house?** And **Hezekiah answered, All that is in mine house have they seen**: there is nothing among my treasures that I have not shewed them.

5 **Then said Isaiah to Hezekiah, Hear the word of the LORD** of hosts:

6 Behold, **the days come, that all that is in thine house**, and that which thy fathers [*ancestors*] have laid up in store until this day, **shall be carried to Babylon**: nothing shall be left, saith the LORD [*prophecy regarding Babylonian captivity, which will take place in about a hundred years*].

7 **And of thy sons** that shall issue from thee, which thou shalt beget, **shall they take away; and they shall be eunuchs** [*servants; they will be made unable to father children—see Bible Dictionary, under "Eunuch"*] **in the palace of the king of Babylon**.

8 Then said Hezekiah to Isaiah, Good is the word of the LORD which thou hast spoken. He said moreover, For there shall be peace and truth in my days.

Some scholars are critical of Hezekiah's response in verse 8, above, but he remained loyal to God and did much good for his people during his reign. Perhaps he did mourn for his people in the future and it is just not recorded here. See 2 Kings 20:19–20. It is possible to be happy and at peace with God despite others' wickedness. For instance, see Mormon in Mormon 2:19 and Lehi in 2 Nephi 1:15.

Isaiah 40–49

"Comfort Ye My People"

As you read and study this block of Isaiah's writings, watch for a change of tone from previous chapters of Isaiah. The dominant theme for these chapters is upbeat. It teaches the Atonement of Christ and the miraculous power it provides to redeem us from the effects of our sins. Chapter 40 sets the tone with the first sentence: "Comfort ye, comfort ye my people, saith your God." You will likely recognize the comforting words in 41:10 as found in our hymn "How Firm a Foundation" (*Hymns*, no. 85). Chapter 42 continues the theme as Isaiah teaches that the Savior will help the weak and the "bruised." Chapters 43–45 continue the theme of redemption and remind us that Jehovah, the God of the Old Testament, is, indeed, the premortal Jesus Christ, our "Saviour" (43:3). Chapters 46–47 prophesy destruction to the wicked. You will likely recognize chapters 48–49 because they are basically 1 Nephi 20 and 21 in the Book of Mormon. As you study these, I hope you will understand why Nephi wanted his brothers to study the words of Isaiah.

NOTES

ISAIAH 40

Selection: all verses

This chapter contains a number of prophecies about the Messiah, and includes a description of the role of John the Baptist. Chronologically, it seems to move around quite a bit, including prophecies of the Savior's mortal mission as well as of His Second Coming. It is a chapter of comfort and witness about the Savior, and teaches beautifully that none on earth can compare to Him.

Isaiah will also point out the absurdity of idol worship, in view of the true power of the true God.

1 **Comfort ye, comfort ye my people**, saith your God.

Verse 2, next, seems to refer to the last days and on into the Millennium.

2 **Speak ye comfortably** [*German: in a friendly manner; Hebrew: tenderly*] **to Jerusalem, and cry unto her, that her warfare** [*time of service*] **is accomplished, that her iniquity is pardoned** [*through repentance and the Atonement*]: for **she hath received of the LORD's hand double for all her sins** [*has paid a heavy penalty for wickedness*].

3 ¶ **The voice of him that crieth in the wilderness, Prepare ye the way of the LORD**, make straight in the desert a highway for our God. [*This fits John the Baptist as described in Matthew 3:1–3. Other "Eliases," or "preparers" and prophets, also fit this passage in the last days as they prepare us for the Second Coming.*]

4 **Every valley shall be exalted** [*raised*], **and every mountain and hill shall be made low**: and the crooked shall be made straight, and the rough places [*mountains*] plain [*changes in the earth at the Second Coming; also can be symbolic of wickedness, being "straightened out" at the Second Coming*]:

5 And the glory of the LORD shall be revealed, and all flesh shall see it together [*at the same time at the Second Coming*]: for the mouth of the LORD hath spoken it.

Verse 6, next, is a course in perspective. Man's power is insignificant compared to that of God. See also verse 18.

6 The voice said, Cry [*preach*]. **And he said, What shall I cry** [*preach*]? [*Answer:*] **All flesh** [*people*] **is** [*are like*] **grass, and all the goodliness thereof is as the flower of the field:** [*Mortality is temporary; not that we are not significant and important—Christ gave His life for us—but just a reminder that God is way ahead of us and we would be wise to follow and obey Him completely. We are nothing, at this point, compared to Him.*]:

7 The grass withereth, the flower fadeth: because the spirit of the LORD bloweth upon it: surely the people is grass [*man's power and wisdom pale against the Lord's*].

8 The grass withereth, the flower fadeth: but the word of our God shall stand for ever [*trust in God, not in the "arm of flesh"*].

9 O Zion, that bringest good tidings [*the gospel*], get thee up into the high mountain; O Jerusalem, that bringest good tidings, lift up thy voice with strength; lift it up, be not afraid; say unto the cities of Judah, Behold your God!

Next, Isaiah bears witness of the Second Coming.

10 Behold, the Lord GOD will come with strong hand [*German: with power*], **and his arm** [*symbolic of power*] **shall rule** for him [*He will rule on earth; Second Coming and Millennium*]: **behold, his reward is with him** [*He will reward the righteous and the wicked, according to what they have earned*], and his work before him [*German: reward precedes Him; that is, Second Coming, Revelation 22:12*].

11 He shall feed his flock like a shepherd [*He knows each of us by name; Millennial reign*]: **he shall gather the lambs with his arm, and carry them in his bosom, and shall gently lead those that are with young** [*peaceful conditions during the Millennium*].

The "course in perspective" concerning the greatness of God continues, leading to verse 18.

12 ¶ Who hath measured the waters in the hollow of his hand, **and meted out heaven** with the span, and comprehended the dust of the earth in a measure, and weighed the mountains in scales, and the hills in a balance? [*Who else do you know who can create worlds and design oceans, continents, mountains, heavens, and so forth?*]

13 Who hath directed [*taught*] **the Spirit of the LORD** [*the Holy Ghost*], or being his counsellor hath taught him [*what mortal could teach God anything!*]?

14 With whom took he [*God*] **counsel** [*from whom does God seek counsel, advice*], and **who instructed him**, and taught him in the path of judgment, **and taught him knowledge**, and shewed to him the way of understanding [*the answer "no one" is implied*]?

NOTES

_____
_____
_____
_____
_____
_____
_____
_____
_____
_____
_____
_____
_____
_____
_____
_____
_____
_____
_____
_____
_____
_____
_____
_____
_____
_____
_____
_____

15 **Behold, the nations** [*of this earth*] **are as a drop of** [*in*] **a bucket** [*compared to God's domain*], **and are counted as** [*like*] **the small dust of the balance** [*are about as significant as a small speck of dust on a scale*]: **behold, he taketh up the isles as a very little thing** [*German: the continents are like the tiniest speck of dust to Him*].

16 **And Lebanon** [*sometimes used to represent all of Palestine*] **is not sufficient to burn, nor the beasts thereof sufficient for a burnt offering** [*all the wood and all the animals in Lebanon wouldn't even begin to make a sacrifice worthy of who God really is*].

17 **All nations** before [*compared to*] him **are as nothing; and they are counted** [*compared*] **to him less than nothing**, and vanity.

Verse 18, next, serves as a transition to the topic of how absurd and foolish it is to use idols as substitutes for God.

18 ¶ **To whom then will ye liken** [*compare*] **God? or what likeness** [*idol*] **will ye compare unto him**?

19 **The workman** [*craftsman*] **melteth** [*uses molten metal to form*] **a graven image, and the goldsmith spreadeth** [*covers*] **it over with gold**, and casteth [*makes*] silver chains [*foolish people make idols and then compare them to God*].

20 **He that is so impoverished that he hath no oblation** [*German: so poor that he can give only the smallest offering*] **chooseth a tree that will not rot** [*selects wood for an idol*]; **he seeketh unto him a cunning workman** [*he hires a skilled craftsman*] **to prepare a graven image** [*idol*], that shall not be moved [*German: becomes a permanent fixture*].

21 **Have ye not known** [*German: Do you not know?*]? **have ye not heard?** hath it not been told you from the beginning? **have ye not understood from the foundations of the earth** [*don't you understand!*]?

22 **It is he** [*the Lord*] **that sitteth upon the circle of the earth** [*is above all*], **and the inhabitants thereof are as grasshoppers** [*compared to God; continues the theme of verse 17*]; **that stretcheth out** [*creates*] **the heavens** as a curtain, and spreadeth them out as a tent to dwell in [*the Lord is the Creator*]:

23 That bringeth the princes [*leaders*] to nothing; he maketh the judges [*rulers*] of the earth as vanity [*nothing*].

24 **Yea, they** [*the wicked rulers and leaders*] **shall not be planted** [*German: shall be as if they hadn't even been planted*]; yea, they shall not be sown: yea, their stock shall not take root in the earth: and **he** [*the Lord*] **shall also blow upon them, and they shall wither,** and the whirlwind shall take them away as stubble [*they are nothing compared to God*].

25 **To whom then will ye liken me, or shall I be equal?** saith the Holy One [*Jehovah: Jesus Christ; same question as in verse 18*].

26 **Lift up your eyes on high** [*look all around you*], **and behold** [*see*] **who hath created these things** [*God's creations*], that bringeth out their host by number: **he calleth them all by names** [*He knows every one of them*] by [*because of*] the greatness of his

might [*German: ability*], for that he is strong in power; not one faileth [*His creations all obey him*].

27 **Why sayest thou, O Jacob** [*you Israelites*], and speakest, O Israel, **My way is hid from the LORD** [*why do you think that you can hide your wickedness from God*], and my judgment [*cause*] is passed over from [*is unknown by*] my God?

28 ¶ **Hast thou not known? hast thou not heard** [*haven't you heard by now*], **that the everlasting God**, the LORD, the Creator of the ends of the earth, **fainteth not** [*German: is not weak*], **neither is weary?** there is no searching of his understanding [*you can't comprehend His understanding*].

29 **He giveth power to the faint**; and to them that have no might he increaseth strength [*Ether 12:27*].

30 **Even the youths** [*with lots of energy*] **shall** [*may grow*] **faint and be weary**, and the young men shall utterly fall [*all mortals have their limitations*]:

31 **But they that wait** [*base their hopes*] **upon the LORD shall renew their strength**; they shall mount up with wings as eagles [*be renewed like molting eagles are as they lose their old feathers each year, then get new ones*]; they shall run, and not be weary; and they shall walk, and not faint [*in pursuing exaltation. See context of Doctrine & Covenants 89:20–21; the righteous receive extra strength on earth, have a glorious resurrection, and receive the strength of the Lord as joint heirs with Christ*].

ISAIAH 41

Selection: all verses

Chapters 41–44 refer mainly to the last days.

There are many different opinions among scholars concerning the meaning of some verses in this chapter. In such cases, I have used the Old Testament Student Manual (Institute of Religion, Religion 302), as the authority for interpretive notes in brackets. I have also made considerable use of the Martin Luther version of the German Bible for clarifications.

1 **Keep silence before me** [*hush, and let me teach you*], **O islands** [*all land masses where scattered Israel live*]; **and let the people renew their strength** [*as mentioned in Isaiah 40:31*]: let them come near; then let them speak: let us come near together to judgment. [*German: dispute, see who is right—see who is more powerful, God or your idols; similar to Elijah and priests of Baal in I Kings 18*];

In verse 2, next, Isaiah asks the question, "Who is more powerful, your idols or our God?"

2 **Who raised up the righteous man from the east** [*the Savior Himself fits this description, coming in from the east wilderness at age thirty to begin His ministry; could also refer to many prophets, including Abraham, who have come from the "East"—on assignment from the Lord, and assisted in "calling the generations from the beginning," verse 4*], **called him to his foot** [*German: to go forth*], **gave** [*him power over*] **the nations before him, and made him rule over kings?** he gave them [*kings*] as the dust to his sword [*they*]

_____
_____
_____
_____
_____
_____
_____
_____
_____
_____
_____
_____
_____
_____
_____
_____
_____
_____
_____
_____
_____
_____
_____
_____
_____
_____
_____
_____
_____
_____
_____
_____
_____
_____

couldn't stop his sword (power) anymore than dust particles could], and as driven stubble to his bow [*nations and kings couldn't stop him*].

3 **He pursued them, and passed safely; even by the way that he had not gone with his feet** [*German: without wearying of his errand, assignment; perhaps ties back to Isaiah 40:31*].

4 **Who hath wrought and done it** [*the things referred to above*], **calling the generations** [*German: calling all people*] **from the beginning?** [*Answer to the question put in verse 2:*] **I the LORD, the first, and with the last; I am he.**

5 **The isles** [*scattered Israel*] **saw it, and feared** [*respected it, responded positively*]; **the ends of the earth were afraid, drew near, and came** [*people from all parts of the earth responded; the gathering of Israel*].

6 **They helped every one his neighbour; and every one said to his brother, Be of good courage**.

7 **So** [*yet, nevertheless*] **the carpenter encouraged the goldsmith, and he that smootheth with the hammer him that smote the anvil, saying,** It [*an idol*] is ready for the sodering: and he fastened it with nails, that it should not be moved [*yet, many foolishly continued with their making and worshipping of idols*].

Next, those who want to be the faithful covenant people of the Lord are encouraged to remember who they are and to remain loyal to God.

8 **But thou, Israel, art my servant, Jacob whom I have chosen, the seed of Abraham my friend.**

9 **Thou whom I have taken** [*gathered*] **from the ends of the earth,** and called thee from the chief men thereof, and said unto thee, Thou art my servant; I have chosen thee, and not cast thee away [*I have not left you*].

Verse 10, next, reminds us of the third verse of our hymn, "How Firm a Foundation" (Hymns, 85).

10 **Fear thou not; for I am with thee: be not dismayed; for I am thy God: I will strengthen thee;** yea, I will **help thee**; yea, I will **uphold thee with the right hand of my righteousness**.

Verse 11, next, reminds us that the wicked will someday face the consequences of their fighting against the Saints.

11 **Behold, all they that were incensed** [*German: prejudiced; angry*] **against thee shall be ashamed** [*shamed*] **and confounded** [*German: humiliated*]: they shall be as nothing; and they that strive with [*fight against*] thee shall perish [*ultimately, your enemies will not succeed against you*].

12 **Thou shalt seek them** [*your enemies*], **and shalt not find them,** even them that contended with thee: they that war against thee shall be as nothing, and as a thing of nought [*eventually, the wicked will all be gone*].

13 **For I the LORD thy God will hold thy right hand** [*covenant hand; in other words, I will strengthen you with covenants*], **saying unto thee, Fear not; I will help thee.**

Have you noticed that most Christians do not believe that Jesus is the God of the Old Testament (under the Father's direction)? Verse 14, next, teaches correct doctrine on this matter. It uses the word "redeemer" in reference to the Lord (the premortal Christ) who is directing Israel in Old Testament times. We will see additional strong evidence in chapter 43 of this doctrine.

14 **Fear not, thou worm** [*meek, humble*] **Jacob**, and ye men of Israel; **I will help thee, saith the LORD, and thy redeemer, the Holy One of Israel** [*Jesus*].

15 Behold, **I will make thee** [*German: into*] **a new sharp threshing instrument having teeth** [*capable of much destruction*]: **thou shalt thresh the mountains** [*your former strong enemies*], **and beat them small**, and shalt make the hills as chaff. [*Israel will triumph over her enemies. Perhaps this verse could also remind us that Israel, as a "sharp threshing instrument," will help gather the wheat—scattered Israel—and separate it from the "chaff," or the wicked.*]

16 **Thou shalt fan** [*German: scatter; as in the threshing process of throwing wheat up into the wind so the chaff is blown away while the wheat drops back to the threshing floor*] **them, and the wind shall carry them away**, and the whirlwind shall scatter them: **and thou shalt rejoice in the LORD**, and shalt glory in the Holy One of Israel [*Israel will once again become righteous and give glory to God*].

17 When the poor and needy seek water, and there is none, and their tongue faileth for thirst, **I the LORD will hear them, I the God of Israel will not forsake them** [*I will help you. I have not left you; see verse 9*].

18 **I will open rivers in high places, and fountains in the midst of the valleys: I will make the wilderness a pool of water, and the dry land springs of water** [*geographical changes will help Israel; could also be symbolic of "living water" (John 4:10), or the gospel, bringing forth new life in an apostate wilderness and satisfying the thirst mentioned in verse 17*].

19 I will plant in the wilderness the cedar, the shittah [*acacia*] tree, and the myrtle, and the oil tree; I will set in the desert the fir [*cypress*] tree, and the pine [*ash*], and the box tree together [*Hebrew prophets often use trees to represent people, for example, Isaiah 2:13; Ezekiel 31:3; thus various types of trees in this verse could be symbolic of the gospel's going to all races of people in the last days*]:

20 **That they may see, and know, and consider, and understand together, that the hand of the LORD hath done this**, and the Holy One of Israel hath created it.

21 **Produce your cause** [*present your case*], saith the LORD; **bring forth your strong reasons** [*arguments against the Lord*], **saith the King of Jacob** [*Christ, Jehovah, the King of Israel*].

22 **Let them** [*idol worshippers*] **bring them** [*their idols*] **forth, and shew us what shall happen** [*predict the future*]: let them [*idols*] shew the former things [*the past*],

NOTES

what they be, that we may consider them, and know the latter end [*the final outcome*] of them; or declare us things for to come [*predict the future*].

23 **Shew the things that are to come hereafter, that we may know that ye are gods** [*let's see if your idols can predict the future like God can; in other words, prove that your idols are gods*]: **yea, do good, or do evil, that we may be dismayed** [*surprised, startled*], and behold it together [*just do anything, good or bad, to demonstrate your power to us*].

24 **Behold, ye** [*idols*] **are of nothing, and your work of nought** [*you are worthless and do absolutely nothing*]: **an abomination is he** [*the wicked who worship idols*] **that chooseth you** [*idols*].

25 **I have raised up one** [*perhaps meaning Christ, referring back to verse 2*] from the north [*possibly meaning coming from Nazareth, north of Jerusalem*], **and he shall come: from the rising of the sun** shall he call upon my name: **and he shall come upon** [*descend upon, destroy*] **princes** [*wicked leaders of nations*] as upon morter, and as the potter treadeth clay [*He will tread upon the wicked and none will stop Him; Doctrine & Covenants 133:50–51*].

26 **Who** [*which of your idols*] **hath declared** [*prophesied this*] **from the beginning, that we may know?** and beforetime, that we may say, He is righteous? yea, there is none that sheweth, yea, there is none that declareth, yea, there is none that heareth your words [*none of your idols do a thing!*].

27 The first shall say to Zion [*the Lord will prophesy it*], Behold, behold them: and I [*the Lord*] will give to Jerusalem one that bringeth good tidings.

28 For I beheld, and there was no man; even among them, and **there was no counsellor, that, when I asked of them, could answer a word** [*idol worship has reduced them to a completely confused people*].

29 **Behold, they are all vanity** [*false*]; their works are nothing: their molten images [*idols*] are wind and confusion.

ISAIAH 42

Selection: all verses

In this chapter, Isaiah continues to prophesy about the Messiah. Considerable emphasis is given to the Restoration of the gospel in the last days and the taking of the gospel to all the world.

1 **Behold my servant** [*Christ—see Matthew 12:18; perhaps in a dual sense could also include the whole house of Israel—see Isaiah 41:8*], **whom I uphold; mine elect** [*Christ; those set apart as a chosen people; Israelites*], **in whom my soul delighteth**; I have put my spirit upon him: he shall bring forth judgment to the Gentiles.

2 **He shall not cry, nor lift up, nor cause his voice to be heard in the street** [*Christ was low-key, designed His preaching to not make great disturbances, often said to those healed, "tell no one"*].

The tenderness of the Savior is described beautifully by Isaiah in verse 3, next.

3 **A bruised reed shall he not break** [*he came to help the weak, the "bruised," not to crush them more*], **and the smoking flax** [*the glowing candle wick that still has a tiny spark of light in it*] **shall he not quench** [*he came to gently fan the spark within into a flame of belief and testimony, not to snuff it out*]: he shall bring forth judgment unto truth [*victory, see Matthew 12:20*].

4 **He shall not fail** [*falter, stop, quit; see Doctrine & Covenants 19:19*] **nor be discouraged** [*German: unable to finish*], till he have set judgment in the earth: and the isles [*all continents, nations*] shall wait for [*trust in*] his law.

5 ¶ **Thus saith God the LORD**, he that created the heavens, and stretched them out; he that spread forth the earth, and that which cometh out of it; he that giveth breath unto the people upon it, and spirit to them that walk therein [*the Creator of all*]:

Verse 6, next, seems to apply mainly to Israel. See Israel's responsibility and mission in Abraham 2:9–11.

6 **I the LORD have called thee in righteousness, and will hold thine hand**, and will keep thee, **and give thee for a covenant of the people, for a light of** [*German: unto*] **the Gentiles**;

7 **To open the blind eyes, to bring out the prisoners from the prison, and them that sit in darkness out of the prison house** [*what Christ and his righteous servants can do*].

8 **I am the LORD: that is my name: and my glory will I not give to another** [*you are still My chosen people*], neither my praise to graven images [*idols*].

9 **Behold, the former things** [*truth and keys from former days—the Restoration of the gospel*] **are come to pass, and new things** [*new knowledge in dispensation of fulness of times*] **do I declare**: before they spring forth I tell you of them [*they have been prophesied*].

10 **Sing unto the LORD a new song**, and his praise from the end of the earth [*to all the world*], ye that go down to the sea, and all that is therein; the isles, and the inhabitants thereof [*restored gospel will be preached to all the world*].

11 **Let the wilderness** [*dual meaning: literal wilderness; apostate Israel*] **and the cities thereof lift up their voice**, the villages that Kedar [*nomadic tribe in the wilderness east of Sea of Galilee; Kedar was a grandson of Abraham through Ishmael, see Genesis 25:13*] doth inhabit: let the inhabitants of the rock [*Sela, a desert town south of the Dead Sea*] sing, let them shout from the top of the mountains [*even remote places like Kedar and Sela will receive the gospel and be able to rejoice in it*].

12 **Let them give glory unto the LORD**, and declare his praise in the islands [*everybody will hear the gospel in the last days*].

NOTES

13 **The LORD shall go forth as a mighty man**, he shall stir up jealousy [*with zeal*] like a man of war: he shall cry, yea, roar; **he shall prevail against his enemies** [*the Lord will ultimately triumph*].

14 **I** [*the Lord*] **have long time holden my peace** [*I have been patient*]; I have been still, and refrained myself [*I have been patient and not shown forth great power*]: now will I cry like a travailing woman [*woman in labor; in other words, delivery time for Israel has come; the restored gospel will go forth with great power that none can stop*]; I will destroy and devour at once.

15 **I will make waste mountains and hills, and dry up all their herbs; and I will make the rivers islands, and I will dry up the pools** [*after the gospel is restored, there will be great destruction, drought, and so forth as the Lord preaches "sermons" via the forces of nature as a way of getting people's attention in the last days—see Doctrine & Covenants 88:87–90*].

16 **And I will bring the blind** [*the spiritually blind scattered of Israel*] **by a way** [*the restored gospel*] **that they knew not; I will lead them in paths** [*truths and covenants of the restored gospel*] **that they have not known: I will make darkness light before them**, and crooked things straight [*effects of the Restoration*]. **These things will I do unto them, and not forsake them.**

17 ¶ They shall be turned back, **they shall be greatly ashamed, that trust in graven images**, that say to the molten images, Ye are our gods [*idol worship will not pay off*].

18 **Hear, ye deaf; and look, ye blind, that ye may see** [*open your eyes and ears to the truth*].

The Joseph Smith Translation makes many changes in verses 19 through 25. We will first examine these verses as they stand in our Bible, and then provide the JST with explanatory notes added to the JST.

19 Who *is* blind, but my servant? or deaf, as my messenger *that* I sent? who *is* blind as *he that is* perfect, and blind as the LORD's servant?

20 Seeing many things, but thou observest not; opening the ears, but he heareth not.

21 The LORD is well pleased for his righteousness' sake; he will magnify the law, and make *it* honourable.

22 But this *is* a people robbed and spoiled; *they are* all of them snared in holes, and they are hid in prison houses: they are for a prey, and none delivereth; for a spoil, and none saith, Restore.

23 Who among you will give ear to this? *who* will hearken and hear for the time to come?

24 Who gave Jacob for a spoil, and Israel to the robbers? did not the LORD, he against whom we have sinned? for they would not walk in his ways, neither were they obedient unto his law.

25 Therefore he hath poured upon him the fury of his anger, and the strength of battle: and it hath set him on fire round about, yet he knew not; and it burned him, yet he laid *it* not to heart.

JST Isaiah 42:19–25

19 For I will send my servant unto you who are blind; yea, a messenger to open the eyes of the blind, and unstop the ears of the deaf;

20 And they [*those who listen and repent*] shall be made perfect [*the power of the Atonement; 2 Nephi 25:23*] notwithstanding their blindness, if they will hearken unto the messenger, the Lord's servant.

21 Thou [*Israel*] art a people, seeing many things, but thou observest not [*you don't obey*]; opening the ears to hear, but thou hearest not [*you don't want to hear the truth*].

22 The Lord is not well pleased with such a people, but for his righteousness' sake he will magnify the law and make it honorable.

23 Thou art a people robbed and spoiled; thine enemies, all of them, have snared thee in holes, and they have hid thee in prison houses; they have taken thee for a prey, and none delivereth; for a spoil, and none saith, Restore [*consequences of Israel's wickedness*].

24 Who among them [*Israel's enemies in verse 23*] will give ear unto thee [*Israel*], or hearken and hear thee for the time to come? and who gave Jacob for a spoil, and Israel to the robbers [*who turned Israel over to her enemies*]? did not the Lord, he against whom they have sinned [*the Lord did, because of Israel's wickedness*]?

25 For they [*Israel*] would not walk in his ways, neither were they obedient unto his law; therefore [*that is why*] he [*the Lord*] hath poured upon them the fury of his anger, and the strength of battle; and they [*Israel's enemies*] have set them [*Israel*] on fire round about [*have caused terrible destruction*], yet they [*Israel*] know not [*won't acknowledge that they are being punished*], and it burned them, yet they laid it not to heart [*refused to repent*].

ISAIAH 43

Selection: all verses

This chapter contains clear doctrine that Jesus Christ, our Savior and Redeemer, is the God of the Old Testament—see, for example, verses 3, 11 and 14.

Having pointed out the foolishness of idol worship and the wisdom of being loyal to the true God, the Savior now reaches out to covenant Israel, inviting them to be gathered to Him. Everyone on earth can become a member of covenant Israel through being baptized, living the gospel, and making and keeping the additional covenants available to faithful members of the Church.

1 But now **thus saith the LORD that created thee, O Jacob**, and he that formed thee, **O Israel** [*emphasis on the words "created" and "formed" as used in Genesis 1:27 and 2:7; in other words, the true God is your Creator as described by Moses; these words will again be repeated for emphasis in verse 7*], Fear not: for **I have redeemed thee**, I have called thee by thy name; thou art mine [*the Savior will succeed in redeeming a remnant of Israel despite their coming problems as described in Isaiah 42:22–25*].

NOTES

2 **When thou passest through the waters, I will be with thee; and through the rivers, they shall not overflow thee** [*referring to the parting of the Red Sea and Jordan River; in other words, I helped you then and the same power and help is still available to you*]: **when thou walkest through the fire, thou shalt not be burned**; neither shall the flame kindle upon thee. [*Perhaps referring to how He will help Shadrach, Meshach, and Abed-nego survive the fiery furnace (Daniel 3). I want to protect and bless you too.*]

3 For **I am** the LORD thy God, the Holy One of Israel, **thy Saviour**: I gave Egypt for thy ransom, Ethiopia and Seba [*a people in southern Arabia*] for thee [*I will ransom you from your enemies—sin, Satan—represented by Egypt. I will pay the price that you might go free. Applies literally also, in terms of protection from physical enemy nations, see Isaiah 45:14*].

4 **Since thou wast** [*art, are*] **precious in my sight**, thou hast been honourable [*honored by me*], and **I have loved thee: therefore will I give men for thee** [*prophets' lives have been sacrificed for us, for our benefit*], **and people for thy life** [*many have given their lives for the benefit of others. Most especially, Christ's Atonement works for us*].

5 **Fear not: for I am with thee**: I will bring thy [*Israel's*] seed from the east, and gather thee from the west [*the gathering of Israel*];

6 **I will say to the north**, Give up [*give up the Israelites you're holding back from the Lord*]; and to the **south**, Keep not back: bring my sons from far, and my daughters from the ends of the earth [*the gathering of Israel is worldwide*];

7 **Even every one that is called by my name** [*that is willing to make and keep covenants*]: for **I have created him for my glory, I have formed him; yea, I have made him** [*carries the connotation of redemption through the Atonement via repentance—being "born again" as discussed in Alma 5. That is how the Savior "creates" us as new people spiritually*].

8 ¶ **Bring forth the blind people that have eyes, and the deaf that have ears** [*spiritually blind and deaf who have ignored prophets' messages and turned to other gods—see verse 9*].

9 Let all the nations be gathered together, and let the people be assembled: who among them can declare this [*the true gospel*], and shew us former things [*such as premortal life details*]? **let them bring forth their witnesses** [*their false gods, sorcerers, and so forth*], **that they may be justified** [*let's see their false gods, sorcerers, etc., do the kinds of things the true God of Israel can do*]: **or let them hear, and say, It** [*Israel's message as given in verses 11–13*] **is truth.**

10 **Ye** [*Israel*] **are my witnesses, saith the LORD, and my servant whom I have chosen** [*to carry the gospel to all the world, see Abraham 2:9*]: that ye may know and believe me, and understand that I am he: **before me there was no God formed, neither shall there be after me** [*no idols ever have, nor ever will, take My place*].

11 I [*Jesus*], even **I, am the LORD; and beside me there is no saviour.** [*This is the message!*]

12 I have declared, and have saved, and I have shewed, when there was no strange god [*idol*] among you [*I have greatly blessed you when you were not worshipping idols*]: therefore ye [*Israel*] are my witnesses [*our calling, responsibility*], saith the LORD, that I am God.

13 Yea, before the day was I am he [*I was God before time began for you and will continue to be God*]; and there is none that can deliver out of my hand: I will work [*perform the Atonement and bless you with the gospel*], and who shall let [*JST: "hinder"*] it?

14 ¶ Thus saith the LORD, your redeemer, the Holy One of Israel; For your sake I have sent to [*I will triumph over*] Babylon [*dual meaning: Symbolically Satan's kingdom; literally Israel's enemies in the nation of Babylon*], and have brought [*will bring*] down all their nobles, and the Chaldeans [*inhabitants of southern Babylon; symbolic of the wicked in all nations*], whose cry is in the ships [*German: whose shouting will turn to lamenting as I hunt them in their ships; in other words, freedom from your enemies comes through the Savior*].

Verse 15, next, summarizes the main point of this chapter.

15 I am the LORD, your Holy One, the creator of Israel, your King.

16 Thus saith the LORD, which maketh a way in the sea [*parted the Red Sea*], and a path in the mighty waters;

17 Which bringeth forth [*German: puts down, dismantles*] the chariot and horse, the army and the power; they [*your enemies*] shall lie down [*die*] together, they shall not rise: they are extinct, they are quenched as tow [*snuffed out like a smoldering candle*].

In verse 18, next, we see, among other things, that the gospel of Jesus Christ allows us to leave the past behind us and put all our energy into the present in order to have a glorious future. This is the essence of the Atonement of Christ.

18 Remember ye not the former things, neither consider the things of old [*forget the past troubles and oppressions; they are now behind you*].

19 Behold, I will do a new thing [*the Restoration of the gospel; the gathering of Israel*]; now it shall spring forth; shall ye not know it [*you will see it plainly*]? I will even make a way in the wilderness, and rivers in the desert [*perhaps dual meaning, referring to physical changes in the earth to help Israel's gathering, and also symbolic of effects of "living water," gospel, bringing life to apostate Israel (referred to as "dry ground" in Isaiah 53:2; 44:3) as water does to the wilderness, desert*].

20 The beast of the field shall honour me, the dragons and the owls [*jackals and ostriches—see footnote 20a in your Bible; in other words, even "unclean" animals and fowls will honor Me*]: because I give waters in the wilderness, and rivers in the desert, to give drink [*"living water" also; John 7:37–38*] to my people, my chosen.

21 This people have I formed [*German: prepared*] for myself; they shall shew forth my praise [*definite, strong prophecy that Israel will return to the Lord and be gathered*].

Next, the topic turns to Israel's past performance, which has not been good.

NOTES

NOTES

22 ¶ **But thou hast not called upon me, O Jacob; but thou hast been weary of me, O Israel** [*you have a poor "track record," a history of disloyalty to Me*].

23 **Thou hast not brought me** the small cattle [*lambs or young goats*] of thy **burnt offerings**; neither hast thou **honoured** me with thy **sacrifices**. I have not caused thee to serve with an offering [*German: I have not been pleased with your offerings of the first fruits, Numbers 18:12*], nor wearied thee with incense [*German: nor taken pleasure in your incense*].

24 **Thou hast bought me no sweet cane** [*spices used in making anointing oil for use in the tabernacle; Exodus 30:23–25*] **with money, neither hast thou filled** [*satisfied*] **me with the fat of thy sacrifices** [*your sacrifices are empty ritual*]: **but thou hast made me to serve** [*burdened me; German: made work for me*] **with thy sins**, thou hast wearied me [*German: caused me trouble and pains*] with thine iniquities.

Next, in verse 25, we see another clear statement that Jesus Christ is the God of the Old Testament, in other words, the one who is speaking and teaching in the Old Testament. Here He teaches about His Atonement.

25 I [*the Savior*], even **I, am he that blotteth out thy transgressions** for mine own sake [*I desire very much to forgive you and save you; Moses 1:39, Isaiah 1:18*], **and will not remember thy sins** [*if you truly repent; Doctrine & Covenants 58:42–43*].

26 **Put me in remembrance** [*remember me*]: **let us plead together** [*German: debate as in a court of law; in other words, let us look at the facts*]: **declare thou** [*state your point of view*], **that thou mayest be justified** [*go ahead, try to justify your wicked behavior*].

27 **Thy first father** [*ancestors; early Israel, the children of Israel under Moses—see footnote 27a in your Bible*] **hath sinned, and thy teachers** [*priests and ministers*] **have transgressed against me.**

28 **Therefore** [*for this reason*] **I have profaned the princes** [*priests and ministers; considered them to be worldly, not acceptable to Me*] of the sanctuary [*probably meaning the tabernacle or the temple in Jerusalem*], **and have given Jacob** [*Israel*] **to the curse** [*German: excommunication, cut off*], **and Israel to reproaches** [*German: become the object of scorn*].

ISAIAH 44

Selection: all verses

Verses 1–8 deal mostly with Christ's role in redeeming Israel. Verses 9–20 deal mainly with pagan idol worship.

1 Yet **now hear, O Jacob** [*another word for Israel*] my servant; and **Israel, whom I have chosen** [*in other words, Israel constitutes the Lord's "chosen people"*]:

There are many things one could say about the word "chosen" in verse 1, above. For example, Israel is chosen to carry the gospel and blessings of the priesthood to all the world (see Abraham 2:9–11). Israel is chosen to carry heavy burdens of persecution and scorn, from time to time. Israel (which can include anyone who is willing to join the Church through baptism and afterwards keep the commandments) is chosen to be exalted. Israel is chosen "to stand as witnesses of God at all times and in all things, and in all places" (Mosiah 18:9). And the list of meanings for the word "chosen" goes on and on.

The thing that "chosen" does not imply is that God arbitrarily chooses some people over others to be saved.

Notice that "Jacob" and "Israel" are often used interchangeably in the scriptures. That is because they are both names of the father of the twelve sons who became the heads of the twelve tribes of Israel.

2 **Thus saith the LORD** that made thee, and formed thee from the womb, which will help thee [*I have been helping you from the beginning and will continue to do so*]; **Fear not, O Jacob, my servant; and thou, Jesurun** [*those who are righteous, Deuteronomy 33:26, footnote 26a*], **whom I have chosen**.

3 **For I will pour water** [*dual meaning: literal; also "living water" (the gospel of Jesus Christ), 2 Nephi 9:50*] **upon him that is thirsty, and floods upon the dry ground** [*apostate Israel; Isaiah 53:2*]: **I will pour my spirit upon thy seed** [*descendants*], and my blessing upon thine offspring [*the "blessings of Abraham, Isaac, and Jacob;" Abraham 2:9–11*]:

4 **And they shall spring up as among the grass, as willows by the water courses** [*there will be righteous Israelites all over the place; Isaiah 49:21, 1 Nephi 21–21*]

5 **One shall say, I am the LORD's; and another shall call himself by the name of Jacob** [*they have both converted to the Lord and are loyal to Him; compare with 19:25*]; **and another shall subscribe with his hand** [*make covenants*] **unto the LORD, and surname himself by the name of Israel** [*take upon himself the name of Christ and become part of righteous covenant Israel*].

6 **Thus saith the LORD** the King of Israel, and **his** [*Israel's*] **redeemer** the LORD of [*heavenly*] hosts; **I am the first, and I am the last** [*Jesus was chosen at the first, in the premortal existence, to be our Redeemer, and He will be around at the last, to be our Judge—see John 5:22*]; **and beside me there is no God** [*there are no idols that are actually gods*].

7 **And who** [*what idols; compare with Isaiah 40:25*], **as I, shall call, and shall declare it, and set it in order for me, since I appointed** [*established*] **the ancient people** [*my people*]? and the things that are coming [*future events*], and shall come, **let them** [*your idols, false gods*] **shew unto them** [*foretell for you; in other words, this whole verse is a challenge for apostate Israel to have their idols do as well as the Lord in leading them and prophesying the future*].

8 **Fear ye not, neither be afraid** [*trust in me*]: have not I told thee from that time [*from the ancient times from the beginning; see verse 7*], and have declared it? ye are even my witnesses [*Israel's calling, stewardship*]. **Is there a God beside me** [*is there an idol that is a god like Me*]? **yea, there is no God; I know not any.**

Verses 9–20 will now deal primarily with the apostate practice of worshiping idols.

NOTES

9 **They that make a graven image** [*an idol*] **are all of them vanity** [*German: vain, conceited, won't take counsel from God*]; **and their delectable** [*German: precious*] **things shall not profit** [*will do them no good*]; **and they are their own witnesses; they see not, nor know** [*those who worship idols are as blind and empty-headed as the idols they worship*]; **that they may be ashamed** [*may be put to shame*].

10 **Who hath formed a god, or molten a graven image that is profitable for nothing** [*good for nothing; in other words, who would do such a foolish thing*]?

11 Behold, **all his fellows** [*fellow idol worshipers*] **shall be ashamed**: and the workmen, they are of men [*are mere mortals*]: let them all be gathered together, let them stand up; yet they shall fear, and they shall be ashamed together [*no matter how many worship idols, it does no good; they will all be put to shame*].

12 **The smith** [*blacksmith*] with the tongs both worketh in the coals, and fashioneth it [*an idol*] with hammers, and worketh it with the strength of his arms: yea, **he is hungry** [*the craftsman is a mere mortal*], and **his strength faileth**: he **drinketh no water, and is faint** [*the craftsmen who make idols for you are mere mortals themselves*].

13 The carpenter stretcheth out his rule; he marketh it [*the idol he is making*] out with a line; he fitteth it with planes, and he marketh it out with the compass [*your craftsmen exercise great care and skill in manufacturing your idols*], and maketh it after the figure of a man, according to the beauty of a man; that it may remain in the house [*your craftsmen put great care into making your idols; implication: if you were as careful worshipping God as you are in making idols . . .*].

14 He heweth him down cedars, and taketh the cypress and the oak, which he strengtheneth [*cultivates and grows*] for himself among the trees of the forest: he planteth an ash [*tree*], and the rain doth nourish it.

15 Then shall it be for a man to burn: for he will take thereof, and warm himself; yea, he kindleth it, and baketh bread; yea, he maketh a god, and worshippeth it [*you use most of the tree's wood for normal daily needs; how can you possibly turn around and worship wood from the same tree in the form of idols!*]; he maketh it a graven image, and falleth down thereto.

16 He burneth part thereof in the fire; with part thereof he eateth flesh; he roasteth roast, and is satisfied: yea, he warmeth himself, and saith, Aha, I am warm, I have seen the fire [*normal uses*]:

17 And **the residue thereof** [*with the rest of the tree*] **he maketh a god**, even his graven image: **he falleth down unto it, and worshippeth it**, and prayeth unto it, and saith, Deliver [*save*] me; for thou art my god [*Isaiah is saying how utterly ridiculous it is to assign part of a tree to have powers over yourselves*].

18 **They** [*idol worshipers; see Isaiah 45:20*] **have not known** [*German: know nothing*] **nor understood** [*German: understand nothing*]: for he hath shut their eyes [*German: they are blind*], that **they cannot see** [*are spiritually blind*]; and **their hearts, that they cannot understand** [*they are as blind and unfeeling, insensitive, as the idols they make and worship*].

19 And **none considereth in his heart** [*if idol worshipers would just stop and think*], **neither is there knowledge nor understanding** [*they don't have enough common sense*] **to say, I have burned part of it** [*the tree spoken of in verse 14*] **in the fire**; yea, also **I have baked bread upon the coals thereof**; I have **roasted flesh, and eaten it**: and **shall I make the residue thereof an abomination** [*is it reasonable to make the leftover portion into an abominable idol*]? **shall I fall down to the stock of a tree** [*is it rational to worship a chunk of wood*]?

20 **He** [*the idol worshiper*] **feedeth on ashes** [*German: takes pleasure in ashes, perhaps referring to ashes left over from some forms of idol worship*]: **a** [*German: his own*] **deceived heart hath turned him aside** [*German: leads him astray*], **that he cannot deliver** [*save*] **his soul, nor say** [*wake up and think*], **Is there not a lie in my right hand** [*covenant hand—am I not making covenants with false gods*]?

21 ¶ Remember these, O Jacob and Israel; for thou art my servant: **I have formed thee** [*the exact opposite of idol worshipers who form their gods*]; **thou art my servant: O Israel, thou shalt not be forgotten of me.**

Next, in verse 22, the Savior assures Israel that their sins can be blotted out completely by His Atonement.

22 **I have blotted out, as a thick cloud, thy transgressions**, and, as a cloud, thy sins [*the Atonement can still work for you*]: **return unto me**; for **I have redeemed thee** [*I have paid the price of your sins; therefore, please repent*].

In verse 23, next, all things in nature are invited to praise the Lord for what He has done for Israel.

23 **Sing, O ye heavens**; for the LORD hath done it: **shout, ye lower parts of the earth** [*German: O earth below*]: break forth into singing, ye **mountains, O forest**, and every tree therein: **for the LORD hath redeemed Jacob, and glorified himself in Israel** [*speaking of the future*].

24 Thus saith the LORD, **thy redeemer**, and he that formed [*German: prepared*] thee from the womb, I am the LORD **that maketh all things**; that stretcheth forth the heavens alone; that spreadeth abroad the earth by myself [*I created heaven and earth; no idols helped Me!*];

One of the evil things rebellious Israelites had done was to go to fortune-tellers, witches, sorcerers, and so forth for "revelation," rather than repenting and going to God for revelation. Verse 25, next, addresses this issue.

25 **That frustrateth** [*causeth to fail*] **the tokens** [*signs*] **of the liars** [*German: fortune tellers*], **and maketh diviners** [*people who deal in the occult*] **mad** [*German: absurd*]; **that turneth** [*so-called*] **wise men backward, and maketh their knowledge** [*German: business of fortune-telling*] **foolish**;

26 [*I am the Lord*] **That confirmeth the word of his servant, and performeth the counsel of his messengers** [*I support My servants, whereas idols don't support theirs*]; **that saith to Jerusalem, Thou shalt be inhabited; and to the cities of Judah, Ye**

shall be built, and I will raise up the decayed places thereof [*when I command, things obey; idols can't command and aren't obeyed*]:

27 [*I am the Lord*] **That saith to the deep** [*the sea, such as the Red Sea when the Israelites crossed through it*], **Be dry, and I will dry up thy rivers** [*as in the case of the Jordan River when the Israelites crossed through it into the promised land; see Joshua 3:17*]:

28 **That saith of Cyrus** [*the Persian*], **He is my shepherd** [*a tool in my hand*]**, and shall perform all my pleasure**: even saying to Jerusalem, Thou shalt be built; and to the temple, Thy foundation shall be laid. [*A specific prophecy! Cyrus conquered Babylon about 538 BC, who had conquered Jerusalem about fifty years earlier in 588 BC. In 537 BC, Cyrus issued a decree to let the Jews return home to Palestine to rebuild Jerusalem and the temple. See 538 BC on the chronology chart in the Bible Dictionary at the back of your Latter-day Saint Bible*].

ISAIAH 45

Selection: all verses

This chapter contains a prophecy about Cyrus the Persian, who conquered Babylon in about 538 BC and subsequently (about 537 BC) allowed the Jews to return to Jerusalem to build up the city again and rebuild the temple. One of the lessons we learn here is that the Lord often uses "nonmember" leaders and individuals to accomplish His purposes. For example, the British helped the Jews return to their homeland in 1948 and establish their own nation.

1 **Thus saith the LORD** to his anointed, **to Cyrus**, whose right hand I have holden [*strengthened*], to subdue nations before him; and I will loose the loins of kings [*German: take the sword of kings away from them*], to open before him the two leaved gates [*main city gates*]; and the gates shall not be shut [*the Lord will open the way for Cyrus and none will stop him*];

2 **I will go before thee**, and make the crooked places straight [*German: will take out the bumps*]: I will break in pieces the gates of brass, and cut in sunder [*cut through*] the bars of iron:

3 And **I will give thee** the **treasures** of darkness, and hidden riches of secret places [*hidden treasures, probably referring to Babylon*], that thou mayest know that I, the LORD, which call thee [*Cyrus*] by thy name, am the God of Israel.

Remember, "Jacob" and "Israel," as used in verse 4, next, are the same thing. In "the manner of prophesying among the Jews" (2 Nephi 25:1), it is common for prophets such as Isaiah to say the same thing in succession, for emphasis. If you don't understand this, you might think that Jacob and Israel are two separate groups in this verse.

4 **For Jacob my servant's sake, and Israel mine elect, I have even called thee** [*Cyrus*] by thy name: I have surnamed thee, **though thou hast not known me** [*although you don't know Me and do not realize that I am using you to fulfill My purposes, I will use you to free the Jews*].

5 **I am the LORD,** and there is none else, there is no God beside me: I girded thee [*dressed you for war and strengthened you*], **though thou hast not known me:**

6 That they may know from the rising of the sun, and from the west [*from east to west—everywhere*], **that there is none beside me** [*that I am the only true God; in other words, idols and man-made deities are not gods*]. **I am the LORD, and there is none else.**

7 I form the light, and create darkness: I make peace, and create evil [*cause calamity, as in 3 Nephi 9:3–12*]: **I the LORD do all these things.**

8 Drop [*drip; rain*] down, ye heavens, from above, and let the skies pour down righteousness: let the earth open [*produce*], and let them [*heaven and earth*] bring forth salvation [*the main purpose of creating the earth*], and let righteousness spring up together [*with it*]; I the LORD have created it [*let the purposes of creating heaven and earth be wonderfully fulfilled*].

9 Woe unto him that striveth with [*fights against*] **his Maker!** Let the potsherd [*vessel of clay; shard, broken piece of pottery*] strive with the potsherds of the earth [*German: a shard like other mortal shards—how foolish of a mere mortal to quarrel with his Creator*]. **Shall the clay say to him that fashioneth it, What makest thou?** or thy work, He hath no hands [*an insolent question, asking, in effect, "Who do you think you are, God?"; compare with Isaiah 29:16*]?

10 Woe unto him that saith unto his father, What begettest thou? or to the woman [*his mother*], **What hast thou brought forth** [*what do you think you're doing; being sassy*]?

11 Thus saith the LORD, the Holy One of Israel [*Jehovah, Jesus Christ*], and his [*Israel's*] Maker, **Ask me of things to come** [*about the future*] concerning my sons, and concerning the work of my hands **command** [*German: acknowledge me as the Creator*] **ye me** [*ask Me, I'll tell you*].

12 I have made the earth, and created man upon it: I, even my hands, have stretched out [*created*] the heavens, and all their host have I commanded [*I am the Creator*].

Having borne strong witness of the fact that none of the pagan gods are real gods, the Lord returns now to the prophecy that He will use a leader named Cyrus (verse 1) to free the Jews from Babylon so that they can return to Jerusalem. Since Isaiah served as a prophet from about 740 BC to 701 BC, and since Cyrus the Persian conquered Babylon in about 538 BC and decreed the Jews' freedom about 537 BC, this prophecy is given by Isaiah over 160 years before it takes place!

13 I have raised him [*Cyrus—see verse 1*] **up** in righteousness [*I will use him to fulfill My righteous purposes*], and I will direct all his ways: **he shall build my city** [*rebuild Jerusalem*], **and he shall let go my captives** [*the Jews*], not for price nor reward [*the hand of the Lord is in it*], saith the LORD of hosts.

14 Thus saith the LORD, The labour of **Egypt**, and merchandise of **Ethiopia** and of **the Sabeans** [*a people in southeastern Arabia*], men of stature, shall come over unto thee, and they **shall be thine**: they shall come after thee [*behind you*]; in chains they shall come over, and they shall fall down unto thee, they shall make supplication unto thee, saying, Surely God is in thee; and there is none else, there is no God [*all nations will recognize that the Lord is with Cyrus and Israel*].

15 Verily **thou art a God that hidest thyself** [*in other words, can't be seen physically on a daily basis like idols can*], O God of Israel, the Saviour.

16 **They** [*nations of the world*] **shall be ashamed** [*put to shame because of their wickedness and corruption*], and also confounded, all of them: they shall go to confusion together **that are makers of idols** [*results of idol worship*].

17 **But Israel shall be saved in the LORD with an everlasting salvation**: ye shall not be ashamed nor confounded world without end [*throughout eternity; results of righteousness*].

18 **For thus saith the LORD** [*in answer to the insolent question in verses 9 and 10*] **that created the heavens**; God himself that formed **the earth** and made it; he hath established it, he created it not in vain, he formed it to be inhabited: **I am the LORD; and there is none else**.

19 **I have not spoken in secret, in a dark place of the earth** [*I have not hidden from you, played "hard to get." I have been open and direct with you.*]: **I said not unto the seed of Jacob** [*the covenant people, Israel*]**, Seek ye me in vain**: I the LORD speak righteousness, I declare things that are right.

20 **Assemble yourselves and come**; draw near together, **ye that are escaped** [*survivors*] of the nations: **they** [*idol worshippers, Isaiah 44:18*] **have no knowledge** [*see notes for Isaiah 44:18*] that set up the wood of their graven image, and pray unto a god [*idol*] that cannot save.

21 **Tell ye** [*spread the word*], and **bring them** [*idol worshippers*] **near**; yea, **let them take counsel** [*plot*] together: **who hath declared** [*explained*] **this from ancient time** [*since time began*]? who hath told it from that time? **have not I the LORD? and there is no God else beside me**; a just God and **a Saviour**; there is none beside me [*there is no comparison between idols and the true God!*].

Next, the Lord invites all people everywhere to repent.

22 **Look unto me** [*German: turn to me; in other words, repent*]**, and be ye saved**, all the ends of the earth [*the Atonement applies to all*]: for I am God, and there is none else.

Next, in verse 23, we are taught that every person who has ever been born or who will be born, will someday acknowledge that Jesus is the Christ.

23 **I have sworn** [*covenanted, promised*] **by myself** [*in My own name*], the word is gone out of my mouth in righteousness, and shall not return [*see Doctrine & Covenants 1:38*], **That unto me every knee shall bow, every tongue shall swear** [*acknowledge Christ; does not mean that everyone will repent and be righteous; for example this phrase refers to inhabitants of the telestial glory as used in Doctrine & Covenants 76:110*].

24 **Surely, shall one say, in the LORD have I righteousness and strength**: even to him shall men come; **and all that are incensed** [*angry*] **against him shall be ashamed** [*put to shame; disappointed, disconcerted*].

25 In the LORD [*Christ*] **shall** [*can*] **all the seed of Israel be justified** [*brought into harmony with God's ways, thus be approved to dwell with God*], **and shall glory** [*in the Lord, 1 Corinthians 1:31*].

It is interesting to note that the word "justified," seen in verse 25 above, is used in current word processing terminology to mean "lined up," as in "justify the margins." In scriptural language, "justified" likewise means "lined up"—in other words, "lined up with God's will," or in harmony with God's commandments and thus worthy to be ratified and approved by the Holy Ghost, the Holy Spirit of Promise, to live with God forever.

ISAIAH 46

Selection: all verses

This chapter continues the comparison of Jehovah with the false gods and idols worshiped by so many people in Isaiah's day. The point is that there is no comparison!

Verse 1 introduces us to two prominent false gods in Isaiah's day. Bel and Nebo were chief gods in Babylon. Ancient cultures such as Babylon believed that each "god" had a territory, and when a city or country was defeated in battle by enemies, it meant that their gods (such as Bel and Nebo) had been defeated by the enemy's gods. Chapter 46 ties in with chapters 13 and 14 concerning Babylon's downfall, and with chapters 40–45 concerning Jehovah's power as compared to the lack of power of idols.

1 Bel boweth down [*German: has been defeated*], **Nebo stoopeth, their idols were upon the beasts, and upon the cattle** [*the idols are powerless; they can't move by themselves and have to be transported upon beasts of burden*]: your carriages were heavy loaden; they [*the idols*] are a burden to the weary beast [*the message, by implication, is that Bel and Nebo are burdens to those who "created" them, in contrast to the true God of Israel, who lightens the burdens of those He created, who worship Him*].

2 They [*Bel and Nebo*] **stoop, they bow down together** [*German: they are both defeated*]; **they could not deliver** [*German: remove*] **the burden** [*they couldn't do the job*], **but themselves are gone into captivity** [*they have failed their worshippers and couldn't even save themselves*].

3 Hearken unto me, O house of Jacob, and all the remnant of the house of Israel, which are borne by me [*note that I the Lord carry you, help you, am not a burden*] from the belly [*from the womb, or from the beginning*], which are carried from the womb [*I have carried you from the beginning, contrasted to idol worshippers who have to transport their "gods"*]:

4 And even to your old age [*throughout your entire life*] **I am he** [*the true God*]; **and even to hoar** [*gray*] **hairs will I carry you: I have made** [*German: I want to do it*], **and I will** [*German: desire to*] **bear**; **even I will carry, and will deliver you** [*I want to help, support and bless you throughout your entire life; I want to be your Redeemer!*].

5 To whom will ye liken me, and make me equal, and compare me, that we may be like [*who among your false gods can compare to Me*]? [*Same question as in 40:18, 25.*]

Next, in verses 6–7, Isaiah again points out how ridiculous it is to make and then worship idols.

NOTES

6 **They** [*idol worshippers*] **lavish gold** out of the bag, **and weigh silver** in the balance [*on the scales; in other words, you pay out much money for your worthless idols*], **and hire a goldsmith; and he maketh it a god** [*turns it into an idol*]: **they fall down, yea, they worship**.

7 **They** [*idol worshippers*] **bear him** [*their idol*] **upon the shoulder, they carry him, and set him in his place** [*put the idol in the room or place they want it to stay*], **and he standeth; from his place shall he not remove** [*the idol can't even move from the place the people put it*]: yea, **one shall cry** [*pray*] **unto him** [*the idol*], **yet can he** [*the idol*] **not answer, nor save him** [*the idol worshiper*] out of his trouble [*idols are totally worthless!*].

8 **Remember this, and shew yourselves men** [*think about this and prove that you are man enough to face the truth*]: **bring it again to mind, O ye transgressors** [*face the issue, you sinners!*].

9 **Remember the former things of old** [*the many miracles I performed for you in the past*]: **for I am God, and there is none else; I am God, and there is none like me,**

10 **Declaring the end from the beginning** [*prophesying the future*], and from ancient times the things that are not yet done [*things prophesied anciently that are yet in the future*], saying, **My counsel shall stand, and I will do all my pleasure** [*everything I have said will happen; this message is also given in Doctrine & Covenants 1:38*]:

11 **Calling a ravenous bird from the east** [*a bird of prey; in other words, Cyrus from Persia—see 45:1*], **the man that executeth** [*carries out*] **my counsel** [*plans*] from a far country [*Persia*]: yea, **I have spoken it, I will also bring it to pass;** I have purposed [*planned*] it, I will also do it.

12 **Hearken unto me, ye stouthearted** [*hardhearted*], **that are far from righteousness** [*as mentioned in verse 8*]:

13 I bring near my righteousness [*victory, triumph*]; it shall not be [*German: is not*] far off, and my salvation shall not tarry [*will not be late*]: and **I will place salvation in Zion for Israel my glory** [*I will succeed in bringing salvation and glory to Israel, and you can be a part of it if you repent*].

ISAIAH 47

Selection: all verses

This chapter is a prophecy about the downfall of Babylon. Remember that Babylon was an actual large city (56 miles around with walls 335 feet high and 85 feet wide—see Bible Dictionary, under "Babylon"), but that Babylon is also used often in the scriptures to symbolize Satan's kingdom.

1 **Come down** [*be humbled*], **and sit in the dust** [*a sign of humiliation in eastern cultures; see Isaiah 3:26, Lamentations 2:10*], **O virgin** [*unconquered*] **daughter of Babylon** [*the Babylonian Empire*], sit on the ground [*humiliation*]: **there is no throne** [*Babylon was to be conquered, overthrown; this prophecy was fulfilled literally by Cyrus the Persian in 538 BC and will be fulfilled symbolically as Christ overthrows Satan's kingdom*], **O daughter**

of the Chaldeans [*inhabitants of southern Babylonia, part of the Babylonian Empire*]: **for thou shalt no more be called tender and delicate** [*German: desirable*].

Using imagery to illustrate a conquered Babylon, Isaiah now describes conditions and tasks of slaves, according to the culture of his day.

2 **Take the millstones, and grind meal** [*flour*]: **uncover thy locks** [*take off your veil, like slaves do*], **make bare the leg, uncover the thigh** [*tie up your skirts and expose your legs so you can get around easily to do the work required of slaves*], **pass over the rivers** [*you'll have to wade through canals to get from one field to another as you do the work of slaves*].

3 **Thy nakedness shall be uncovered** [*dual meaning: sexual abuse suffered by slaves; also the "true colors"—in other words, the wickedness of Babylon will be uncovered, exposed*], **yea, thy shame shall be seen: I** [*the Lord*] **will take vengeance, and I will not meet thee** [*Babylon and all things represented by Babylon*] **as a man** [*you won't be able to stop Me because I'm not a mortal man*].

4 **As for** [*German: thus doeth*] **our redeemer**, the LORD of hosts is his name, the Holy One of Israel.

5 **Sit thou** [*Babylon*] **silent**, and get thee into darkness, O daughter of the Chaldeans [*Babylon*]: for **thou shalt no more be called, The lady of kingdoms** [*you've been conquered*].

Next, in verse 6, the Lord explains why He allowed Babylon to conquer the Jews (the main portion of Israel affected by this prophecy). Remember that Isaiah is prophesying of the future as if it had already happened. The events foretold here didn't actually take place until over one hundred years later.

6 **I** [*God*] **was wroth** [*angry*] **with my people, I have polluted** [*German: disowned*] **mine inheritance** [*wicked Israel*], **and given them** [*prophecy of future*] **into thine** [*Babylon's*] **hand: thou didst shew them** [*Israel, especially the Jews*] **no mercy; upon the ancient hast thou very heavily laid thy yoke** [*in other words, you abused the power I allowed you to have over Israel*].

7 **And thou** [*Babylon*] **saidst** [*boasted*], **I shall be a lady** [*German: a queen*] **for ever**: so that **thou didst not lay these things to thy heart** [*you didn't take My warnings seriously*], **neither didst remember the latter end of it** [*you didn't stop to consider the consequences of your behavior*].

8 **Therefore hear now this**, thou [*Babylon*] **that art given to pleasures** [*lustful and riotous living*], **that dwellest carelessly** [*NIV: "lounging in your security"*], **that sayest in thine heart, I am, and none else beside me** [*I am the most powerful of all!*]; **I shall not sit as a widow** [*have my kingdom taken away from me*], **neither shall I know the loss of children** [*Babylon boasts she will never be conquered; however, she will be depopulated and her king destroyed*]:

9 **But these two things** [*the loss of your king and your inhabitants*] **shall come to thee in a moment** [*suddenly*] **in one day**, the **loss of children**, and **widowhood**: they shall come upon thee in their perfection [*in full measure*] for [*despite*] the multitude of thy

NOTES

sorceries, and for [*despite*] the great abundance of thine enchantments [*the so-called "magic" of your false religions will not save you*].

10 **For thou hast trusted in** [*relied on*] **thy wickedness**: thou hast said, None seeth me [*I can get away with it*]. Thy wisdom and thy knowledge, it hath perverted thee [*German: has led you astray*]; and thou hast said in thine heart, I am, and none else beside me [*I am all-powerful*].

11 **Therefore** [*because of the things mentioned above*] **shall evil come upon thee**; thou shalt not know [*German: expect it*] from whence it riseth [*the source of your demise will surprise you*]: and mischief [*ruin*] shall fall upon thee; thou shalt not be able to put it off [*German: atone for it via sacrifices to false gods; see verse 12*]: and **desolation shall come upon thee suddenly**, which thou shalt not know [*foresee*].

12 **Stand now with thine enchantments**, and with the multitude of thy sorceries, wherein thou hast laboured from thy youth [*like you've done all your lives*]; if so be thou shalt be able to profit, if so be thou mayest prevail [*go ahead, try to stop this destruction with your false gods and enchantments; see if they help or not*].

13 **Thou art wearied in the multitude of thy counsels** [*you have spent many boring hours with your counselors, stargazers, and so forth*]. **Let now the astrologers**, the **stargazers**, the monthly **prognosticators** [*those who predict the future*], **stand up, and save thee from these things that shall come upon thee** [*call their bluff*].

14 **Behold, they** [*your religious leaders, soothsayers, wizards, and so forth, as mentioned in verse 13*] **shall be as stubble; the fire shall burn them**; they shall not deliver themselves from the power of the flame: there shall not be a coal to warm at, nor fire to sit before it [*your soothsayers are utterly powerless to save themselves, let alone you*].

The whole message of this chapter, that no one can save Babylon, is summarized in verse 15, next.

15 **Thus** [*like straw in a fire*] **shall they be unto thee** with whom thou hast laboured, even thy merchants [*religious leaders*], from thy youth: they shall wander every one to his quarter; **none shall save**.

ISAIAH 48

Selection: all verses

In this chapter, "Babylon" is used in the symbolic sense. It means wickedness and evil, in other words, Satan's kingdom. This is one of the two chapters of Isaiah that Nephi read to his people in First Nephi, including his rebellious brothers, Laman and Lemuel (1 Nephi 20 and 21). Nephi explained to us why he chose to read these words of Isaiah. He said (bold added for emphasis):

1 Nephi 19:23–24

23 And I did read many things unto them which were written in the books of Moses; but **that I might more fully persuade them to believe in the Lord their Redeemer I did read unto them that which was written by the prophet Isaiah**; for I did liken all scriptures unto us, that it might be for our profit and learning.

24 Wherefore I spake unto them, saying: Hear ye the words of the prophet, ye who are a remnant of the house of Israel, a branch who have been broken off; hear ye the words of the prophet, which were written unto all the house of Israel, and liken them unto yourselves, **that ye may have hope** as well as your brethren from whom ye have been broken off; for after this manner has the prophet written.

Every verse of 1 Nephi, chapter 20, has at least one thing that is different than what we will read here in Isaiah, chapter 48. This is a reminder that the Book of Mormon text of Isaiah was translated from the Brass Plates of Laban, which Lehi and his family had obtained. The Isaiah passages found in the Book of Mormon come from records much closer to the original source (Isaiah only lived about one hundred years before Lehi's departure from Jerusalem). In contrast, Isaiah in the Bible is derived from sources much farther removed from the original. Therefore, we will use 1 Nephi chapter 20 often for clarification as we study this chapter.

As we begin, we see that Isaiah is pointing out the empty worship and hypocrisy of Israel. After doing so, he issues an invitation from the Lord for these people to repent, to flee from Babylon (wickedness), and come unto Him. He finishes with a stern warning that there is no peace for the wicked.

1 **Hear ye this, O house of Jacob** [*the twelve tribes of Israel*], **which are called by the name of Israel** [*who are known as the Lord's covenant people*], **and are come forth out of the waters of Judah** [*waters of baptism, 1 Nephi 20:1*], **which swear by the name of the LORD** [*who make covenants in the name of Jesus Christ*], **and make mention of the God of Israel, but not in truth, nor in righteousness** [*you make covenants but don't live the gospel; empty worship is the problem*].

2 **For they call themselves of the holy city** [*they claim to be the Lord's people*], **and stay themselves upon** [*pretend to rely upon*] **the God of Israel**; The LORD of hosts [*Jehovah*] is his name.

In the next several verses, the Lord reminds Israel that there is no lack of evidence that He exists.

3 **I have declared the former things from the beginning** [*I've had prophets prophesy*]; **and they** [*their prophecies*] **went forth out of my mouth, and I shewed them** [*fulfilled them, so you would have solid evidence that I exist*]; I did them suddenly, and they came to pass [*so you can know I am God; Isaiah 42:9*].

4 **Because I knew that thou art obstinate, and thy neck is an iron sinew** [*your necks won't bend; you are not humble*], **and thy brow brass** [*you are thickheaded; can't get things through your skulls*];

5 **I have even from the beginning declared it** [*prophecies*] **to thee; before it** [*prophesied events*] **came to pass I shewed it thee:** lest thou shouldest say, Mine idol hath done them, and my graven image, and my molten image, hath commanded them [*so you couldn't claim your idols, false gods, did it*].

6 **Thou hast heard, see all this; and will not ye declare it** [*acknowledge it*]? **I have shewed thee new things** from this time, even hidden things, and **thou didst not know them** [*German: that thou hadst no way of knowing*].

7 **They** [*the prophesied events*] **are created** [*happening*] **now, and not from the beginning;** even before the day when thou heardest them not [*without my prophecies, you couldn't*

_____
_____
_____
_____
_____
_____
_____
_____
_____
_____
_____
_____
_____
_____
_____
_____
_____
_____
_____
_____
_____
_____
_____
_____
_____
_____
_____
_____
_____

have known in advance]; lest thou shouldest say, Behold, I knew them [*I did it this way so you would have obvious evidence that I exist*].

8 Yea, **thou heardest not**; yea, thou knewest not; yea, from that time that **thine ear was not opened** [*you wouldn't listen*]: for **I knew that thou wouldest deal very treacherously** [*the Lord knew right from the start that it would be hard to "raise" us. Great potential for good inherently has great potential for evil, but it was worth the risk!*], **and wast called a transgressor from the womb** [*I've had trouble with you Israelites right from the start*].

9 **For my name's sake** [*because I have a reputation to uphold—mercy, patience, love, and so forth*] **will I defer mine anger**, and for my praise will I refrain for thee, that I cut thee not off [*I will not cut you off completely*].

In verse 10, next, the Lord is speaking of the future as if it has already happened. The message is that He will yet have a people who are righteous and worthy of celestial glory. They will have gone through the refiner's fire to get there, just as pure gold must go through the refiner's fire in order to be set free from the impurities of the ore in which it is found.

10 **Behold, I have refined thee**, but not with [*German: "as"*] silver [*"but not with silver" is deleted in 1 Nephi 20:10. Perhaps this phrase in the Bible implies that we are not being refined to be "second-best"—in other words, silver—but rather to be gold, the best, celestial. See Revelation 4:4*]; **I have chosen thee** [*German: I will make you*] **in the furnace of affliction**.

11 **For mine own sake, even for mine own sake, will I do it**: for how should my name be polluted [*German: lest My name be slandered for not keeping My promise*]? and I will not give my glory unto another [*the Lord will stick with Israel*].

12 **Hearken unto me, O Jacob** and Israel, my called [*chosen people*]; **I am he; I am the first, I also am the last** [*I am the Savior*].

13 **Mine hand also hath laid the foundation of the earth** [*I am the Creator*], **and my right hand** [*the covenant hand; the hand of power*] **hath spanned** [*spread out; created*] **the heavens**: when I call unto them, they stand up together.

14 All ye, assemble yourselves, and hear; which among them hath declared these things? **The LORD hath loved him** [*Israel*]: he [*God*] **will do his pleasure on** [*will punish*] **Babylon**, and his arm shall be on the Chaldeans [*southern Babylon*].

15 I, even I, have spoken; yea, I [*Jesus speaking for Heavenly Father?*] **have called him** [*Jesus?*]: **I have brought him, and he shall make his way prosperous**.

16 **Come ye near unto me, hear ye this; I have not spoken in secret** [*I have been open about the gospel*] **from the beginning; from the time that it was** [*declared, 1 Nephi 20:16*], **there am I** [*from the time anything existed, I have spoken*]: and now the Lord GOD, and his Spirit, hath sent me.

17 **Thus saith the LORD, thy Redeemer**, the Holy One of Israel [*Jesus*]; **I am the LORD thy God** which teacheth thee to profit [*German: for your profit, benefit*], **which leadeth thee by the way that thou shouldest go**.

18 **O that thou** [*Israel*] **hadst hearkened** [*if you had just listened and been obedient*] **to my commandments! then had thy peace been as a river** [*you would have had peace constantly flowing unto you*], **and thy righteousness as the waves of the sea** [*you would have been steady, constant*]:

19 **Thy seed also had been as the sand** [*your posterity could have been innumerable; exaltation*], **and the offspring of thy bowels like the gravel thereof** [*like the sand of the seashore*]; his name should not have been cut off nor destroyed from before me [*Israel could have had it very good and would not have been conquered*].

Next, in verse 20, the Lord invites all people to flee from wickedness. Remember, Babylon is often used in the scriptures to mean wickedness.

20 **Go ye forth of Babylon** [*quit wickedness*], **flee ye from the Chaldeans** [*Babylonians*], **with a voice of singing** [*be happy in your righteousness*] declare ye, tell this, utter it even to the end of the earth; **say ye, The LORD hath redeemed his servant Jacob** [*spread the word everywhere you go that the Atonement of Christ works*].

Next, the Savior reminds Israel that just as He brought forth water for the children of Israel in the desert, so also He can provide the refreshing living water of the gospel for all who are willing to partake.

21 And **they thirsted not when he led them through the deserts** [*perhaps symbolic of the results of drinking "living water" (the gospel) as you follow the Savior through the barren world of the wicked*]: **he caused the waters to flow out of the rock** [*Exodus 17:6; symbolic of the Savior*] for them: he clave the rock also, and the waters gushed out.

One of the major messages of Isaiah's writings is summarized in verse 22, next.

22 **There is no peace, saith the LORD, unto the wicked.**

ISAIAH 49

Selection: all verses

1 Nephi 21 is the Book of Mormon version of this chapter of Isaiah. As was the case with Isaiah 48, we will draw heavily from the Book of Mormon as we study Isaiah 49, here.

Isaiah continues his prophecy about the Messiah, and of the gathering of Israel in the last days. The prophecy includes the fact that the governments of many nations will assist in this gathering. In the last days, Israel will finally do the work she was originally called to do but failed to accomplish.

This particular chapter contains one of my personal favorite verses, verse 16, which contains beautiful Atonement symbolism. Beginning with verse 1, we will be taught about the foreordination of covenant Israel and the responsibilities we have as the Lord's chosen people. Remember that "chosen" includes the concept that we are chosen to carry whatever burdens are necessary in order to spread the gospel and the priesthood throughout the earth.

Isaiah sets the stage for this prophecy by having us think of Israel as a person who is thinking about her past and feels like she has been a failure as far as her calling and mission from the Lord is concerned. Then she is startled by her success in the last days. Note that Isaiah says the same thing twice in a row, using different words, several times in this chapter. In verse 1, for example, he says "Listen, O isles unto me; and hearken . . ."

As previously mentioned in this study guide, this was typical repetition for emphasis in biblical culture.

1 **Listen, O isles** ["isles" means "continents and nations throughout the world;" symbolic of scattered remnants of Israel throughout the world—see 1 Nephi 21:1], **unto me**; and hearken, ye people, from far; **The LORD hath called me** [Israel; see verse 3] **from the womb** [before I was born; foreordination]; from the bowels of my mother [from my mother's womb] hath he made mention of my name [Israel was foreordained in premortality to assist the Lord in His work].

2 And **he hath made my mouth like a sharp sword** [Israel is to be an effective instrument in preaching the gospel; the imagery of a sharp sword implies that the gospel is hard on the wicked but helps the righteous by cutting through falsehood]; in the shadow [protection] of his hand hath he hid me, and made me a polished shaft; in his quiver hath he hid me [Israel has been refined and prepared by the Lord to fulfill its calling];

3 And said unto me, **Thou art my servant, O Israel, in whom I will be glorified** [a prophecy that Israel will yet fulfill its stewardship].

In verses 4–12, Isaiah portrays Israel's loneliness and regrets because of rebellion and apostasy in times past. The prophecy also shows us the glorious blessings and responsibilities that await her as she repents.

In order to better appreciate what Isaiah is doing to portray Israel to us, you might picture an actor, representing Israel, dressed in black, sitting all alone on stage, with a single spotlight on her, speaking to the audience as she discusses her past failure to fulfill the mission the Lord gave her.

4 **Then I** [Israel] **said** [to myself], **I have laboured in vain, I have spent my strength for nought, and in vain** [uselessly, in apostasy, false religions, and so on]: **yet surely my judgment is with the LORD** [German: the case against me is in God's hands], **and my work** [German: my office, my calling] **with my God** [German: is from God].

5 **And now, saith the LORD that formed** [foreordained] **me** [Israel, Abraham's posterity through Isaac] **from the womb to be his servant, to bring Jacob** [Israel] **again to him,** Though Israel be not gathered, yet shall I be glorious in the eyes of the LORD, and my God shall be my strength [those who try valiantly to convert and gather Israel will be blessed, whether or not Israel responds; similar to Nephi with respect to Laman and Lemuel in 1 Nephi 2:18–21].

Next, in verse 6, Israel tells us that the Lord not only wants her to bring the gospel to the scattered remnants of Israel, but to the whole world also.

6 **And he said, It is a light thing** [German: not enough of a load] **that thou shouldest be my servant** to raise up the tribes of Jacob [Israel], and **to restore the preserved** [remnants or survivors] **of Israel: I will also give thee for a light to the Gentiles** [you must also bring the gospel to everyone else; quite a prophecy in Isaiah's day when almost any enemy nation could walk all over Israel], **that thou mayest be my salvation unto the end of the earth** [the responsibility of members of the Church today; compare with Abraham 2:9–11].

7 **Thus saith the LORD, the Redeemer of Israel,** and ["and" is deleted in 1 Nephi 21:7] his [Israel's] Holy One, **to him** [Israel] **whom man despiseth, to him whom the nation**

abhorreth [*German: to the people despised by others*], **to a servant of rulers** [*you have been servants and slaves to many nations*], **Kings shall see** [*the true gospel as you fulfill your stewardship*] **and arise** [*out of respect for God*], **princes** [*leaders of nations*] **also shall worship** [*German: fall down and worship*], **because of the LORD** that is faithful, and the Holy One of Israel, **and he shall choose thee** [*German: who chose you*].

Next, Isaiah speaks prophetically of the future as though it had already happened. We are watching this prophecy being fulfilled.

8 **Thus saith the LORD, In an acceptable time** [*when the time is right, beginning with Joseph Smith and the Restoration*] **have I heard thee, and in a day of salvation have I helped thee**: and I will preserve thee, and give thee for a covenant of the people, **to establish the earth** [*to establish the gospel on the earth again*], **to cause to inherit the desolate heritages** [*the spiritual wildernesses caused by apostasy, in other words, the Lord will gather Israel and help Israel fulfill its stewardship as described in verse 6 above*];

9 **That thou mayest say to the prisoners** [*including the living and the dead in spiritual darkness*], **Go forth** [*Go free*]; to them that are in darkness, Shew yourselves [*German: Come out!*]. They shall feed in the ways, and their pastures shall be in all high places [*they will have it good when they repent and follow the true God*].

10 They shall not hunger nor thirst; neither shall the heat nor sun smite them: **for he** [*Christ*] that hath mercy on them **shall lead them**, even by the springs of water shall he guide them [*benefits of accepting and living the gospel*].

11 And **I will make all my mountains a way, and my highways shall be exalted** [*the high road of the gospel will be available to all; "mountains" could symbolize temples in the last days and during the Millennium, where the Lord teaches us the plan of salvation and provides ordinances of exaltation*].

12 Behold, **these** [*remnants of scattered Israel*] **shall come from far**: and, lo, these from the north and from the west [*the gathering will be from all parts of the world*]; and these from the land of Sinim [*perhaps China but not certain; see Bible Dictionary, under "Sinim"*].

13 Sing, O heavens; and be joyful, O earth; and break forth into singing, O mountains: for **the LORD hath comforted his people, and will have mercy upon his afflicted** [*the Lord will eventually redeem Israel*].

With verse 14, next, Isaiah takes us back to Israel, who says, in effect, "Don't waste your effort trying to comfort me. I have failed and the Lord has given up on me."

14 **But Zion said** [*Israel hath said*], **The LORD hath forsaken me, and my Lord hath forgotten me** [*wicked Israel's complaint; 1 Nephi 21:14 adds "but he will show that he hath not" to this verse*].

Next, Isaiah says, in effect, "You think that a mother's bond to her nursing child is strong, but that is nothing compared to how much the Lord cares for Israel."

NOTES

_____
_____
_____
_____
_____
_____
_____
_____
_____
_____
_____
_____
_____
_____
_____
_____
_____
_____
_____
_____
_____
_____
_____
_____
_____
_____
_____
_____
_____
_____
_____

15 **Can a woman forget her sucking** [*nursing*] **child**, that she should not have compassion on the son of her womb? yea, **they** [*Israel*] **may forget, yet will I** [*the Lord*] **not forget thee** [*Israel*].

Verse 16, next, contains beautiful Atonement symbolism and demonstrates how much the Savior cares for all of us.

16 Behold, **I have graven thee upon the palms of my hands** [*In effect, I will be crucified for you. Just as a workman's hands bear witness of his profession, his type of work, so shall nail prints in My hands bear witness of My love for you.*]; **thy walls are continually before me** [*I know where you live, see you continuously, and I will not forget you*].

17 **Thy children** [*descendants*] **shall make haste;** [*"haste against," 1 Nephi 21:17*] **thy destroyers and they that made thee waste shall go forth of** [*flee from*] **thee** [*the tables will be turned in the last days*].

18 **Lift up thine eyes round about, and behold** [*look into the future*]: **all these** [*Israelites*] **gather themselves together, and come to thee** [*you thought you had no family left, but look at all your descendants in the future*]. **As I live** [*the strongest Hebrew oath or promise possible was to promise by the Living God*], saith the LORD, **thou shalt surely clothe thee with them all, as with an ornament, and bind them on thee, as a bride doeth** [*a bride puts on her finest clothing for the occasion; in other words, Israel will have many of her finest descendants in the last days*].

19 **For thy waste and thy desolate places, and the land of thy destruction** [*where you've been trodden down for centuries*], **shall even now be too narrow by reason of the inhabitants** [*you will have so many Israelites, you'll seem to be running out of room for them all; latter-day gathering of Israel*], **and they** [*your former enemies*] **that swallowed thee up shall be far away.**

20 **The children** [*converts to the true gospel*] **which thou shalt have, after thou hast lost the other** [*child; through apostasy, war and so on*], **shall say again in thine ears, The place is too strait for me: give place to me that I may dwell** [*there is not enough room for us all*].

We see evidence of the rapid growth of the Church, as prophesied in these verses, in the ever expanding need for new chapels, temples, MTC's, etc. in our day.

21 **Then shalt thou** [*Israel*] **say in thine heart, Who hath begotten me these, seeing I have lost my children** [*where in the world did all these Israelites come from*], **and am desolate, a captive, and removing to and fro** [*scattered all over*]? and who hath brought up these? Behold, I was left alone [*I thought I was done for*]; **these, where had** [*have*] **they been?**

In verses 22–26, next, the Lord answers the question asked in verse 21, above, as to where all these future faithful Israelites will come from. The answer is simple and powerful. The Lord will use His power to gather them.

22 Thus saith the Lord GOD, Behold, **I will lift up mine hand to the Gentiles, and set up my standard** [*the true Church, gospel*] **to the people: and they** [*the Gentiles or non-Jews*] **shall bring thy sons in their arms, and thy daughters shall be carried**

upon their shoulders [*the Lord will open the way and inspire people everywhere to help in gathering Israel*].

23 **And kings shall be thy nursing fathers, and their queens thy nursing mothers** [*leaders of nations will help gather Israel; for instance, as mentioned previously, Great Britain sponsored the return of the Jews to Palestine in 1948*]: they shall bow down to thee with their face toward the earth, and lick up the dust of thy feet [*the tables will be turned and they will show respect for you*]; and **thou shalt know that I am the LORD: for they shall not be ashamed** [*disappointed*] **that wait for** [*trust in*] **me.**

24 **Shall the prey be taken from the mighty, or the lawful** [*the Lord's covenant people*] **captive delivered** [*Israel asks how they can be freed from such powerful enemies*]?

25 **But thus saith the LORD,** Even **the captives** [*Israel*] **of the mighty** [*Israel's powerful enemies*] **shall be taken away** [*from the enemy*], **and the prey** [*victims*] **of the terrible** [*tyrants*] **shall be delivered** [*set free*]: **for I** [*the Lord*] **will contend with him that contendeth with thee, and I will save thy children** [*the covenant people; see 2 Nephi 6:17*].

26 **And I will feed them that oppress thee with their own flesh** [*your enemies will turn on each other and destroy themselves*]; and they shall be drunken with their own blood, as with sweet wine: and **all flesh shall know that I the LORD am thy Saviour and thy Redeemer,** the mighty One of Jacob.

NOTES

Isaiah 50–57

"He Hath Borne Our Griefs, and Carried Our Sorrows"

In these Isaiah chapters, you will see more about the Atonement of Jesus Christ, along with many prophecies about our day, the last days before the Second Coming. For example, in chapter 50, regarding the Atonement, you will be told by Isaiah that just before the Savior's crucifixion, He was scourged and his tormentors pulled His beard out. You will see much of joy and gladness in chapter 51 as Zion is gathered in the last days. Chapter 52 is a joyful chapter with many prophecies and much counsel, including "be ye clean that bear the vessels of the Lord." You may recognize some phrases from chapter 53, including Isaiah's prophecy that the Savior would be "despised and rejected of men." Pay attention to the prophetic fact that the Church and her stakes will experience tremendous growth in the last days, as summarized in chapter 54. You will see much symbolism in chapter 55, which will be explained verse-by-verse as you read along. You will see Isaiah abruptly switch topics (which he typically does) in chapter 56 as he suddenly changes from counseling the righteous to condemning the wicked leaders of Isaiah's day. In chapter 57, Isaiah delivers a scathing rebuke of the rampant sexual immorality of his day, which applies equally to our day. Verse 21 of chapter 57 clearly warns that wickedness brings no peace.

NOTES

ISAIAH 50

Selection: all verses

This chapter can be compared with 2 Nephi 7. As with many other portions of Isaiah, this chapter speaks of the future as if it had already taken place. A major question here is who has left whom when people apostatize and find themselves far away from God spiritually. Another question that Isaiah asks is, essentially, "Why don't you come unto Christ? Has He lost His power to save you?"

It is in this chapter that we learn that one of the terrible tortures inflicted upon the Savior during His trial and crucifixion was the pulling out of His whiskers (see verse 6).

At the beginning of verse 1, the Lord asks, in effect, "Did I leave you, or did you leave Me?"

1 Thus saith the LORD, **Where is the bill of your mother's divorcement, whom I have put away** [*where are the divorce papers, decreeing that I left you? In other words, do you think I would divorce you (break My covenants with you) and send you away from Me like a man who divorces his wife*]? **or which of my creditors is it to whom I have sold you** [*was it I who sold you into slavery*]? Behold, for your iniquities have **ye sold yourselves** [*the real cause*], **and for your transgressions is your mother put away** [*you brought it upon yourselves*].

2 **Wherefore** [*why*], **when I** [*Jesus*] **came** [*to save My people*], **was there no man** [*who accepted Me as Messiah; in other words, why did My people reject Me*]? **when I called** [*"Come unto Me"*], **was there none to answer** [*German: no one answered*]? **Is my hand shortened at all, that it cannot redeem? or have I no power to deliver** [*have I lost My power*]? **behold, at my rebuke** [*command*] **I dry up the sea** [*as with the parting of the Red Sea*], **I make the rivers a wilderness**: their fish stinketh, because there is no water, and dieth for thirst [*no, I have not lost My power!*].

3 **I clothe the heavens with blackness, and I make sackcloth** [*a sign of mourning*] **their covering** [*I can cause the sky to be dark during the day, as if it were mourning the dead (which it will do at Christ's death; see Matthew 27:45)*].

NOTES

4 **The Lord GOD** [*the Father*] **hath given me** [*Jesus*] **the tongue of the learned** [*Father taught Me well*], **that I should know how to speak a** [*strengthening*] **word in season to him** [*Israel; see 2 Nephi 7:4*] **that is weary**: he wakeneth morning by morning, he wakeneth mine ear to hear as the learned [*German: the Father is constantly communicating with Me and I hear as His disciple*].

5 **The Lord GOD** [*the Father*] **hath opened mine ear, and I was not rebellious, neither turned away back** [*I was obedient and did not turn away from accomplishing the Atonement*].

In verses 6–7, next, Isaiah prophesies some details surrounding Christ's crucifixion. In verse 6, especially, He speaks of the future as if it is past.

6 **I gave my back to the smiters** [*allowed Himself to be flogged; see Matthew 27:26*], **and my cheeks to them that plucked off the hair** [*pulled out the whiskers of My beard*]: **I hid not my face from shame and spitting** [*see Matthew 26:67*].

Here is a quote from Bible scholar Edward J. Young, (n≠ot a member of the Church) concerning the plucking of the beard, in verse 6, above:

"In addition the servant [*Christ, in Isaiah 50:6*] gave his cheeks to those who pluck out the hair. The reference is to those who deliberately give the most heinous and degrading of insults. The Oriental regarded the beard as a sign of freedom and respect, and to pluck out the hair of the beard (for *cheek* in effect would refer to a beard) is to show utter contempt." (Book of Isaiah, vol. 3, page 300.)

7 For **the Lord GOD** [*the Father*] **will help me; therefore shall I not be confounded** [*I will not be stopped*]: **therefore have I set my face like a flint** [*I brace Myself for the task*], **and I know that I shall not be ashamed** [*I know I will not fail*].

8 **He** [*the Father*] **is near that justifieth me** [*approves of everything I do*]; **who will** [*dares to*] **contend with me? let us** [*Me and those who would dare contend against Me*] **stand together** [*go to court, as in a court of law—go ahead and present your arguments against Me*]: **who is mine adversary? let him come near to me** [*face Me*].

9 **Behold, the Lord GOD** [*the Father*] **will help me** [*the Savior*]; **who is he that shall condemn me? lo, they** [*those who contend against Me*] **all shall wax old as a garment; the moth shall eat them up** [*the wicked will have their day and then fade away and reap the punishment*].

Next, in verse 10, the question is asked, in effect, "Who is loyal to the Lord and is not supported by Him?" The answer, as you will see, is no one.

10 **Who is among you that feareth** [*respects*] **the LORD,** that obeyeth the voice of his servant, **that walketh in darkness, and hath no light?** [*Answer: No one, because the Lord blesses His true followers with light.*] **let him trust in the name of the LORD, and stay upon** [*be supported by*] **his God.**

Verse 11, next, addresses all who decide that they can get along fine without God.

11 **Behold, all ye that kindle a fire, that compass** [*surround*] **yourselves about with sparks: walk in the light of your fire** [*try to live without God, according to your own philosophies*], **and in the sparks that ye have kindled** [*rather than Christ's gospel light*]. **This shall ye have of mine hand** [*German: you will get what you deserve*]; **ye shall lie down in sorrow** [*misery awaits those who try to live without God*].

ISAIAH 51

Selection: all verses

The Lord now speaks to the righteous in Israel. Compare with 2 Nephi 8.

One of Satan's goals is to get people to believe that they have no basic worth, that they are simply a biological accident that has somehow developed an ability to think and move about. He teaches that there is no God and that when people die, that is the absolute end of them. In this chapter, Isaiah begins with an invitation for us to consider our origins, the marvelous heritage we have from Abraham and Sarah, and the reality of the hand of the Lord in our lives.

1 **Hearken to me, ye that follow after righteousness**, ye that seek the LORD: **look unto the rock whence** [*from whence; 2 Nephi 8:1*] **ye are hewn** [*look at the top-quality stone from which you originate*], **and to the hole of the pit** [*the rock quarry*] **whence ye are digged** [*consider your origins; you come from the finest stock*].

2 **Look unto Abraham your father, and unto Sarah** [*note that Abraham and Sarah are of equal importance*] **that bare you** [*your ancestors; in other words, your heritage is the finest*]: **for I called him alone** [*of his family, to renew the covenant line*], **and blessed him** [*see Abraham 2:9–11*], **and increased him.**

3 For **the LORD shall comfort Zion: he will comfort all her waste places; and he will make her wilderness like Eden, and her desert like the garden of the LORD** [*the Garden of Eden*]; **joy and gladness shall be found therein, thanksgiving, and the voice of melody** [*wonderful reward for the righteous*].

4 Hearken unto me, my people; and give ear unto me, O my nation: for a law shall proceed from me, and **I will make my judgment to rest for a light of the people** [*My laws will bring light to the nations*].

5 **My righteousness** [*triumph; ability to save*] **is near** [*is available to you*]; my salvation is gone forth, and mine arms shall judge the people [*I will personally rule over the nations*]; the isles [*nations of the world*] shall wait [*trust; rely*] upon me, and on mine arm [*My power*] shall they trust.

6 **Lift up your eyes to the heavens, and look upon the earth beneath**: for the heavens shall vanish away like smoke, and the earth shall wax old like a garment, and they that dwell therein shall die in like manner: but **my salvation** [*the salvation I bring*] **shall be for ever** [*will last forever*], and my righteousness [*triumph*] shall not be abolished [*compare Doctrine & Covenants 1:38*].

7 **Hearken unto me, ye that know righteousness** [*you who are righteous*], the people **in whose heart is my law** [*you who have taken My gospel to heart*]; **fear ye not the reproach** [*insults*] **of men, neither be ye afraid of their revilings** [*stinging criticism*].

NOTES

8 For **the moth shall eat them** [*the wicked who revile against the righteous*] **up like a garment, and the worm shall eat them like wool** [*they are just like moth-eaten clothing that will disintegrate and disappear*]: **but my righteousness** [*salvation and deliverance*] **shall be** [*will last*] **for ever**, and my salvation from generation to generation [*throughout eternity*].

The righteous now reply and invite the Lord's blessings and help in their lives, leading to salvation.

9 **Awake, awake** [*German: Now then, come, Lord*], **put on strength, O arm** [*symbolic of power*] **of the LORD; awake, as in the ancient days**, in the generations of old [*please, Lord, use Thy power to save us like You did in olden days*]. Art thou not it that hath cut Rahab [*German: the proud; hath trimmed the proud down to size. Rahab can refer to the sea monster, Leviathan, in Isaiah 27:1, which represents Satan and any who serve him, such as Egypt when the Israelites escaped them via the Red Sea.*], **and wounded the dragon** [*in other words, defeated Satan, see Revelation 12:7–9*]?

10 **Art thou not it which hath dried the sea** [*the Red Sea*], the waters of the great deep; **that hath made the depths of the sea a way** [*a path*] **for the ransomed** [*the children of Israel, whom the Lord ransomed from Egypt*] **to pass over**?

Next, Isaiah prophesies about the gathering of Israel in the last days.

11 **Therefore** [*because of the Lord's power*] **the redeemed of the LORD** [*Israel; those who will be saved*] **shall return** [*the gathering of Israel in the last days*], **and come with singing unto Zion; and everlasting joy shall be upon their head**: they shall obtain gladness and joy; and sorrow and mourning shall flee away [*the results of righteousness*].

Now the Lord speaks to righteous Israel, responding to their plea for help and reminding them again that He is their God and the One who will help them return.

12 **I, even I, am he that comforteth you: who art thou, that thou shouldest be afraid of a man that shall die** [*mortal men*], and of the son of man [*mortal men*] which shall be made as grass [*short-lived glory of evil mortal men; fear God, not man*];

13 **And forgettest the LORD thy maker**, that hath stretched forth the heavens, and laid the foundations of the earth [*how could you forget Me, your Creator!*]; and hast feared continually every day because of the fury of the oppressor, as if he were ready to destroy [*why should you live in fear of mortal men*]? and where is the fury of the oppressor [*the day will come when their fury won't be able to touch you*]?

14 **The captive exile hasteneth that he may be loosed, and that he should not die in the pit, nor that his bread should fail** [*the day will come when Israel will be set free, no more to die in captivity, and will have plenty*].

15 But **I am the LORD thy God, that divided the sea** [*parted the Red Sea*], whose waves roared: The LORD of hosts is his name [*is My name, 2 Nephi 8:15*].

16 And **I have put my words in thy mouth** [*I have given you My teachings*], and **I have covered thee in the shadow** [*protection*] **of mine hand**, that I may plant the heavens,

NOTES

and lay the foundations of the earth [*I created heaven and earth for you*], **and say unto Zion, Thou art my people** [*you are My covenant people*].

17 **Awake, awake, stand up, O Jerusalem**, which hast drunk at the hand of the LORD the cup of his fury; thou hast drunken the dregs [*the bitter, coarse stuff that settles in the bottom of the cup*] of the cup of trembling, and wrung them out [*you have "paid through the nose" for your wickedness*].

Next, we are reminded that in times of apostasy, the people lose direction.

18 **There is none to guide her** among all the sons whom she [*Israel*] hath brought forth [*you have spent many years without prophets*]; neither is there any that taketh her by the hand of all the sons that she hath brought up.

The Book of Mormon provides much-needed help for understanding verse 19, next.

19 These two things are come unto thee; who shall be sorry for thee [*2 Nephi 8:19 changes this line considerably: "These two sons are come unto thee, who shall be sorry for thee"*]? desolation, and destruction, and the famine, and the sword: by whom shall I comfort thee? [*This verse in the Book of Mormon seems to refer to the two prophets in the last days who will keep the enemies of the Jews from totally destroying them. See Revelation 11.*]

20 Thy sons [*your people*] have fainted [*German: are on their last leg, save these two, 2 Nephi 8:20*], they lie at the head of all the streets, as a wild bull in a net [*your wicked people are being brought down like a wild animal by a net of wickedness*]: they are full of the fury of the LORD [*they are catching the full fury of the Lord*], the rebuke of thy God [*the consequences of sin have caught up with them*].

21 Therefore hear now this, thou afflicted, and drunken [*out of control*], but not with wine [*rather with wickedness*]:

22 Thus saith thy Lord the LORD, and thy God that pleadeth the cause of his people [*I have not deserted you*], Behold, I have taken out of thine hand the cup of trembling [*I suffered the Atonement for you; see Doctrine & Covenants 19:15–19*], even the dregs of the cup of my fury; thou shalt no more drink it again [*Christ will save the Jews in the last days, see 2 Nephi 9:1–2*]:

23 But I will put it [*the cup of his fury in verse 22*] into the hand of them [*your enemies*] that afflict thee; which have said to thy soul [*have said to you*], Bow down, that we may go over [*lie down so we can walk on you*]: and thou hast laid thy body as the ground [*you did*], and as the street, to them that went over [*you have been walked all over, treated like dirt*].

ISAIAH 52

Selection: all verses

Most of this chapter is essentially contained in 3 Nephi 20:30–44, although in different order. It is an invitation to come unto Christ and be gathered to Him with His covenant people, Zion. It begins with a focus on the gathering of the Jews to Jerusalem. The imagery is that of clothing oneself in the gospel of Jesus Christ.

1 **Awake, awake; put on thy strength** [*repent and take Christ's name upon you*], O Zion; **put on thy beautiful garments** [*return to proper use of the priesthood; see Doctrine & Covenants 113:7–8*], **O Jerusalem**, the holy city: for henceforth there shall no more come into thee the uncircumcised and the unclean [*the wicked*].

2 **Shake thyself from the dust; arise** [*from being walked on, Isaiah 51:23*], **and sit down** [*in dignity, redeemed at last*], **O Jerusalem: loose thyself from the bands of thy neck** [*come forth out of spiritual bondage*], O captive daughter of Zion.

Next, we get a brief review of why Israel has had troubles in the past.

3 For thus saith the LORD, **Ye have sold yourselves for nought** [*for nothing of value; in other words, apostatized*]; **and ye shall be redeemed without money** [*the hand of the Lord is in it*].

4 For thus saith the Lord GOD [*Jehovah*], **My people went down aforetime** [*a long time ago*] **into Egypt to sojourn** [*live*] there; **and the Assyrian oppressed them without cause** [*were not justified in how they treated Israel; they abused their power as did Babylon; see 47:6*].

Verse 5, next, emphasizes the need for redemption.

5 Now therefore, **what have I here**, saith the LORD, **that my people is taken away for nought** [*why have My people sold themselves into spiritual bondage for such worthless things (such as pride, wickedness, worshiping false gods, materialism)]*]? **they that rule over them make them to howl**, saith the LORD; and **my name continually every day is blasphemed**.

Verse 6, next, foretells the day when Israel, including the Jews, will return to the Lord.

6 Therefore **my people shall know my name**: therefore they shall know in that day [*in the last days*] that I am he that doth speak: behold, it is I.

7 [*"**And then shall they say**," 3 Nephi 20:40, referring to the last days*] **How beautiful upon the mountains are the feet of him that bringeth good tidings**, that publisheth peace; that bringeth good tidings of good, that publisheth salvation; that saith unto Zion, Thy God reigneth [*missionary work, gathering, etc.*]!

8 [*Compare with 3 Nephi 20:32*] **Thy watchmen** [*prophets, leaders*] **shall lift up the voice; with the voice together shall they sing: for they shall see eye to eye,** <u>when the LORD shall bring again Zion</u>. [*The underlined phrase is replaced in 3 Nephi 20:33 with "Then will the Father gather them together again and give unto them Jerusalem for the land of their inheritance."*]

9 [*"**Then shall they**," 3 Nephi 20:34*] **Break forth into joy**, sing together, ye waste places of Jerusalem: **for the LORD** hath comforted his people, he **hath redeemed Jerusalem** [*will likely occur in the last days, near or at the beginning of the Millennium*].

10 The LORD [*the Father, 3 Nephi 20:35*] **hath made bare his holy arm** [*shown forth His power*] **in the eyes of all the nations**; and **all the ends of the earth shall see the salvation** [*the power to save and redeem*] of our God [*"of the Father; and the Father and I are one." 3 Nephi 20:35*].

Verse 11, next, provides direction for being among those who are gathered to the Father through the Savior.

11 [*And then shall a cry go forth, 3 Nephi 20:41; referring to the last days*] **Depart ye, depart ye, go ye out from thence** [*from among the wicked, Doctrine & Covenants 38:42*], **touch no unclean thing**; **go ye out of the midst of her** [*Babylon, or wickedness*]; **be ye clean, that bear the vessels of the LORD** [*a major message of Isaiah*].

12 For **ye shall not go out with haste, nor go by flight** [*the gospel brings calmness*]: for **the LORD will go before you; and the God of Israel will be your rereward** [*rearward, protection; see Doctrine & Covenants 49:27*].

13 Behold, **my servant** [*could be Joseph Smith Jr. (3 Nephi 21:10–11; page 428 of* Religion 121 Book of Mormon Student Manual); *or Christ; or modern servants and prophets of God; or all of the above working together to fulfill verse 15*] **shall deal prudently**, he shall be exalted and extolled, and be very high.

14 **As many were astonied** [*astonished*] **at thee; his visage was so marred more than any man** [*the Savior as well as most prophets are highly praised by some, see verse 13, and much maligned by others*], and his form more than the sons of men:

15 **So shall he sprinkle** [*JST: gather*] **many nations; the kings shall shut their mouths at him**: for that which had not been told them shall they see; and that which they had not heard shall they consider [*see 3 Nephi 21:8; kings (powerful leaders) will not be able to stop the Lord's work in the last days*].

ISAIAH 53

Selection: all verses

This chapter compares with Mosiah 14 in the Book of Mormon. It is a wonderful chapter, showing that a dominant part of the work of Old Testament prophets was teaching and prophesying about Christ.

Isaiah gives specific details about the Savior's mortal mission and gives a beautiful description of the blessings of the Atonement for each one of us. Among other insights, he teaches us that Jesus Himself derived great personal satisfaction in having performed the Atonement for us (verse 11).

Isaiah starts out with a bit of frustration over how few people take him and his fellow prophets seriously.

1 **Who hath believed our report** [*German: Who listens to us prophets anyway*]? and **to whom is the arm of the LORD revealed** [*who sees God's hand in things*]?

Beginning with the last part of verse 2, next, Isaiah speaks prophetically about the future, as if it has already taken place.

2 **For he** [*Jesus*] **shall grow up before him** [*possibly referring to the Father but could also refer to mankind as implied in the last phrase of verse 1*] **as a tender plant** [*a new plant, a restoration of truth*], **and as a root out of a dry ground** [*"dry ground" symbolizes apostate Judaism*]: **he** [*Jesus*] **hath no form nor comeliness** [*no special, eye-catching attractiveness*]; **and when we shall see him, there is no beauty that we should desire him** [*normal people couldn't tell He was the Son of God just by looking at Him*].

3 **He** [*Jesus*] **is despised and rejected of men; a man of sorrows** [*sensitive to people's troubles and pain*], **and acquainted with grief** [*He endured much suffering and pain*]: **and we hid as it were our faces from him** [*wouldn't even look at Him*]; **he was despised, and we** [*people in general*] **esteemed him not** [*German: paid no attention to him; even his own brothers rejected him at first; see John 7:5*].

4 **Surely he hath borne our griefs, and carried our sorrows** [*the Atonement*]: **yet we did esteem him stricken, smitten of God, and afflicted** [*we didn't recognize Him as the Great Atoner; we rather thought He was just another criminal receiving just punishment from God*].

5 But **he was wounded for our transgressions** [*He suffered for our sins; see 2 Nephi 9:21*], **he was bruised for our iniquities** [*He suffered for our sins (double emphasis)*]: **the chastisement of** [*required for*] **our peace was upon him** [*He was punished so that we could have peace*]; and **with his stripes** [*wounds and punishments*] **we are healed** [*from our sins, upon repentance*].

6 **All we** like sheep **have gone astray; we have turned every one to his own way** [*every one of us has sinned; we all need the Atonement*]; **and the LORD** [*the Father*] **hath laid on him** [*the Savior*] **the iniquity of us all** [*2 Nephi 9:21*].

Isaiah continues to speak prophetically as if the future events he is foretelling have already taken place, thus emphasizing the fact that they will take place.

7 **He** [*Christ*] **was oppressed, and he was afflicted, yet he opened not his mouth** [*for instance, He wouldn't even speak to Pilate; see Mark 15:3*]: **he is brought as a lamb to the slaughter, and as a sheep before her shearers is dumb** [*doesn't speak*], **so he openeth not his mouth.**

8 **He was taken from prison and from judgment** [*He was refused fair treatment*]: and who shall declare his generation? for **he was cut off out of the land of the living: for the transgression of my people was he stricken** [*He was punished for our sins*].

9 And **he made his grave with the wicked** [*He died with convicted criminals*], **and with the rich in his death** [*a rich man (Joseph of Arimathaea) donated his tomb; see John 19:38–42*]; **because he had done no violence** [*German: no wrong*], **neither was any deceit in his mouth** [*Christ was perfect*].

10 **Yet it pleased the LORD to bruise him** [*it was the Father's will to allow the Atonement to be performed by His Son*]; he hath put him to grief: **when thou** [*He, Christ*] **shalt make** [*makes*] **his soul** [*German: life*] **an offering for sin, he shall see his seed** [*His loyal followers, success; see Mosiah 15:10–12*], he shall prolong his days, and **the pleasure of the LORD** [*the Father's plan*] **shall prosper in his hand** [*will succeed through Christ's mission and Atonement*].

NOTES

_____
_____
_____
_____
_____
_____
_____
_____
_____
_____
_____
_____
_____
_____
_____
_____
_____
_____
_____
_____
_____
_____
_____
_____
_____
_____
_____
_____
_____
_____

11 **He** [*Jesus*] **shall see** [*the results*] **of the travail** [*suffering*] **of his soul, and shall be satisfied** [*shall have joy—the Savior will have personal joy because of having performed the Atonement for us*]: **by his knowledge** [*by the knowledge He brings*] **shall my righteous servant** [*Christ*] **justify** [*save; prepare them to be approved by the Holy Ghost, sealed by the Holy Spirit of Promise*] **many; for he shall bear their iniquities**.

12 **Therefore will I divide him a portion with the great** [*He will receive His reward*], and **he shall divide the spoil** [*share the reward, in other words, we can be joint heirs with Him; see Romans 8:17*] **with the strong** [*the righteous*]; **because he hath poured out his soul unto death** [*laid down His life*]: and he was numbered with the transgressors; and he bare the sin of many, and made intercession for the transgressors.

ISAIAH 54

Selection: all verses

This chapter deals with the last days and compares with 3 Nephi 22. A major message of this chapter is that in the last days, Israel will finally be righteous and successful.

1 **Sing, O barren** [*one who has not produced children; Israel, who has not produced righteous children*], thou that didst not bear; **break forth into singing, and cry aloud, thou that didst not travail** [*go into labor*] **with child** [*in former days, you did not succeed in bringing forth righteous children, loyal to Christ*]: **for more are the children** [*righteous converts*] **of the desolate** [*perhaps meaning scattered Israel*] **than the children of the married wife** [*perhaps meaning Israelites who remained in the Holy Land; in other words, now in the last days, you've got more righteous Israelites than you ever thought possible, with almost all the converts coming from outside the land of Israel*], saith the LORD.

2 **Enlarge the place of thy tent** [*make more room*], and let them stretch forth the curtains of thine habitations: spare not, **lengthen thy cords, and strengthen thy stakes** [*the Church will greatly expand in the last days as righteous Israel is gathered*];

3 **For thou shalt break forth on the right hand and on the left** [*righteous Israel will show up everywhere*]; and **thy seed shall inherit the Gentiles, and make the desolate cities** [*cities without the true gospel*] **to be inhabited** [*Church membership will grow throughout the world*].

4 Fear not; for **thou shalt not be ashamed** [*you will not fail in the last days*]: neither be thou confounded; for thou shalt not be put to shame: for **thou shalt forget the shame of thy youth, and shalt not remember the reproach of thy widowhood any more** [*you can forget the failures of the past when Israel was apostate; the once "barren" Church is going to bear much fruit in the last days*].

5 For **thy Maker is thine husband** [*you have returned to your Creator in the last days*]; the LORD of hosts is his name; and **thy Redeemer** the Holy One of Israel; The God of the whole earth shall he be called.

6 For **the LORD hath called thee as a woman forsaken and grieved in spirit** [*Israel has been through some very rough times*], **and a wife of youth, when thou wast refused** [*when you didn't bear righteous children*], saith thy God.

7 **For a small moment have I forsaken thee** [*because you apostatized*]; **but with great mercies will I gather thee** [*in the last days*].

8 In a little wrath I hid my face from thee for a moment [*when you rejected me*]; but **with everlasting kindness will I have mercy on thee**, saith the LORD thy Redeemer.

9 For **this** [*your situation*] **is as the waters of Noah** unto me: **for as I have sworn** [*promised*] **that the waters of Noah should no more go over the earth; so have I sworn that I would not be wroth with thee, nor rebuke thee** [*just as I promised not to flood the earth again, so I have promised to accept you back as you return to Me in the last days*].

10 For the mountains shall depart, and the hills be removed; but **my kindness shall not depart from thee**, neither shall the covenant of my peace be removed, saith the LORD that hath mercy on thee. [*Isaiah reminds us here of the true nature of God, a very kind and merciful God indeed! Unfortunately, many people have not been correctly taught this truth.*]

Next, the Lord promises to prepare fine accommodations for righteous Israel in the last days, as well as in the celestial kingdom.

11 **O thou** [*Israel*] **afflicted, tossed with tempest, and not comforted** [*you have been through some very rough times*], behold, **I will lay thy stones with fair colours** [*I will use the finest "materials" for the Restoration of the gospel in the last days and to build your "celestial homes"*], and lay thy foundations with sapphires [*precious gemstones*].

12 And I will make thy windows [*German: battlements*] of agates [*gemstones*], and thy gates of carbuncles [*bright, glittering gemstones*], and all thy borders of pleasant stones [*similar to the description of the celestial city in Revelation 21; you Israelites will have it very good, even better than you can imagine, when you repent and return unto Me to dwell*].

13 And **all thy children shall be taught of the LORD; and great shall be the peace of thy children** [*likely referring to the Millennium; see Doctrine & Covenants 45:58–59*].

14 **In righteousness shalt thou be established**: thou shalt be far from oppression; for thou shalt not fear: and from terror; for it shall not come near thee [*seems to refer to millennial conditions*].

15 Behold, they [*enemies of righteousness*] shall surely gather together, but not by me: **whosoever shall gather together against thee shall fall for thy sake** [*I will protect you, you will finally have peace*].

16 Behold, **I have created the smith** that bloweth the coals in the fire, and that bringeth forth an instrument for his work; **and I have created the waster** [*German: the Destroyer*] to destroy [*I created all things and have power over Satan. I can control all things; you are safe with Me*].

17 **No weapon that is formed against thee shall prosper**; and every tongue that shall rise against thee in judgment thou shalt condemn. **This is the heritage of the servants of the LORD**, and their righteousness is of me, saith the LORD [*there is safety for the righteous with Me*].

ISAIAH 55

Selection: all verses

The Lord here invites all to come partake of the bounties of the gospel (which are equally available to all, either here on earth or afterward in the spirit world), and to enjoy eternity with Him.

1 **Ho** [*German: come now!*], **every one that thirsteth, come ye to the waters** [*the "living water"; in other words, Christ; see John 4:14, 7:37–38*], **and he that hath no money; come ye, buy** [*with your good works, keeping the commandments, and so forth*], **and eat; yea, come, buy wine and milk without money and without price** [*the gospel is available to all without regard to economic status*].

2 **Wherefore** [*why*] **do ye spend money for that which is not bread** [*not of true value*]? **and your labour for** *that which* **satisfieth not** [*why are you so materialistic*]? **hearken diligently unto me** [*the Lord*], **and eat ye that which is good** [*that which comes of Christ*], **and let your soul delight itself in fatness** [*the best; in other words, the richness of the gospel*].

3 **Incline your ear** [*listen carefully*], **and come unto me** [*Christ*]: hear, and your soul shall live [*you will receive salvation*]; **and I will make an everlasting covenant** [*the fulness of the gospel; see Doctrine & Covenants 66:2*] **with you, even the sure mercies of David** [*German: the mercies and pardons of Christ spoken of by David; "David" is often used symbolically for Christ—see Isaiah 22:22; hence, "sure mercies of David" can mean the "sure mercies of Christ"*].

4 **Behold, I have given him** [*Christ*] **for a witness to the people**, a leader and commander to the people.

There could be many different interpretations of verse 5, next. One possibility is presented here.

5 Behold, **thou** [*Christ*] **shalt call a nation that thou** [*Israel*] **knowest not, and nations** [*the true Church in the last days*] **that knew not thee** [*weren't personally acquainted with ancient Israel*] **shall run unto thee** [*shall gather Israel*] **because of the LORD** thy God [*under the direction of the Lord*], and for the Holy One of Israel; **for he** [*Israel*] **hath glorified thee** [*God*]. [*In the last days, Israel will be gathered, will return to God, and be saved.*]

Verses 6–7, next, are an invitation to repent and return to a kind, merciful God.

6 **Seek ye the LORD while he may be found**, call ye upon him while he is near:

7 **Let the wicked forsake his way, and the unrighteous man his thoughts: and let him return unto the LORD, and he** [*the Lord*] **will have mercy upon him; and to our God, for he will abundantly pardon**.

Next, in verses 8–9, Isaiah again uses chiasmus in order to make a point. You may wish to read the background notes accompanying Isaiah chapter 3 in this study guide for some insights about chiasmus. In this case, the chiastic structure is brief, consisting

NOTES

of A, B, C, C,' B,' A.' You'll notice that C and C' are not the same; rather, they are related ideas, and thus still work in a chiasmus.

8 For my <u>thoughts</u> **[A]** are not your thoughts, neither are your <u>ways</u> **[B]** my ways, saith the LORD.

9 For as the <u>heavens</u> **[C]** are higher than the <u>earth</u> **[C']**, so are my <u>ways</u> **[B']** higher than your ways, and my <u>thoughts</u> **[A']** than your thoughts [*come unto Me and live as I do, which way of life is much more satisfying than you can possibly comprehend*].

10 For **as the rain cometh down, and the snow from heaven, and returneth not thither, but watereth the earth, and maketh it bring forth and bud, that it may give seed to the sower, and bread to the eater:**

11 **So shall my word be** [*designed to bring forth exaltation*] **that goeth forth out of my mouth**: it shall not return unto me void, but **it shall accomplish that which I please**, and it shall prosper in the thing whereto I sent it [*My gospel will ultimately succeed; can also mean that those who receive the gospel into their lives will be greatly blessed*].

12 **For ye shall go out** [*from premortality to earth*] **with joy, and be led forth** [*to return home to God*] with peace: **the mountains and the hills shall break forth** before you **into singing, and all the trees of the field shall clap their hands** [*God's creations rejoice as their role in helping man achieve exaltation is fulfilled*].

13 **Instead of the thorn shall come up the fir tree, and instead of the brier shall come up the myrtle tree** [*the earth will eventually be celestialized; see Doctrine & Covenants 130:9*]: **and it** [*the earth and many of its inhabitants' achieving celestial glory*] **shall be to the LORD for a name** [*will increase God's glory and dominion*], **for an everlasting sign** [*that God's promises are fulfilled and that man can achieve exaltation*] **that shall not be cut off** [*that will never end*].

ISAIAH 56

<u>Selection: all verses</u>

Verses 1–8 extend the invitation (given in chapter 55) to exaltation to all, including Gentiles.

1 Thus saith the LORD, **Keep ye judgment, and do justice** [*be righteous*]: for my salvation is near to come, and my righteousness to be revealed.

2 **Blessed is the man that doeth this** [*the good mentioned in verse 1*], and the son of man that layeth hold on it [*who follows My counsel to live righteously*]; **that keepeth the Sabbath from polluting it, and keepeth his hand from doing any evil.**

3 **Neither let the son of the stranger** [*the Gentiles*], **that hath joined himself to the LORD** [*that has joined the Church, accepted and follows Christ*], **speak, saying, The LORD hath utterly separated me from his people** [*the Lord has made me a second-class citizen forever*]: **neither let the eunuch** [*see Bible Dictionary, under "eunuch"*] **say, Behold, I am a dry tree** [*I will never have children; eunuchs were not allowed into the congregation of Israel; see Deuteronomy 23:1*].

NOTES

_____
_____
_____
_____
_____
_____
_____
_____
_____
_____
_____
_____
_____
_____
_____
_____
_____
_____
_____
_____
_____
_____
_____
_____
_____
_____
_____
_____
_____
_____
_____

4 **For thus saith the LORD unto the eunuchs** [*symbolically represent a class of people that the Israelites despised and would never consider to be potential citizens of heaven*] **that keep my sabbaths, and choose the things that please me** [*keep my commandments*], **and take hold of my covenant** [*make and keep covenants of exaltation with Me*];

5 **Even unto them will I give in mine house** [*temple; celestial kingdom*] **and within my walls** [*perhaps dual, meaning temples or heavenly home*] **a place and a name** [*King Benjamin promised his people a "name" in Mosiah 1:11; in other words, the name of Christ, Mosiah 5:8*] **better than of sons and of daughters** [*they will have more honor and glory in exaltation than they would have had from having sons and daughters on earth*]: **I will give them an everlasting name** [*a new name (see Revelation 2:17, Doctrine & Covenants 130:11), symbolic of covenants of exaltation*], **that shall not be cut off** [*eunuchs and all "outcasts" can be exalted too!*].

6 **Also the sons of the stranger** [*Gentiles*], **that join themselves to the LORD** [*make covenants*], **to serve him, and to love the name of the LORD, to be his servants, every one that keepeth the Sabbath from polluting it, and taketh hold of my covenant** [*all Gentiles can receive exaltation if they keep the commandments*];

7 **Even them will I bring to my holy mountain** [*God's kingdom*], **and make them joyful in my house** of prayer: their burnt offerings and their sacrifices shall be accepted upon mine altar; for mine house shall be called an house of prayer for all people [*celestial exaltation is available for all people who make covenants with the Lord and keep His commandments*].

8 **The Lord GOD which gathereth the outcasts of Israel** [*the gathering of scattered Israel*] **saith, Yet will I gather others** [*Gentiles*] **to him** [*Israel*], **beside those** [*Israelites*] **that are gathered unto him** [*Israel*].

Isaiah switches topics now to the Gentile "beasts" who will come to "devour" (destroy) the wicked of Israel.

9 **All ye beasts** [*Gentile armies*] **of the field, come to devour** [*come to devour Israel*], **yea, all ye beasts in the forest.**

10 **His watchmen** [*Israel's wicked leaders*] **are blind: they are all ignorant** [*of the dangers of wickedness*], **they are all dumb dogs** [*not doing their job of warning the people of danger*], **they cannot bark** [*they won't sound the alarm*]; **sleeping, lying down, loving to slumber** [*they are asleep on the job*].

11 Yea, **they are greedy dogs which can never have enough** [*are never satisfied*], **and they are shepherds that cannot understand** [*leaders who don't understand the seriousness of the situation*]: **they all look to their own way** [*look only after their own interests*], **every one for his gain**, from his quarter.

12 **Come ye, say they, I will fetch wine, and we will fill ourselves with strong drink** [*"Let's party!"*]; and to morrow shall be as this day, and much more abundant [*"And tomorrow we will have even a bigger and better party!"*].

ISAIAH 57

Selection: all verses

In this chapter, Isaiah gives comfort to the righteous and a warning to the wicked. In verse 1, he addresses the issue that the righteous often suffer and no one seems to care. In verse 2, Isaiah gives counsel and comfort to the righteous.

1 **The righteous perisheth** [*the righteous suffer when the wicked rule; see Doctrine & Covenants 98:7*], **and no man layeth it to heart** [*no one seems to care*]: and merciful men are taken away, none considering that the righteous is taken away from the evil to come.

2 **He** [*the righteous*] **shall enter into peace**: they shall rest in their beds [*or on their couches*], each one walking in his uprightness [*personal righteousness leads to inner peace here and peace in eternity*].

Beginning with verse 3, next, Isaiah addresses the wicked.

3 **But draw near hither, ye sons of** [*followers of*] **the sorceress** [*people who live wickedly*], **the seed of** [*followers of*] **the adulterer and the whore** [*gross wickedness; used in 1 Nephi 22:14 to represent Satan's kingdoms*].

4 **Against whom do ye sport yourselves** [*whom are you mocking*]? **against whom make ye a wide mouth** [*making faces*], **and draw out the tongue** [*sticking your tongues out*]? **are ye not children of transgression** [*totally caught up in sin*], **a seed of falsehood** [*a bunch of liars*],

5 **Enflaming yourselves** [*sexually arousing yourselves*] **with idols under every green tree** [*German: You run to your gods with sexual arousal, referring to the use of prostitutes as part of pagan worship*], **slaying the** [*your*] **children in the valleys under the clifts of the rocks** [*killing your children as human sacrifices*]?

6 **Among the smooth stones of the stream** [*used for building altars for idol worship*] **is thy portion** [*German: you base your whole existence on your false gods, idols*]; they, **they are thy lot** [*you have chosen them over Me, therefore, you will have to depend on them for your reward*]: **even to them hast thou poured a drink offering** [*part of idol worship that was originally revealed for worship of the true God—see Exodus 29:40; they have perverted proper worship ceremonies over to their idol worship*], **thou hast offered a meat offering** [*to your idols; see Exodus 29:41*]. Should I receive comfort in these [*do you expect Me to be happy about such perversions of true worship*]?

In verses 7 and 8, the Lord chastises Israel for breaking the seventh commandment literally by having sexual intercourse with temple prostitutes as part of pagan worship services. Symbolically, the Lord is the husband and Israel is the bride in the covenant relationship, symbolized by marriage. In these next verses, Isaiah uses the imagery of a wife being unfaithful to her husband and committing adultery.

7 **Upon a lofty and high mountain hast thou set thy bed**: even thither wentest thou up to offer sacrifice.

8 **Behind the doors also and the posts hast thou set up thy remembrance** [*German: statue*]: for **thou hast discovered** [*uncovered, exposed, undressed*] **thyself to another than me** [*you have "stepped out on Me," been unfaithful to Me*], and art gone up; **thou hast enlarged thy bed** [*made room for many false gods in your life*], **and made thee a covenant with them** [*you have given your loyalty to many false gods*]; thou lovedst their bed where thou sawest it.

9 **And thou wentest to the king** [*Molech, a large, brass idol with a hollow fire-pit stomach, used for sacrificing children*] **with ointment, and didst increase thy perfumes** [*you have worshipped the idol, Molech, with ointment and perfumes*], and didst send thy messengers far off, **and didst debase thyself even unto hell.** [*"You have traveled all the way to hell to find new and worse ways to commit sin!"; the Lord implies that they have made covenants with Satan himself.*]

10 **Thou art wearied in the greatness of thy way** [*you got tired trying to find worse ways to sin*]; **yet saidst thou not, There is no hope** [*but you didn't give up; rather, you said to yourself, "There has got to be something more wicked we can do!"*]: **thou hast found the life of thine hand** [*renewal of strength*]; **therefore thou wast not grieved** [*you kept striving for worse wickedness against all odds*].

11 **And of whom hast thou been afraid or feared, that thou hast lied** [*why have you respected false gods instead of Me*], **and hast not remembered me, nor laid it to thy heart** [*you don't even seem to be aware of Me*]? **have not I held my peace even of old, and thou fearest me not** [*have I been too kind and gentle with you*]?

12 **I will declare** [*German: point out*] **thy** [*so-called*] **righteousness, and thy works; for they shall not profit thee** [*I will expose your so-called righteousness and good works; they won't save you*].

13 **When thou criest** [*cry out for help when you are in trouble*], **let thy companies** [*of idols*] **deliver** [*save*] **thee**; but the wind shall carry them all away [*your idols and false gods are no more secure and stable than a tumbleweed in the wind*]; vanity shall take them [*a puff of breath will blow them away*]: **but he that putteth his trust in me shall possess the land, and shall inherit my holy mountain** [*I do have power to save you and can give you great blessings*];

14 **And** [*I, the Lord*] **shall say**, Cast ye up, cast ye up [*German: make a highway, make a highway*], prepare the way [*clear the way*], take up the stumbling block out of the way of my people [*prepare the way for the return of My people—certainly foreshadowing the Restoration*].

15 For thus saith the high and lofty One [*the Lord*] that inhabiteth eternity, whose name is Holy; **I dwell in the high and holy place, with him also that is of a contrite and humble spirit** [*the contrite and humble will find safety and security with Me*], **to revive** [*German: refresh*] **the spirit of the humble, and to revive the heart of** [*give new courage to*] **the contrite ones.**

The word "contrite," used at the end of verse 15, above, not only means "humble," but also carries with it the connotation of "desiring to be corrected as needed."

16 For **I will not contend** [*against you*] **for ever**, neither will I be always wroth [*angry*]: for the spirit should fail before me [*if I did, all mankind would perish*], and the souls [*people*] which I have made [*no one would survive*].

17 **For the iniquity** [*because of the wickedness*] **of his** [*Israel's*] **covetousness** [*wicked greediness*] **was I wroth, and smote him**: I hid me [*I withdrew My spirit*], and was wroth, and he [*Israel*] went on frowardly in the way of his heart [*kept right on in his wicked ways*].

18 **I have seen his ways** [*probably referring to Israelites who repent with a contrite and humble spirit as mentioned in verse 15*], **and will heal him**: I will lead him also, and restore comforts [*comfort him*] unto him and to his mourners [*those Israelites who mourn for their sins, who repent*].

19 **I create the fruit of the lips** [*speech; German: I will create fruit of the lips that preaches:*]; **Peace, peace to him** [*the righteous*] that is far off, and to him that is near, saith the LORD; and I will heal him [*the repentant, anywhere he is found*].

20 **But the wicked are like the troubled sea, when it cannot rest, whose waters cast up mire and dirt**.

21 **There is no peace, saith my God, to the wicked** [*a major message from the Lord through Isaiah*].

Isaiah 58–66

"The Redeemer Shall Come to Zion"

These chapters are rich with doctrine and gospel applications that can make our lives and worship deeper and more fulfilling. Chapter 58 gives us powerful help for increasing the effectiveness of our fasting and helps us make the Sabbath "a delight." Chapter 59 warns us that unrepented-of sin separates us from God. Chapter 60 contains many prophecies of Isaiah, including that the last day's gathering of Israel will take place in amazing ways even though gross spiritual darkness will be prevalent upon the earth. You may have heard a well-known phrase in chapter 61 as Isaiah prophesies of the glorious benefits of the Atonement of Christ in the last days. The phrase is "beauty for ashes," describing the results of the Savior's Atonement in our lives. Chapter 62 describes many of the blessings of living on the covenant path. Chapter 63 describes the Second Coming and tells us why the Lord will wear red when He comes. In chapter 64, Israel implores Christ to come, and chapter 65 tells us how old people will live to be during the Millennium and describes Millennial conditions. Chapter 66 gives some details about the Second Coming, the destruction of the wicked, and the preaching of the gospel to the Gentiles.

NOTES

ISAIAH 58

Selection: all verses

Verses 1–3 imply that the people have been complaining about not getting the blessings they want from the Lord, even though they keep the letter-of-the-law ordinances. The Lord responds in verses 4–5.

Verses 6–12 are some of the most beautiful found anywhere in scripture regarding the purposes of fasting and detailing some of the blessings of fasting as the Lord intends it to be.

Verses 13–14, likewise, describe the desired attitude about keeping the Sabbath holy.

1 **Cry aloud, spare not, lift up thy voice like a trumpet, and shew my people their transgression,** and the house of Jacob their sins [*go ahead, Isaiah, tell the people why they aren't getting the desired blessings; tell them of their sins*].

2 **Yet they seek me daily** [*are going through the motions, doing all the rituals*], **and** [*appear to*] **delight to know my ways, as a nation that did righteousness, and forsook not the ordinance of their God** [*German: as if they were a nation who had not forsaken the ordinances of their God*]: **they ask of me the ordinances of justice** [*German: they demand their rights*]; **they take delight in approaching to God** [*German: want to debate with God and demand their rightful blessings*].

3 **Wherefore** [*why*] **have we fasted, say they, and thou seest not** [*You don't seem to notice*]? **wherefore have we afflicted our soul** [*why do we put our bodies through this pain*], **and thou takest no knowledge** [*You ignore it*]? [*God now answers their question:*] **Behold, in the day of your fast ye find pleasure** [*German: you do what you desire*], **and exact all your labours** [*German: make your employees work*].

4 Behold, **ye fast for strife and debate** [*your way of fasting causes contention*], and to smite with the fist of wickedness: **ye shall not fast as ye do this day, to make your voice to be heard on high** [*you cannot expect the Lord to bless you for such hypocritical fasting*].

5 Is it such a fast that I have chosen [*do you really think such fasting pleases Me*]? a day **for a man to afflict his soul** [*German: do evil to his body*]? is it to bow down his head as a bulrush, and to spread sackcloth and ashes under him? **wilt thou call this a fast, and an acceptable day to the LORD** [*do you really think outward appearance is everything*]?

Next, in verses 6–12, we are taught principles of true fasting.

6 Is not this the fast that I have chosen [*let Me tell you the real purpose of the fast*]? **to loose the bands of wickedness** [*to help you grow in righteousness*], **to undo the heavy burdens** [*including those that are brought on by sin*], **and to let the oppressed** [*by sin*] **go free, and that ye break every yoke** [*break loose from every burden*]?

7 Is it not to deal thy bread to the hungry [*to feed the hungry*], **and that thou bring the poor that are cast out to thy house** [*to take care of the homeless*]? **when thou seest the naked, that thou cover him** [*to clothe the naked*]; **and that thou hide not thyself from thine own flesh** [*to help your own family and relatives*]?

8 Then [*when you do the above*] **shall thy light break forth as the morning,** and **thine health shall spring forth speedily:** and **thy righteousness shall go before thee; the glory of the LORD shall be thy rereward** [*rear guard; protection*].

9 Then shalt thou call, and the LORD shall answer; thou shalt cry [*pray*], and he shall say, Here I am. **If thou take away from the midst of thee the yoke** [*root out the evils from among you*], **the putting forth of the finger** [*pointing in a gesture of scorn*], **and speaking vanity** [*maliciously*];

10 And if thou draw out thy soul [*German: heart*] **to the hungry** [*help the hungry*], **and satisfy the afflicted soul** [*help the afflicted*]; **then shall thy light rise in obscurity** [*shine in the darkness*], and thy darkness be as the noonday [*instead of darkness, you will have light*]:

11 And the LORD shall guide thee continually, and satisfy thy soul in drought, and make fat thy bones [*strengthen you*]: and **thou shalt be like a watered garden, and like a spring of water, whose waters fail not** [*never cease*].

12 And they that shall be of thee shall build the old waste places [*German: and through you shall the old waste places be built*]: **thou shalt raise up the foundations of many generations; and thou shalt be called, The repairer of the breach, The restorer of paths to dwell in** [*perhaps indicating that as Israel returns to the Lord and does the things prescribed in verses 6 and 7, then they will be the means of restoring the Church*].

Next we are taught the proper attitude about keeping the Sabbath day holy.

13 If thou turn away thy foot from the Sabbath, **from doing thy pleasure on my holy day** [*if you will do My will rather than your will on the Sabbath*]; **and call the Sabbath a delight** [*have a good attitude about the Sabbath*], the holy of the LORD, honourable; **and shalt honour him** [*the Lord*], **not doing thine own ways, nor finding thine own pleasure, nor speaking thine own words:**

14 **Then shalt thou delight thyself in the LORD** [*then you will have joy in the Lord*]; **and I will cause thee to ride upon the high places of the earth, and feed thee with the**

_____

_____

_____

_____

_____

_____

_____

_____

_____

_____

_____

_____

_____

_____

_____

_____

_____

_____

_____

_____

_____

_____

_____

_____

_____

_____

_____

_____

_____

heritage of Jacob thy father [*you will receive the Lord's choicest blessings, the blessings of Abraham, Isaac, and Jacob*]: for the mouth of the LORD hath spoken it [*this is a promise!*].

ISAIAH 59

Selection: all verses

In this chapter Isaiah teaches us a lesson on the behaviors of the wicked and the motives and thought processes found in their minds and hearts. Then he teaches us about the Messiah and His role in intervening for our sins, if we choose to repent. Isaiah concludes by strongly emphasizing that the Lord will indeed save those who repent from their sins (verse 20).

Verse 1 explains that the Lord has not lost His power to save, and verses 2–8 explain that the Israelites have put distance between themselves and the Lord by their wicked behaviors.

1 Behold, **the LORD's hand is not shortened, that it cannot save**; neither his ear heavy [*deaf*], that it cannot hear [*the Lord has not lost His power to save, perhaps referring back to the people's questions in Isaiah 58:3*]:

2 But **your iniquities have separated between you and your God**, and your sins have hid his face from you, that he will not hear [*your wickedness has separated you from God*].

3 For **your hands are defiled with blood** [*perhaps referring to their killing the prophets and others as implied in verse 7*], **and your fingers with iniquity** [*you've got your hands in all kinds of wickedness*]; **your lips have spoken lies** [*you are dishonest*], **your tongue hath muttered perverseness** [*German: unrighteousness; you are wicked through and through*].

4 **None calleth** [*seeks*] **for justice, nor any pleadeth for** [*desires; advocates*] **truth: they trust in vanity** [*man rather than God*], **and speak lies** [*are dishonest*]; **they conceive mischief** [*they are constantly dreaming up more ways to sin*], **and bring forth iniquity** [*their desires are to do evil continually*].

5 **They hatch cockatrice' eggs** [*they "hatch" all kinds of wickedness, like hatching poisonous snake eggs in their minds*], **and weave the spider's web** [*design entanglements in sin*]: **he that eateth of their eggs dieth, and that which is crushed breaketh out** [*hatches*] **into a viper** [*they are creating a menu for spiritual death and going from bad to worse*].

6 **Their webs** [*the things they've surrounded themselves with*] **shall not become garments** [*they cannot clothe themselves comfortably in wickedness*], **neither shall they cover themselves** [*"insulate" themselves*] **with their works** [*they will not "insulate" themselves from consequences of wickedness; they can't get completely comfortable in wickedness; see Isaiah 28:20*]: **their works are works of iniquity, and the act of violence is in their hands.**

7 **Their feet run to evil** [*they are anxious to sin*], **and they make haste to shed innocent blood** [*they are anxious to kill their true prophets and others of the righteous*]: **their thoughts are thoughts of iniquity** [*evil desires are constantly on their minds*]; **wasting**

and destruction are in their paths [*they are wasting away their lives, heading for disaster*].

8 **The way of peace they know not**; and **there is no judgment** [*justice*] **in their goings: they have made them** [*for themselves*] **crooked paths** [*they have created a very wicked and perverse lifestyle for themselves*]: **whosoever goeth therein shall not know peace** [*there is no peace for the wicked; compare with Isaiah 57:21*].

In verses 9–15, Israel admits guilt and faces the issue that they are behaving wickedly, like Alma the Younger did as described in Alma 36:13–14. This paves the way for the Atonement to work in their lives.

9 **Therefore** [*for this reason*] **is judgment** [*fairness, integrity in our dealings with others*] **far from us, neither doth justice** [*charity, righteousness*] **overtake us**: we wait for [*look forward to*] light, but behold obscurity [*darkness*]; for brightness, but we walk in darkness [*because of our wickedness*].

10 **We grope for the wall like the blind, and we grope as if we had no eyes** [*we are stumbling around in the dark (spiritual darkness)*]: **we stumble at noonday** as in the night; we are in desolate places as dead men [*we are as good as dead, we've about had it*].

11 **We roar all like bears** [*we are fierce*], **and mourn sore** [*plaintively*] **like doves** [*and have our sorrows*]: **we look for judgment** [*pleasant treatment*], **but there is none; for salvation, but it is far off from us** [*we are a long way away from God*].

12 For [*because we are so wicked*] **our transgressions are multiplied before thee, and our sins testify against us**: for our transgressions are with us [*we are dragging our sins around with us*]; **and as for our iniquities, we know** [*German: feel*] **them** [*we are aware of and acknowledge our sins*];

13 In **transgressing** and **lying** against the LORD [*making and then breaking covenants*], and **departing** away from our God, **speaking oppression** and **revolt, conceiving and uttering from the heart words of falsehood** [*our hearts have not been right before God*].

14 And **judgment is turned** away backward, and **justice standeth afar off**: for truth is fallen in the street [*our lifestyle is completely out of line*], and **equity** [*honesty*] **cannot enter** [*into our lives the way we are living them now*].

15 Yea, **truth faileth** [*is lacking*]; and **he that departeth from evil maketh himself a prey** [*When a person repents and turns from evil, he is mocked and becomes a victim in a wicked society. From here to the end of verse 21, Isaiah says that the Lord can now start redeeming Israel, because they have faced guilt, verses 9–15, and are turning from transgression, verse 20.*]: **and the LORD saw it, and it displeased him that there was no judgment**.

16 And **he saw that there was no man** [*no one besides Christ could do the job of redeeming Israel; similar to Revelation 5:3–4*], **and wondered that there was no intercessor: therefore his** [*the Lord's*] **arm brought salvation unto him** [*German: himself, Christ*

had the power within Himself; see Isaiah 63:5]; **and his** [_Christ's personal_] **righteousness, it sustained him** [_Christ_].

17 **For he** [_Christ_] **put on righteousness** as a breastplate, and an helmet of salvation upon his head [_breastplate and helmet are armor and imply intense attacks by the enemies of righteousness_]; and he put on the garments of vengeance for clothing [_Christ can save us through His righteousness and power of salvation (the law of mercy), or punish us (according to the law of justice, sometimes referred to as "vengeance"), depending on our deeds as stated in verse 18_], and was clad with zeal as a cloke [_Christ is completely able to be the Intercessor desired in verse 16_].

18 According to their deeds, accordingly he will repay [_the law of the harvest_], fury to his [_Christ's_] adversaries, recompence [_Alma 41:4_] to his enemies; to the islands [_all continents, nations_] he will repay recompence [_emphasis is on "recompence," or giving them what they have earned_].

19 **So shall they fear** [_includes the idea of respect, reverence_] **the name of the LORD** from the west, and his glory from the rising of the sun [_from east to west, everywhere_]. When the enemy [_German: the Lord_] shall come in like a flood [_the judgments of God will come quickly to the whole earth, "islands" in verse 18_], the Spirit of the LORD shall lift up a standard against him [_the enemies; the wicked in verse 18_].

20 And **the Redeemer shall come to Zion, and unto them that turn from** [_repent from_] **transgression** in Jacob [_among the house of Israel_], saith the LORD [_the righteous will live with Christ; implies Millennium_].

21 **As for me** [_the Lord_], **this is my covenant with them** [_those who have turned away from sin, verse 20_], saith the LORD; **My spirit** that **is upon thee**, and **my words** [_the fulness of the gospel_] which I have put in thy mouth, **shall not depart out of thy mouth**, nor out of the mouth of thy seed, nor out of the mouth of thy seed's seed, saith the LORD, from henceforth and for ever [_an everlasting covenant which will see ultimate fulfillment with those who attain exaltation in the celestial kingdom_].

ISAIAH 60

Selection: all verses

Isaiah now prophesies that in the last days the Church of Jesus Christ will arise, shine forth, and be a light to the nations as taught in Isaiah 5:26, as well as other places. Ultimately, all those who have chosen to join with the Lord and become part of covenant Israel will enjoy celestial glory with Him forever.

1 **Arise, shine; for thy light is come** [_the time for the Restoration of the gospel through the Prophet Joseph Smith has come_], **and the glory of the LORD is risen upon thee.**

2 **For, behold, the darkness** [_spiritual darkness in the last days, see_ Teachings of the Prophet Joseph Smith, _page 47_] **shall cover the earth**, and gross darkness the people: **but the LORD shall arise upon thee, and his glory shall be seen upon thee** [_the restored Church; Zion in the last days_].

3 And **the Gentiles shall come to** [*German Bible: walk in*] **thy light, and kings to the brightness of thy rising** [*German: to the brightness that has come upon you*].

4 Lift up thine eyes round about, and see: **all they gather themselves together, they come to thee** [*Israel, Zion*]: **thy sons** [*converts*] **shall come from far, and thy daughters** [*converts*] **shall be nursed at thy side** [*people will gathered to Zion from far and near, and will be nourished by the true gospel of Jesus Christ*].

5 **Then thou shalt see, and flow together** [*be radiant, be happy*], **and thine heart shall fear** [*German: be surprised, thrill*], **and be enlarged** [*swell; rejoice*]; because the abundance of the sea [*multitude*] shall be converted unto thee [*Zion*], the forces [*wealth*] of the Gentiles shall come unto thee.

In these verses, we see, among other things, that the restored Church will become prosperous in the last days.

6 The multitude of camels shall cover thee, the dromedaries [*young camels*] of Midian and Ephah [*parts of Jordan and Saudi Arabia*]; all they from Sheba [*part of Saudi Arabia*] shall come: **they shall bring gold and incense** [*similar to when the Wise Men came to Christ; perhaps symbolic of when people come to Christ*]; **and they shall shew forth the praises of the LORD** [*people from these Arabic countries will come unto Christ; symbolic of people from all nations coming to Christ in the last days*].

7 All the flocks [*perhaps symbolic of converts*] of Kedar [*Syria*] shall be gathered together unto thee, the rams [*strong men, leaders, chiefs*] of Nebaioth shall minister unto thee [*Israel in the last days*]: **they** [*people out of all nations*] **shall come up with acceptance on mine altar** [*shall become acceptable to Me*], and I will glorify the house of my glory.

8 **Who are these that fly as a cloud,** and as the doves to their windows [*who are these people who flock into the Church from over the sea (the gathering)*]?

9 Surely **the isles** [*nations*] **shall wait** [*German: trust in; look forward eagerly*] **for me,** and the ships of Tarshish first, to bring thy sons [*converts*] from far, **their silver and their gold with them,** unto the name of the LORD thy God, and **to the Holy One of Israel,** because he hath glorified thee [*Israel; the true Church*].

10 **And the sons of strangers** [*foreigners*] **shall build up thy walls** [*will help build up Zion*], and **their kings shall minister unto thee** [*leaders of foreign governments will help the spread of the Church in the last days*]: for in my wrath I smote thee [*in times past, I've had to severely discipline you*], but in my favour have I had mercy on thee [*but in the last days as you (Israel) return to Me, you will partake of My mercy*].

11 **Therefore thy gates** [*as in city gates, closed as needed for defense*] **shall be open continually** [*you will not fear attack by enemies*]; they shall not be shut day nor night; that men may bring unto thee the forces [*wealth*] of the Gentiles, and that their kings may be brought [*German: that their kings may be brought to you also*].

12 For **the nation and kingdom that will not serve thee** [*Zion, in the last days, and as the Millennium begins*] **shall perish**; yea, those nations shall be utterly wasted.

NOTES

Remembering that Isaiah often uses trees to symbolize people is helpful in understanding verse 13, next.

13 **The glory** [*the best of*] **of Lebanon** [*the Holy Land*] **shall come unto thee**, the fir tree, the pine tree, and the box together, to beautify the place of my sanctuary [*temple*]; and I will make the place of my feet [*footstool, earth, temple*] glorious.

14 **The sons also of them** [*your former enemies*] **that afflicted thee shall come bending unto thee**; and all they that despised thee shall bow themselves down at the soles of thy feet [*your former enemies and oppressors will humbly respect you*]; **and they shall call** [*acknowledge*] **thee, The city of the LORD, The Zion of the Holy One of Israel.**

15 **Whereas thou hast been forsaken and hated** [*in the past*], so that no man went through thee [*people hated you and avoided you*], **I will make thee an eternal excellency, a joy of many generations**.

16 **Thou shalt also suck the milk of** [*be nourished and assisted by*] **the Gentiles, and** shalt suck the breast of [*be nourished and assisted by*] **kings**: and **thou shalt know that I the LORD am thy Saviour and thy Redeemer**, the mighty One of Jacob [*in other words, the God of Abraham, Isaac, and Jacob*].

The basic message of verse 17, next, is that the gospel of Jesus Christ brings the very best into our lives.

17 **For** [*instead of*] **brass I will bring gold**, and **for** [*instead of*] **iron** I will bring **silver**, and for [*instead of*] wood brass, and for [*instead of*] stones iron [*you will prosper*]: **I will also make thy officers** [*leaders*] **peace, and thine exactors** [*rulers*] **righteousness** [*righteous leaders will bless our lives in the Church in the last days; also, during the Millennium, Christ will be assisted by the righteous Saints as leaders and rulers; see Revelation 20:4*].

18 **Violence shall no more be** heard in thy land, wasting nor destruction within thy borders [*wonderful peace awaits the righteous*]; but thou shalt call thy walls Salvation [*you will be surrounded with peace and salvation*], and thy gates Praise.

19 The sun shall be no more thy light by day; neither for brightness shall the moon give light unto thee: but **the LORD shall be unto thee an everlasting light**, and thy God thy glory [*some conditions in New Jerusalem will be similar to conditions in the celestial glory as described in Revelation 21:23 and 22:5*].

20 Thy sun shall no more go down; neither shall thy moon withdraw itself: for the LORD shall be thine everlasting light, and **the days of thy mourning shall be ended** [*your earthly sorrows will be over*].

Next, we are taught that the righteous will inherit the earth forever. We know that this earth will be celestialized and become the celestial kingdom for those from our world who are worthy of it (see Doctrine & Covenants 130:9).

21 Thy people also shall be all righteous: they shall inherit the land [*earth*] **for ever** [*Doctrine & Covenants 88:17–20; 130:9*], the branch of my planting, the work of my hands [*the righteous*], that I may be glorified.

22 **A little one** [*a seemingly unimportant, insignificant person*] **shall become a thousand**, and a small [*insignificant*] one **a strong nation** [*perhaps referring to "a continuation of the seeds (children) forever," Doctrine & Covenants 132:19; eternal posterity for those who gain exaltation*]: I the LORD will hasten it [*act quickly*] in his [*My*] time [*the Lord will act quickly to bestow these blessings when the time is right*].

ISAIAH 61

Selection: all verses

Isaiah here describes Christ's authority, power, and the purposes of His earthly ministry. The Savior quoted verse 1 and the first phrase of verse 2 in Luke 4:18–19 as He stood and read from Isaiah, identifying Himself as the Messiah to those assembled in the synagogue at Nazareth. They were incensed and attempted to throw Him off a cliff.

1 **The Spirit of the Lord GOD** [*Jehovah—see footnote 1b in your Bible*] **is upon me**; because **the LORD hath anointed me** [*My mission, calling, is*] **to preach good tidings** [*the gospel*] **unto the meek; he hath sent me to bind up** [*apply first aid; to heal*] **the brokenhearted, to proclaim liberty to the captives** [*those in spiritual bondage here and in spirit prison*], **and the opening of the prison** [*spirit prison; spiritual blindness*] **to them that are bound;**

2 **To proclaim the acceptable year** [*the time designated by the Father for Me to perform My earthly missions—see Bruce R. McConkie,* Doctrinal New Testament Commentary, *vol. 1, page 161*] **of the LORD, and the day of vengeance of our God;** [*this phrase refers to the destruction of the wicked at the Second Coming*] **to comfort all that mourn;**

3 **To appoint** [*extend compassion*] **unto them that mourn in Zion,** to give unto them **beauty for** [*in place of*] **ashes,** the **oil of joy for** [*in place of*] **mourning,** the garment of **praise for** [*in the place of*] **the spirit of heaviness** [*depression*]; **that they might be called trees of righteousness,** [*righteous people in the Lord's garden*] **the planting** [*people, work*] **of the LORD, that he might be glorified** [*that He might bring people to live in exaltation with Him eternally; compare with Moses 1:39*].

4 And they [*the righteous in the last days*] shall build the old wastes, they shall raise up the former desolations, and **they shall repair the waste cities, the desolations of many generations** [*in the last days, Zion will be built up again*].

5 **And strangers** [*foreigners, your former enemies*] **shall stand and feed your flocks,** and the sons of the alien [*foreigner*] shall be your plowmen and your vinedressers [*the tables are turned, former enemies will be your servants now*].

6 **But ye shall be named the Priests of the LORD:** [*make covenants leading to exaltation*] men shall call you **the Ministers of our God:** [*you will have priesthood authority*] ye shall eat the riches of the Gentiles, and in their glory [*wealth*] shall ye boast [*German: enjoy*] yourselves.

NOTES

7 **For** [*in place of*] **your shame** [*German: humiliation in times past*]; **ye shall have double** [*a reference to the birthright blessing; in other words, exaltation; see Doctrine & Covenants 132:20*]; **and for** [*in place of*] **confusion they** [*righteous Israel in the last days and beyond*] **shall rejoice in their portion** [*reward*]: therefore in their land they shall possess the double [*birthright blessing; see Deuteronomy 21:17*]: **everlasting joy shall be unto them.**

8 **For I the LORD love judgment** [*justice, righteousness*], **I hate robbery** [*plundering*] **for** [*in place of*] **burnt offering** [*I hate hypocrisy, evil lifestyles, combined with empty worship rituals with which people try to look righteous*]; **and I will direct their work in truth, and I will make an everlasting covenant with them.**

9 **And their seed** [*the righteous*] **shall be known among the Gentiles** [*the gospel will spread to all nations*], **and their offspring among the people: all that see them shall acknowledge** [*recognize*] **them, that they are the seed which the LORD hath blessed** [*they are the people of the Lord, those who receive the blessings of Abraham as promised in Abraham 2:8–11*].

Next, in verses 10–11, we see rejoicing and singing songs of praise to the Lord. This can have dual or triple or quadruple meaning, which is typical of Isaiah's words. For example, it can be Isaiah who is rejoicing, or Zion, or any of the righteous in the last days, or anyone who attains exaltation. And, no doubt, you can come up with additional possibilities.

10 **I** [*Isaiah or Zion or other*] **will greatly rejoice in the Lord, my soul shall be joyful in my God; for he hath clothed me with the garments of salvation** [*2 Nephi 4:33–35, similar to Nephi's rejoicing in the Lord*], **he hath covered me with the robe of righteousness, as a bridegroom decketh himself with ornaments** [*German: priestly clothing; Hebrew: mitre or cap; see Exodus 39:28 footnote b*], **and as a bride adorneth herself with her jewels.**

Reference to garments, robes, priestly "ornaments" or cap, in verse 10, above, points one's mind to ordinances of exaltation in temples today.

11 **For as the earth bringeth forth her bud, and as the garden causeth the things that are sown in it to spring forth; so the Lord GOD will cause righteousness** [*victory of Zion*] **and praise** [*of Zion, Israel*] **to spring forth before** [*among*] **all the nations** [*the Lord will restore Israel and will again make the blessings of exaltation available in the last days*].

ISAIAH 62

Selection: all verses

This chapter deals with the gathering of Israel in the last days, and the fact that the earth will have true prophets of God again. The gathering will be the result of the preaching of the gospel throughout the world. People will once again become part of the covenant people of the Lord, which is another way of saying that they will be saved.

1 **For Zion's sake will I not hold my peace** [*remain silent*], **and for Jerusalem's sake I will not rest** [*remain silent*], **until the righteousness thereof** [*victory of Zion*] **go forth as brightness** [*very noticeable, beautifully conspicuous*], **and the salvation thereof as**

a lamp that burneth [*flaming torch; in other words, the restored gospel will be a light for all who chose to come unto Christ*].

2 **And the Gentiles shall see thy** [*Zion's*] **righteousness, and all kings** [*world leaders*] **thy glory**: and **thou shalt be called by a new name** [*symbolic of having made covenants with God, which, when kept, lead to life in celestial glory; see Doctrine & Covenants 130:11; Revelation 2:17*], which the mouth of the LORD shall name.

3 **Thou shalt also be a crown of glory** [*symbolic of exaltation; see Revelation 4:4; 2 Timothy 4:8*] **in the hand of the LORD**, and a royal diadem [*crown, symbolic of royal power and authority*] in the hand of thy God.

4 **Thou shalt no more be termed Forsaken** [*you will never again be forsaken*]; neither shall thy land any more be termed Desolate: **but thou shalt be called Hephzi-bah** [*JST: delightful*], **and** thy land **Beulah** [*the married wife; you will belong to the Lord and the Lord to you*]: for the LORD delighteth in thee, and **thy land shall be married** [*you will belong to the Lord; you will be His covenant people*].

5 **For as a young man marrieth a virgin, so shall thy sons** [*JST: God*] **marry thee**: and as the bridegroom rejoiceth over the bride, so shall thy God rejoice over thee.

Remember that Isaiah is speaking prophetically of the future as if it has already happened.

6 **I have set watchmen** [*latter-day prophets*] **upon thy walls, O Jerusalem, which shall never hold their peace** [*remain silent*] **day nor night** [*in other words, there will again be continuous revelation*]: **ye that make mention of the LORD** [*you who pray and worship the Lord*], **keep not silence,**

7 And **give him** [*the Lord*] **no rest** [*don't stop praying*], **till he** [*the Lord*] **establish, and till he** [*the Lord*] **make Jerusalem** [*Zion, the Lord's covenant people in the last days*] **a praise in the earth** [*highly respected throughout the earth*].

Verses 8–9, next, appear to describe conditions during the Millennium.

8 **The LORD hath sworn by his right hand** [*has covenanted*], and by the arm of his strength, **Surely I will no more give thy corn** [*crops*] **to be meat** [*food*] **for thine enemies**; and the sons of the stranger [*foreigners, Gentiles*] shall not drink thy wine, for the which thou hast laboured [*in other words, you will live in peace with Me*]:

9 **But they that have gathered** [*harvested*] **it shall eat it, and praise** [*give thanks to*] **the LORD**; and they that have brought it [*made it*] together shall drink it in the courts of my holiness [*you will enjoy the fruits of your labors in peace in My holy kingdom*].

10 **Go through, go through the gates** [*come to Zion, via the gates—baptism and other gospel ordinances, coupled with righteous living*]; **prepare ye the way of the people; cast up, cast up the highway** [*the highway to Zion, the way to God, will be built up*]; **gather out the stones** [*remove the stumbling blocks*]; **lift up a standard** [*ensign, or the restored gospel of Jesus Christ*] **for the people.**

_____
_____
_____
_____
_____
_____
_____
_____
_____
_____
_____
_____
_____
_____
_____
_____
_____
_____
_____
_____
_____
_____
_____
_____
_____
_____
_____
_____
_____
_____
_____
_____

11 **Behold, the LORD hath proclaimed unto the end of the** [all of the] **world, Say ye to the daughter of Zion** [Jerusalem, the righteous], **Behold, thy salvation** [your Deliverer] **cometh; behold, his** [Christ's] **reward** [He brings your reward with Him when He comes] **is with him, and his work before him.**

12 **And they shall call them** [the righteous will be referred to as], **The holy people, The redeemed of the LORD**: and thou [righteous Israel] **shalt be called, Sought out, A city not forsaken** [chosen by the Lord to be blessed and enjoy His help].

ISAIAH 63

Selection: all verses

This is one of the better-known chapters of Isaiah, particularly because it informs us that the Savior will wear red (either literally or symbolically) when He comes at the time of the Second Coming (see verses 1–2). The red represents the blood of the wicked, who are destroyed at His coming. Verses 3–6 continue the theme of the destruction of the wicked at that time.

Isaiah is a master at using comparison and contrast for teaching purposes. Thus, beginning with verse 7, he contrasts the horror of the wicked, depicted in the first six verses, with the blessed state of the righteous, who will receive the promised blessings of peace and safety when the Lord returns.

1 **Who is this** [Christ] **that cometh** [the Second Coming] **from Edom** [from the east; travelers from the east to Jerusalem usually came north past the Dead Sea and then west to Jerusalem. From Edom could also mean from the east, or heaven; see Doctrine & Covenants 133:46], **with dyed** [red—see verse 2] **garments** [clothing] **from Bozrah** [the capital city of Edom]? this **that is glorious in his apparel** [Christ comes in glory], **travelling in the greatness of his strength** [Christ comes in great power at the Second Coming]? **I** [Christ; "It is I," the Savior] **that speak in righteousness, mighty to save** [the repentant].

2 **Wherefore** [why] **art thou red in thine apparel** [what is the red spattered all over Your clothing; see Doctrine & Covenants 133:51], **and thy garments like him that treadeth in the winefat** [Hebrew: press, in other words, the wine press and the vat for collecting the juice of the grapes or olives]?

Next, the Savior answers the question posed in verses 1–2, above, as to who He is.

3 **I have trodden the winepress alone** [I was the only one capable of doing the Atonement]; and of the people **there was none with me** [I had to do it alone]: **for** [the reason that My clothing is red is that] **I will tread them** [the wicked] **in mine anger, and trample them in my fury; and their blood** [the blood of the wicked—see Doctrine & Covenants 133:51] **shall be sprinkled upon my garments**, and I **will stain all my raiment** [judgment will be thorough].

4 **For the day of vengeance is in mine heart** [German: is part of My task, My responsibility], **and the year of my redeemed is come** [the time has come for the righteous to be set free from the cares of a wicked world, perhaps referring to the Millennium].

Another way to look at the phrase "the day of vengeance is in mine heart," in verse 4, above, is to say "the law of justice is also in My heart"; in other words, the law of justice is a vital part of the plan of salvation (see Alma 42:25).

5 And **I looked, and there was none to help** [*no mortal; no one could help Me do the Atonement*]; and **I wondered that there was none to uphold** [*I had to do it alone—see Matthew 27:46*]: **therefore mine own arm** [*the power was within Me*] **brought salvation unto me**; and my fury [*My own divine strength*], it upheld me.

6 And **I will tread down the people** [*the wicked*] **in mine anger, and make them drunk in my fury** [*judgment, the law of justice, will fall upon the wicked*], **and I will bring down their strength to the earth** [*I will humble the wicked*].

Isaiah now switches topics and turns to the kindness and blessings of the Lord to the righteous. In so doing, he will review some of Israel's rebellious past.

7 **I will mention the lovingkindnesses of the LORD**, and the praises of the LORD, according to all that the LORD hath bestowed on us, and the great goodness toward the house of Israel, which he hath bestowed on them according to his mercies, and according to the multitude of his lovingkindnesses.

8 For he said, **Surely they are my people**, children that will not lie [*German: people of integrity*]: **so he was their Saviour.**

9 **In all their affliction he was afflicted** [*He suffered and paid for their sins*], **and the angel of his presence saved them** [*the Lord rescued the children of Israel from Egypt*]: in his love and in his pity **he redeemed them; and he bare them, and carried them all the days of old** [*see Doctrine & Covenants 133:53–55, referring to righteous*].

10 **But they** [*the children of Israel*] **rebelled, and vexed his holy Spirit: therefore he was turned to be their enemy, and he fought against them.** [*He had to discipline them severely*]

11 **Then he remembered,** [*His people remembered—see footnote 11a in your Bible*] **the days of old, Moses, and his people, saying, Where is he that brought them** [*us*] **up out of the sea** [*the parting of the Red Sea*] **with the shepherd** [*leaders—see footnote 11c in your Bible*] **of his flock? where is he that put his holy Spirit within him?** [*within them—see footnote 11e in your Bible*];

Isaiah is reminding the people that they had been greatly blessed by the Lord in times past (verses 11–14), in contrast to wicked Israel's punishments in Isaiah's day and for centuries since then.

12 **That led them by the right hand of Moses** with his glorious arm, dividing the water [*parting the Red Sea*] before them, to make himself an everlasting name?

13 **That led them** [*children of Israel*] **through the deep** [*Red Sea*], as [*easily as a*] an horse in the wilderness [*walks along in the desert*], **that they should not stumble** [*be stopped*]?

14 **As a beast goeth** [*as cattle walk easily*] **down into the valley, the Spirit of the LORD caused him** [*them, the Israelites*] **to rest**: so didst thou lead thy people, to make thyself a glorious name [*You led Your people and became famous among surrounding nations as a result*].

NOTES

Next, Isaiah pleads with the Lord to bless Israel.

15 **Look down from heaven, and behold from the habitation of thy holiness** [*German: from Your heavenly home*] **and of thy glory: where is thy zeal and thy strength, the sounding of thy bowels** [*Thy tenderness*] **and of thy mercies toward me? are they restrained?**

16 **Doubtless thou art our father, though Abraham be ignorant of us, and Israel acknowledge us not** [*Abraham is long since dead, can't help us. Jacob is long since dead, can't help us*]: **thou, O LORD, art our father, our redeemer**; thy name is from everlasting [*German: You have been our Redeemer since the beginning*].

17 **O LORD, why hast thou made** [*JST: "suffered," (allowed)*] **us to err from thy ways, and hardened** [*allowed us to harden*] **our heart from thy fear** [*German: to the point that we no longer feared You*]? **Return for thy servants' sake, the tribes of thine inheritance** [*let us be Thy people again*].

18 **The people of thy holiness** [*covenant Israel*] **have possessed it** [*the temple*] **but a little while**: our adversaries have trodden down thy sanctuary [*the temple, Doctrine & Covenants 64:11; in other words, enemies have possessed the temple more than we have through the ages*].

19 **We are thine: thou never barest rule over them** [*German: we have become just like people over whom You have never ruled*]; **they were not called by thy name** [*like people who are not Your covenant people, not bearing Your name*].

ISAIAH 64

Selection: all verses

Isaiah continues the theme of 63:15, desiring that the Lord would come down now and rule over Israel. Isaiah, in effect, has Israel pleading with the Lord to come again, as promised (the Second Coming—see heading to this chapter in your Bible).

1 **Oh that thou wouldest** rend the heavens, that thou wouldest **come down**, that the mountains might flow down at thy presence [*the Second Coming*],

2 As when the **melting fire burneth**, the fire causeth the waters to boil, **to make thy name known to thine adversaries** [*the wicked*], that the nations may tremble at thy presence!

3 **When thou didst terrible things** [*German: because of the miracles you do*] which we looked not for [*German: which we didn't expect*], **thou camest down, the mountains flowed down at thy presence.**

4 For since the beginning of the world **men have not heard, nor perceived by the ear, neither hath the eye seen**, O God, beside thee, **what he hath prepared for him that waiteth for him** [*trusts in Him; no one can even imagine the blessings the Lord has in store for the righteous*].

The JST makes significant changes in verse 5, next. We will give it as it stands in the King James Version of the Bible and then give it from the Joseph Smith Translation of the Bible.

5 Thou meetest [*guidest*] him that rejoiceth and worketh righteousness, those that remember thee in thy ways: behold, thou art wroth; for we have sinned: in those is continuance, and we shall be saved.

JST Isaiah 64:5

5 Thou meetest him that worketh righteousness, and rejoiceth him that remembereth thee in thy ways; in righteousness there is continuance, and such shall be saved.

6 **But** [*JST: "we have sinned"*] **we are all as an unclean thing**, and all our righteous-nesses are as filthy rags [*the few things we do right are of little value because of our gross wickedness*]; **and we all do fade as a leaf** [*we are fading away as a covenant people because of wickedness*]; and **our iniquities**, like the wind, **have taken us away** [*our wickedness has separated us from Thee*].

7 And **there is none that calleth upon thy name** [*no one turns to the Lord*], that stirreth up himself to take hold of thee: for **thou hast hid thy face from us, and hast con-sumed us, because of our iniquities** [*we have separated ourselves from You*].

8 **But now** [*and yet*], **O LORD, thou art our father; we are the clay, and thou our potter** [*our Maker*]; **and we all are the work of thy hand.**

9 **Be not wroth very sore** [*please don't be too angry with us*], O LORD, **neither re-member** [*our*] **iniquity for ever** [*please forgive us*]: behold, see, we beseech thee, we are all thy people.

10 **Thy holy cities are a wilderness, Zion is a wilderness, Jerusalem a desolation** [*much destruction has come to us already because of our wickedness*].

11 **Our holy and our beautiful house** [*the temple in Jerusalem*], where our fathers praised thee, **is burned up with fire**: and **all our pleasant** [*German: beautiful-to-look-at*] **things are laid waste.**

12 **Wilt thou refrain thyself for these things** [*will You continue to withhold blessings despite our pleas*], **O LORD? wilt thou hold thy peace** [*keep silent*], **and afflict us very sore** [*continue to punish us severely—please have mercy on us!*]?

ISAIAH 65

Selection: all verses

This chapter summarizes the reasons the Lord rejected ancient Israel and explains in some detail the consequences of rejecting the Lord. In contrast, it also gives some details about the Millennium and the blessings for the righteous at that time, including the fact that mortals then living will live to be one hundred years old (verse 20).

The JST makes several changes in verses 1, 2, 4, and 20. We will point these out as we go along.

Verse 1 in the JST seems to answer the question in Isaiah 64:12, namely, how long the Lord will remain silent and keep punishing rebellious Israel.

1 I am sought of them that asked not for me [*JST:* "*I am found of them who seek after me. I give unto all them that ask of me*"]; I am [*JST:* "*I am not*"] found of them that sought me not [*JST:* "*or that inquireth not after me*"]: I said [*JST:* "*unto my servant*" (*probably meaning Isaiah*)], Behold me, behold me [*JST:* "*look upon me; I will send you*"], unto a nation that was not called by my name [*JST:* "*is not called after my name*"]; [*that has not taken upon them My name*].

2 I have spread out my hands [*invited them to come unto me—compare with Jacob 6:4–5*] all the day [*constantly*] unto a rebellious people, which walketh in a way that was not good, after their own thoughts [*they are rebellious and wicked*];

JST Isaiah 65:2

2 For I have spread out my hands all the day to a people who walketh not in my ways, and their works are evil and not good, and they walk after their own thoughts.

3 A people that provoketh me to anger continually to my face [*in other words, blatantly disobey God*]; that sacrificeth in gardens, and burneth incense upon altars of brick [*the Israelites were commanded in Exodus 20:25 to use unhewn (uncut) stones in making altars; in other words, they just won't obey God*];

4 Which remain [*German: sit*] among the graves [*implies that they were breaking the commandment in Leviticus 19:31: they were attempting to commune with spirits of the dead*], and lodge in the monuments [*German: hang around the graveyards overnight*], which eat swine's flesh [*strictly forbidden by Mosaic law*], and broth of abominable [*unclean*] things is in their vessels [*they are breaking every rule in the book*];

JST Isaiah 65:4

4 Which remain among the graves, and lodge in the monuments; which eat swine's flesh, and broth of abominable beasts, and pollute their vessels;

5 Which say, Stand by thyself [*stay away from me*], come not near to me; for I am holier than thou. These are a smoke in my nose [*such hypocrites are a constant source of irritation*], a fire that burneth all the day.

6 Behold, it is written before me [*it is written in the scriptures*]: I will not keep silence, but will recompense [*pay back, reward*], even recompense into their bosom [*drop their sins right back into their own laps; they will be held accountable for their wickedness*],

7 Your iniquities, and the iniquities of your fathers [*ancestors*] together [*along with yours*], saith the LORD, which have burned incense upon the mountains [*worshiped idols*], and blasphemed me upon the hills [*worshiped false gods*]: therefore will I measure their former work into their bosom [*I will drop their sins right back into their laps*].

8 Thus saith the LORD, As the new wine [*fresh grape juice*] is found in the cluster [*of grapes; there is still potential for good in Israel*], and one saith, Destroy it not; for a

blessing is in it [*Israel still has potential*]: **so will I do for my servants' sakes, that I may not destroy them all** [*a remnant of Israel will remain*].

9 **And I will bring forth a seed** [*descendants; a remnant*] **out of Jacob** [*Israel*]**, and out of Judah** [*the Jews*] **an inheritor of my mountains** [*God's kingdom and blessings*]: and mine elect shall inherit it, and my servants shall dwell there.

10 **And Sharon** [*part of the Holy Land*] **shall be a fold of flocks** [*a peaceful place*]**, and the valley of Achor** [*a part of the Holy Land, near Jericho*] **a place for the herds to lie down in, for my people that have sought me** [*the righteous will receive wonderful peace and blessings*].

11 **But ye are they that forsake the LORD, that forget my holy mountain** [*the gospel*], that prepare a table for that troop [*Gad, an idol of fortune—see footnote 11a in your Bible*], and that furnish the drink offering unto that number [*Meni, an idol of fate or destiny—see footnote 11b in your Bible*].

12 **Therefore** [*because of your wickedness*] **will I number you** [*turn you over*] **to the sword, and ye shall all bow down to the slaughter** [*great destruction will come upon you*]**: because when I called, ye did not answer**; when I spake, ye did not hear; **but did evil** before mine eyes, and did choose that [*wickedness*] wherein I delighted not.

Isaiah now contrasts rewards for the righteous with punishments for the wicked.

13 **Therefore thus saith the Lord GOD, Behold, my servants** [*the righteous*] **shall eat, but ye** [*the wicked*] **shall be hungry**: behold, **my servants shall drink, but ye shall be thirsty**: behold, **my servants shall rejoice, but ye shall be ashamed** [*put to shame, devastated*]:

14 Behold, **my servants shall sing for joy** of heart, **but ye shall cry for sorrow** of heart, and shall howl for vexation of spirit.

15 **And ye** [*the wicked*] **shall leave your name for a curse unto my chosen** [*it is you, the wicked, who will be cursed*]**: for the Lord GOD shall slay thee** [*you will be destroyed*]**, and call his servants by another name** [*a new name; see Isaiah 62:2, Doctrine & Covenants 130:11, Revelation 2:17; symbolic of celestial glory*]:

16 That **he who blesseth himself** [*asks for blessings from the Lord*] in the earth **shall bless himself in the God of truth** [*will pray to God, not idols*]; and **he that sweareth** [*makes covenants*] in the earth **shall swear by the God of truth** [*rather than idols*]; because **the former** [*past*] **troubles are forgotten** [*over*], and because they are hid from mine eyes [*your troubles will then be over, gone*].

17 For, behold, **I create new heavens and a new earth** [*paradisiacal conditions during the Millennium—see footnote 17c in your Bible*]: and the former shall not be remembered, nor come into mind [*because past troubles will be completely overshadowed by the beauties of millennial life*].

18 But be ye glad and rejoice for ever in that which I create: for, behold, **I create Jerusalem a rejoicing, and her people a joy** [*the Jews in Jerusalem will become a righteous covenant people of the Lord during the Millennium*].

19 And **I will rejoice in Jerusalem, and joy in my people**: and **the voice of weeping shall be no more heard in her**, nor the voice of crying [*millennial conditions*].

20 **There shall be no more thence** [*during the Millennium*] an infant of days [*German: an infant who lives just a few days*], **nor an old man that hath not filled his days** [*lived out his years completely*]: for **the child shall die an hundred years old**; but the sinner being an hundred years old shall be accursed.

JST Isaiah 65:20

20 In those days there shall be no more thence an infant of days, nor an old man that hath not filled his days; for **the child shall not die, but shall live to be an hundred years old; but the sinner, living to be an hundred years old, shall be accursed**.

Elder Joseph Fielding Smith taught the following about the age of mortals during the Millennium (bold added for emphasis):

"When Christ comes the Saints who are on the earth will be quickened and caught up to meet him. This does not mean that those who are living in mortality at that time will be changed and pass through the resurrection, for mortals must remain on the earth until after the thousand years are ended. A change, nevertheless, will come over all who remain on the earth; they will be quickened so that they will not be subject unto death until they are old. Men shall die when they are one hundred years of age, and the change shall be made suddenly to the immortal state. Graves will not be made during this thousand years, and Satan shall have no power to tempt any man. Children shall grow up 'as calves of the stall' unto righteousness, that is, without sin or the temptations that are so prevalent today. Even the animal kingdom shall experience a great change, for the enmity of beasts shall disappear, as we have already stated, 'and they shall not hurt nor destroy in all my holy mountain: for the earth shall be full of the knowledge of the Lord, as the waters cover the sea.'—Isaiah 11:9." (The Way to Perfection, pages 298–99)

21 **And they shall build houses, and inhabit them; and they shall plant vineyards, and eat the fruit of them** [*no one will attack and take things away during the Millennium*].

22 **They shall not build, and another inhabit; they shall not plant, and another eat: for as the days** [*age; see Doctrine & Covenants 101:30*] **of a tree** [*one hundred years, Isaiah; see 65:20*] **are the days of my people, and mine elect shall long enjoy the work of their hands**.

23 **They shall not labour in vain, nor bring forth** [*German: bear children*] **for trouble** [*into a world of trouble*]; for they [*the children you bring forth during the Millennium*] are the seed [*children*] of the blessed [*you, the righteous*] of the LORD, and their offspring [*descendants*] with them.

24 And it shall come to pass, that **before they call, I will answer**; and while they are yet speaking, I will hear [*conditions during the Millennium will be even better than you can imagine*].

25 The **wolf and the lamb shall feed together, and the lion shall eat straw like the bullock**: and dust shall be the serpent's meat [*food*]. **They shall not hurt nor destroy in all my holy mountain, saith the LORD** [*peace will abound during the Millennium*].

ISAIAH 66

Selection: all verses

The Lord now says that everything He has created is designed for the purpose of developing humble, righteous people.

1 Thus saith the LORD, **The heaven is my throne, and the earth is my footstool**: where is the house that ye build unto me? and where is the place of my rest?

2 For **all those things hath mine hand made**, and those things [*everything I have created*] have been [*created*], saith the LORD: but **to this man** [*the humble, righteous person*] **will I look** [*with this type of person I am pleased*], even **to him that is poor** [*humble*] **and of a contrite spirit, and trembleth at my word** [*takes God's word seriously*].

Isaiah now switches topics and speaks of hypocrites.

3 **He** [*the type of person who wants to look good by offering sacrifices to God, yet intentionally lives in sin*] **that killeth an ox is as if he slew a man** [*is like a murderer*]; **he that sacrificeth a lamb, as if he cut off** [*German: broke*] **a dog's neck** [*see Exodus 13:13; his efforts are useless, just as an animal with a broken neck is useless*]; **he that offereth an oblation** [*a grain offering*], **as if he offered swine's blood; he that burneth incense, as if he blessed** [*worshipped*] **an idol.** Yea, **they have chosen** [*they have their agency*] **their own ways, and their soul delighteth in their abominations** [*they are wicked and like to be so*].

4 **I also will choose** [*they have "chosen" to have the Lord "choose" to punish them*] **their delusions** [*punishments*], **and will bring their fears** [*German: that which they dread*] **upon them; because when I called, none did answer; when I spake, they did not hear** [*they have been intentionally disobedient*]: but **they did evil before mine eyes, and chose that in which I delighted not** [*they chose wickedness*].

5 **Hear the word of the LORD, ye** [*the righteous*] **that tremble at his word** [*that take His word seriously*]; **your brethren** [*your own people*] **that hated you, that cast you out for my name's sake** [*that persecuted you because you obeyed Me*], **said, Let the LORD be glorified** [*let the Lord come and show His power—we're not afraid; the haughty attitude of the wicked*]: **but he** [*the Lord*] **shall appear to your joy** [*to the joy of the righteous*], **and they** [*the wicked*] **shall be ashamed** [*put to shame, devastated*].

6 A voice of noise from the city, a voice from the temple, a voice of **the LORD** that **rendereth recompence to his enemies** [*the punishments spoken of will surely come upon the wicked*].

NOTES

Verses 7 and 8 seem to parallel Isaiah 49:21, "Who hath begotten me these . . .?" In other words, "Where in the world did all these Israelites come from?" Isaiah is describing the rapid growth of Zion as the earth is prepared for the Millennium (see verse 22, near the end of this chapter).

7 **Before she travailed** [*went into labor*], **she brought forth** [*her child was born*]; **before her pain** [*labor pains*] **came, she** [*perhaps the Church of God (see JST Revelation 12:7); in other words, the Church brings forth the kingdom of God very rapidly upon the earth in the last days and on into the Millennium*] **was delivered of a man child** [*the kingdom of God (see JST Revelation 12:7); in other words, the kingdom of God will grow much faster than expected*].

8 **Who hath heard such a thing?** who hath seen such things? **Shall the earth be made to bring forth in one day** [*it will seem to happen overnight!*]? or **shall a nation** [*righteous Israel*] **be born at once?** for as soon as Zion travailed, she brought forth her children [*can refer to rapid progress of the work of the Lord in the last days, or the righteousness brought suddenly by the Second Coming, or both*].

9 **Shall I bring to the birth, and not cause to bring forth** [*would the Lord get everything ready and then not follow through with what He has revealed*]? saith the LORD: shall I cause to bring forth, and shut the womb [*stop it at the last moment*]? saith thy God.

10 **Rejoice ye with Jerusalem** [*the Lord's people*], and be glad with her, **all ye that love her** [*the Lord's kingdom*]: **rejoice for joy with her**, all ye that mourn for her [*the day will come when joy and peace will reign supreme*]:

Isaiah now describes wonderful blessings that will come to those who join Zion and seek nourishment from the Lord therein.

11 **That ye may** suck, and be satisfied with the breasts of her consolations; that ye may milk out, and **be delighted with the abundance of her glory**.

12 **For thus saith the LORD, Behold, I will extend peace to her** [*Zion, the righteous*] **like a river** [*a constant supply*], and the glory [*wealth*] of the Gentiles like a flowing stream: **then shall ye suck** [*the righteous will be nourished*], ye shall be borne upon her sides [*German: in her arms*], **and be dandled** [*German: held happily*] **upon her knees.**

13 **As one whom his mother comforteth, so will I comfort you** [*the righteous will feel right at home with the Savior; millennial conditions*]; and ye shall be comforted in Jerusalem [*God's kingdom*].

14 **And when ye** [*the righteous*] **see this, your heart shall rejoice, and your bones shall flourish like an herb** [*German: you will green up like lush grass*]: and the hand of the LORD shall be known toward his servants [*great blessings will come to the righteous*], and his indignation toward his enemies [*but the wicked will be punished*].

15 For, behold, **the LORD will come with fire**, and with his chariots like a whirlwind, **to render his anger with fury, and his rebuke with flames of fire** [*the destruction of the wicked at the Second Coming*].

16 **For by fire and by his sword will the LORD plead with all flesh** [*judge all people*]: **and the slain of the LORD shall be many** [*there will be large numbers of wicked in the last days, and they will be destroyed at His coming*].

Isaiah now refers again to forbidden practices among the wicked of Israel, as already mentioned in verse 3.

17 **They** [*the wicked*] **that sanctify themselves, and purify themselves in the gardens** behind one tree in the midst [*attempting to make themselves holy via false gods, idol worship located in groves of trees, and so on*], **eating swine's flesh** [*strictly forbidden*], and the abomination, **and the mouse** [*a forbidden food; see Leviticus 11:29*], **shall be consumed together** [*suddenly, at the same time, at the Second Coming*], saith the LORD.

18 **For I know their** [*the wicked*] **works and their thoughts** [*and that is why they will be destroyed*]: [*Isaiah begins a new topic now, namely the gathering of Israel in the last days and on into the Millennium*] **it shall come, that I will gather all nations and tongues; and they shall come, and see my glory.**

19 **And I will set a sign** [*ensign (see Isaiah 5:26); the true gospel, certainly including the Book of Mormon as explained in 3 Nephi 21:1–7*] **among them** [*the remnant of Israel*], **and I will send those that escape of them** [*a righteous remnant of Israel; see Isaiah 37:32; missionary work*] **unto the nations,** to Tarshish [*Spain?*], Pul [*Lybia*], and Lud, that draw the bow [*famous for skilled archers*], to Tubal [*Turkey*], and Javan [*Greece; Isaiah has thus described basically all the commonly known world in his day*], **to the isles** [*continents*] **afar off** [*to all nations*], that have not heard my fame, neither have seen my glory; **and they shall declare my glory among the Gentiles** [*the gospel will be preached to all nations*].

20 **And they** [*the missionaries; the true Church*] **shall bring all your brethren** [*Israelites; the gathering*] **for an offering** [*righteous lives; see 1 Samuel 15:22*] **unto the LORD out of all nations** upon horses, and in chariots [*with great power—compare with Jeremiah 23:3*], and in litters, and upon mules, and upon swift beasts, **to my holy mountain** Jerusalem [*to the true gospel*], saith the LORD, as the children of Israel bring an offering in a clean vessel into the house of the LORD.

21 **And I will also take of them for priests and for Levites,** saith the LORD [*the priesthood will be restored to men in the last days*].

22 **For as the new heavens and the new earth** [*can refer to millennial earth, Doctrine & Covenants 101:25; and celestial earth, Doctrine & Covenants 130:9; 88:18, 19, 25, 26*], which I will make, **shall remain** [*will be eternal*] before me, saith the LORD, **so shall your seed** [*families*] **and your name** [*symbolic of celestial glory, Doctrine & Covenants 130:11*] **remain** [*you and your families can be with Me forever*].

23 **And it shall come to pass, that from one new moon** [*special Sabbath ritual among the Israelites at the beginning of the month; see Bible Dictionary, under "New Moon"*] **to another, and from one Sabbath to another, shall all flesh come to worship before**

NOTES

NOTES

me, saith the LORD [*the righteous are those who will be completely consistent and faithful during the Millennium and beyond*].

24 **And they** [*the righteous*] **shall go forth, and look upon the carcases of the men that have transgressed against me** [*they will be aware that the judgments of God did finally come upon the wicked*]: **for their worm shall not die** [*"Worm" refers to a scarlet dye that was made from the dried body of a certain type of female worm* (Coccus ilicis). *Scarlet was considered a "colorfast" dye—permanent, lasting. Hence, "their worm shall not die" implies that, even though their dead bodies can be seen, the "permanent" part of them (spirit up until the resurrection of the wicked, then their resurrected bodies) will live forever and they will thus face the consequences of their wicked choices.*] **neither shall their fire be quenched; and they shall be an abhorring unto all flesh** [*a final warning from Isaiah that wickedness does not pay at all*].

Jeremiah 1–3; 7; 16–18; 20

"Before I Formed Thee in the Belly I Knew Thee"

When Lehi was called to be a prophet in the Jerusalem area, Jeremiah had already been preaching to the apostate Jews for about twenty-six to twenty-eight years. You will see in chapter 1 that Jeremiah was foreordained in the premortal life to be a prophet. In fact, this chapter helps our missionaries teach the reality of our premortal existence. The chapters of Jeremiah selected for this week's Come, Follow Me study describe the wickedness of the citizens of Judah and Israel at the time of Jeremiah's preaching. You will see that corruption permeated every aspect of society. In chapter 7, an invitation to repent is issued to the Jews, but they reject it. In chapters 16–18, Jeremiah prophesies the destruction of the Jews and their being carried away captive into Babylon and their subsequent return. He also prophesies that in the last days, Israel will be gathered again. First, symbolically, fishermen will gather many in the gospel net as converts, and afterward, "hunters" will come along and gather individuals. Many sins, including violation of the Sabbath, caused the downfall of the Jews. In chapter 20, you will see Jeremiah put in stocks and prophesy that the Jews will be carried away captive into Babylon.

Jeremiah is a well-known prophet in the Old Testament. There are at least sixty-two prophecies given in his writings. The book of Jeremiah has almost twenty-two thousand words, making it somewhat longer than Isaiah, and making it the second longest book in the Old Testament (only Psalms is longer). Just so you know, if you were to count the pages of Jeremiah and Isaiah in our Latter-day Saint Bible, in English, you would come up with more pages for Isaiah than for Jeremiah. That is because there is more space taken up for footnotes in Isaiah. In a page count in a King James Bible without footnotes, Jeremiah is several pages longer than Isaiah.

The book of Jeremiah can be divided roughly into the following sections:

Chapters 1–25
Prophecies about Judah and Jerusalem

Chapters 26–35
Prophecies about the restoration of Israel and Judah

Chapters 36–45
History and life story **of Jeremiah**

Chapters 46–51
Prophecies against foreign nations

Chapter 52
Basically an appendix giving some details of the Babylonian captivity of Jerusalem and wicked King Zedekiah's downfall, including the carrying of the Jews into Babylon.

Jeremiah was born into a priestly family in the Levite town of Anathoth (see Jeremiah 1:1 and Bible Dictionary under "Jeremiah"), which was located about three miles northeast of Jerusalem and is known today as Anata. According to the Bible Dictionary in our Latter-day Saint English edition of the Bible, he served as a prophet in Jerusalem for over forty years, from about 626 BC to 586 BC. After the fall of Jerusalem to Babylonian captivity in about 587 BC, a group of Jews who escaped into Egypt took Jeremiah with them (Jeremiah 43:5–7), and, according to tradition, later stoned him to death.

Jeremiah was a contemporary of Lehi and several other prophets who preached during the same time period when the wickedness of the people in and around Jerusalem was setting the stage for the Babylonian captivity of Jerusalem, in about 587 BC, when the Jews were carried captive to Babylon. Babylon was a very large city located about fifty

NOTES

371

miles south of modern-day Bagdad, Iraq. It was nearly six hundred miles directly east of Jerusalem, across the desert, and was about nine hundred miles away from Jerusalem by land travel routes. As you will perhaps recall, Lehi and his family fled Jerusalem in 600 BC, as directed by the Lord, and journeyed to the promised land of America.

In 1 Nephi 1:4, Nephi mentions "many prophets" who prophesied at the time Lehi, his father, was prophesying and preaching. You might wish to go to the Chronology in your Bible Dictionary (in the back of your Latter-day Saint Bible) and note several of these prophets in the "Internal History" column, beginning with 642 BC. You will see Nahum (with a ?), Jeremiah, Zephaniah, Obadiah (with a ?), and Habakkuk, as well as Daniel and Ezekiel who prophesied while in Babylonian captivity.

Jeremiah was one of the few ancient prophets who prophesied destruction for the people and then saw the fulfillment of his prophecies during his own lifetime. In a way, he was a lot like Mormon, in the Book of Mormon, who was called by the Lord to work with a people for whom there was little hope, because of their extreme wickedness (see Mormon 2:15, 19; 3:12; 5:2).

Jeremiah ministered as a prophet during the reign of the last five kings of Judah, which kingdom came to an end in 587 BC with the final wave of the Babylonian captivity. Remember that the kingdom of Israel (the northern ten tribes) had previously been carried away into captivity by the Assyrians about 722 BC, and had thus become the "lost ten tribes." The two remaining tribes, Judah and part of Benjamin, were known collectively as "Judah," with headquarters in Jerusalem.

Three of these last kings of Judah are mentioned in Jeremiah 1:2–3. A more detailed study of biblical history shows that there were actually five kings who reigned during Jeremiah's ministry, but two of them ruled for only three months apiece. They were Jehoahaz, who reigned for three months before being exiled to Egypt in 609 BC, and Jehoiachin, who ruled three months before he was exiled to Babylon in 598 BC.

Of these kings, all but King Josiah were wicked, and led their people deeper into depravity and toward destruction. The last, King Zedekiah, is probably most familiar to members of the Church because Nephi mentions him as being the king in Jerusalem when Lehi began preaching (see 1 Nephi 1:4). Zedekiah was twenty-one years old at the time he began ruling as king (see 2 Kings 24:18), and reigned for eleven years before his captivity. One of his sons, Mulek, somehow escaped captivity and was brought by the Lord to America (see Helaman 6:10; 8:21). We know his descendants in the Book of Mormon as Mulekites.

We will provide a quote used in the Old Testament Student Manual: 1 Kings–Malachi, for the Church's institutes of religion (page 235) that describes the conditions under which Jeremiah served as a prophet:

"With the exception of Josiah, all of the kings of Judah during Jeremiah's ministry were unworthy men under whom the country suffered severely. Even during the reign of an earlier king, the wicked Manasseh, the Baal cult was restored among the Jews, and there was introduced the worship of the heavenly planets in accordance with the dictates of the Assyro-Babylonian religion. Jeremiah therefore found idolatry, hill-worship, and heathen religious practices rampant among his people. Heathen idols stood in the temple (Jeremiah 32:34), children were sacrificed to Baal-Moloch (7:31; 19:5; 32:35), and Baal was especially invoked as the usual heathen deity. The worship of the 'queen of Heaven' ought also to be mentioned (7:18; 44:19). The corruption of the nation's religious worship was, of course, accompanied by all manner of immorality and unrighteousness, against which the prophet had continually to testify. The poor were forgotten. Jeremiah was surrounded on all sides by almost total apostasy. But professional prophets there were aplenty. Says Dr. H. L. Willett:

"'He was surrounded by plenty of prophets, but they were the smooth, easy-going, popular, professional preachers whose words awakened no conscience, and who assured the people that the nation was safe in the protecting care of God. This was a true message in Isaiah's day, but that time was long since past, and Jerusalem was destined for captivity. Thus Jeremiah was doomed to preach an unwelcome message, while the false prophets persuaded the people that he was unpatriotic, uninspired, and pessimistic (14:13, 14).' " (Sidney B. Sperry, The Voice of Israel's Prophets, page 153.)

As you study Jeremiah's writings, you will see much symbolism and imagery (as is the case with studying Isaiah). For example, we will look ahead at three verses that describe the people of Judah during Jeremiah's time as hardened clay, no longer moldable by the Lord. This image basically sums up the description of Judah given by Brother Sperry in the above quote. We will use bold, as usual, to point things out to you.

Selection: Jeremiah 19:1, 10–11

1 THUS saith the LORD, Go and get a potter's **earthen bottle** [*a hardened clay jar, no longer moldable; symbolic of the people of Judah who are no longer willing to be molded and shaped by the hands of the Lord*], and *take* of the ancients of the people, and of the ancients of the priests;

10 Then shalt thou **break the bottle** [*symbolic of the fact that Judah will soon be "broken" by the Babylonian captivity—see verse 11, next*] in the sight of the men that go with thee,

11 And shalt say unto them, **Thus saith the LORD of hosts; Even so will I break this people** [*the kingdom of Judah*] **and this city** [*Jerusalem*], **as** *one* **breaketh a potter's vessel** [*a clay jar*]**, that cannot be made whole again**: and they shall bury *them* in Tophet [*a location south of Jerusalem where human sacrifices were offered*], till *there be* no place to bury.

During King Zedekiah's wicked rule, Jeremiah spent much time in prison. The king kept him in a dismal dungeon with deep mud, bringing him out of the dungeon from time to time to see if he had anything new to say or had changed his mind about the things he had prophesied concerning the kingdom of Judah. We read especially about these most difficult conditions for this humble prophet in Jeremiah, chapters 38–39.

Jeremiah was probably a relatively young man when he began his ministry (in approximately 628–626 BC, depending on which historical sources used), preaching and prophesying about the rampant evils of society among the people of Judah. We read about his call in chapter 1. One of the major doctrines taught in this chapter is that of premortal life. Few, if any, Christian denominations teach that we lived before we were born on earth, even though it is so clearly taught in Jeremiah 1:5.

We will now proceed with chapter 1.

JEREMIAH 1

Selection: all verses

In this chapter, Jeremiah records his call to serve as a prophet. He records his feelings of inadequacy. His call as a true prophet is immediately apparent as he teaches the doctrine of premortality and tells us of two visions he was given.

1 **THE words of Jeremiah** the son of Hilkiah, of the priests that *were* in Anathoth [*a town about three miles northeast of Jerusalem*] in the land of Benjamin [*the area given to the tribe of Benjamin when the twelve tribes of Israel arrived in the land of Canaan*]:

Next, in verse 2, Jeremiah, without additional explanation, humbly and simply tells us that he was called by the Lord to be a prophet in the thirteenth year of the reign of Josiah, king of Judah, which, according to most sources, would be approximately 627 BC (about twenty-seven years before Lehi and his family left Jerusalem).

Jeremiah's Call

2 To whom the word of the LORD came in the days of Josiah the son of Amon king of Judah, in the thirteenth year of his reign.

Next, in verse 3, Jeremiah states, in effect, that he continued to receive and deliver the word of the Lord to the people of Judah, as a prophet, for over forty years, until Jerusalem was taken captive by Babylon at the end of King Zedekiah's reign.

3 It [*the word of the Lord to Jeremiah*] **came also in the days of Jehoiakim** the son of Josiah king of Judah, **unto the end of the eleventh year of Zedekiah** the son of Josiah king of Judah, unto the carrying away of Jerusalem captive in the fifth month.

Few if any other Christian churches teach the doctrine of premortality as a vital part of the plan of salvation. Perhaps you have been surprised or even amazed that they do not teach it, since Jeremiah teaches it clearly here in verses 4–5.

Doctrine

We lived in premortality before we were born into mortality.

4 Then the word of the LORD came unto me, saying,

5 Before I [*the Lord*] **formed thee in the belly** [*before you were conceived and grew in your mother's womb; in other words, in the premortal life*] **I knew thee**; and **before thou camest forth out of the womb** I sanctified thee, *and* **I ordained thee a prophet unto the nations** [*Before Jeremiah was born, he was foreordained to be a prophet*].

Doctrine

In addition to the doctrine of premortality in verse 5, we also see the doctrine of fore-ordination.

Verse 5, above, tells us that Jeremiah was "ordained," in other words, "foreordained" to be a prophet on earth, while he was yet in his premortal existence. He was no doubt one of the "noble and great ones" spoken of in Abraham 3:22–23.

Being foreordained does not imply loss of agency, nor does it mean "predestined." Rather, it means that we were set apart or ordained in our premortal lives to accomplish certain tasks in the work of the Lord here on earth. Joseph Smith explained this. He taught:

"Every man who has a calling to minister to the inhabitants of the world was ordained to that very purpose in the Grand Council of heaven before this world was. I suppose I was ordained to this very office in that Grand Council" (Teachings of the Prophet Joseph Smith, page 365).

Foreordination is very similar in concept to patriarchal blessings. Direction is given and potential to do good and fulfill specific work in the Lord's plan is revealed, yet agency is preserved.

Jeremiah was overwhelmed by this call from the Lord, as has been the case with countless others throughout the ages who have been called to fulfill the Lord's will in unexpected ways. This would include Moses (see Exodus 3:11), Isaiah (see Isaiah 6:5), Enoch (Moses 6:31), and Mary (Luke 1:34). You have very likely experienced similar feelings. We see Jeremiah's reaction to the call in verse 6, next, and the Lord's response to his concerns, in verses 7–9.

6 Then said I, **Ah, Lord GOD! behold, I cannot speak** [*perhaps meaning "I am speechless." Could also mean "I am not old enough to be taken seriously by the people"*]: **for I** *am* **a child**.

7 ¶ **But the LORD said** unto me, **Say not, I** *am* **a child: for thou shalt go to all that I shall send thee, and whatsoever I command thee thou shalt speak.**

8 **Be not afraid** of their faces: **for I** *am* **with thee** to deliver thee, saith the LORD.

Next, the Lord (the premortal Jesus Christ, who is the God of the Old Testament—see for example Ether 3:6 and 14) gives Jeremiah the gift of speaking the mind and will of God clearly.

9 Then **the LORD put forth his hand, and touched my mouth**. And the LORD said unto me, Behold, **I have put my words in thy mouth**.

This scene with Jeremiah is very similar to the scene with Enoch at the time he was called to preach the gospel. We will take a moment to read two verses about Enoch's call from the book of Moses:

Moses 6:31–32

31 And **when Enoch had heard these words** [*his call from the Lord*], **he** bowed himself to the earth, before the Lord, and **spake** before the Lord, saying: Why is it that **I** have found favor in thy sight, and **am but a lad**, and all the people hate me; for **I am slow of speech**; wherefore [*why*] am I thy servant?

32 **And the Lord said** unto Enoch: Go forth and do as I have commanded thee, and no man shall pierce thee. **Open thy mouth, and it shall be filled, and I will give thee utterance**, for all flesh is in my hands, and I will do as seemeth me good.

Next, the Savior describes the scope of Jeremiah's mission for him.

10 See, **I have this day set thee over the nations and over the kingdoms, to root out** [*to expose and destroy evil*], and to **pull down**, and to **destroy**, and to **throw down** [*to destroy wickedness and the wicked—see Jeremiah 12:17 and 18:7*], to **build** [*righteousness*], and to **plant** [*including planting the seeds of the gospel in peoples' lives*].

Next, the Lord shows Jeremiah two visions, one described in verses 11–12, and the other in verses 13–16.

Vision

11 ¶ Moreover **the word of the LORD came unto me, saying**, Jeremiah, **what seest thou?** And I said, **I see a rod of an almond tree** [*the first tree to blossom in the spring in the Jerusalem area of Jeremiah's day*].

NOTES

_____
_____
_____
_____
_____
_____
_____
_____
_____
_____
_____
_____
_____
_____
_____
_____
_____
_____
_____
_____
_____
_____
_____
_____

12 Then said the LORD unto me, Thou hast well seen: for **I will hasten my word to perform it** [*perhaps meaning that the Lord will fulfill Jeremiah's prophecies about coming destruction of Judah sooner than expected*].

Vision

13 And **the word of the LORD came unto me the second time**, saying, **What seest thou?** And I said, **I see a seething pot** [*a boiling cauldron*]; **and the face thereof** *is* **toward the north** [*the invading Babylonian armies will come from Babylon (about six hundred miles across the desert directly east of Jerusalem). But their route will be the trade route which will bring them northwest up over the Arabian Desert and then west and then south, down to Jerusalem; therefore, the "seething pot" would likely symbolize the conquering enemy armies of Babylon who will come from the north as they swoop down on the wicked people of Judah*].

14 Then the LORD said unto me, **Out of the north an evil** [*probably referring to the Babylonian armies, which will come upon the people of Judah in about forty years*] **shall break forth upon all the inhabitants of the land**.

15 For, lo, **I will call all the families of the kingdoms of the north** [*most likely the Babylonians*], saith the LORD; and **they shall come**, and they **shall set every one his throne at the entering of the gates** [*symbolic of conquering a city*] of Jerusalem, and against all the walls thereof round about, and against all the cities of Judah.

16 And **I will utter my judgments** [*the punishments of God*] **against them** [*the people of Judah*] touching all their wickedness, **who have forsaken me**, and have **burned incense unto other gods** [*who have turned to idol worship*], and **worshipped the works of their own hands** [*idols, which they have made with their own hands*].

Verses 17–19, next, appear to be a repetition of the Lord's instructions to Jeremiah in verses 7–8, above, with a bit more detail as to how the Lord will enable him to accomplish his mission, if he exercises faith.

17 ¶ Thou therefore **gird up thy loins** [*prepare for action*], and **arise**, and **speak unto them** [*the inhabitants of the kingdom of Judah*] **all that I command thee: be not dismayed at their faces**, lest I confound thee before them [*if you falter in faith, you will not be blessed to succeed*].

18 For, behold, **I have made thee this day a defenced city**, and **an iron pillar**, and **brasen walls** [*in other words, the Lord will defend Jeremiah*] against the whole land, against the kings of Judah, against the princes [*leaders*] thereof, against the priests thereof, and against the people of the land.

Next, in verse 19, the Savior prophesies that Jeremiah will face much opposition during his ministry.

19 And **they shall fight against thee; but they shall not prevail** [*win*] **against thee; for I** *am* **with thee**, saith the LORD, to deliver thee.

One of the important messages for us in verse 19, above, is that, with the Lord on our side, our enemies cannot ultimately triumph over us spiritually. Such was the case with

Jeremiah. Although he was subjected to much physical misery during mortality, his enemies did not win against him spiritually. And that is everything, as we view things from the perspective of the eternal truths given in the plan of salvation.

JEREMIAH 2

Selection: all verses

In this chapter, Jeremiah basically says that the Lord loves His people and that they once had a loyal, tender relationship with Him. But now they have deserted Him and are worshipping false gods. The prophet rebukes the people, describing their apostasy in some detail.

1 MOREOVER **the word of the LORD came to me** [*Jeremiah*]**, saying,**

Next, in verses 2–3, Jeremiah speaks for the Lord, reminding the people of the Lord's love for them and of good times in the past when the Israelites kept the commandments and were close to Him.

2 Go and cry in the ears of Jerusalem [*the people of Judah*], saying, Thus saith the LORD; **I remember thee, the kindness of thy youth** [*the love and tenderness of the earlier days of our relationship*]**, the love of thine espousals** [*when you made covenants of loyalty to Me*]**, when thou wentest after me in the wilderness** [*when you followed Me in the wilderness, a cloud by day and a pillar of fire by night*]**, in a land** *that was* **not sown** [*in the unplanted wilderness, when I provided manna for you*].

3 **Israel** *was* **holiness unto the LORD,** *and* **the firstfruits of his increase** [*you belonged to Me and were dedicated to being My covenant people*]**: all that devour him shall offend; evil shall come upon them, saith the LORD** [*it was said at that time that any enemies who came upon Israel were held guilty by the Lord and disaster came upon them*].

The implication in verse 3, above, is that the Lord protected covenant Israel in times past, but now, because of their wickedness, He will allow their enemies (Babylon) to come upon them. In other words, disastrous punishments will no longer come upon Judah's enemies, rather, they will be allowed to conquer and humble Judah, because of wickedness among her people.

Perhaps you've noticed that we keep using the terms "Israel," "Judah," "Israelites," and other terms somewhat interchangeably. This can be a bit confusing. Let's have a brief review:

"Israel" is a general term for the twelve tribes of Israel. These twelve tribes were descendants of the twelve sons of Jacob (son of Isaac and grandson of Abraham), whose name was later changed to "Israel." The Lord made a covenant with Abraham (see Abraham 2:9–11). Part of the covenant was that he and his descendants, through Isaac, were to carry the gospel and the blessings of the priesthood to all the world. Thus, the descendants of Abraham, through Isaac and Jacob, are often referred to as "the covenant people of the Lord." They are also referred to as "Israel." Likewise, they are "Israelites," and were also called "the children of Israel," especially when Moses was leading them in the wilderness.

"Judah" was one specific group of Israelites, headquartered in Jerusalem. When Joshua led the children of Israel across the Jordan River and into the promised land (the land of Canaan), he divided the land up among the twelve tribes. Eventually, these twelve tribes broke up and formed two nations, one consisting of ten tribes and the other consisting of two tribes. The ten tribes, with Ephraim as the dominant tribe, became known as the "Northern Kingdom" and retained the name, "Israel." The other two tribes, with Judah as the dominant tribe, became known as the "Southern Kingdom," or "Judah," and were headquartered in Jerusalem.

In about 722 BC, the Assyrians conquered the northern ten tribes, headquartered in Samaria, and carried most of them away into captivity. They became the "lost ten tribes of Israel."

The two remaining tribes, Judah and Benjamin, known collectively as "Judah," remained. Jeremiah was sent to warn them and preach to them. He continued to preach and prophesy to Judah until the Babylonians conquered them in about 587 BC.

Remember that the people of Judah are from the "house of Jacob," in other words they are descendants of Jacob (Israel), and, therefore, are Israelites. Thus, in verse 4, next, Jeremiah addresses them as the "house of Jacob." In verse 5 the Lord will ask these wicked people what wickedness they have found in Him that has caused them to leave Him.

Details of Israel's apostasy (Verses 4–13)

4 **Hear ye the word of the LORD, O house of Jacob** [*Israel*], and all the families of the **house of Israel**:

5 ¶ Thus saith the LORD, **What iniquity have your fathers** [*ancestors*] **found in me** [*the Lord*], **that they are gone far from me** [*that has given them a reason to have left Me, apostatized*], and **have walked after vanity** [*things that have no value—see verse 11*], and **are become vain** [*have lost their value as a covenant people of the* Lord]?

One of the causes of apostasy is not remembering past blessings from the Lord. This is pointed out in verses 6–8, next.

6 **Neither said they, Where** *is* **the LORD that brought us up out of the land of Egypt,** that **led us through the wilderness,** through a land of **deserts** and of **pits,** through a land of **drought,** and of the **shadow of death,** through a land [*the deserts of Sinai*] that no man passed through, and **where no man dwelt?**

7 And **I brought you into a plentiful country** [*Canaan, the promised land*], **to eat the fruit thereof and the goodness thereof;** but when ye entered, **ye defiled my land** [*polluted the promised land with wickedness*], and **made mine heritage an abomination** [*you polluted your inheritance given to you by Me*].

8 **The priests said not, Where** *is* **the LORD?** [*In other words, were not faithful to God.*] and **they that handle the law knew me not** [*your priests and leaders led you astray*]: **the pastors also transgressed against me,** and **the prophets prophesied by Baal** [*you accepted and followed false religious leaders and prophets who led you to worship Baal, a major false religion of the day*], and **walked after** *things that* **do not profit.**

The word "plead," in verse 9, next, means "to bring charges against" as in a formal court of law. In other words, sadly, Israel is guilty of leaving God and turning instead to false gods and the abominable practices associated with their worship. The Lord, operating under the law of justice, is, in effect, formally charging wicked Judah with apostasy.

9 ¶ Wherefore [*this is the reason*] **I will yet plead with you** [*bring charges against you*], saith the LORD, **and with your children's children will I plead**.

10 For pass over the isles of Chittim [*Cyprus and beyond*], and see; and send unto Kedar [*in the Arabian Desert*], and consider diligently, and **see if there be such a thing** [*look far and wide and see if you can find such a thing as people changing gods*].

11 **Hath a nation changed *their* gods**, which *are* yet no gods [*can you find a nation who has changed their false gods, who have no power at all*]? **but my people** [*Israel*] **have changed their glory** [*have exchanged the glory and blessings of their God, who does have power*] **for *that which* doth not profit**.

12 **Be astonished**, O ye heavens, **at this**, and **be horribly afraid**, be ye very desolate, saith the LORD.

13 For **my people have committed two evils**; they have **forsaken me** [*Jehovah, Jesus Christ*] the fountain of living waters [*the source of the true gospel—see John 4:10, 14*], and hewed them out cisterns, broken cisterns, that can hold no water [*and have replaced Me with leaky containers (false gods) that are incapable of holding "living water," in other words, that cannot save*].

Next, in verse 14, the Lord asks why Israel is being so foolish. What could possibly lead the covenant people to abandon their True God and worship powerless false gods? What reasons could they have?

14 ¶ *Is* **Israel a servant?** *is* he **a homeborn** *slave* [*does he not stand a chance of "promotion" to exaltation*]? **why is he spoiled** [*why has Israel become easy prey for their enemies*]?

Perhaps you have noticed that ancient prophets among the Israelites often spoke of the future as if it had already taken place. This is part of the "manner of prophesying among the Jews" (2 Nephi 25:1) spoken of by Nephi which is difficult for many modern students of the scriptures to grasp. We see examples of this in the next verses as the Lord speaks of coming destruction upon Israel because of wickedness, as if it had already taken place.

15 **The young lions** [*symbolic of terrible destruction*] **roared upon him** [*Israel*], *and* yelled, and **they made his land waste: his cities are burned without inhabitant**.

16 Also **the children of Noph** [*the men of Memphis, an ancient city in Egypt not far south of modern Cairo*] **and Tahapanes** [*in Egypt*] **have broken the crown of thy head** [*have cracked your skull*].

17 **Hast thou not procured this unto thyself** [*did you not ask for this*], **in that thou hast forsaken the LORD** thy God, when he led thee by the way [*in spite of the fact that He led you in safety in times past*]?

NOTES

Next, in verse 18, the Lord refers to the fact that Israel has adopted the wicked practices common in the world, symbolized by Egypt and Babylon. In other words, they have sunk to the level of spiritual depravity that existed in that day in these nations.

Have you noticed that Egypt and especially Babylon are often used elsewhere in the scriptures to symbolize worldly wickedness?

18 And now **what hast thou to do in the way of Egypt, to drink the waters of Sihor** [*the Nile River; in other words, can the Nile (symbolic of Egypt) provide you with "living water—verse 13*]? **or what hast thou to do in the way of Assyria, to drink the waters of the river** [*why have you turned to the spiritually lifeless waters of idolatrous Babylon*]?

Major Message (verse 19)

We are often punished "by" our sins as well as "for" them.

19 **Thine own wickedness shall correct** [*punish*] **thee, and thy backslidings shall reprove thee:** know therefore and see that *it is* **an evil** *thing* **and bitter, that thou hast forsaken** [*abandoned*] **the LORD thy God,** and that **my fear** [*respect, reverence, awe before God*] *is* **not in thee,** saith the Lord GOD of hosts.

A scathing rebuke of Judah (Verses 20–37)

20 ¶ For **of old time** [*in days gone by*] **I** [*the Lord*] **have broken thy yoke,** *and* **burst thy bands** [*I set you free from the bondage of Egypt (symbolic of being set free from the bondage of sin)*]; **and thou saidst, I will not transgress; when upon every high hill and under every green tree thou wanderest, playing the harlot** [*you promised to keep the commandments while at the same time you were engaging in worshiping false gods*].

"Under every green tree," in verse 20, above, has reference to sexual immorality engaged in with temple prostitutes used in the worship of idols of the day, especially in Baal worship. The phrase "playing the harlot" refers to "spiritual adultery" in the sense that the people, who had made covenants of loyalty to God, were "stepping out on Him" as they worshipped false gods.

21 Yet **I had planted thee a noble vine, wholly a right seed** [*I gave you the best possible start, as My covenant people with the true gospel*]: **how then art thou turned into the degenerate plant of a strange vine unto me** [*how could you possibly leave Me and become an apostate people, producing bitter fruit*]?

In verse 22, next, the word "nitre" means lye, carbonate of soda—see footnote 22b in your Latter-day Saint Bible. It was a strong cleansing agent used in ancient times. The point is that the people of Judah cannot continue in wickedness and hope to still be clean.

22 For **though thou wash thee with nitre, and take thee much soap,** *yet* **thine iniquity** [*wickedness*] **is marked before me,** saith the Lord GOD.

23 **How canst thou say** [*claim*], **I am not polluted,** I have not gone after Baalim [*I have not worshiped Baal*]? **see thy way in the valley** [*look back at your tracks*], know what thou hast done: *thou art* a swift dromedary traversing her ways;

We will quote from the Old Testament Student Manual: 1 Kings–Malachi for the explanation of the "dromedary" (camel) in verse 23, above, and the wild ass in verse 24, next.

"The imagery indicates that as a camel or a wild ass in heat runs back and forth during the mating season, so did Israel run after false gods" (Old Testament Student Manual, page 236).

24 A wild ass used to the wilderness, *that* snuffeth up the wind at her pleasure; in her occasion [*when she is in heat*] who can turn her away? all they that seek her will not weary themselves; in her month they shall find her.

The JST (Joseph Smith Translation of the Bible) of verse 24, above, changes the position of "not," implying that the wicked wear themselves out in evil pursuits, but do not ultimately find satisfaction.

JST Jeremiah 2:24

24 A wild ass used to the wilderness, that snuffeth up the wind at her pleasure; in her who can turn her away? all they that seek her will weary themselves; in her month they shall not find her.

The imagery in verse 25, next, is that of people so anxious to get on with the sinful life of worshipping false gods that they won't even take time to put on shoes or get a drink of water to slake their thirst before they run out of their houses to pursue idolatry.

25 **Withhold thy foot from being unshod** [*at least take time to put on your shoes*], **and thy throat from thirst** [*at least get a drink*]: **but thou saidst, There is no hope** [*I am hopeless*]: no; for I have loved strangers [*I am an idol worshiper*], and **after them will I go** [*and that is what I want to keep doing*].

We see from verse 26, next, that Judah is corrupt, through and through.

26 **As the thief is ashamed** [*put to shame, disgraced*] **when he is found** [*caught*], **so is the house of Israel ashamed; they, their kings,** their **princes,** and their **priests,** and their **prophets** [*their false prophets*],

In verses 27–28, Jeremiah points out how ridiculous idol worship is.

27 **Saying to a stock** [*a piece of wood which they have carved into an idol*], **Thou *art* my father;** and **to a stone** [*an idol*], **Thou hast brought me forth** [*you are my creator*]: for **they** [*Judah*] **have turned** *their* **back unto me** [*have rejected the Lord*], and not *their* face: **but in the time of their trouble they will say, Arise, and save us** [*Israel has a track record of turning to the Lord only in times of trouble*].

28 But **where *are* thy gods that thou hast made** thee? **let them** arise, if they can **save thee in the time of thy trouble**: for *according to* the number of thy cities are thy gods [*you have as many idols, false gods, as you have cities*], O Judah.

It was common practice for each city to have its own god, represented by a specific idol. And when one city prevailed over another, it was thought that their god was more powerful than the losing city's god.

The Lord goes on in verse 29 to ask, in effect, what complaint Judah has against Him which caused the people to turn to other gods.

29 **Wherefore** [*why*] **will ye plead** [*quarrel, argue—see footnote 29a in your Latter-day Saint Bible*] **with me?** ye all have transgressed against me, saith the LORD.

Next, in verse 30, the Lord tells Judah that it has not done a bit of good for Him to punish Israelites, such as the northern ten tribes, who are gone now. Judah has not repented at all.

30 **In vain have I smitten your** [*Israel's*] **children; they received no correction**: your own sword hath devoured your prophets [*you have destroyed the prophets I have sent to correct you*], like a destroying lion.

31 ¶ O generation, see ye the word of the LORD. **Have I been a wilderness unto Israel** [*have I not blessed Israel abundantly*]? a land of darkness? **wherefore say my people, We are lords; we will come no more unto thee** [*why do My people arrogantly say that they will no longer consider Me to be their God*]?

32 **Can a maid forget her ornaments,** *or* **a bride her attire** [*her wedding gown, her finest clothing; in other words, have you ever known a bride to forget to prepare for her wedding? Symbolic of covenant Israel keeping covenants in preparation to meet the Groom (the Savior)*]? **yet my people have forgotten me days without number** [*they have a long track record of forgetting Me*].

33 **Why trimmest thou thy way to seek love** [*why do you demonstrate such skill in pursuing false gods*]? **Therefore** [*because of your skill in evil ways*] **hast thou also taught the wicked ones thy ways** [*even the most wicked can learn more evil from you*].

34 Also **in thy skirts is found the blood of the souls of the poor innocents** [*your guilt against the righteous is obvious, is written all over you*]: I have not found it by secret search, but upon all these.

Verse 35, next, is very applicable today. The wicked claim that what they are doing is not against God's will. Therefore, they are innocent, and thus God's punishments will not come upon them.

In the second half of the verse, the Lord says that He will indeed bring them to accountability and punishment for their wickedness.

35 Yet **thou** [*Judah*] **sayest, Because I am innocent, surely his anger shall turn from me**. Behold, I [*the Lord*] will plead with thee [*will bring charges against you*], because thou sayest, I have not sinned.

36 **Why gaddest thou about so much to change thy way** [*why do you go back and forth so much, constantly changing your loyalties*]? **thou also shalt be ashamed of Egypt** [*Egypt will provide no protection for you*], **as thou wast ashamed of Assyria** [*just as Assyria was no protection for your brethren of the Northern Kingdom, when they tried to make alliances with them for protection*].

37 Yea, **thou shalt go forth from him, and thine hands upon thine head** [*you will be enslaved*]: for **the LORD hath rejected thy confidences** [*your trust in other gods*], **and thou shalt not prosper in them**.

JEREMIAH 3

Selection: all verses

In this chapter, Jeremiah uses the imagery of a wife being unfaithful to her husband and divorcing him to represent Judah's apostasy from the Lord. In other words, the wife is symbolic of Judah (and Israel in general), and the husband is symbolic of the Lord. The phrase "played the harlot" (in verse 1) is a phrase that means "committed adultery." In this case, it is used to mean "spiritual adultery," in other words, breaking covenants made with the Lord through personal and national wickedness. Actual physical sexual immorality is a major player in the spiritual adultery committed by Israel and Judah against the Lord.

In spite of the extreme wickedness of the people in Jeremiah's day, you will see an invitation to repent and return to God in several verses within the chapter, thus reminding us of the tender love of the Savior and His desire to have sinners return to Him and thus to His Father. It is also a reminder of the power of the Atonement to cleanse and heal.

In this chapter, you will also see a prophecy that Israel will be gathered again in the last days, some one at a time, and sometimes just a few members of a family at a time. They will be brought into the latter-day Zion through the restored gospel of Jesus Christ.

Watch now as Jeremiah points out the wickedness of Judah and the open invitation, still in place, for them to repent.

1 **THEY say, If a man put away his wife** [*it is said that if a man divorces his wife (implying that she has been unfaithful to him)*], **and she go from** [*leave*] **him, and become another man's** [*symbolic in this case of worshipping idols*], **shall he return unto her again** [*do you think he would ever take her back (answer: No, according to the Law of Moses—see Deuteronomy 24:3–4)*]? **shall not that land be greatly polluted** [*wouldn't that ruin that nation*]? **but thou** [*Judah specifically, Israel in general*] **hast played the harlot with many lovers** [*you have worshiped many false gods; you have broken covenants made with God*]; **yet return again to me**, saith the LORD [*please return, it is not too late*].

Next, in verse 2, Jeremiah invites the people of wicked Judah to look all around them to see obvious evidence of their apostasy. The "high places" are the mountains and groves of trees on them where idolatry typically takes place, including literal adultery with temple prostitutes as a part of idol worship, especially Baal worship.

2 **Lift up thine eyes unto the high places, and see where thou hast not been lien with** [*see if you can find any places where idol worship and associated adultery has not taken place; symbolically, look all around you and see if you can find any people of Judah who have not been involved in idolatry*]. **In the ways hast thou sat for them** [*you have waited by the side of the road for idols to worship just like a harlot waits along the path for potential lovers*], as the Arabian in the wilderness [*as is the common practice*]; and **thou hast polluted the land** [*the promised land*] with thy whoredoms [*unfaithfulness to God*] and with thy wickedness.

We will quote from the Bible Dictionary (in the back of your Latter-day Saint Bible) for a general statement on the subject of sexual immorality commonly associated with idol worship. We will use bold for emphasis:

NOTES

_____

_____

_____

_____

_____

_____

_____

_____

_____

_____

_____

_____

_____

_____

_____

_____

_____

_____

_____

_____

_____

_____

_____

_____

_____

_____

_____

_____

_____

_____

Bible Dictionary: Idol

Among the nations of Canaan and W. Syria Baal was the sun god or source of life, and Ashtoreth was the corresponding female deity. In addition each nation had its own peculiar god to whom it ascribed its prosperity and misfortunes (see Chemosh; Molech). The idolatry into which the Israelites so often fell consisted either in making images that stood for Jehovah, such as the calves of Jeroboam (1 Kgs. 12:28); or in worshipping, in addition to Jehovah, one of the gods of the heathen nations around them (1 Kgs. 11:7, 33; 2 Kgs. 21:3–6; 23:10; Jer. 7:31; Ezek. 20:26–49), such idolatry being some form of nature worship, which encouraged as a rule immoral practices.

Next, in verse 3, the Lord tells the people that their wickedness is the cause of drought in their land. Then, He points out that the people of Judah are not even ashamed of their wickedness.

3 **Therefore** [*because you have "played the harlot"*] **the showers have been withholden**, and there hath been no latter rain [*the spring rains have been withheld by the Lord*]; and **thou hadst a whore's forehead** [*you advertised your wickedness like a prostitute marks her forehead (a cultural practice of that day) to attract lovers*], **thou refusedst to be ashamed** [*and you weren't even embarrassed at your public display of wickedness*].

4 **Wilt thou not from this time cry unto me, My father, thou** *art* **the guide of my youth** [*won't you please return to Me and seek guidance from Me as in times past*]?

Next, the people ask, in effect, how long the Lord will be angry with them. Jeremiah then points out their shallowness and hypocrisy, noting that even while they are asking the question about the Lord's anger, they continue in their evil ways.

5 **Will he** [*the Lord*] **reserve** [*keep*] *his anger* **for ever? will he keep** *it* **to the end?** Behold, thou [*Judah*] hast spoken [*asked the above questions*] **and done evil things as thou couldest** [*the people ask how long the Lord will be angry with them but they keep right on being wicked*].

Next, Jeremiah tells the people what the Lord had called his attention to previously during the reign of King Josiah. Jehovah had used Israel (the ten tribes who were carried away captive by the Assyrians about one hundred years ago, in 722 BC) as an example of what happens to covenant people who get completely caught up in wickedness. Judah should look at what happened to Israel, wake up and repent.

6 ¶ **The LORD said also unto me** in the days of Josiah the king, **Hast thou seen** *that* **which backsliding Israel hath done?** she is gone up upon every high mountain and under every green tree, and there hath played the harlot [*apostate Israel was deeply involved with idol worship before their destruction by the Assyrians*].

The Lord points out that in spite of Israel's wickedness, He had still invited them to repent. But they refused.

7 **And I said after she** [*Israel—the northern ten tribes*] **had done all these** *things,* **Turn thou unto me. But she returned not.** And her treacherous sister Judah saw *it.*

In verses 8–11, next, the Lord continues to point out that the people of Judah have not learned a lesson from what happened to their fellow Israelites, the northern ten tribes (referred to as "Israel" in this context).

8 **And I** [*the Lord*] **saw, when for all the causes whereby backsliding Israel committed adultery** [*broke her covenants with Me*] **I had put her away, and given her a bill of divorce** [*I rejected her and let her be carried away into Assyrian captivity*]; **yet her treacherous sister Judah feared not, but went and played the harlot also** [*Judah did not learn from what happened to Israel, rather, continued breaking covenants*].

As has been previously stated, the word, "adultery," as used in verse 8, above, often means "apostasy." We will quote from the Bible Dictionary on this subject (bold added for emphasis):

Bible Dictionary: Adultery

While adultery is usually spoken of in the individual sense, **it is sometimes used to illustrate the apostasy of a nation or a whole people from the ways of the Lord**, such as Israel forsaking her God and going after strange gods and strange practices (Ex. 20:14; Jer. 3:7–10; Matt. 5:27–32; Luke 18:11; Doctrine & Covenants 43:24–25).

9 **And it came to pass through the lightness of her whoredom** [*she did not consider her disloyalty to God to be a serious matter*], that she defiled the land, and **committed adultery with stones and with stocks** [*she committed spiritual adultery by worshiping idols of rock and wood*].

10 And **yet for all this** [*in view of all this evidence*] her treacherous sister **Judah hath not turned unto me** with her whole heart, but feignedly [*merely pretended*], saith the LORD.

11 And the LORD said unto me [*Jeremiah*], The **backsliding Israel hath justified herself more than treacherous Judah** [*even apostate Israel was not as wicked as Judah has become*].

Unless we realize that verses 12–18, next, are a prophecy about the future, we can become confused. As we read verse 12, we might think, "Wait a minute. Israel is gone. The Assyrians took the people away over one hundred years ago. How can Jeremiah talk to them?" But when we understand that it is a prophecy about the future gathering of Israel (see heading to this chapter in your Bible), it makes sense. And we realize that we are watching a major portion of the fulfillment of this prophecy in our day.

12 ¶ Go and **proclaim these words toward the north** [*address this message to Israel*]**, and say,** Return, thou backsliding Israel, saith the LORD; *and* I will not cause mine anger to fall upon you: for **I *am* merciful, saith the LORD,** *and* I will not keep *anger* for ever.

In verses 13–14, next, the Lord explains in the simplest terms how Israel will someday be enabled to return to Him.

13 Only **acknowledge thine iniquity, that thou hast transgressed against the LORD thy God,** and hast scattered thy ways to the strangers [*you have joined the ways of the world, participated in their evil ways*] under every green tree [*a reference to the immoral*

NOTES

practices associated with ancient idol worship], and ye have not obeyed my voice [*the problem*], saith the LORD.

14 Turn, O backsliding children, saith the LORD; for I am married unto you [*I am your God; you can be My covenant people again*]: and **I will take you** [*gather you*] **one of a city, and two of a family, and I will bring you to Zion:**

> In times past, wicked priests and false prophets led Israel astray. Verse 15, next, prophesies that in conjunction with the gathering of Israel in the last days, we will once again have righteous leaders whose hearts are in tune with God. They will nourish us with correct doctrine.

15 And **I will give you pastors** [*leaders*] **according to mine heart** [*whose hearts are in harmony with the Lord's heart*], which **shall feed you with knowledge and understanding**.

> Verse 16, next, appears to be saying that, in the last days when the gospel is restored and Israel is being gathered, the focus will no longer be on the Law of Moses, with the ark of the covenant, etc. Rather the emphasis will be on the restored gospel of Jesus Christ.

16 And it shall come to pass, **when ye be multiplied and increased in the land, in those days** [*when Israel is gathered in the last days*], saith the LORD, **they shall say no more, The ark of the covenant** of the LORD: neither shall it come to mind: neither shall they remember it; **neither shall they visit** *it;* neither shall *that* be done any more [*the people will no longer live by the Law of Moses*].

> Verse 17, next, appears to refer to the Millennium, when the Savior will be "KING OF KINGS AND LORD OF LORDS" (Revelation 19:16) as He rules and reigns on earth during the Millennium. During the one thousand years of peace, there will be two headquarters of the Church on earth, one in Zion (Independence, Jackson County, Missouri) and one in Old Jerusalem. We will say a bit more about this and give a reference for it, after verse 17.

17 **At that time** [*during the Millennium*] **they shall call Jerusalem the throne of the LORD** [*Jerusalem will be a headquarters for the Savior during the Millennium*]; and all the nations [*people from all nations*] shall be gathered unto it, to the name of the LORD, to Jerusalem: **neither shall they walk any more after the imagination of their evil heart** [*the people will not be wicked*].

> Joseph Fielding Smith (who became the tenth president of the Church) taught about the two cities that would become headquarters of the kingdom of God during the Millennium. He said:

> "ZION AND JERUSALEM: TWO WORLD CAPITALS. When Joseph Smith translated the Book of Mormon, he learned that America is the land of Zion which was given to Joseph and his children and that on this land the City Zion, or New Jerusalem, is to be built. He also learned that Jerusalem in Palestine is to be rebuilt and become a holy city. These two cities, one in the land of Zion and one in Palestine, are to become capitals for the kingdom of God during the millennium" (Doctrines of Salvation, vol. 3, page 71).

Verse 18, next, contains an additional prophecy. As you perhaps recall, after settling in the Holy Land, the twelve tribes of Israel eventually broke up into two nations, Israel (ten tribes) and Judah (two tribes). This happened after King Solomon's death. There was much hatred and animosity between the two nations. Verse 18 foretells the day when Judah and Israel will once again be united in peace and harmony.

18 In those days **the house of Judah shall walk with the house of Israel**, and they shall come together out of the land of the north to the land that I have given for an inheritance unto your fathers.

Verse 19, next, gives a simple answer as to how Israel and Judah can someday live in peace and be the Lord's covenant people.

19 But I said, How shall I put thee among the children, and give thee a pleasant land, a goodly heritage of the hosts of nations? and I said, **Thou shalt call me, My father; and shalt not turn away from me** [*they will accept the gospel of Jesus Christ and remain faithful to Him*].

Verses 20–22, next, review once again what got these people into such a mess and the invitation to repent is given yet again.

20 ¶ Surely *as* **a wife treacherously departeth from her husband, so have ye dealt treacherously with me, O house of Israel**, saith the LORD.

21 A voice was heard upon the high places, weeping *and* supplications of **the children of Israel**: for they **have perverted their way, *and* they have forgotten the LORD their God**.

22 **Return, ye backsliding children, *and* I will heal** your backslidings. Behold, we come unto thee; for thou *art* the LORD our God.

The last half of verse 22, above, and verses 23–25, next, may be understood to be Israel's reply to the Lord, in the last days, as they repent and return to Him, affirming that He is the only one who can provide salvation.

23 **Truly in vain *is salvation hoped for* from the hills** [*salvation is not available through the worship of false gods*], *and from* the multitude of mountains: **truly in the LORD our God *is* the salvation of Israel**.

24 **For shame hath devoured the labour of our fathers from our youth** [*we have long since apostatized from the foundations laid by our ancestors*]; their flocks and their herds, their sons and their daughters.

25 We lie down in our shame, and our confusion covereth us: for **we have sinned against the LORD our God, we and our fathers, from our youth even unto this day, and have not obeyed the voice of the LORD** our God.

NOTES

_____
_____
_____
_____
_____
_____
_____
_____
_____
_____
_____
_____
_____
_____
_____
_____
_____
_____
_____
_____
_____
_____
_____
_____
_____
_____
_____
_____
_____
_____

JEREMIAH 4

Selection: all verses

In Helaman in the Book of Mormon we are informed that Jeremiah prophesied of the destruction of Jerusalem. We read:

Helaman 8:20

20 And behold, also Zenock, and also Ezias, and also Isaiah, and Jeremiah, (**Jeremiah** being that same prophet who **testified of the destruction of Jerusalem**) and now we know that Jerusalem was destroyed according to the words of Jeremiah. O then why not the Son of God come, according to his prophecy?

We read one of Jeremiah's many prophecies of Jerusalem's coming destruction, starting with verse 7 here in chapter 4 and going through chapter 5, verse 13. But first, beginning with verse 1, we read another invitation to repent. You will see that the first requirement for returning to God is a desire to repent.

1 **IF thou wilt** [*if you have a desire to*] **return**, O Israel, saith the LORD, **return unto me** [*just do it*]: and **if thou wilt put away thine abominations out of my sight** [*if you will stop being wicked; this is the next step*], then shalt thou not remove [*then you will remain My covenant people*].

The next step, as given in verse 2, is for the people to sincerely and seriously commit to Jehovah as their God.

2 And **thou shalt swear** [*pledge, commit*], The LORD liveth, in truth, in judgment, and in righteousness; and the nations shall bless themselves in him, and in him shall they glory.

Did you notice the phrase in verse 2, above, which says, in effect, that we are doing ourselves a tremendous favor when we are loyal to the Lord? It is "the nations shall bless themselves in him."

Verses 3 and 4, next, appear to be an invitation to the men of Judah, with headquarters in Jerusalem, to repent and become clean. The Lord uses considerable symbolism to get the message across.

3 ¶ For thus saith the LORD to the men of Judah and Jerusalem, **Break up your fallow** [*unplowed*] **ground** [*perhaps meaning you have yet another chance to become productive as the Lord's covenant people*], and **sow** [*plant*] **not among thorns** [*don't try to mix the gospel and wickedness together in your lives*].

4 **Circumcise yourselves to the LORD** [*dedicate yourselves to the Lord*], and **take away the foreskins of your heart** [*dedicate your hearts to the Lord*], ye men of Judah and inhabitants of Jerusalem: **lest my fury come forth like fire**, and burn that none can quench *it*, [*otherwise, the punishments of the Lord will come upon you and none will stop them*] because of the evil of your doings.

5 Declare ye in Judah, and publish in Jerusalem [*spread the word throughout the people of Judah*]; and say, Blow ye the trumpet in the land: cry, gather together, and say, Assemble yourselves, and let us go into the defenced [*fortified*] cities [*in other words, spread the word that we must gather to the Lord for protection against the enemies*].

6 Set up the standard [*sound the alarm, raise the flag, signaling to gather*] toward Zion [*symbolic of returning to the Lord*]: retire, stay not [*don't hesitate*]: for I will bring evil from the north [*the Babylonians are coming*], and a great destruction.

Next, Jeremiah uses fearsome images to warn the people of Judah of the destruction that is coming if they don't repent.

7 **The lion** [*the King of Babylon and his armies; symbolic of Satan and his evil hosts*] **is come up from his thicket** [*has come out of hiding*], and the destroyer of the Gentiles [*the Babylonian armies have destroyed many Gentile cities*] is on his way; he is gone forth from his place to make thy land desolate; *and* thy cities shall be laid waste, without an inhabitant.

8 For this [*because of this*] **gird you with sackcloth** [*clothe yourselves with course, uncomfortable cloth to symbolize that you are going into mourning*], **lament and howl**: for the fierce anger of the LORD is not turned back from us [*we are still in trouble with the Lord, (because, as a nation, they have not repented)*].

9 And **it shall come to pass at that day** [*when the punishments and destructions come*], saith the LORD, *that* **the heart** [*courage*] **of the king shall perish, and the heart of the princes** [*the leaders of the land will lose courage*]; and the priests shall be astonished [*the false priests will be horrified*], and the prophets shall wonder [*the false prophets will be appalled*].

Verse 10, next, is a problem as it stands. Surely, Jeremiah would not say such a thing to the Lord. Either something is missing or the translation is wrong. Let's read the verse and then look at an alternate translation.

10 Then said I, Ah, Lord GOD! surely thou hast greatly deceived this people and Jerusalem, saying, Ye shall have peace; whereas the sword reacheth unto the soul.

The Martin Luther translation of the German Bible may provide some help for us regarding verse 10, above. It has Jeremiah saying, in effect, "Lord, thou has allowed these people and Jerusalem to be led far astray, because their false prophets and priests said to them that they would have peace [*in spite of their wickedness*], whereas in reality the sword is about to destroy their souls."

Verses 11–20, next, carry on the prophetic theme of coming destruction.

11 At that time [*when destruction comes to Judah and Jerusalem*] shall it be said to this people and to Jerusalem, **A dry wind** [*symbolic of destruction*] of the high places in the wilderness **toward the daughter of my people** [*Jerusalem*], not to fan, nor to cleanse [*not a pleasant, cleansing breeze*],

12 *Even* **a full wind** [*a very devastating destruction*] from those *places* shall come unto me: now also will I give sentence against them.

13 Behold, he shall come up as clouds, and his chariots *shall be* **as a whirlwind**: his horses are swifter than eagles. Woe unto us! for we are spoiled.

14 O Jerusalem, **wash thine heart from wickedness** [*repent and be baptized*], that thou mayest be saved. **How long shall thy vain thoughts lodge within thee** [*how long will your wicked and foolish thinking stay with you*]?

> Joseph Fielding Smith indicated that verse 14, above, is a reference to baptism. Speaking of the fact that the Jews were not surprised by the baptisms performed by John the Baptist, because it was a common Old Testament ordinance, he said:

> "John stood forth in the spirit of the prophets of old to preach his baptism of repentance symbolized by cleansing with water. (See Jer. 4:14; Ezek. 36:25; Zech. 13:1.)" (Answers to Gospel Questions, vol. 2, page 68)

> It is helpful for understanding verse 15, next, to know that the land of Dan was the farthest north among the inheritances of the twelve tribes when they arrived in the promised land.

15 For a voice declareth from Dan [*the news of destruction is coming from the north*], and publisheth affliction from mount Ephraim.

16 **Make ye mention to the nations** [*spread the news*]; behold, publish against Jerusalem, *that* **watchers** [*NIV: "a besieging army"*] come from a far country [*Babylon*], and **give out their voice against** [*are enemies to*] **the cities of Judah.**

17 As keepers of a field, are they against her round about [*they will surround Judah*]; **because she hath been rebellious against me**, saith the LORD.

18 **Thy way and thy doings have procured these *things* unto thee** [*you have brought this destruction upon yourselves*]; this *is* thy wickedness, because it is bitter, because it reacheth unto thine heart [*you are wicked through and through (ripe in iniquity)*].

> Verse 19, next, can describe the terror that will engulf the wicked inhabitants of Judah as the Babylonian armies descend upon them. However, it can also describe the deep anguish and sorrow in Jeremiah's heart as he sees the vision of coming destruction upon the wicked people of Judah.

19 ¶ My bowels, my bowels [*a phrase meaning "deepest anguish"*]! I am pained at my very heart [*deepest agony*]; my heart maketh a noise in me [*my heart is pounding*]; I cannot hold my peace [*I cry out*], because thou hast heard, O my soul, the sound of the trumpet, the alarm of war.

20 Destruction upon destruction is cried; for **the whole land is spoiled** [*ruined, ravaged*]: suddenly are my tents spoiled, *and* my curtains [*dwelling places*] in a moment.

21 How long shall I see the standard, *and* hear the sound of the trumpet [*how long do I have to look at this scene of horror, this scene of battle and destruction*]?

> It appears that verse 22, next, could represent the feelings of the Lord about Judah at this time.

22 For **my people *is* foolish**, they have not known me [*they have apostatized, left Me*]; they *are* sottish [*senseless; do not think*] children, and they have none understanding: **they *are* wise to do evil, but to do good they have no knowledge.**

Verses 23–29 seem to describe the devastation and desolation that will come upon Judah and Jerusalem when the invading Babylonian armies finish with them.

23 I beheld the **earth, and, lo,** *it was* **without form, and void** [*the land was "empty and desolate"—see Abraham 4:2*]; and the heavens, and **they** *had* **no light** [*perhaps meaning that the dust from the battles obscured the sunlight; could also symbolize that the light of the gospel is gone*].

24 I beheld the mountains, and, lo, they trembled, and all the hills moved lightly.

25 I beheld, and, lo, *there was* no man [*the people were slaughtered or taken away into captivity*], and all the birds of the heavens were fled.

26 I beheld, and, lo, **the fruitful place** [*the once-beautiful Jerusalem and surrounding area*] *was* **a wilderness**, and all the cities thereof were broken down at the presence of the LORD, *and* **by his fierce anger.**

In verse 27, next, the Lord says that the land will be desolate, but the Jews will not be completely destroyed.

27 For thus hath the LORD said, The whole land shall be desolate; **yet will I not make a full end.**

In the context of this chapter and prophecy, verse 28, next, states emphatically that unless the people of Judah repent (verse 14), the destruction will come as described.

By the way, since the Lord is sinless, He has no need to repent. Thus, the word "repent" in this verse is not a good translation in view of the normal use of the word.

28 For this [*because of this destruction*] shall the earth mourn, and the heavens above be black: because **I have spoken** *it,* **I have purposed** *it,* **and will not repent** [*relent nor change My mind*], **neither will I turn back from it.**

29 **The whole city** [*Jerusalem*] **shall flee** for [*because of*] the noise of the horsemen and bowmen [*the Babylonian armies*]; they shall go into thickets, and climb up upon the rocks: **every city** [*of Judah*] *shall be* **forsaken** [*deserted*], and not a man dwell therein.

Verses 30–31 conclude this chapter with the question, "What will you do when all this happens?" And the basic answer is that Judah will still seek help from her false gods, her idols. Verse 30 is a description of a harlot attempting to make herself attractive for her lovers. The imagery is that Judah (the "harlot," symbolic of "stepping out on God," in other words, disloyalty to her covenants with Jehovah) attempts to get help from her false gods and gets none.

30 And *when* **thou** *art* **spoiled** [*ruined by the Babylonians*], **what wilt thou do?** Though thou clothest thyself with crimson, though thou deckest thee with ornaments of gold, though thou rentest thy face with painting [*use makeup to make your eyes look bigger—see footnote 30b, in your Latter-day Saint Bible*], in vain shalt thou make thyself fair [*your attempts to make yourself look attractive won't work*]; *thy* **lovers** [*false gods*] **will despise thee,** they will seek thy life [*they will not help you at all against your enemies*].

Part of the imagery in verse 31, next, is that there is no way (in Jeremiah's day) to stop childbirth labor once it starts. So also, once the coming armies descend upon Jerusalem, there will be no way to stop them. The pain and anguish of a woman having her first child is compared to the anguish of the people of Judah, as the stark reality of their destruction hits them.

31 For **I have heard a voice as of a woman in travail** [*childbirth labor*], *and* the **anguish** as of her that bringeth forth her first child, the voice of the daughter of Zion [*Jerusalem*], *that* **bewaileth herself**, *that* spreadeth her hands, *saying,* **Woe** *is* **me now!** for my soul is wearied because of murderers [*my life is in the hands of murderers*].

JEREMIAH 5

Selection: all verses

In this chapter, Jeremiah describes the corruption that has permeated every facet of society by this point in the history of Judah.

We will move rather quickly through this chapter, using bold to let the scriptures themselves point out this corruption to you. The hope is that you will gain more skill and confidence in capturing the basic meaning of Jeremiah's writing without having to understand every detail. We will intentionally add very few notes in this chapter. Try going through first, just reading the bolded words and phrases. Remember, we are looking for various types of corruption that can ruin society and lead to downfall and destruction, as well as the consequences of such behavior, as described by Jeremiah.

1 **RUN ye to and fro through the streets of Jerusalem, and see** now, and know, and seek in the broad places thereof, **if ye can find a man**, if there be *any* that executeth judgment, **that seeketh the truth**; and I will pardon it.

2 And **though they say, The LORD liveth; surely they swear falsely** [*break covenants and contracts; don't keep their word*].

3 O LORD, *are* not thine eyes upon the truth? **thou hast stricken them, but they have not grieved; thou hast consumed them,** *but* **they have refused to receive correction**: they have made their faces harder than a rock; **they have refused to return**.

4 Therefore I said, Surely these *are* poor; they are foolish: for **they know not the way of the LORD**, *nor* the judgment of their God.

5 I will get me unto the great men, and will speak unto them; for they have known the way of the LORD, *and* the judgment of their God: but **these have altogether broken the yoke** [*the covenants that bind them to Jehovah*], *and* burst the bonds.

6 **Wherefore a lion** out of the forest **shall slay them,** *and* **a wolf** of the evenings **shall spoil them**, a leopard shall watch over their cities: every one that goeth out thence shall be torn in pieces [*the Lord will allow their destruction*]: **because their transgressions are many,** *and* their backslidings are increased.

7 ¶ **How shall I pardon thee for this? thy children have forsaken me, and sworn by** *them that are* **no gods** [*have worshiped idols*]: when I had fed them to the full, they

then **committed adultery**, and **assembled themselves by troops in the harlots' houses**.

8 **They were** *as* **fed horses** in the morning: **every one neighed after his neigh-bour's wife** [*sexual immorality is rampant throughout society*].

9 **Shall I not visit** [*punish*] **for these** *things*? **saith the LORD**: and shall not my soul be avenged on such a nation as this?

10 ¶ Go ye up upon her walls, and destroy; but make not a full end: take away her battlements; for they *are* not the LORD's.

11 **For the house of Israel and the house of Judah have dealt very treacherously against me**, saith the LORD.

12 **They have belied** [*lied about*] **the LORD, and said**, *It is* not he; **neither shall evil come upon us; neither shall we see sword nor famine**:

13 And **the prophets shall become wind, and the word** *is* **not in them** [*the prophe-cies against us will not be fulfilled*]: thus shall it be done unto them.

14 Wherefore thus saith the LORD God of hosts, **Because ye speak this word** [*verse 13*], behold, **I will make my words in thy mouth fire**, and this people wood, **and it shall devour them**.

15 Lo, **I will bring a nation upon you from far**, O house of Israel, saith the LORD: **it** *is* **a mighty nation, it** *is* **an ancient nation, a nation whose language thou knowest not, neither understandest what they say**.

16 Their quiver *is* as an open sepulchre, **they** *are* **all mighty men**.

17 And **they shall eat up thine harvest, and thy bread**, *which* thy sons and thy daugh-ters should eat: they shall eat up **thy flocks and thine herds**: they shall eat up **thy vines and thy fig trees**: they shall impoverish thy fenced cities, wherein thou trust-edst, with the sword.

18 **Nevertheless** in those days, saith the LORD, **I will not make a full end with you** [*I will preserve a remnant of Judah*].

19 ¶ And it shall come to pass, when ye shall say, Wherefore [*why*] doeth the LORD our God all these *things* unto us? then shalt thou answer them, Like as **ye have forsak-en me**, and served strange gods in your land, **so shall ye serve strangers in a land** *that is* **not yours** [*you will be taken into slavery to a foreign country (Babylon)*].

20 **Declare this** in the house of Jacob [*Israel*], and **publish it in Judah**, saying,

21 Hear now this, **O foolish people**, and without understanding; which have eyes, and see not; which have ears, and hear not:

NOTES

22 **Fear ye not me?** saith the LORD: **will ye not tremble at my presence**, which have placed the sand *for* the bound of the sea by a perpetual decree, that it cannot pass it: and though the waves thereof toss themselves, yet can they not prevail; though they roar, yet can they not pass over it?

23 But **this people hath a revolting and a rebellious heart**; they are revolted and gone.

24 **Neither say they in their heart, Let us now fear the LORD our God**, that giveth rain, both the former and the latter, in his season: he reserveth unto us the appointed weeks of the harvest.

25 ¶ **Your iniquities have turned away these *things*, and your sins have withholden good *things* from you**.

26 For **among my people are found wicked *men***: they lay wait, as he that setteth snares; they set a trap, they catch men.

27 As a cage is full of birds, so *are* **their houses full of deceit**: therefore they are become great, and waxen rich.

28 **They are waxen fat** [*they have grown rich on corruption*], they shine: yea, **they overpass** [*ignore*] **the deeds of the wicked**: they judge not the cause, the cause of the fatherless, yet they prosper; and the right of the needy do they not judge.

29 **Shall I not visit** [*punish*] **for these *things*?** saith the LORD: shall not my soul be avenged on such a nation as this?

30 ¶ **A** wonderful [*astonishing*] and **horrible thing is committed in the land;**

31 **The prophets** [*false prophets*] **prophesy falsely**, and the priests bear rule by their means [*take authority unto themselves; are not authorized by God*]; and **my people love *to have it* so**: and what will ye do in the end thereof?

How did you do? This approach to reading the Old Testament can be quite helpful. Even though you may not understand everything, you get the big picture and can benefit much from the major messages.

JEREMIAH 6

Selection: all verses

This chapter continues the theme of the destruction of Jerusalem by the Babylonians, because of gross wickedness among the covenant people. We will add a few more notes here than we did for chapter 5, in hopes that you will continue to get a better feel for the "manner of prophesying among the Jews" (2 Nephi 25:1), including the use of words and symbolism to create pictures in the minds of the readers.

1 O YE children [*descendants*] **of Benjamin** [*remember that the tribes of Judah and Benjamin stayed together at the time the twelve tribes split into two nations, after King Solomon died; they became known as "Judah"*], gather yourselves to **flee out of the midst**

of Jerusalem, and blow the trumpet [*sound the alarm*] in Tekoa [*a Judean city, about six miles south of Bethlehem, which is about five miles southwest of Jerusalem*], and set up a sign of fire in Beth-haccerem: **for evil appeareth out of the north, and great destruction**.

Next, the siege of Jerusalem by Babylon is described.

2 I have likened [*compared*] the **daughter of Zion** [*Jerusalem*] to a comely [*beautiful*] and delicate *woman*.

3 **The shepherds** [*the Babylonians*] with their flocks shall come unto her; they **shall pitch *their* tents against her round about**; they shall feed every one in his place.

4 **Prepare ye war against her** [*Jerusalem*]; arise, and let us [*Babylon*] go up at noon [*let's attack Jerusalem at noon*]. Woe unto us! for the day goeth away [*the daylight is fading*], for the shadows of the evening are stretched out [*are getting longer*].

5 Arise, and let us go by night [*let us also attack Jerusalem at night*], and **let us destroy her palaces**.

6 ¶ For thus hath the LORD of hosts said, **Hew ye down trees, and cast a mount against Jerusalem** [*throw up a mound of dirt outside the walls of Jerusalem for the siege and build battlements*]: **this is the city to be visited** [*punished*]; she *is* wholly oppression in the midst of her [*Jerusalem is completely corrupt*].

Next, Jerusalem is described as a fountain of filthy water, spewing forth wickedness all around.

7 **As a fountain** casteth out her waters, so **she casteth out her wickedness**: violence and spoil is heard in her; before me continually *is* grief and wounds.

8 **Be thou instructed** [*heed the warnings*], **O Jerusalem**, lest my soul depart from thee; **lest I make thee desolate, a land not inhabited**.

The symbolism in verse 9, next, is that of being thoroughly harvested. The "gleaners" went through the vineyards again, after the main harvest was gathered, and completely stripped the vines of any remaining grapes. Thus, the inhabitants of Jerusalem and the surrounding cities of Judah are going to be thoroughly "gleaned" by their enemies.

9 ¶ Thus saith the LORD of hosts, **They** [*the Babylonians*] **shall thoroughly glean the remnant of Israel** [*Judah*] as a vine: turn back thine hand as a grapegatherer into the baskets.

Next, the question is, in effect, who is there in all of Judah to whom this urgent message might get through? Answer: nobody.

10 **To whom shall I speak, and give warning**, that they may hear? behold, **their ear *is* uncircumcised** [*they don't even recognize the word of God; they are wicked to the point that they are completely spiritually deaf*], and **they cannot hearken** [*they cannot obey because they cannot hear*]: behold, **the word of the LORD is unto them a reproach** [*they consider the word of the Lord to be a negative thing*]; **they have no delight in it**.

NOTES

In verse 11, next, we are told that destruction will come upon all the inhabitants of Jerusalem, regardless of age and circumstance.

11 **Therefore** [*this is why*] **I am full of the fury of the LORD**; I am weary with holding in [*holding it back*]: I will pour it [*the fury of the Lord*] out upon the children abroad [*playing in the streets*], and upon the assembly of young men together [*simultaneously*]: for even the husband with the wife shall be taken, the aged with *him that is* full of days [*those who are bent over with age*].

12 And their houses shall be turned unto others [*others will inhabit their homes*], *with their* fields and wives together: for I will stretch out my hand upon [*I will punish*] the inhabitants of the land, saith the LORD.

Perhaps you've noticed that Jeremiah is saying the same basic thing many different ways. This is typical of prophetic utterances of his day. Repetition for emphasis is typical of Isaiah's writings also, likewise with many other prophets in the Old Testament.

Next, Jeremiah again repeats that society in and around Jerusalem is completely riddled with corruption. (This is one of the reasons Lehi and his family were commanded to leave the Jerusalem area.)

13 For from the least of them even unto the greatest of them **every one *is* given to covetousness**; and from the prophet [*false prophet*] even unto the priest [*false, corrupt priest*] **every one dealeth falsely**.

14 **They** [*the false prophets and false priests supported by these corrupt people*] **have healed also the hurt *of the daughter* of my people slightly** [*have superficially addressed the moral corruption and coming destruction and war*], saying, Peace, peace; when *there is* no peace.

Next, in verse 15, we see that the people had lost their ability to blush and be embarrassed at wickedness. It had become so common and accepted among them that it was no longer a big deal.

15 **Were they ashamed** when they had committed abomination? **nay, they were not at all ashamed, neither could they blush**: therefore they shall fall among them that fall: at the time *that* I visit [*punish*] them they shall be cast down, saith the LORD.

Once again, in verse 16, next, the people are invited to repent. But they refuse.

16 **Thus saith the LORD, Stand ye in the ways** [*repent and stand in holy places; in other words, live righteously*], and see, and **ask for the old paths** [*the old ways of truth and righteousness*], where *is* the good way, **and walk therein, and ye shall find rest for your souls**. But **they said, We will not walk *therein***.

Have you noticed that the Lord reminds us over and over that He has given these people plenty of warning? One of the great blessings in our lives is that we hear the same warning messages time and time again in our lives, thus giving us many opportunities to repent and continually improve.

Once again, these wicked people of Judah refuse to listen to the warning.

17 Also **I set watchmen** [*prophets*] over you, *saying,* Hearken to the sound of the trumpet [*listen to the warning of approaching danger and destruction*]. **But they** [*the people of Judah*] **said, We will not hearken.**

18 ¶ **Therefore hear, ye nations**, and know, O congregation, **what** *is* **among them** [*all nations are called to serve as witnesses against Judah*].

19 Hear, O earth: behold, **I will bring evil upon this people**, *even* the fruit [*product*] of their thoughts [*their evil thoughts have produced wicked deeds*], **because they have not hearkened unto my words, nor to my law, but rejected it.**

As you can see, the main message of verse 20, next, is that empty ritual and empty worship is of no value. The incense and offerings mentioned were part of normal religious worship under the Law of Moses.

20 **To what purpose** cometh there to me incense from Sheba, and the sweet cane from a far country [*in other words, what good does your ritual and worship do*]? **your burnt offerings** *are* **not acceptable, nor your sacrifices sweet unto me**.

The theme of destruction continues in verse 21, next.

21 Therefore thus saith the LORD, Behold, **I** [*the Lord*] **will lay stumblingblocks** before this people, and **the fathers and the sons together shall fall upon them; the neighbour and his friend shall perish.**

More repetition. Remember, repetition for emphasis is a major component of the Jewish culture at the time of Jeremiah. Sometimes, "westerners" (including most of us) struggle a bit with such repetition, because we start thinking, "Wait a minute. He already said that. Is he saying something else here and I am missing it?" No. You are not missing it. It is just part of the manner of speaking and prophesying among the Jews.

22 Thus saith the LORD, Behold, **a people** [*the Babylonian armies*] **cometh from the north country**, and **a great nation** [*Babylon*] shall be raised **from the sides of the earth** [*the ends of the earth; in other words, from far away*].

23 **They shall lay hold on bow and spear** [*they will be well-armed*]; **they** *are* **cruel**, and have no mercy; their voice roareth like the sea; and they ride upon horses, set in array as men for war against thee, O daughter of Zion [*Jerusalem*].

24 **We have heard the fame thereof: our hands wax feeble** [*we get weak and faint just hearing about them*]: anguish hath taken hold of us, *and* pain, as of a woman in travail.

25 Go not forth into the field [*don't leave the house*], nor walk by the way; for the sword of the enemy *and* **fear** *is* **on every side.**

26 ¶ O daughter of my people, **gird** *thee* **with sackcloth** [*start mourning now*], and **wallow thyself in ashes** [*roll in ashes; putting ashes upon one's self was a sign of mourning in the Jewish culture of the day*]: **make thee mourning**, *as for* an only son, **most bitter** lamentation: for the spoiler [*Babylon*] shall suddenly come upon us.

NOTES

_____

_____

_____

_____

_____

_____

_____

_____

_____

_____

_____

_____

_____

_____

_____

_____

_____

_____

_____

_____

_____

_____

_____

_____

_____

_____

_____

_____

_____

Next, the Savior reassures Jeremiah of his calling to be a prophet (compare with Jeremiah 1:18).

27 **I have set thee** *for* **a tower** *and* a fortress among my people, that thou mayest know and try their way.

The imagery of the "tower," in verse 27, above, is that of the watchtowers which were built in those days. A person standing upon the watchtower could spot trouble coming a long way off. Our prophets, as inspired men of God, serve as "watchtowers" among us to spot coming danger and warn us of it while there is still time to prepare to defend ourselves from it.

Next, Jeremiah is reminded of the kind of people he is to serve, as one of the Lord's prophets shortly before the downfall of Jerusalem. The Lord uses the imagery of a refiner attempting to smelt precious metal from available ore to describe the wicked residents of Judah. In the normal refining process, the ore is placed in a crucible that is then heated with fire until the ore melts.

As the ore melts, the impurities float to the top and are removed as slag. The precious metal is heavier, so it sinks to the bottom of the crucible. The impurities are, in effect, burned out of the mix and all that remains is the precious metal, in other words, the desired product of the refiner's fire.

Symbolically, the Lord is the Refiner. We are the ore. We have many imperfections that need to be burned out of us in the "furnace of affliction." If we are willing, the "fire of the Holy Ghost" will burn the imperfections out of our souls. We can thus be cleansed by the Atonement of Christ, and become pure gold in the hands of the Refiner.

In the case of Israel, and Judah specifically in this example, they are not allowing the Refiner's fire to work on them successfully. They remain "brass and iron" (verse 28). In fact, they get "consumed" by the fire (verse 29), rather than refined. It is an agency choice whether to be purged and cleansed by the refiner's fire, or destroyed by it. The people of Judah have chosen to be destroyed at this time in their history.

28 **They** *are* **all grievous revolters,** walking with slanders: *they are* **brass and iron**; they *are* all **corrupters**.

29 The bellows are burned [*the bellows of the refiner's fire blow fiercely; see footnote 29a in your Latter-day Saint Bible*], **the lead is consumed of** [*by*] **the fire** [*in effect, the Jews have decided they want to be "lead" rather than gold (symbolic of godliness) and thus are destroyed by the refiner's fire*]; **the founder melteth in vain** [*the Lord works in vain to redeem these people*]: for **the wicked are not plucked away** [*the imperfections are not purged out of the people; in other words, there are not just a few wicked people of Judah, rather, the whole nation is corrupt; therefore, if the Lord takes out the "impurities," there will be almost no one left in Judah*].

30 Reprobate [*rejected*] silver shall *men* call them, because **the LORD hath rejected them**.

JEREMIAH 7

Selection: all verses

Chapters 7 through 10 go together. Chapter 26 contains the same basic prophecy but is somewhat shorter. In these chapters, sometimes called "the temple sermon" or "the temple prophecy" by scholars, Jeremiah is told by the Lord to stand in the gate of the temple in Jerusalem and deliver the messages that follow.

You will see that yet another invitation to repent is given to these wicked and foolish people. It is another reminder to all of us that it is not too late to repent, but can become so. The sweet message is that we can repent still. The sad fact is that these people opt to refuse to return to the Lord. Consequently, additional detail is provided regarding the coming destruction.

Perhaps you have noticed that it is often difficult to determine who is speaking here, Jeremiah or the Lord. Sometimes it is quite clear, but in many instances it is not. We won't worry too much about this because we are familiar with the quote from the Doctrine and Covenants which says (bold added for emphasis):

Doctrine & Covenants 1:38

38 What I the Lord have spoken, I have spoken, and I excuse not myself; and though the heavens and the earth pass away, my word shall not pass away, but shall all be fulfilled, **whether by mine own voice or by the voice of my servants, it is the same**.

Again, we will make frequent use of bold for emphasis.

1 **THE word that came to Jeremiah** from the LORD, saying,

2 **Stand in the gate of the LORD's house** [*the temple in Jerusalem*], and proclaim there this word, **and say**, **Hear the word of the LORD**, all *ye of* Judah, that enter in at these gates to worship the LORD.

    Did you notice that even though they are wicked, they are still "going to church," so to speak?

3 Thus saith the LORD of hosts, the God of Israel, **Amend your ways** and your doings, **and I will cause you to dwell in this place** [*and you can stay here*].

4 **Trust ye not in lying words**, saying, The temple of the LORD, The temple of the LORD, The temple of the LORD, *are* these [*don't trust in the physical temple, nor in going there to worship, to save you (unless you repent)*].

5 For **if ye thoroughly** [*through and through; genuinely*] **amend your ways and your doings**; if ye throughly execute judgment [*fairness; integrity*] between a man and his neighbour;

6 *If* ye oppress not the stranger, the fatherless, and the widow, and shed not innocent blood in this place, **neither walk after other gods** [*worship idols*] to your hurt:

7 **Then will I cause you to dwell in this place**, in the land that I gave to your fathers, **for ever and ever.**

NOTES

8 ¶ Behold, ye trust in lying words, that cannot profit [*you trust in the words of false prophets and priests, corrupt leaders, etc., which do you no good*].

9 **Will ye steal, murder, and commit adultery,** and **swear falsely,** and **burn incense unto Baal,** and **walk after other gods** whom ye know not;

10 **And come and stand before me in this house** [*the temple in Jerusalem*], which is called by my name, and say, We are delivered to do all these abominations [*as long as we attend the temple, we are free to be wicked*]?

11 **Is this house** [*the temple*], which is called by my name, **become a den of robbers** in your eyes? Behold, even **I have seen** *it,* **saith the LORD.**

Next, the people are told to go to Shiloh and be reminded what happened there to wicked Israel. By way of quick review, after Joshua led the children of Israel into the promised land, the Tabernacle was set up in Shiloh (about twenty miles north of Jerusalem). Thus, Shiloh, in effect, was the site of their temple. Eventually, Israel became so wicked that they set up idols and worshipped them there (Judges 18:30–31). They lost the protection of the Lord and the Philistines conquered Shiloh and took the ark of the covenant (1 Samuel 4:10–12).

12 But **go ye now unto my place which** *was* **in Shiloh,** where I set my name at the first, **and see what I did to it for** [*because of*] **the wickedness of my people Israel.**

13 And now, because ye have done all these works, saith the LORD, and **I spake unto you**, rising up early and speaking, **but ye heard not** [*you would not listen*]; and **I called you, but ye answered not;**

14 **Therefore will I do unto** *this* **house** [*the temple in Jerusalem*], which is called by my name, wherein ye trust, and unto the place which I gave to you and to your fathers, **as I have done to Shiloh.**

15 And **I will cast you out of my sight, as I have cast out all your brethren,** *even* **the whole seed of Ephraim** [*Israel, the lost ten tribes, which were commonly referred to as "Ephraim"*].

Verse 16, next, is a dramatic way of saying that the people are so wicked that it is hopeless for Jeremiah to try to get the Lord to save them. This can remind us of the hopeless situation Mormon faced, when his people fell to the same spiritual low as Jeremiah's people here. Let's read what Mormon said about the Nephites of his day and then look at verse 16 in Jeremiah:

Mormon 5:2

2 But behold, **I was without hope,** for I knew the judgments of the Lord which should come upon them; for they repented not of their iniquities, but did struggle for their lives without calling upon that Being who created them.

16 Therefore **pray not thou for this people,** neither lift up cry nor prayer for them, **neither make intercession to me: for I will not hear thee** [*in other words, in effect, the Lord will not be able to answer Jeremiah's prayers for them, because He cannot violate their agency; see also verse 27*].

17 ¶ **Seest thou not what they do in the cities of Judah and in the streets of Je-rusalem?**

Verse 18, next, says, in effect, that everyone in Judah is participating in idol worship, including every member of every family. Various activities involved in preparing for and performing idol worship are described.

18 The **children gather wood** [*to be used in pagan sacrifices*], and the **fathers kindle the fire**, and the **women** knead *their* dough, to **make cakes to the queen of heaven** [*the goddess of fertility, such as Ishtar, whom the Babylonians worshiped—see footnote 18a in your Latter-day Saint Bible*], and to **pour out drink offerings unto other gods**, that they may provoke me to anger.

19 Do they provoke me to anger? saith the LORD: *do they* **not** *provoke* themselves **to the confusion of their own faces** [*aren't they bringing shame and disgrace upon themselves by so doing—see footnote 19a in your Latter-day Saint Bible*]?

20 Therefore [*this is why*] thus saith the Lord GOD; Behold, **mine anger and my fury shall be poured out upon this place**, upon man, and upon beast, and upon the trees of the field, and upon the fruit of the ground; and it shall burn, and shall not be quenched.

Verses 21–24, next, say, in effect, that a major purpose of burnt offerings and sacrifices for the children of Israel under the Law of Moses was to teach obedience to God. The problem with Judah is that the people are continuing the ritual sacrifices of the Law of Moses but they are disobeying the Lord in their daily lives. Their ritual worship of Jeho-vah is empty and meaningless.

21 ¶ Thus saith the LORD of hosts, the God of Israel; **Put your burnt offerings unto your sacrifices, and eat flesh** [*go ahead and continue with your empty rituals, offering sacrifices and eating the meat from the animal sacrifices as always*].

22 For I spake not unto your fathers, nor commanded them in the day that I brought them out of the land of Egypt, concerning burnt offerings or sacrifices [*NIV: "I did not just give them commands about burnt offerings and sacrifices"*]:

23 But this thing commanded I them, saying, Obey my voice, and I will be your God, and ye shall be my people: and **walk ye in all the ways that I have com-manded** you, **that it may be well unto you.**

24 But they hearkened not, nor inclined their ear [*wouldn't listen*], but walked in the counsels *and* in the imagination of their evil heart, and **went backward, and not forward.**

Next, the Savior reminds these people that He has constantly tried to save them.

25 Since the day that your fathers [*forefathers, ancestors*] came forth out of the land of Egypt unto this day **I have even sent unto you all my servants the prophets**, daily rising up early [*I have warned you constantly, ahead of the coming destruction*] and sending *them:*

NOTES

26 **Yet they hearkened not unto me, nor inclined their ear**, but hardened their neck [*remained prideful*]: they did worse than their fathers [*they are worse than their ancestors—compare with Jeremiah 16:12*].

Next, Jehovah reminds Jeremiah that the people will not listen to him and change their ways. He gives him more specific things to say to them.

27 Therefore **thou shalt speak all these words unto them** [*the call to repentance*]; **but they will not hearken to thee**: thou shalt also call unto them; but they will not answer thee [*respond positively*].

28 **But thou shalt say unto them, This** *is* **a nation that obeyeth not the voice of the LORD** their God, nor receiveth correction [*they refuse to repent*]: truth is perished, and is cut off from their mouth [*they no longer live truth nor speak it*].

Verse 29, next, can well have several meanings. It is typical of Jeremiah, Isaiah, and others to embed several symbolic meanings into a word or phrase in their writings. For example, in verse 29, it says, in effect, that the Jews of Jeremiah's day should go into mourning now in anticipation of the coming destruction. It says for Jerusalem to cut off her hair. This can have many possible meanings:

1. Conquering armies of the day often shaved their prisoners bald, to identify them as slaves as well as to humiliate them (compare with Isaiah 3:24).

2. Shaving one's head was symbolic of grief as in Job 1:20.

3. In Jewish culture of the time, one's hair was considered to be a diadem, a crown symbolizing royalty and dignity. And having it cut off by an enemy was demeaning and a terrible insult.

4. In a religious sense, long hair could symbolize the vow of a Nazarite and his consecration to Jehovah (Numbers 6:2–8.) Intentionally cutting off one's hair could be symbolic of abandoning Jehovah and His commandments.

29 ¶ **Cut off thine hair**, *O Jerusalem,* and cast *it* away, and **take up a lamentation** [*go into mourning*] on high places; for the LORD hath rejected and forsaken the generation of his wrath [*because you are no longer under the protection of the Lord*].

Several reasons as to why the Lord can no longer bless and protect these wicked people are reviewed again in verses 30–31, next. Verse 31 informs us that they had gone so far as to sacrifice their children to their false gods.

30 **For the children of Judah** [*the Jews*] **have done evil in my sight**, saith the LORD: they **have set their abominations in the house** [*they have placed idols in the temple at Jerusalem*] which is called by my name, **to pollute it**.

31 And **they have built the high places of Tophet**, which *is* in the valley of the son of Hinnom, **to burn their sons and their daughters in the fire**; which I commanded *them* not, neither came it into my heart.

In verses 32–34, next, we see that the coming Babylonian armies will cause such slaughter that there will not be room to bury all the dead of Jerusalem and Judah.

32 ¶ Therefore, behold, the days come, saith the LORD, that **it shall no more be called Tophet, nor the valley of the son of Hinnom** [*the site where the Jews sacrificed their children to their false gods—see verse 31*], **but the valley of slaughter**: for **they shall bury in Tophet, till there be no place**.

The Bible Dictionary gives us a bit of additional information about Tophet (verse 32, above).

Bible Dictionary: Tophet

A spot in the valley of the son of Hinnom, south of Jerusalem, where human sacrifices were offered to Molech (2 Kgs. 23:10; Isa. 30:33; Jer. 7:31 f.; 19:6, 13).

33 And the carcases of this people [*the people of Judah and Jerusalem*] shall be meat [*food*] for the fowls of the heaven, and for the beasts of the earth; and none shall fray [*frighten*] *them* away.

Verse 34, next, is a prophetic description of the devastating aftermath resulting from the Babylonian captivity of the Jews.

34 **Then will I cause to cease** from the cities of Judah, and from the streets of Jerusalem, the voice of **mirth**, and the voice of **gladness**, the voice of the **bridegroom**, and the voice of the **bride**: for **the land shall be desolate**.

JEREMIAH 8

Selection: all verses

Jeremiah's description of the destruction of Judah and Jerusalem continues in this chapter. Verses 1–2 describe one of the ultimate insults heaped upon a nation by its conquerors, namely the desecration of their dead by the triumphant enemies.

1 **AT that time** [*when Jerusalem and Judah are defeated*], saith the LORD, **they** [*the enemies*] **shall bring out the bones** of the kings of Judah, and the bones of his princes, and the bones of the priests, and the bones of the prophets, and the bones of the inhabitants of Jerusalem, **out of their graves**:

2 **And they shall spread them** before the sun, and the moon, and all the host of heaven, whom they have loved, and whom they have served, and after whom they have walked, and whom they have sought, and whom they have worshipped: **they shall not be gathered, nor be buried; they shall be for dung upon the face of the earth**.

We will include a quote from the Old Testament Student Manual that helps us understand verses 1–2, above.

"In order to pour the utmost contempt upon the land, the victorious enemies dragged out of their graves, caves, and sepulchers, the bones of kings, princes, prophets, priests, and the principal inhabitants, and exposed them in the open air; so that they became, in the order of God's judgments, a reproach to them in the vain confidence they had in the sun, moon, and the host of heaven—all the planets and stars, whose worship they had set up in opposition to that of Jehovah. This custom of raising the bodies of the dead, and scattering their bones about, seems to have been general. It was the

_____
_____
_____
_____
_____
_____
_____
_____
_____
_____
_____
_____
_____
_____
_____
_____
_____
_____
_____
_____
_____
_____
_____
_____
_____
_____
_____
_____
_____
_____
_____
_____

highest expression of hatred and contempt" (Adam Clarke, *The Holy Bible . . . with a Commentary and Critical Notes,* 4:276).

Verse 3, next, indicates that the fate of those who survive the slaughter will be worse than death. They will desire to die rather than to continue living in such horrible conditions.

3 And **death shall be chosen rather than life by all the residue of them that remain of this evil family** [*Judah*], which remain in all the places whither I have driven them, saith the LORD of hosts.

From here to the end of the chapter, we see the sins of these people described. You will no doubt see many parallels between them and the world in which we live.

In verses 4–5, next, the question is asked, in effect, "Why don't these people return to the Lord?"

4 ¶ Moreover [*in addition*] thou [*Jeremiah*] shalt say unto them, Thus saith the LORD; **Shall they fall, and not arise** [*don't people normally get up after they fall*]? **shall he turn away, and not return?**

5 **Why** *then* **is this people of Jerusalem slidden back by a perpetual backsliding** [*why do these people live lives of continual apostasy*]? **they hold fast deceit** [*they hold on tightly to wickedness and evil, to self-deception*], they refuse to return [*repent*].

6 **I hearkened and heard** [*the Lord has listened carefully for them to ask for forgiveness*], *but* **they spake not aright** [*but they don't ask*]: **no man repented him of his wickedness, saying, What have I done?** every one turned to his course [*they all walk in their own paths*], as the horse rusheth into the battle [*like a horse running into battle*].

Next, in effect, we are told that creatures are wiser than these people. The creatures sense when to migrate, etc., and do it. But the covenant people of the Lord do not sense the coming destruction.

7 Yea, the stork in the heaven knoweth her appointed times; and the turtle and the crane and the swallow observe the time of their coming [*follow their migratory patterns*]; **but my people know not the judgment of the LORD.**

Next, in verse 8, we are told that the scribes (who interpret the laws of God among these Jews) have led them astray with their false and evil interpretations of the law of the Lord.

8 **How do ye say** [*how can you say*], **We** *are* **wise, and the law of the LORD** *is* **with us** [*we have the law of God among us*]? Lo, certainly in vain made he *it;* **the pen of the scribes** *is* **in vain** [*the scribes have misinterpreted the Laws of Moses*].

9 **The wise** *men* **are ashamed** [*your supposedly wise men will be put to shame*], they are dismayed and taken: lo, **they have rejected the word of the LORD; and what wisdom** *is* **in them** [*why listen to them*]?

The message of verse 10, next, is that the wicked leaders of Jerusalem will be gone. Another message is that their society is completely corrupt. Greed is a major problem.

10 Therefore will I give their wives unto others, *and* their fields to them [*new owners*] that shall inherit *them:* for every one from the least even unto the greatest is given to covetousness, from the prophet [*false prophet*] even unto the priest [*corrupt priests*] every one dealeth falsely.

Next, we see that the leaders of the Jews at this point in their history have treated corruption and wickedness lightly, telling the people that destruction is not coming and that peace will continue. The imagery used is that of treating a serious wound as if it were just a scratch.

11 For **they have healed the hurt of the daughter of my people slightly,** saying, Peace, peace; when *there is* no peace.

Next, we see that one of the problems of this corrupt society is that nobody blushes at evil anymore.

12 Were they ashamed when they had committed abomination? nay, they were not at all ashamed, neither could they blush: therefore shall they fall among them that fall: in the time of their visitation [*punishment*] they shall be cast down, saith the LORD.

13 ¶ I will surely consume them, saith the LORD: *there shall be* no grapes on the vine, nor figs on the fig tree [*none will escape*], and the leaf shall fade; and *the things that* I have given them shall pass away from them [*the Lord's former blessings will disappear*].

Verses 14–16, next, appear to be the answer from the inhabitants of Jerusalem and Judah in response to what the Lord has said above about the coming destruction. Verses 15–16 seem to be in the future, as if the Babylonian captivity is already under way or is completed.

14 Why do we sit still [*why are we sitting here*]? **assemble yourselves, and let us enter into the defenced cities** [*let's all retreat into our fortified cities*], **and let us be silent there** [*NIV: "and perish there"*]: for the LORD our God hath put us to silence [*NIV: "For the Lord our God has doomed us to perish"*], and given us water of gall [*bitter water*] to drink, **because we have sinned against the LORD.**

15 We looked for peace [*perhaps meaning that they looked for peace in wickedness*], **but no good** *came; and* for a time of health, and behold trouble!

16 The snorting of his horses [*the enemy armies; horses are symbolic of military might and power in Jewish symbolism*] was heard from Dan [*was heard in the far north*]: **the whole land trembled at the sound of the neighing of his strong ones**; for they are come, and **have devoured the land, and all that is in it; the city, and those that dwell therein.**

17 For, **behold, I** [*the Lord*] **will send serpents, cockatrices** [*poisonous serpents; vipers; symbolic of the coming enemy armies*], **among you, which *will* not *be* charmed** [*which you cannot talk out of destroying you*], and **they shall bite you,** saith the LORD.

Opinions vary among scholars as to whether verses 18–22 represent the Lord's words or Jeremiah's. We will use verse 19 to sway us to believe that they represent

NOTES

_____
_____
_____
_____
_____
_____
_____
_____
_____
_____
_____
_____
_____
_____
_____
_____
_____
_____
_____
_____
_____
_____
_____
_____
_____
_____
_____
_____
_____
_____
_____

the mourning of the Lord for His wayward people. But remember, it could represent Jeremiah's feelings too. We know from the record of Enoch in Moses that the Lord weeps for His people when they go astray.

Moses 7:28 (see also 28–44)

28 And it came to pass that the God of heaven looked upon the residue of the people, and he wept; and Enoch bore record of it, saying: How is it that the heavens weep, and shed forth their tears as the rain upon the mountains?

18 ¶ *When* I would comfort myself against sorrow, **my heart *is* faint in me** [*German Bible: "my heart is sick"*].

19 Behold the voice of **the cry of the daughter of my people** [*Jerusalem*] **because of them that dwell in a far country** [*apparently representing the future cries of the Jews far away in Babylonian captivity*]: *Is* not the LORD in Zion? *is* not her king in her? **Why have they provoked me to anger** with their graven images, *and* with strange vanities [*idol worship; pride, sin*]?

20 The harvest is past, the summer is ended, and we are not saved.

21 **For** [*because of*] **the hurt** [*suffering*] **of the daughter of my people** [*Judah and Jerusalem*] **am I hurt** [*I suffer*]; **I am black** [*gloomy—see footnote 21a in your Bible; I am heartbroken, in mourning*]; astonishment hath taken hold on me.

You will see the phrase, "balm in Gilead," in verse 22, next. It is a reference to a healing gum or spice found in a large area east of the Jordan River, extending north of the Dead Sea. The balm was highly prized and was used, among other things, to heal wounds. It appears to be a reference to Christ and the healing power of His Atonement. You are probably familiar with this phrase because "balm of Gilead" is used in verse 3 of our hymn, "Did You Think to Pray," which begins with "Ere you left your room this morning" (Hymns, no. 140).

22 *Is there* **no balm in Gilead** [*is healing not available*]; *is there* no physician there [*can no one heal; is the Physician (the Savior) not available*]? **why then is not the health of the daughter of my people recovered** [*perhaps meaning why don't the people turn to the Savior and be healed*]?

JEREMIAH 9

Selection: all verses

Verses 1–3 of this chapter appear to be a continuation from chapter 8, bemoaning the coming destruction. Remember that the language of the Old Testament is often that of painting pictures and feelings with words. We see that here as the Lord (or possibly Jeremiah), as indicated in verse 3, expresses deep-felt sorrow for apostate Judah.

1 **OH that my head were waters, and mine eyes a fountain of tears**, that I might weep day and night for the slain of the daughter of my people [*Jerusalem and the cities of Judah*]!

2 **Oh that I had in the wilderness a lodging place of wayfaring men** [*a place where travelers could obtain temporary lodging*]; that I might leave my people, and go from them! for **they *be* all adulterers, an assembly of treacherous men**.

In addition to the rampant sexual immorality mentioned in verse 2, above, the people of Jerusalem and its surroundings were also filled with dishonesty. Their whole lifestyle was one of seeking greater and greater evil in which to participate, as indicated in verse 3, next.

3 And they bend their tongues *like* **their bow** *for* **lies**: but they are not valiant for the truth upon the earth; for **they proceed from evil to evil, and they know not me, saith the LORD.**

The next several verses point out more sins of these wicked people and give us a feel for what their wickedness has done to their society. As stated previously, this could be either the Lord or Jeremiah speaking or both. It is difficult to tell since they both share the same feelings, and also since a prophet can speak for the Lord as if the Lord were the one doing the talking (D&C 1:38).

The first thing that is pointed out is the distrust that permeates a dishonest society.

4 Take ye heed [*beware*] every one of his neighbour, and **trust ye not in any brother**: for every brother will utterly supplant [*deceive you at every opportunity to do so*], and every neighbour will walk with slanders [*gossips*].

5 And **they will deceive every one his neighbour, and will not speak the truth**: they have taught their tongue to speak lies, *and* weary themselves [*wear themselves out*] to commit iniquity.

6 **Thine habitation** *is* in the midst of deceit [*you are surrounded by deception*]; **through deceit they refuse to know me, saith the LORD.**

Verse 7, next, says, in effect, that the Lord will have to send them through the "refiner's fire" in order to once again have a pure people.

7 Therefore thus saith the LORD of hosts, Behold, **I will melt them** [*as a refiner does with gold ore in order to extract impurities and have pure gold as the end product of the re-fining process*], and try them; **for how shall I do for the daughter of my people** [*what else can I do in light of the sins of My people in Jerusalem*]?

8 **Their tongue** *is as* **an arrow shot out; it speaketh deceit** [*they are constantly shooting off their mouths with lies*]: *one* **speaketh peaceably to his neighbour with his mouth, but in heart he layeth his wait** [*he sets a trap for him; he says one thing but thinks another*].

9 ¶ **Shall I not visit** [*punish*] **them for these** *things*? **saith the LORD**: shall not my soul be avenged [*should not the law of justice take over*] on such a nation as this?

Verses 10–11, next, prophesy emptiness and desolation, rubble and loneliness where a once-prosperous people lived.

10 **For the mountains will I take up a weeping and wailing, and for the habitations of the wilderness a lamentation** [*I will mourn for the mountains and wilderness where many people once lived and traveled*], because they are burned up [*they have become like a barren desert*], so that **none can pass through** *them*; neither can *men*

hear the voice of **the cattle**; both **the fowl** of the heavens **and the beast** are fled; they **are gone**.

11 And **I will make Jerusalem heaps** [*a pile of rubble*], ***and* a den of dragons** [*a place where desert animals (jackals) live*]; and **I will make the cities of Judah desolate, without an inhabitant**.

12 ¶ **Who *is* the wise man, that may understand this** [*who is wise enough to get the picture*]? and ***who is he* to whom the mouth of the LORD hath spoken, that he may declare it** [*who can explain why this has happened*], for what [*why*] the land perisheth *and* is burned up like a wilderness [*has become like a desert*], that none passeth through?

In verse 12, above, the Lord asked a question, in effect, "Who can explain why this happened to Jerusalem?" In verses 13–16, He now answers His own question. In effect, He says, "I will tell you why."

13 And the LORD saith, **Because they have forsaken my law which I set before them, and have not obeyed my voice, neither walked therein;**

14 **But have walked after the imagination of their own heart**, and after Baalim [*Baal worship, an extremely wicked form of idol worship*], which their fathers taught them:

15 **Therefore** thus saith the LORD of hosts, the God of Israel; Behold, **I will feed them**, *even* this people, **with wormwood** [*extremely bitter*], and **give them water of gall to drink** [*in other words, the Lord will give them bitter medicine*].

16 **I will scatter them** also among the heathen [*foreign nations*], whom neither they nor their fathers have known: and I will send a sword after them, till I have consumed them.

"Consumed," as used in verse 16, above, does not mean to become extinct. We will quote from the Old Testament Student Manual for clarification on this:

"To be consumed does not mean to become extinct. Being consumed and destroyed, in the context of the prophecies of the scattering of Israel, meant to be utterly disorganized and disbanded so that Israel's power, influence, and cohesiveness as a nation was gone. Moses, in Deuteronomy 4:26, told all Israel that they would 'utterly be destroyed.' Yet the verses following show that Israel still existed as homeless individuals" (*Old Testament Student Manual*, page 238).

Next, these unrepentant people are told to get ready to mourn.

17 ¶ Thus saith the LORD of hosts, Consider ye, and **call for the mourning women**, that they may come; and **send for cunning *women*** [*skilled mourners*]*,* that they may come:

18 And let them make haste [*have them hurry, you will need them soon*], and **take up a wailing** [*mourning*] **for us**, that our eyes may run down with tears, and our eyelids gush out with waters [*tears*].

As stated previously, part of the "manner of prophesying among the Jews" (2 Nephi 25:1) was to speak of the future as if it had already taken place. Verse 19, next, is an example of this. It speaks of the coming destruction of Jerusalem as if it had already occurred.

19 For **a voice of wailing is heard out of Zion** [*Jerusalem and the other cities of Judah*], **How are we spoiled** [*see how completely we are ruined*]! **we are greatly confounded**, because we have forsaken the land, because our dwellings have cast *us* out.

20 Yet hear the word of the LORD, O ye women, and let your ear receive the word of his mouth, and **teach your daughters wailing**, and every one her neighbour lamentation.

21 For **death is come** up into our windows, *and* is entered into our palaces, to cut off the children from without, *and* the young men from the streets.

22 Speak, Thus saith the LORD, Even **the carcases of men shall fall as dung** [*animal droppings*] **upon the open field**, and as the handful [*the few remaining*] after the harvestman, and none shall gather *them*.

Do you know what the backward "P" at the beginning of verse 23, next, (and many other places throughout the King James Version of the Bible—the version we use in English) means? It indicates that the Bible is now turning to another topic or a new aspect of the topic already under consideration.

In this case, it is a very short course in how to avoid wickedness.

23 ¶ Thus saith the LORD, **Let not the wise *man* glory in his wisdom** [*avoid being prideful*], **neither let the mighty *man* glory in his might** [*let powerful people avoid pride*], **let not the rich *man* glory in his riches**:

24 **But let him** that glorieth **glory in this, that he understandeth and knoweth me, that I *am* the LORD** which exercise lovingkindness, judgment, and righteousness, in the earth: for in these *things* I delight, saith the LORD.

The topic now turns to hypocrisy, claiming to be the Lord's people through outward ordinances, but inwardly being the "natural man" (Mosiah 3:19). The Lord says that the day is coming when His people, who have been circumcised according to the Law of Moses (a token of loyalty and dedication to the Lord, from Abraham to the end of the Old Testament), will be punished by other wicked nations, referred to as "the uncircumcised" at the end of verse 25. The cause of this punishment is given at the end of verse 26.

25 ¶ Behold, the days come, saith the LORD, that I will punish all *them which are* circumcised [*who have entered into outward covenants with the Lord, but are wicked*] **with the uncircumcised;**

26 Egypt, and Judah, and Edom, and the children of Ammon, and Moab, and all *that are* in the utmost corners, that dwell in the wilderness: for **all *these* nations *are* uncircumcised**, and **all the house of Israel *are* uncircumcised in the heart** [*are not faithful to God*].

NOTES

_____
_____
_____
_____
_____
_____
_____
_____
_____
_____
_____
_____
_____
_____
_____
_____
_____
_____
_____
_____
_____
_____
_____
_____
_____
_____
_____
_____
_____
_____

The point in verses 25–26, above, seems to be that even though the people of Judah, as part of Israel, are outwardly the Lord's covenant people, they are in fact no better off than any other nation or people because they have broken their covenants with God.

JEREMIAH 10

Selection: all verses

In this chapter, the people are counseled to learn to distinguish between false gods and the true God. Jeremiah points out how absurd idol worship is and teaches the people to worship the Lord. We will quote from the Old Testament Student Manual:

"In a profound and yet simple chain of reasoning, Jeremiah showed the stupidity and sheer illogic of worshiping an idol. Men take such materials as wood and precious metals which they work and shape at their own will, making all kinds of objects of service. Then they take those same materials, make them into an idol by the work of their own hands, and suddenly expect the idol to be filled with supernatural power and be able to provide miraculous aid for the person who made it" (Old Testament Student Manual, pages 238–39).

1 HEAR ye the word which the LORD speaketh unto you, O house of Israel:

2 **Thus saith the LORD, Learn not the way of the heathen** [_don't join with the heathen in their false religions, including idol worship_], and **be not dismayed** [_terrified_] **at the signs of heaven** [_at signs in the sky, such as eclipses and falling stars_]; for the heathen are dismayed at them.

Watch now as Jeremiah points out how ridiculous it is to make idols with their own hands and then worship them.

By the way, some have interpreted verse 3, next, to be a direct reference to Christmas trees in our day, and have thus come to the conclusion that the Bible is against them. Not so. The word of the Lord here is against idols, as a replacement for the true God. Trees were often cut down and idols made from the wood.

3 For the customs of the people _are_ vain [_useless_]: for _one_ cutteth a tree out of the forest, **the work of the hands of the workman**, with the axe.

4 **They deck it with silver and with gold**; they **fasten it with nails** and with hammers, **that it move not** [_so that it doesn't fall over_].

5 **They** [_the idols_] _are_ upright as the palm tree, but **speak not**: they **must needs be borne** [_they have to be carried from place to place_], **because they cannot go** [_because they can't move themselves_]. **Be not afraid of them; for they cannot do evil, neither also** _is it_ **in them to do good.**

Next, in verses 7–8, Jeremiah points out that neither idols nor the greatest among men can begin to compare with the true God.

6 Forasmuch as _there is_ **none like unto thee, O LORD**; thou _art_ great, and thy name _is_ great in might.

7 Who would not fear [*revere and respect*] thee, O King of nations? for to thee doth it appertain [*reverence and honor are properly due You*]: forasmuch as among all the wise *men* of the nations, and in all their kingdoms, ***there is* none like unto thee.**

8 **But they** [*people who make and worship idols*] **are altogether brutish** [*are completely without sense*] **and foolish**: the stock [*the idol made from a portion of a tree trunk or limb*] *is* a doctrine of vanities [*is a worthless doctrine*].

9 Silver spread into plates is brought from Tarshish, and gold from Uphaz, the work of the workman, and of the hands of the founder: blue and purple *is* their clothing: **they** [*idols*] ***are* all the work of cunning** *men* [*skilled craftsmen*].

10 **But the LORD** *is* **the true God, he** *is* **the living God, and an everlasting king**: at his wrath the earth shall tremble, and the nations [*wicked nations*] shall not be able to abide his indignation.

11 Thus shall ye say unto them, **The gods** [*idols and other false gods*] that have not made the heavens and the earth, *even* they **shall perish from the earth**, and from under these heavens.

12 **He** [*Jehovah; Jesus Christ*] **hath made the earth by his power**, he hath established the world by his wisdom, and hath stretched out the heavens by his discretion.

Verse 13, next, gives a very brief summary of the creation. The point is that when the Living God speaks, He is obeyed by nature. Contrast this to the lack of power in idols, as described in verse 14.

13 **When he uttereth his voice,** *there is* a multitude of waters in the heavens [*see Genesis, chapter 1*], and he causeth the vapours to ascend from the ends of the earth; he maketh lightnings with rain, and bringeth forth the wind out of his treasures.

14 Every man is brutish [*behaving like an animal*] in *his* knowledge [*every man who makes and then worships an idol, is totally without common sense in applying knowledge*]: every founder [*goldsmith, silversmith, etc., who shapes precious metal overlays for idols*] is confounded [*put to shame*] by the graven image: for his molten image *is* falsehood [*the resulting idol is a lie*], and ***there is* no breath in them** [*idols*].

15 They *are* vanity [*worthless*], *and* the work of errors [*the product of false doctrine*]: in the time of their visitation [*when God's punishments come*] they shall perish.

16 **The portion of Jacob** [*Jehovah, the God of Israel*] *is* **not like them** [*idols*]: for **he** *is* **the former** [*creator*] **of all** *things;* and Israel *is* the rod [*NIV: "tribe"*] of his inheritance: **The LORD of hosts** *is* **his name.**

In verse 17, next, the people of Judah are told to gather their belongings in preparation for the coming siege. And in verse 18, they are told that after the siege (verse 17), they will be scattered.

17 ¶ **Gather up thy wares** out of the land, O inhabitant of the fortress [*the besieged city*].

NOTES

_____
_____
_____
_____
_____
_____
_____
_____
_____
_____
_____
_____
_____
_____
_____
_____
_____
_____
_____
_____
_____
_____
_____
_____
_____
_____
_____
_____
_____
_____

18 For **thus saith the LORD**, Behold, **I will sling out the inhabitants of the land** at this once [*the Jews will be scattered by the Babylonians*], and will distress them, that they may find *it so* [*and will cause that they can be captured*].

Verses 19–22, next, describe the mourning and devastation that will accompany the conquering and scattering of the Jews at this point in their history.

19 ¶ Woe is me for my hurt! **my wound is grievous**: but I said, Truly this *is* a grief, and I must bear it.

20 **My tabernacle** [*dwelling*] **is spoiled**, and all my cords [*the ropes that hold the tent up*] are broken [*in other words, economic and spiritual support are gone*]: **my children are gone forth of me** [*scattered*], and they *are* not [*they are gone*]: *there is* none to stretch forth my tent any more, and to set up my curtains.

We will use verses 19–20, above, as a reminder that there is more than one way in which Jeremiah's writings can be interpreted. We will mention three possibilities for these verses. No doubt there are more.

One

If it is Jeremiah who is speaking, then we might interpret them as follows:

19 ¶ Woe is me [*Jeremiah*] for my hurt! my wound is grievous [*it makes me very sad to see this happen to my people*]: but I said, Truly this is a grief, and I must bear it.

20 My tabernacle is spoiled [*my home and homeland are ruined*], and all my cords are broken [*all the support for my people is gone*]: my children are gone forth of me [*my family and followers are scattered*], and they are not [*they are gone*]: there is none to stretch forth my tent any more, and to set up my curtains [*no one is left in the land*].

Two

These two verses could represent the mourning of the Lord for His people.

19 ¶ Woe is me [*the Lord*] for my hurt! my wound is grievous [*it makes Me very sad to see this happen to My people*]: but I said, Truly this is a grief, and I must bear it.

20 My tabernacle is spoiled [*My temple in Jerusalem is ruined*], and all my cords are broken [*all the covenants with My people have been broken*]: my children are gone forth of me [*my people have been scattered*], and they are not [*they are gone*]: there is none to stretch forth my tent any more, and to set up my curtains [*there are none left in Jerusalem and the cities of Judah to establish My Church*].

Three

These two verses could even represent the mourning of Jerusalem for her people. Such personification of a city or land is often found in ancient writings.

19 ¶ Woe is me [*Jerusalem*] for my hurt! my wound is grievous [*it makes me very sad to see this happen to my people*]: but I said, Truly this is a grief, and I must bear it.

20 My tabernacle is spoiled [*my land is devastated*], and all my cords are broken [*I have fallen down, crumbled*]: my children are gone forth of me [*my inhabitants have been*

scattered], and they are not [*they are gone*]: there is none to stretch forth my tent any more, and to set up my curtains [*no one is left in me*].

As you continue to read and study the writings of the Old Testament prophets, keep in mind that many of their writings can be understood in more than one way. Such is the beauty as well as the difficulty of writings that involve much use of symbolism.

We will continue now with some possible explanations of these next verses.

21 For **the pastors** are become brutish, and **have not sought the LORD** [*the leaders of the Jews are senseless and have not come to the Lord for guidance*]: **therefore they shall not prosper, and all their flocks shall be scattered** [*the scattering of the Jews*].

22 Behold, the noise of the bruit [*news*] is come [*the news of the coming armies has arrived*], and **a great commotion out of the north country, to make the cities of Judah desolate,** *and* a den of dragons [*jackals; in other words, jackals will move into the ruins of Jerusalem and Judah; symbolic of the desolation and emptiness left by the invading armies*].

Verse 23, next, says, in effect, that man, when he opts to do things on his own, without God, is not capable of governing himself successfully. Most scholars consider verses 23–25 to be Jeremiah speaking.

23 ¶ O LORD, I know that **the way of man** *is* **not in himself:** *it is* **not in man that walketh to direct his steps.**

Joseph Smith explained the principle in verse 23, above. He taught (bold added for emphasis):

"It has been the design of Jehovah, from the commencement of the world, and is His purpose now, to regulate the affairs of the world in His own time, to stand as a head of the universe, and take the reins of government in His own hand. When that is done, judgment will be administered in righteousness; anarchy and confusion will be destroyed, and 'nations will learn war no more.' It is for want of this great governing principle, that all this confusion has existed; 'for it is not in man that walketh, to direct his steps;' this we have fully shown" (Teachings of the Prophet Joseph Smith, pages 250–51).

In verse 24, next, Jeremiah humbly requests that the Lord correct him as needed. This attitude is described by the word "contrite." It appears that what Jeremiah has seen in vision by way of the coming punishments that will come upon Jerusalem has caused him to be a bit concerned about the anger of the Lord. Thus, he asks that he not be punished in anger. We know that the Lord does not punish righteous people in anger, but it may be that Jeremiah is still learning.

24 **O LORD, correct me, but with judgment** [*justice; fairness*]; **not in thine anger,** lest thou bring me to nothing [*perhaps meaning "for fear that Thou destroy me too"*].

The enemies of Israel and Judah were cruel and wicked people themselves. In verse 25, next, Jeremiah invites the Lord to exercise punishment upon them too.

25 **Pour out thy fury upon the heathen** [*referring to the enemies of Israel, in this context*] that know thee not, and upon the families that call not on thy name: for **they**

NOTES

have eaten up Jacob [*they have destroyed the house of Israel*], and devoured him, and consumed him, **and have made his habitation desolate.**

JEREMIAH 11

<u>**Selection: all verses**</u>

In this chapter we see emphasis on the fact that, anciently, Israel was chosen to be the Lord's covenant people, but they rejected Him and the covenant. Remember, the covenant involved being blessed themselves with the blessings of potential exaltation, and the responsibility of taking the priesthood and the blessings of the gospel to all people (Abraham 2:9–11).

As we begin, the people of Judah are reminded that they and their ancestors rejected the covenant through their wickedness. (Remember that the people of Judah, which includes part of the small tribe of Benjamin, are all that remain of the Israelites, as a group in the Holy Land, since the ten tribes were conquered and carried away captive about one hundred years ago at this point of Jeremiah's prophesying.)

1 **THE word that came to Jeremiah from the LORD, saying,**

2 Hear ye the words of this covenant, and **speak unto the men of Judah**, and to the inhabitants of Jerusalem;

3 And say thou unto them, Thus saith the LORD God of Israel; **Cursed** [*stopped in progression*] ***be* the man that obeyeth not the words of this covenant,**

The covenant (known to us as the Abrahamic covenant) is briefly described in verses 4–5, next.

4 Which I commanded your fathers [*ancestors*] in the day *that* I brought them forth out of the land of Egypt, from the iron furnace [*symbolic of affliction*], saying, **Obey my voice**, and do them [*keep the commandments—see verse 3, above*], according to all which I command you: **so shall ye be my people, and I will be your God:**

5 **That I may perform the oath** [*in other words, as you obey the commandments, you enable the Lord to keep His part of the bargain—compare with D&C 82:10*] which I have sworn [*promised*] unto your fathers, **to give them a land flowing with milk and honey** [*symbolic of prosperity on earth and eventual celestial exaltation*], as *it is* this day. **Then answered I** [*the children of Israel answered—compare with Deuteronomy 26:17; Exodus 6:7*], and said, **So be it, O LORD.**

We see yet another invitation to the wicked people of Judah to repent and renew their covenant, delivered through Jeremiah by the Lord, in verse 6, next.

6 Then the LORD said unto me, Proclaim all these words in the cities of Judah, and in the streets of Jerusalem, saying, **Hear ye the words of this covenant, and do them.**

Verse 7, next, reminds us that the Lord had given these rebellious Israelites many, many chances to repent and return to Him.

7 For **I earnestly protested** [*witnessed—see footnote 7a in your Bible*] **unto your fathers** [*ancestors*] in the day *that* I brought them up out of the land of Egypt, *even* **unto this day**, rising early and protesting, **saying, Obey my voice**.

8 **Yet they obeyed not**, nor inclined their ear, **but walked every one in the imagination of their evil heart**: therefore **I will bring upon them all the words of this covenant** [*they will be held accountable for breaking this covenant*], which I commanded *them* to do; but they did *them* not.

9 And the LORD said unto me [*Jeremiah*], **A conspiracy** [*deliberate disobedience*] **is found among the men of Judah**, and among the inhabitants of Jerusalem.

10 **They are turned back to the iniquities of their forefathers**, which refused to hear my words; and they **went after other gods** to serve them: **the house of Israel and the house of Judah have broken my covenant** which I made with their fathers.

11 ¶ **Therefore** thus saith the LORD, Behold, **I will bring evil upon them**, which they shall not be able to escape; and **though they shall cry unto me, I will not hearken unto them** [*it will get to the point that it is too late to be saved by the Lord from their enemies*].

12 **Then shall the cities of Judah and inhabitants of Jerusalem** go, and **cry unto the gods** [*their idols*] unto whom they offer incense: **but they shall not save them at all** in the time of their trouble.

Next, we see that Jewish society of the day was completely riddled with idolatry. They had idols for every city, with altars to them in every street. Baal was worshiped everywhere. Remember that Baal worship involved sexual immorality with temple prostitutes. Sexual immorality destroys societies as well as individuals.

13 For *according to* **the number of thy cities were thy gods**, O Judah; and *according to* **the number of the streets of Jerusalem have ye set up altars** to *that* shameful thing, *even* altars to burn incense unto Baal.

The hopelessness of Judah's situation is again symbolized by the Lord's requesting that Jeremiah no longer pray for these people.

14 **Therefore pray not thou for this people**, neither lift up a cry or prayer for them: for I will not hear *them* in the time that they cry unto me for their trouble.

15 **What hath my beloved to do in mine house** [*in effect, what is Judah thinking?*], *seeing* **she hath wrought lewdness** [*adultery*] **with many** [*in other words, has stepped out on God with spiritually illicit relationships with many false gods, as well as literal adultery*], and the holy flesh [*righteous, acceptable sacrifices—see footnote 15a in your Bible*] is passed from thee? **when thou doest evil, then thou rejoicest**.

Verses 16–17, next, remind us of the allegory of the tame and wild olive trees, taught by Zenos and quoted by Jacob in the Book of Mormon, in Jacob, chapter 5. We wonder in fact if Zenos lived before Jeremiah and these verses are a reference to his writings. We don't know the answer, but the question is interesting.

NOTES

We will continue by giving one possible interpretation of verses 16–17, next.

16 The LORD called thy name, **A green olive tree, fair, *and* of goodly fruit** [*Judah is compared to an olive tree that once produced good people*]: **with the noise of a great tumult** [*with the coming destruction at the hands of the Babylonians*] **he** [*the Lord*] **hath kindled fire upon it** [*has destroyed Judah*], **and the branches of it are broken** [*the Jews are broken and scattered*].

17 For the LORD of hosts, **that planted thee** [*who established you as part of covenant Israel*], **hath pronounced evil against thee** [*the punishments of God are upon you*], **for** [*because of*] **the evil of the house of Israel and of the house of Judah**, which **they have done against themselves** to provoke me to anger in offering incense unto Baal [*they have brought great evil upon themselves because of their apostasy*].

Did you notice, in verse 17, above, that when we sin against God, we sin against ourselves?

Major Message

(Verse 17)

When we sin against God, we sin against ourselves.

Next, Jeremiah reports to us that the men of his hometown, Anathoth, hatched a plot to kill him. He was unaware of it until the Lord revealed it to him.

18 ¶ And the LORD hath given me knowledge *of it,* and I know *it:* **then thou shewedst me their doings** [*the plot devised by the men of Anathoth—see verse 21*].

19 But **I** *was* **like a lamb** *or* **an ox** *that* **is brought to the slaughter**; and **I knew not that they had devised devices against me**, *saying,* Let us destroy the tree with the fruit thereof, and let us cut him off from the land of the living, that his name may be no more remembered.

20 But, O LORD of hosts, that judgest righteously, that triest the reins [*kidneys; symbolic, in Jewish culture of the day, of the deepest thoughts and feelings*] and the heart, let me see thy vengeance on them: for unto thee have I revealed my cause.

Verse 21, next, tells us that the men of Jeremiah's hometown threatened to kill him if he did not stop prophesying.

21 Therefore thus saith the LORD of **the men of Anathoth**, that seek thy life, **saying, Prophesy not in the name of the LORD, that thou die not by our hand**:

22 Therefore **thus saith the LORD** of hosts, Behold, **I will punish them**: the young men shall die by the sword; their sons and their daughters shall die by famine:

23 And **there shall be no remnant of them** [*they will be wiped out*]: for **I will bring evil** [*punishment*] **upon the men of Anathoth**, *even* the year of their visitation [*the day of their punishment will come*].

JEREMIAH 12

Selection: all verses

In this chapter, Jeremiah asks a question that many people would like to hear the Lord's answer to. It is important to understand correct doctrine on this matter. The question is, in effect, why do the wicked prosper and the righteous suffer? (The same question is asked in Habakkuk, chapter 1, and answered in Habakkuk 2:1–4.)

We appreciate that Jeremiah's relationship with the Savior was such that he could be open about his concerns on this issue. In the heading to chapter 12, in your Latter-day Saint Bible, you will note that the wording is "Jeremiah complains of the prosperity of the wicked." Let's dive right in and see how the Lord responds to his concerns about fairness.

1 **RIGHTEOUS** *art* **thou, O LORD**, when I plead with thee: **yet let me talk with thee of** *thy* **judgments** [*in effect, "I have a concern about how You are running things*]: **Wherefore** [*why*] **doth the way of the wicked prosper** [*why do the wicked prosper*]? *wherefore* **are all they happy that deal very treacherously** [*why are the wicked so happy*]?

2 **Thou hast planted them** [*You established them in this land*], yea, they have taken root: they grow, yea, **they bring forth fruit** [*they prosper*]: **thou** *art* **near in their mouth** [*they do lip service to You*], **and far from their reins** [*but You are far from their inner thoughts and desires*].

3 **But thou, O LORD, knowest me**: thou hast seen me, and tried [*tested*] mine heart toward thee: pull them out like sheep for the slaughter, and prepare them for the day of slaughter [*a prophecy of coming destruction for the wicked in Judah*].

In verse 4, next, and also in verse 11, below, Jeremiah's concerns remind us of Enoch's witness of the earth's mourning because of the suffering she goes through due to the wickedness upon her.

Moses 7:48

48 And it came to pass that Enoch looked upon the earth; and he heard a voice from the bowels thereof, saying: Wo, wo is me, the mother of men; I am pained, I am weary, because of the wickedness of my children. When shall I rest, and be cleansed from the filthiness which is gone forth out of me? When will my Creator sanctify me, that I may rest, and righteousness for a season abide upon my face?

4 **How long shall the land mourn**, and the herbs of every field wither [*because of famine sent to punish the wicked*], **for** [*because of*] **the wickedness of them that dwell therein?** the beasts are consumed, and the birds; **because they said, He shall not see our last end** [*because the wicked say that God will not punish and destroy them*].

In verses 5–17, the Lord answers Jeremiah's question as to why the wicked seem to prosper. In effect, He says that punishment will come upon the wicked, in the Lord's due time. He also reminds Jeremiah that He does know what is going on.

5 ¶ **If thou hast run with the footmen, and they have wearied thee, then how canst thou contend with horses** [*perhaps saying to Jeremiah that he is getting in a bit over his head in wondering if the Lord is slipping up where the wicked are concerned*]? and *if* **in the land of peace,** *wherein* **thou trustedst,** *they wearied thee,* **then how wilt**

thou do in the swelling of Jordan [*perhaps saying, in effect, to Jeremiah that if he is having trouble while peace is still upon the land, how will he handle it when the flood of enemies takes over the land*]?

6 For **even thy brethren, and the house of thy father** [*the members of your own family*], even they **have dealt treacherously with thee**; yea, **they have called a multitude after thee** [*it sounds like a mob came after Jeremiah*]: **believe them not**, though they speak fair words unto thee [*even though they try to convince you that you are in no danger from them*].

Next, it appears that the Lord is saying that Jeremiah is not the only one who has been deserted by his family. The Lord's people have likewise deserted Him, causing Him not to be able to bless them.

7 ¶ I have forsaken mine house, I have left mine heritage; **I have given the dearly beloved of my soul into the hand of her enemies.**

8 **Mine heritage** [*My people*] is unto me as a lion in the forest; it **crieth out against me** [*they cry loudly, like the roar of a lion, against Me*]: **therefore have I hated it** [*I could no longer bless them*].

When you see the phrase "the Lord hated them," or something to that effect in the scriptures, it often means "He could no longer bless them," rather than that He literally hates them.

Have you ever seen birds, for example, baby chicks, peck at one that is odd or wounded, until they kill it? This seems to be the imagery used in verse 9, next, where the "speckled bird" (Judah, which should be different than other people because she is the covenant people of the Lord) is attacked by other birds (enemies).

9 **Mine heritage** [*the Jews and the land of Judah*] *is* unto me *as* **a speckled bird**, the **birds round about** *are* **against her**; come ye, assemble all the beasts of the field [*symbolic of the armies of Babylon—see footnote 9a in your Bible*], **come to devour**.

Verse 10, next, points out the damage done to a society by false political and religious leaders.

10 **Many pastors have destroyed my vineyard**, they have trodden my portion under foot, they have **made my pleasant portion** [*Jerusalem and the land of Judah*] **a desolate wilderness.**

11 They have made it desolate, *and being* desolate **it mourneth unto me**; the whole land is made desolate, because no man layeth *it* to heart [*no one pays attention—see footnote 11a in your Bible*].

12 The spoilers [*enemies*] are come upon all high places through the wilderness: for **the sword of the LORD shall devour from the *one* end of the land even to the *other* end** of the land: no flesh shall have peace.

13 They have sown wheat, but shall reap thorns [*they will harvest disappointment*]: they have put themselves to pain [*they work hard to be wicked*], *but* shall not profit: and they

shall be ashamed of your revenues [*they will be put to shame because of the products of their wickedness*] because of the fierce anger of the LORD [*the law of justice*].

Next, in verses 14–17, we see a prophecy that the gospel will eventually be taught to all people, including the nations who attack the Lord's people. This reminds us that all people will have a completely fair chance to be taught the gospel, understand it, and accept it or reject it, before the day of final judgment.

14 ¶ Thus saith the LORD against all mine evil neighbours [*all enemies of the Lord's covenant people*], that touch the inheritance which I have caused my people Israel to inherit; Behold, I will pluck them out of their land, and pluck out the house of Judah from among them [*the gathering of the Jews*].

15 And it shall come to pass, after that I have plucked them out **I will return, and have compassion on them**, and will bring them again, every man to his heritage, and every man to his land.

16 **And it shall come to pass** [*a prophecy*], **if they** [*all people in the world*] **will diligently learn the ways of my people** [*will learn the gospel of Jesus Christ*], to **swear by my name** [*make covenants with God*], The LORD liveth; as they taught my people to swear by Baal [*in place of the counterfeit covenants of false philosophies and false religions*]; **then shall they be built in the midst of my people** [*then they too will become the Lord's chosen people*].

17 **But if they will not obey, I will utterly pluck up and destroy that nation**, saith the LORD.

JEREMIAH 13

Selection: all verses

Have you noticed by now that the same basic messages are being repeated over and over in these chapters of Jeremiah? One of the benefits of studying some chapters in considerable detail is that it prepares you to understand the basic messages in other chapters, even though you may not understand all the details.

One of my friends recently observed that although he did not understand everything he was listening to in Isaiah (on a portable recorder while walking), he discovered that he understood far more than he anticipated, just by paying attention to the main messages and words of the Lord and thinking how they might apply to him and the world today. This approach can be of great help to all of us as we study the writings of Old Testament prophets.

In this chapter, Israel and Judah are compared to a linen girdle or sash (verse 1) which is hidden or buried in a crevice of some rocks and later dug up (verse 7). Through this treatment, it becomes useless. We don't know if what the Lord commanded Jeremiah to do here, with respect to the linen sash, is literal, or if it is symbolic, a type of parable. Either way, the lesson is the same: Israel and Judah have become so marred by "hiding" from the Lord that they have basically become of no use as the covenant people.

1 THUS saith the LORD unto me [*Jeremiah*], **Go and get thee a linen girdle, and put it upon thy loins** [*put it around your waist*], and put it not in water.

2 **So I got a girdle** according to the word of the LORD, **and put** *it* **on my loins.**

NOTES

3 And the word of the LORD came unto me the second time, saying,

4 **Take the girdle** that thou hast got, which *is* upon thy loins, **and arise, go to Euphrates, and hide it there in a hole of the rock**.

It may be that "Euphrates," in verse 4, above, symbolizes Babylon, since a river by that name flows through that country. If so, this could symbolize the Babylonian captivity of Judah, which is just around the corner at this time in the history of the Jews.

5 **So I went, and hid it by Euphrates**, as the LORD commanded me.

6 And it came to pass **after many days**, that **the LORD said** unto me, Arise, **go to Euphrates, and take the girdle from thence**, which I commanded thee to hide there.

7 Then **I went to Euphrates, and digged, and took the girdle from the place where I had hid it**: and, **behold, the girdle was marred, it was profitable for nothing** [*it was ruined, good for nothing*].

8 Then the word of the LORD came unto me, saying,

The meaning of verses 1–7 is given in the next verses.

9 Thus saith the LORD, **After this manner will I mar the pride of Judah, and the great pride of Jerusalem**.

10 **This evil people**, which refuse to hear my words, which walk in the imagination of their heart [*pridefulness, stubbornness*], and walk after other gods, to serve them, and to worship them, **shall even be as this girdle, which is good for nothing**.

In verse 11, next, the Lord explains the symbolism. Just as a sash or girdle is wrapped around a man's waist, so also the house of Israel was invited to be the Lord's covenant people, and to "stick to Him" tightly, just as a girdle sticks tightly to the person wearing it. But when a girdle rots (see heading to this chapter in your Bible), it is of no use. Israel (the northern ten tribes in this context) and Judah (the tribes of Judah and Benjamin) could have been a glorious people, a credit to the Lord and to themselves, but they refused.

11 For **as the girdle cleaveth to the loins of a man, so have I caused to cleave unto me the whole house of Israel and the whole house of Judah**, saith the LORD; that they might be unto me for a people, and for a name, and for a praise, and for a glory: **but they would not hear**.

Verses 12–14, next, basically say that these people will become drunk with wickedness, in other words, out of control with wickedness, and will be destroyed.

12 ¶ Therefore thou shalt speak unto them this word; Thus saith the LORD God of Israel, Every bottle [*symbolic of every person in Jerusalem and the other cities of Judah*] shall be filled with wine: and they shall say unto thee, Do we not certainly know that every bottle shall be filled with wine?

13 Then shalt thou say unto them, Thus saith the LORD, Behold, **I will fill all the inhabitants of this land, even the kings that sit upon David's throne, and the priests** [*false priests*]**, and the prophets** [*false prophets*]**, and all the inhabitants of Jerusalem, with drunkenness.**

14 **And I will dash them one against another**, even the fathers and the sons together, saith the LORD: I will not pity, nor spare, nor have mercy, but **destroy them**.

Next, the Lord issues yet another invitation to these people to repent, before it is too late and destruction comes upon them.

15 ¶ **Hear ye**, and give ear; **be not proud**: for the LORD hath spoken.

16 **Give glory to the LORD your God**, before he cause darkness, and before your feet stumble upon the dark mountains, and, while ye look for light, he turn it into the shadow of death, *and* make *it* gross darkness.

17 **But if ye will not hear it, my soul shall weep** in secret places **for** *your* **pride; and mine eye shall weep sore, and run down with tears, because the LORD's flock is carried away captive**.

18 Say unto the king and to the queen, **Humble yourselves**, sit down: for your principalities shall come down, *even* the crown of your glory [*if you don't repent*].

19 The cities of the south shall be shut up, and none shall open *them:* **Judah shall be carried away captive all of it**, it shall be wholly carried away captive.

20 Lift up your eyes, and behold them [*the Babylonian armies*] that come from the north: where *is* the flock *that* was given thee, thy beautiful flock?

Verse 21, next, in effect asks the question "What will you have to say for yourselves, how will you explain your foolishness in ignoring the call from the Lord to repent, when all that is prophesied happens to you?"

21 **What wilt thou say when he shall punish thee?** for thou hast taught them *to be* captains, *and* as chief over thee: shall not sorrows take thee, as a woman in travail? [*In other words, unless you repent, the coming sorrows and destructions are as sure as the labor of a woman who is expecting a child.*]

22 ¶ And **if thou say in thine heart, Wherefore come these things upon me** [*why am I being punished*]**? For the** [*the answer is because of the*] **greatness of thine iniquity** are thy skirts discovered, *and* thy heels made bare [*you will be ravished and reduced to bondage*].

23 **Can the Ethiopian change his skin, or the leopard his spots?** *then* may ye also do **good, that are accustomed to do evil** [*in effect, if the impossible can happen, then people like you can do good who are completely caught up in wickedness*].

Next, we see another direct prophecy of the scattering of the Jews.

24 **Therefore** [*because of the above-mentioned wickedness*] **will I scatter them** as the stubble that passeth away by the wind of the wilderness.

25 **This** *is* **thy lot** [*this is what you have coming*], the portion of thy measures from me, saith the LORD; **because thou hast forgotten me, and trusted in falsehood.**

26 Therefore will **I discover thy skirts upon thy face** [*I will pull your skirts up over your face*], **that thy shame may appear** [*in effect, your protection, your false façade will be taken off and your sins will be exposed for all to see*].

Verse 27, next, contains a very brief summary of the sins of Judah, which will lead to Babylonian captivity. They are already spiritually in bondage to the devil.

27 I have seen thine **adulteries**, and thy **neighings** [*chasing after other men's wives— see Jeremiah 5:8*], the **lewdness** of thy **whoredom**, *and* thine **abominations on the hills** [*symbolic of idol worship*] in the fields. **Woe unto thee, O Jerusalem!** wilt thou not be made clean? **when** *shall it* **once be** [*when will the day finally come*]?

JEREMIAH 14

Selection: all verses

This chapter deals with a devastating drought that will come to the Jerusalem area. Verses 1–6 describe how serious the drought will be and the famine that will ensue.

1 THE word of the LORD that came to Jeremiah **concerning the dearth** [*famine*].

2 **Judah mourneth**, and the gates thereof languish [*are wasting away*]; they are black [*dejected, discouraged*] unto the ground; and the cry of Jerusalem is gone up [*their desperate cry is heard everywhere*].

3 And their nobles have sent their little ones to the waters: they came to the pits [*wells*], *and* **found no water**; they returned with their **vessels empty**; they were ashamed [*dismayed*] and confounded [*in deep despair*], and covered their heads.

4 Because **the ground is chapt** [*cracked, parched*], for there was **no rain** in the earth, the plowmen were ashamed [*dismayed, desperate to know what to do*], they covered their heads.

5 Yea, **the hind** [*deer*] also **calved** [*had its baby*] in the field, **and forsook** *it* [*deserted its newborn fawn*], because there was **no grass.**

6 And the wild asses did stand in the high places, they snuffed up the wind [*pant*] like dragons [*jackals; wild dogs*]; their eyes did fail, because *there was* **no grass.**

In the next several verses, Jeremiah prays for his people, but is told that the Lord cannot answer his prayers because of the wickedness of Judah. In verse 7, it appears that Jeremiah humbly includes himself with his people.

7 ¶ **O LORD, though our iniquities testify against us, do thou** *it* [*please turn Thy wrath aside*] **for thy name's sake** [*for the sake of Your reputation as a merciful God*]: **for our backslidings are many; we have sinned against thee.**

8 O the **hope of Israel** [*another name for the Savior*], the **saviour thereof in time of trouble**, why shouldest thou be as a stranger in the land [*must You be far from us in our time of need*], and as a wayfaring [*traveling*] man *that* turneth aside to tarry for a night?

9 **Why shouldest thou be** as a man astonied [*astonished, paralyzed with surprise, unable to act*], **as a mighty man** *that* **cannot save** [*why can't You show your power for us*]? yet thou, O LORD, *art* in the midst of us, and we are called by thy name; **leave us not.**

Next, the Lord answers the questions raised above and explains why He cannot help them while they are wicked with no intent to repent.

10 ¶ Thus saith the LORD unto this people, **Thus have they loved to wander** [*in sin*], **they have not refrained their feet** [*they have not stopped wandering in the paths of sin*], **therefore the LORD doth not accept them**; he will now remember their iniquity, and visit [*punish*] their sins.

11 **Then said the LORD** unto me [*Jeremiah*], **Pray not for this people** for *their* good.

12 When they fast, **I will not hear their cry**; and when they offer burnt offering and an oblation, **I will not accept them**: but **I will consume them** by the sword, and by the famine, and by the pestilence.

13 ¶ Then said I, Ah, Lord GOD! behold, **the prophets** [*the false prophets among the Jews*] **say unto them, Ye shall not see the sword, neither shall ye have famine**; but I will give you assured peace in this place [*in effect, the false prophets have told the people that sin is not really sin and that there can be peace in wickedness*].

Sometimes we think of false prophets, such as those in verse 13, above, as being various religious leaders gone astray. But we would do well to think of political leaders, media idols, philosophers, teachers, in fact any who lead us away from the teachings of the gospel of Jesus Christ, as being false prophets also.

In verse 14, next, the Savior delivers a stern rebuke against such false prophets.

14 Then the LORD said unto me, **The prophets prophesy lies in my name** [*in other words, there are many who teach falsehoods in the name of God*]: **I sent them not**, neither have I commanded them, neither spake unto them: **they prophesy unto you a false vision** and divination, and a thing of nought, **and the deceit of their heart** [*they teach the wicked thoughts and intents of their own hearts as the word of God*].

15 **Therefore thus saith the LORD concerning the prophets that prophesy in my name, and I sent them not** [*in other words, concerning false prophets*], yet they say, Sword and famine shall not be in this land; **By sword and famine shall those prophets be consumed.**

16 **And the people to whom they prophesy shall be cast out in the streets of Jerusalem because of the famine and the sword**; and they shall have none to bury them, them, their wives, nor their sons, nor their daughters: **for I will pour their wickedness upon them**.

In verses 17–18, we see that the Lord weeps when His people become wicked.

17 ¶ Therefore thou shalt say this word unto them; **Let mine eyes run down with tears night and day**, and let them not cease: **for the virgin daughter of my people** [*Jerusalem*] **is broken with a great breach** [*is conquered*], with a very grievous blow.

18 If I go forth into the field, then **behold the slain** with the sword! and if I enter into the city, then **behold them that are sick with famine!** yea, both the prophet and the priest [*false prophets and priests*] go about into a land that they know not [*will be taken captive into a foreign land*].

Next, Jeremiah asks heartrending questions. He has the ability to love the wicked even though he has been told that they will be destroyed because of their rejecting the Lord.

19 **Hast thou utterly rejected Judah?** hath thy soul lothed [*loathed*] Zion? why hast thou smitten us, and *there is* no healing for us? we looked for peace, and *there is* no good; and for the time of healing, and behold trouble!

20 **We acknowledge, O LORD, our wickedness**, *and* the iniquity of our fathers: for **we have sinned against thee**.

21 **Do not abhor** *us,* for thy name's sake, do not disgrace the throne of thy glory: remember, break not thy covenant with us.

22 **Are there** *any* **among the vanities** [*false gods*] **of the Gentiles that can cause rain?** or can the heavens give showers? **art not thou he, O LORD our God?** therefore we will wait upon thee: for thou hast made all these *things*.

JEREMIAH 15

Selection: all verses

This chapter gives more prophetic detail about the destruction and scattering of the Jews in Jeremiah's day. Because of their intentional rebellion, there is no stopping the coming famine and captivity.

First, in verse 1, the Lord tells Jeremiah that even if the great prophets Moses and Samuel asked Him to stop the coming destruction upon Judah, it would not happen. We are seeing the law of justice in action. One of the lessons we are taught here is that mercy cannot "rob justice" (see Alma 42:25).

Major Message

Mercy cannot rob justice

1 THEN said the LORD unto me, **Though Moses and Samuel stood before me,** *yet* **my mind** *could* **not** *be* **toward this people** [*in other words, He could not bless them*]: cast *them* out of my sight, and let them go forth [*they will be scattered*].

As mentioned several times already in this study guide, the "manner of speaking and prophesying among the Jews" is to repeat things many times for emphasis and to use words skillfully to paint pictures in our minds and create deep emotion in our hearts. We see this again in the next several verses.

2 And it shall come to pass, **if they say unto thee, Whither shall we go forth** [*if they ask you, "Where are we going"*]? then thou shalt **tell them**, Thus saith the LORD; Such as *are* for death, **to death**; and such as *are* for the sword, **to the sword**; and such as *are* for the famine, **to the famine**; and such as *are* for the captivity, **to the captivity**.

3 And I will appoint over them four kinds, saith the LORD: **the sword to slay**, and **the dogs to tear**, and **the fowls** [*carrion birds, such as vultures*] **of the heaven, and the beasts** of the earth, **to devour and destroy.**

4 And I will cause them to be **removed into all kingdoms of the earth** [*scattered to all nations of the earth*], because of Manasseh [*a very wicked king of Judah*] the son of Hezekiah king of Judah, for *that* which he did in Jerusalem.

5 For **who shall have pity upon thee, O Jerusalem?** or who shall bemoan thee? or who shall go aside to ask how thou doest?

6 **Thou hast forsaken me, saith the LORD**, thou art gone backward [*have gone away from the Lord*]: therefore will I stretch out my hand against thee, and destroy thee; **I am weary with repenting** [*since the Lord has no need to repent, this phrase is saying, in effect, I am tired of "relenting" and giving you chance after chance to repent; it doesn't do a bit of good*].

7 And **I will fan them with a fan** in the gates of the land [*I will scatter them, as a fan scatters chaff from wheat*]; I will bereave *them* of children [*they will lose their children*], **I will destroy my people,** *since* **they return not from their ways** [*since they refuse to repent*].

8 **Their widows are increased** to me above the sand of the seas [*there will be more widows than you can count*]: I have brought upon them against the mother of the young men **a spoiler at noonday** [*the enemy armies will be so powerful that they don't have to sneak up on you, rather, they can approach in broad daylight*]: I have caused *him* to fall upon it suddenly, and terrors upon the city.

9 She that hath borne seven languisheth [*grows weak*]: she hath given up the ghost [*has died*]; her sun is gone down while *it was* yet day [*all her hopes are suddenly dashed to pieces*]: she hath been ashamed and confounded [*confused and stopped*]: and the residue of them [*those who don't die of the famine*] will I deliver to the sword before their enemies, saith the LORD.

Next, Jeremiah laments the fact that he was born to be such a focal point of contention to the wicked. Even though he has lived righteously, everyone hates him.

10 ¶ **Woe is me**, my mother, that thou hast borne me **a man of strife and a man of contention to the whole earth!** I have neither lent on usury, nor men have lent to me on usury [*in effect, I have faithfully kept the laws of God*]; **yet** **every one of them** [*the wicked*] **doth curse me.**

NOTES

Verse 11, next, could have several fulfillments. It could refer to Jeremiah, or it could be a prophecy that many of the Jews who are captured and carried away will be treated such that they survive. It could also be a prophecy about the return of the Jews from Babylonian captivity, or all of the above.

If it refers to Jeremiah, then it can remind us of the words of the Lord to Joseph Smith when he was in Liberty Jail (D&C 121 and 122). He will eventually be delivered from his enemies. This can be literal on earth or literal in eternity.

If it refers to the Jews and their eventual return, then it prophesies that their captors will eventually take pity on them and allow them to return.

11 The LORD said, **Verily it shall be well with thy remnant**; verily I will cause the enemy to entreat thee *well* in the time of evil and in the time of affliction.

12 Shall iron break the northern iron and the steel?

The Martin Luther German Bible roughly translates verse 12, above, as saying, "Don't you know that such iron exists that can break iron and brass from the north?" Perhaps this could mean, in effect, that the Lord has power over the strong "iron hand" of nations (including Babylon who came from the north) who hold the Jews captive, and He can cause their captors to treat them well and eventually let them go free.

Verse 13, next, seems to refer to the Jews and be yet another reminder as to why many of them are to be slaughtered and the remainder carried away into captivity at this point of their history.

13 Thy substance and thy treasures will I give to the spoil without price, and *that* **for all thy sins**, even in all thy borders [*the whole nation of Judah is riddled with wickedness*].

Verse 14, next, tells Jeremiah that he too will be carried away captive into a foreign country. He was eventually taken by a group of Jews to Egypt as they escaped the conquerors of Jerusalem, and then, according to tradition, stoned to death by them. (See Bible Dictionary under "Jeremiah." It appears that Jeremiah is being reminded that the righteous also suffer when the wicked rule and incur the wrath of God [*compare with D&C 98:9*].)

14 And **I will make** *thee* **to pass with thine enemies into a land** *which* **thou knowest not**: for a fire is kindled in mine anger, *which* shall burn upon you.

Verse 15, next, reminds us of the words of the Prophet Joseph Smith in Liberty Jail, as he pled with the Lord. He said:

D&C 121:5

5 Let thine anger be kindled against our enemies; and, in the fury of thine heart, with thy sword **avenge us of our wrongs**.

15 ¶ O LORD, thou knowest: remember me, and visit [*bless*] me, and **revenge me of my persecutors**; take me not away in thy longsuffering: know that for thy sake I have suffered rebuke.

16 **Thy words were found** [*were given to me*], **and I did eat them** [*internalized them, made them a part of me*]; and **thy word was unto me the joy and rejoicing of mine heart**: for I am called by thy name, O LORD God of hosts.

17 **I sat not in the assembly of the mockers, nor rejoiced** [*I did not join in wickedness and take pleasure in it with the wicked*]; **I sat alone** because of thy hand: for thou hast filled me with indignation [*against sin and wickedness*].

18 **Why is my pain perpetual, and my wound incurable**, *which* refuseth to be healed? wilt thou be altogether unto me as a liar, *and as* waters *that* fail [*perhaps meaning, in effect, "Are You not going to keep Your word? Why aren't Your promises of peace and protection and help fulfilled?"*]? [*Perhaps similar to Joseph Smith's pleading— see Doctrine and Covenants 121:1–6.*]

The Lord responds to Jeremiah's pleading.

19 ¶ Therefore thus saith the LORD, If thou return, then will I bring thee again, *and* **thou shalt stand before me**: and if thou take forth the precious from the vile, **thou shalt be as my mouth**: let them return unto thee; but return not thou unto them [*perhaps meaning for Jeremiah to stand firm, and if the people want the word of the Lord, let them come to him*].

The Lord's word to Jeremiah, in verses 20–21, next, seems to be that of being saved spiritually rather than physically. Spiritual salvation is the only thing that counts in the perspective of eternity.

20 And I will make thee unto this people a fenced brasen wall [*a fortified wall of brass or bronze*]: and **they shall fight against thee, but they shall not prevail against thee**: for I *am* with thee to save thee and to deliver thee, saith the LORD.

21 And **I will deliver thee out of the hand of the wicked, and I will redeem thee out of the hand of the terrible**.

JEREMIAH 16

Selection: all verses

This chapter contains a prophecy that is quite often referred to in our lessons and talks on missionary work in the last days. It is verse 16. We will say more about it when we get there.

Verse 2, if taken literally, would mean that Jeremiah was told not to marry. As we proceed, we will take the viewpoint that this was symbolic, rather than literal. One possible message is that Jerusalem has become so polluted with wickedness that it is no longer a safe place to attempt to raise children. Another possible message is that the coming enemy armies from Babylon will show no mercy to the inhabitants, including children.

1 THE word of the LORD came also unto me, saying,

2 **Thou shalt not take thee a wife, neither shalt thou have sons or daughters in this place.**

We will quote from the *Old Testament Student Manual* for help with verse 2, above (**bold** added for emphasis):

"Jeremiah's day was a sad one for Judah. To symbolize that truth, the Lord told his prophet three things that he was not to do:

"1. He was not to marry or father children (see Jeremiah 16:2). So universal was the calamity bearing down upon the people that God did not want children to suffer its outrage. **This commandment,** however, like the one to Hosea (see Hosea 10), who was commanded to take a wife of whoredoms, **was probably not a literal one; rather, it probably was allegorical, that is, Jeremiah was not to expect that his people would marry themselves to the covenant again, nor was he to expect to get spiritual children (converts) from his ministry.**

"2. He was not to lament those in Judah who died by the sword or famine (see Jeremiah 16:5), since they brought these judgments upon themselves.

"3. He was not to feast or eat with friends in Jerusalem (see verse 8), since feasting was a sign of celebration and eating together a symbol of fellowship.

"In addition, Jeremiah was commanded to explain very clearly to the people the reasons for his actions as well as the reasons for their coming punishment" (Old Testament Student Manual, page 241).

3 For thus saith the LORD **concerning the sons and concerning the daughters that are born in this place**, and concerning their mothers that bare them, and concerning their fathers that begat them in this land;

4 **They shall die of grievous deaths**; they shall not be lamented; **neither shall they be buried**; *but* they shall be as dung upon the face of the earth: and they shall be **consumed by the sword**, and by **famine**; and their carcases shall be **meat for the fowls of heaven, and for the beasts of the earth**.

Verse 5, next, is another reminder that if people do not repent, the law of mercy cannot take over from the law of justice.

5 For thus saith the LORD, Enter not into the house of mourning, neither go to lament nor bemoan them: for **I have taken away my peace from this people, saith the LORD,** *even* **lovingkindness and mercies**.

6 Both **the great** [*the famous and prominent in their society*] **and the small shall die in this land**: they shall **not be buried** [*implying a terrible slaughter*], neither shall *men* lament for them, **nor cut themselves, nor make themselves bald for them** [*signs of deep mourning and grief in their culture*]:

Verses 6 and 7, here, seem to indicate that everyone will be in such distress because of their own circumstances that they will not take time nor have inclination to mourn for others being ravished by the famines and conquering enemy armies.

7 Neither shall *men* tear *themselves* for them in mourning, to comfort them for the dead [*no one will comfort those who mourn*]; neither shall *men* give them the cup of consolation to drink for their father or for their mother.

NOTES

8 Thou shalt not also go into the house of feasting, to sit with them to eat and to drink.

In verse 9, next, Jeremiah is told that these terrible devastations will come upon the Jews in his lifetime.

9 For thus saith the LORD of hosts, the God of Israel; Behold, I will cause to cease out of this place in your eyes, and **in your days**, the voice of mirth, and the voice of gladness, the voice of the bridegroom, and the voice of the bride.

Verse 10, next, warns Jeremiah that the wicked people against whom he preaches will act as if they are righteous and do not deserve such warnings and condemnation.

10 ¶ And it shall come to pass, when thou shalt shew this people all these words, and they shall say unto thee, **Wherefore** [*why*] **hath the LORD pronounced all this great evil against us?** or **what** *is* **our iniquity** [*what have we done wrong*]? or what *is* our sin that we have committed against the LORD our God?

11 **Then shalt thou say** unto them, **Because your fathers** [*parents; ancestors*] **have forsaken me**, saith the LORD, and have walked after other gods, and have served them, and have worshipped them, and have forsaken me, **and have not kept my law**;

12 **And ye have done worse than your fathers**; for, behold, ye walk every one after the imagination of his evil heart, that they may not hearken unto me:

13 **Therefore will I cast you out of this land** into a land that ye know not, *neither* ye nor your fathers; and there shall ye serve other gods day and night; where I will not shew you favour [*I will not be able to bless you with the choicest gospel blessings*].

Next, we see a major prophecy concerning the gathering of Israel in the last days. The prophecy includes the fact that the deliverance of the children of Israel from Egypt, by the Lord, will no longer be the most spectacular event spoken of among the people. Rather, the gathering of Israel from all nations will become the focus of effort and conversation.

Major Prophecy

The Lord will gather scattered Israel in the last days.

14 ¶ Therefore, behold, **the days come, saith the LORD, that it shall no more be said, The LORD liveth, that brought up the children of Israel out of the land of Egypt**;

15 **But, The LORD liveth, that brought up the children of Israel** from the land of the north, and **from all the lands whither he had driven them**: and I will bring them again into their land that I gave unto their fathers.

Notice the order of the missionary work in the last days, as given in verse 16, next. First, large numbers of converts will come into the Church, in various nations. This is represented by "fishers" who fish with nets and catch large numbers with them. These mass conversions are followed by missionaries who are depicted as "hunters" who search the once-fertile mission field for anyone else who will join the Church.

_____
_____
_____
_____
_____
_____
_____
_____
_____
_____
_____
_____
_____
_____
_____
_____
_____
_____
_____
_____
_____
_____
_____
_____
_____
_____
_____
_____
_____
_____
_____

16 ¶ Behold, **I will send for many fishers**, saith the LORD, and **they shall fish them**; and **after will I send for many hunters**, and they shall hunt them [*converts*] **from every mountain**, and from every **hill**, and out of the **holes of the rocks**.

One example of "fishers," in verse 16, above, might be Wilford Woodruff and other early missionaries who baptized thousands of converts in England in the early days of the Church. Another example could be the missionary work in South America in our day, where tens of thousands of converts are being baptized. Yet other examples might be found in any one of several countries or areas, including Africa, where initial missionary efforts have resulted in abundant baptisms in our day.

Now, though, in some areas of the world, convert baptisms are very few in number. The missionaries serving in such areas might be considered to be the "hunters," prophesied of by Jeremiah, who search everywhere for just a few who are willing to be taught the gospel.

Next, the topic turns to the fact that the Lord sees all, including the supposedly "secret" doings of the wicked.

17 For **mine eyes *are* upon all their ways: they are not hid from my face**, neither is their iniquity hid from mine eyes.

18 **And first** [*before the great latter-day gathering*] **I will recompense** [*punish*] **their iniquity** and their sin double; because they have defiled my land [*polluted it with wickedness*], they have filled mine inheritance with the carcases of their detestable and abominable things [*such as idol worship*].

Next, in verse 19, we see a prophecy that Gentiles from all nations will join the Church also in the last days.

19 O LORD, my strength, and my fortress, and my refuge in the day of affliction, **the Gentiles shall come unto thee from the ends of the earth**, and **shall say, Surely our fathers have inherited lies, vanity, and *things* wherein *there is* no profit** [*these converts will discard the false traditions and beliefs of their parents and ancestors in order to join the Church*].

Verse 20, next, is yet another reminder that it is completely ridiculous to make idols with one's own hands, and then worship them.

20 **Shall a man make gods unto himself, and they *are* no gods?**

The Lord says, in verse 21, next, that through the coming punishments, the wicked will know once and for all that there is just one true God.

21 Therefore, behold, **I will this once cause them to know**, I will cause them to know mine hand and my might; and they shall know **that my name *is* The LORD** [*that I am the only true God, in other words, that their idols are not gods*].

JEREMIAH 17

Selection: all verses

This chapter continues emphasizing the sins that will lead to the destruction of Jerusalem and the cities of Judah as a nation in Jeremiah's day. Among other things, we are shown comparison and contrast between the lives of the wicked and the righteous.

First, in verse 1, we are told that they are hardened sinners, and that the deepest desire of their hearts is to be wicked.

1 **THE sin of Judah** *is* **written with a pen of iron,** *and* **with the point of a diamond** [*the fact that they are deeply wicked is irrefutable*]: *it is* **graven upon the table of their heart** [*the innermost desire of their heart is to be wicked*], **and upon the horns of your altars** [*their religions are dedicated to wickedness, rather than protection and blessings from the Lord*];

The "horns of the altar," mentioned in verse 1, above, served as a place of protection and refuge for anyone who was being pursued by another. If they could get to the altar, and grab hold of one of the horns built on the four corners of it, they were safe from their enemy (see 1 Kings 1:50).

2 Whilst their children remember their altars and their groves by the green trees upon the high hills [*the children have been led astray by their idol-worshiping parents*].

Verse 3, next, says, in effect, that everything the people of Judah treasure in their wicked hearts will be given to their enemies.

3 O my mountain in the field, **I will give thy substance** *and* **all thy treasures to the spoil** [*to your enemies*], *and* thy high places for sin, throughout all thy borders.

4 And **thou,** even thyself, **shalt discontinue from thine heritage that I gave thee** [*you will be taken from the Holy Land*]; and **I will cause thee to serve thine enemies in the land which thou knowest not**: for ye have kindled a fire in mine anger, *which* shall burn for ever.

5 ¶ Thus saith the LORD; **Cursed** *be* **the man that trusteth in man, and maketh flesh his arm, and whose heart departeth from the LORD.**

6 For **he shall be like the heath** [*juniper tree—see footnote 6a in your Bible*] **in the desert**, and shall not see when good cometh; but **shall inhabit the parched places in the wilderness**, *in* a salt land and not inhabited.

The "wilderness," spoken of in verse 6, above, is obviously literal, representing their trials in the land of Babylon. But it can also be symbolic of their apostasy, living in a "spiritual wilderness" without the gospel of Jesus Christ.

Verses 7–8, next, are a beautiful representation of the blessings of living the true gospel, in contrast to the devastations of apostasy depicted above.

7 **Blessed** *is* **the man that trusteth in the LORD, and whose hope the LORD is.**

NOTES

8 **For he shall be as a tree planted by the waters, and** *that* **spreadeth out her roots by the river, and shall not see when heat cometh, but her leaf shall be green; and shall not be careful in the year of drought, neither shall cease from yielding fruit.**

Verse 9, next, is a reminder of how devastating a heart that is filled with wicked desires can be. A question is asked and an answer is given.

Question

9 ¶ The heart *is* deceitful above all *things,* and desperately wicked: **who can know it** [*who can tell what is in it*]?

Answer

10 I the LORD search the heart, *I* try the reins [*the innermost thoughts and feelings*], even to give every man according to his ways, *and* according to the fruit of his doings.

11 As the partridge sitteth *on eggs,* and hatcheth *them* not; *so* he that getteth riches, and not by right [*dishonestly*], shall leave them in the midst of his days, and at his end shall be a fool.

Next, Jeremiah praises the Lord.

12 ¶ **A glorious high throne from the beginning** *is* **the place of our sanctuary** [*the Lord is above all and is the only safe refuge*].

13 O LORD, the hope of Israel, **all that forsake thee shall be ashamed** [*will come up empty; will be disappointed, put to shame*], *and* they that depart from me shall be written in the earth, **because they have forsaken the LORD, the fountain of living waters.**

14 **Heal me, O LORD, and I shall be healed; save me, and I shall be saved: for thou** *art* **my praise.**

In verses 15–18, next, Jeremiah stands firm and faithful before the Lord, and prays for protection from his enemies.

15 ¶ Behold, **they** [*Jeremiah's enemies*] **say unto me, Where** *is* **the word of the LORD** [*where are all the destructions you have prophesied*]? **let it come now.**

16 As for me, **I have not hastened from** *being* **a pastor** to follow thee [*I have been faithful to my calling*]: neither have I desired the woeful day [*the coming destruction*]; **thou knowest: that which came out of my lips was** *right* **before thee.**

17 **Be not a terror unto me: thou** *art* **my hope in the day of evil.**

18 Let them be confounded that persecute me, but let not me be confounded: let them be dismayed, but let not me be dismayed: bring upon them the day of evil, and destroy them with double destruction.

Next, in verses 19–22, we are reminded of the importance of keeping the Sabbath holy.

Major Message

Keep the Sabbath Day holy.

19 ¶ Thus said the LORD unto me; **Go and stand in the gate** [*entrance*] of the children of the people, whereby the kings of Judah come in, and by the which they go out, and in **all the gates of Jerusalem** [*in other words, chose locations where everyone can hear your message*];

20 And say unto them, **Hear ye the word of the LORD**, ye kings of Judah, and all Judah, and **all the inhabitants of Jerusalem**, that enter in by these gates:

21 Thus saith the LORD; Take heed to yourselves, and **bear no burden on the sabbath day**, nor bring *it* in by the gates of Jerusalem;

22 Neither carry forth a burden out of your houses on the sabbath day, **neither do ye any work, but hallow ye the sabbath day**, as I commanded your fathers.

The reaction of the people to Jeremiah's message about the Sabbath is given in verse 23, next.

23 **But they obeyed not**, neither inclined their ear [*wouldn't listen*], but made their neck stiff [*they were full of pride, not humble enough to be taught*], that they might not hear, nor receive instruction.

Verses 24–26 explain the great blessings which could have come to these people, had they listened and repented.

24 And it shall come to pass, **if ye diligently hearken unto me, saith the LORD**, to bring in no burden through the gates of this city on the sabbath day, but **hallow the sabbath day, to do no work therein**;

25 Then shall there enter into the gates of this city kings and princes sitting upon the throne of David, riding in chariots and on horses, they, and their princes, the men of Judah, and the inhabitants of Jerusalem: and **this city shall remain for ever** [*in other words, great prosperity, protection and peace will be yours*].

26 **And they shall come** from the cities of Judah, and from the places about Jerusalem, and from the land of Benjamin, and from the plain, and from the mountains, and from the south, **bringing burnt offerings, and sacrifices, and meat offerings, and incense, and bringing sacrifices of praise, unto the house of the LORD.**

NOTES

27 **But if ye will not hearken unto me to hallow the sabbath day**, and not to bear a burden, even entering in at the gates of Jerusalem on the sabbath day; **then will I kindle a fire in the gates thereof, and it shall devour the palaces of Jerusalem, and it shall not be quenched**.

Did you see the message in the above verses about the importance of keeping the Sabbath day holy? Among other things, when individuals and nations keep the Sabbath holy, it serves to remind them of God and the importance of keeping His commandments in their daily living. When people forget the Sabbath, they tend to forget God.

JEREMIAH 18

Selection: all verses

A problem comes up in this chapter where the King James version (the Bible we use for English-speaking areas of the Church) has the Lord repenting in verses 8 and 10. The Lord does not repent since He does not sin. As you will see, when you come to these two verses, the JST makes corrections in both instances.

This chapter starts out by using the symbolism of a potter creating a pot from clay on a potter's wheel. While the clay is pliable, he can form it according to his plans. He can even start over with the clay, if necessary. This symbolizes what the Lord (the Potter) desires to do with His people (the clay). He desires to mold and shape them to become His people.

Jeremiah is told to go to the potter's house in his neighborhood where this message and lesson from the Lord can be demonstrated.

1 **THE word which came to Jeremiah from the LORD**, saying,

2 Arise, and **go down to the potter's house, and there I will cause thee to hear my words**.

3 Then I went down to the potter's house, and, behold, he wrought a work on the wheels [*the potter was making a clay pot on a potter's wheel*].

4 And **the vessel that he made of clay was marred** [*damaged; was not shaping according to plan*] in the hand of the potter: **so he made it again** another vessel [*so he started over with it and made another pot with it*], as seemed good to the potter to make *it*.

Next, the Lord explains the symbolism of the potter throwing (making) a pot.

5 **Then the word of the LORD came to me**, saying,

6 O house of Israel [*the twelve tribes of Israel; the Lord's covenant people*], cannot I do with you as this potter? saith the LORD. Behold, **as the clay *is* in the potter's hand, so *are* ye in mine hand**, O house of Israel.

Next, the Lord explains that He, as the Potter, will do whatever it takes to shape and form His covenant people, even if it means destroying them in order to start over with them. If they will then use their agency to repent (see verse 8), He will be enabled to form them into a covenant people, in other words, a people whom He can bless with exaltation.

7 *At what* instant [*NIV: "if at any time"*] **I shall speak concerning a nation**, and concerning a kingdom, to pluck up, and to pull down, and **to destroy** *it* [*like a potter as he starts over with a failed pot by kneading it back into lump of clay*];

> As mentioned in the background to this chapter, the idea that the Lord "repents" on occasions is not correct. We will first read verse 8, next, and will then use the JST to correct the translation.

> (By the way, someone asked me recently where I get these JST quotes from, since they are not all in the footnotes or in the back of our Latter-day Saint Bible. The answer is that there is not room in our Latter-day Saint Bible to include all the JST corrections. You can see all of them in Joseph Smith's "New Translation" of the Bible, published by Herald Publishing House, Independence, Missouri. I use the 1970 edition. Most Latter-day Saint bookstores have it or can get it for you.)

8 If that nation, against whom I have pronounced, turn from their evil, **I will repent** of the evil that I thought to do unto them.

JST Jeremiah 18:8

> 8 If that nation, against whom I have pronounced, turn from their evil, **I will withhold the evil** that I thought to do unto them.

9 **And** *at what* **instant** [*whenever*] **I shall speak concerning a nation**, and concerning a kingdom, **to build and to plant** *it;*

10 If it do evil in my sight, that it obey not my voice, then **I will repent of the good**, wherewith I said I would benefit them.

JST Jeremiah 18:10

> 10 If it do evil in my sight, that it obey not my voice, then **I will withhold the good**, wherewith I said I would benefit them.

> Next, in verse 11, the Lord instructs Jeremiah to once again invite these wicked people to repent.

Major Message

> Even when it may appear that it is far too late to repent, there can still be hope.

11 ¶ Now therefore **go to, speak to the men of Judah, and to the inhabitants of Jerusalem**, saying, Thus saith the LORD; Behold, I frame evil against you, and devise a device against you [*your destruction looms before you*]: **return ye now every one from his evil way, and make your ways and your doings good** [*please repent*].

> As we look at the phrase "there is no hope" in the context of verse 12, next, we understand that the people are not saying that there is no hope for them. Rather, they are saying, in effect, "Don't get your hopes up. There is no reason for us to repent. We like wickedness and we want to continue the way we are going."

NOTES

12 And they said, There is no hope: but **we will walk after our own devices, and we will every one do the imagination of his evil heart**.

The basic question in verses 13–14, next, is "Have you ever heard of such a thing as a people leaving a God who has power to bless them?" Even the heathen are wiser than that!

13 Therefore thus saith the LORD; Ask ye now among the heathen, **who hath heard such things: the virgin of Israel** [*Jerusalem*] **hath done a very horrible thing**.

14 Will *a man* leave the snow of Lebanon *which cometh* from the rock of the field? *or* shall the cold flowing waters that come from another place be forsaken?

JST Jeremiah 18:14

14 Will you not leave the snow of the fields of Lebanon; shall not the cold flowing waters that come from another place from the rock, be forsaken?

It may be that verse 14, above, in the context of verse 13, is saying, in effect, "Would you not be better off not to leave a sure thing, like the God of Israel?"

The Lord goes on to describe the "horrible thing" mentioned in verse 13.

15 Because **my people hath forgotten me**, they have **burned incense to vanity** [*idols*], and **they** [*their false gods and idols*] **have caused them to stumble in their ways** *from* the ancient paths, to walk in paths, *in* a way not cast up [*in a path which has not been graded and maintained*];

16 **To make their land desolate** [*their choices are setting up their land for destruction*], *and* a perpetual hissing; every one that passeth thereby shall be astonished, and wag his head [*there will be much negative and derisive gossip in the future about what happened to Judah and Jerusalem*].

17 **I will scatter them** as with an east wind [*symbolic of rapid and terrible devastation*] before the enemy: I will shew them the back, and not the face [*the Lord will turn His back to them*], in the day of their calamity.

The people don't like what Jeremiah is saying, so they plot to discredit him (verse 18). Verse 23 indicates that they plotted to kill him.

18 ¶ Then said they, **Come, and let us devise devices against Jeremiah**; for the law shall not perish from the priest, nor counsel from the wise, nor the word from the prophet [*the things he is prophesying will not come to pass*]. **Come, and let us smite him with the tongue**, and let us not give heed to any of his words.

Next, Jeremiah petitions the Lord for help and protection against his enemies. He asks that the Lord's punishments be upon them.

19 **Give heed to me**, O LORD, **and hearken to the voice of them that contend with me** [*be sure to hear the threats my enemies are giving out against me*].

20 Shall evil be recompensed for good? for **they have digged a pit for my soul**. Remember that **I stood before thee to speak good for them,** *and* **to turn away thy wrath from them** [*I have tried to save them*].

Verse 21, next, can serve to remind us of the application of the law of justice. It may also reflect the Lord's law of self-defense, as described in D&C 98.

21 Therefore deliver up their children to the famine, and pour out their *blood* by the force of the sword; and let their wives be bereaved of their children, and *be* widows; and let their men be put to death; *let* their young men *be* slain by the sword in battle.

22 Let a cry be heard from their houses, when thou shalt bring a troop suddenly upon them: for **they have digged a pit to take me, and hid snares for my feet.**

23 Yet, LORD, **thou knowest all their counsel against me to slay** *me:* forgive not their iniquity, neither blot out their sin from thy sight, but **let them be overthrown before thee; deal** *thus* **with them in the time of thine anger.**

As mentioned in our note before verse 21, above, D&C 98 may shed some light on verses 21–23, above. Jeremiah's life has been in danger and his enemies have tried to stop him a number of times by now. It may be that the "one, two, three" of D&C 98:23–27 have, in effect, been fulfilled, and he is now seeking to stop them, according to the law of self-defense that the Lord gave to the ancient prophets (D&C 98:32). We will quote some relevant verses from the Doctrine and Covenants, using bold for emphasis:

D&C 98:23–35

23 Now, I speak unto you concerning your families—**if men will smite you, or your families, once**, and ye bear it patiently and revile not against them, neither seek revenge, ye shall be rewarded;

24 But if ye bear it not patiently, it shall be accounted unto you as being meted out as a just measure unto you.

25 And again, if your enemy shall smite you **the second time**, and you revile not against your enemy, and bear it patiently, your reward shall be an hundred fold.

26 And again, if he shall smite you **the third time**, and ye bear it patiently, your reward shall be doubled unto you four–fold;

27 And these three testimonies shall stand against your enemy if he repent not, and shall not be blotted out.

28 And now, verily I say unto you, if that enemy shall escape my vengeance, that he be not brought into judgment before me, then ye shall **see to it that ye warn him in my name**, that he come no more upon you, neither upon your family, even your children's children unto the third and fourth generation.

29 And then, **if he shall come upon you or your children**, or your children's children unto the third and fourth generation, **I have delivered thine enemy into thine hands;**

30 And then if thou wilt spare him, thou shalt be rewarded for thy righteousness; and also thy children and thy children's children unto the third and fourth generation.

31 Nevertheless, thine enemy is in thine hands; and if thou rewardest him according to his works thou art justified; **if he has sought thy life, and thy life is endangered by him, thine enemy is in thine hands and thou art justified.**

NOTES

32 Behold, **this is the law I gave unto my servant Nephi, and thy fathers, Joseph, and Jacob, and Isaac, and Abraham, and all mine ancient prophets and apostles.**

33 And again, this is the law that I gave unto mine ancients, that they should not go out unto battle against any nation, kindred, tongue, or people, save I, the Lord, commanded them.

34 And if any nation, tongue, or people should proclaim war against them, they should first lift a standard of peace unto that people, nation, or tongue;

35 And **if that people did not accept the offering of peace, neither the second nor the third time, they should bring these testimonies before the Lord;**

JEREMIAH 19

Selection: all verses

In this chapter, we see that the inhabitants of Jerusalem and the cities of Judah had arrived at the point where they were sacrificing their own children to idols. Such sacrifice is the ultimate blasphemy against the voluntary sacrifice of the Son of God for our sins.

Again, as in the case of the potter and the potter's wheel (chapter 18), Jeremiah is requested by the Lord to go to a certain place to obtain this message. This time, he is asked to pick up a clay jar and go to the "valley of the son of Hinnom" (verse 2), and await the word of the Lord. This valley was just south of Jerusalem and was the site of human sacrifices (see Bible Dictionary under "Topheth.") These sacrifices included their own children (verse 5). The breaking (verse 10) of the clay jar (mentioned in verse 1) is symbolic of the destruction of Jerusalem.

1 THUS saith the LORD, **Go and get a potter's earthen bottle** [*a clay jar*], and *take* of the ancients of the people, and of the ancients of the priests [*take some of the city elders and old priests with you*];

2 And **go forth unto the valley of the son of Hinnom**, which *is* by the entry of the east gate, and proclaim there the words that I shall tell thee,

3 **And say,** Hear ye the word of the LORD, O kings of Judah, and inhabitants of Jerusalem; **Thus saith the LORD** of hosts, the God of Israel; Behold, **I will bring evil upon this place,** the which whosoever heareth, his ears shall tingle [*whoever hears about it will hardly believe their ears*].

4 **Because they have forsaken me, and have estranged this place** [*have desecrated this place; made it no longer a "Holy Land"*], and **have burned incense in it unto other gods** [*worshiped idols*], whom neither they nor their fathers have known, nor the kings of Judah, and **have filled this place with the blood of innocents** [*have offered human sacrifices, including children*];

5 They have built also the high places of Baal [*they have built altars to Baal*], to **burn their sons with fire** *for* **burnt offerings unto Baal,** which I commanded not, nor spake *it,* neither came *it* into my mind:

Verses 6–9 are yet another prophecy concerning the coming destruction of Jerusalem and the surrounding area.

6 **Therefore** [*because of gross wickedness*], behold, **the days come**, saith the LORD, **that this place shall no more be called** Tophet, nor **The valley of the son of Hinnom, but The valley of slaughter.**

7 And **I will make void the counsel of Judah and Jerusalem in this place** [*they will no longer have political clout*]; and **I will cause them to fall by the sword** before their enemies, and by the hands of them that seek their lives: **and their carcases will I give to be meat for the fowls of the heaven, and for the beasts of the earth**.

8 And **I will make this city desolate**, and an hissing [*an object of scorn and gossip*]; every one that passeth thereby shall be astonished and hiss [*deride them*] because of all the plagues thereof.

Next, in verse 9, we see a frightful prophecy of cannibalism during the coming siege of Jerusalem.

9 And **I will cause them to eat the flesh of their sons and the flesh of their daughters, and they shall eat every one the flesh of his friend** in the siege and straitness [*dire circumstances*], wherewith their enemies, and they that seek their lives, shall straiten them.

The above prediction of hunger and cannibalism was fulfilled during the siege of Jerusalem by Nebuchadnezzar, king of Babylon. We read of it in Lamentations:

Lamentations 4:8–10

8 Their visage is blacker than a coal; they are not known in the streets: their skin cleaveth to their bones; it is withered, it is become like a stick.

9 They that be slain with the sword are better than they that be slain with hunger: for these pine away, stricken through for want of the fruits of the field.

10 The hands of the pitiful women have sodden [*boiled, cooked*] their own children: they were their meat [*food*] in the destruction of the daughter of my people [*during the destruction of Jerusalem*].

Next, Jeremiah is instructed to break the clay jar (representing the people of Judah) that he was instructed (in verse 1) to take with him to the site of human sacrifices.

10 **Then shalt thou break the bottle** [*symbolic of the "breaking" of Jerusalem and the scattering of the Jews in pieces—see verse 11*] **in the sight of the men** [*the city elders and leaders—see verse 1*] that go with thee,

11 And shalt **say unto them, Thus saith the LORD of hosts; Even so will I break this people and this city, as *one* breaketh a potter's vessel**, that cannot be made whole again: and they shall bury *them* in Tophet [*a spot in the Valley of Hinnon—see verse 2*], till *there be* no place to bury [*in other words, there will be a great slaughter of the Jews in that valley*].

12 **Thus will I do unto this place, saith the LORD**, and to the inhabitants thereof, and *even* make this city as Tophet [*a place of great slaughter*]:

There is symbolism in the phrase "make this city as Tophet" in verse 12, above. As noted above, Tophet was a place in the valley, south of Jerusalem, where human sacrifice was practiced, including the sacrifice of children to the fire god Molech. (See Bible Dictionary under "Molech.") Therefore, to make Jerusalem like Tophet means that the wicked will be sacrificed to their wickedness, just like they wickedly sacrificed others to their false gods.

13 And **the houses of Jerusalem**, and the houses [*palaces*] of the kings of Judah, **shall be defiled as the place of Tophet**, because of all the houses upon whose roofs they have burned incense unto all the host of heaven [*all the false gods and idols imaginable*], and have poured out drink offerings unto other gods.

14 **Then came Jeremiah from Tophet**, whither the LORD had sent him to prophesy; **and he stood in the court of the LORD's house** [*the outer courtyard of the Jerusalem Temple*]; **and said to all the people,**

15 Thus saith the LORD of hosts, the God of Israel; **Behold, I will bring** upon this city and upon all her towns **all the evil that I have pronounced** [*prophesied*] against it, **because they have hardened their necks** [*refused to humble themselves*]**, that they might not hear my words.**

JEREMIAH 20

Selection: all verses

In this chapter, Pashur, the senior officer or chief overseer of the temple in Jerusalem, vents his anger against Jeremiah because of the things he is teaching and prophesying about the wickedness of the Jews and their leaders (see, for example, Jeremiah 19:14–15). He beats Jeremiah (verse 2) and has him placed in the stocks.

1 NOW **Pashur** the son of Immer the priest, who *was* also **chief governor in the house of the LORD, heard that Jeremiah prophesied these things**.

2 **Then Pashur smote Jeremiah** the prophet, **and put him in the stocks** that *were* in the high gate of Benjamin, which *was* by the house of the LORD.

We will quote from the Old Testament Student Manual for a description of being "put in the stocks." We will add bold for emphasis.

"Jeremiah 19:14–15 records Jeremiah's standing in the court of the temple, again reminding the people of the troubles that lay ahead because of their wickedness. When Pashur, the chief overseer of the temple, heard of the incident, he had Jeremiah beaten and placed in stocks. Stocks were an instrument of torture by which the body was forced into an unnatural position, much as the wooden stocks of medieval times confined certain parts of the body, such as the arms, legs, or head, by means of wooden beams that locked the parts of the body into place" (Old Testament Student Manual, page 245).

In verse 3, next, Jeremiah, under the direction of the Lord, uses the common technique (in their culture) of changing a person's name as a means of confirming a change in status, either good or bad. In this case, it is bad. "Pashur" means "free." But watch what the change of names denotes for Pashur's future, at the end of the verse.

3 And it came to pass **on the morrow** [*the next day*], that **Pashur brought forth Jeremiah out of the stocks**. Then said Jeremiah unto him, **The LORD hath not called thy name Pashur, but Magor-missabib** [*"terror all around"—see footnote 3a in your Bible*].

4 For thus saith the LORD, **Behold, I will make thee a terror to thyself, and to all thy friends**: and **they shall fall by the sword** of their enemies, and **thine eyes shall behold** *it* [*you will see this prophecy fulfilled*]: and **I will give all Judah into the hand of the king of Babylon, and he shall carry them captive into Babylon, and shall slay them with the sword**.

5 **Moreover** [*in addition*] **I will deliver all the strength of this city**, and all the labours thereof, and **all the precious things** thereof, and **all the treasures** of the kings of Judah will I give **into the hand of their enemies**, which shall spoil them, and take them, and carry them to Babylon.

6 **And thou, Pashur, and all that dwell in thine house shall go into captivity**: and thou shalt come **to Babylon, and there thou shalt die**, and shalt be buried there, thou, and all thy friends, to whom thou hast prophesied lies.

The scene in verse 6, above, reminds us of Abinadi in King Noah's court (Mosiah 17:16–18).

The word, "deceived," in verse 7, next, can be a problem. We will read it and then get some help on the matter.

7 ¶ O LORD, thou hast **deceived** me, and I was deceived: thou art stronger than I, and hast prevailed: I am in derision daily, every one mocketh me.

"The great stress the prophetic calling caused Jeremiah is particularly discernible in Jeremiah 20:7–8, 14–18. The Hebrew word translated in verse 7 as "deceived" means literally "enticed" or "persuaded." The power that persuaded the prophet to continue to preach God's word at such great personal cost was 'as a burning fire shut up in [*his*] bones' (verse 9). It could not be stayed. Verses 14–18 reflect Jeremiah's despair over the lonely ministry he was given" (Old Testament Student Manual, page 245).

We will now repeat verse 7, above, and incorporate the helps given in the student manual. We catch a glimpse of Jeremiah's personality.

Jeremiah 20:7 (repeated)

¶ O LORD, thou hast deceived me [*persuaded me to serve as a prophet*], and I was deceived [*and I have been successfully persuaded*]: thou art stronger than I, and hast prevailed [*You win*]: I am in derision daily, every one mocketh me [*this is a most difficult calling*].

8 **For since I spake, I cried out, I cried violence and spoil** [*ever since I began to prophesy, I have had to say much about violence and devastation*]; **because the word of the LORD was made a reproach unto me, and a derision, daily** [*and it has caused me to be mocked and brought much personal pain*].

NOTES

We continue to see insights into Jeremiah's personality. He is without guile and rather straightforward with the Lord. Next, he confesses that he considered not delivering the messages, but his burning testimony compelled him to be faithful to his calling as a prophet.

9 **Then I said, I will not make mention of him, nor speak any more in his name** [*I said to myself, "I will not do any more prophesying for the Lord"*]. **But *his word* was in mine heart as a burning fire shut up in my bones**, and **I was weary with forbearing, and I could not** *stay* [*I just could not hold back any more*].

Jeremiah continues, sharing his frustrations and confirming his absolute commitment to be true to the Lord. According to the first part of verse 10, next, it appears that there were many attempts to discredit Jeremiah through slander against his name. People were constantly watching to catch him in any kind of slip up.

10 ¶ For **I heard the defaming** [*slander*] **of many**, fear on every side [*paranoia everywhere*]. Report, *say they,* and we will report it. **All my familiars** [*close acquaintances*] **watched for my halting** [*watched, hoping to see me slip up*], *saying,* **Peradventure he will be enticed** [*perhaps he will compromise his standards*], **and we shall prevail against him, and we shall take our revenge on him.**

11 But **the LORD** *is* **with me** as a mighty terrible one [*NIV: "like a mighty warrior"*]: **therefore my persecutors shall stumble, and they shall not prevail**: they shall be greatly ashamed [*disgraced*]; for **they shall not prosper**: *their* everlasting confusion shall never be forgotten.

Again, we see Jeremiah plead with the Lord for help against his enemies, much the same as Joseph Smith did as recorded in D&C 121:2–5.

12 But, O LORD of hosts, that triest [*tests*] the righteous, *and* seest the reins and the heart [*and sees the innermost feelings and desires of the heart*], **let me see thy vengeance on them: for unto thee have I opened my cause.**

Next, Jeremiah reaffirms his faith that the Lord has power to deliver him from the wicked.

13 Sing unto the LORD, praise ye the LORD: for **he hath delivered the soul of the poor** [*those in need*] **from the hand of evildoers.**

This seems to be a low point in Jeremiah's life (understatement). We feel his discouragement and frustration in verses 14–18.

14 ¶ **Cursed** *be* **the day wherein I was born**: let not the day wherein my mother bare me be blessed.

15 **Cursed** *be* **the man who brought tidings to my father, saying, A man child is born unto thee**; making him very glad.

16 And let that man be as the cities which the LORD overthrew, and repented not: and **let him hear the cry in the morning, and the shouting at noontide** [*in other words, in effect, if the man who told my father that I was born could just hear what I hear everyday, he would be sorry he even announced my birth*];

17 Because he slew me not from the womb; **or that my mother might have been my grave, and her womb** *to be* **always great** *with me* [*if I could just not have been born; if my mother could have remained pregnant with me forever*].

18 **Wherefore came I forth out of the womb** [*why did I have to be born*] to see labour and sorrow, that my days should be consumed with shame [*perhaps meaning "that my life should be spent as a social outcast"*]?

NOTES

_____
_____
_____
_____
_____
_____
_____
_____
_____
_____
_____
_____
_____
_____
_____
_____
_____
_____
_____
_____
_____
_____
_____
_____
_____
_____
_____
_____
_____
_____
_____
_____
_____
NOTES
_____

Book of Mormon Student Manual. Salt Lake City: The Church of Jesus Christ of Latter-day Saints, 1982.

Bryant, T. Alton. *The New Compact Bible Dictionary.* Grand Rapids, Mich.: Zondervan, 1981.

Clark, James R., comp. *Messages of the First Presidency of The Church of Jesus Christ of Latter-day Saints.* 6 vols. Salt Lake City: Bookcraft, 1965–75.

Conference Reports of The Church of Jesus Christ of Latter-day Saints. Salt Lake City: The Church of Jesus Christ of Latter-day Saints, 1898 to present.

Doctrines of the Gospel Student Manual. Salt Lake City: The Church of Jesus Christ of Latter-day Saints (Institutes of Religion), 2000.

Dummelow, J. R. *A Commentary on the Holy Bible.* New York: Macmillan, 1937.

Encyclopedia of Mormonism. Edited by Daniel H. Ludlow. 5 vols. New York: Macmillan, 1992.

German Bible, The Martin Luther Edition of. Wien (Vienna), Austria, 1960.

Hymns of The Church of Jesus Christ of Latter-day Saints. Salt Lake City: The Church of Jesus Christ of Latter-day Saints, 1985.

International Bible Society. *The Holy Bible: New International Version (NIV).* Grand Rapids, Mich.: Zondervan, 1984.

Josephus. *Antiquities of the Jews.* Philadelphia: John C. Winston Co., n.d.

Journal of Discourses. 26 vols. London: Latter-day Saints' Book Depot, 1854–86.

Kiel, C. F., and F. Delitzsch. *Commentary on the Old Testament.* 10 vols. Grand Rapids, Mich.: William B. Eerdmans Publishing, 1991.

Kimball, Spencer W. *Faith Precedes the Miracle.* Salt Lake City: Deseret Book, 1972.

Ludlow, Victor L. Isaiah: Prophet, Seer, and Poet. Salt Lake City: Deseret Book, 1982.

Maxwell, Neal A. *Deposition of a Disciple.* Salt Lake City: Deseret Book, 1976.

McConkie, Bruce R. *A New Witness for the Articles of Faith.* Salt Lake City: Deseret Book, 1985.

————. Doctrinal New Testament Commentary. 3 vols. Salt Lake City: Deseret Book, 1972.

————. *Mormon Doctrine.* 2d ed. Salt Lake City: Bookcraft, 1966.

————. *The Millennial Messiah.* Salt Lake City: Deseret Book, 1982.

————. *The Promised Messiah—The First Coming of Christ.* Salt Lake City: Deseret Book, 1978.

Nyman, Monte S. *Great Are the Words of Isaiah.* Salt Lake City: Bookcraft, 1980.

Ogden, Kelly D., and Andrew C. Skinner. *Verse by Verse—The Old Testament*, Volume 2, 1 Kings through Malachi. Salt Lake City, Deseret Book, 2013.

Old Testament Gospel Doctrine Teacher's Manual. Salt Lake City: The Church of Jesus Christ of Latter-day Saints (Institutes of Religion), 2001.

Old Testament Student Manual: Genesis–2 Samuel. Salt Lake City: The Church of Jesus Christ of Latter-day Saints (Institutes of Religion), 1981.

Old Testament Student Manual, I Kings–Malachi (Religion 302). Salt Lake City: The Church of Jesus Christ of Latter-day Saints, 1981.

Petersen, Mark E. *Moses, Man of Miracles.* Salt Lake City: Deseret Book, 1977.

Rasmussen, Ellis T. *An Introduction to the Old Testament and its Teachings.* 2d ed. 2 vols. Provo, Utah: BYU Press, 1972–74.

——————. *A Latter-day Saint Commentary on the Old Testament.* Salt Lake City: Deseret Book, 1993.

Richards, LeGrand. *Israel! Do You Know?* Salt Lake City: Deseret Book, 1954.

Smith, Joseph. *History of The Church of Jesus Christ of Latter-day Saints.* Edited by B. H. Roberts. 2d ed. rev., 7 vols. Salt Lake City: The Church of Jesus Christ of Latter-day Saints, 1932–1951.

——————. Joseph Smith's "New Translation" of the Bible. Independence, Missouri: Herald Publishing House, 1970.

——————. *Teachings of the Prophet Joseph Smith.* Selected by Joseph Fielding Smith. Salt Lake City: Deseret Book, 1977.

David J. Ridges

David J. Ridges was raised in southeastern Nevada until his family moved to North Salt Lake City, Utah, when he was in fifth grade. He is the second of eight children.

Brother Ridges graduated from Bountiful High, served a two-and-a-half-year German-speaking mission to Austria, attended the University of Utah and BYU, and then graduated from BYU with a major in German and a physics minor. He later received a master's degree in educational psychology with a Church History minor from BYU.

He taught seminary and institute of religion as his chosen career for thirty-five years. He taught BYU Campus Education Week, Especially for Youth, Adult Religion, and Know Your Religion classes for over twenty-five years.

Brother Ridges has served as a Sunday School and seminary curriculum writer. He has had many callings, including Gospel Doctrine teacher, bishop, stake president, and patriarch. He and Sister Ridges have served two full-time, eighteen-month CES missions. He has written over forty books, which include several study guides for the standard works, Isaiah, Revelation, and many doctrinal publications on gospel topics such as the signs of the times, plan of salvation, and temples.

Brother and Sister Ridges met at the University of Utah. They were married in the Salt Lake Temple, are the parents of six children, and have sixteen grandchildren and one great-granddaughter so far. They make their home in Springville, Utah.

Scan to visit

www.davidjridges.com